CORNERSTONE
BIBLICAL
COMMENTARY

Job
August H. Konkel

Ecclesiastes
Song of Songs
Tremper Longman III

GENERAL EDITOR
Philip W. Comfort

with the entire text of the
NEW LIVING TRANSLATION

TYNDALE HOUSE PUBLISHERS, INC. CAROL STREAM, ILLINOIS

Cornerstone Biblical Commentary, Volume 6

Visit Tyndale's exciting Web site at www.tyndale.com

Designed by Luke Daab and Timothy R. Botts.

Job copyright © 2006 by August H. Konkel. All rights reserved.

Ecclesiastes copyright © 2006 by Tremper Longman III. All rights reserved.

Song of Songs copyright © 2006 by Tremper Longman III. All rights reserved.

Library of Congress Cataloging-in-Publication Data

Cornerstone biblical commentary.
   p. cm.
  Includes bibliographical references and index.
  ISBN-13: 978-0-8423-3432-7 (hc : alk. paper)
  ISBN-10: 0-8423-3432-7 (hc : alk. paper)
  1. Biblical—Commentaries.
  BS491.3.C67 2006
  200.7'7—dc22   2005026928

Printed in China

12 11 10 09 08 07 06
 9   8   7   6   5   4   3   2   1

CONTENTS

CONTRIBUTORS TO **VOLUME 6**

Job: August H. Konkel
BRE, Providence College;
MDiv, Providence Theological Seminary;
PhD, Westminster Theological Seminary;
President, Providence College and Theological Seminary.

Ecclesiastes & Song of Songs: Tremper Longman III
BA, Ohio Wesleyan University;
MDiv, Westminster Theological Seminary;
PhD, Yale University;
Robert H. Gundry Proferssor of Biblical Studies, Westmont College.

GENERAL EDITOR'S PREFACE

The *Cornerstone Biblical Commentary* is based on the second edition of the New Living Translation (2004). Nearly 100 scholars from various church backgrounds and from several countries (United States, Canada, England, and Australia) participated in the creation of the NLT. Many of these same scholars are contributors to this commentary series. All the commentators, whether participants in the NLT or not, believe that the Bible is God's inspired word and have a desire to make God's word clear and accessible to his people.

This Bible commentary is the natural extension of our vision for the New Living Translation, which we believe is both exegetically accurate and idiomatically powerful. The NLT attempts to communicate God's inspired word in a lucid English translation of the original languages so that English readers can understand and appreciate the thought of the original writers. In the same way, the *Cornerstone Biblical Commentary* aims at helping teachers, pastors, students, and lay people understand every thought contained in the Bible. As such, the commentary focuses first on the words of Scripture, then on the theological truths of Scripture—inasmuch as the words express the truths.

The commentary itself has been structured in such a way as to help readers get at the meaning of Scripture, passage by passage, through the entire Bible. Each Bible book is prefaced by a substantial book introduction that gives general historical background important for understanding. Then the reader is taken through the Bible text, passage by passage, starting with the New Living Translation text printed in full. This is followed by a section called "Notes," wherein the commentator helps the reader understand the Hebrew or Greek behind the English of the NLT, interacts with other scholars on important interpretive issues, and points the reader to significant textual and contextual matters. The "Notes" are followed by the "Commentary," wherein each scholar presents a lucid interpretation of the passage, giving special attention to context and major theological themes.

The commentators represent a wide spectrum of theological positions within the evangelical community. We believe this is good because it reflects the rich variety in Christ's church. All the commentators uphold the authority of God's word and believe it is essential to heed the old adage: "Wholly apply yourself to the Scriptures and apply them wholly to you." May this commentary help you know the truths of Scripture, and may this knowledge help you "grow in your knowledge of God and Jesus our Lord" (2 Pet 1:2, NLT).

PHILIP W. COMFORT
GENERAL EDITOR

ABBREVIATIONS

GENERAL ABBREVIATIONS

b.	Babylonian Gemara	Gr.	Greek	no.	number
bar.	baraita	Heb.	Hebrew	NT	New Testament
c	*circa,* around, approximately	ibid.	*ibidem,* in the same place	OL	Old Latin
				OS	Old Syriac
cf.	*confer,* compare	i.e.	*id est,* the same	OT	Old Testament
ch, chs	chapter, chapters	in loc.	*in loco,* in the place cited	p., pp.	page, pages
contra	in contrast to			pl.	plural
DSS	Dead Sea Scrolls	lit.	literally	Q	Quelle ("Sayings"
ed.	edition, editor	LXX	Septuagint		as Gospel source)
e.g.	*exempli gratia,* for example	𝔐	Majority Text	rev.	revision
		m.	Mishnah	sg.	singular
ET	English translation	masc.	masculine	*t.*	Tosefta
et al.	*et alli,* and others	mg	margin	v., vv.	verse, verses
fem.	feminine	MS	manuscript	vid.	*videur,* it seems
ff	following (verses, pages)	MSS	manuscripts	viz.	*videlicet,* namely
		MT	Masoretic Text	vol.	volume
fl.	flourished	n.d.	no date	*y.*	Jerusalem Gemara
		neut.	neuter		

ABBREVIATIONS FOR BIBLE TRANSLATIONS

ASV	American Standard Version	NCV	New Century Version	NKJV	New King James Version
CEV	Contemporary English Version	NEB	New English Bible	NRSV	New Revised Standard Version
ESV	English Standard Version	NIV	New International Version	NLT	New Living Translation
GW	God's Word	NIrV	New International Reader's Version	REB	Revised English Bible
HCSB	Holman Christian Standard Bible	NJB	New Jerusalem Bible	RSV	Revised Standard Version
JB	Jerusalem Bible	NJPS	The New Jewish Publication Society Translation (*Tanakh*)	TEV	Today's English Version
KJV	King James Version				
NAB	New American Bible			TLB	The Living Bible
NASB	New American Standard Bible				

ABBREVIATIONS FOR DICTIONARIES, LEXICONS, COLLECTIONS OF TEXTS, ORIGINAL LANGUAGE EDITIONS

ABD *Anchor Bible Dictionary* (6 vols., Freedman) [1992]

ANEP *The Ancient Near East in Pictures* (Pritchard) [1965]

ANET *Ancient Near Eastern Texts Relating to the Old Testament* (Pritchard) [1969]

ANF *Ante-Nicene Fathers*

BAGD *Greek-English Lexicon of the New Testament and Other Early Christian Literature,* 2nd ed. (Bauer, Arndt, Gingrich, Danker) [1979]

BDAG *Greek-English Lexicon of the New Testament and Other Early Christian Literature,* 3rd ed. (Bauer, Danker, Arndt, Gingrich) [2000]

BDB *A Hebrew and English Lexicon of the Old Testament* (Brown, Driver, Briggs) [1907]

BDF *A Greek Grammar of the New Testament and Other Early Christian Literature* (Blass, Debrunner, Funk) [1961]

BHS *Biblia Hebraica Stuttgartensia* (Elliger and Rudolph) [1983]

CAD *Assyrian Dictionary of the Oriental Institute of the University of Chicago* [1956]

COS *The Context of Scripture* (3 volumes, Hallo and Younger) [1997–2002]

DBI *Dictionary of Biblical Imagery* (Ryken, Wilhoit, Longman) [1998]

DBT *Dictionary of Biblical Theology* (2nd edition, Leon-Dufour) [1972]

DCH *Dictionary of Classical Hebrew* (5 volumes, D. Clines) [2000]

DJD *Discoveries in the Judean Desert* [1955–]

DJG *Dictionary of Jesus and the Gospels* (Green, McKnight, Marshall) [1992]

DOTP *Dictionary of the Old Testament: Pentateuch.* (T. Alexander, D.W. Baker) [2003]

DPL *Dictionary of Paul and His Letters* (Hawthorne, Martin, Reid) [1993]

EDNT *Exegetical Dictionary of the New Testament* (3 vols., H. Balz, G. Schneider. ET) [1990–1993]

HALOT *The Hebrew and Aramaic Lexicon of the Old Testament* (L. Koehler, W. Baumgartner, J. Stamm; trans. M. Richardson) [1994–1999]

IBD *Illustrated Bible Dictionary* (3 vols., Douglas, Wiseman) [1980]

IDB *The Interpreter's Dictionary of the Bible* (4 vols., Buttrick) [1962]

ISBE *International Standard Bible Encyclopedia* (4 vols., Bromiley) [1979–1988]

KBL *Lexicon in Veteris Testamenti libros* (Koehler, Baumgartner) [1958]

LCL Loeb Classical Library

L&N *Greek-English Lexicon of the New Testament: Based on Semantic Domains* (Louw and Nida) [1989]

LSJ *A Greek-English Lexicon* (9th edition, Liddell, Scott, Jones) [1996]

MM *The Vocabulary of the Greek New Testament* (Moulton and Milligan) [1930; 1997]

NA^{26} *Novum Testamentum Graece* (26th edition, Nestle-Aland) [1979]

NA^{27} *Novum Testamentum Graece* (27th edition, Nestle-Aland) [1993]

NBD *New Bible Dictionary* (2nd edition, Douglas, Hillyer) [1982]

NIDB *New International Dictionary of the Bible* (Douglas, Tenney) [1987]

NIDBA *New International Dictionary of Biblical Archaeology* (Blaiklock and Harrison) [1983]

NIDNTT *New International Dictionary of New Testament Theology* (4 vols., C. Brown) [1975–1985]

NIDOTTE *New International Dictionary of Old Testament Theology and Exegesis* (5 vols., W. A. VanGemeren) [1997]

PGM *Papyri Graecae magicae: Die griechischen Zauberpapyri.* (Preisendanz) [1928]

PG *Patrologia Graecae* (J. P. Migne) [1857–1886]

TBD *Tyndale Bible Dictionary* (Elwell, Comfort) [2001]

TDNT *Theological Dictionary of the New Testament* (10 vols., Kittel, Friedrich; trans. Bromiley) [1964–1976]

TDOT *Theological Dictionary of the Old Testament* (8 vols., Botterweck, Ringgren; trans. Willis, Bromiley, Green) [1974–]

TLOT *Theological Lexicon of the Old Testament* (3 vols., E. Jenni) [1997]

TWOT *Theological Wordbook of the Old Testament* (2 vols., Harris, Archer) [1980]

UBS^3 *United Bible Societies' Greek New Testament* (third edition, Metzger et al) [1975]

UBS^4 *United Bible Societies' Greek New Testament* (fourth corrected edition, Metzger et al) [1993]

WH *The New Testament in the Original Greek* (Westcott and Hort) [1882]

ABBREVIATIONS FOR BOOKS OF THE BIBLE

Old Testament

Gen	Genesis	1 Sam	1 Samuel	Esth	Esther
Exod	Exodus	2 Sam	2 Samuel	Ps, Pss	Psalm, Psalms
Lev	Leviticus	1 Kgs	1 Kings	Prov	Proverbs
Num	Numbers	2 Kgs	2 Kings	Eccl	Ecclesiastes
Deut	Deuteronomy	1 Chr	1 Chronicles	Song	Song of Songs
Josh	Joshua	2 Chr	2 Chronicles	Isa	Isaiah
Judg	Judges	Ezra	Ezra	Jer	Jeremiah
Ruth	Ruth	Neh	Nehemiah	Lam	Lamentations

Ezek	Ezekiel	Obad	Obadiah	Zeph	Zephaniah
Dan	Daniel	Jonah	Jonah	Hag	Haggai
Hos	Hosea	Mic	Micah	Zech	Zechariah
Joel	Joel	Nah	Nahum	Mal	Malachi
Amos	Amos	Hab	Habakkuk		

New Testament

Matt	Matthew	Eph	Ephesians	Heb	Hebrews
Mark	Mark	Phil	Philippians	Jas	James
Luke	Luke	Col	Colossians	1 Pet	1 Peter
John	John	1 Thess	1 Thessalonians	2 Pet	2 Peter
Acts	Acts	2 Thess	2 Thessalonians	1 John	1 John
Rom	Romans	1 Tim	1 Timothy	2 John	2 John
1 Cor	1 Corinthians	2 Tim	2 Timothy	3 John	3 John
2 Cor	2 Corinthians	Titus	Titus	Jude	Jude
Gal	Galatians	Phlm	Philemon	Rev	Revelation

Deuterocanonical

Bar	Baruch	1–2 Esdr	1–2 Esdras	Pr Man	Prayer of Manasseh
Add Dan	Additions to Daniel	Add Esth	Additions to Esther	Ps 151	Psalm 151
Pr Azar	Prayer of Azariah	Ep Jer	Epistle of Jeremiah	Sir	Sirach
Bel	Bel and the Dragon	Jdt	Judith	Tob	Tobit
Sg Three	Song of the Three Children	1–2 Macc	1–2 Maccabees	Wis	Wisdom of Solomon
Sus	Susanna	3–4 Macc	3–4 Maccabees		

MANUSCRIPTS AND LITERATURE FROM QUMRAN

Initial numerals followed by "Q" indicate particular caves at Qumran. For example, the notation 4Q267 indicates text 267 from cave 4 at Qumran. Further, 1QS 4:9-10 indicates column 4, lines 9-10 of the *Rule of the Community*; and 4Q166 1 ii 2 indicates fragment 1, column ii, line 2 of text 166 from cave 4. More examples of common abbreviations are listed below.

CD	Cairo Geniza copy of the *Damascus Document*	1QIsa[b]	Isaiah copy [b]	4QLam[a]	Lamentations
		1QM	*War Scroll*	11QPs[a]	Psalms
		1QpHab	*Pesher Habakkuk*	11QTemple[a,b]	*Temple Scroll*
1QH	*Thanksgiving Hymns*	1QS	*Rule of the Community*	11QtgJob	*Targum of Job*
1QIsa[a]	Isaiah copy [a]				

IMPORTANT NEW TESTAMENT MANUSCRIPTS

(all dates given are AD; ordinal numbers refer to centuries)

Significant Papyri (𝔓 = Papyrus)

𝔓1 Matt 1; early 3rd
𝔓4+𝔓64+𝔓67 Matt 3, 5, 26; Luke 1-6; late 2nd
𝔓5 John 1, 16, 20; early 3rd
𝔓13 Heb 2-5, 10-12; early 3rd
𝔓15+𝔓16 (probably part of same codex) 1 Cor 7-8, Phil 3-4; late 3rd

𝔓20 James 2-3; 3rd
𝔓22 John 15-16; mid 3rd
𝔓23 James 1; c. 200
𝔓27 Rom 8-9; 3rd
𝔓30 1 Thess 4-5; 2 Thess 1; early 3rd
𝔓32 Titus 1-2; late 2nd
𝔓37 Matt 26; late 3rd

𝔓39 John 8; first half of 3rd
𝔓40 Rom 1-4, 6, 9; 3rd
𝔓45 Gospels and Acts; early 3rd
𝔓46 Paul's Major Epistles (less Pastorals); late 2nd
𝔓47 Rev 9-17; 3rd

𝔓49+𝔓65 Eph 4-5; 1 Thess
  1-2; 3rd
𝔓52 John 18; c. 125
𝔓53 Matt 26, Acts 9-10;
  middle 3rd
𝔓66 John; late 2nd
𝔓70 Matt 2-3, 11-12, 24; 3rd
𝔓72 1-2 Peter, Jude; c. 300

𝔓74 Acts, General Epistles; 7th
𝔓75 Luke and John; c. 200
𝔓77+𝔓103 (probably part of
  same codex) Matt 13-14,
  23; late 2nd
𝔓87 Phlm; late 2nd
𝔓90 John 18-19; late 2nd
𝔓91 Acts 2-3; 3rd

𝔓92 Eph 1, 2 Thess 1; c. 300
𝔓98 Rev 1:13-20; late 2nd
𝔓100 James 3-5; c. 300
𝔓101 Matt 3-4; 3rd
𝔓104 Matt 21; 2nd
𝔓106 John 1; 3rd
𝔓115 Rev 2-3, 5-6, 8-15; 3rd

Significant Uncials

א (Sinaiticus) most of NT; 4th
A (Alexandrinus) most of NT;
  5th
B (Vaticanus) most of NT; 4th
C (Ephraemi Rescriptus) most
  of NT with many lacunae;
  5th
D (Bezae) Gospels, Acts; 5th
D (Claromontanus), Paul's
  Epistles; 6th (different MS
  than Bezae)
E (Laudianus 35) Acts; 6th
F (Augensis) Paul's Epistles; 9th
G (Boernerianus) Paul's
  Epistles; 9th

H (Coislinianus) Paul's
  Epistles; 6th
I (Freerianus or Washington)
  Paul's Epistles; 5th
L (Regius) Gospels; 8th
Q (Guelferbytanus B) Luke,
  John; 5th
P (Porphyrianus) Acts—
  Revelation; 9th
T (Borgianus) Luke, John; 5th
W (Washingtonianus or the
  Freer Gospels) Gospels; 5th
Z (Dublinensis) Matthew; 6th
037 (Δ; Sangallensis) Gospels;
  9th

038 (Θ; Koridethi) Gospels;
  9th
040 (Ξ; Zacynthius) Luke; 6th
043 (Φ; Beratinus) Matt,
  Mark; 6th
044 (Ψ; Athous Laurae)
  Gospels, Acts, Paul's
  Epistles; 9th
048 Acts, Paul's Epistles,
  General Epistles; 5th
0171 Matt 10, Luke 22;
  c. 300
0189 Acts 5; c. 200

Significant Minuscules

1 Gospels, Acts, Paul's
  Epistles; 12th
33 All NT except Rev; 9th
81 Acts, Paul's Epistles,
  General Epistles; 1044
565 Gospels; 9th
700 Gospels; 11th

1424 (or Family 1424—a
  group of 29 manuscripts
  sharing nearly the same
  text) most of NT; 9th-10th
1739 Acts, Paul's Epistles; 10th
2053 Rev; 13th
2344 Rev; 11th

f¹ (a family of manuscripts
  including 1, 118, 131, 209)
  Gospels; 12th-14th
f¹³ (a family of manuscripts
  including 13, 69, 124, 174,
  230, 346, 543, 788, 826,
  828, 983, 1689, 1709—
  known as the Ferrar group)
  Gospels; 11th-15th

Significant Ancient Versions

SYRIAC (SYR)
syrᶜ (Syriac Curetonian)
  Gospels; 5th
syrˢ (Syriac Sinaiticus)
  Gospels; 4th
syrʰ (Syriac Harklensis) Entire
  NT; 616

OLD LATIN (IT)
itᵃ (Vercellenis) Gospels; 4th
itᵇ (Veronensis) Gospels; 5th
itᵈ (Cantabrigiensis—the Latin
  text of Bezae) Gospels, Acts,
  3 John; 5th
itᵉ (Palantinus) Gospels; 5th
itᵏ (Bobiensis) Matthew, Mark;
  c. 400

COPTIC (COP)
copᵇᵒ (Boharic—north Egypt)
copᶠᵃʸ (Fayyumic—central Egypt)
copˢᵃ (Sahidic—southern Egypt)

OTHER VERSIONS
arm (Armenian)
eth (Ethiopic)
geo (Georgian)

TRANSLITERATION AND NUMBERING SYSTEM

Note: For words and roots from non-biblical languages (e.g., Arabic, Ugaritic), only approximate transliterations are given.

HEBREW/ARAMAIC

Consonants

א	aleph	= '	מ, ם	mem	= m
ב, ב	beth	= b	נ, ן	nun	= n
ג, ג	gimel	= g	ס	samekh	= s
ד, ד	daleth	= d	ע	ayin	= '
ה	he	= h	פ, פ, ף	pe	= p
ו	waw	= w	צ, ץ	tsadhe	= ts
ז	zayin	= z	ק	qoph	= q
ח	heth	= kh	ר	resh	= r
ט	teth	= t	שׁ	shin	= sh
י	yodh	= y	שׂ	sin	= s
כ, כ, ך	kaph	= k	ת, ת	taw	= t, th
ל	lamedh	= l			(spirant)

Vowels

	patakh	= a		qamets khatuf	= o
ח	furtive patakh	= a		holem	= o
	qamets	= a	ו	full holem	= o
ה	final qamets he	= ah		short qibbuts	= u
	segol	= e		long qibbuts	= u
	tsere	= e	ו	shureq	= u
	tsere yod	= e		khatef patakh	= a
	short hireq	= i		khatef qamets	= o
	long hireq	= i		vocalic shewa	= e
	hireq yod	= i		patakh yodh	= a

Greek

α	alpha	= a	ε	epsilon	= e
β	beta	= b	ζ	zeta	= z
γ	gamma	= g, n (before γ, κ, ξ, χ)	η	eta	= ē
			θ	theta	= th
δ	delta	= d	ι	iota	= i

κ	kappa	= k		τ	tau	= t
λ	lamda	= l		υ	upsilon	= u
μ	mu	= m		φ	phi	= ph
ν	nu	= n		χ	chi	= ch
ξ	ksi	= x		ψ	psi	= ps
ο	omicron	= o		ω	omega	= ō
π	pi	= p			rough	= h (with
ρ	rho	= r (ῥ = rh)			breathing	vowel or
σ, ς	sigma	= s			mark	diphthong)

THE TYNDALE-STRONG'S NUMBERING SYSTEM

The Cornerstone Biblical Commentary series uses a word-study numbering system to give both newer and more advanced Bible students alike quicker, more convenient access to helpful original-language tools (e.g., concordances, lexicons, and theological dictionaries). Those who are unfamiliar with the ancient Hebrew, Aramaic, and Greek alphabets can quickly find information on a given word by looking up the appropriate index number. Advanced students will find the system helpful because it allows them to quickly find the lexical form of obscure conjugations and inflections.

There are two main numbering systems used for biblical words today. The one familiar to most people is the Strong's numbering system (made popular by the *Strong's Exhaustive Concordance to the Bible*). Although the original Strong's system is still quite useful, the most up-to-date research has shed new light on the biblical languages and allows for more precision than is found in the original Strong's system. The Cornerstone Biblical Commentary series, therefore, features a newly revised version of the Strong's system, the Tyndale-Strong's numbering system. The Tyndale-Strong's system brings together the familiarity of the Strong's system and the best of modern scholarship. In most cases, the original Strong's numbers are preserved. In places where new research dictates, new or related numbers have been added.[1]

The second major numbering system today is the Goodrick-Kohlenberger system used in a number of study tools published by Zondervan. In order to give students broad access to a number of helpful tools, the Commentary provides index numbers for the Zondervan system as well.

The different index systems are designated as follows:

TG	Tyndale-Strong's Greek number	ZH	Zondervan Hebrew number
ZG	Zondervan Greek number	TA	Tyndale-Strong's Aramaic number
TH	Tyndale-Strong's Hebrew number	ZA	Zondervan Aramaic number

So in the example, "love" *agapē* [TG26, ZG27], the first number is the one to use with Greek tools keyed to the Tyndale-Strong's system, and the second applies to tools that use the Zondervan system.

---

1. Generally, one may simply use the original four-digit Strong's number to identify words in tools using Strong's system. If a Tyndale-Strong's number is followed by capital a letter (e.g., TG1692A), it generally indicates an added subdivision of meaning for the given term. Whenever a Tyndale-Strong's number has a number following a decimal point (e.g., TG2013.1), it reflects an instance where new research has yielded a separate, new classification of use for a biblical word. Forthcoming tools from Tyndale House Publishers will include these entries, which were not part of the original Strong's system.

Job

AUGUST H. KONKEL

INTRODUCTION TO
Job

THE BOOK OF JOB belongs to that category of writings typically termed "wisdom literature." This is not a specific genre designation but is a term of convenience, derived apparently from ecclesiastical usage and used to designate the biblical books of Proverbs, Job, and Ecclesiastes (Murphy 1981:3). Biblical wisdom may be defined as the exposition of a fundamental order within the universe (Crenshaw 1981:66). Wisdom is to know and follow this order, and folly is to contravene and ignore it. Traditional wisdom sought to provide direction for understanding order, but the wisdom writers recognized that the divine order contains mystifying paradoxes. Reflective wisdom addressed realities that appeared to be a contradiction of the traditional understanding of the creative order. The book of Job is a profound reflection on the mysteries of the divine order.

Fundamental to Old Testament revelation is the affirmation that the sovereignty of the Creator is absolute and that his providence for his creation is uncompromisingly beneficent. Traditional Hebrew wisdom asserts that wisdom and knowledge begin with a reverence for the Creator and a loyalty to the covenant that he has given: the fear of the LORD is the beginning of wisdom (Prov 1:7; 9:10). Such knowledge is the means to a good life: "Joyful is the person who finds wisdom, the one who gains understanding. . . . She offers you long life in her right hand, and riches and honor in her left. . . . Wisdom is a tree of life to those who embrace her; happy are those who hold her tightly" (Prov 3:13, 16, 18). The basic premise is that righteousness contains its own reward in the operative providence of God.

The reality of life is that the affirmations of traditional wisdom often contradict the experience of the faithful. Bad things happen to good people; and, conversely, good things often happen to bad people. The book of Job confronts the tension between the idea that virtue has its own reward and the reality that the virtuous often suffer. However, the book of Job does not sever the connection between conduct and consequences. It is not adequate to say that the world is "amoral." Tsevat has argued that there is no realization of moral values except those affected by people, so there is no relation between fate and religio-moral actions (1980:26-33). This amounts to a denial of the sovereign providence of God, so fate operates as a cruel, arbitrary force that may as readily punish good as reward it. Job indeed suffered as an innocent person, but this does not imply that we are to expect nothing from our behavior. The prologue is not meant to teach us that piety, as far as it is possible, is disinterested in personal good. Certainly, it does not insure safety, nor is personal benefit the primary motivation for good conduct; but there are temporal rewards for moral behavior. In the end, the fortunes of Job are restored as a reminder that the author is not oblivious to the consequences of our actions and the truth about a moral universe (Clines 1989:xlvii). Thus, we should conclude that the author was not seeking to undermine all traditional values.

The book of Job does not resolve the rational question of the problem of the innocent suffering.[1] The story of Job suggests that, in human experience, the cause of individual suffering may remain forever a mystery. Readers are privy to the reason for Job's anguish, but Job himself will never learn of the challenge in the courts of heaven that so drastically changed his life. The quest for wisdom does not lead us to explain the order of the universe but to live within it under the sovereign control of God. A large portion of the dialog is an attempt to explain the order of the world in terms of justice and retribution; but in the end this effort is condemned by God. "Job's friends cherished religious conviction more than a vital relationship with the living God, for they believed in a rational deity who was enslaved by a greater principle: justice" (Crenshaw 1981:118).

Job is a solemn reminder that our attempts to defend the order of God may not be honoring to him at all. Although Job is overwhelmed by God to the point that he is brought to silence and submission, God, in the end, takes his side—the side of the man who had challenged the divine rule—and Job must offer sacrifices for his three friends (42:7-8; cf. Barr 1971:46). The profound lesson of the book of Job would seem to be that the fear of the Lord is the beginning of wisdom.

Humans face the problem of suffering on both a rational and an existential level. On a rational level, the problem is one of justice; on an existential level, the question is one of how to respond to inexplicable suffering. The question of why innocent people suffer is intellectual; the practical question is what the innocent should do when suffering comes upon them.[2] In the book of Job we see more than one response. In the prologue Job is reverent and accepting, but in the dialog we find him rejecting his very life (9:21). The fundamental issue is Job's relationship to God. When Job could not bow in submission to the divine "theft" of his property, family, and health, there was still no question but that he must plead his innocence before God and find his hope and life there.

The lament of Job "unfolds a curious situation which bristles with irony" (Crenshaw 1981:109). On the one hand, Job endeavored to escape God's constant vigilance; on the other, he longed to find the God who concealed himself from his former friend. God could not be responsible for such antagonism, but Job knew that such misfortune must be a part of the ruling hand of God. The speeches of God removed Job from the center of the picture and destroyed the illusion that he was at the heart of the universe. Job was not able to determine the order of the universe, nor did he understand his suffering. He was, however, able to meet God as someone other than a hostile enemy and to submit to him as a child of the earth (42:6).

Job, who earlier had rejected his life, saw God and rejected his former attitude (42:5-6). "Seeing God" was not a sensory perception but a personal encounter. The crucible of life experience led to a more profound reverence for God.

The book of Job excels as an example of wisdom literature. The search for wisdom must begin on the path of understanding the fear of the Lord as the beginning of wisdom (Prov 1:7; 9:10). Job began as an individual uncompromising in his integrity and his desire to revere God. No effort may be spared in the search for wisdom (Prov 2:1-4). Job was relentless in his pursuit of God, even in his pain and anguish. The end result of wisdom is not some new rational insight but a more profound comprehension of the fear of the Lord (Prov 2:5-6). Skladny defines the fear of the Lord as the instinctive and intuitive recognition of the total claim of God in religious and moral issues (1961:15). In the end, Job came to terms with this claim in a way that was not possible at the beginning; he was able to speak rightly about God (42:7-8). The theodicy of Job's friends proved to be their liability. Job had no such answers for the moral problem of evil in the world, but he was rewarded for his uncompromising submission to the claim of God upon his life. This is true wisdom.

AUTHOR

As is the case with a large portion of the literature of the Old Testament, the book of Job is anonymous. We know nothing of the identity or the life circumstances of the author, but from his work we do know something about him as a person. The book of Job has its origin among the wise. In ancient Israel, there were three primary means of revelation: law, prophecy, and wisdom. This is observed when those who rejected the prophetic warnings of Jeremiah laid plot against him, assuring themselves that the "law will not fail from the priest, nor counsel from the wise man, nor the word from the prophet" (Jer 18:18, my translation). Similarly, Ezekiel's warning to the rebels of Jerusalem mentions these same three means: "They will look in vain for a vision from the prophet, the law will fail from the priest, and counsel from the wise" (Ezek 7:26, my translation). The author of Job speaks from within the circles of the wise rather than from the ranks of the priests or prophets.

It is often assumed that there was a professional class of wise men in Israel as was the case in Egypt and Mesopotamia. A royal court of wise men responsible for the education of the royal family and other bureaucrats was indispensable to aspiring rulers. They needed to learn proper speech, correct etiquette, interpersonal relationships, and all the skills that enabled them to function as elites. This was less necessary in Israel for at least two reasons: they did not have the complex writing systems of Egypt and Mesopotamia, and the whole specialized technique of reading omens was excluded in Israel (Crenshaw 1981:28). There probably was a class of wise men in Israel, such as the men of Hezekiah who collected proverbs (Prov 25:1). However, in Israel the wise, as a class, were those who stood in opposition to fools. Their instruction had less to do with the finer details of court life and more to do with the ordinary struggles of living a good life. The setting for the vast majority of proverbs and wisdom sayings was the family. The continuity of the wisdom tradition is expressly said to rest within the family (Prov 4:1-5). The purveyors of wisdom did not necessarily have a particular affiliation with a recognized group of scholars. Their inspiration and authority was recognized in the exercise of their craft; the author of a magisterial work like that of Job would be known as one of the wise regardless of any particular social position or function.

There have been various proposals suggesting that the book of Job originated outside of Israel. Humbert argued that the book was of Egyptian origin, based on the extensive development of wisdom literature in Egypt.[3] He notes the detailed and knowledgeable descriptions of the hippopotamus and the crocodile in the God speeches (40:15–41:34) and the reference to ships of papyrus plying the waters (9:26). Though wisdom was highly advanced in Egypt, nothing in that literature begins to approach the profundity and the scope of Job. Another suggestion is that the book of Job was originally Arabic, which would account for its universal spirit and the difficulty of its language.[4] However, the polytheism of the pre-Islamic, Arabic-speaking world could hardly have furnished the background for the spiritual and intellectual concerns which inspired the author of Job. Pfeiffer, who believed that Edomite tradition served as one source for the documents of the Pentateuch, insisted that Job was thoroughly Edomite wisdom.[5] Altogether, these observations of influences outside of Israel merely indicate the inclusive nature of the material in the composition (Fohrer 1989:42-43); the author used all manner of information from Egypt and Mesopotamia, and drew on the full resources of the Hebrew language, which was far more extensive than that preserved in the pages of the Bible.

It can readily be seen that the writers of the wisdom literature of the Bible, as a whole, drew on material from the common cultural environment. For example, the thirty sayings referred to in Proverbs 22:20 are not only modeled on the thirty sayings of the Egyptian work of Amenemope, but there is also an overlap of form and content. It is also true that wisdom made much use of observations from the natural world. This, however, does not make it less theological. Wisdom embodied timeless, universal principles via concrete illustrations from and applications to a particular historical life situation. Religion and faith were present in every experience, for the wise did not divide their world into the sacred and profane. Even the most profane experience was religious, for it was always a part of life within the divine order (Nel 1978:34). Wisdom derived its authority from its theological context within the religious community of Israel. In bringing a wide variety of experiences and information to the text, the author of Job was completely within this Hebrew wisdom tradition.

Another observation that appears to favor authorship from outside of Israel is that Job, the hero, is depicted as living in north Arabia or possibly Edom. Furthermore, in most of the book God is not addressed by his Israelite name, Yahweh. The author made no direct reference to any of the historical traditions of the Hebrew people. But these facts only mean that he succeeded in disguising his own age and background in the portrayal of his hero (Clines 1989:lvii). There is no question that the poet had deep roots in the traditions of Israel and that the universalism of Job is authentically Hebrew. The evidence for the Hebrew background of the author is all the more impressive because it is incidental and unconscious (Gordis 1965:214). The national name for God appears at Job 12:9, betraying a reminiscence of a familiar passage in Isaiah 41:20: "it is the LORD [Yahweh] who has done this." In describing a hippopotamus lying placidly in the stream, the proper name Jordan is parallel to the generic reference to a river: "It is not disturbed by the raging river, not concerned when the swelling Jordan rushes around it" (40:23).

Though the search for allusions to other biblical literature can become too speculative, it seems that the poet was familiar with other passages of the Hebrew Scriptures. For example, the touching lament of Job in 7:17-18 is even more moving when it is recognized as a conscious parody of the triumphant declaration of the glory of humankind expressed in Psalm 8:4-5. The psalmist could say, "What are people that you should think about them, mere mortals that you should care for them? Yet you made them only a little lower than God and crowned them with glory and honor." Job can only lament, "What are people, that you should make so much of us, that you should think of us so often? For you examine us every morning and test us every moment." Eliphaz mocked Job's claim to wisdom (15:7-8): "Were you the first person ever born? Were you born before the hills were made?" In the book of Proverbs, Wisdom boasts of being the first and most beloved of God's works: "The LORD formed me from the beginning . . . Before the mountains were formed, before the hills, I was born" (Prov 8:22, 25).

The ethical code of Job's confession of integrity (ch 31) is a statement of the ideals of justice, equality, reverence, and consideration for the weak enjoined in the law and the prophets. The three basic violations of murder, theft, and adultery are mentioned in 24:14-16 just as in the covenant stipulations (Exod 20:13-15). Though the author of Job drew on a vast array of experience and education, his fundamental view of life was shaped by the Hebrew precept that "the fear of the LORD is the foundation of wisdom."

Though we do not know of an official guild of the wise, their education and experience certainly set them apart from more ordinary folk. As Andersen aptly expresses it, a book like Job "was not written in a vacuum. Only God creates out of nothing. His creatures use the materials he gives them, and the work of the mind is done with what flows into a man's life from his own experience and from the culture of his people" (1976:23). The author of Job appears to have had firsthand experience of such foreign countries as Egypt and of such varied areas as the desert, the mountains, and the sea. Such opportunities for travel were most likely limited to the members of the upper classes. The writing also reveals the author's high degree of familiarity with the arts and sciences of his time. He created vivid images of wild beasts, birds, and sea monsters (38:39-41:34). He was familiar with sea and clouds, snow and hail, rain and ice (38:16-30); and he could talk about the constellations (38:31-33). He knew about the science of mining (28:6-11) and was familiar with the craft of the hunter, referring to six different types of traps (18:8-10). Not only must the author have been an individual of some means, he must have had a keen mind of diverse interests—gaining knowledge from reading and discussion as well as from travel.

It is not surprising that the author of Job should have chosen an upper-class figure as his hero, since this was probably the life that he himself understood best. Perhaps it was those who had experienced some of the best of life who could reflect more philosophically on the suffering of the less fortunate. Job demonstrates that there were those among the wise who were not satisfied with the conventional wisdom of collective retribution and the general operation of justice. In order to depict the tragedy of human suffering, the author of Job posed the problem in a way that he might experience it—or perhaps even did experience it. He selected an individual of great prosperity who was hurled to the lowest depths of misfortune rather than one who suffered a lifetime of poverty, misery, and rejection. From this vantage point he was able to contemplate the meaning of righteousness and justice in relation to people and God.

DATE AND OCCASION OF WRITING

There are no historical allusions in the book that indicate the times or circumstances of the author, so even from ancient times there has been a great disparity in suggestions for the time and occasion of writing. Rabbinic opinion ranged from the era of the patriarchs down to the Persian period. The Babylonian Talmud records an opinion to the effect that Job lived in the time of Abraham and that he was married to the daughter of Jacob (*b. Bava Batra* 15b). Another tradition of the Talmud connects Job with Jethro and Balaam, who were consulted by Pharaoh on the question of the genocide of the Israelites. This tradition says that Job was punished because he failed to protest this crime (*b. Sanhedrin* 106a; *b. Sotah* 11a). The Tannaitic rabbis Johanan and Eleazar supposed that Job was one of those who returned from the Babylonian captivity (*b. Bava Batra* 15a). In another tradition, the Greek appendix to the book of Job identifies the man Job with Jobab the king of Edom, grandson of Esau (Gen 36:33). The early datings no doubt reflect the patriarchal setting of the book's hero, which is presented in authentic detail and coloring. However, this is not necessarily the life circumstance of the author, who made use of this story just as he did the other ancient material with which he was familiar.

The earliest reference to the person Job outside the book is found in Ezekiel 14:14, 20. Ezekiel singles out three paragons of virtue whose righteousness could save none but themselves in such a corrupt land: Noah, Daniel, and Job. It is not certain, however, that the references to these three individuals are based on the biblical narratives as we know them, for Ezekiel may have had traditions that were different from what we know of these three in the present biblical accounts. This would seem to be necessarily true in the case of Daniel, since the prophetic writing of Ezekiel precedes that of the biblical book of Daniel.[6] Noth attempted to show that all three individuals used as examples of righteousness by Ezekiel were ancient figures known outside of Israel who were deliberately chosen by the prophet as non-Israelites to prove the universal execution of divine recompense (1951:253-

259). Noth allows that Ezekiel could have had in mind the approximate content of the biblical accounts of Job and Noah as we know them. Whether or not Noth's hypothesis is right, it would seem that the author of Job used a familiar story about an ancient hero, the type of figure that would correspond to Noah, as his main character. In the composition, Job is simply introduced as an individual of the ancient past from outside of Israel without specific chronological reference: "There was once a man named Job who lived in the land of Uz" (1:1).

An indication of the date of Job could be found in its literary features—that is, if sufficient distinctives could be found to point to a particular period. Orthography—corroborated by other features of poetic style, mythological allusions, vocabulary, and syntax—led Freedman to propose that Job was composed among the Diaspora of northern Israel in the seventh or early sixth century BC. A more drastic date was proposed by David Robertson in his doctoral thesis,[7] in which, on the basis of relative dates of Hebrew poetry, he argued for a date about the time of Solomon or earlier, in the tenth or eleventh century BC. In contrast, a study by Hurvitz (1974) comparing postexilic Hebrew with the frame story led him to require an exilic or postexilic date. None of the evidence is sufficiently consistent to provide any helpful parameters for dating.

Attempts have also been made to date Job on the basis of allusions to other portions of Scripture. Many of these can be found, and at times the resemblance is sufficient to indicate a direct literary dependency.[8] As suggested earlier, Job 7:17 is certainly later than Psalm 8:4, which it parodies (Driver and Gray 1921:lxvii). There are, however, two problems with such allusions: (1) it is often difficult to decide in which direction the dependence lies, and (2) there is often no agreement on the dates of the passages compared. Williams (1985:22-23) lists a number of authors, beginning with T. K. Cheyne (1882), who have adopted the view that Isaiah 40–55 is later than Job, some even suggesting Isaiah was attempting to respond to Job's questions. Gordis, however, argues that the author of Job used Isaiah and extended the idea that suffering is not a sign of sin from the circumstance of the nation to that of the individual (1965:216). Wolfers states his case adamantly: "The dependence of the book of Job on Deuteronomy is crucial, not only to the comprehension of the book, but to its dating. It is scarcely going too far to describe the book of Job as an elaborate midrash on Deuteronomy 28. . . . It is, however, almost beyond comprehension that innumerable commentaries on Job have been written, and almost all without even passing reference to the many close resemblances, amounting again and again to direct quotation" (1995:53). Wolfers interprets Job as an allegory of the Assyrian defeat of Israel in 701 BC, and therefore dates it to the seventh century BC. These observations are all complementary to each other to the extent that they demonstrate that the author of Job is thoroughly Hebrew, quite obviously steeped in his own literature, and consciously writing as a part of it. He could deliberately write with archaisms and in the partially epic style of the prologue and epilogue, or he could incorporate foreign material and write with the sophistication and skill of the best of Hebrew poets as in the majority of the book. We must conclude that the author of Job was able to conceal his time and circumstances in the style of his writing just as readily as he did in his use of the frame story, so the very expression of his profound ideas has become all the more timeless.

The book of Job has often been thought to have been composed in the fifth century (c. 450 BC) on the basis of developments within Old Testament literature. John Gray (1974:333) follows Dhorme (1984:clxviii) in relating the composition of Job to the scandal caused by the prosperity of the ungodly. The prophet Malachi in particular referred to blasphemous words that deny any concern of God for justice in human affairs (Mal 2:17; 3:13-15). Dhorme suggests that the sincere insistence on the good fortune of the wicked in Job (e.g., 21:7-33) caused false conclusions to be drawn even by the pious, causing alarm to prophets such as Malachi. Gray further suggests that Job is a censure on the inflexible doctrine of sin and retribution, virtue and reward, as found in Chronicles. The book of Chronicles portrays each of the kings of Judah in terms of immediate reward and punishment, often in considerable contrast with the author's primary source, the book of Kings.[9] These evidences face the same difficulties already noted in connection with verbal allusions regarding the priority and dependence of such relationships. It is quite possible that Chronicles, in part, responds to the skepticism of wisdom writers regarding the justice of God. The retribution of Chronicles certainly continues as a predominant doctrine.

Gordis (1965:216) dates the book of Job in the fifth century on the basis of an assumed monotheism in Job, which he believes was not yet evident in exilic times. For example, Isaiah 40–55 has repeated diatribes against idolatry (e.g., Isa 44:12-20), as Isaiah describes Israel at the time of the rise of Cyrus the Persian (cf. Isa 45:1-3). This demonstrates a general pluralism in Israel's societal assumptions as opposed to a purely monotheistic view.

Further evidence for this date, also referred to by Dhorme (1984:clxvii), is the development of the Hebrew word *satan* [TH7854/7854A, ZH8477]. This term has the simple meaning of "adversary" and is used to describe the messenger of the Lord against Balaam (Num 22:22, 32), David when he is among the Philistines (1 Sam 29:4), and Rezon the enemy of Solomon (1 Kgs 11:25). In later references, *satan* comes to have the specific meaning of a particular instigator of evil, such as the accuser of Joshua the high priest (Zech 3:1-2). The references in Zechariah, like those in the prologue of Job (1:6-9, 12), occur with the article (*hasatan*) indicating a recognized or well-known adversary. However, this adversary is not an independent figure but simply one of the members of the divine council. When David numbered the people in Chronicles, *satan* seems to appear as a proper name without the article (1 Chr 21:1), in reference to a well-known individual (cf. 2 Sam 24:1, where it is the Lord who incites David). By the time Wisdom of Solomon was written (c. 100 BC), Satan is pictured as a fallen angel through whom death entered the world (Wis 2:24). In Job *hasatan* (the Accuser) has neither a proper name nor a cosmic function; in Chronicles he appears to have a proper name, which would place Job's date before Chronicles in the first half of the Persian period (538–323 BC).

The unity of the book, its eloquent poetry, and its profound reflections suggest that it is the product of one mind steeped in a rich literary and theological heritage. On rare occasions, the author's resources are revealed, as in the case of his use of Isaiah 41:20 in Job 12:9 (cf. the Heb. of these passages). Job appears to have been composed after Isaiah's prophecy concerning the time of Cyrus and before Chronicles, which places its date in the exilic or early postexilic period, sometime between the sixth and fourth centuries. Much of the terminology is compatible with this period, such as the reference to kings, prime ministers, and princes (3:14-15), though the book does not show a strong Aramaic influence (Fohrer 1989:42). Wisdom came to be an important application of the divine instruction, as seen in Psalm 1, and certainly came to be predominant in the postexilic period, as demonstrated by the deuterocanonical books Wisdom of Solomon and Wisdom of Jesus Son of Sirach (Ecclesiasticus).[10] It is likely that the magisterial work of Job was composed early in the process of such application of divine revelation and served as an inspiration to the movement.

AUDIENCE

Consistent with wisdom thinking, the book of Job was intended for all people of all times, as expressed in the call of wisdom: "Listen to this, all you people! Pay attention, everyone in the world! High and low, rich and poor—listen! For my words are wise, and my thoughts are filled with insight" (Ps 49:1-3). In his selection of an ancient non-Israelite hero, his deliberate avoidance of the usual Israelite names for God, and his lack of allusion to any known historical events, the author has created a universal and timeless perspective. The book does not address a particular historical situation or even a theological issue relevant only to a specific time.

As expressed by Gordis (1965:7), the literary greatness of Job is only one element—and perhaps a less important element—of the universal appeal of this book. The enduring significance of Job lies in its theme and in the way that theme is addressed. The mystery of evil is perhaps the most agonizing issue confronting people of faith; it has been a stumbling block through the centuries. The author of Job was an open-minded genius with all-embracing sympathies; he was able to give fair and eloquent expression to the accepted religious doctrines of his day but was also able to challenge the adequacy of those views. He did not answer the problem of how a good God could allow evil to exist in the world; but he did present the truth of God and the world in a manner that not only stimulates pondering of the ancient puzzle but also brings comfort to all those in the throes of pain.

It must, however, be said that there is a specific audience of interest to the poet—namely, those who can appreciate profound philosophical questions cast in cryptic poetic lines and enigmatic imagery. One might compare it to a more contemporary English masterpiece such as Milton's *Paradise Lost*. Those who read it generally do so in an edited version with explanatory notes. No matter how intensely it is studied, there is more to be learned. Translations of Job necessarily simplify the enigmas of its poetic expression. This is as it should be, and the author of Job would not be disappointed to have his masterpiece in a simplified form that all should read. He would be disappointed, however, if his readers failed to do more than just expose themselves to a simplified translation. Those who wish to fully appreciate the magnificent book of Job must spare no intellectual effort; their effort will be rewarded, not only by the impact of the power of its expression but also with a fuller understanding of the mind of its inspired author.

CANONICITY AND TEXTUAL HISTORY

The book of Job has been well preserved in the Masoretic Text of the Hebrew Bible. The form of the Masoretic Text was determined in the Middle Ages and included establishing both the letters and the vocalization of the text, which determined words and meanings. The earliest complete manuscript, which serves as the base for interpretation, is Codex Leningrad B19A, which is dated to AD 1009 (Tov 1992:47). The actual manuscript variations of the Masoretic Text in Job are very few, including the variants preserved by indicating a different word by an alternate pronunciation (technically called Kethiv-Qere). However, the Hebrew of the text of Job is at times difficult, and it is impossible to know for certain if certain problems are the result of textual corruption or simply modern ignorance of the Hebrew. According to Jenni and Westermann, the book of Job has 170 words that occur only once in the Hebrew Bible (technically called *hapax legomena*) out of a total of 8,343 words in the book[11]; that is one out of every 49 words. Only Song of Songs has a higher proportion of rare words; it has 43 hapax legomena out of a total of 1,250 words, or one out of every 29 words in the book. The average for the Old Testament is one hapax legomena for every 185 words.

Difficulties in understanding the Hebrew text lead most commentators to propose changes to the Masoretic Text, assuming either the corruption of some letters or larger problems such as missing lines, misplaced lines, explanatory glosses, and expansions (e.g., Fohrer 1989:55, who provides a tabulation of his own conclusions). In most such instances no consensus is possible, so such proposals must be tentatively adopted or rejected. It is usually best to try to understand the Masoretic Text as it is, a method adopted resolutely by Wolfers (1995:44-46), who has yielded surprisingly creative and positive results in numerous instances, as shall be noted in the commentary.

The earliest evidence of the Hebrew text of Job comes from Qumran. Three copies of Job have been found at Qumran written in the traditional Hebrew square script, and one written in the old Hebrew script (Tov 1992:105). The old Hebrew script is found in the fragments of 11-14 biblical scrolls, all of them from either the Torah or Job. Analysis of this script indicates that these manuscripts were not the oldest at Qumran, but they do reflect ancient traditions since they were no doubt copied from manuscripts written in the old Hebrew script (Tov 1992:106).

The Masoretic manuscripts of Job we possess derive from a tight group of texts at Qumran known as the proto-Masoretic texts. The proto-Masoretic texts are unvocalized, but their consonantal framework is more or less identical with that of the medieval manuscripts, though the earlier scrolls have more deviances than the later ones (Tov 1992:27). Almost all the texts in the old Hebrew script are of the proto-Masoretic type, indicating the early origins of this text; the antiquity of this tradition is also indicated by the use of scribal dots as word dividers in the old Hebrew texts of Qumran. The origin of the proto-Masoretic texts is unknown; and though there was always a concern for conformity, there never was a single text to represent the group. Because these texts already differed from each other in very early times, the wish to preserve a unified textual tradition was an abstract ideal that, in reality, could not be accomplished.

It must further be remembered that though the proto-Masoretic text was preferred by a central stream in Judaism, it was not always the best text (Tov 1992:24). Other texts like the Hebrew parent of the Greek translation, or other text types at Qumran, often offer a better reading than the Masoretic. For this reason, all textual evidence must be taken into consideration in reading the book of Job.

The Greek text of Job is a particularly unusual phenomenon. The oldest translation into Greek, dating from the first century BC, frequently omits lines or verses, and even passages of six or seven verses in length (e.g., 21:28-33; 26:5-11; 28:14-19, etc.). Later revisions of the Greek, particularly that of Theodotion, were used by Origen to supplement the much shorter original text and basically replaced it. However, at least five manuscripts preserve Origen's markings of the additions, so the original Greek is substantially known. The original Greek translation has only about five-sixths of the volume of the Masoretic Text. The abbreviations are not evenly distributed, increasing from the prologue to the epilogue (Dhorme 1984:ccii-cciii): the Greek translation is 4% briefer up to chapter 15; 16% in chapters 15–21; 25% in chapters 22–31; 35% in the speeches of Elihu (chs 32–37); and 16% in the speeches of God and the epilogue (chs 38–42). As the text was shortened, it was done with a sensitivity for continuity—in the end being a work of artistic deliberation.

While the Greek translation of Job is substantially shorter, it often reads like a paraphrase or even a virtual commentary in its choice of words and rendering of some grammatical constructions (Orlinsky 1958:229-271). In many instances, a vague or purely Hebrew idiom was turned into clear idiomatic Greek, and at times the Greek appears to be an excellent dynamic equivalent rendering. In addition to the idiomatic and at times highly interpretive nature of the Greek translation, there were deliberate midrashic expansions. In the prologue the righteousness of Job is enhanced by making him a careful observer of the law, and an addition to the speech of Job's wife (at 2:9) heightens the religiosity of her husband. In the epilogue, a substantial addition (following 42:17) historicizes Job so he is no longer a shadowy legendary individual. He is made to be a fifth generation descendant of Abraham and a king of Edom. The epilogue also makes Eliphaz a son of Esau and a king of the Temanites. Further, righteous Job is said to be waiting for the resurrection—a view consistent with some Hellenistic Jewish expectations. The result is that the original Greek translation of Job is quite a different book and stands in its own social and theological world.

In spite of the distinct and idiomatic nature of the Greek version of Job, its importance for understanding the Masoretic Text of Job should not be underestimated. The translation of Job was made from a Hebrew text substantially similar to the Masoretic Text, and often the differences in the Greek are because of corruptions in its own transmission; once the original Greek is restored we often find it translates the Hebrew text we possess in the Masoretic tradition (Orlinsky 1962:125-151 provides numerous examples). At the same time, it is clear the Hebrew *Vorlage* (or exemplar) of the Greek translator was different from the Hebrew text we know, thereby giving us a different textual tradition, which antedates the Masoretic tradition. This simply confirms the phenomena already observed about the plurality of Hebrew text types at Qumran. Though it is not possible to know what relationship may have existed between these texts, or even how they came about, in many instances the Hebrew behind the Greek is preferable to that of the Masoretic Text (Orlinsky 1962:58-78 evaluates numerous examples).

It is possible that prior to the Greek translation of Job there was an Aramaic version. A substantial fragment of an Aramaic Targum of Job has been found among the scrolls of cave 11 at Qumran, officially published by Van der Ploeg and Van der Woude (1971). The fragment consists of portions of 17:14–42:11, but it is only from 37:10–42:11 that the text is reasonably continuous. This includes God's speeches and the epilogue—in many ways the critical part of Job. The script of the Targum is the type known as Herodian, a very precise kind of writing that began around 50 BC. The grammar and orthography of the Targum is close to that known as imperial Aramaic, the type that is found in Daniel. This is older than the Aramaic of another Qumran work known as the *Genesis Apocryphon*, which is dated to the first century BC. The editors suggest that the origin of this Targum may be as early as the last half of the second century BC (Van der Ploeg and Van der Woude 1971:3-4). This unquestionably pre-Christian Targum is a literal translation of the Hebrew, though it does have a few added phrases or periphrastic renderings. The variances from the Masoretic Text are usually at those places where the Hebrew was suspect, scarcely intelligible, or where other versions also differed (Gray 1974:344-350 provides a number of examples). The Targum confirms the structure of the Hebrew text, including the controversial third section of the dialog, which is often thought to be in disarray. Verses and parts of verses that are missing are indicative of a different recensional activity.[12]

The canonicity of Job, attested by both the Greek and Aramaic versions, was never questioned in Jewish tradition. Perhaps the reason for this is that the disturbing ideas of the debate were couched in difficult poetry that would not readily offend the average reader. Job is singled out for mention in the Wisdom of Ben Sirach (Ecclesiasticus) in his praise of famous men. The Greek translation of Sirach 49:9 is not clear (cf. RSV), but the Hebrew text found in the Cairo synagogue evidently refers to Job in connection with Ezekiel (cf. NRSV). This reference to Job (c. 190 BC) is almost certainly derived from the biblical composition and sets the limit for the latest date of the composition (Fohrer 1989:42). It is probable, however, that the composition was considerably earlier and may have already been considered as canonical by this time. The reference to wisdom in Sirach 39:1 in the context of the law and the prophecies would seem to include wisdom writings as having an equal authority with the others.

Orlinsky has provided a strong defense for the idea that the concept of canon is evident in the prologue to Sirach (1991:483-490). In this prologue, the grandson of Ben Sirach refers to the law, the prophets, and those that followed them. Those that followed them in many translations are given as other writers or authors, but it is clear that the grandson is designating books or writings. The text of the prologue is describing the material that had been mastered by the author of the book; it then compares the law, the prophets, and the others with the work produced by the author. Further, David, as author of the Psalms (Sir 47:8-10), or Solomon, as author of Proverbs (Sir 47:14-17), cannot be thought to succeed the prophets as individuals. The prologue is explicit: "the Law itself, the Prophecies, and the rest of the books" (NRSV) are the works that were translated. Within the composition of Sirach, the law and the prophets are handled as collections indicating canonical divisions and should be capitalized (as in the NRSV). The other writings then must refer to a third division of books considered canonical, as we find in later references (e.g., Lk 24:44). The mention of Job within Sirach and the affirmation of canonical books outside the collections of the law and the prophets indicate the canonical status of the composition of Job at this early period.

The linking of wisdom to the earlier authoritative writings in this manner had a double effect. If wisdom was grounded in the canonical tradition, it could retain a religious significance comparable to the earlier traditions such as the Torah (law). Conversely, the use of the Torah in this manner validated its claim to continued and pervasive authority as it informed the concerns of wisdom. The affinity of the poetry of Job with other canonical Hebrew literature was a way of extending the teaching of the received Scriptures and a means of validating the book of Job as Scripture.

LITERARY STYLE

The book of Job has rightly been compared with the greatest of literary works, such as Dante's *Divine Comedy* or Goethe's *Faust*.[13] As with great literature of this type, there is no adequate genre classification, for all the usual conventions are transformed and transcended to meet particular artistic goals. In Job, language has been extended to the very limits of its capabilities in the unusual use of vocabulary; the use of allusion, imagery, and analogy; and the use of rhetoric, cryptic references, and figures of speech. One feature used a great deal in the book is lament and the element of complaint. Usually lament involves the complaintant, God, and the enemy; in Job there is no third party, for God himself is the enemy and the object of complaint from Job's limited perspective. Another literary feature used extensively is the legal metaphor—the book is a type of disputation. A wide variety of technical forensic terms are employed by the author at strategic points. Habel provides a structure for the entire composition with the major components of a lawsuit

(1985:54) but freely admits Job may not be thought of as a "lawsuit drama." The lawsuit is one of the common forms used in the prophets (e.g., Isa 1:2-20; Mic 6:1-8), but the book of Job is a radical adaptation of the metaphor. In the prophets, God takes his people to trial for violation of the covenant; in Job it is God who is the defendant called to trial. Job speaks eloquently of the power of God, but his paean of praise stresses the negative and destructive aspects of God's might (chs 9–10) and becomes a searing attack upon God's irresponsible and unjust power. This masterful adaptation and integration of known literary forms is creativity at its best, a work of art truly *sui generis.*

The challenging language of Job has led some to the radical proposal that it must have become confused in a process of translation. The medieval exegete Abraham ibn Ezra in his famous commentary on Job said "It seems probable to me that it is a translated book and that this is why, like all translated books, it is difficult to interpret" (II, 12, cited in Torczyner 1967:111). After a lifetime of struggling with the problems of Job, Torczyner produced a vast number of new and unusual meanings for words, which he provided in his introduction (1967:viii-xxx) to serve as the basis for his extensive commentary. (The English translation of 1967 is somewhat revised from the earlier Hebrew edition.) Torczyner's detailed lexical and exegetical analysis led to an interpretation based on the assumption that the book was translated from Aramaic and that frequently the translator erred, so the original meaning could only be derived by reconstructing the original. Most of his examples, however, have proven to be unconvincing. Further, the notion involves a number of unlikely assumptions, including the complete loss of a canonical document in its original language and the adoption of a somewhat incompetent translation in its place. Aramaic is a language closely related to the Hebrew; they are both northwest Semitic languages. There are a number of reasons for the apparent Aramaic influence in Job: many words are the same because they emerged from a common language; words were borrowed in preexilic and postexilic times; idioms and forms were introduced into Hebrew by speakers familiar with both languages. No doubt the author was very familiar with Aramaic.

The book of Job consists of a very abbreviated narrative of Job's story, contained in a prologue (1:1–2:13) and epilogue (42:11-17), which serves as the basis for a lengthy poetic disputation. Many literary affinities make it clear that in the Masoretic text of Job the prologue and epilogue belong together. Job is the servant of God, he offers sacrifices to assuage God's anger, and his material possessions are restored in multiple proportions of what he originally had. There is much exact repetition of unusual vocabulary, such as the expressions for consolation in 2:11 and 42:11. Though the prologue and epilogue are often described as prose, they have many poetic features: assonance and alliteration, parallelism, poetic words, phrases, and unique expressions (examples are given by Sarna 1957:15-18). The story is given in the repetitious style of the epic, the type of composition usually done for a live audience. The commentary will develop the symmetrical scheme of the repetition found in descriptions of the celestial council (1:6-12; 2:1-7), the character of Job (1:1, 8,

22; 2:3), and the misfortunes of Job (1:13-19). These are further examples of the "epic law of iteration."

Good poetry has the ability to transport the reader into other worlds through its power to evoke images, ideas, and moods beyond its explicit content. Figures of speech are the very essence of the pattern. The poetry in Job is a wealth of metaphors, with power to move the reader into the very minds of the characters. At the same time, all analogy leaves a certain ambiguity so that the reader must supply the implications. Job declares that he is the innocent victim and that God pursues him like a lion so that he can demonstrate his prowess as a hunter (10:16). The ear tests arguments as the palate tastes food (12:11). The cloud represents the ephemeral nature of mortals (7:9) and the mysteries of the heavens (37:15-16). The poet extends his analogies to those drawn from the mythological domain. Job summoned Leviathan as the ancient primordial destroyer to negate his birth (3:8); God challenged Job to subdue the fire-breathing crocodile portrayed in the manner of Leviathan (41:1-34) as God himself had destroyed the sea monster at the creation of the world (26:10-12). But perhaps the most important analogy comes on a comprehensive scale. The speeches of God reveal a universe with beauty and order, though full of danger. The universe is full of mysteries incomprehensible to the human mind. In application to the question of justice, which is at the heart of the poem, it is reasonable to believe there is also a moral order, but it is not predictable and is often incomprehensible to finite humans.

Finally, we must note that the book of Job is filled with aphorisms. Williams has appropriately described aphoristic discourse as a tension of literary and conceptual elements (Williams 1981:86); it is both poetic and philosophical. On the philosophical side, wisdom is concerned with order. The breakdown of order results in a disorientation, which requires an intuition or a vision of a counterorder, a dimension of reality that goes beyond the traditional. The literary form is a means of reaffirming the received tradition or challenging it but always in a manner that presents wisdom as an authority that transcends the immediate experience of the individual. This reflective poetic expression is a response to the deeply felt tension of order and disorder. It is intended to illumine by bringing particular experience into cognitive contact with general truth; it is an aesthetic movement between representing truth and paradoxical questioning. The literary style of Job can best be described as a twofold linguistic organization: literary and conceptual, poetic and philosophical.

MAJOR THEMES

Readers of every level of sophistication have found the primary theme of the book of Job to be the problem of suffering—or, stated more comprehensively, it is about the mystery of evil. In the book of Job the problem of evil is presented in terms of justice, which is to say that if something is considered to be unjust, it is regarded as evil. Justice and goodness are the products of God's sovereign rule; they are manifest in his provision for his people. According to the prologue, God took away the wall of protection he had placed around Job (1:10-12). Consequently, Job experienced calamity from what we call natural disaster (lightning and storm) and human maliciousness (plunder and murder). The problem of the mystery of evil is herein explicitly set out in terms of the relationship between God and humans.

Since the book of Job does not resolve the question of the justice of God, it has been assumed that God is not just (Tsevat 1980) or that the real theme of the book is not about the problem of suffering. Steinmann (1996:98-99) suggests that the actual theme of Job is the struggle to maintain integrity of faith in time of suffering. Steinmann proposes a restructuring of the book of Job in which the poem about wisdom (ch 28 in Job's final speech) serves as a transition to Job finding his way back to faith. The speeches of Elihu and God lead Job back to simple faith and make it clear that questions of theodicy are irrelevant for human beings. Inasmuch as the book of Job is fundamentally about the relationship between God and humans, it involves questions of faith and integrity. In the end, the resolution for Job is indeed to submit himself in faith to the order of God's world (42:6).

The book, however, cannot be reduced to this one aspect of God's relationship with humans. Having set out the question of justice in the divine order, it becomes the central point of the debates that form the largest portion of the book. These great debates, though certainly somewhat repetitious, cannot be marginalized as being nothing more than a foil for the theme of faith. Whether or not there is an answer to the question of justice in the divine order, it certainly is the theme we are meant to ponder as we struggle with the mystery of evil. The question of theodicy or the justice of God is not only relevant, it is inevitable. If the problem of evil could be resolved through reason, there would be no need for faith. Though our response to the mystery of evil can only be one of faith, either in God or in denying God, faith cannot be isolated from the function of reason.

The dialog appears to revolve around a specific question that occurs four times in slightly different forms and highlights the question of God's justice. It is first seen in the initial address of Eliphaz: "Can a mortal be innocent before God? Can anyone be pure before the Creator?" (4:17). Job himself asks the question when pondering who could challenge God (9:2). Then this question is repeated in Eliphaz's second speech (15:14) and finally in the last speech of Bildad (25:4). Whatever the precise meaning of the question and the argument that follows in each instance, it strikes at the heart of the relationship between an absolutely sovereign God and finite, mortal humans and advances a view different from that of the traditional wisdom of its day. It is the question of justice and the problem of evil, and its repetition indicates its significance. It is critical to determine the identity of the person asking this question and the premise on which it is based in order to understand how it expresses the major theme of the book.

Although the dialog formally indicates that Eliphaz and, later, Bildad are the main speakers when this question occurs, it is important to note that within the speeches one speaker may quote another in order to respond to an argument or bring a word of wisdom to his own argument. Also, the question is first posed as the content of a revelatory vision. Who is it that lays claim to such a revelation? Who is arguing for the validity of that revelation? At times, the dialog within a speech has formal indications of quotation, but at other times these do not suit the development of the poetry, so the recognition of quoted material is much more subtle. Formal indicators of quotation do not necessarily require an actual verb of speaking or thinking. There may simply be the presence of another subject, the presence of a verb that implies speech, or the expression of another's point of view indicated by a change in person (Fox 1980:422).

It seems likely, then, that after speaking about Job's words in 15:12-13 ("What has taken away your reason? What has weakened your vision, that you turn against God and say all these evil things?"), Eliphaz quotes Job's words in verse 14: "Can any mortal be pure? Can anyone born of a woman be just?" After summing up Job's argument, Eliphaz reasserts his own argument (15:17-18): "If you will listen, I will show you. I will answer you from my own experience. And it is confirmed by the reports of wise men who have heard the same thing from their fathers." It is clear here that Eliphaz was responding to something Job himself had said.

This analysis of the second speech of Eliphaz helps to clarify the introduction of the question in the vision of the first speech (4:12-21). This terrifying vision is introduced abruptly after the imagery of the lions, which appear to illustrate the fate of the wicked. Following the recapitulation of the vision, Eliphaz directly addressed Job with a question about the source of his knowledge (5:1): "Cry out, but is there one to answer you? To whom rather than the Holy One would you turn?"[14] Again Eliphaz appears to attribute the preceding revelation to Job. If the translation above is followed, Eliphaz is insinuating that the source of the vision must be other than God, even though Job apparently claimed it to be divine in origin. This stands in contrast to his own knowledge, which was derived from traditional wisdom and which Eliphaz emphasized did come from God (5:8): "As for me, I would seek after God, and to God entrust my cause."[15] It seems from his insinuations that Eliphaz knew of a vision, purported to be divine in origin, which he vigorously contested (the Heb. adversative 'ulam [TH199, ZH219] in 5:8 is very forceful; cf. 2:5). Job must be the source of this vision since he is addressed immediately following it. If the vision belonged to Job, as proposed, it answers two problematic questions about the response of Eliphaz in the above translation of 5:1, 8 (Smith 1990:454-455): (1) why would he think Job wished to appeal to another source of revelation (5:1), and (2) why would he condemn such a source of revelation—pointing Job to God, in contrast (5:8)—if he had just received such a vision? The formal markers of quotation that follow the vision (Eliphaz's use of the imperative and his emphatic contrasts between "you" and "I" in 5:1, 8) actually serve to indicate that the question of whether humans can be righteous before God belongs to Job, not Eliphaz.

Similarly, Eliphaz challenged the authority of Job's source of knowledge in contrast to that of traditional wisdom in 15:7-10: "Were you the first person ever born? Were you born before the hills were made? Were you listening at God's secret council? Do you have a monopoly on wisdom? What do you know that we don't? What do you understand that we do not? On our side are aged, gray-haired men much older than your father!" Eliphaz disputed Job's claim to knowledge that was derived from some sort of revelation within the council of God. Ginsberg has cogently demonstrated that at issue in the dialog is a conflict over the source of authority (1969:95-107). Thus, it would appear that the author of Job, in addressing his main theme, was challenging the simplicity of retribution in traditional wisdom through the claim of an alternate revelation also given to the wise and expressed through Job's question, "Can any mortal be pure?"

The final occurrence of the question appears to be truncated (25:4-6). It may be that Bildad was deliberately interrupted right at the point where he would have repeated the traditional response to the question; in his rebuttal, Job asks sarcastically whose help Bildad had in uttering his words (26:4a). It was clear Bildad had no original ideas whatever in relation to the problem. It has often been argued that the third cycle of the debate must be in disarray at this point, as there is a very extended speech by Job and no further word from Zophar. This may, however, have been a very deliberate technique on the part of the author. The interruption of the speech in traditional order brings an end to those arguments and shows their failure. Leaving the question as the basic content of the last speech on traditional wisdom may be another way the author focuses on the main theme of his treatise.

The author also implies that Job had received a divine revelation previously and made it known to his friends in Job's first response to Eliphaz. That response began with a longing for release from the arrows of the Almighty with one assurance: "I have not [concealed] the words of the Holy One" (6:10c). As in 5:1, it is not clear whether God was directly the source of this knowledge or whether it was simply from the heavenly realm; but it does seem clear that Job had received some sort of revelation. Smith (1990:456) suggests that 6:26 is a further reference to the words of the Spirit of the vision (4:15). It is probable that 6:25-26 is a chiasm that contrasts the revelation with the knowledge of the friends: "How painful are the words of truth. But how does your reproof correct? Do you think that mere words convince? The words of the despairing one are of the Spirit" (so Smith 1990:456). Job speaks true words; his despair stems from a revelation that came by the Spirit and with the sensation of a wind sweeping by his face (4:15). Job complained that God terrified him with visions and shattered him with dreams (7:14). Job's first reply to Bildad began with the question of the vision: "How can a person be declared innocent in God's sight?" (9:2b). And later in the chapter, Job uses the words that described the vision in a complaint about his inability to confront God: "When he comes near, I cannot see him. When he moves by, I do not see him go." (9:11; cf. 4:15-16). By presenting the truth of the vision through the person of the suffering hero in a somewhat oblique manner, the author of Job was able to challenge traditional order without controverting it directly. Furthermore, the author presented an alternative counterorder with the authority of divine revelation.

If this revelation is an argument of counterorder, just what is the premise of that order? An explanation follows the question of 4:17 in the form of a rhetorical argument from the greater to the lesser (*a maiore ad minus*): "If God does not trust his own angels and has charged his messengers with foolishness, how much less will he trust people made of clay! They are made of dust, crushed as easily as a moth" (4:18-19). It is often assumed that these lines are an assertion of the depravity of all mankind, so none can hope to escape suffering—in the words of Ginsberg, "Your righteousness is no guarantee against total ruin, because God recognizes no such category as righteous men" (1969:107). Job certainly never made the claim to be sinless, but he denied that his sin was the cause of his suffering. Job asked why God would not simply forgive his sin (7:20-21) or why God must ordain him to bitterness and make him inherit the sins of his youth (13:26). Job knew that purity cannot come from impurity (14:4); he only wished that God would not maintain constant vigilance for his sins (14:16-17). The fact of universal sin did not explain Job's problem or address the significance of the question, "Can any mortal be innocent?" The problem was that Job had not sinned in proportion to his suffering (10:3-7). Andersen suggests the argument emphasizes the weakness of God's creatures in relation to his infinite power (1976:114-116), but again it is not the relative weakness of God's creatures that explains suffering like that of Job. The problem is that God's dealings with his creatures are not readily understood. If even the heavenly messengers may be charged with folly, how much more guilty of folly are those of the earthly realm? As Gibson observes, "the implication is clearly of a capricious deity, who sows discord in the heavenly places and permits only ignorance on earth" (1975:267). How can any person be righteous before God (9:2b) when all end up with a similar fate (9:22) regardless of their relative merits? The vision confirms Job's worst fears about his suffering; he indeed has no means of determining the reason for his fate.

The teaching of the vision contradicts the basic premise of traditional wisdom asserted by the friends. The vision cannot belong to Eliphaz, who assured Job that his piety should be his confidence, that the innocent do not perish, that a person reaps what he sows (4:6-9). Though the vision undermines the simple theology of retribution, it does not provide an explanation for the relationship that exists between God and his creatures. The freedom of God and the freedom of humans is terrifying, for we do not know what to expect. This is not to deny a belief in God's justice, but it is to deny that we have the ability to prescribe how it functions. We are unable to provide a defense of God's ways because we do not understand them. Knowing the limits of reason does not lead to an abandonment of it but rather to the proper use of it in wisdom. Reason does not lead to the conclusion that justice is nonexistent and that evil has free reign. The author asserts that reason leads us to see beauty, power, and goodness in creation and that if we can submit the limits of our knowledge to God's sovereign rule (42:6), we can be assured that our faith will be rewarded.

THEOLOGICAL CONCERNS

The central theological concern of Job is the character of God. The character of God is known through his activity in the world and his relationship with his creatures. In the book of Job, God is the God of the covenant, the God proclaimed in Isaiah as sovereign over all places, including the distant stars of the universe and all peoples, whose great rulers are as nothing to him (Isa 40:12-26). The poet used seven different names for God: *yhwh* [TH3068, ZH3378] (Yahweh, LORD), *'elohim* [TH430, ZH466] (God), *'el* [TH410A, ZH446] (God), *'eloah* [TH433, ZH468] (God), *shadday* [TH7706, ZH8724] (the Almighty), *'adonay* [TH136, ZH151] (Lord; 28:28 in most MSS), and *qadosh* [TH6918/6918A, ZH7705] (the Holy One; 6:10; and possibly 5:1). The covenant name Yahweh is reserved for the prologue, the God speeches, and the epilogue, but in no way does this suggest we are dealing with a different God or different characteristics of God in the dialogs (de Wilde 1981:29). The dialog is set in a non-Israelite context, so it is only natural that more generic names for God be used. All of these names are well known in the other Hebrew Scriptures. For the author of Job, there is only one God, and his sovereignty over all events is uncontested. Even the accuser, Satan, in the prologue is completely subject to God; he does nothing without divine sanction. There is no dualism in Job, no notion that there is a contest between the forces of good and the forces of evil which battle against each other. The problem of evil in Job pertains directly to God and his rule.

The book of Job assumes that God has created the world out of the original chaos, as is typical in other Creation references. While the ancient monster of the sea is powerless to alter any divine activities (9:13), God has set the boundaries of the waters and stilled chaos (Rahab the fleeing serpent) forever (26:12). This is the same God the psalmist calls upon to restore the desolate sanctuary (Ps 74:1-11), whose ability to do so is demonstrated in his crushing of Leviathan and creating the orderly world (Ps 74:12-17). It is the same God Isaiah says will bring the exiles back from Babylon, conquering the great monster of the captivity, just as he conquered Rahab at creation and the Egyptians at the Red Sea (Isa 51:9-11). The poet of Job, however, used different imagery, portraying the beauty of creation as a birth in which the sea burst forth from the womb and the clouds became its swaddling garments (38:8-9); here there is no thought of chaos or conquest. The poet showed that the imagery of ancient myths can provide only a partial and inadequate conception of the beginning of the world. The home of light (38:12, 19-20), the depths of the underworld (38:16-18), and the treasures of the snow and hail (38:22-23) are all familiar to God. It is unfortunate that the book of Job is seldom consulted for the doctrine of creation, for the theology of creation is nowhere else expressed with more beauty and power.

The universe of the book of Job introduces us to personal and accountable beings that belong to the heavenly realm. It is not simply the winds which are God's messengers and the clouds his chariots (Ps 104:3-4). The celestial servants in Job are accountable to God (4:18); these holy ones depend on God for their purity, for in themselves they are untrustworthy (15:15). In this respect they are not different than the stars whose purity cannot be compared with God's (25:5).

Most significantly, however, in the prologue we are introduced to the heavenly court, described in common ancient Near Eastern terminology as "the sons of God"

(1:6, etc.). This terminology is not unique to Job; in the Psalms God takes his stand in the divine assembly and proclaims judgment upon its members (Ps 82:1-2); he is terrifying in the midst of the holy ones (Ps 89:6-7). Though the terminology comes from ancient myth, the concepts bear no parallels. These beings are utterly subordinate, and their function is only vaguely described. They have assigned responsibilities within the divine rule and seemingly never act on their own accord.

The most important figure of the heavenly beings in Job is a challenger called "the satan" who appears with the sons of God. This figure does not have the same function as "the old serpent," called the devil, who will come to bear the name Satan in the New Testament (Rev 12:9). This is generally misleading in translations since the antagonist of the prologue is usually called "Satan." The Hebrew terminology, however, forbids such a simple equation. Whatever the etymology of the word *satan*, it has the general meaning "stumble" in its earlier contexts in the Old Testament (Hurvitz 1974:19). Block charts the similarities between the Accuser in Job and the spirit sent from God's court to deceive Ahab (1 Kgs 22:10-28). The sequences of the divine discourse are the same (Block 2005). Later apocryphal and Qumran literature tends to insert the name when referring to an evil power, indicating the development of the use of the word. For instance, the prayer of the psalmist in Ps 119:133 is "Guide my steps by your word, so I will not be overcome by evil;" the equivalent in a Qumran manuscript (11QPsᵃ) is "Let not Satan rule over me." In the time of Ahab, when the heavenly court was gathered and a seducer was called upon (1 Kgs 22:21), he was simply referred to as a spirit (*ruakh* [ᵀᴴ7307, ᶻᴴ8120]). In Job, the word *satan* has become suitable as an appellation (used with the definite article) for one of the members of the divine assembly. The concept of the divine assembly in heavenly affairs is found throughout the Old Testament. In Job one member serves as a protagonist who is specifically addressed by God. Though he is the immediate agent of Job's suffering, Job directs none of his antagonism against such an individual. God is the enemy who allows Job to suffer.

The main concern of God in the book of Job is people, not other heavenly beings. He sets his mind on them continually, tests them every moment, does not look away long enough to let them swallow their spit (7:17-19). They are guilty of sin, which will result in God's chastisement, as stated most eloquently by Elihu (e.g., 36:7-11). Chastisement is redemptive; it enables the righteous to live in prosperity. This was also the theology of the friends, and in this they were right. The comforters of Job have been given a bad reputation—beyond what they deserve (Ginsberg 1969:107-111). Their primary error was in assuming they were able to explain all of the justice of God's ways, and in this respect they were Job's tormentors.

An understanding of God's justice is not possible for humans, but they are assured of the ultimate triumph of that justice. "Job cannot conceive of life in an immoral universe, and so behind the present manifestation of God's power he sees the future revelation of God's justice" (Gordis 1965:88). Though Job attacks God's power (e.g., 9:4-17), he also appeals to God's mercy (10:8-12). In his darkest moments, Job was confident of his vindication. Job longed for an arbiter who might judge for him (9:32-33); he expressed the firm conviction that there is in heaven a witness to testify on his behalf (16:19). In a moment of triumph, Job was assured of justice: "But as for me, I know that my Redeemer lives, and he will stand upon the earth at last. And after my body has decayed, yet in my body I will see God!" (19:25-26). The "redeemer" means a kinsman, the one who was bound by law to see that justice was done to an injured brother. This redeemer can be none other than God; the idea that some other being should or could come to vindicate Job would, in the theology of the book, be more than blasphemy—it would be the ultimate absurdity. Job's affirmation of faith during his affliction was realized when God both confronted and comforted Job. The children of dust and ashes are secure in the arms of a loving and just God.

OUTLINE
  I. Prologue: The Misfortunes of Job (1:1–2:13)
    A. The Integrity of Job (1:1-5)
    B. The First Test (1:6-22)
      1. The challenge in heaven (1:6-12)
      2. The loss of family and possessions (1:13-19)
      3. Job's confession and confidence (1:20-22)
    C. The Second Test (2:1-10)
      1. The challenge in heaven (2:1-6)
      2. Job's affliction and confession (2:7-10)
    D. Job's Comforters (2:11-13)
 II. Dialog (Job and His Friends): The Question of Retribution (3:1–25:6)
    A. Job: Despair for the Day of Birth (3:1-26)
      1. The universe should not have Job's day (3:1-10)
      2. Job should have died at birth (3:11-19)
      3. Job should be allowed to die now (3:20-26)
    B. Eliphaz: The Harvest of Sorrows (4:1–5:27)
      1. You reap what you sow (4:1-11)
      2. Can a person be righteous before God? (4:12-21)
      3. Evil is the root of trouble (5:1-7)
      4. God judges evil (5:8-16)
      5. God delivers the righteous (5:17-27)
    C. Job: Life Is Futile (6:1–7:21)
      1. Faithfulness brings no relief (6:1-13)
      2. Friends betray the sufferer (6:14-30)
      3. Life is miserable and brief (7:1-10)
      4. God vigilantly watches humans (7:11-21)
    D. Bildad: The Wisdom of the Sages (8:1-22)
      1. Judgment is justice (8:1-7)
      2. Lessons from the plants (8:8-22)

ENDNOTES

1. Tsevat (1980:26) argues that while Job "is not only a theoretical treatise, it is certainly that, and basically that." This must be so because the disputants share a common premise: the world is founded upon justice, or the principle of retribution. If this principle is given up, "the problem of Job, the man and the book, disappears." He further argues that the response to the problem must be seen in the speeches of God, where there is no provision for retribution. For instance, the dawn of every day provides an occasion to punish the wicked (38:15), but this is not realized in practice. Such arguments are precarious, for this passage may well indicate there is a sovereign control of evil with the arrival of light each day. Tsevat regards the epilogue as merely solving the spiritual problem in that it provides for the vindication of Job. However, to demonstrate Job's piety in this manner is to affirm in some way the reward of piety. The epilogue undermines the thesis that there are no consequences to piety.

2. The questions of wisdom were primarily those of life and conduct. Fohrer has summarized well the final answer of the book of Job: "Job endures his fate in unconditional devotion to God and personal communion with him. . . . Job participates in the great life and suffering of the world, but at the same time is raised above it through communion with the divine fundamental principle of the world. This is the correct understanding of suffering and the right conduct of people in it: humble and devoted silence comes from peace in God." (1989:558).

3. See P. Humbert, *Recherches sur les sources Aegyptiennes de la littérature sapientiale d'Israël* (Neuchâtel: Secrétariat de l'Université, 1929).

4. The medieval grammarian Abraham ibn Ezra in his Job commentary already suggested the difficulty in interpreting Job was because it was translated. Thomas Carlyle suggested it originated in an Arabic region of the world, as it reflected a noble universality different from patriotism or sectarianism (*On Heroes, Hero Worship and the Heroic in History* [New York: Scribners, 1905], 69). Gordis points out (1965:210) that this tendency to admire Hebrew literature but denigrate its writers is also seen in Renan (*Le livre de Job* [Paris: Calmann Levy, 1864], xvii) and Voltaire in his article on Job in the *Dictionnaire Philosophique*. A linguistic argument based on Arabisms in Job was advanced by F. H. Foster in "Is the Book of Job a Translation from an Arabic Original?" *American Journal of Semitic Languages and Literature* 49 (1932–1933): 21-45.

5. See his *Introduction to the Old Testament* (London: A & C Black, 1966), 680-681; in note 13 he names some eighteenth-century scholars such as Herder, Dessau, and Ilge as advancing similar arguments.

6. Another reason to question whether it is the Daniel of the Bible that Ezekiel is referring to is that the passage seems to be referring to the integrity of a well-known historical figure rather than a little-known contemporary. Ezekiel 28:3 reports that the king of Tyre claimed to be wiser than Daniel, apparently a reference to a well-known figure of ancient Phoenician tradition. Though a hero named Danel is known in the Ugaritic story of Aqhat, it is unlikely Ezekiel is directly referring to that story; but it may be that a righteous Danel was the impetus of that Canaanite story and was also known in Israelite circles. For discussion see J. Day, "The Daniel of Ugarit and Ezekiel and the Hero of the Book of Daniel," *Vetus Testamentum* 30 (1980): 174-184 and H. H. P. Dressler, "The Identification of the Ugaritic DNIL and the Daniel of Ezekiel," *Vetus Testamentum* 29 (1979): 152-161.

7. The thesis was published as *Linguistic Evidence in Dating Early Hebrew Poetry* (Atlanta: Society of Biblical Literature, 1972).

8. Driver and Gray provide a lengthy list of references (1921:lxiii) with bibliography in which they are discussed; virtually every commentary has a list of such references.

9. In Chronicles, God reacts immediately to the behavior of the king, granting what he deserves; however, before punishment there is a mandatory warning. The story of Asa (2 Chr 14:1–16:14) is a remarkable example of this viewpoint, as the whole chronology of the war with Baasha (cf. 2 Chr 16:1 and 1 Kgs 15:16) appears to be altered in order

to explain the death of Asa from illness (see further R. B. Dillard, "The Reign of Asa (2 Chr 14–16): An Example of the Chronicler's Theological Method," *Journal of the Evangelical Theological Society* 23 [1980]: 207-218).

10. Psalm 1 shares the characteristics of wisdom poetry in its appeal to heed the divine instruction (v. 2), and it is generally recognized as a wisdom psalm in the same spirit as Psalm 49 (see especially vv. 1-4). It is appropriate that it should so introduce the Psalter, and in general tradition the whole of the third section of the canon, which contains the three major books of wisdom (Job, Proverbs, and Ecclesiastes). Sheppard (1980:141-142) regards Psalm 1 as an exilic or postexilic didactic instruction to use the Torah as a guide to the righteous life. By their close association with Psalm 2, the psalms of David were set forth as having an authority derived from the Torah as a guide to righteous living, like that found in the wisdom traditions.

11. The statistics are derived from Jenni and Westermann 1976:2.541.

12. The Qumran Targum (11QtgJob) does differ in two substantial ways from the received Masoretic Text. The first instance is found in Job's responses to God. The submission of Job in 40:3-5 is missing in the Targum (van der Ploeg and van der Woude 1971:78). The response of Job in 42:2-5 is substantially different in the Targum as it lacks the equivalent of 42:3 in the Masoretic Text; in its place is the equivalent of 40:5 in the Masoretic Text. In effect, in the Targum Job makes only one response to God. However, we must be dealing with a damaged text in the missing portion of 40:3-5 in the Targum, because 40:6 begins with God answering Job; this must continue some response of Job in the previous section. The case is more questionable in the epilogue of the Targum. The Targum ends with a blank line at 42:11, indicating the end of a paragraph (as seen in column x, line 6, which is 26:14). The bottom of the Targum is damaged at that point, but the remainder of the scroll, which could have contained another column, is blank. It is not certain that the Targum ended with 42:11, as a few lines could have been included in the lost portion following the break, but certainly not the full equivalent of the Heb. of 42:12-17 (van der Ploeg and van der Woude 1971:87). Many have regarded the content of the epilogue in which the fortunes of Job are restored as a later midrashic expansion, and the Targum would provide textual evidence for such a conclusion (Gray 1974:335). On the other hand, the Targum may simply be omitting or abbreviating some of the original Hebrew text as seen in the Greek translation. In any case there is some fluidity in the tradition of Job at this point.

13. This comparison is made by Carl Cornill in *Introduction to the Canonical Books of the Old Testament* (New York: Putnam, 1907), 421. As in these famous works, the book of Job is a lengthy poem of several parts incorporating a great array of literary elements and an immense variety of cultural material.

14. The identity of the source of the vision is here obscure. The "holy ones" (*qedoshim* [TH6918/6918A, ZH7705]) may be a reference to God as the Holy One (cf. Heb. of Prov 9:10; Hos 12:1), or it may refer to the heavenly court. The translation given follows the syntactical and lexical suggestions of Gordis (1978:52). This is an abbreviation of the expression found in Esth 6:6, "Whom would the king wish to honor more than me?"

15. This translation also comes from Gordis (1978:52).

COMMENTARY ON
Job

◆ **I. Prologue: The Misfortunes of Job (1:1–2:13)**
   A. The Integrity of Job (1:1–5)

There once was a man named Job who lived in the land of Uz. He was blameless— a man of complete integrity. He feared God and stayed away from evil. ²He had seven sons and three daughters. ³He owned 7,000 sheep, 3,000 camels, 500 teams of oxen, and 500 female donkeys. He also had many servants. He was, in fact, the richest person in that entire area.

⁴Job's sons would take turns preparing feasts in their homes, and they would also invite their three sisters to celebrate with them. ⁵When these celebrations ended— sometimes after several days—Job would purify his children. He would get up early in the morning and offer a burnt offering for each of them. For Job said to himself, "Perhaps my children have sinned and have cursed God in their hearts." This was Job's regular practice.

NOTES

1:1 *There once was a man.* Noth is correct in observing that the Heb. perfect is deliberately ambiguous in its temporal reference (1951:258). The phrase translated "There once was a man" does not imply that Job is a literary creation, as the English expression "Once upon a time" does.

named Job. Apart from Ezek 14:14, 20, the name is found only in the book of Job in the Heb. Bible. The Heb. form *'iyyob* [TH347, ZH373] follows an inflection pattern in nouns that indicates a characteristic activity or profession. If it is linked to the root *'ayab* [TH340, ZH366] "enemy," it could be interpreted as "inveterate foe." The name derives from Semitic tradition and is well known outside the Bible. One of the Amarna letters (no. 256), dating from about 1350 BC, names the prince of Ashtaroth in Bashan as *'ayyab*, an older form of the biblical name. Still earlier, an Egyptian execration text (c. 2000 BC) mentions a Palestinian chief named *'ybm*. The name *'ayyabum* is found in Akkadian documents from Mari and Alalakh dating from the early second millennium BC (Albright [1954] has explained this as a contracted form of *'ayya 'abu(m)*, meaning "Where is my father?"). An Ugaritic version of the name in the form *ayab* is also found in a list of palace personnel.

the land of Uz. Job is ambiguous in location as well as time. He is situated outside the land of Israel to the east (1:3), which, from the point of view of an Israelite, could be anywhere from Midian in the south (Judg 6:3) to the northern part of Syria ("Paddan-aram"; cf. Gen 28:2; 29:1). To the east lay the desert and the edge of civilization. It was the domain of nomadic shepherds such as the Midianites, but it was also the home of wealthy farmers such as Job who resided in the few fertile areas. Uz may be connected to Aram in the more northern area of the east (Gen 10:22-23), the location of the relatives of Abraham (Gen 22:21), but the name is also found among the descendants of Esau in the southern area of Edom (Gen 36:28), a territory that came under judgment for its role in the fall of Jerusalem (Jer 25:20; Lam 4:21). Later traditions maintain both southern and northern locations. Josephus (*Antiquities* 1.6.4) says Uz, one of the four sons of Aram, founded Trachonitis and Damascus (the area of Syria in the north). The appendix to the Greek translation of Job places Uz on the borders of Edom and Arabia and makes Job one of the kings of Edom at a city named Dennaba. However, tradition has also identified Job's city Dennaba with Karnaim (cf. Amos 6:13) in the territory of Hauran, the modern *Sheikh Sa'ad* just to the east of the Sea of Galilee (Pope 1965:4).

1:2 *seven sons and three daughters.* Seven is a number symbolic of completeness applied to the full number of children in the song of Hannah (1 Sam 2:5). The ratio of seven sons to three daughters is apparently ideal (cf. Job 42:13). Three added to seven provides ten, which according to Elkanah is also a complete family (1 Sam 1:8). The same ratio applies to sheep and camels (Job 1:3) and in another context to Solomon's wives and concubines (1 Kgs 11:3).

1:5 *sometimes after several days.* The Heb. refers to the completion of the festival cycle and does not indicate the number of days involved. Although the course of such a festival could be seven days (Judg 14:12, 15), there is no reason to imagine a week of celebration with each brother hosting a day, as suggested by the medieval Jewish commentators Rashi and Ibn Ezra.

COMMENTARY

There is little point in speculating on the form of the story of Job known to the author. It has numerous archaic elements of language and style, which indicate it was an old story (Sarna 1957), but these have been integrated into the work both linguistically and literarily. The prologue contains poetic elements (e.g., 1:21) as well as dialog, which unites it with the main sections of the book. Theological unity between the prologue and main sections is demonstrated in the shared perspective that the idea of retributive justice does not adequately explain God's providence. The difficulty of reading Job does not arise out of the diverse form of the original story of Job, whatever we may conceive that to have been. The real tension between the prologue and the rest of the book is in the diverse portrayal of its characters; but, as Cheney observes, it is this very feature that is quintessential to the structure and the meaning of the book as a whole (1994:1). The prologue presents Job as a paragon of virtue who survives the test of integrity; Job worshiped God in spite of the testing that deprived him entirely of God's blessing. However, this is not all there is to Job. The virtuous Job provides the perspective from which we can observe the contradictions of human character and faith and evaluate what it means to have integrity of both reason and faith in times of trial.

There is no reason to doubt that Job was a historical individual whose story was well known. The prophet Ezekiel (Ezek 14:14) refers to Noah, Daniel, and Job as three historical individuals. Though they may have been known through the biblical stories, Ezekiel does not refer to them as existing only in stories. The prologue of Job, however, does not tell us his story in the manner of a biography. Instead Job is presented without reference to historical circumstances. He is given no genealogy and no reference point in biblical chronology. His life circumstances are left deliberately vague so that they can represent any person at any point in time; people of any era in any location can identify with Job and learn the lessons that wisdom has for them.

It is often proposed that Job was an individual created by the author. As early as the Babylonian Talmud, the opinion was expressed that Job was created as a parable, that he never really existed (*b. Bava Batra* 15a). The same opinion was followed by Maimonides, who affirmed in his commentary that the book of Job was based on fiction. This is a misunderstanding of the intent of the author, who does not wish to present Job as fictitious but to make him representative of a universal human problem. The land of Uz apparently formed a link with the Aramean, Edomite, and Arabic regions, as the name is found with all these associations. Job is located at the confluence of the great civilizations of Arabia and Syria. His name is one that transverses a great time span and numerous languages. Job was known as a venerable nobleman of ancient times.

The most important aspect of Job's life is his character; "he was blameless—a man of complete integrity" (1:1). The terms used suggest uncompromising ethical conduct. This is not perfection (as is frequently ascribed to Job), for that is beyond human capability; but it signifies a person of impeccable morality. The conduct of Job was based on his reverence for God, which inspired a desire to perform God's will at all times. Such a man was blessed, not only in terms of his relationship with God and others but also in the material provision of life. In Hebrew thought these aspects of blessedness were never separated from each other: Job's family was the first item of blessedness, for children are a heritage from the Lord, a reward and a source of strength (Ps 127:3-5). All those who fear the Lord will be blessed; all those who walk in God's ways will eat of the fruit of their labor. They will be prosperous— their children around the table will be like olive shoots (Ps 128:1-3). Job's wealth is given in terms of cattle and servants in keeping with the patriarchal setting. The numbers are perfectly realistic for a wealthy person; Nabal had 3,000 sheep and 1,000 goats (1 Sam 25:2). Nevertheless, it is not the author's concern to provide a precise inventory of Job's wealth; the number seven, a symbol of fullness, is added to three to provide the number ten, another symbol of fullness. Job's greatness does not consist of his wealth; his greatness is his character, which is seen in all the accruements that pertain to such a person.

Job was scrupulous in his conduct to the point of offering sacrifices for his sons and daughters after their celebrations. This is not to be thought of as neurotic behavior done out of fear of punishment but rather as a desire to exemplify the fullest reverence for God. Neither is this to suggest that Job may be vicariously pious for his children. As the head of a patriarchal household, it would be his responsibility to take the initiative in spiritual leadership. Job invited his children to the central location of the family home in order to offer sacrifices on behalf of the collective family, symbolizing the purification of sins.

Job was afraid that one of his children may have "cursed God in their hearts" (1:5). The question here is just what sort of sin it was that Job feared. This is the first of four occurrences in the prologue in which the Hebrew word that normally means "bless" (*barak* [TH1288A, ZH1385]) has the sense of "curse" (cf. 1:11; 2:5, 9). This has often been treated as a euphemism to avoid the word "curse" (*qalal* [TH7043, ZH7837]) in speaking about God, but Cheney is certainly correct in his observation that this is an antiphrastic idiom that has a major role in the narrative (1994:52-77). *Antiphrasis* is a common technique in many languages in which a word is used opposite to its normal sense. Usually it is done for the sake of humor or irony, as when speaking of "a giant of 3 feet 4 inches." (Other examples of antiphrases in English include the use of *wicked* and *deadly* in the statements "That was a wicked game" and "That was a deadly dessert.") The word *barak* is used antiphrastically in contemporary Hebrew. In Yiddish the *misheberak* (a noun form of the word *barak*) normally is a blessing that someone asks to be said, usually on behalf of someone else, on being called to read the Scriptures (Torah). Antiphrastically, it means a tirade against someone (this example was posted by Francis Landy on the Enkidu list [a now defunct online forum], June 18, 1995). Further evidence that the use of the word *barak* for "curse" is not a case of euphemism but of antiphrasis is that the direct expression for cursing God (using the Heb. word *qalal* for "curse") is found elsewhere in Scripture (Exod 22:28; Lev 24:15-16) and could have been used here. In each of its four occurrences in the prologue of Job, *barak* is used to mean "curse" for literary effect. The use of "bless" raises theological questions about our relationship to an all-powerful and all-knowing God when, as humans, we are so limited in knowledge and ability. Using the term "bless" instead of "curse" suggests that we do not always know the effects of our actions.

Our relationship toward God is not always knowable or certain. It may be that our intentions to honor God lead to what is in reality an offense; our blessing may be a curse. In turn, there is the possibility that God's blessing to us will be experienced as a curse. There is no reason to contemplate deliberate blasphemy on the part of the children of Job. It instead seems that Job was seeking to make amends for any inadvertent sins that would undermine the piety of his children. Cheney suggests that in this verse the Hebrew may be read as a relative sequence: Job thinks that his children may have sinned and then blessed God in their hearts (1994:72). Their words of blessing would then be a blasphemy without their even knowing it. Job's offering is not out of fear that the children were willfully sinning or secretly cursing God.

Job's offering on behalf of his children introduces a central theological issue in the book of Job: well-intending mortals, in their finite knowledge, may offend God and not realize it; their words of blessing may be a mockery. If this is the case, God's blessing is much less predictable than the traditional wisdom asserted. This already begins to raise the recurring question of the dialog: "Can a mortal be pure before God?" (4:17; 9:2; 15:14; 25:4).

◆ **B. The First Test (1:6–22)**
   1. The challenge in heaven (1:6–12)

⁶One day the members of the heavenly court* came to present themselves before the LORD, and the Accuser, Satan,* came with them. ⁷"Where have you come from?" the LORD asked Satan.

Satan answered the LORD, "I have been patrolling the earth, watching everything that's going on."

⁸Then the LORD asked Satan, "Have you noticed my servant Job? He is the finest man in all the earth. He is blameless—a man of complete integrity. He fears God and stays away from evil."

⁹Satan replied to the LORD, "Yes, but Job has good reason to fear God. ¹⁰You have always put a wall of protection around him and his home and his property. You have made him prosper in everything he does. Look how rich he is! ¹¹But reach out and take away everything he has, and he will surely curse you to your face!"

¹²"All right, you may test him," the LORD said to Satan. "Do whatever you want with everything he possesses, but don't harm him physically." So Satan left the LORD's presence.

1:6a Hebrew *the sons of God.* 1:6b Hebrew *and the satan;* similarly throughout this chapter.

NOTES

1:6 *the members of the heavenly court.* As indicated by the NLT mg, the lit. expression is "sons of God"; it is used to describe a royal council in which a king is surrounded by his courtiers (cf. 15:8; Ps 29:1; Isa 6:1-8). The Heb. idiom "sons of" indicates a group belonging to their "father" as their leader (cf. the "father" of a band of prophets in 1 Sam 10:12).

the Accuser, Satan. The Heb. word *satan* [TH7854, ZH8477], in this context, is not the devil but the Accuser. That old serpent, the devil, is given the name Satan in the New Testament (Rev 12:9). It is important to be aware of how the usage of the word develops in the Heb. Scriptures. In Job and Zechariah, a member of the divine court appears in the role of "the accuser." The meaning of the term is evident in the Zechariah passage (Zech 3:1) where the noun and verb occur together: the accuser (*hasatan*) was standing at the right hand of Joshua (the priest) to accuse him (*lesitno* [TH7853, ZH8476]). The term does come to be used as a proper name for the devil in later Hebrew, and it is probably used that way in Chronicles: Satan stood against Israel and tempted David to number Israel (1 Chr 21:1). Satan, however, does not appear in the Samuel account (2 Sam 24:1). It is notable that the Heb. word *satan* never refers to a tempter in the heavenly realms in the kingdom period (Samuel) but does in the postexilic period (Chronicles). When it does refer to such a tempter in the later writings, it is always in terms of a specific test that God allows or initiates, a function quite unlike that of the devil in the New Testament. Should we think of the devil as being a member of the divine assembly as the *satan* (the Accuser) is introduced in Job and Zechariah? John, in Revelation, does speak of the devil as being cast out of heaven at the triumph of Jesus (Rev 12:5-9), suggesting that the role of the devil did change with the work of Christ. In Job it may be the devil that stands before God as part of the divine council; but if so, in this passage he does not have the role of an angel of light seeking to deceive, as we find him in the New Testament. Rather, his task here is to call God's attention to a situation that ought to be tested. He accuses Job of serving God only because God has blessed Job.

1:10 *You have made him prosper.* The Heb. has the word "bless" (*barak* [TH1288A, ZH1385]), the usual way of speaking of prosperity. The common meaning in this verse is subtly used in contrast to the opposite meaning of the same verb in verse 11, where it is translated "he will surely curse you to your face." This accentuates the accusation: God's blessing of Job is in reality a bribe to get a blessing from Job; if God removes his blessing, the blessing Job returns will be the opposite as well.

COMMENTARY

The narrator shifts the scene to the assembly of the heavenly council, where God is pictured as a king surrounded by his courtiers receiving reports, taking counsel, and dispensing orders. The heavenly sphere is depicted entirely in terms of the earthly human experience of authoritative persons taking counsel and devolving functions. The Accuser is a member of the divine court; his role in the council is specific, so the question about Job's integrity is directed immediately to him. The point of the narrator in introducing the reader to this heavenly scene is not to suggest that God is less than fully aware of Job's sincerity or how he will respond. Rather, God was able to make his declaration about Job without hesitation because he knew Job. There could, however, have been doubt about Job's integrity both in the heavenly realm and in the earthly, even in the mind of Job himself. In the heavenly court, it was the function of the Accuser to remove all such doubt.

The Accuser pointed out that God's blessing upon Job's life cast doubt on Job's motives for so conscientiously blessing God. God's blessing (*barak*) had the effect of a hedge around Job's life so he could suffer no harm (1:10; *sakta ba'ado* [TH7753/1157, ZH8455/1237]). So long as the hedge God placed around Job kept difficulty away, there was no question about Job's response to God. However, should God remove that hedge, Job would then "bless" God in quite the opposite manner, the Accuser explained. In verse 11, the verb *barak* must be meant in the sense of curse, just as it is when king Ahab incited two malevolent individuals to incriminate Naboth by insisting that he had "blessed" God and the king (1 Kgs 21:10, 13). God agreed to remove the hedge from around Job and gave the Accuser license to remove Job's blessings. The Accuser's question in 1:11 then becomes acute: what kind of blessing would God now receive from Job? The hedge of God's blessing is an uncertain kind of providence; it may be wealth or loss. In turn, Job's blessing of God is an uncertain kind of praise. Job may say, "The LORD gave me what I had, and the LORD has taken it away. Praise the name of the LORD!" (1:21); or he may say, "Why give light to those in misery, and life to those who are bitter?" (3:20). The challenge of the Accuser concerning the life of Job defies the usual assumptions about God's protection and his blessing. It also calls into question the sense in which those who suffer will bless God. The motives for piety come under scrutiny as the usual axioms of reward and punishment are altered.

As expressed by Clines, the prologue "is a beguilement of the reader, a strategy that, if it seduces naive readers into finding a reflection of their own shallowness in the text, equally entrances more perceptive readers into an exploratory journey into its depths" (1985:127-128). The introduction of the Accuser and the antiphrastic use of the word "bless" contribute to both the beguilement and the entrancement. The Accuser serves to remind naive readers that they cannot trust their own judgment of themselves. The use of the word "bless" causes the more perceptive to reflect on their own motives and how their words and actions may be perceived by God (cf. 1:5).

◆   ## 2. The loss of family and possessions (1:13-19)

¹³One day when Job's sons and daughters were feasting at the oldest brother's house, ¹⁴a messenger arrived at Job's home with this news: "Your oxen were plowing, with the donkeys feeding beside them, ¹⁵when the Sabeans raided us. They stole all the animals and killed all the farmhands. I am the only one who escaped to tell you."

¹⁶While he was still speaking, another messenger arrived with this news: "The fire of God has fallen from heaven and burned up your sheep and all the shepherds. I am the only one who escaped to tell you."

¹⁷While he was still speaking, a third messenger arrived with this news: "Three bands of Chaldean raiders have stolen your camels and killed your servants. I am the only one who escaped to tell you."

¹⁸While he was still speaking, another messenger arrived with this news: "Your sons and daughters were feasting in their oldest brother's home. ¹⁹Suddenly, a powerful wind swept in from the wilderness and hit the house on all sides. The house collapsed, and all your children are dead. I am the only one who escaped to tell you."

NOTES

1:15 the Sabeans. Sheba is the name of the South Arabian people whose capital was Marib, about 1,200 miles south of Jerusalem. The Sabean inscriptions record many kings and buildings that give testimony to the wealth and power of ancient Sheba (Driver and Gray 1921:16). Sheba was famous for its trade in frankincense, gold, and precious stones; this is the subject of most of the Old Testament references to it (Isa 60:6; Jer 6:20; Ezek 27:22). The visit of the queen of Sheba to Solomon (1 Kgs 10:1-9) portrays the enormity of Solomon's wealth by means of comparison with that of the queen. The author of Job, however, does not have such a distant country in mind (Dhorme 1984:xxiii, xxv). Sheba is related to Dedan (Gen 10:7; 25:3; Ezek 38:13); Uz and Buz are described as sons of Nahor (Gen 22:21); and the prophet Jeremiah connects Buz, Tema, and Dedan as the cities of one territory (Jer 25:23). Job will speak of the caravans from Tema and Sheba (6:19). Dedan and Tema are both identified with the oasis of al-'Ula in the northwest region of the Arabian peninsula, about 350 miles south of Jerusalem and 250 miles north of Medina. Fohrer thinks the reference to the northern location indicates the great age of the Job narrative, and that later readers would have been inclined to think the Accuser went to the ends of the world to summon Job's attackers (1989:90). However, it is also possible that there were trading stations of the distant, southern Sheba in northern Arabia in the area of Edom (Driver and Gray 1921:16).

1:16 The fire of God. The literal translation at this point retains the ambiguity of the original. In Heb., lightning is regularly called the "fire from heaven" (2 Kgs 1:10, 12, 14) or the "fire from the LORD" (cf. Num 11:1; 16:35; 1 Kgs 18:38). The term "fire of God" is often used in Heb. to express the superlative, i.e., "a very great fire" (see Waltke and O'Conner 1990:14.5b for examples), but clearly more than that is in mind here. Though the expression is a natural one for lightning, its use in this context reminds the reader that Job's calamities are a part of divine intervention in his life.

1:17 bands of Chaldean raiders. This is not a reference to the imperial race of Aramaic-speaking descendants who formed the nucleus of Nebuchadnezzar's army and empire (cf. 2 Kgs 24:1-2). The Chaldeans first appear in ninth-century BC Assyrian records, from the time of Ashurnasirpal II (884–859 BC); they settled west of the Tigris. Several times they gained control of Babylon in the late eighth century BC, before Nabopolassar formed the neo-Babylonian empire (626 BC). Marauding Aramaic nomads roamed the deserts of the whole area between the Persian Gulf and north Arabia.

COMMENTARY

The cryptic and stylized description of the four simultaneous catastrophes heightens the impact of the total devastation of all that God had blessed Job with. As the
owner and manager of a large farm, Job received the reports of destruction from
every aspect of his operation in immediate succession. The pattern of the reports is
very similar to that underlying the ten plagues of Exodus (Sarna 1957:19-20). As in
the plague story, stereotyped phrases demarcate the catastrophes and provide a
symmetrical pattern. In the Job sequence, the messenger arrives, reports that only
he has escaped, and while he is speaking another messenger arrives. Each of the first
three reports mentions two things: first the total loss of Job's livestock and then the
complete loss of human life; in six blows Job has lost all of his possessions and servants. The fourth report comes as a climactic seventh blow, in which Job discovers
that he has lost his entire family with the exception of his wife. The calamities alternately are caused by human and natural agency: Sabeans, lightning, Chaldeans, and
wind. In each case, disaster strikes without warning. The disasters come from all
directions: the Arabic Sabeans from the south, the Aramaic Chaldeans from the
north; the lightning storm from the west, and the violent sirocco wind from the
desert in the east. The seven blows emphasize the symbolic significance of the utter
totality of the loss that Job endured.

Except for the plundering of the Chaldeans, each of the catastrophes is described
as a disaster that fell (*napal* [TH5307, ZH5877]) upon Job. On the one hand, this provides
a unified depiction of the fortuity of the events that happened to Job; but on the
other, it reinforces the portrayal of pious Job in the face of the divine onslaught
against him (Cheney 1994:57-58). After hearing these reports without interruption,
Job fell (*napal*) to the ground and worshiped God (1:20). The succinct sequence of
tragic events created a kind of "domino effect," which ends with Job falling in reverence and blessing the author of his tragedies (1:21). This action counters the Accuser's anticipation of the way in which Job would "bless God" (1:11).

Neither God nor the Accuser is implicated in the reports of the disasters. The absence of the heavenly figures establishes a dichotomy between the heavenly and
earthly spheres; this absence replicates the human experience in which things simply happen. The calamities in themselves are cold and mute, which has the effect of
amplifying the profundity of Job's confession (1:21). Job fell to the ground before
God as an acknowledgment of divine control over his life, even though he was totally ignorant of the actual cause behind his troubles.

The reports of the catastrophes are also surreal in their depiction, heightening the
impact on Job as the recipient, but reminding the reader that these events were designed for total destruction according to the agreement of the divine council. The
object of the Sabeans was to plunder, but they also killed all the farm hands except
for one. A lightning strike might devastate a herd, but it is only preternatural fire
that can destroy a flock of 7,000 along with all of their attendants except for one.
The Chaldeans employ the strategy of striking from three directions simultaneously
so there is no possibility of any escape, except for one. And finally the sirocco wind

strikes all four sides at once, more in the fashion of a tornado though in description it simply "swept in from the wilderness," an accurate portrayal of life on the desert fringe.

The life of Job is moved in an instant from uneventful normalcy to utter chaos (Clines 1989:31). In the early winter, after the early rains, the oxen were plowing Job's vast acreage, while the donkeys that carried the gear and the seeds were quietly grazing alongside. The shepherds were out on the hills unmolested. The camels were on the caravan trail carrying out the business of Job's extensive enterprise. Job's family was gathered in the mansion of the eldest brother, as was their custom. In spite of all Job's care and precaution, he suddenly fell prey to unpredictable tragedy.

◆   ## 3. Job's confession and confidence (1:20-22)

²⁰Job stood up and tore his robe in grief. Then he shaved his head and fell to the ground to worship. ²¹He said,

"I came naked from my mother's womb, and I will be naked when I leave.

The LORD gave me what I had, and the LORD has taken it away. Praise the name of the LORD!"

²²In all of this, Job did not sin by blaming God.

NOTES
1:20 *fell to the ground to worship.* The Heb. *khwh* [TH2331.1, ZH2556] describes a reverential act of worship as a sequel to bowing down (cf. Josh 5:14; 2 Chr 20:18).

1:21 *I will be naked when I leave.* The Heb. is necessarily paraphrased at this point. Job's confession is a beautifully balanced poem with correspondence in each of the elements of the first two lines, literally: "Naked I came from my mother's womb, and naked I shall return there." The use of "there" (or, "over there") as a euphemism for one's place after death corresponds to the mother's womb as one's place before birth.

1:22 *Job did not sin by blaming God.* This line, a paraphrase, corresponds to the third line of Job's confession: "The LORD gave (*nathan* [TH5414, ZH5989]); the LORD has taken away"; this line says, "Job gave (*nathan*) nothing unseemly to God." The noun meaning "unseemliness" (*tiplah* [TH8604, ZH9524]) is a virtual homonym for the word for prayer (*tepillah* [TH8605, ZH9525]), though both come from different roots; the former is related to the noun *tapel* [TH8602B, ZH9522] meaning "insipid thing" (cf. 6:6), the latter to the root for prayer (*palal* [TH6419A, ZH7137]). The verse emphasizes the genuine nature of the blessing as a prayer without irreverence of any kind.

COMMENTARY
Job responded to the disasters that befell him with ritualistic mourning. His actions were customary and deeply symbolic. Tearing one's garments and putting ashes on one's head are frequently attested in Scripture as rites of mourning (2:12; Gen 37:29; Josh 7:6; 2 Sam 1:2; 3:31; 13:19). Shaving the head was also a widespread custom (Isa 15:2; 22:12; Jer 7:29; 16:6), though it was censured in Deuteronomic law (Deut 14:1), probably because of pagan associations. All of these actions signify an identification of the living with the dead (Clines 1989:35). The tearing of the outer mantle or robe would require considerable strength and might be something

of a cathartic exercise and could signify that a significant part of one's own life had been ripped away. The disfigurement of the mourner is a stark portrayal of the disruption of life. The nonverbal actions of Job were not impulsive and hasty; they required forethought and significant activity.

Job's falling to the ground "does not describe an immediate half-involuntary physical action against distressing news . . . but an act of reverential obeisance or worship" (Driver and Gray 1921:18). Job's falling to the ground extended beyond ritualistic mourning; it involved his worship of God. Job's response to disaster falling upon him was to fall down and worship. It was an act of deliberate piety in which the worshiper drops gently to his knees, places his hands upon the ground, and touches the ground with his forehead between his hands. This is one of the postures of prayer; Job, however, did not offer a prayer but made a confession.

Job's confession (1:21) recognized the utter dependence of human life upon God as the giver of life: he arrived in this world with nothing and would leave it the same way. The psalmist spoke of being formed in the womb of his mother (Ps 139:13), as well as being woven together in the heart of the earth (Ps 139:15; NLT's "utter seclusion"). Both time and place are drawn together in this image, both the individual and the whole of humankind. At the time of death we are as at the time of birth; at the time of death we return to the earth, just as we as humans were first formed from the earth. This is not to suggest that the earth is "mother earth," but rather that it represents our origin and our destiny as recipients of the gift of life from the good hand of God. It should be noted that the personal name for God (*yhwh* [TH3068, ZH3378]) appears in the formula: "Yahweh has given, Yahweh has taken away." It is a reminder that Job's faith is in the God of the covenant and is evidence of a Hebrew confession.

Job's reference to birth in the confession of verse 21 may be contrasted with that of the lament of the day of his birth. In his lament, he declared that his birth was not a gift of life but a misfortune that ought not to have happened (3:10-11). In this confession Job accepted the situation of his life until he would return "there"—that is, to death (see note on 1:21). In the lament, Job complained that he was denied his desire to return "there" (3:19), inasmuch as he longed for death but it would not come. Job expressed no irreverence for God in this response. The Accuser had suggested that Job's words would blaspheme God (1:11), but Job did not assert any unseemliness at all on God's part (1:22). Misfortune had led Job to bless God in the true sense of the word.

◆   C. The Second Test (2:1-10)
     1. The challenge in heaven (2:1-6)

One day the members of the heavenly court* came again to present themselves before the LORD, and the Accuser, Satan,* came with them. 2"Where have you come from?" the LORD asked Satan.

Satan answered the LORD, "I have been patrolling the earth, watching everything that's going on."

3Then the LORD asked Satan, "Have you noticed my servant Job? He is the finest man in all the earth. He is blameless—a man of complete integrity. He fears God and stays away from evil. And he has maintained his integrity, even though you urged me to harm him without cause."

⁴Satan replied to the LORD, "Skin for skin! A man will give up everything he has to save his life. ⁵But reach out and take away his health, and he will surely curse you to your face!"

⁶"All right, do with him as you please," the LORD said to Satan. "But spare his life."

2:1a Hebrew *the sons of God.* 2:1b Hebrew *and the satan*; similarly throughout this chapter.

NOTES

2:3 *even though you urged me to harm him without cause.* This translation is correct, contrary to various translations and commentators who connect "without cause" to the verb translated "urged," giving the sense that the Accuser inciting God against Job was to no avail or without effect (Rowley 1970:37; Dhorme 1984:15). The point is not that testing Job was baseless or futile (Andersen 1976:90) but rather that Job had done nothing to deserve such an attack. This is also grammatically preferable, as the phrase modifies the verb nearest to it (Gordis 1978:19; Fohrer 1989:91; Clines 1989:5).

urged me. The verb here has the sense of incitement, as in 1 Sam 26:19: "If the LORD has stirred you up against me." The action is an attempt to persuade rather than the actual act of persuasion; the Lord does not allow the Accuser to have responsibility for the experiment (Gordis 1978:19).

to harm him. Lit. "to swallow him up" (*bala'* [TH1104, ZH1180]), a vivid image of destruction. It is found more commonly in epic or poetic texts and may be an expression derived from Canaanite mythology (Sarna 1957:16). In Ugaritic texts, the god of death (Mot) typically swallows his victims.

2:4 *skin for skin.* The metaphor is enigmatic. The common translation might suggest it is derived from the language of bartering, where one item is exchanged for another of equal value, perhaps derived from a Bedouin practice of using pelts as a measure of value. In support of this, Fohrer cites an Ugaritic legal document that has the phrase "house for house" (1989:97). The parallel is weakened by the fact that the Ugaritic uses the preposition *kima* (which logically expresses equality), while the Heb. has *ba'ad* [TH1157, ZH1237] (around, after). Both prepositions are common in both languages, so the difference is significant. The use of *ba'ad* in Hebrew, coupled with the following explanation "a man will give up everything he has to save his life," is notable in Job. We have been told that God put a protective wall around (*ba'ad*) everything Job had (1:10). The Accuser here seems to be insinuating that the hedge had only been partially removed and that which matters most had not yet been touched. The expression may have the sense of "skin around skin" (which is more natural for the preposition used) with the sense that that which is most important is most carefully protected (cf. Torczyner 1967:23-24). The sense is that one must use all one has to protect one's life.

COMMENTARY

The second dialog of the heavenly council follows the pattern of the first with virtually identical wording. The simplicity of the scene and the similarity of the expressions may be described as naive but subtle (Clines 1985:130-131). The Lord is the first to speak, indicating that the initiative belongs to him. His question, "Where have you come from?" may seem redundant in the second scene, but it enhances the mystique of the council as it proceeds in a familiar pattern. The response of the Accuser, "I have been patrolling the earth," is identical to that of the first scene, but the implications are now different. In the first scene the Accuser had nothing to report; the initiative of the conversation was thrown back to the Lord. In the second scene the answer is evasive, for surely the Accuser had acted on the liberties he was granted when he left the presence of the Lord (1:12). The question "have you noticed?" is in its repetition even more provocative than in the original dialog, for the outcome of the test, quite apparently known to all, had intensified the challenge to the Accuser.

The new situation of the second scene is further developed by subtle differences from the original scene. In the first scene we are told that the members of the divine council present themselves to the Lord and the Accuser is among them (1:6); in the second scene the Accuser is not simply among them but also presents himself to the Lord (2:1). Though these two verses have been translated identically as early as the ancient Greek, and continue to be in modern translations (NEB, TEV, NLT), the difference in the Hebrew is significant. The Accuser now appears as someone on a mission. The Lord repeats his assertion of the integrity and piety of Job but with an intensified provocation: this in spite of the fact that the Accuser had incited an attack against Job for no reason. This elicited a new response from the Accuser, expressed enigmatically in the phrase "skin for skin," and explained by saying one will give up all one's possessions to protect one's life (2:4). The explanation can be read in reference to the test Job had endured, or it may be introducing what the Accuser was about to propose. Looking back, this would suggest that Job had quite readily given up his possessions and his family in order to spare his own life. Job, of course, did not willingly give up his possessions or family, but it could be argued that Job did not protest (i.e., curse God) in order to protect his own life. The argument of the Accuser, however, is even more poignant if it looks forward to the test being proposed. God had only partially lowered the hedge around Job; that which was of most vital interest to Job, namely his own life, had remained protected. The Accuser was asking that the protective hedge around Job be removed entirely in order that the test be without compromise. Taken this way, "skin for skin" does not have the sense of equal value in an exchange; it would rather have the sense of "skin around skin," suggesting that the test had not yet penetrated to the deepest level of pain and vulnerability. The Accuser suggests that perhaps Job knew he could not stand against God's power and refrained from cursing God simply because he valued his own life. The question, then, would be whether Job would still bless God if his own life became totally miserable and seemed worthless. In other words, there was still a skin around Job, and Satan was proposing it be removed—literally.

The second scene in heaven closes in a manner similar to the first, but with the frightening concession that the Lord allowed this new challenge. In the first scene, the Lord dismissed the Accuser saying all Job possessed was given over to the power of the Accuser; now it is Job himself given over to the power of the Accuser. The sparing of Job's life is not a mercy and is not merely a concession necessary to the test, but in reality it is also a part of the test. The most difficult of life's sorrows are perhaps found when even the mercy of death is denied (cf. 3:20-23). Thus, this was the ultimate test.

♦   2. Job's affliction and confession (2:7-10)

⁷So Satan left the LORD's presence, and he struck Job with terrible boils from head to foot.

⁸Job scraped his skin with a piece of broken pottery as he sat among the ashes. ⁹His wife said to him, "Are you still trying to maintain your integrity? Curse God and die."

¹⁰But Job replied, "You talk like a foolish woman. Should we accept only good things from the hand of God and never anything bad?" So in all this, Job said nothing wrong.

NOTES

2:8 *as he sat among the ashes*. The Heb. would suggest that the Accuser's second attack on Job came while he was still sitting on the ash heap lamenting the first disasters (Driver and Gray 1921:24). The sequences in the Heb. are closely joined, so the final temporal phrase can refer to either of the previous clauses; the logical sequence is that "he struck Job . . . as he sat among the ashes."

2:9 *His wife said*. The Greek text has a considerable expansion at this point, which presents Job's wife as sharing his misery and wishing his death so as to end his unbearable suffering speedily. This becomes the basis of a speech attributed to her in the apocryphal *Testament of Job*; there she is given the name Sitides and sympathetically supports Job, even selling her hair to buy him three loaves of bread.

COMMENTARY

The increasing intensity of the experiment against Job is indicated both by the speed with which the Accuser carried out his gruesome task and his direct involvement in it. Though the scene in heaven ends with the Accuser leaving the presence of the Lord exactly as the first time, there is no delay of calamity, as in the first instance (cf. 1:13). The immediate involvement of the Accuser as agent removes all uncertainty about the relationship of events in heaven to those on earth; there is a direct causal connection. The second affliction of Job resembles the first calamities in its suddenness and completeness: his entire body was smitten from head to foot. The nature of the disease is left ambiguous, except to say that it afflicted Job's skin (cf. 2:4). Its description as a boil is similar to that of a contagious skin disease which rendered one unclean (cf. Lev 13:12-15, 18-20), but in this case it did not prevent Job's friends from coming to see him. The disease made Job repugnant, as one too loathsome to be human (Ps 22:6). These features about the disease are all that is relevant.

Sitting on the ash heap was a common ritual of lamentation. Rituals of lament included the throwing of dust (2:12) as well as rending the garments and shaving one's head (1:20). The narrative does not make clear what length of time was involved after the previous disasters and Job's lamentation or what his subsequent actions were, but the silence provided the impression that this personal scourge came even as he sat among the ashes. The immediacy of this further plague would be in harmony with the suddenness of the first disasters, which came as each messenger was still speaking. The usual assumption is that the ash heap was part of a rubbish dump outside the city, as is asserted in the Greek translation. The dung heap was the resort of outcasts and persons with infectious diseases; a mourner would go there to identify with the rejected and destitute.[1] However, the narrative does not specificy whether Job made a public display of his grief, though it might seem to have been a part of the mourning ritual.

The second response of Job did not follow as immediately as in the first instance (cf. 1:20). His response was elicited by his wife, who may be viewed in a negative light because she urged her husband to take the course of self-damnation anticipated by the Accuser. The church fathers viewed her negatively: Augustine described her as "the assistant of Satan," and Chrysostom commented that one of Job's trials was that his wife did not die. Such sentiments are unduly harsh. Her role was to raise the question of Job's integrity. Her first words echo verbatim the affirmation of the Lord after the first test, but now apparently as a rhetorical question: "Are you still trying to maintain your integrity?" (cf. 2:3). "Curse God" translates another antiphrastic use of the Hebrew word for "bless" encountered earlier (1:5, 11), now echoing verbatim the words of the Accuser (2:5). However, the double meaning of the word *barak* as "bless" or "curse" makes the statement somewhat ambiguous (Cheney 1994:76). The imperative "die" may be viewed as a consequence or as an unavoidable end; it may be that Job should curse God so he will die, or it may mean Job should praise (bless) God and face the bitter end. In any case, unlike the friends, Job's wife expected the inevitability of his death. She affirmed the connection between righteousness and blessing and, ironically, reflected on the uselessness of piety. Though her thoughts were impious, they did not arise out of impiety but out of pity. Death was the merciful end that Job himself sought (3:20-21).

Job's wife was not a foolish woman, but she spoke as if she were. The only question for Job was the proper human response to divine providence—in whatever form it is experienced. Job's answer was that the only possible human response is submissive faith, trust that God knows what he is doing. His response affirms the sovereign providence of God. This is the same piety witnessed in Job's blessing the God who gives and takes away (1:21).

At this point it might seem that another scene in heaven should resolve the question about Job (Clines 1985:129-130). It might further seem that the question of the significance of Job's suffering is settled (Clines 1985:133-134) and that there is the possibility of piety for its own sake. However, at this point the heavens remain sealed, and it is clear this is not just a story of the ancient hero Job. The meaning of Job's suffering serves as an inquiry into the problem of suffering, for Job knew nothing of the moral conundrum discussed in the heavenly council. The reader knows the reason for Job's suffering and now identifies with Job for whom suffering is full of mystery.

ENDNOTES

1. The best clues we have regarding this tradition are found in the Tell Fekheriyah curse (lines 28-29; COS 2.34, p. 154). For discussions of the word *qlqlt'*, "rubbish heap," see Jonas Greenfield and A. Shaffer, "Qlqlt'" *Revue Biblique* 92 (1985): 56-57.

◆ D. Job's Comforters (2:11-13)

11When three of Job's friends heard of the tragedy he had suffered, they got together and traveled from their homes to comfort and console him. Their names were Eliphaz the Temanite, Bildad the Shuhite, and Zophar the Naamathite. 12When they saw Job from a distance, they scarcely recognized him. Wailing loudly, they tore their robes and threw dust into the air over their heads to show their grief. 13Then they sat on the ground with him for seven days and nights. No one said a word to Job, for they saw that his suffering was too great for words.

NOTES

2:11 *to comfort.* The Heb. indicates an action of shaking the head. It is usually understood to be a sympathetic gesture of consolation, but Fohrer thinks it is an apotropaic gesture to ward off evil (1989:104).

Eliphaz the Temanite. Teman is always represented as one of the principal localities of Edom (Gen 36:11, 15; Ezek 25:13; Amos 1:11-12). It was legendary for its wisdom (Jer 49:7).

Bildad the Shuhite. Shuah is mentioned as the son of Abraham and Keturah, the brother of Midian and the uncle of Sheba and Dedan (Gen 25:2; 1 Chr 1:32), a locale in Edom or Arabia. The name Bildad occurs in this form only in Job.

Zophar the Naamathite. Naamah is the name of a female descendant of Cain, who is the eponymous ancestor of the wandering tribe of the Kenites (Gen 4:22). The Kenites are associated with the Midianites in the Sinai and Arabian deserts (Num 10:29; Judg 4:11). The name Zophar is also known only in Job.

2:12 *they scarcely recognized him.* The Heb. says they did not recognize Job, usually taken to mean they could not recognize Job at a distance (RSV, NRSV, NEB, TEV). One does not normally expect to recognize another at a distance; it is more logical to say they did know this was Job as they approached him (NIV, NLT), implying they were close enough to recognize him. The Heb. disjunctive and the general sense suggest that their ability to recognize Job was unrelated to distance.

COMMENTARY

The identity of the three friends and their habitats are given only in a general manner, but there is no reason to doubt that they were real people. As suggested in the notes, the places are likely to be identified with similar names found in Genesis and related passages; each are associated with a region in northwest Arabia near Edom. Though the names Bildad and Zophar are unique to Job, they consist of elements of Hebrew names known elsewhere.[1] The fact that they met by appointment suggests that they were acquaintances and agreed it was best they come together to mourn with Job.

The way in which Job's friends responded to his condition indicates Job's utter desolation. It is often thought that apotropaic rites to ward off evil were involved, either in the shaking of the head (see note on 2:11) or in the throwing of dust toward heaven (Gordis 1978:24). Fohrer interprets the throwing of dust toward heaven as an action protesting a disaster of heavenly origin or an attempt to stir up the heavens in revenge (1989:104-106), similar to the action of Moses in the plagues (Exod 9:8-10). Not recognizing Job could also be part of a ritual, where a mourner arrives in disbelief and only later acknowledges the reality of the loss (Clines 1989:60-61). Clines argues that the friends actually treat Job as if he were dead (1989:61-62); their silence is explained as representative of their refusal to acknowledge Job as being alive. Thus, their rituals of mourning were not for Job's children but for Job himself. However, the focus of the passage is not on the attitude of the friends. Their responses demonstrate the extreme nature of the effect of the test on Job. Seeing Job from afar means they knew the distant figure in lonely vigil on the ash heap to be Job. But they could no longer recognize him; either Job himself was disfigured beyond recognition (cf. Isa 52:14), or his situation was now so altered that no semblance of his status as the greatest of all the men of the east remained.

The sincerity of the friends is not to be questioned. Though the gestures of grief—such as the loud wailing, the tearing of garments, and sitting in the dust—are conventional, they are also genuine and are a way of empathizing with the mourner in the disruption of ordinary life. However, this empathy should not be overstated. Nothing in the narrative suggests that throwing dust in the air was a means of summoning, as Moses did (Exod 9:8, 10), afflictions of boils on the mourners themselves (Habel 1985:97). Whatever the precise meaning of this gesture of mourning, it is found in other contexts of death and anger (cf. Acts 22:23). The silence of seven days represents a complete period of mourning in a time of utter disaster; in a similar manner, Ezekiel sat stunned for seven days when he met the exiles (Ezek 3:15). This is not morbid rejection or distinguished wisdom but simply a means by which Job's friends come alongside him as true companions within the customs of their culture.

The appearance of the friends in the narrative is not only a means of indicating the severity of the trial, but it provides a transition to the dialog by introducing those who genuinely wanted to support a friend. It further allows the reader to identify with them in a response to suffering. Severe suffering that transfigures individuals such that we can no longer recognize them is a sad phenomenon throughout history. It can be the physical distortions of severe illness or accident. It can also be economic and financial so that we no longer recognize the abode of a former friend. These transformations can happen with the suddenness experienced by Job.

At such times, it is important to be a friend, most importantly by simply being present. The custom followed by the friends in being silent is prudent; we must not presume we have something to tell people in such circumstances. It is best to let the sufferer speak first, for the comforter has much to learn from the afflicted. When the afflicted does speak, a response must be judicious and not presume too much knowledge, particularly in efforts to defend God or provide explanations. The negative example of the friends in this latter regard becomes the means by which our own thoughts on suffering are tested and refined.

ENDNOTES
1. A concise and helpful discussion is found in Gordis (1978:23). De Wilde provides a helpful chart in which the land of Uz and the friends are linked to Terah the father of Abram (1981:92). Pope provides possible broader Semitic associations of the names (1965:23-24).

◆ II. Dialog (Job and His Friends): The Question of Retribution (3:1–25:6)
    A. Job: Despair for the Day of Birth (3:1-26)
        1. The universe should not have Job's day (3:1-10)

At last Job spoke, and he cursed the day of his birth. ²He said:

³ "Let the day of my birth be erased,
    and the night I was conceived.
⁴ Let that day be turned to darkness.
    Let it be lost even to God on high,
    and let no light shine on it.
⁵ Let the darkness and utter gloom
    claim that day for its own.
    Let a black cloud overshadow it,
    and let the darkness terrify it.
⁶ Let that night be blotted off the
    calendar,
    never again to be counted among
    the days of the year,
    never again to appear among
    the months.
⁷ Let that night be childless.
    Let it have no joy.
⁸ Let those who are experts at cursing—
    whose cursing could rouse
    Leviathan*—
    curse that day.
⁹ Let its morning stars remain dark.
    Let it hope for light, but in vain;
    may it never see the morning light.
¹⁰ Curse that day for failing to shut my
    mother's womb,
    for letting me be born to see all this
    trouble.

3:8 The identification of Leviathan is disputed, ranging from an earthly creature to a mythical sea monster in ancient literature.

NOTES

3:1 This verse begins a dialog that concludes in 25:6. The dialog is generally considered to consist of three cycles that begin and end with Job. The problem is that the third cycle is incomplete, with a very short speech for Bildad and none for Zophar. Various proposals have been made concerning the structure of the dialog, usually involving rearrangement of the Heb. text to create a complete third cycle. Since the third speech of Job is very long (chs 26–31) and portions of it contain sentiments expressed by the friends, it is thought the text has been disrupted. A minimal rearrangement is to assign 26:5-14 to Bildad and 27:13-23 to Zophar. Such a speculative rearrangement, however, creates more problems than it solves: the final speeches of Bildad and Zophar remain fragmentary, and the hymn to wisdom (ch 28) with the following soliloquy does not contain a response to Zophar. It must be concluded that there is not a complete third cycle because the dialog has broken down.

An alternate proposal by Wolfers is that there are really only two cycles, each of which begin and end with Eliphaz (1995:225-255). The first cycle begins with chs 4–5 and ends with 15:2-16; the second cycle begins with 15:17-35 and ends with ch 22. The theme of the first cycle is the inevitable association of suffering and sin in the function of justice; the second cycle describes the terrible state in which the wicked are condemned to live (Wolfers 1995:254). But, such a division of ch 15 is totally unjustified. It fails to take account of the quotation in 15:14-16, which contains the central question of the dialog. This quote is introduced in a direct rebuke to Job in verses 12-13; verse 17 begins the response of Eliphaz to the question and can scarcely introduce a whole new round of speeches.

Wolfers is correct in suggesting that there is not a complete third cycle. The last speech of Bildad (ch 25), which also quotes the question, appears to be interrupted by Job because evidently traditional wisdom has nothing further on the matter. The third cycle then dissolves, and a monologue of Job ensues, which opens the way for other responses to the key question. The dialog is also opened by Job, as he begins with a lament of his wretched life.

3:2 *He said.* The dialog continues the technique of exact repetition of phrases already observed in the prologue. "He said" in Heb. expression is identical to the introduction of each of the speeches that will follow as a reply (4:1; 6:1; 8:1; etc.). These are not simply statements, as is often suggested by the translations in the latter references (RSV, NIV), but rather are responses to the situation. This verse introduces us to Job's second response to his calamity (cf. 1:21-22).

3:5 *utter gloom.* Lit. "the shadow of death," a phrase found in Ps 23:4; it refers to death itself or the place of death (10:21-22). A day dies when it is overcome by the deepest darkness in which no light is possible.

claim that day. The expression is commonly used for a relative laying claim to property that belonged to the family. Job is asking that death take possession of his day. The meaning "stain" (KJV) is not appropriate as a metaphor in this verse.

let the darkness terrify it. The meaning "darkness" for the Heb. *kimrir* [TH3650, ZH4025] is obtained from the Semitic root *kmr*. Though this use is attested only in Syriac, it is to be preferred in this context. The Masoretic vocalization supposes the root *marar* [TH4843, ZH5352] meaning "bitterness." The ancient Jewish commentators Rashi and Ibn Ezra understood this to be a reference to a Canaanite deity, based on Deut 32:24, where *meriri* [TH4815, ZH5321] is parallel to *resep*, the Canaanite god of the underworld (cf. Heb. of Job 5:7).

3:6 *never again to be counted.* This meaning, based on the root *yakhad* [TH3161, ZH3479] (joined), is preferable. The NLT seems to agree with repointing the vowels from the MT to the stative stem (niphal) and assigning it the lexical form *khadah* [TH2302A, ZH2526] ("to appear"; cf. root II, HALOT 1:292). The translation "let it not rejoice" (RSV) is based on the *khadah* root I [TH2302, ZH2525].

3:8 *Leviathan.* The sea monster, often called Leviathan, was a way of referring to the unruly chaotic waters before creation, which had to be quashed before the emergence of created order (cf. Ps 74:13-14).

COMMENTARY

Job begins his speech by cursing "his day" (cf. "day of his birth"; 3:1, NLT). This day is not just that of Job's birth, though he does begin with the wish that that day would have never been. The expression "his day" is more inclusive, carrying the sense of "his time," making reference to the period of his life. Job laments the time he was conceived, the fact that he was born, and the time in which he is living and suffering. His curse was in reality a complaint, for the curse was directed against that which cannot be changed—namely, past events. His curse was an imprecation against the hard circumstances of his life.

The words of Job that follow are a further response to his situation. Job earlier expressed his trust in God as one who gives and one who takes (1:21), as one who is sovereign over both good and evil (2:10). Job now responds with a wish that his very existence in the universe be obliterated. This ought not to be taken as a sign that Job had cracked under the strain (Andersen 1976:100). The fiery outburst of passion is not a weakness but an expression of Job's humanity and his deepest desires. Self-control (Gal 5:23) is not a repression of all feeling and desire but rather a self-mastery that leads to the highest possible level of achievement. A man made of stone and bronze might remain unmoved (6:12), but this Job cannot be. Job is "bereaved, humiliated, and in pain. His skin is festering and his nerves are on fire"

(Andersen 1976:101). The test was not to see if Job could remain as unmoved as a piece of wood but whether he would curse God. Job's "volcanic outbursts" (Andersen 1976:98) are startling in comparison to the tranquility of the prologue, but his strength of faith remained intact. Job did not bewail the losses of wealth, family, or health. His concern from beginning to end was his life with God, which, from his circumstances, appeared to be lost. It was the apparent alienation of God himself that led Job to wish that he should be excluded from God's universe.

In Hebrew thought, it was impossible to isolate a relationship with God from the ordinary concerns of work, family, and body. God was known through these ordinary things of life; these things were the means by which the presence of God could be experienced. The loss of these ordinary things was both a loss of humanity and a loss of God. One's relationship with God did not lead to indifference toward bereavement, poverty, and pain. The only conclusion Job could draw from his situation was that he had lost God; and if this was true, then his life had no place in God's world.

Job did not ask for answers to his agony, nor did he question or reproach God in his passionate expression of grief. He could only wish that his life had been denied, that he had not been born to this trouble (3:10). The day of birth and the night of conception are two aspects of the same event: the beginning of Job's life. Job first addressed the day (3:4-5), then the night (3:6-9). God should not have called that day into being; light should never have come to it (3:4); it should have been obliterated by a darkness of death (3:5). That night should never have entered time (3:6); it should have remained barren and joyless (3:7); it should have been annihilated by the very forces that destroy creation itself (3:8). That night should never have survived to welcome the light of dawn (3:9). Grief is not rational—no one can wish away the past. Grief does not seek answers but seeks to come to terms with the present.

Though Job did not curse God, he felt that he no longer had any place in God's creation or purposes. Job did not deny the goodness of God's creation, but he did deny that all of God's creation is good. He used the language of creation to challenge the goodness of his own existence, which is to implicitly challenge the goodness of God. As happens so often in human passion, his grief made him presumptuous about his relationship with God. His losses led him to assume God was not present with him and therefore that his own presence within creation was not good.

What is automatically recognized in this section is that this "Job" seems quite different from the Job in the prologue. The Job of the prologue accepted life as experienced in God's providence: "The LORD gave me what I had, and the LORD has taken it away. Praise the name of the LORD!" (1:21). In chapter three Job laments his existence, decrying the very possibility of his life. Later in the dialog he will explicitly reject his life: "I am innocent, but it makes no difference to me—I despise my life" (9:21; cf. 7:16). This contrast is actually a key element that binds the entire book together and contributes to its point. After God speaks (later in the book), Job will reverse his attitude entirely: "I take back everything I said, and I sit in dust and ashes to show my repentance" (42:6). The Job of the prologue accentuates the intellectual and existential dilemma encountered by the children of faith. The Job of the dialog freely vents the anguish and anger caused by this dilemma. Eventually, Job repents after being challenged by God and thereby becomes a model of faith and integrity. Job received God's rebuke, but he also received his commendation.

◆   2. Job should have died at birth (3:11-19)

11 "Why wasn't I born dead?
Why didn't I die as I came from the womb?
12 Why was I laid on my mother's lap?
Why did she nurse me at her breasts?
13 Had I died at birth, I would now be at peace.
I would be asleep and at rest.
14 I would rest with the world's kings and prime ministers,
whose great buildings now lie in ruins.
15 I would rest with princes, rich in gold, whose palaces were filled with silver.
16 Why wasn't I buried like a stillborn child,
like a baby who never lives to see the light?
17 For in death the wicked cause no trouble,
and the weary are at rest.
18 Even captives are at ease in death,
with no guards to curse them.
19 Rich and poor are both there,
and the slave is free from his master.

NOTES

3:14 *whose great buildings now lie in ruins.* It has been suggested, on the basis of Arabic parallels, that this is a reference to pyramids. However, this is very tenuous. The rebuilding of ancient ruins was a mark of success (Isa 58:12; 61:4). The records of the prestigious accomplishments of great kings include the rebuilding and improvement of the cities of their ancestors, particularly their fortifications and temples (e.g., Sargon in Sumer, Nabonidus in Babylon).

3:17 *in death the wicked cause no trouble.* The Heb. refers to death obliquely: "There the wicked cease their troubling; there the weary are at rest." This is a common euphemism for the place of the dead (cf. 1:21; 3:19).

the weary. This is forcefully expressed as those exhausted and without strength.

3:18 *Even captives are at ease in death.* More precisely, all the prisoners will rest without fear from their taskmaster.

3:19 *Rich and poor are both there.* The point is not equality of status after death but that death claims all people. The Heb. refers to the small and the great, which would include status and achievement, as well as wealth.

COMMENTARY

For one whose life was a struggle, death would be release. Death was described by Job as the place where one lies in quiet, where there is sleep and rest. In death those taken captive as slaves are at ease; they are set free from the taskmaster. Though it might seem that Job desired to be set free from pain, the focus of this section is rather on the conflict of human relations. Job had suffered the entire loss of his position and influence; he had come to be at the opposite end of the social spectrum. He had begun to experience the powerlessness of the poor and could understand their suffering at the hands of their masters.

Job looked to death not so much as the equalizer of status but rather as the means by which conflict would be removed, resulting in peace. The description of death as peace is given in two complementary sections, the second of which explains the first. Job began by asking why he could not have died at birth (3:11-12), a question he repeats (3:16). The repetition of the question divides Job's observations on the preferability of death. In the first section (3:13-15), Job describes the powerful rulers who amass wealth and undertake great restorations. In the second section (3:17-19), Job describes the wicked in conflict with the weak and the slaves in conflict with their taskmasters. In ancient societies kings amassed their wealth through enslavement of their subjects. The idea of the wicked troubling others (3:17) is readily perceived as the rulers afflicting the powerless. In death the great conflict of this disparity is removed, for both the great and the small are there, the place where none has power over another. Death removes the conflict caused by social disparity between peoples and provides peace.

The suffering and loss experienced by Job are not on the same level as ordinary suffering. The exceptional suffering of the exceptionally pious shakes the very foundations of order in the world and within society (Clines 1989:91). Job now realized as never before that the order of society is not secure and does not provide peace. The wicked may be the wealthy who throw life into turmoil in their great accomplishments, and the righteous may suffer, powerless to change their lot in this life. Job found his lot with the poor—he was helpless in the great conflict of life. Only in death is there escape from this struggle. If death had been granted to Job at birth, he might have had peace.

3. Job should be allowed to die now (3:20-26)

20 "Oh, why give light to those in misery,
   and life to those who are bitter?
21 They long for death, and it won't come.
   They search for death more eagerly
      than for hidden treasure.
22 They're filled with joy when they
      finally die,
   and rejoice when they find the grave.
23 Why is life given to those with no
      future,

those God has surrounded with
   difficulties?
24 I cannot eat for sighing;
   my groans pour out like water.
25 What I always feared has happened
      to me.
   What I dreaded has come true.
26 I have no peace, no quietness.
   I have no rest; only trouble
      comes."

NOTES

3:20 *to those in misery.* The Heb. word *'amel* [TH6001, ZH6664] has the sense of toil, a fitting descriptor for the labor of life that brings exhaustion not only from exertion but also from turmoil, conflict, and worry.

3:21 *They search for death.* The Heb. verb has the connotation of digging; the image is that of a grave robber looking for buried treasure. Job searched for his own grave more eagerly than a grave robber.

3:22 *They're filled with joy when they finally die.* It is probable that there is a double entendre in the choice of idiom; the word *gil* [TH1524A, ZH1637] means rejoice, but *gal* [TH1530, ZH1643] (a heap of stones) could be a type of burial marker. Job would rejoice to see his own marked grave.

3:24 *I cannot eat for sighing.* The import of the line is quite powerful; it suggests that sighs have become food for Job. Since Job cannot eat, his only nourishment is sighing. It does not mean "sighing comes before I eat" (KJV).

COMMENTARY

In this section, we see a man so miserable that he feeds on nothing but his own sighs. Job lamented that life denied him the very thing he desired most, that which he could surely find in death: peace. He was grieved that God gave him light and life when he was in such a miserable condition.

Light is a common metaphor for life (cf. Eccl 11:7), but it is particularly appropriate for Job, the person whose greatest longing was that his day never be allowed in creation, never permitted to see the dawn. Though Job's question as to why he should see the light is a lament of anguish, there is no escaping the implication that Job's groaning is a reproach against God, for the God of Job is the only source of life. This becomes even clearer when Job asks why life should be given to those without a future, whose lives God has hedged in with trouble. The loss of everything could only signify that Job's plight was hidden from God (Isa 40:27). Job could not triumphantly wait for renewed strength, as Isaiah had exhorted Israel (Isa 40:31); Job could wait only for death, which would not come. Israel could look to the broken covenant as the cause of her suffering, but for Job there was no possible explanation; he could only long for escape.

Though Job brought this reproach against God in the exasperation caused by his suffering, he could not doubt the sovereign provision of the one who continued to give him life. The story of Job is a story of resolute faith, however much Job might have been compelled to challenge the Almighty. He did not contemplate suicide. Such an act would have been a failure of faith, a taking into his own hands a life that was not his to take, for it was a gift. Job came to feel that the gift was cruel, but that did not grant him the power to deny that gift. Though his plight seemed to be hidden from God, the fact of his life was an undeniable testimony of God's sovereign purpose.

All of us are very aware of the troubles that beset life, and we seek to live so we may avoid them. Job's fears may have been those he had in the time of his prosperity, for even then he lived with scrupulous care (1:5), but he most certainly described even further his present dilemma and his lack of peace. It would seem the worst he imagined was a continual reality, so completely had his life been hid from God's care. Yet he continued to have life, undesirable though it was. His situation demanded an explanation.

Two possible solutions to Job's dilemma are provided in the dialog that follows. One is to assume that we understand God's ways and are obligated to defend them. The other is to conclude that we do not understand the ways of God. This brings us to realize what is perhaps the worst of all fears: we have no means of determining our fate and avoiding suffering. This will be Job's position, but it is not one he will accept without challenging the God who continued to give him life.

B. Eliphaz: The Harvest of Sorrows (4:1–5:27)
1. You reap what you sow (4:1-11)

Then Eliphaz the Temanite replied to Job:

2 "Will you be patient and let me say a word?
For who could keep from speaking out?

3 "In the past you have encouraged many people;
you have strengthened those who were weak.
4 Your words have supported those who were falling;
you encouraged those with shaky knees.
5 But now when trouble strikes, you lose heart.
You are terrified when it touches you.
6 Doesn't your reverence for God give you confidence?

Doesn't your life of integrity give you hope?

7 "Stop and think! Do the innocent die?
When have the upright been destroyed?

8 My experience shows that those who plant trouble
and cultivate evil will harvest the same.
9 A breath from God destroys them.
They vanish in a blast of his anger.
10 The lion roars and the wildcat snarls,
but the teeth of strong lions will be broken.
11 The fierce lion will starve for lack of prey,
and the cubs of the lioness will be scattered.

NOTES

4:2 Will you be patient? Eliphaz actually begins in the most considerate manner possible. His first words are a conditional sentence in the form of a question: "Should one venture a word with you, could you endure?" Eliphaz is politely asking Job whether he could endure a conversation or whether he would become exasperated; the Heb. *la'ah* [TH3811, ZH4206] means either to be "unable" or to be "weary." This is in contrast with the next line, where Eliphaz says one is not able to refrain from speech. It is probable that the word to be "able" (*yakol* [TH3201, ZH3523]) in the second line is parallel to *la'ah* (to be "unable") in the first, so the contrast is between the words Job might not be able to bear and the words that cannot be constrained.

4:3 you have strengthened. Unless the Heb. word *yasar* [TH3256B, ZH3580] is being used as an alternate form of '*ashar*, the sense is not really that of "strengthening" but "correction"; the emphasis is more on the way Job has been of assistance as a counselor. The verb *yasar* does not refer to intellectual instruction but education of a moral nature; the sense of discipline is not appropriate here but rather the sense of counsel in a time of distress.

4:5 you lose heart. The translation "lose heart" for the Heb. verb *la'ah* [TH3811, ZH4206] assumes the meaning "to be weary"; the sense is probably that Job is unable to endure, as in verse two.

4:10 The Heb. has five words for "lion" in verses 10 and 11. The distinguishing feature appears to be the young of the lions referred to in the second half of each verse. Though the adult lion is a fierce animal, the teeth of its young may be broken (4:10), or the cubs may be scattered for lack of food (4:11). The violence of the lion is frequently applied as a metaphor for the wicked (Pss 7:2; 22:13; 34:10; 35:17; 58:6).

COMMENTARY

Eliphaz began his speech with a sympathetic spirit, fully supportive of his friend. His opening remark, however, was balanced by his closing remark, which is a subtle rebuke (5:27). He could not constrain his speech, for he had to affirm that which Job should already know. The question at this point was not one of intellectual information; rather, it was a question of whether Job could apply this information to his situation. Would he be unable to bear it should one remind him (4:2)? Would he be able to recognize for himself what he knew about others (5:27)? Eliphaz remembered Job as a wise counselor (4:3) and, no doubt, as a firm disciplinarian who would correct those in error but who would never fail to encourage. The physician, however, appeared to be unable to heal himself. Job was horrified at what had happened to him. His worst fears had become a reality. But in Eliphaz's thinking, Job's reverence for God and the integrity of his life should be a consoling confidence at such a time. This is what Job had always affirmed, and it should now be truer than ever.

Eliphaz provided a simple reminder of the facts. If Job was upright, as there was every reason to assume, there was nothing to fear. What he was experiencing would yet turn out to be a blessing, and Job must not seek to escape the experience (5:17). Evil and trouble do not just happen; they are the result of human conduct (4:8). The analogy of Eliphaz is assisted by the fact that iniquity or wrongdoing (*'awen* [TH205, ZH224]) and trouble or sorrow (*'amal* [TH5999, ZH6662]) can refer to both the act and its consequences. The action is like sowing, and its consequence is the reaping; sinfulness brings about wrong and vanity, making trouble brings about sorrow and misery. This is a part of the divine order in this world (4:9); it is the manner in which judgment operates. The breath of God's fury is like the hot desert wind that scorches all vegetation. The breath of God may either be a life-giving force (Gen 2:7) or it may snuff life out so it perishes. The wicked not only reap the consequences of their own actions, they also find themselves the object of destructive wrath. This simple truth can also be observed in the animal world (4:10-11; cf. Ps 34:10). The violent can never survive by the strength that enables them to be violent. If the violent could survive by the power of their violence, the whelps of the lion would never come to grief. In nature we see both the mighty lion and its young die. We may, therefore, conclude that our destiny is not in our hands; the innocent do not perish, but the violent do perish. The repetition of the word perish (*'abad*) forms an introduction and conclusion to the simple lesson Job knew so well.

The central point of Eliphaz's lecture is that one reaps what one sows. All analogies, like this one—"you reap what you sow"—are very useful in their power to make a point, but that which is their strength also makes them dangerous. An analogy is not applicable in all respects. The comparison of sowing and reaping with the consequences of human conduct is self-evident (cf. Gal 6:7), but the complexities of human conduct go far beyond one analogy. Although the one aspect that the analogy illustrates may be powerfully relevant in the instances where it is true, it may not be at all relevant in other instances. Though it is not evidently the intent of Eliphaz, the implications of his analogies make him a truly miserable comforter. Not only must Job be a sinner but so must his sons and daughters whom he so deeply loved, for they were all cut off, which is something that does not happen to the innocent (4:7). Job's efforts on their behalf were of no avail. However much Eliphaz may have believed that Job was upright and that his punishment would correct his failings, his assurance that the innocent are not cut off was not much comfort to one who wanted his life to end (3:22). The words of Eliphaz did not soothe the wounded Job; rather, they were salt on his wounds. In this way, the author of Job succeeded in exposing this "doctrine" and its oversimplified analogies.

2. Can a person be righteous before God? (4:12-21)

12 "This truth was given to me in secret,
   as though whispered in my ear.
13 It came to me in a disturbing vision
   at night,
   when people are in a deep sleep.
14 Fear gripped me,
   and my bones trembled.
15 A spirit* swept past my face,
   and my hair stood on end.*
16 The spirit stopped, but I couldn't see
   its shape.
   There was a form before my eyes.
   In the silence I heard a voice say,
17 'Can a mortal be innocent before
   God?

Can anyone be pure before the
   Creator?'
18 "If God does not trust his own angels
   and has charged his messengers
   with foolishness,
19 how much less will he trust people
   made of clay!
   They are made of dust, crushed
   as easily as a moth.
20 They are alive in the morning but
   dead by evening,
   gone forever without a trace.
21 Their tent-cords are pulled and the
   tent collapses,
   and they die in ignorance.

4:15a Or wind; also in 4:16.   4:15b Or its wind sent shivers up my spine.

NOTES

4:13 *a disturbing vision at night.* The vision is described as one of confusing and disturbing thoughts. The Heb. se'ippim [TH5587A, ZH8546] is probably a metaphorical usage of the word "branch" (se'appah [TH5589, ZH6190]), as suggested by Rowley (1970:53): "Just as the boughs branch off from the trees, so thoughts and opinions can branch off in more than one direction, leading to bewilderment and indecision."

deep sleep. This sleep (tardemah [TH8639, ZH9554]) was not ordinary, but a very deep sleep (Prov 19:15), often one with a supernatural dimension (Gen 2:21; 1 Sam 26:12). This vision is described in the same terms as when God came to Abraham to confirm his promise (Gen 15:1, 12).

4:15 *A spirit swept.* The word ruakh [TH7307, ZH8120] can be either wind or spirit; this verse suggests there was a wind, but in that wind was the divine presence as in other theophanies. In his response, Job will imply that he received divine words (6:10c, 26).

my hair stood on end. The NLT mg reads, "Or, *its wind sent shivers up my spine.*" The Heb. is a homonym which can mean either "hair" (*sa'arah* [TH8185, ZH8553]) or "wind, gale" (*se'arah* [TH8183, ZH8554]), so the phrase is often translated "the hair of my body bristled." But the meaning with "wind" is preferable for several reasons (Blommerde 1969:40): (1) wind forms a parallel with *ruakh* in the previous line (cf. Pss 107:25; 148:8); (2) in the only other occurrence of the word "bristle" (*samar* [TH5568, ZH6169]), it speaks of the body trembling in fear (Ps 119:120); and (3) the form of the word is not genitive but absolute (cf. Gesenius §80b).

4:17 *Can a mortal be innocent before God?* The translation of this phrase as a comparative, asking if one can be more just than God (NIV, KJV, ASV), is decidedly incorrect. The preposition *min* [TH4480, ZH4946] simply indicates presence before God, equivalent to its use in Num 32:22: "fulfilled your duty to the LORD." The comparative does not make sense in the present argument, and the question cannot be translated this way in any of its other occurrences (9:2; 15:14; 25:4).

4:20 *gone forever without a trace.* They disappear with no awareness of what has happened. The question is whether it is the moth itself that is unaware, or whether others take no notice. Almost certainly this line is meant to be parallel with 21b (Gordis 1978:51); moths die without wisdom—that is, they learn nothing about their own existence. The expression of verse 20 (*mibbeli mesim*) is elliptical for turning the mind to something (*sim leb* [TH7760/3820, ZH8492/4213]), a favorite expression of Haggai (Hag 1:5, 7; 2:15, 18). Before the moth can give attention to its life or death, it is gone.

COMMENTARY

Eliphaz spoke as though the truths he had just uttered came to him via a vision. This vision was related as a disturbing and frightful experience. It may have been the apparition itself that produced the fright, as might be expected from the sudden experience of a divine encounter. It would seem to be a preternatural sleep that was described, as in the experience of Adam (Gen 2:21) or Abraham (Gen 15:12). Below, it will be argued that he is actually recounting a vision that Job has reported, but first we will examine the content of the vision.

In this vision, a question is raised: "Can a mortal be innocent before God?" (4:17; cf. 9:2; 15:14; 25:4). The meaning of the question must be determined through the explanation that follows (4:18-21). The question has often been assumed to describe the universal sinfulness of humanity, with the result that suffering will come to all. This, however, is not the problem in the book of Job, nor is it the point of the following argument. The problem is the complete disproportion of suffering Job must endure. If sin were the problem, then it could be forgiven (7:20-21). The explanation is provided in a traditional form of wisdom disputation, in which the argument is made from the greater to the lesser. Essentially it points out the frailty and vulnerability of all created beings. Even the heavenly servants do not escape God's scrupulous attention and may be suddenly charged with folly; the inference to be made is that even they cannot understand or control what may happen to them. How much less, then, can those whose formation was from the dust understand or control what happens to them? In the words of Gibson, "The implication is clearly of a capricious deity, who sows discord in the heavenly places and permits only ignorance on earth" (1975:267).

Job's complaint is that he is simply God's target, and the watchful eye of God allows him no moment of relief (7:19-20). This point is driven home by the comparison of the human experience with the moth. In a moment without warning the moth is crushed. It knew no significance to its life or its death; it dies in ignorance. The painful truth is that human experience is no different. In the end it is impossible to comprehend the destiny of our earthly lives; we are cut off before we are any wiser about what has happened.

This understanding of the vision and its explanation is not only in harmony with Job's later perceptions (7:19-21) but also with what we know from the prologue. Job's troubles began in the heavenly court in dealing with the Accuser. What happened to Job was completely under the sovereign control of God, and there was nothing that Job could have known or done to prevent its occurrence. This is precisely what the vision affirms. We do not have the power to determine that goodness will come to our lives.

This first speech of Eliphaz is a crux in understanding the argument and structure of the dialog. It is here that the major theme of Job, the mystery of evil, is discussed in response to a question that will be repeated throughout the dialog: "Can a mortal be innocent before God?" (4:17; cf. 9:2; 15:14; 25:4). The question is introduced in a vision (4:12-21) in this first speech of Eliphaz. The dialog progresses with formal indicators of speech (e.g., 4:1; 6:1), which mark the change of speaker, but quotations are found within the speeches as reference is made to the arguments of opposing speakers. Sometimes these have the explicit marks of citation (15:12-13 introduces 15:14-15 in this way and 15:16 closes the quote), but at other times the reference to the thoughts of an opponent is more subtle. In the first speech Eliphaz begins politely (4:1-11), but following the vision and its interpretation (4:12-21) his speech resumes with a rebuke to Job for seeking someone other than God. In 5:1 he says, "Cry for help, but will anyone answer you? Which of the angels will help you?" He continues with what must be regarded as a further rebuke (5:8); using a strong adversative ('ulam [TH199, ZH219]), Eliphaz contrasts himself to Job: "If I were you, I would go to God." To this point Job had not made any statements about the problem of evil. Why does Eliphaz think Job is consulting someone other than God for answers? Eliphaz speaks as if the vision contained a message contrary to what he believes but one that Job does believe. The direct challenge to Job (5:1, 8) indicates that the vision reflects the thoughts of Job, and Eliphaz is responding to this in his speech.

Since Job himself asks the question of the vision (9:2), and the last word of Bildad is the same question (25:4-6), the reader must ask about the source of this question. The origin of the question is also important to understanding its significance in the dialog. As discussed under "Major Themes" in the Introduction, the question must be answered negatively; mortals cannot be righteous before God. The question is not suggesting mortals can be sinless, since it is implicitly evident that Job and the friends know that no mortal is sinless (cf. 7:20-21). The question is asking whether it is possible for humans to live in a manner so righteous that they will be assured of blessing. The answer is that humans cannot guarantee blessing for themselves through their righteousness; they will die like moths, not knowing the time or the reason for the events of their lives. This is the position that Job maintains in the dialog. He is righteous, but he is not blessed; instead he is suffering, and he will soon die. The friends assert that the righteous are blessed, so they exhort Job to determine a future of blessing for himself. The dialog revolves around these two intransigent positions. Thus, the dialog makes the most sense if the vision with the question in the first speech is one Eliphaz has been told by Job. This is the reason Eliphaz rebukes Job immediately following his description of the vision. Understanding this clarifies the meaning and importance of the question, explains why Job asks the question, why Eliphaz twice reacts negatively to the question (5:1-8; 15:12-18), and why Bildad is cut short by Job when he raises the question in his last abbreviated speech.

Eliphaz introduces the cause and effect relationship with two analogies from nature. The first is drawn from agriculture (you reap what you sow), and the second from the wilds of nature (even the mightiest of the violent die). Having illustrated this self-evident truth, Eliphaz reports a terrifying vision concerning the mystery of evil. His first response is to assert again that people are the source of their own trouble (5:2-7), then he declares that God always punishes the wicked (5:8-16); therefore, if the righteous do suffer, it is to correct them so they are blessed in the end (5:17-27).

◆   ## 3. Evil is the root of trouble (5:1-7)

1 "Cry for help, but will anyone answer you?
  Which of the angels* will help you?
2 Surely resentment destroys the fool,
  and jealousy kills the simple.
3 I have seen that fools may be successful for the moment,
  but then comes sudden disaster.
4 Their children are abandoned far from help;
  they are crushed in court with no one to defend them.
5 The hungry devour their harvest, even when it is guarded by brambles.*
  The thirsty pant after their wealth.
6 But evil does not spring from the soil, and trouble does not sprout from the earth.
7 People are born for trouble as readily as sparks fly up from a fire.

5:1 Hebrew *the holy ones.*   5:5 The meaning of the Hebrew for this phrase is uncertain.

NOTES

5:1 *Which of the angels will help you?* The difficulties in translating this verse are both semantic and contextual. The adjective *qadosh* [TH6918A, ZH7705] can be used nominatively to refer to God as the Holy One in the singular (6:10) or in the honorific "plural" form (Prov 9:10; 30:3).[1] The plural is also used to refer to the saints as holy people (Ps 34:9) or to members of the divine council (Ps 89:5-7; Zech 14:5). Contextually, it is not clear whom Eliphaz thinks Job is calling on for help. He does, however, sharply contrast Job with himself, for he instead would appeal to God (5:8). Since Eliphaz used the plural to refer to members of the divine council in 15:15, it is likely he also had them in mind here. Perhaps he considered them to be the source of the vision (cf. 4:18) and that Job was using them to justify his situation. It may be possible to translate this as an appeal to turn to God, as Eliphaz himself would do: "To whom other than the Holy One can you turn?" (see Introduction, endnote 14). The syntax for such a translation, however, is not well supported.

5:3 but then comes sudden disaster. This is a paraphrase of a personal pronouncement from Eliphaz that the dwelling of the wicked is under a curse.

5:5 Even when it is guarded by brambles. This difficult Heb. line is usually translated with a reference to thorns (KJV, RSV, NIV, TEV), but the meaning is obscure (cf. NLT mg). The previous line says the hungry eat the harvest of the wicked, and this line is best taken as parallel to it, saying they take away his shriveled sheaf. This involves a redivision of the words in the MT and the addition of repeated letters easily lost in copying. The consonantal text *'l mtsnym* ("to thorns") becomes *'lmym tsnmym* ("withered sheaves"); the result is the vocabulary of sheaves found elsewhere in Scripture (cf. Gen 37:7; 41:23).

5:7 People are born for trouble. Habel (1985:117) translates verse 6 to say that trouble surely springs from the soil (taking the negative particle *lo'* [TH3808, ZH4202] as the asseverative *lu'* [TH3863, ZH4273]), referring to the fact that people are born to the hardship of the hostile ground (Gen 3:17-19). Eliphaz's point is not that trouble happens to people but rather that people create their own trouble (5:6). The word *yalad* [TH3205, ZH3528] can be vocalized as a passive or as a causative; in this case it should be the latter: "people *beget* trouble."

sparks. Lit. a reference to the mythological "sons of Resheph," a god of pestilence (cf. Heb. of Deut 32:24; Hab 3:5). The Phoenician god Resheph appears with lightning bolts. The "sons of Resheph" could refer to either the sparks of lightning or the shafts of pestilence. The latter would say, "People make trouble and a plague takes flight." According to Eliphaz, the actions of humans set free the powers of evil to cause trouble.

COMMENTARY

Eliphaz has been arguing the case for retribution. He introduced the cause-and-effect relationship of retribution with two analogies from nature. The first was drawn from agriculture (you reap what you sow) and the second from the wilds of nature (even the mightiest of the violent die). After illustrating this self-evident truth, Eliphaz recounted Job's terrifying vision concerning the mystery of evil (4:12-21). His first response to the revelation of the vision was to assert again that people are the source of their own trouble (5:2-7). Then he declared that God always punishes the wicked (5:8-16) and that if the righteous do suffer it is to correct them so they are blessed in the end (5:17-27).

Two questions face the reader as Eliphaz continues his speech in verse 1: why should Eliphaz imagine that Job would want to appeal to the "holy ones," and why should such appeal be futile or wicked? In answer to the first question, the reader might go back to the words of Job's lament. Clines (1981:186) suggests that Eliphaz has misunderstood Job's wish for death (3:21-22) and assumes that Job is in reality appealing to the "holy ones" for a calm and peaceful existence, the kind Eliphaz is about to describe (5:19-26). In answer to the second question, Eliphaz would regard such an appeal as futile because he believed Job was responsible for his own sufferings, and no external agency can remove that pain. There is, however, no reason to impute to Eliphaz a misunderstanding of Job's wish for death.

Job's appeal to the "holy ones" must refer to what immediately precedes it, namely, the vision he has just reported. His response shows that he learned about the vision from Job. Eliphaz rejects the message of this vision, but Job will affirm it. Job, in his reply to Eliphaz, asserts that he does have a word he received from God

(6:10), and he avers that he will not conceal it. This word is painful but true (6:25).
The only divine word that has been given is in this vision, and this is the word Job
refuses to conceal. Job believes this word is from God, but Eliphaz responds to the
vision by denying that it is from God.

The message of the vision is that humans are not pure enough in the eyes of God
to determine the destiny of their lives. Eliphaz contested such an assertion; he had
already made clear that humans are the cause of their own misery (4:8), a claim that
he illustrated in 5:3-5 and reiterated in 5:6-7. Contrary to the claim of the vision,
Eliphaz asserted that Job's fate lay entirely within his own power.

Eliphaz tried to persuade Job not to be a fool (5:2). The fool (*'ewil* [TH191A, ZH211])
is not simply one who is unwise but one who is morally bankrupt, one who has rejected the fear of the Lord, which is the beginning of wisdom. Eliphaz did not contend that Job was such a fool, for he had instructed many (4:3), but that his passion
could lead him into the irreversible self-destruction of the fool. Eliphaz knew such a
person, one who had been well established, but whom he recognized at once to be
accursed even while the signs of wealth were present.[2] The children of the fool
would never enjoy his wealth; both the court and the needy or greedy would go
against them; in short, they would be plundered by others. Eliphaz may have been
thinking of the seminomadic plunderers who would ravage the farmers' crops, as
happened in the days of Gideon (Judg 6:3-5). What happened to the fool was not
simply the result of natural forces. Evil and trouble do not spring from the soil as an
uncontrollable seed; they are a harvest that humans themselves have sown (4:8).
People bring about the birth of trouble themselves (5:7); their own actions set free
the powers of pestilence and destruction.

Eliphaz was not saying that trouble is the inevitable result of birth. Eliphaz's
argument is that the fool is the cause of his own downfall; he is not the victim of
being born into an unfriendly world. In verse 7 Eliphaz seals his argument with this
"astounding and provocative generalization" (Clines 1989:141) that presumes he
has explained the cause of all human suffering.

ENDNOTES
1. Grammatically this is traditionally referred to as *pluralis majestatis* or an intensive plural;
   cf. Waltke & O'Conner 7.4.3b.
2. The Heb. says Eliphaz pronounced the dwelling of the wicked accursed; this does not
   mean Eliphaz pronounced a curse upon the fool, but rather that Eliphaz could declare
   the fool accursed even though the evidence was not yet present.

◆   4. God judges evil (5:8-16)

8 "If I were you, I would go to God
   and present my case to him.
9 He does great things too marvelous to
   understand.
   He performs countless miracles.
10 He gives rain for the earth

   and water for the fields.
11 He gives prosperity to the poor
   and protects those who suffer.
12 He frustrates the plans of schemers
   so the work of their hands will not
   succeed.

¹³He traps the wise in their own
  cleverness
so their cunning schemes are
  thwarted.
¹⁴They find it is dark in the daytime,
  and they grope at noon as if it
  were night.

¹⁵He rescues the poor from the cutting
  words of the strong,
and rescues them from the clutches
  of the powerful.
¹⁶And so at last the poor have hope,
  and the snapping jaws of the wicked
  are shut.

NOTES

5:8 *If I were you, I would go to God.* Eliphaz spoke for himself: "As for me, this is what I do." His correction of Job was polite, not confrontational.

and present my case to him. Eliphaz was asking Job to leave his cause with God. Unlike Job, he did not think Job had a legal case as one who had been wronged (cf. 9:2-3). Eliphaz has already said there is no one to whom Job can appeal (5:1). He now begins a doxology extolling the marvelous providence of God for his creation. Eliphaz's message: Job should rest in the assurance that God does everything right.

5:16 *the snapping jaws of the wicked are shut.* The metaphor of the Heb. is that wickedness must shut its mouth; that is, the wicked sit in stunned silence at the reversal of fortune. This verse shares a line with Ps 107:42.

COMMENTARY

In contrast to Job, who appeared to be following false or futile wisdom, Eliphaz described how he himself would approach God. In doing so, he showed how little he understood Job. Eliphaz began with the typical theme of the unfathomable works of God (5:9). Job, of course, accepted this; Job will ironically repeat this exact line in his own speech (9:10). But for Job these great works of God have a destructive side. As Eliphaz contemplated the works of God, he saw two complementary aspects: God sustains and restores creation (5:10), and in the same way he maintains moral and social order by redressing evil (5:11-16). In the arid east, rain is the greatest of wonders (5:10); it has the power to transform the world (cf. 36:27-28; 38:26-27; Ps 147:8). The former and the latter rains are the mark of the changing seasons and the sign of divine providence (Joel 2:23). Just as rain transforms the ground, God reverses the situation of the poor (5:11). The crafty are taken in their own cunning (5:12-13); they are caught in their own trap—a sentiment expressed elsewhere in Scripture (Pss 7:14-15; 10:2; 35:7-8; Prov 26:27). Though their tongues are sharp swords (5:15)—a reference to the calumny of the unscrupulous— their mouths will be silenced in astonishment (5:16). Eliphaz intended his view of God to be a source of hope for Job, just as it was for himself. Not only should this certainty of justice have been an assurance for Job (cf. 4:6), but Job should have considered his "chastisement" a blessing, as Eliphaz would go on to explain.

◆   5. God delivers the righteous (5:17-27)

¹⁷"But consider the joy of those
  corrected by God!

Do not despise the discipline of the
  Almighty when you sin.

18 For though he wounds, he also
    bandages.
  He strikes, but his hands also heal.
19 From six disasters he will rescue you;
    even in the seventh, he will keep
    you from evil.
20 He will save you from death in time
    of famine,
    from the power of the sword in time
    of war.
21 You will be safe from slander
    and have no fear when destruction
    comes.
22 You will laugh at destruction and
    famine;
    wild animals will not terrify you.
23 You will be at peace with the stones
    of the field,

and its wild animals will be at peace
    with you.
24 You will know that your home
    is safe.
  When you survey your possessions,
    nothing will be missing.
25 You will have many children;
    your descendants will be as plentiful
    as grass!
26 You will go to the grave at a ripe
    old age,
    like a sheaf of grain harvested at
    the proper time!

27 "We have studied life and found all
    this to be true.
  Listen to my counsel, and apply
    it to yourself."

NOTES

5:19 *From six disasters he will rescue you; even in the seventh, he will keep you from evil.* This is the Heb. poetic device known as the numerical saying; these use a sequence of two numbers—here six disasters, seven calamities.

5:20-23 It is possible that the catalog of calamities uses seven calamities as a symbol of completeness, and that the parallelism of the poetry has resulted in a certain duplication. Job 5:22b and 5:23b appear to say the same thing, and it is unlikely that destruction in line 22a is to be distinguished from the calamity of famine. The seven calamities would then be famine (20a), war (20b), fire (21a; NLT's "slander"), flood (21b), "ravaging famine" (22a), drought (23a) and animal destruction (23b).

5:21 *safe from slander.* The Heb. elliptically refers to "the roving tongue." This may be the human tongue, or it may be a tongue of fire. It is somewhat odd that a personal attack should be included in a list of natural calamities, and we should more likely think of fire here. As destruction is mentioned in the following line, it is possible that "destruction" here is a reference specifically to a flood, parallel with fire (Gordis 1978:59); the Aramaic cognate of *shod* [TH7701, ZH8719] (destruction) frequently has the meaning "flow" or "pour."

5:22 *destruction and famine.* This may be a hendiadys for "ravaging famine."

5:23 *peace with the stones . . . animals.* The verse distinguishes two threats of the field: drought and destruction by animals. "Peace with the stones" is covenant language; the fields take a vow promising good crops. Peace with the animals means the crops will be safe from their plunder.

COMMENTARY

Eliphaz cited traditional wisdom to explain Job's present situation: the Lord disciplines those he loves (Prov 3:12). Such discipline should not be rejected (Job 5:17b parallels Prov 3:11a) because even in discipline, we should recognize that we are blessed (Job 5:17a parallels Ps 94:12a). If God injures, we know he will bandage (cf. Hos 6:1); if he strikes, he will heal (cf. Deut 32:39). God may be the agent of suffering, but it is for our greater good. The verbal allusion to the glib response of unrepentant Israel in Hosea 6:1, that though the Lord had injured he would heal, may be an indication that in the mouth of Eliphaz this well-known axiom similarly lacked moral depth.

Eliphaz mentions seven items of calamity as a way of including every kind of disaster. There appears to be a certain intensification of assurance, moving from deliverance (5:20) to protection (5:21), from protection to derision at the possibility of danger (5:22), and to the assurance that there is a covenant with the fields that they will produce (5:23). Famine, war, pestilence or fire, and flood (5:20-21) are the typical calamities that bring alarm. Crops need protection from disease or drought; animals and insects can also destroy crops, from which they must be protected (5:22); finally there is the possibility that the soil itself may be resistant (5:23). The last three distresses are a listing of varieties of famine. From Eliphaz's perspective, the righteous in the present time may be at total peace with the earth.

Not only did Eliphaz promise protection from disaster, he provided assurance that the family of a righteous man would be both prosperous (*shalom* [TH7965, ZH8934], which includes material well-being) and protected; furthermore, his family would be large, and he would live to a good old age. These are the important indications of divine blessing. Eliphaz concluded (5:27) as he began (4:2); these are the facts of life known to the wise, and they must be spoken.

◆   ## C. Job: Life Is Futile (6:1–7:21)
1. Faithfulness brings no relief (6:1–13)

Then Job spoke again:

² "If my misery could be weighed
  and my troubles be put on the scales,
³ they would outweigh all the sands of
  the sea.
  That is why I spoke impulsively.
⁴ For the Almighty has struck me down
  with his arrows.
  Their poison infects my spirit.
  God's terrors are lined up against me.
⁵ Don't I have a right to complain?
  Don't wild donkeys bray when they
  find no grass,
  and oxen bellow when they have no
  food?
⁶ Don't people complain about unsalted
  food?
  Does anyone want the tasteless
  white of an egg?*

⁷ My appetite disappears when I look
  at it;
  I gag at the thought of eating it!

⁸ "Oh, that I might have my request,
  that God would grant my desire.
⁹ I wish he would crush me.
  I wish he would reach out his hand
  and kill me.
¹⁰ At least I can take comfort in this:
  Despite the pain,
  I have not denied the words of the
  Holy One.
¹¹ But I don't have the strength to
  endure.
  I have nothing to live for.
¹² Do I have the strength of a stone?
  Is my body made of bronze?
¹³ No, I am utterly helpless,
  without any chance of success.

6:6 Or *the tasteless juice of the mallow plant?*

NOTES

6:2 *misery . . . troubles.* The language here is very forceful, including both mental anguish (*ka'as* [TH3708A, ZH4089]) and external calamity (*hawwah* [TH1942A, ZH2095], following the Qere; cf. the Kethiv *hayyah* [TH1962, ZH2119]).

6:4 *has struck me down with his arrows.* Illness or disaster is often described as being struck by arrows (cf. Deut 32:23; Ps 38:2), which may be poisonous or incendiary (Ps 7:12-13). Here the metaphor is applied in terms of Job's mental anguish, as his spirit absorbs the poison (cf. 21:20).

6:5 *Don't I have a right to complain?* This phrase is not in the Hebrew but sums up the point of vv. 5-6, which are rhetorical questions derived from common experience that appear to have become proverbial.

6:6 *the tasteless white of an egg.* This traditional English translation is based on a rabbinic interpretation of the obscure words *rir khallamuth*. The word *rir* [TH7388, ZH8202] is found in 1 Sam 21:13 [21:14] where it means spittle; the rabbis took the unknown word *khallamuth* [TH2495, ZH2733] to be the equivalent of *khlmwn*, their word for "yolk," and the whole expression to be "the slime of the yolk" or egg white. However, *khallamuth* is a Canaanite word for a plant, and most modern interpreters take this to be the unsavory secretion of a mallow, a very mucilaginous wild plant.

6:7 *I gag at the thought.* This is a paraphrase of an emendation of the Heb. in accordance with the similar expression of 33:20; it provides a parallel to the first line of the verse. The Heb. text begins with the pronoun "they" (*hemmah* [TH1992A, ZH2160]), which has no antecedent in the previous line; if *hemmah* is emended to "loathe" (*zaham* [TH2092, ZH2299]) a good sequence is formed.

6:10 *Despite the pain.* This is the preferred sense of this verse (cf. CEV). Most of the English versions provide the sense of "joy in unrelenting pain" (NIV; cf. "exult" in ASV, RSV, NRSV, or "leap for joy" in NEB, TEV). The problem arises with the word *salad* [TH5539, ZH6134], found only here in the Hebrew Bible. It should be taken with the sense of "recoil" from pain or discomfort as found in Talmudic usage (Jastrow 993; cf. Gordis 1978:72) rather than "leap" for joy as in most English versions. "I would harden myself in sorrow" is based on a comparison with Arabic, but the verb is not reflexive as required by the translation.

the words of the Holy One. "The Holy One" (*qadosh* [TH6918A, ZH7705]) is an abbreviation of "the Holy One of Israel," found frequently in the prophets; here it is a response to the accusation of Eliphaz that Job is turning to some other holy ones (*qedoshim*) for wisdom (5:1). Though the character Job is not an Israelite, Job's author is; and at points, he makes subtle connections with the literature of Israel (e.g., 12:9; 40:23). Israelite readers would recognize his heritage, and non-Israelites would not be bothered by such allusions.

6:13 *No, I am utterly helpless.* Other English versions indicate that the form is that of a question (KJV, ASV, NIV). The expression, found elsewhere only in Num 17:13 [17:28] must be the equivalent of an asseverative introduced by a rhetorical question (Gesenius §150g, note 1): "isn't there any help for me?"

COMMENTARY

This section divides into two parts: first, Job declares that his lament is well founded (6:2-7); second, he finds no mercy though he has been faithful to the words of the Holy One (6:8-13). Eliphaz did not understand the physical anguish or moral dilemma that tormented Job (cf. 5:8-16). The situation was exacerbated by the fact that Job and Eliphaz substantially agreed theologically (Andersen 1976:127). Our most intense conflict is often with those most closely in agreement with us; for they, of all people, should affirm our point of view. The supreme sovereignty of God and the wonder of his providence are not in question. For Job, however, there were deeper questions about the character of God and the exercise of justice.

For the first time, Job distinctly named God as the cause of his suffering (6:4). It was as if God had attacked him with arrows. Job will later complain that he seemed to be a target at which God aimed his shafts (16:12-13). Though the physical suffering of Job was beyond comprehension, it was the denial of God's favor that made him speak so rashly. This should have been self-evident to Eliphaz. Using an analogy, Job told him that, like an ox or donkey, he would not complain if he were partaking of God's usual providence. For Job, however, even the necessary food for physical sustenance had become insipid and rotten (6:7). This was not just a sign of the severity of his illness; it showed how despondent he had become in the absence of God's favor.

Job was reduced to seeking only one last favor from God. Since he had totally fallen out of favor with God, so far as he could tell, God should end his existence (6:9). Job could not carry on without divine care and provision; one last comfort would be to know that God would grant the favor of ending his life. Job did not have the strength to endure any longer; his body was not made of stone or brass. Job had no hope left and anticipated no deliverance.

Job had confidence in this last request because he was sure of his standing with God. He had not denied the words of the Holy One (6:10). God must be true to Job even as Job has been true to God; for Job, that could not be in question. This line should not be paraphrased to say "I have never opposed what he commands" (TEV) or "I have never disobeyed God" (CEV). In this very speech, Job did not deny his sin (7:20-21), but he knew that his sin was not the problem. What Job affirmed was God's revelation; he knew he had the truth about God while Eliphaz did not understand it.

It was Job who had received a word of wisdom in a vision (4:17-21), as is evident in the negative response of Eliphaz to the vision (cf. 5:1-8). The message came in the form of a question: "Can a mortal be pure before God?" The question did not suggest that humans could be sinless; it was asking whether the righteousness of mortals could assure them they would be blessed. The answer was that humans are like the moths; they do not know when or why they will die. To Eliphaz, this was blasphemous, but to Job it was a word from God (6:10), and he would not deny that word. Job knew that he could not change the lot that had fallen to him. His only longing, as a person true to what he knew of God, was that God would grant him one last comfort in ending his life.

◆   ## 2. Friends betray the sufferer (6:14-30)

14 "One should be kind to a fainting friend,
but you accuse me without any fear of the Almighty.*

15 My brothers, you have proved as unreliable as a seasonal brook that overflows its banks in the spring

16   when it is swollen with ice and
      melting snow.
17 But when the hot weather arrives, the
      water disappears.
   The brook vanishes in the heat.
18 The caravans turn aside to be
      refreshed,
      but there is nothing to drink, so
      they die.
19 The caravans from Tema search for
      this water;
      the travelers from Sheba hope to
      find it.
20 They count on it but are disappointed.
      When they arrive, their hopes are
      dashed.
21 You, too, have given no help.
      You have seen my calamity, and you
      are afraid.
22 But why? Have I ever asked you for a
      gift?
   Have I begged for anything of yours
      for myself?

23 Have I asked you to rescue me from
      my enemies,
      or to save me from ruthless
      people?
24 Teach me, and I will keep quiet.
      Show me what I have done wrong.
25 Honest words can be painful,
      but what do your criticisms
      amount to?
26 Do you think your words are
      convincing
      when you disregard my cry of
      desperation?
27 You would even send an orphan into
      slavery*
      or sell a friend.
28 Look at me!
      Would I lie to your face?
29 Stop assuming my guilt,
      for I have done no wrong.
30 Do you think I am lying?
      Don't I know the difference between
      right and wrong?

6:14 Or friend, / or he might lose his fear of the Almighty.   6:27 Hebrew even gamble over an orphan.

NOTES

6:14 *a fainting friend.* The translation of this verse is disputed. The first word (*lammas* [TH4523, ZH4988]) is uncertain; it is generally related to the word *masas* [TH4549, ZH5022] meaning melt and is metaphorically translated as one afflicted (KJV) or despairing (NIV). The difficulty is that a verb must then be inferred, e.g., "pity *should be shown*" (KJV). It may be, however, that a weak letter (aleph) has been dropped, a not infrequent occurrence (Gesenius §23f). Omitting the first letter, the first word would be the verb "refuse" (*ma'as* [TH3988, ZH4415]). The verse would then be translated, "One who withholds loyalty from a friend forsakes the fear of the Almighty" (RSV, NRSV). This interpretation is supported by the Greek, the Latin, the Syriac, and the Targums. A further suggestion is that two alephs have been dropped (Clines 1989:160), assuming a negative was also present. The verse should say, "One does not withhold (*lo' ma'as* [TH3808/3988, ZH4202/4415]) loyalty from his friend."

6:15 *that overflows its banks.* The metaphor is clear, but the translation of this particular line is uncertain; the verb *'abar* [TH5674, ZH6296] can mean "overflow" (NIV) or it may mean "pass away, vanish" (KJV, ASV, RSV). The former meaning leads to the next verse, the latter forms a parallel to the first line (6:15a).

6:16 *when it is swollen with ice.* The Heb. is again obscure; it speaks of the streams that grow dark (*qadar* [TH6937, ZH7722]) with ice in which the snow hides itself (KJV, ASV, RSV). The thawing ice and snow bring torrents in the gullies, but this does not hide the snow. The NLT rendering follows the probability that the word "hide" (*'alam* [TH5956A, ZH6623]) is a variant spelling of the word for "swell" (*'aram* [TH6192, ZH6890]), as the interchange of liquid consonants is quite common (Gordis 1978:75).

6:18 *The caravans turn aside.* It is not clear if this verse is describing the paths of the streams (6:17) or of the caravans (6:19); the word *'arkhoth* [TH736, ZH785] could refer to the courses or paths of either. In 6:19, *'arkhoth* is clearly used to refer to the travelers; however, 6:18 may very logically refer to the water courses of 6:17 that dry up and vanish (cf. KJV).

6:21 have given no help. This translation adopts the enigmatic Heb. adverbial negative *lo'* [TH3808A, ZH4202] as nominal, meaning "you have become nothing." Though this has been defended on grammatical grounds by Blommerde (1969:48), the evidence is unconvincing. Gordis prefers the variant reading *lo* [TH3807.1/2050.2, ZH4200/2257] (as it), meaning that the friends are like the stream (1978:76). Most commentators prefer a small emendation to *li* (to me), so the line explicitly completes the metaphor (so you have come to be to me). Though this emendation might appear to be supported by the Gr. (Orlinsky 1965:39), the history of the Gr. translation is very complicated in this verse (Orlinsky 1962:130-132), and it is entirely possible the Gr. translator was influenced by the similarity of 30:21a (Heater 1982:47-48); if the translator used 30:21a to help him, it is evident that his Heb. text was identical to what we have. Even so, it is probable that at some point an original Heb. *li* was inadvertently changed to the virtually identical *lu,* and that the translation should say "so you have become to me."

6:25 honest words can be painful. Although many English translations adopt the sense of "forceful" for the word *marats* [TH4834, ZH5344] in describing "honest words" (KJV, ASV, RSV, NRSV), the true sense of the word is "grievous" or "bitter," as can be seen in these translations at the other occurrences of this word (1 Kgs 2:8; Mic 2:10; cf. Job 16:3 for a related form). The Akkadian cognate *mrs* describes the pain of a wound, a curse, or a word.

6:26 you disregard my cry of desperation. More lit., "the speech of the despairing man is wind" (RSV). Two ambiguities in this verse can be resolved only by the larger context: (1) the relationship of the second line to the first, and (2) the meaning of *ruakh* [TH7307, ZH8120], which can be wind or spirit. If the poetic unit (strophe) is four lines (rather than the usual two), the result is a balanced structure in which the last line (6:26b) parallels the first (6:25a) with reference to spoken words, and the two middle lines (6:25b, 26a) both refer to correction. Further, the words in view would logically be the words Job had not denied (6:10), which are not those of mere wind but are of the Spirit (the Holy One).

6:29 Stop assuming my guilt. The Heb. *shub* [TH7725, ZH8740] is a polysemous word, and several of its possible meanings are possible here: "turn to me," "think it over," "change your attitude" (i.e., "repent"), "cease your attack" (i.e., "relent"). "Relent" makes most sense with the following phrase (Koehler and Baumgartner 4:1328), which asks that wrong not be done. Though it is possible the phrase is an affirmation ("there is no wrong in me"), it is logical as a plea following the previous verse: "relent, let there be no wrong."

6:30 Do you think I am lying? The word "wrong" (*'awlah* [TH5766B, ZH6406]) is repeated from the previous verse. Job asked that they do no wrong (6:29a) because there was no wrong in what he had said (6:30a).

right and wrong. Though the *hawwah* [TH1942A, ZH2095] may mean falsehood or malice (as it is taken in the NLT), it is likely that in this verse the sense of disaster should be retained. As Job drew his appeal to a close, he recalled his opening words (6:2). Job understood the disaster that had befallen him, but his friends did not.

COMMENTARY

Having pointed out the failure of his friends to understand his situation, Job explained how the speech of Eliphaz had impacted him. Simply put, he considered Eliphaz to be a traitor. This section falls into two very distinct parts: first Job graphically illustrated the way in which he had been betrayed (6:14-21), then he asked that his friends reconsider his situation and their response to him (6:22-30).

The second part begins and ends with a series of rhetorical questions (6:22-23, 30). Had Job somehow wronged his neighbors by acting in self-interest? It was evident he had not done so. Did Job not understand wrong and disaster? The very thought was preposterous. It was painful to Job that his friends didn't understand his disaster. Eliphaz had spent his whole speech pointing out that what happened to Job was not wrong; in fact, he was convinced that in reality it was good because the outcome would be good. For Job, such attempted comfort was total betrayal.

The metaphor of the desert streams would have been poignant to experienced desert travelers such as Job's friends. Caravans from distant places such as Sabea (cf. 1:15) or Teman (cf. 2:11) could never carry enough canisters of water to suffice for them and their animals through the vast stretches of desert. Such travelers had to be experts at spotting potential sources of water wherever there was evidence of plant life. Their search could be frustrating, for not only might they fail to find water, but they would use what precious reserves they had in the effort. In the time of spring and melting snow, rivulets quickly spring up in the gullies, but they drain quickly and in the hot sun the remaining water is immediately evaporated. Job seems to have compared the travelers and the streams; just as the streams trail off into the desert and disappear (6:18), so the desert travelers wander in hope of water (6:19) only to discover that the signs had betrayed them entirely (6:20). Job's friends are like such streams (6:21a); not only do they fail to bring any water, but they evaporate any life there might have been. They see disaster and they fear; they are afraid to be loyal to Job and, no doubt, are afraid to assume any identity with him, for then such calamity might be theirs as well.

Rather than showing true sympathy for Job, their harsh judgment appeared to be defensive. They refused to believe that they, too, could be like Job; they preferred to live in denial. Even if Job could provide good evidence that he had been speaking the true words of God, they refused to accept it. Their failure to make their case prompted Job's exclamation: "Honest words can be painful" (6:25)—that is, the kind Job spoke. Such words were too painful for the friends to accept. The rebuke of the friends corrected nothing; they seemed to think that their thoughts, unconnected to the experience of the suffering of the righteous, could somehow be convincing. Job returned to his own words, those of the despairing one, those that are true though they be painful. His friends may have regarded these as "wind," but Job knew better. These were the words of the Spirit, as Job had earlier affirmed, the words he could not deny (6:10). If these friends, in their denial, could so betray a sufferer such as Job, would they callously gamble over an orphan or a friend (6:27)? If such an accusation seems unduly harsh, it only shows how hurt Job was by his friends.

Job, however, did not believe that these friends were truly beyond the capability of understanding him. He asked them to look him in the eye; surely, they could see that Job in his misery sat naked before them. There were no hidden thoughts, no secret agendas; Job had nothing to lose. If he could hope that this punishment was somehow corrective of something wrong, he would have the most to gain by clinging to that promise. If they looked at him, they had to see his sincerity and his integrity. They had to relent; they had to stop the wrong they were inflicting on him. If they would just stop their attack, they would see that Job was still righteous. The problem with their understanding was that when they saw disaster and wrong, they failed to recognize it for what it really was. Instead, they contrived explanations as to why it was not really a disaster.

In conclusion, Job asked, "Was there anything wrong in what I said?" It is true that he spoke rashly (6:3), but this was not wrong. His speech was compelled by the calamities that were more burdensome than all the sands of the sea. After all, Job was only a man; the Holy One does not expect a man to be more than a man can be. If only Job's calamities could be put on a scale and weighed, others could begin to discern the enormity of the loss he had endured. Then they could begin to understand the pain of God's attack; then they could begin to know the agony of the loss of God's favor. They, too, would understand that as mortals such things are outside of their control.

◆ 3. Life is miserable and brief (7:1-10)

¹ "Is not all human life a struggle?
   Our lives are like that of a hired
   hand,
² like a worker who longs for the shade,
   like a servant waiting to be paid.
³ I, too, have been assigned months
   of futility,
   long and weary nights of misery.
⁴ Lying in bed, I think, 'When will it be
   morning?'
   But the night drags on, and I toss
   till dawn.
⁵ My body is covered with maggots
   and scabs.
   My skin breaks open, oozing with
   pus.

⁶ "My days fly faster than a weaver's
   shuttle.
   They end without hope.
⁷ O God, remember that my life is but
   a breath,
   and I will never again feel
   happiness.
⁸ You see me now, but not for long.
   You will look for me, but I will
   be gone.
⁹ Just as a cloud dissipates and
   vanishes,
   those who die* will not come back.
¹⁰ They are gone forever from their
   home—
   never to be seen again.

7:9 Hebrew *who go down to Sheol.*

NOTES

7:5 *My body is covered with maggots.* The terminology of the entire verse is obscure, with particular words given diverse meanings, though the resultant translations tend to be similar. The word *rimmah* [TH7415, ZH8231] usually denotes a maggot found in decaying flesh or food (e.g., Exod 16:24). In this verse, *rimmah* may be a metonymy for putrid and festering skin, or it may even be a homonym with the meaning rottenness, as indicated by an Arabic cognate. The idea of rotting flesh forms a suitable balance with the closing description, "oozing with pus" (Clines 1989:163).

and scabs. The words *gush 'apar* [TH1487/6083, ZH1599/6760] lit. denote lumps or clods of dust, but it is not likely that this is a metaphor for "dirty scabs" (Dhorme 1984:100). More plausibly, *gush* is here used metaphorically as a medical term meaning pustules or the like, and the whole expression refers to rough, scabby skin (Driver 1969:73-74).

skin breaks open, oozing with pus. The word *raga'* [TH7280B, ZH8090] does not really mean "break open" (contra Driver 1969:75); it more likely means "harden" or "become scabby" (Delekat 1964:57). "Oozing with pus" translates the word *ma'as* [TH3988A, ZH4416], here a variant form of *masas* [TH4549, ZH5022] meaning "flow" (as in Ps 58:7), describing skin that oozes or festers. The whole verse, then, has two balanced lines: Job is covered with putrid flesh and scabs; his skin hardens and festers.

7:6 *without hope.* The word *tiqwah* [TH8615A, ZH9536] is a homonym; it means both thread and hope. Job's life ends without hope, just as a weaver's shuttle runs out of thread.

COMMENTARY

In this section, Job turns from his friends and directs his attention to God. Though he does not directly address God until verse 7, it is clear that his initial words are a reflection on his existence in the presence of God. Job now sees human existence in terms of his own experience: life is miserable and it has no significance; it is like a vapor—it is over before any good can happen.

Job compares the drudgery and struggle of life to the harsh experience of the laborer, the person who had no property and was dependent on his creditors whom he served. Such a person earned about enough in one day to live to the next day. Such a worker was occupied with thoughts of shade that would arrive with the evening and waited for the pay that would provide the day's basic necessities. The ancient laborer's experience went along like the lyric that says all we get each day is "another day older and deeper in debt." Just so, Job was assigned months of futility and nights of misery. There was no progress and there was no relief. The nights that should have been for restoration and refreshment of life were worse than the days, for the pain allowed no sleep and the hours dragged on endlessly. Job could only long for the time when morning would come and his tossing would end. For Job, the ultimate reality of life is that it brings suffering rather than joy and futility rather than fulfillment.

The inevitable end of Job's life was fast approaching. His life was both too long and too short. Though days dragged on endlessly, they were gone so quickly that there was no opportunity for the realization of his desires. Days passed by as quickly as the shuttle moving through the warp in the work of weaving cloth. Without warning, the thread (*tiqwah*) comes to an end and the weaving is over; in the same way the end of Job's life was fast approaching and all hope (*tiqwah*) would abruptly be at an end. In a moment, Job would be gone from his place; no one would see him again—he would vanish like a cloud. The grave is the place of no return; once people have descended there, all memory of the place they had on earth is forgotten. This irony of life is heightened through a reflection on the psalms in 7:10; "never to be seen again" is more literally "his place will know him no more" and shares exactly the same words as Psalm 103:16b. In the psalm the brevity of human life is compared to the grass, which disappears when the wind blows over it. The psalm assures us that the merciful God remembers the brevity of our life. He understands that we are dust, and his loyalty to us will never end. For Job, the brevity of life is not a way to be reminded of God's constant providence; his impending death is simply a reminder that his hopes for success are gone forever—that his life was like the passing wind.

4. God vigilantly watches humans (7:11-21)

11 "I cannot keep from speaking.
    I must express my anguish.
    My bitter soul must complain.
12 Am I a sea monster or a dragon
    that you must place me under
    guard?
13 I think, 'My bed will comfort me,
    and sleep will ease my misery,'
14 but then you shatter me with dreams
    and terrify me with visions.
15 I would rather be strangled—
    rather die than suffer like this.
16 I hate my life and don't want to go
    on living.
    Oh, leave me alone for my few
    remaining days.
17 "What are people, that you should
    make so much of us,
    that you should think of us so
    often?
18 For you examine us every morning
    and test us every moment.
19 Why won't you leave me alone,
    at least long enough for me to
    swallow!
20 If I have sinned, what have I done
    to you,
    O watcher of all humanity?
    Why make me your target?
    Am I a burden to you?
21 Why not just forgive my sin
    and take away my guilt?
    For soon I will lie down in the dust
    and die.
    When you look for me, I will
    be gone."

NOTES

7:15 *rather die than suffer like this.* Lit., "death rather than these bones" (cf. Ps 22:17). Bones is a graphic description of the present state of Job's life. The emendation of "bones" (*'atsemoth* [TH6106, ZH6795]) to "pains" (*'atsevoth* [TH6089A, ZH6776]), adopted by many commentators, is unwarranted.

7:16 *I hate my life.* The object for the verb "hate" (*ma'as* [TH3988, ZH4415]) must be supplied, as in other instances with this verb (34:33; 36:5; 42:6). In this instance, the object is clearly Job's life (cf. 9:21), which has now been reduced to bones.

7:20 *Am I a burden to you?* This is no doubt the correct translation, though the Heb. text actually asks, "Am I a burden to myself?" Though some have preferred the Heb. reading as having more impact, it is textually questionable. The Gr. translator had the words "to you" before him (Orlinsky 1964:66). The best explanation for the textual discrepancy is that of rabbinic tradition, which maintains that this was one of eighteen deliberate "changes of the scribes" (*tiqqune sopherim*) in order to avoid any possible irreverence in reference to God.

COMMENTARY

In times of distress it may seem that God has forgotten us, that we have escaped his notice; such, at least, were the thoughts of the Israelites in captivity (Isa 40:27). Their plea was that God would turn his attention to them, that he would rise up as in the days of old and slay the great monster of the waters (Isa 51:9-10), just as he had slain the monster of the primeval floods before Creation or that of the

Egyptians who threatened the lives of his people. For Job, however, the problem was that God was indeed watching him, and that with scrupulous vigilance. It was as if Job were the monster of the waters that threatened all created order, one who must be guarded at all times. Job asked that God would leave him alone for the brief moments of life still left to him. Job gives two reasons for this astonishing request (Clines 1989:187): the misery and the brevity of his life; his misery was due to God relentlessly attacking him. What Job desired was a little less attention from God; only a few days remained for him to enjoy some respite.

In this first section of his plea for relief, Job again turns his attention to his bed (7:13-14). The place that should offer him rest is one where he again receives the attention he does not desire. Instead of providing rest, God disturbed him with visions. Job could have been terrified by nightmares or visions from the stress of his terrible ordeal, but he referred to visions as something given by God. There is only one frightening vision reported in the book—the one shared by Eliphaz in his first speech. That vision testifies to the fearful truth that Job affirms; he cannot live in a manner so righteous that he can avoid disasters like those he has experienced. It is not the vision itself but the message of the vision that is so terrifying. The word that Job had received from God was not at all comforting. Job could bear this no longer; again he complained that his days were a vapor, not only in terms of their brevity but in terms of their utterly irreversible vanity.

Job knew some psalms and reflected on them, but they were not a comfort to him. He continued his protest in a bitter parody of Psalm 8, a poem that extols human dignity. Who are mortals that God should be mindful of them (Ps 8:4)? As those made in God's image, they are supposed to make known the majesty of God in all the earth (Ps 8:1, 9). For Job, the question of God's attention to mortals has only to do with the fact that God can examine them every morning and test them every moment. God does not even leave them alone long enough to swallow their own spit. Why should Job be of such great interest to God? God may well be concerned about Job's sin, but is this a reason why he should become God's target? It is not that Job would consider sin to be trivial or a matter of indifference to God, nor is it that Job considers himself to be sinless. Job was simply protesting his suffering; God's vigilant attention to him has been only suffering for him. He complained that his life would end in a moment, and he would lie in the dust where none give glory to God. His destiny with death is nothing but the empty conclusion of his futile life.

◆   D. Bildad: The Wisdom of the Sages (8:1-22)
           1. Judgment is justice (8:1-7)

Then Bildad the Shuhite replied to Job:

2 "How long will you go on like this?
    You sound like a blustering wind.
3 Does God twist justice?

Does the Almighty twist what
    is right?
4 Your children must have sinned
    against him,

so their punishment was well
deserved.
5 But if you pray to God
and seek the favor of the Almighty,
6 and if you are pure and live with
integrity,

he will surely rise up and restore
your happy home.
7 And though you started with
little,
you will end with much.

NOTES

8:4 *Your children must have sinned.* This is exactly what the Heb. conveys. The use of the same particle (*'im* [TH518, ZH561]) as in vv. 5 and 6 has led various translations to make this verse conditional (KJV, ASV, RSV, NRSV), but Bildad was not making a conditional statement. There is no doubt about the fate of Job's children, and Bildad intended to explain the cause. Gordis has shown conclusively (1965:352) that this particle is used in a variety of ways in succession in Job.

8:6 *he will surely rise up.* The Heb. phrase conveys a sense of immediacy; God would act in a moment if Job were righteous.

COMMENTARY

Bildad responded vehemently against the idea that life is futile and unfulfilled, that God vigilantly watches people in order to mercilessly afflict them. While Eliphaz began sympathetically, with an affirmation of Job's reputation as a teacher of right and an assurance that God will restore those who are right, Bildad began with accusation and stern rebuke. The death of Job's children was irrefutable proof of their guilt. If Job were pure, God would act immediately on his behalf, so by implication his sorry state testified to his guilt. Bildad saw life in black and white. There are two kinds of people, the blameless and the godless; for the former there is reward, but the latter will be punished.

For Bildad, justice was a matter of simple and immediate retribution. This is the premise of his accusations and his advice. He considered Job's words to be a tempestuous or perhaps even a destructive wind (8:2). To Bildad, Job's rejection of the words of the wise (6:25-26) was an audacity of pure arrogance and virtually blasphemous—Job's words were really only wind (*ruakh* [TH7307, ZH8120]). Job, however, claimed he had maintained the words of the Holy One (6:10) and suggested that his words were of the Spirit (*ruakh*), as implied in verse 6:26. As Bildad understood it, Job's view implied that God must be unjust; since that was unthinkable, for both Bildad and Job, the inevitable conclusion must be accepted: Job's children were incorrigible sinners who received their just reward. Job may as well stop his objections and accept the facts. All his efforts on behalf of his children (cf. 1:5) were by implication a failure. Job had to accept this.

According to Bildad, Job should also learn from the facts. Seeing the justice of God in his own family, he should appeal to the mercy of the Almighty. In purity there is not only hope but full assurance, for God would immediately spring into action and Job would be rewarded. He would again inhabit his righteous abode; and though he had virtually nothing, he could be sure that God would give him great blessings in the future. The fact that Bildad could not promise the restoration of Job's dead children appears to be no issue for him. The restoration of Job's estate would be justice enough and testimony to his restored righteousness.

Bildad thought of mercy in a limited sense; there may be mercy for sins confessed, those for which the ultimate penalty of death had not yet come, but the blessings he promised Job are the reward of righteousness. Once sins are forgiven, justice demands that the blessings of righteousness will follow immediately.

◆ 2. Lessons from the plants (8:8-22)

8 "Just ask the previous generation.
Pay attention to the experience
of our ancestors.
9 For we were born but yesterday and
know nothing.
Our days on earth are as fleeting
as a shadow.
10 But those who came before us will
teach you.
They will teach you the wisdom
of old.
11 "Can papyrus reeds grow tall without
a marsh?
Can marsh grass flourish without
water?
12 While they are still flowering, not
ready to be cut,
they begin to wither more quickly
than grass.
13 The same happens to all who forget
God.
The hopes of the godless evaporate.
14 Their confidence hangs by a thread.
They are leaning on a spider's web.
15 They cling to their home for security,
but it won't last.

They try to hold it tight, but it will
not endure.
16 The godless seem like a lush plant
growing in the sunshine,
its branches spreading across the
garden.
17 Its roots grow down through a pile
of stones;
it takes hold on a bed of rocks.
18 But when it is uprooted,
it's as though it never existed!
19 That's the end of its life,
and others spring up from the earth
to replace it.
20 "But look, God will not reject a person
of integrity,
nor will he lend a hand to the
wicked.
21 He will once again fill your mouth
with laughter
and your lips with shouts of joy.
22 Those who hate you will be clothed
with shame,
and the home of the wicked will be
destroyed."

NOTES

8:13 *The same happens.* This is certainly the sense of the Heb. (cf. REB, NJB, NIV) and is preferable to "so are the paths" (KJV, ASV, RSV, NRSV). The expression is formally equivalent to Prov 1:19, where it also has the idea of "fate" or "destiny" (cf. Ps 37:5; Isa 40:27). The Gr. version of Job, however, indicates that instead of the word "paths" (*'arkhoth* [TH734, ZH784]) the translator found the word "end" or "outcome" (*'akharith* [TH310C, ZH339]), the same word Bildad used to describe the destiny of Job if he repents (8:7). Though either word has much the same sense in this context, the latter may be regarded as preferable, as Bildad was consciously contrasting the end of the wicked with what would be true for a righteous, repentant Job.

8:14 *hangs by a thread.* The Heb. *'asher yaqot* [TH6962A, ZH7753] is obscure. It seems best to follow the lead of the ancient Aramaic and Syriac versions, as is done in the traditional

English translations, which provide the meaning "cut off" (KJV; cf. RSV, ASV "break in sunder"). The unknown word *yaqot* may be derivative of the root *qwt* or *qtt* (the orthography is uncertain), which can be related to an Arabic cognate meaning "cut" or "carve" (Koehler and Baumgartner 3:1012). The rendering "their confidence is gossamer" (NEB, NRSV), while forming a parallel with "spider's web" in the next line, involves a dubious etymology to the Aramaic *qyt* (summer) and an interpretive expansion not otherwise attested (Reider 1954:288-289). Other suggestions include an emendation of the text to a word meaning "thread," either *qur* [TH6980, ZH7770] as in Isa 59:5-6 (cf. Driver and Gray 1921:2.52) or *qwym*, which might be related to *qaw* [TH6057, 7H7742] meaning "line" or "thread" (Gordis 1978:91).

8:15 They cling to their home. This assumes the subject of the verse is the godless and that the preceding analogy is now applied to them. The verbs, however, are impersonal, and the verse may actually continue the description of the hope of the godless (8:13) which has been likened to a spider's home (8:14b): one might grasp at such hope, but it will not endure.

8:16 The godless. The subject is not specified in the Heb. and is supplied by the translation. The verse describes a flourishing plant, which Gordis (1985:521) argues is intended to contrast with the previous plant (8:11-12) in order to describe the suffering of the righteous. In spite of the fact that it may be uprooted (8:18), it will flourish again. Verse 20 is a summary of the two plants, one representing the survival of the righteous, the other the destruction of the wicked. Though this is an attractive parallel, the interpretation requires an abrupt switch of the subject by means of a pronoun without an antecedent (Gordis 1985:92). It is better to assume the pronoun continues the subject already introduced, namely the wicked whose prosperity is temporary.

8:17 grow down through. Some older translations provide a literal translation of the Hebrew: "it sees the place of the stones" (KJV, ASV). This assumes the verb *khazah*, [TH2372, ZH2600] which hardly fits the metaphor. It is probable that the verb is *'akhaz* [TH270, ZH296], assuming an orthographical practice that did not reproduce a silent aleph (cf. 6:14); this provides the very acceptable sense of "takes firm hold among the rocks." Best among numerous other suggestions is the meaning "cut through" or "divide" (NLT), either assuming a cognate of an Arabic verb (*khzz*) meaning "cut" (Driver and Gray 1921:2.53), or a phonetic equivalence of *khatsah* (cut, divide) with *khazah* (Gordis 1978:92). Less likely is an emendation to follow the Gr., "it lives (*khayah* [TH2421, ZH2649]) among the rocks" (RSV, NRSV).

8:18 it's as though it never existed! The Heb. provides a very colorful personification; the place where the plant once existed denies it had ever seen the plant.

8:19 the end of its life. "This is the joy of his way" (KJV, ASV, RSV) and the rather surprising "these are their happy ways" (NRSV) take this to be Bildad's satirical comment on the good life of the wicked. If this is not irony, *mesos* [TH4885, ZH5375] (joy) must be regarded as the phonetic equivalent of *mesos* [TH4549, ZH5022] meaning "dissolution" or "end" (NLT), though the literal "melting of its way" is a questionable metaphor (Driver and Gray 1921:2.54). Gordis finds here the root *mwsh*, which he translates as "it goes on its way" (1978:93); though the plant is torn away, it will spring up elsewhere from its roots. He regards this as the example of the righteous who flourish again though decimated by suffering.

COMMENTARY

Bildad continued his argument with an appeal to wisdom, which he fortified by analogies from nature in typical wisdom style. He then provided a summary conclusion on the doctrine of retribution and an assurance that Job would yet come to experience the joy of life, while all that was against him would come to nothing. Both Job and Bildad agreed that knowledge comes from wisdom, and there is no doubt what traditional wisdom has to say on the matter; wisdom is unambiguous on this question.

Wisdom derives its knowledge from tradition, from past experience where the outcome is already known and the lessons have been learned. This tradition is received from the former generations. Those not yet advanced in years are unable to analyze their own experience, for their time is like a passing shadow. They have no context from which to interpret events. Experience by itself can teach us nothing; knowledge is required to understand the significance of the things that happen. Only the aged have this knowledge; they are the source from which the young must learn. Job claimed that he had knowledge the ancients did not know about, but Bildad had already dismissed this as a blustering wind. Bildad was trapped in his own circular reasoning: tradition interprets experience, so each new experience is interpreted by tradition the same old way. For Bildad all we need to know is found in the traditions of the wise, and to alter that tradition would be to twist the justice of God; it would be virtually blasphemous.

Wisdom conveyed its truths through analogies from nature. That which is observed in one realm of life has applicability in another. This application, of course, is governed through certain views of the world handed down through tradition. However, this did not prevent the analogies from being offered as proof of the position maintained, and that is exactly what Bildad did. Typically, wisdom drew its analogies from that which was distant and mysterious; thus, Bildad looked to the marshes of Egypt. One may observe the lofty papyrus plant that grows to a height of ten to fifteen feet, and the tall grasses that grow in the swamp. Though they appear to be the most vigorous of plants, they are actually the most vulnerable. They are dependent on a constant supply of water. Should the marsh dry up, these are the first plants to wither. The hope of the wicked is just that vulnerable; they do not realize that they depend on what is outside their control. Bildad developed this analogy with a double application to the godless person, who is the real subject of the next scene. The wicked depend on their properties, their dwellings, but they do not realize that this is like relying on a spider's web. No matter how sturdy their dwelling, it cannot provide the security they seek; it is too fragile to support life.

To clinch the argument, Bildad returned to the image of the flourishing plant. Under the warm sun, the plant sends out roots that can penetrate the rockiest soil and extend far enough for the plant to survive in arid and dry earth. Even this does not protect the plant from destruction. The plant can be uprooted, and there won't even be evidence it was ever there. Another plant will grow up in its place, and no one will ever even miss it. There is nothing as futile as being totally unnoticed— worthless and insignificant. Such, Bildad assured Job, is the futility of the wicked.

Job must not think of life as being futile and unfulfilled. Bildad asserted (8:20) that God would never reject those who have integrity (*tam* [TH8535, ZH9447]). Bildad was completely oblivious to the fact that he was speaking to just such a person, but the reader knows this very well from the prologue where Job is repeatedly described as a man of integrity using this very same word (1:1, 8; 2:3). The poet introduced this touch of irony to point out the inadequacies of traditional wisdom as represented by Bildad. Simple retribution is not adequate to describe the complexities of life. Bildad not only assured Job that he would yet have joy but also that his enemies would be destroyed. In this Bildad was again incriminating himself. In the lament psalms, enemies are most often those who judge one to be guilty because some misfortune has overcome them (e.g., Pss 35:26; 109:29). Bildad has adopted the very role of such an accusing enemy, who will be disgraced (Fohrer 1989:194).

◆ **E. Job: Can a Mortal Be Just before God? (9:1–10:22)**
    1. Mortals cannot challenge God (9:1-24)

Then Job spoke again:

2 "Yes, I know all this is true in
    principle.
    But how can a person be declared
    innocent in God's sight?
3 If someone wanted to take God to
    court,*
    would it be possible to answer him
    even once in a thousand times?
4 For God is so wise and so mighty.
    Who has ever challenged him
    successfully?

5 "Without warning, he moves the
    mountains,
    overturning them in his anger.
6 He shakes the earth from its place,
    and its foundations tremble.
7 If he commands it, the sun won't rise
    and the stars won't shine.
8 He alone has spread out the heavens
    and marches on the waves of the sea.
9 He made all the stars—the Bear and
    Orion,
    the Pleiades and the constellations
    of the southern sky.
10 He does great things too marvelous
    to understand.
    He performs countless miracles.

11 "Yet when he comes near, I cannot
    see him.
    When he moves by, I do not see
    him go.

12 If he snatches someone in death,
    who can stop him?
    Who dares to ask, 'What are you
    doing?'
13 And God does not restrain his anger.
    Even the monsters of the sea* are
    crushed beneath his feet.

14 "So who am I, that I should try to
    answer God
    or even reason with him?
15 Even if I were right, I would have
    no defense.
    I could only plead for mercy.
16 And even if I summoned him and
    he responded,
    I'm not sure he would listen to me.
17 For he attacks me with a storm
    and repeatedly wounds me without
    cause.
18 He will not let me catch my breath,
    but fills me instead with bitter
    sorrows.
19 If it's a question of strength, he's the
    strong one.
    If it's a matter of justice, who dares
    to summon him to court?
20 Though I am innocent, my own mouth
    would pronounce me guilty.
    Though I am blameless, it* would
    prove me wicked.

21 "I am innocent,
    but it makes no difference to me—
    I despise my life.

²²Innocent or wicked, it is all the same
  to God.
  That's why I say, 'He destroys both
  the blameless and the wicked.'
²³When a plague* sweeps through,
  he laughs at the death of the
  innocent.

²⁴The whole earth is in the hands
  of the wicked,
  and God blinds the eyes of the
  judges.
  If he's not the one who does it,
  who is?

9:3 Or *If God wanted to take someone to court.*   9:13 Hebrew *the helpers of Rahab,* the name of a mythical sea monster that represents chaos in ancient literature.   9:20 Or *he.*   9:23 Or *disaster.*

NOTES

9:2 *Yes, I know all this is true.* The Heb. is particularly emphatic: this is *certainly* true. The adverb (from the root *'aman,* [TH539, ZH586], "amen" in English) is forcefully ironic at 12:2, but here it is more ambiguous. Job may have been affirming the justice of God as affirmed by Bildad (8:3), or he may have been somewhat ironically permitting Bildad's basic premise. However, it may be that the affirmation was looking ahead to Job's words, which begin with his question. In that case, Job was asserting that the revelation he received was true and could not be controverted.

can a person be declared innocent? It should be observed that the question in this verse uses the exact vocabulary (*'enosh* [TH582, ZH632], "mortal"; *tsadaq* [TH6663, ZH7405], "be innocent") as when posed in the speech of Eliphaz in 4:17, but it is here condensed to one line. The variation of the interrogative (*mah* [TH4100, ZH4537]) does not emphasize the means (*"how* can one be just?") as put forth by Clines (1989:227) but rather suggests the impossibility of being just with God (Koehler and Baumgartner 2:523). The question has the same significance as it did previously (4:17).

9:4 *God is so wise.* The subject of this line is not specified. The line may describe God, but it could also describe the best of mortals: "Though one be wise in thought and mighty in strength, who could contend with God?" (Gordis 1978:102).

9:9 *the Bear.* This rare word (*'ash* [TH5906A, ZH6933]; cf. Jastrow 1124) is the equivalent of the Aramaic *yotha'* (see *'atha,* Jastrow 132); it is often taken to be a reference to Pleiades (cf. Job 38:32).

constellations of the southern sky. This is the proper understanding of the Heb., traditionally translated too literally as "the chambers of the south" (KJV, NASB, NRSV).

9:12 *If he snatches someone in death.* The Heb. *khathap* [TH2862, ZH3166] is a rare word and more likely has the sense of "plunder" than "kill" (cf. Prov 23:28 for the noun form), though the Akkadian cognate (*hatapu*) does mean "kill." The root is sufficiently well attested that emendations or reinterpretations are unwarranted (Grabbe 1977:60-63).

9:15 *were right.* Job knew he was innocent; in this case the word *tsadaq* [TH6663, ZH7405] has the sense of being right, particularly in his assessment of his situation.

plead for mercy. The Heb. indicates that Job must plead with his opponent (*limshopeti* [TH8199, ZH9149]) or for his rights (*lemishpati* [TH4941, ZH5477]). The MT provides the former vocalization; and though it is an unusual form, it should probably be accepted (Gesenius §55b, c) with the more forceful sense of accuser (RSV, NEB) rather than the neutral sense of judge (KJV, NASB, NIV). It could also be read to say that Job could appeal only to God's justice (Blommerde 1969:53).

9:16 *I'm not sure he would listen to me.* Job was expressing uncertainty; since God does not need to answer for any of his actions, Job could not believe that God would actually answer.

9:19 *who dares to summon him to court?* The Heb. says "who will summon me"—that is, "who will bring me to court for justice," giving the sense that God is speaking (Driver and Gray 1921:2.58), a paraphrase followed in some English translations (e.g., ASV). Both lines are cryptic Heb.—the first containing "a very pregnant construction" (Gesenius §147b)—and require some paraphrase in translation. It is probable that the second line should say "who will challenge him," as it is in the Gr.; the pronoun may have been altered to show respect for God (Gordis 1978:107).

9:20 *it would prove me wicked.* Though grammatically the subject "it" is ambiguous, it is not Job's intention to suggest that God would condemn a righteous person. The subject is continued from the previous line: "[my own mouth] would prove me wicked."

9:21 *it makes no difference to me.* Lit. "I don't know my soul." Similar statements are found elsewhere in Heb., and a variety of interpretations are suggested for Job's disregard of his own life. Gordis suggests Job is beside himself (1978:107; cf. Song 6:12a); Dhorme suggests Job does not know himself and cannot be confident of his own integrity (1984:139). Gray seems to have captured the best sense in the context (1921:1.92): Job does not have concern for his own life (cf. Gen 39:6; Deut 33:9), whether he lives or dies is not the critical issue.

9:22 *it is all the same.* The Heb. is ambiguous; this may refer to whether one is innocent or guilty, or whether one lives or dies. Clines suggests the phrase qualifies the previous verse about Job, and that blamelessness and hopelessness are both found in the same individual (1989:236)—a situation Job says implies God's indiscriminate hostility to humans.

9:23 *When a plague sweeps through, he laughs at the death of the innocent.* Each of the two lines in Heb. contains a word for calamity that is somewhat uncertain in meaning. The first word (*shot* [TH7752A, ZH8766]) may have either the sense of a scourge (KJV, NASB, NIV) or a flood (NEB). The second word (*massah* [TH4531A, ZH5000]) may be related to the word "test" (*nasah*) and be translated "trial" (KJV, ASV). More probably, it is derived from the word for "melt" or "flow" (*masas* [TH4549, ZH5022]) and refers to dissolution as a metaphor either for discouragement (NASB, NIV) or calamity (RSV, NRSV). The general sense is not affected, but it is important to notice that the vocabulary deliberately recalls the speech of Eliphaz concerning the safety of the righteous (5:21-22). There he says the righteous will laugh (*sakhaq* [TH7832, ZH8471]) at calamity (5:22a); here Job says God mocks (*la'ag* [TH3932, ZH4352]) the calamity of the innocent (9:23b). Both are parallel in meaning (cf. Ps 2:4), and the word *shot* is found in both contexts.

COMMENTARY

Job did not even bother to address the inflexible thinking of Bildad. His opening line possibly acknowledges his agreement with Bildad that God is just (8:3), but from that point on Job turned his attention to his own burden, that of the relationship between an almighty God and frail mortals. Job should not be seen as launching a "vigorous attack upon the moral government of the world," accusing God of "irresponsible and unjust power" (Gordis 1978:95). Rather, he protested his own inability to be vindicated before God (Clines 1989:225-226). Job was not challenging Bildad's assertion that God is just by suggesting that with God "might makes right," so that the human can never be right (Fohrer 1989:203). Job's suffering branded him a sinner; he contested this, but he was powerless to gain a sense of worth and acceptance before God.

Justice is normally perceived to be a matter of appropriate retribution—the way it would be decided in a court. Job recognized that this could never be a satisfactory procedure in dealing with God. Though Job considered a court case, it is not clear if he would be the plaintiff or the defendant; it seems that Job here considered reversing the normal roles and making God the defendant. Job knew that such a disputation would be futile, for God could advance a thousand charges or pose a thousand questions for every one a human could devise. A second problem—and this may be the real issue—is that we simply do not understand justice the way God does, so our ideas of righteousness do not receive recognition from God (Andersen 1976:144). What do any of us know of the wisdom of God? How can anyone resist the knowledge and the strength of God? Though Job deserved vindication, he was powerless to pursue it. This does not mean justice does not exist, but it certainly cannot be obtained through the normal channels in dealing with God.

Somewhat sardonically, Job took up the theme introduced by Eliphaz (5:9) to affirm that God does indeed do mighty and marvelous things (9:10). Divine providence in the world inspires awe, but it is not always kind to humans. Some things are unsearchable, not because of the mysterious forces that produce them, but because of the inexplicability of their destructive power. Landslides and earthquakes are certainly notable for the awesome forces released, but they are remembered for the destructive havoc they produce. Sandstorms, grasshopper plagues, storm clouds, and various other phenomena cause the sun to turn dark, but they are remembered primarily in terms of horror and devastation by their victims. For the prophet Joel, these very phenomena were a sign of the divine judgment of the Day of the Lord (Joel 2:10-11); they served as a warning for the people to repent, to tear their hearts and not their garments. But Job observed these phenomena in quite another way, for they appear to happen in an arbitrary manner.

Creation is indeed marvelous in its grandeur, but from the perspective of mortals, the marvel of providence often appears to fail. Job used the very words of the prophets to speak of the power of the Creator: God alone stretches out the heavens (the exact words of Isa 44:24); God is the creator of the constellations (the very expression found in Amos 5:8); God is the one who began his creative work treading on the waters (expressed in Isa 51:9 as the slaying of the sea monster Rahab). Job affirmed all this but added that creation also has a sinister and dark side that does not always serve mortals well.

From these general observations about God, Job moved to his particular case. It is impossible to apprehend God, to confront him concerning his actions, or to escape his anger. God cannot be recognized even if he were to pass by, and if someone loses his belongings and family through disaster, no one can challenge God. Further, Job asserted that God never relents in his anger; ever since God unleashed his powers to crush the unruly waters and subdue them, he continues to be on the attack. Just as no one can turn God back (*shub* [TH7725, ZH8740]) from his acts of plunder (9:12), so God does not hold back (*shub*; 9:13) his own rage—he would continue to assault Job.

Job then returned to the question of entering into a legal disputation with God and the quest for justice. Even if it were possible to find God, how could a mortal such as Job plead his case, even when he was completely right? The problem is that the wrath of God continues unabated. The point is not that the world suffers under an arbitrary and amoral judgment that cannot be contested, as argued by Fohrer (1989:207), but that under such circumstances a rational defense becomes impossible. Job could not formulate a defense of himself against the hostile interrogation of an angry God. In such circumstances, Job could only plead with his opponent. Bildad had implored Job to seek God's mercy (8:5). Job could not do this without abandoning his integrity (Clines 1989:234); at the same time, he had to pursue his vindication from God.

Job then considered a reversal of the situation (9:16), in which he would ask God the questions and God would be the defendant. This might be less threatening in that Job would not need to defend himself, but it is no less hopeless in terms of its results. God is elusive and is not obligated to give an account of any of his actions. How could Job be sure that God would take the trouble to vindicate him? God, in his wrath, might not address Job's dilemma. Job's experience with God offered no assurance that he should expect God to hear his concern. God had attacked him mercilessly for no reason, and he was allowed no respite in which there might be opportunity for him to even present his case. Job was completely at God's mercy; he could make no claim upon God whatsoever. Yet Job continued to pursue vindication lest he lose the one thing he knew he had—his integrity. He emphatically repeated this point: "I am blameless" (*tam 'ani* [TH8535, ZH9447]). Still, Job can imagine an even worse scenario than God not answering his voice: it could be that if Job were allowed to speak to God, he would end up condemning himself. Then he would lose his integrity—the one thing still left to him. God would not need to give an answer at all, for Job would no longer be innocent.

Job went on to consider the implications of his personal situation. More important than his life itself was the truth (Habel 1985:194): his situation showed that both the righteous and the unrighteous suffer destruction because God relentlessly attacks humans. Here again, the language of Job is intended to directly contest the point made by Eliphaz concerning the righteous (5:21-22). The righteous do not mock fire, flood, and famine; instead, it is God who mocks the guiltless when they are destroyed by sudden calamity (9:23). It is understandable that God would mock those who willfully deny his sovereignty and vainly imagine they will control their own destiny (Ps 2:4). But in his suffering, Job could only conclude that the righteous are treated with the same scorn. Job did not suggest that God is the agent of the suffering in the world; in fact, he asserted the opposite (9:24). But God's response to the suffering of the righteous gives wicked judges free reign in the land. Though God is not the agent of such suffering, his failure to intervene means righteous and wicked alike are consumed. For righteous Job, this indifferent attitude of God could only be taken as a mockery, and it was none other than God who must be held accountable for having this attitude. In Job's mind, this was the undeniable truth that emerged from the fact that a man of integrity was left in such hopeless despair.

◆   ## 2. Mortals are mercilessly subject to God (9:25-31)

25 "My life passes more swiftly than
a runner.
It flees away without a glimpse of
happiness.
26 It disappears like a swift papyrus boat,
like an eagle swooping down on its
prey.
27 If I decided to forget my complaints,
to put away my sad face and be
cheerful,
28 I would still dread all the pain,

for I know you will not find me
innocent, O God.
29 Whatever happens, I will be found
guilty.
So what's the use of trying?
30 Even if I were to wash myself with soap
and clean my hands with lye,
31 you would plunge me into a muddy
ditch,
and my own filthy clothing would
hate me.

NOTES

9:25 *My life passes.* Job described his life in terms of completed action: it had been swift, it had fled, and there had been no good.

9:26 *like a swift papyrus boat.* Lit. "the reed boat," a reference to the Egyptian skiffs made of papyrus, built light for fast travel.

9:27 *to put away my sad face.* The meaning is clear, but the sense of the verb used (*'azab* [TH5800, ZH6440]) is debated. Driver (1969:76) distinguishes five homonyms for this verb and, based on a possible Arabic cognate, translates it as "I will make pleasant" rather than "I will put off."

9:29 *I will be found guilty.* According to Gesenius §107n, the tense here expresses "an obligation or necessity according to the judgment of another person."

9:30 *wash myself with soap.* Some translations refer here to snow (KJV, NASB, RSV), but a reference to snow (*sheleg* [TH7950, ZH8920]) would not be a metaphor for purity as in other passages (Ps 51:7; Isa 1:18). This is because it occurs parallel to "lye" in the following line, and because although snow has a clean appearance, it is not an actual cleansing agent as the context demands. It is generally accepted that this word has the meaning "soap" as in later Mishnaic Heb. (*'ashleg* [cf. TH7950A, ZH8921]), which then makes it parallel with the next line, which refers to the cleansing of lye. Lye was a caustic potash made from the ashes of wood or vegetable matter.

9:31 *muddy ditch.* A pit was a muddy and miry hole in the ground. The experience of Jeremiah (Jer 38:6), who sank in the mud at the bottom of an old well, is the type of experience envisioned here.

COMMENTARY

Job now turns to address God directly. He abandons his monologue (which may have been intended for the friends), in which he contemplated his case in legal terms, and adopts the form of lament, with the result that some of his sentiments seem to contradict what he has just said. Job has just said that he did not care about himself, that he rejects his life in the greater interest of making evident his innocence. He also decried the fact that both innocent and wicked alike suffer destruction under the wrath of God (9:22). Now he laments the brevity of his life.

In considering his own life, Job could only lament the manner in which it had escaped his grasp. Job expanded on the metaphors that describe the way in which his life had gone by (9:25-26; cf. 7:6): the runner is the swift messenger, the skiff is similarly used to transport those who have urgent information, and the swooping vulture is a classic example of precipitous motion. The point, of course, was not the actual length of time involved, which for Job had often been too long (cf. 7:3-4), but the fact that the days passed without the good that ought to accompany life. Days come and go, but nothing changes. Job, of course, could determine that he must make the most of his lot, that within each of the miserable days there must be some potential for good. But he also knew that it simply would not change. He would continue to suffer the pains of one who was regarded as guilty. Job did not say he was declared guilty, for that had not happened, but he was not regarded as innocent. Nothing could be gained from an effort to deny this, for he was continually miserable.

Further, nothing could be gained if Job should attempt to purify himself (9:30-31). Job described this futility in terms of a symbol of holiness—the cleansing of water. Even if Job were to cleanse himself thoroughly, God would throw him right back into the miry pit while he was still naked. Even his own clothing would abhor him as unclean. The rigor of the cleansing would not be relevant (lye would be extreme in terms of bodily cleansing). The meaning of this is as follows: Job was innocent; he was not suffering because of sin. So to try to alleviate the suffering by confession would be futile. Confession would simply not be getting to the real cause of the problem. His suffering would continue unabated, so there could be no evidence of cleansing whatsoever; he would be right back in the miry pit.

So Job's life seems about to pass without any hope of good. Again, he laments that the long days have breezed by, his life has fled, and death is upon him. All Job can say is that a proper experience of life has escaped him.

◆   ## 3. Mortals need a mediator (9:32-35)

³² "God is not a mortal like me,
    so I cannot argue with him or take
    him to trial.
³³ If only there were a mediator
    between us,
    someone who could bring us
    together.

³⁴ The mediator could make God stop
    beating me,
    and I would no longer live in terror
    of his punishment.
³⁵ Then I could speak to him without fear,
    but I cannot do that in my own
    strength.

NOTES

9:33 *If only there were.* This translation requires a minor emendation of the Heb. text to the particle *lu'* [TH3863, ZH4273] from the negative *lo'* [TH3808, ZH4202] (KJV, NASB, RSV, NRSV). The emendation is preferable syntactically because it provides the protasis (the "if" statement) required for the apodosis (the "then" statement) in 9:35.

9:35 *in my own strength.* The Heb. is ambiguous, in part because of the homonym *ken* [TH3651/3651A, ZH4026/4027], which may mean either "fair" or "in such a way." The verse may be literally translated "for I am not this way (*ken*) with myself." It is often emended to say "he [God] is not fair (*ken*) with me" (Fohrer 1989:200). The emendation, however, is unwarranted, since Job was referring to himself. Job may be saying he was not what he was thought to be, namely guilty. More logical is a reference to fear, the immediate antecedent; Job was not normally fearful.

COMMENTARY

Job interrupted the lament of his hopeless situation to return to his musings on justice through legal disputation. If there were a mediator in a legal confrontation with God, it might be possible that the rod of God's wrath would be lifted sufficiently so that Job would not condemn himself. This is the first glimmer of hope, the first level of confidence Job attains (Gordis 1978:111). He will later acknowledge God as his witness (16:19) and finally even as his redeemer (19:25). So far, God has not answered Job at all, and Job has realized that if God were to respond, the result would not be positive for him. Now Job considers another possibility: if there were someone to intervene so that his anguish might be alleviated for a moment, perhaps his fears could be relieved sufficiently enough for him to defend himself before God. Such a mediator is a kind of redeemer figure or advocate who delivers people from unjust condemnation in a court of law. Though such a mediator did not exist for Job, he hoped that such a person might be found. If Job were able to prove his innocence, there would be at least that much good. If Job were vindicated, he could face the end of his life with a certain sense of satisfaction. Job could then be known for the courageous and innocent man he really was, rather than being remembered as a fearful individual suffering in terror at the hands of an angry God.

◆   ## 4. Mortals are humiliated by their Maker (10:1-22)

1 "I am disgusted with my life.
   Let me complain freely.
   My bitter soul must complain.
2 I will say to God, 'Don't simply
      condemn me—
   tell me the charge you are bringing
      against me.
3 What do you gain by oppressing me?
   Why do you reject me, the work of
      your own hands,
   while smiling on the schemes of the
      wicked?
4 Are your eyes like those of a human?
   Do you see things only as people
      see them?
5 Is your lifetime only as long as ours?
   Is your life so short
6 that you must quickly probe for my
      guilt
   and search for my sin?
7 Although you know I am not guilty,
   no one can rescue me from your
      hands.

8 "'You formed me with your hands;
   you made me,

yet now you completely destroy me.
9 Remember that you made me from
      dust—
   will you turn me back to dust so
      soon?
10 You guided my conception
   and formed me in the womb.*
11 You clothed me with skin and flesh,
   and you knit my bones and sinews
      together.
12 You gave me life and showed me your
      unfailing love.
   My life was preserved by your care.

13 "'Yet your real motive—
   your true intent—
14 was to watch me, and if I sinned,
   you would not forgive my guilt.
15 If I am guilty, too bad for me;
   and even if I'm innocent, I can't hold
      my head high,
   because I am filled with shame and
      misery.
16 And if I hold my head high, you hunt
      me like a lion

and display your awesome power
against me.
¹⁷ Again and again you witness against
me.
You pour out your growing anger
on me
and bring fresh armies against me.

¹⁸ "'Why, then, did you deliver me from
my mother's womb?
Why didn't you let me die at birth?
¹⁹ It would be as though I had never
existed,

going directly from the womb to the
grave.
²⁰ I have only a few days left, so leave
me alone,
that I may have a moment of comfort
²¹ before I leave—never to return—
for the land of darkness and utter
gloom.
²² It is a land as dark as midnight,
a land of gloom and confusion,
where even the light is dark as
midnight.'"

10:10 Hebrew *You poured me out like milk / and curdled me like cheese.*

NOTES

10:8 *you completely destroy me.* The Heb. has been traditionally translated (KJV, ASV, NASB) to say that God made Job "altogether, on all sides" (*yakhad sabib* [TH3162/5439, ZH3480/6017]). The clause division however is not clear, so the phrase may be taken as modifying the first line, which describes Job being fashioned, or the second line, which describes Job's destruction. In the latter case, the text would say that Job is being destroyed on every side (Dhorme 1984:149; cf. NLT). Most contemporary translations (RSV, NRSV, NIV) further emend *sabib* to the verb form *sabbota* [TH5437, ZH6015] (Koehler and Baumgartner 3:699) to say "you now turn and destroy me."

10:9 *will you turn me back to dust so soon?* Though this line is often translated as a question, there is no formal indication of an interrogative. The line makes perfectly good sense as a statement of fact—"from dust to dust" being a common association (Gen 3:19; Eccl 12:7). In this case, however, Job was objecting to the untimely nature of his return to the dust.

10:10 *formed me in the womb.* The Heb. has a metaphor of gestation: "you curdled me like cheese." The word translated "cheese" (*gebinah* [TH1385, ZH1482]) is found only here in the Heb. Bible but is well known in later Heb. and Aramaic (Jastrow 206).

10:14 *you would not forgive my guilt.* This is the same expression used earlier when Job laments that he would not be held innocent (9:28). This is not to say he would not be forgiven but rather that he would suffer punishment, be regarded as guilty.

10:15 *filled with shame and misery.* This is certainly preferable to the rendering, "look on my affliction" (KJV, RSV, NRSV). Rather than the word "see" (*ra'ah* [TH7200, ZH8011]) there is an orthographic variant of the word meaning "sated" (*rawah* [TH7301, ZH8115]).

10:16 *I hold my head high.* The translation involves emending the verb from third person to first person, but this is warranted by the context and is preferable to the attempt to make "head" the subject (ASV, NASB; cf. KJV). Pope (1965:81) emends the verb to the adjective "proud" (*ge'eh* [TH1343, ZH1450]), which then modifies the subject of "hunt," yielding the translation "bold as a lion you hunt me."

10:17 *you witness against me.* On the basis of the Arabic comparisons, Pope (1965:81) suggests here a word meaning "attack" ('*adi*) rather than witness ('*ed* [TH5707, ZH6332]), which he says continues the metaphor of God hunting Job as a lion (cf. NEB). However, a reference to witnesses is perfectly in place; according to the theology of retribution, each new wave of suffering is further testimony to Job's guilt.

bring fresh armies. The expression may be taken from the military (Gordis 1978:115), referring to changes of a military guard, used here in the metaphorical sense of new waves of struggle. The word "army" or "host" (*tsaba'* [TH6635, ZH7372]) frequently has the sense of forced service (Koehler and Baumgartner 3:934) as a metaphor for punishment (cf. Isa 40:2).

10:20 leave me alone. The verbs of this verse must be read as imperatives (as vocalized in the MT) rather than as indicatives. Job asked to be left alone, exactly as he had previously (7:16).

10:22 a land of gloom and confusion. This is literally expressed as a negative, "a land where there is no order" (*seder* [TH5468, ZH6043]). Though this is the only occurrence of the word *seder* in the Heb. Bible, it is common in later Heb. to describe order in a great variety of ways (Jastrow 958-959). Driver (1969:76-77) finds the meaning "beam of light" for *seder*, based on an Arabic word, and then a second meaning for "show dark clouds" instead of the common meaning "show light" for the next word (*yapha'* [TH3313, ZH3649]), providing the translation "a land without a ray of light, gloomy as the deep darkness." This conjecture is highly improbable.

COMMENTARY

Job returned to his lament and his complaint against God. He could not escape the fact that his life had become repulsive (10:1). He had earlier complained that he could not bring God to trial (9:32) but was certain that God had brought him to trial and already had passed a verdict (10:2). Job was treated as guilty—a fact he could not deny (9:29) or change (9:30-31). Still he demanded to know why he was condemned (10:2). The question concerning Job's guilt frames the first section; what possible reason could there be for Job to be treated as guilty when God knew full well he was innocent?

Job explored this question with a series of rhetorical questions. There could be any number of reasons why Job must suffer if certain human limitations were true of God, but these were definitely not true. Humans might take some sinister delight in oppression, they might have limited understanding, or they might be constrained by the limited time of their life to search for a possible wrong. In raising these questions, Job went back to Creation (10:8-12). The conclusion of the creation story (Gen 1:31) was that all things were "very good" (*tob me'od*); the creation of humans in particular was also good (Gen 1:25). Since Job was human, what possible benefit or good (*tob*) could come from God's attack on Job? God was destroying the very thing he had declared good. Though Job often used his own situation to describe the general human condition (7:1-2), here he had in mind God's creation of himself as an individual (10:8-12). Furthermore, Job considered it rather ironic that God should ignore the wicked in their schemes, while Job, the one who has been faithful, was treated as guilty. Since God is not in any sense deceived or limited in power, Job's situation remained inexplicable. Job understood his own conception and birth to have been the result of the personal creative activity of God: he was knit together by the hands of God and molded out of the clay. But now Job is "swallowed up" in death; he is turned back to the clay from which he was made. Conception, gestation, and birth are a mystery and a marvel. How can one explain the multiplication of cells consistently of the right type and proportion? Each part performs its proper function. Not only does God create life, he is loyal to his creation and preserves it, watching for each breath.

If this is a proper description of God's genius and his compassion, could there possibly be some other sinister purpose behind God's actions? What was really in God's mind, and what were his real motives? Behind the smile of God's providence was the frown of his wrath. The protective care of God might be watching (*shamar* [TH8104, ZH9068]) for every breath, but Job surmised that in reality God was watching (*shamar*) for Job's sin so that his guilt would not be left unpunished. The great watcher of mankind (7:20) is not nearly so interested in being loyal to human life (10:12) as he is in scrutinizing it. It would seem Job's lament expresses a depth of despair beyond the irony he had expressed earlier about God's attention to mortals (7:17-21). It is not that God does not distinguish the innocent and the guilty; it is rather that he treats them all the same (cf. 9:22). From Job's perspective, the design of God appears to be to destroy life and reputation; even the innocent cannot have a modicum of self-respect but instead are filled with shame and contempt. Should Job seek a bit of self-worth, God would hunt him like a lion. Thus, his wonders were seen in his destructive judgment (cf. 9:5-10). Any effort on Job's part to clear his name could only mean more suffering.

As Job contemplated his destiny in the land of death, he could only wish that he had not been born. In his first speech, Job had already expressed this desire (3:11), but there he did not credit his birth to God's personal activity on his behalf. His complaint was that he was born. But now his complaint becomes a direct accusation against God. Job's birth and its outcome are all part of a divine plan that is perverse in its design. Given the fact of his birth, he can only repeat his request that he be allowed some relief in the few days of life left to him (10:20; cf. 7:16). This is the most he can hope for as he goes to the land of no return.

Earlier, Job had eulogized death as a land of peace where the struggles of life would be over (3:13-19). Here, he describes it as the place of darkness, where the light and order of creation are utterly destroyed. The expression "the shadow of death" (10:21b, 22b), used in earlier translations (KJV, ASV), can be taken as a superlative, a way of speaking about the deepest shadows (Waltke and O'Conner 1990:14.5b), as expressed in most translations (RSV, NIV, NRSV, TEV, NEB). In Job, however, it describes the totality of darkness in death. Even the light there is darkness. Whatever the marvels of God in creating Job's body, it would soon be utterly destroyed. All he could hope was that God would turn away and give his body a little relief before it disintegrated in the darkness of death.

◆   F. Zophar: Repent (11:1-20)
        1. God knows guilt better than the guilty (11:1-12)

Then Zophar the Naamathite replied to Job:

2 "Shouldn't someone answer this
    torrent of words?
Is a person proved innocent just by
    a lot of talking?

3 Should I remain silent while you
    babble on?
When you mock God, shouldn't
    someone make you ashamed?
4 You claim, 'My beliefs are pure,'
    and 'I am clean in the sight of God.'

⁵If only God would speak;
   if only he would tell you what he
      thinks!
⁶If only he would tell you the secrets
   of wisdom,
   for true wisdom is not a simple
      matter.
   Listen! God is doubtless punishing
      you
   far less than you deserve!

⁷"Can you solve the mysteries of God?
   Can you discover everything about
      the Almighty?
⁸Such knowledge is higher than the
   heavens—

and who are you?
   It is deeper than the underworld*—
      what do you know?
⁹It is broader than the earth
   and wider than the sea.
¹⁰If God comes and puts a person in
      prison
   or calls the court to order, who
      can stop him?
¹¹For he knows those who are false,
   and he takes note of all their sins.
¹²An empty-headed person won't
      become wise
   any more than a wild donkey can
      bear a human child.*

11:8 Hebrew than Sheol.   11:12 Or than a wild male donkey can bear a tame colt.

NOTES

11:6 *is not a simple matter.* A comparison of translations will indicate the difficulty of this line: "the secrets of wisdom . . . are double to that which is" (KJV); "wisdom is many-sided" (RSV, NRSV); "he is manifold in understanding" (ASV); or "wisdom has two sides" (NASB, NIV). All these translations are an interpretation of the word *kapal*, which usually means "a doubling." Gesenius suggests that in this instance *kepel* [TH3718, ZH4101] is a multiplicative with the meaning "manifold" (§134r, note 2), but Driver and Gray call this "very doubtful" (1921:2.68). Pope suggests that there are two sides to every matter, one hidden and one open (1965:84-85), and it is the former, of course, that God must reveal to Job. Dhorme proposes the sense of "two-fold for the understanding" (1984:159), a way of describing ambiguous matters that may be interpreted two ways. De Wilde (1981:157) takes the word in the sense of "fold," saying that the mysteries of wisdom are "folded" or "hidden to our understanding." The advantage of this translation is that it provides a natural sequence to the first line without altering the consonantal text (*kplym*). However, it is more likely that *kapal* is a case of quiescent aleph (cf. 6:14) and that the word is actually *pele'* [TH6382, ZH7099] (wonder), preceded by *ke*, the particle of comparison (Fohrer 1989:221; cf. Koehler and Baumgartner 2:469; Clines 1989:254; Gordis 1978:121). The word "wonder" (*pele'*) is similarly used together with "understanding" (*tushiyah* [TH8454, ZH9370]) in Isa 28:29b. This analysis of the word forms a complementary parallel to the first line of the verse: God declares the mysteries of wisdom (*khokmah* [TH2451, ZH2683]), for there are marvels to insight (*tushiyah*).

Listen! The Heb. imperative following an expressed wish (11:5-6) denotes a consequence to be expected with certainty (Gesenius §110i).

11:7 *everything about the Almighty.* There is a contrast here between the inmost mystery of God (11:7a) and the outer fullness of his being (11:7b). The Heb. word for "fullness" (*taklit* [TH8503, ZH9417]) indicates the complete extent of God's greatness (Jenni and Westermann 1971:1.831); the preposition (*'ad* [TH5704, ZH6330]) expresses measure or degree (Waltke and O'Conner 1990:11.2.12c). The expression "up to the whole [of God]" is a way of indicating full and complete knowledge of God. The expression should not be taken adverbially, as in "are you able to discover God perfectly?" (cf. KJV, ASV), nor does the noun here have the sense of edge or limit (RSV, NRSV, NASB, NIV). "Can you fathom the perfection of the Almighty" (NEB) might suggest only a specific knowledge of one particular fact about God (i.e., his "perfection").

11:8 *higher than the heavens.* This requires a small emendation of the Heb., which rather elliptically says "heights of the heavens." The emendation is in accordance with the ancient Latin and is parallel with the second half of the verse.

11:11 *he takes note.* Most translations make this a question (e.g., RSV, NIV) because it concludes by saying "he does not consider it." The thought could be that God can recognize evil without even taking thought (Driver and Gray 1921:1.108). Others would change the negative (*lo'* [TH3808, ZH4202]) to an asseverative (*lu'* [TH3863, ZH4273]) to say God will mark it well.

11:12 *wild donkey can bear a human child.* The subject of the verb "be born" (*yiwwaled* [TH3205, ZH3528]) can be either the human or the donkey; the Heb. may say "a man is born as a wild ass" (cf. KJV, ASV), or "a wild ass is born a man" (cf. RSV, NASB, NIV). Part of the problem lies with understanding the expression "wild ass's colt" (KJV, ASV, RSV, NASB, NIV). These two words should not be in the genitive relationship as commonly translated; a colt (*'ayir* [TH5895A, ZH6555]) is a domesticated male donkey, a wild ass (*pere'* [TH6501, ZH7230]) is a wild donkey (Pope 1965:86); a wild donkey could not have a domesticated colt as its offspring (cf. NLT mg). A further complication is the relation between the wild donkey (*pere'*) and the man (*'adam* [TH120, ZH132]); these two words do occur together as an expression. Ishmael is called a "wild donkey of a man" (*pere' 'adam*), in constant hostility with his brothers (Gen 16:12). However, the same metaphor may not be present in this verse. It may be that *'adam* is really a reference to the ground (usually *'adamah* [TH127, ZH141]), that from which man was taken. The meaning "ground" for the form *'adam* may be found again in the Heb. of 36:28b. In this case, the phrase is simply a way of referring to the "donkey of the open field." The form *'adam* for "ground" would suggest only the application of the phrase to humans, as in the description of Ishmael (Gen 16:12) as a "wild donkey," whose hand is against everyone. If this is the case, the second line of 11:12 does not refer to a human at all; rather, it speaks of the wild donkey *becoming* a tame donkey.

The verb "be born" (*yiwwaled*) can be used to describe one acquiring the nature of another (as in the expression "born again"). The "hollow head" gaining some intelligence is compared to a wild donkey being trained. It is sometimes proposed that instead of the word "be born" (*yiwwaled*) we should read "be taught" (*yelammed* [TH3925, ZH4340]), an emendation that would specifically describe the taming of a wild donkey (Fohrer 1989:222), but the change is unnecessary. The verse is certainly a proverb, indicated by the assonance between the words within the first line (*nabub* [TH5014, ZH5554], "hollow head"; *yillabeb* [TH3823, ZH4220], "get understanding") and between the last word of each line (*yillabeb*, "get understanding"; *yiwwaled*, "be born"). The proverb serves as a conclusion to this section on our inability to understand God. Either Zophar was saying that it is impossible to train a fool, just as a donkey cannot become human, or he was saying that a fool must gain intelligence just as a wild donkey must be trained. The latter is the more likely direction of Zophar's thought; a person that comes to understand God will be as a wild donkey that has been tamed.

COMMENTARY

Though Zophar is the least sympathetic of the three friends and comes across as very harsh and impatient, his thoughts are not to be summarily dismissed. Though he is far too self-assured in his theological analysis, he has just enough truth to foster this self-confidence. In this respect, Zophar is at times representative of each of us. Confident of the truth we know and oblivious to what we do not know, we respond with biting criticism to those we perceive as being in the wrong. When we are suffering, it is easy to ignore such individuals or even despise them, but this may be to our own peril. We need to be sure we have fully appreciated the truth they do represent. As Zophar points out, it is true that all of us have unconscious sins (Ps 19:12) for which we are culpable and that we never do fully suffer the consequences of our actions. None of us can afford to receive what we deserve; we live always by grace. The mysteries of providence are indisputably beyond our comprehension.

The problem with Zophar is that while he was quick to see the rashness of the speech of others, he was much less sensitive to being guilty of the same problem. Certainly Job had already been more than a little rash (10:8-19), a point he will come to admit (42:6), but he had a genuine and profound theological dilemma thrust upon him by the crucible of his experience. Though Zophar insisted on the profundity of providence to assure Job he did not understand it all, Zophar had a consistent but oversimplified concept of providence. This concept is in harmony with his sense of justice—namely, that retribution is always proportionate to the fault and that it is immediate (though, as he mentions in 11:6, God exacts less than we deserve). This compelled him to make assertions about Job that were completely unwarranted but for which he felt completely justified. He was even less capable than Job of realizing the implications of what he was saying—that the working of God in this world is beyond our comprehension.

This first section of Zophar's speech can be divided into two parts (11:2-6, 7-12), each of which concludes with a very difficult saying. In the first section, Zophar would silence the words of Job while professing to represent God. Job had pled for vindication; he had asked that his case be considered so that he might be shown to be right before God (9:3-4, 11-21). This was in response to his own question about whether it is possible for a mortal to be just before God (9:2). In asking this question, Job agreed in a sense with what Zophar was saying: we do not know our own sin. This led Job to conclude that we cannot know or control how God will deal with us. However, Job knew his friends had made false assumptions about the enormity of his guilt, and he demanded that he be vindicated.

Zophar grasped the teaching Job had given in his own defense (11:4). Zophar might even concede that there was a logic to Job's position that would allow him to claim his innocence, but he was convinced that Job was pursuing a self-righteous justification. If God were to have words with Job, as he desired (9:3), he would reveal how thoroughly he knows us and rewards us. Zophar enforced the reality of this retribution with an imperative (11:6), the most forceful way of indicating the consequence of the conditions he had outlined.

Zophar went on to provide a reminder of the vastness of God's knowledge. He introduced this in terms of its mystery and its fullness, much the way the praise of God is expressed in Psalm 95:4. The mystery of God is that which we search out or explore (the term *kheqer* [TH2714, ZH2984] is used in both Ps 95:4a and Job 11:7a). The praise of God is expressed in terms of his creative works, so his greatness is seen as far as the tops of the mountains (Ps 95:4b); Zophar spoke of knowing God himself, and asked if Job could discover the fullness (*taklith* [TH8503, ZH9417]) of the Almighty (11:7b). This, of course, includes his entire domain, which extends beyond the heavens above and the underworld below—it is greater than what we ourselves can observe in the world. Job couldn't possibly be so pretentious as to think he could comprehend things greater than creation and somehow confute the known order within creation.

Zophar continued to argue that God is fully present in the world and mortals will encounter that presence. Job had complained that he would not even recognize God if he passed by, but Zophar assured Job that he would know when God passed by, for God would arrest him. Job had complained that no one could confront God for his mighty and destructive acts (9:12), but Zophar maintained that you cannot confute God when he arraigns you and assembles the court. God knows our deception fully—that our empty words often masquerade as the truth making them worthless (*shawe'* [TH7723, ZH8736], "false"; 11:11), a misleading testimony (Deut 5:20). Such empty teaching is really a way of making the good name of God worthless; taking the name of the Lord in vain is a fundamental violation of the covenant (Deut 5:11). Zophar said that this was a great evil that God would note well and one that would add to Job's sufferings.

Job, however, was not a willful fool, a mocker who scorned the good teaching of the wise. He was more of a "hollow-head," who needed to be taught (Prov 9:9). Zophar had hope that such teaching would take place. Just as a wild donkey can be "reborn" through training so that it becomes tame, so Job and his torrent of ranting words must be brought under control. If Job were an incorrigible scorner (Prov 9:7), Zophar himself would be the fool for allowing such a one to shame him. Job was a person who needed to accept the human limits of understanding (11:7), but who also needed to learn the truth of God—that is, the teaching of the wise (*leqakh* [TH3948, ZH4375]; cf. Prov 1:5; 4:2; 9:9; 16:21, 23), that men such as Zophar knew fully well.

2. God restores the repentant (11:13-20)

13 "If only you would prepare your heart
    and lift up your hands to him in
        prayer!
14 Get rid of your sins,
    and leave all iniquity behind you.
15 Then your face will brighten with
        innocence.
    You will be strong and free of fear.
16 You will forget your misery;
    it will be like water flowing away.
17 Your life will be brighter than the
        noonday.

Even darkness will be as bright
    as morning.
18 Having hope will give you courage.
    You will be protected and will rest
        in safety.
19 You will lie down unafraid,
    and many will look to you for
        help.
20 But the wicked will be blinded.
    They will have no escape.
    Their only hope is death."

NOTES

11:14 *Get rid of your sins.* The Heb. is actually conditional; it is parallel in form with the previous verse: "If iniquity is in your hand . . ." (RSV). This makes verse 14 a parenthesis, since it does not continue the conditionals of verse 13; the apodosis of verse 13 is found in verse 15. There was no doubt in Zophar's mind that Job committed sin, and he was telling him to remove it.

11:15 brighten with innocence. The expression "lift your face" describes an appearance of confidence and cheer—in this case, because the person is free from any blemish of sin. **You will be strong.** The image implied is that of hardened metal after casting (*yatsaq* [TH3332, ZH3668]); "a man of iron" (NEB) captures the sense very well.

11:16 like water flowing away. The poetry has an antithetic parallelism. "You will *forget* your misery" in the first half of the verse is complemented by "you will *remember* it like water flowing away."

11:18 be protected. "Dig about" (KJV) is a common meaning for *khapar* [TH2658, ZH2916], but an obscure metaphor in this verse; "search about" (ASV, NASB, NIV) is a somewhat rare metaphor based on the idea of digging for treasure. "You will be protected" (NLT, RSV, cf. NEB) is based on an Arabic homonym (Dhorme 1984:166); this would be the only occurrence of such a meaning in Heb. (Koehler and Baumgartner 1:327), but it is generally adopted as it is the sense required for this verse.

11:19 many will look to you. "Great" is equally as possible as "many" for the meaning of the Heb. adjective *rab* [TH7227, ZH8041]. Cf. "Great men will seek your favor" (NEB).

11:20 Their only hope is death. This expression is lit. "a breathing out," often taken to mean "giving up the ghost" (Koehler and Baumgartner 2:584; cf. ASV, NASB, NIV, RSV), and in this regard, the line is conceptually similar to "murdered its owners" in Job 31:39 (Dhorme 1984:167). In rabbinic literature this idiom has the meaning of exhaustion or despair (Jastrow 820), which is the most likely concept in both verses in Job (Gordis 1978:125).

COMMENTARY

In an unremarkable and traditional manner, Zophar made his appeal for this "wild donkey" of a man to change his ways. Instead of being empty-headed, Job needed to prepare his mind and his heart. The first half of the verse unquestionably refers to Job's mind. Zophar had insisted that Job needed to gain intelligence (he used the verb *labab* [TH3823, ZH4220]) so he would not speak so irrationally (11:12); now he asks Job to settle his mind (using the noun *leb* [TH3820, ZH4213]) so he can begin to become wise. Of course, there was a spiritual problem as was evident by Job's suffering, but Job could not get to the moral problem before he dealt with the intellectual. If Job continued to insist on vindication for his situation, he would never acknowledge the moral problem. The teaching of the wise could put Job's mind in the proper order, so he would recognize his need to spread his hands out to God and beg forgiveness. Zophar's appeal for Job to distance himself from his sin comes as a type of extended apposition and is actually expressed in the same conditional terms as the previous verse. The literal "if there is iniquity" of 11:14a does not suggest the possibility of innocence but rather declares what Job must do to prepare his heart and get wisdom (see note on 11:14). If Job would get wisdom—that is, if he would remove the evil of his life—then his situation would change. The Hebrew says that sin must not "live in his tent" (v. 14b); if Job would remove that sin, "leave it behind," then he would be secure and need not fear. If Job would pray, if he would not allow his sin to live in his house with him, then he would be secure and need not fear. This is the way that Job could get his situation to brighten.

Job had complained that there was nothing he could do to change his situation (9:27-31); if he attempted to cheer up, he would only be afflicted with more suffering, and if he were to try to cleanse himself, God would simply throw him back in the pit. To Zophar these were the rantings of a man too overcome with emotion to think straight. God would cheer Job up, so there was no reason for him to be so despondent. Job could become an "iron man" with no need to have any fear of pain at all. Job's fears of how he would suffer if he tried to cheer up (9:28) were totally unwarranted and unfounded.

By Zophar's account, Job would be surprised how quickly his suffering would become a distant memory, if only he could bring his mind to lift his hands in prayer. Now he could only wait for the darkness and the disorder of death to envelop him (10:20-22); but if he would repent, he would discover the time of his life would be as bright as the noonday. Job had expected that he would soon be in the place where even the light is darkness. Zophar said that he should have an experience where even the darkness of night comes to be as morning light. When Job lay down at night even his bed was a place of terror (7:13-14); it was a place where he tossed until the morning (7:4). Zophar said that Job could and should lie down in security; he should be able to trust in hope rather than despair over his inability to contend with God. God is the good shepherd who makes us lie down (rabats [TH7257, ZH8069]) in green pastures and leads us by quiet waters (Ps 23:2); Job should lie down (rabats) with no fear of alarm. Zophar told Job that God desired to raise Job's face, for God is the one who casts down the face of the wicked, not the righteous. Job had it all wrong, Zophar said: the wicked have no place of refuge; their hope will become despair. If the conditions of the wicked describe Job, then Job should know what he needs to do. It was all a matter of Job getting things right in his mind so that he could get them right in his life.

◆   G. Job: A Challenge to Wisdom (12:1–14:22)
      1. Wisdom belongs to God alone (12:1-25)

Then Job spoke again:

2 "You people really know everything, don't you?
And when you die, wisdom will die with you!
3 Well, I know a few things myself—
and you're no better than I am.
Who doesn't know these things you've been saying?
4 Yet my friends laugh at me,
for I call on God and expect an answer.
I am a just and blameless man,
yet they laugh at me.
5 People who are at ease mock those in trouble.
They give a push to people who are stumbling.
6 But robbers are left in peace,
and those who provoke God live in safety—
though God keeps them in his power.

7 "Just ask the animals, and they will teach you.
Ask the birds of the sky, and they will tell you.

⁸Speak to the earth, and it will instruct
you.
Let the fish in the sea speak to you.
⁹For they all know
that my disaster* has come from the
hand of the LORD.
¹⁰For the life of every living thing is in
his hand,
and the breath of every human
being.
¹¹The ear tests the words it hears
just as the mouth distinguishes
between foods.
¹²Wisdom belongs to the aged,
and understanding to the old.
¹³"But true wisdom and power are found
in God;
counsel and understanding are his.
¹⁴What he destroys cannot be rebuilt.
When he puts someone in prison,
there is no escape.
¹⁵If he holds back the rain, the earth
becomes a desert.
If he releases the waters, they flood
the earth.
¹⁶Yes, strength and wisdom are his;
deceivers and deceived are both in
his power.
¹⁷He leads counselors away, stripped of
good judgment;

wise judges become fools.
¹⁸He removes the royal robe of kings.
They are led away with ropes around
their waist.
¹⁹He leads priests away, stripped of
status;
he overthrows those with long years
in power.
²⁰He silences the trusted adviser
and removes the insight of the
elders.
²¹He pours disgrace upon princes
and disarms the strong.
²²"He uncovers mysteries hidden in
darkness;
he brings light to the deepest
gloom.
²³He builds up nations, and he destroys
them.
He expands nations, and he
abandons them.
²⁴He strips kings of understanding
and leaves them wandering in
a pathless wasteland.
²⁵They grope in the darkness without
a light.
He makes them stagger like
drunkards.

12:9 Hebrew *that this.*

NOTES

12:2 *You people really know everything.* The syntax of this verse has generated much discussion concerning the meaning of the Heb. word "people" ('*am* [TH5971A, ZH6639]), which must in some sense be applied to the wise. The word is defined in the second line by a paratactic relationship. Supplying the usual conjunctions, it would say "you are the people with whom wisdom will die." The cryptic line arrangement makes the poetry very forceful.

12:3 *no better than I.* Lit. "I am not inferior to you." "Not inferior" is litotes for saying that something is actually superior. Job does not view his friends' statements as any terrific revelation.

12:5 *give a push.* This is the correct translation of *nakon* [TH5221A, ZH5787], which is derived from the word for "strike" (*nakah* [TH5221, ZH5782]). The translations along the lines of "it is ready" (ASV, NASB, RSV, NRSV) mistakenly relate *nakon* to the word prepare (*kun* [TH3559, ZH3922]). The translation "he that is ready to slip with *his* feet *is as* a lamp" (KJV) is a further misunderstanding of the word *lappid* [TH3940, ZH4365] in the first line, which is a prepositional form of the noun *pid* [TH6365, ZH7085] (misfortune) and not the word for "torch" (*lappid*).

12:6 *God keeps them in his power.* This translation is to be preferred over the many variations found in other translations: God gives abundantly into their hand (cf. KJV, ASV);

those whom God brings under the power (control) of the violent (cf. NASB); those who
bring their god (i.e., idol) in hand (cf. RSV, NRSV, NIV). All of these translations assume
that the "hand" is that of those who provoke God yet still appear to be blessed by God. In
Hebrew, "hand" is a common way of referring to power; however, the last line of the verse
does not say that God prospers the robbers (12:6a) by giving into their hand but rather
that God has them in his hand. This may be taken in a concessive sense (God does nothing, even though he obviously could) or in a causative sense (they are secure because God
has them in his power).

12:7 ask the animals. These next two verses appear to be a wisdom proverb quoted by Job.
Job's response to the proverb comes in 12:9 with a rhetorical question, "Who does not
know this?" (cf. NLT: "For they all know"). Job used the proverb to refute the traditional
arguments of the friends. Job accepted the mysteries of nature as evidence for wisdom;
what he rejected was the sweeping conclusions of traditional wisdom, especially as his
friends had applied it to him.

12:8 the earth. "Plants of the earth" (RSV, NRSV) reads the noun *siakh* [TH7880, ZH8489]
(shrub) instead of the verb *siakh* [TH7878, ZH8488] (consider), in the interest of making a better parallel to animals, birds, and fish (12:7-8).

12:9 they all know. The application of the proverb would suggest it is the wise who are the
subject: "who does not know through all these things?" Nature was an important means of
understanding the divine order of the universe.

the LORD. This is the only use of the divine name (Yahweh) outside of the prologue and
the God speeches. This is probably because this line is quoted from Isa 41:20c.

12:12 Wisdom belongs to the aged. This verse is sometimes translated as an interrogative
(NIV, NRSV) meant to challenge tradition (cf. 8:8-10) since it is hardly Job's own opinion,
but this is unwarranted; Job is quoting another wisdom proverb (cf. 12:7), which he will
refute. The translation of "aged" (*yashish* [TH3453, ZH3813]) as "the Old One" and "those of
many years" as "the Long Lived" (Blommerde 1969:62-63) is not only a false application
of epithets for God (Ugaritic and Heb.) but also an inadequate attempt to understand the
verse.

12:13 true wisdom and power. Using the vocabulary of Isa 11:2, Job begins his argument
that true wisdom belongs to God alone. His use of Scripture to point out the inadequacy
of human wisdom serves as a rebuttal to the claims of wisdom.

12:15 flood the earth. This negative view of rain (contrast Eliphaz in 5:10) as "ravaging"
the land describes the effects of flooding (erosion and destruction of buildings).

12:16 strength and wisdom. This verse has synonymous terms to 12:13; the word wisdom
(*khokmah* [TH2451, ZH2683]) of 12:13 is replaced here by "understanding" (*tushiyah* [TH8454,
ZH9370]; cf. 11:6 and the discussion there).

deceivers and deceived are both in his power. This is a merism in which opposites indicate
totality; this description of all humanity expresses Job's negative view of God's power.

12:17 stripped of good judgment. The meaning barefoot (NASB) assumes that the word
sholal [TH7758, ZH8768] comes from the root *nashal* [TH5394, ZH5970] (draw off), sometimes
used with reference to the shoe (Koehler and Baumgartner 4:1338). More likely, *sholal* is
related to the verb *shalal* [TH7997A, ZH8964] (strip away), usually used in the sense of plunder; from this comes the noun "booty" (*shalal* [TH7998, ZH8965]). In Mic 1:8 (the only occurrence of *sholal* outside of Job 12:17, 19), the adjective is a synonym with "naked" (*'arom*
[TH6174, ZH6873]). Rather than the meaning "barefoot," it should have the sense of
"stripped" (RSV, NRSV, NIV). In Job, the metaphor must be inferred from the manner in
which the adjective "stripped" (*sholal*) modifies its referent (Gordis 1978:139). In 12:17,

counselors are stripped of sense, and in v. 19 priests are stripped of their ordination. The translation "behave like idiots" (NEB) for both verses fails to understand the metaphor.

12:18 *with ropes around their waist.* The verse might imply that defeated kings are led away into captivity (Clines 1989:300), but the Heb. speaks only of the divesture of royal clothing, which is replaced by rudimentary garments.

12:19 *he overthrows those with long years in power.* This line must refer to the priests named in the first line. The Heb. refers to the perpetuity (*'ethanim* [TH386, ZH419]) of their ordained status; "the renderings *mighty, strong, strength* are in reality only guesses" (Driver and Gray 1921:2.79). God "overthrows those long in office" (REB; cf. NIV).

12:21 *disarms the strong.* The metaphor in Heb. is clear: to "loose the belt" is to disable or "disarm" a soldier (e.g., Isa 5:27). "Belt" (*maziakh* [TH4206B, ZH4653]) is an Egyptian loan-word also known in Akkadian (Koehler and Baumgartner 2:535). The meaning "strong" for the root *'apaq* is known in both Heb. and Akkadian (*epequ*). Cf. NIDOTTE 1:479.

12:23 *He expands nations.* The verb *shatakh* [TH7849, ZH8848] (scatter, spread about) may have the negative sense of dispersing and destroying nations (Reider 1954:290-291).

and he abandons them. The MT says he "leads them" (*wayyankhem*). This is often taken in a negative sense (he leads them away), but the verb *nakhah* [TH5148, ZH5697] is never used negatively. The word may be related to the root *nuakh* [TH5117, ZH5663] (rest) which can mean "put down, leave" (vocalized as *wayyannikhem*), but when used of nations it means "to leave" in a good sense. Rather than synonymous parallelism with the first line (as the NLT implies), the second line is more logically antithetic to the first (Blommerde 1969:64); sometimes God disperses nations and then leads them to order (or gives them peace)— i.e., they go from ruins to greatness.

COMMENTARY

This section begins Job's longest speech (12:1–14:22) outside of his concluding monologue. It is connected by some scholars to the second cycle of speeches (Fohrer 1989:232), but others take it as the conclusion to the first cycle (e.g., Gordis 1978:127). It functions as a transition between the two cycles, serving as a reply to the friends collectively and as cause for further discussion (Clines 1989:285). The poet has formally structured his thoughts as a dialog of speech-response but not in a rigid symmetric pattern of argument-response. This is not a formal debate with equal time for all, as a glance at the chapter lengths makes clear, nor does each response necessarily relate to the speech immediately preceding it. Though Zophar may be picking up on particular aspects of the preceding speech of Job, as noted above, for the most part the debate is carried on only in general principle in the formal dialog. Job addresses God as much as the friends because, for him, God is the real antagonist. The friends are only witnesses of this controversy, so they have a somewhat subsidiary role in the Job speeches.[1]

This long speech of Job breaks down into two main sections; in the first Job addresses the friends (12:1–13:19), and in the second Job addresses God (13:20–14:22). The main point that Job makes in response to the friends is that true wisdom belongs to God alone, so even wise mortals cannot pretend to know what God is doing. This may, in part, be a direct challenge to Zophar who speaks of the mysteries of wisdom (11:7-9). If Zophar was right, he should stop passing judgment on Job, for he didn't know any better than Job what God was doing. The argument that wisdom is mysterious supports the case for Job, not against him, for what wisdom anyone truly does have is only partial and insufficient to defend God to a suffering man. This then led Job to address his true antagonist, the silent sovereign of the realms of earth and heaven. Job could only plead for mercy and lament his helplessness.

In this section, Job begins his address with biting sarcasm against his friends. His statement is not a characterization of the friends so much as a criticism of the mentality that they represent. It is particularly ironic to say that wisdom will die, because the very basis of wisdom was in passing its traditions and teachings on from the oldest living member of a generation to those who would carry it forward (8:8). This irony is particularly poignant for those who regard themselves as the very embodiment of wisdom; if they are the only ones truly wise, then wisdom must die with them. Job's friends would have recognized the implications of such arrogant presumption. Whatever their opinions of themselves as the true bearers of wisdom, they were wrong. Zophar had called Job an empty-headed person (11:12) who needed to "get some intelligence"; Job would remind Zophar that his intelligence was not in any sense inferior to any other (see note on 12:3). The perspective of wisdom presented by Job's friends so far was, in reality, common knowledge. Job knew some things the friends did not know, but since they didn't know that they didn't know, they were unwilling to listen. The friends are all too typically representative of some who presume to dispense knowledge and wisdom for other people.

Job's friends' ignorance had a negative impact. Though his friends may not have actually derided him, he had become vulnerable to their scorn, for they held him guilty and unrepentant. They could not see the real Job. He was a person whose integrity was uncompromised, a person who should have been able to laugh at the calamity that was coming upon the wicked. Instead, he had become a laughingstock to his friends. Job is not alone in history in this predicament. The Psalms frequently lament the case of an innocent person being mocked by enemies. The high priest Pashhur threw the prophet Jeremiah into the stocks for preaching the truth of God's judgment, so the prophet felt deceived by God for being made a laughingstock (Jer 20:7-8). Though the enemies of Jeremiah were religious leaders, they obviously were enemies. Job's detractors professed to be godly friends. They told him he should call out to God. Job could and did call out to God; that was not the problem. The problem was the inadequate wisdom of these friends who thought that simple, immediate retribution is somehow the sum total of justice, that it is the very foundation of the divine order, and therefore the basis for all application of wisdom. With their rhetoric they made Job into a proverbial example of self-righteousness under judgment. These friends rewarded calamity with derision; they kicked their friend while he was down. Job could only lament this supreme injustice. He imagined that those who do not have his innocence, even those who are violent plunderers and provoke God, were safe and secure in their homes. This is true even though they, as well, were fully under God's control. If God was not actively protecting them, he was certainly allowing them to continue in their violent ways, and no one was laughing at them. Some admire them, others fear them, but no one saw them so humiliated as a just and righteous man like Job was.

Job challenged the sort of wisdom that can justify such a situation by quoting the arguments of wisdom itself. Wisdom typically drew its advice from the realm of nature; by analogy, the same rules applied to the human sphere. If you wish to know about male and female relations, consider the snake, the eagle, and the ship (Prov 30:18-20); if you wish to know about work and success, consider the ant, the coney, the grasshopper, or the lizard (Prov 30:24-28). Wisdom is to be found in all realms of nature as everyone knows, said Job (12:7-9). Then, somewhat bitterly, he responded with a prophetic line found in Isaiah 41:20. The prophet could triumphantly proclaim a new redemption, a second journey through the vast wilderness, a return to the Promised Land, because both the desert and the Babylonian powers were fully under the control of their creator. Job knew all about such deliverance and all about the divine control of all life (12:10). Job, however, knew that there is another side to the activity of God within the created order. This knowledge is critical to true wisdom, and here his friends were particularly deficient.

The assumption of the wise was that they were capable of fully understanding the natural order and therefore God's activity within it. You can understand food through tasting it, so also you can evaluate wisdom by hearing it. This is another platitude of wisdom that Job had been taught long ago. Further, such knowledge derived from observation and experience was by no means limited to one individual or even one generation. Those who have barely begun to live, said Eliphaz (8:9), should not begin to pass judgment on all these things. Wisdom is with the aged (12:12). The aged represent the distillation of truth, not just of each one's own lifetime, nor only of their collective lifetimes, but of all the generations that have preceded them. This is another of those great wisdom truths Job had been taught all too well. For Job, this great truth of wisdom, which he quoted, is also its Achilles heel. If no human can understand all the workings of God in creation, then some of that working remains a mystery to all humans. Collecting what humans can know over generations is still only pooling human ignorance. Job responded to this claim by repeating a phrase that opens and closes the main point: only God has wisdom and strength (12:13, 16), and only God can provide true counsel and understanding. Job expressed this particular observation in the vocabulary of the prophet Isaiah, so that its validity could not be questioned. The prophet spoke of the one who has the spirit of wisdom, strength, counsel, and understanding (Isa 11:1-2), who will bring about the restoration of the divine order. This is the one who would restore peace to the garden, who would bring the wolf and the lamb together, the calf and the lion, even the child and the snake (Isa 11:6-8). This is wisdom and power, but this is not ordinary human wisdom and power. The only way humans can get a lion and a lamb to cohabit is to provide a new lamb every day.

Though such conflict within what we euphemistically call the "balance of nature" may cause a certain amount of dismay among some environmentalists, it was no problem for ancient wisdom. Violence in the natural world was not particularly

Job's problem, but this conflict was a symptom of that violence that also extends into the human realm and directly affects people. What God tears down is not rebuilt; God imprisons and there is no freedom (12:14). These destructive actions might be the work of humans themselves, acting as their own worst enemy. Even so, that is still a problem for Job because God does not intervene against the wicked. However, the natural order, which is completely outside of human control, is no kinder toward humans. If there is no rain, there is drought, and then if the rain does come it ravages the land, overturning the earth and everything built upon it. Again, Job emphasized, this happens indiscriminately; both the deceivers and the deceived are affected the same way. The theology of retribution has not explained this problem; their experience has not come to terms with it—the wise and aged are dumbfounded. In the end, we must admit that understanding and strength are found only with God. Wisdom can be wise only in so far as it knows its limits. When wisdom pontificates on what it cannot understand, it mocks the innocent.

Job focused on the destructive side of God's activity. Job systematically reviewed the various levels and function of social order, and he found them all to be askew. Fundamental to the poetic author was the role of the wise in maintaining good order—especially those who served as counselors to kings, the kings themselves, and the priests who represent an eternal order to maintain the divine covenant. Job used the word "stripped" to describe counselors and priests. They simply were not what they are supposed to be. Political advisers end up being stripped of sense (i.e., completely mad), and priests are stripped of status (i.e., the perpetual order is simply brought to an end). This latter observation may be an oblique acknowledgement of the fact that in the days of the author of the book of Job, the Temple had been razed to the ground and its officials taken into exile. If that is the case, it also provides a national historical circumstance for the observation that kings were divested of their royal robes and instead had only the most basic garments or, even worse, had their royal sash replaced with a rope by which they were led into exile. Even the elders lost their sagacity; scorn came upon the nobles, and the soldiers were disarmed. One cannot help but feel here the kind of situation described in Isaiah 3:1-7, where God removed all leadership and support from his people, where the chiefs were children, where the fools mocked the wise, where everyone fought their neighbor, where not even the lowliest individual assumed responsibility for the ruin that had taken place. Such was the society Job observed.

The poetic author, through Job's character, again made his point by expressing himself in terms of Scripture. His phrase concerning the shame heaped on nobles is derived from Psalm 107:40a. He concluded his thoughts on the decay of human society by saying that leaders of the land were robbed of reason and were left to wander in the trackless wasteland (12:24). The last half of that verse is also derived from Psalm 107:40. Job said that God unveils the deep secrets of darkness, that he brings light to the deepest gloom (12:22). This is expressed in the words of Psalm 107:10a and 14a. Those imprisoned and in gloom were the ones who defied God, but then they cried out to him and were delivered (Ps 107:10-14). In the psalm, it is the enemy princes who were shamed and led into a trackless wilderness in order to bring redemption for those humiliated. Job, however, did not see these things in simple redemptive terms. When society falls into disorder, everyone suffers; it does not result in the deliverance of the afflicted. Why should nobles be shamed and soldiers disarmed? These seem to be part of the dark secrets of God's own order, the ominous aspects of the providence of the Creator. Those who sit in prison in darkness are there because they are within God's power, and they are helpless whatever their guilt or innocence. Sometimes God raises up nations then destroys them; sometimes he scatters nations and then leads them back into power. The whole progression of human government is an inexplicable madness; it is a wandering in the wilderness with no path. Humans are simply left to grope in the darkness; they stagger like a drunk with no more hope of obtaining sense than someone intoxicated. As the drunk sees the horizons sway, so they sway for Job, and there is nothing wisdom can say to bring hope to the situation.

ENDNOTES

1. Much of this speech of Job has been treated as secondary because of perceived irrelevancies or contradictions, at times almost to the point of eliminating it. Gordis provides some striking examples of older critical analyses (1978:523); although most more recent commentators are less radical, Fohrer regards 12:7-11 and 12:12-25 as two later expansions (1989:240). This is a misunderstanding of the poet's procedure. The real dialog often takes place within the speeches, where positions are quoted and specifically rebutted, so contradictions are not a sign of secondary material. This technique creates a stimulating and tight argument, but it requires constant alertness on the part of the reader. At times, there are fairly obvious formal indications of quotation by the change of pronouns or use of proverbs (Gordis 1978:523-524), but even these are not always preserved in translation.

◆   ## 2. Wisdom cannot defend God (13:1-19)

1 "Look, I have seen all this with my own eyes
and heard it with my own ears, and now I understand.
2 I know as much as you do.
You are no better than I am.
3 As for me, I would speak directly to the Almighty.
I want to argue my case with God himself.
4 As for you, you smear me with lies.
As physicians, you are worthless quacks.
5 If only you could be silent!
That's the wisest thing you could do.
6 Listen to my charge;
pay attention to my arguments.

7 "Are you defending God with lies?
Do you make your dishonest arguments for his sake?
8 Will you slant your testimony in his favor?
Will you argue God's case for him?
9 What will happen when he finds out what you are doing?
Can you fool him as easily as you fool people?
10 No, you will be in trouble with him if you secretly slant your testimony in his favor.
11 Doesn't his majesty terrify you?
Doesn't your fear of him overwhelm you?

12 Your platitudes are as valuable as ashes.
   Your defense is as fragile as a clay
   pot.
13 "Be silent now and leave me alone.
   Let me speak, and I will face the
   consequences.
14 Yes, I will take my life in my hands
   and say what I really think.
15 God might kill me, but I have no other
   hope.
   I am going to argue my case with
   him.

16 But this is what will save me—I am not
   godless.
   If I were, I could not stand before
   him.
17 "Listen closely to what I am about
   to say.
   Hear me out.
18 I have prepared my case;
   I will be proved innocent.
19 Who can argue with me over this?
   And if you prove me wrong, I will
   remain silent and die.

NOTES

13:4 *smear me with lies*. The word smear (*tapal* [TH2950, ZH3260]) is well known in later
Heb. and Aramaic as a term for pasting or plastering (Jastrow 547); it can describe the
repair of a cracked pot. Metaphorically, it is used to describe calumny, vilifying someone
with lies, just as in Ps 119:69.

13:10 *you will be in trouble*. The language is legal: if the friends were secretly partisan,
God would charge them for their offense. This whole section contains a series of questions
hurled at the friends intended to make them see the fallacy of their thinking. It is possible
that this verse should be formulated as a question (Gordis 1978:142): Would God argue
the case of your innocence, if you secretly show partiality?

13:11 *Doesn't his majesty terrify you?* The traditional interpretation of this line is based
on taking the noun *se'eth* [TH7613, ZH8420] as a common derivative of the verb *nasa'* [TH5375,
ZH5951] (lift up), meaning "exaltation" or "majesty" (Koehler and Baumgartner 4:1213).
However, in this context it is more likely a synonym of "fear" (*pakhad* [TH6343, ZH7065])
in the next line, and should instead be read as the noun *sho'ah* [TH7722A, ZH8739] (storm,
destruction) from the verb *sha'ah* [TH7582, ZH8615] (to lay waste). It would then have the
sense of "dread" because of impending destruction as in Prov 3:25, where it is also parallel
to *pakhad* (cf. Ps 35:8). In these speeches, Job consistently emphasizes the destructive side
of God's greatness rather than the majestic.

13:12 *Your platitudes*. The Heb. *zikkaron* [TH2146, ZH2355] (memories, memorial) here
refers to the traditional arguments of wisdom, typically expressed as proverbial analogies,
here described as maxims of "ashes" (*mishle 'eper* [TH4912/665, ZH5442/709]). Wisdom arguments appeal to the recollections of the elders (cf. 8:8-10).

Your defense. There are two problems with this almost universal translation: it needs to
be paradigmatically related to the word "proverb" (*mashal*) of the first line and syntag-
matically related to the word "clay" (*khomer* [TH2563, ZH2817]). A further difficulty is that
the meaning must be metaphorically derived from the word meaning "back" (*gab* [TH1354,
ZH1461]). "Your bodies" (KJV) has taken *gab* to refer to the human back (as in Ps 129:3) and
used it as synecdoche for the whole body, perhaps under the influence of the Gr. translation and the link to the word "clay." The usual translation is based on the well-known use
of *gab* for the boss of a shield (cf. 15:26), used here metaphorically for words spoken in
one's defense (Driver and Gray 1921:2.83). However, this forms an awkward connection to
clay, since it is strange to speak of a clay boss or shield. Such a metaphor is also a strained
parallel for the word "proverb" (*mashal*) in the first line. Most commentators believe *gab*
has a Heb. homonym related to the root *gabab* known in later Heb. and Aramaic and used
as a term for frivolous arguments (Jastrow 203).

13:14 Yes, I will take. The Heb. begins with an interrogative (NASB, NIV), though it is often proposed the pronoun be deleted or attached to the previous verse (RSV, NRSV; cf. Driver and Gray 1921:2.84) since Job determined to take his life by his own hands. It may be, however, that this was an indirect question (Gordis 1978:143-144) used for rhetorical effect in speaking to the friends (cf. Isa 1:5). The question is answered in the next verse: Job must make his case before God because this would be his salvation, even if he lost his life.

13:15 I have no other hope. Though this implies Job has hope, the word "other" is not derived directly from the Heb. text. Another issue in this verse is that while the Heb. consonants indicate an adverbial negative (lo' [TH3808, ZH4202], "no"), yielding "I have no hope" (RSV, NRSV), the Qere in the MT proposes lo (to/in him), yielding the well-known statement "Though he slay me, yet will I trust in him" (KJV), but more correctly "I will hope in him" (NASB, NIV). The question is whether Job really has hope at this point. Though the thought of such a hope is beautiful and is what Job ought to have said, and would say in the end (cf. Clines 1989:313; see also 19:25-26), it is not the attitude of Job in his present lament. The verb yakhal [TH3176, ZH3498] has the primary sense of "wait"; waiting with expectation would be hope (cf. "hope," NLT). In this verse, however, Job says he has no hope and cannot wait.

argue my case. This is the same legal term for disputing a case that appears in 13:10 (see note).

13:16 this is what will save me. The pronoun "this" is ambiguous. It may refer back to verse 15: "And (gam) this (hu') will be my salvation" (NASB, NIV, RSV, NRSV, NLT). However if the particle (gam) is taken as emphatic (as in Koehler and Baumgartner 1:188), the pronoun (hu') would point to God as the savior: "He also shall be my salvation" (KJV). Gordis (1978:144-145) defends the latter interpretation, but it is more likely that gam is a connective; the salvation Job seeks is found in coming before God to make the case for his innocence. The translation "This at least assures my success, that no godless person may appear . . ." (NEB) is too weak, for Job would not be satisfied merely to appear before God.

COMMENTARY

In this section Job continues his argument that he has as much wisdom as his friends, if not more (cf. 12:2). He wanted to prove that they were the ones who did not understand. In their ignorance they had smeared him with lies; their counsel was as empty as pursuing an idol for help. It would be wise for them to be absolutely silent, for their speech betrayed their utter ignorance about Job and the mysteries of God. Job could only wish that they would be silent long enough to realize their foolishness. Job had a series of questions for them that might enable them to recognize the inadequacy of their traditions and understand their folly in attempting to defend God.

The friends needed to recognize the seriousness of their own role in the "trial" that Job was entering with God (13:7-10, 15). Before Job entered this litigation with God, he had a contention with the friends who were the witnesses of what had happened. Though this trial might put Job himself in grave danger, there was also great risk for the friends who had been speaking on behalf of God. Lies cannot serve in any defense, yet his friends had been speaking lies about Job. Not only had these lies made the friends "quack doctors" as far as providing any help for Job, they also falsified the person and character of God. The friends had apparently spoken these lies because they thought the reputation of God was in danger and they needed to defend it. They were willing, in a legal disputation, to show favoritism on behalf of one of the litigants. Now if there is one characteristic about the King of kings and Lord of lords that needs to be remembered, it is that he never shows partiality (Deut 10:17). The awesome God expects justice, will accept no bribes, and is particularly vigilant on behalf of the weak (Deut 10:18). Israel was reminded to love God by exemplifying this conduct at all times (Deut 10:19). In this instance, Job was indisputably the one disadvantaged, but the friends lied about Job to defend his oppressor. Even though Job viewed God as his oppressor, he could not doubt the consistency of God's character. God would not accept favoritism on his behalf since he would not accept it for others. How would it be if God should examine the friends? In a human court, such partiality might go genuinely undetected by the judge, but this would not happen in the trial Job anticipates. The friends would necessarily be a part of the trial, for they had involved themselves in the case, and they seemed to have forgotten the justice of the God they professed to serve.

Job anticipated the end result about his friends (cf. 42:7-8), which apparently did not come as any surprise to him. The friends must reconsider their position. In terms of the Hebrew Scriptures familiar to the poet, they needed to heed the passages of the covenant that warn against partiality (e.g., Deut 10:17-20). If so, the dread of the divine would surely come upon them. The traditional wisdom of the friends did not defend God but reduced God. The friends did not understand the majesty of God; they tried to explain God rather than learn to fear him. They spoke platitudes, as useless as dusty ashes; they gave frivolous arguments as fragile as pottery. There was no doubt in Job's mind that his wisdom was better than that of his friends (cf. 13:2) and that in the end his position would be vindicated, for it was based on faithfulness to the truth, not on lies and a shallow view of God.

The friends, of course, did not think they were speaking lies, and so they refused to hear differently. Job could only enjoin them to maintain their silence so that he could make his defense. Though Job still spoke to the friends in calling for attentiveness, he was preparing the way for his address to God, which was about to begin.

The course that Job was undertaking might prove suicidal, but Job could wait no longer. Hopelessness engenders a courage of its own kind; desperation provides its own kind of opportunity. For Job this was the right course of action. Though indeed he must risk his own body, graphically expressed as "take my flesh in my teeth," this was the decision that would lead to his salvation. For Job, there was one thing more important than life itself—that was to show that he was righteous. Proving that he was not godless would be his salvation. Job was not expecting to be saved from death; his salvation was to be faithful to the truth that he knew, what he earlier referred to as his consolation (6:10). The salvation Job was talking about could be nothing less than making the case of his innocence before God. He could not hope for more, but he would not accept less.

Job knew that coming before God would not only save him from the vilification of his friends and restore his reputation, it would also result in reconciliation with God. Whatever the immediate result of this encounter with God, he would find

God to be his deliverer. Job had no doubt about his innocence; there was no one who could make a case against him. If such a case were possible, the friends would have succeeded. They did not succeed and must remain silent, as Job turned his attention to speak to God directly. As a righteous person, he was about to exercise his privileges, then he would be silent until his last breath (13:19). The irony is that in the end God does what the friends could not do; Job is "worsted by his heavenly interlocutor" (Clines 1989:315). Job then proves to be as good as his word and puts his hand on his mouth. God turns out to be his deliverer in a way Job did not anticipate—he restored Job's health and his family.

◆   3. God must defend his ways (13:20-27)

20 "O God, grant me these two things,
   and then I will be able to face you.
21 Remove your heavy hand from me,
   and don't terrify me with your
   awesome presence.
22 Now summon me, and I will answer!
   Or let me speak to you, and you
   reply.
23 Tell me, what have I done wrong?
   Show me my rebellion and my sin.
24 Why do you turn away from me?

Why do you treat me as your enemy?
25 Would you terrify a leaf blown by the
   wind?
   Would you chase dry straw?

26 "You write bitter accusations
   against me
   and bring up all the sins of
   my youth.
27 You put my feet in stocks.
   You examine all my paths.
   You trace all my footprints.

N O T E S

13:20 *O God.* These words are not in the Heb., which shifts the address to God without warning. The vocative address is appropriately provided in translation to make the transition more apparent in English (cf. NIV).

13:26 *bitter accusations.* The Heb. is more ambiguous: "bitter things." Did Job mean to say by this that God charged Job with wrongs (Gordis 1978:146), that God prescribed punishment (NEB), or that he ordained suffering (Clines 1989:277)? In the context of Job asking about his sins and paying for the sins of his youth, it is appropriate to see here an indictment of wrongdoing as in the rendering "accusations" (NLT).

13:27 *trace all my footprints.* The "roots of my feet" is an unusual expression variously taken to be "heels" (KJV), "soles" (NASB, NIV, RSV), "arch" (NEB), or "footprint." A further problem is the significance of what it means for God to "mark this for himself" (*tithkhaqqeh* [TH2707, ZH2977]). This is variously translated as "settest a print" (KJV), "putting marks on" (NIV), "setting a slave mark" (NEB), or "set a limit" (NASB), "set a bound" (NRSV). The first set of translations apparently takes this to be the branding of a slave; the second set of translations treats this as a type of confinement. Either concept fits the first line of the verse (you put my feet in the stocks) very well, but neither provides the appropriate emphasis. Fohrer would reinterpret the first line to say "God puts chalk on Job's feet so he can follow his footprints" (1989:239, 253). The vocabulary of Fohrer's reinterpretations is unlikely, but the general idea is correct (NLT), as is indicated by the phrase "you examine all my paths" (13:27b). All three lines express the vigilant manner in which God was guarding Job (so closely that he could not even swallow in peace; cf. 7:19), whether by confinement or by following his every move.

COMMENTARY

When Job laid out his case before God, he (surprisingly) did not give a systematic presentation of his innocence. Such a defense would be given when Job brought his monologue to a close—with the code of a man of honor in chapter 31. In a series of oaths, Job called down punishment if he had violated any of his standards of integrity, listing fourteen possible transgressions that include even the more subtle sins. In this speech the tone is much less about justice and more about mercy. When Job focused on his suffering, he spoke in terms of his vindication and his innocence; but when Job addressed his heavenly opponent he sought reconciliation and mercy. He began by asking for mercy so that he would not shrink from this confrontation with God. Though earlier he bravely spoke of taking his life in his hands in order to prove his innocence, he then asked that God relent from the punishment that such boldness might merit and that he not be overwhelmed by the majesty of the divine (13:21). Job did not so much declare his innocence as ask that God show him his sin. The formulation of the question implicitly allows that Job is not perfect (13:23); he does not ask if he's sinned at all but literally "how great (kammah) are my iniquities and my sins?" Job could not claim absolute innocence, and his point was not that he did not deserve punishment at all but rather that his punishment was out of proportion and God should have mercy. Job may expect to pay for the sins of his youth, but the fact that they were done in the inexperience and ignorance of youth should make him less culpable. Instead, it seems that God hounded him relentlessly, ever vigilant for further evidence of sin. This does not seem to be the confidence of a man who could allege his absolute innocence to his friends.

There are elements of litigation in this first section of Job's speech. If God had been offended, let him call and Job would answer. However, God's complaint was known only in the suffering that Job must endure; therefore, Job as the complainant must call in the hope that as plaintiff he may receive a reply. As plaintiff, Job did not directly demand a vindication of his innocence. Instead, he asked only that he may know the sins with which he had been charged. These charges have an exceedingly bitter result, for Job must now "inherit" the legacy accumulated for all his previous wrongs. Though Job's tone was somewhat more contrite than the strident stance he had adopted earlier, he required that God justify the bitter suffering that he was still enduring.

Though Job had never assumed he could win his case against God—that he would be recompensed and God shown to be wrong—he demanded that his righteousness be made public. This would be his salvation. As Job confronted God, his priorities were altered. He wished that God would not treat him as an enemy and that God would not reject him, for he recognized that before God he was as powerless as chaff driven in the wind. He was terrified, driven as a leaf, but God still pursued him without mercy. God scrutinized Job either by confining him or watching his every move. The demand that God justify his ways abruptly shifted to a lament for the lot of humanity. As such, the need for mercy supersedes the need for justice.

◆   4. Mortals are no match for God (13:28–14:22)

28 I waste away like rotting wood,
  like a moth-eaten coat.

CHAPTER **14**

1 "How frail is humanity!
  How short is life, how full of
    trouble!
2 We blossom like a flower and then
    wither.
  Like a passing shadow, we quickly
    disappear.
3 Must you keep an eye on such a frail
    creature
  and demand an accounting from me?
4 Who can bring purity out of an impure
    person?
  No one!
5 You have decided the length of our
    lives.
  You know how many months we
    will live,
  and we are not given a minute
    longer.
6 So leave us alone and let us rest!
  We are like hired hands, so let us
    finish our work in peace.

7 "Even a tree has more hope!
  If it is cut down, it will sprout again
  and grow new branches.
8 Though its roots have grown old in
    the earth
  and its stump decays,
9 at the scent of water it will bud
  and sprout again like a new seedling.

10 "But when people die, their strength
    is gone.
  They breathe their last, and then
    where are they?
11 As water evaporates from a lake

and a river disappears in drought,
12 people are laid to rest and do not rise
    again.
  Until the heavens are no more, they
    will not wake up
  nor be roused from their sleep.

13 "I wish you would hide me in the
    grave*
  and forget me there until your
    anger has passed.
  But mark your calendar to think
    of me again!
14 Can the dead live again?
  If so, this would give me hope
  through all my years of struggle,
  and I would eagerly await the
    release of death.
15 You would call and I would answer,
  and you would yearn for me, your
    handiwork.
16 For then you would guard my steps,
  instead of watching for my sins.
17 My sins would be sealed in a pouch,
  and you would cover my guilt.

18 "But instead, as mountains fall and
    crumble
  and as rocks fall from a cliff,
19 as water wears away the stones
  and floods wash away the soil,
  so you destroy people's hope.
20 You always overpower them, and they
    pass from the scene.
  You disfigure them in death and
    send them away.
21 They never know if their children grow
    up in honor
  or sink to insignificance.
22 They suffer painfully;
  their life is full of trouble."

14:13 Hebrew *in Sheol.*

N O T E S

13:28 *I waste away.* The Heb. has the third person "he wastes away," apparently in reference to mortals born of a woman (14:1). Though the Gr. does have the first person, it is best explained as an adaptation of the more difficult Heb. Some translations supply the word "man" for the pronoun "he" (NIV, RSV). Though it is often proposed that this verse follow 14:2 (cf. Habel 1985:226; de Wilde 1981:72), it introduces a foreign image to that context (Driver 1921:2.87). Fohrer (1989:253-54) suggests the abrupt shift is because the poet has adopted the image of the moth from typical poetic expression (Isa 50:9; 51:8). The style is unusual, but the verse is a transition to Job's thoughts on the fleeting life of a mortal spent under God's watchful eye (cf. 13:27; 14:3).

14:6 leave us alone and let us rest. The verb *khadal* [TH2308, ZH2532] means to cease or desist. Job has used this verb in the imperative to ask that God leave him alone (7:16), and on a second occasion (10:20) the Qere reading in the MT calls for an emendation to an imperative for the same expression (see note on 10:20). Though the indicative here might be provided with an object to say "let one cease |to complain or to suffer|," it seems better to provide an imperative as suggested by the Masoretes in 10:20: "let them alone."

let us finish our work. Translations vary between "enjoy" (RSV, NRSV, TEV, CEV) and "accomplish" (KJV), "fulfill" (NASB), or "put in time" (NIV). There are two verbs with the same spelling (*ratsah* [TH7521/7521A, ZH8354/8355]); the first means "enjoy," the second means "count" or "pay off" (Lev 26:41, 43). It may be that both verbs derive from the basic meaning of receiving a due (Jenni and Westermann 1976:2.810-811), either in the positive sense of a type of inheritance (a benefit or enjoyment) or the negative sense of an obligation that must be reckoned (counted). In at least two instances, *ratsah* is used in the second sense with the meaning "complete" (Lev 26:34; 2 Chr 36:21)—that is, to count to completion or count fully. "Counting the hours day by day" (NEB) is "an impossible translation of the Hebrew" (Clines 1989:284). The request may be that God would allow humans to complete the necessary work of the day like a hired hand (NLT). In a more ironical sense, the request would be that God should allow at least the kind of enjoyment a worker receives from daily toil. Either thought follows v. 5 logically; the same two thoughts are present in 10:20.

14:10 their strength is gone. The correct meaning of *khalash* [TH2522, ZH2764] is to become weak (cf. Joel 3:10c); "waste away" (KJV) treats the Heb. as if "any word may mean anything" (Driver and Gray 1921:2.90). "Lies prostrate" (NASB) and "laid low" (RSV, NRSV, NIV) are figurative interpretations that somewhat miss the point; "he disappears" (NEB) is based on an Arabic homonym and is not relevant here. The contrast is between the impotence of humans in death with the ability of a tree to revive in new life.

14:12 will not wake up. "Until the very sky splits open" (NEB) is based on a speculative second root for *quts* [TH6973A, ZH7763] (Koehler and Baumgartner 3:1019); the common word *qits* [TH6974, ZH7810] (awake) is most appropriate here.

14:18 but instead, as mountains fall. The contrast of reality to the ideal is given with a strong adversative "but" ('*ulam* [TH199, ZH219]) in 14:18. The adversative confirms the correctness of taking the previous verses (14:16-17) as describing the hypothetical ideal introduced in 14:15 (see NLT) rather than a description of Job's present reality.

14:20 always overpower. Though the word *netsakh* [TH5331, ZH5905] commonly means "forever," it may be used for the superlative. In this verse it logically would say, "you utterly overpower," or "you overpower him once for all" (NIV), a sense particularly fitting for death.

COMMENTARY

As Job contemplated the future of his life before God, it seemed that a common proverb abruptly shifted his thinking toward the human experience (13:28). The truth is that all people perish like moth-eaten cloth (cf. Pss 39:11; 102:26). In Psalm 39, the psalmist lamented the chastening hand of God, which was taking away everything that was dear to him; all human life is a mere breath. In a similar manner in Psalm 102, the psalmist lamented that his strength was gone and his time cut short, but he realized that even the earth and heavens must perish, so humans, like a garment, grow old and pass on. Job described humans as overcome by God's power once for all (14:20); he makes them old and then sends them off.

Having abruptly introduced this thought, switching from how God always watched him to how everyone wears out as if in a state of decay, Job directed his thoughts to mortals (14:1), those born of woman. Human life is like a flower (Pss 90:5-6; 103:15), the time of human life is like a fleeting shadow (14:2). Given the frail nature of humanity, why should God watch them so closely?

Humans are helpless to change their condition; there are none that can make themselves pure (14:4). Though the language is that of cultic purity, where cleansing could be possible, it is used here for the morality that the cultic symbols represented. As a righteous man, Job found himself helpless before God, for he could not change who he was. It seemed that all God had done was fix a term of service for frail humans, during which time they must pay their dues.

Job here appeared to have given up on the idea of vindicating himself before God in a court setting. The trials of God had overcome him, and he simply pled that God look away, that he desist—a plea he had uttered before (cf. 7:16; 10:20). Let the laborers complete their term and enjoy what respite they may find in this frail and fleeting life. In a touching metaphor, Job compared human life to that of a tree. A tree has tremendous power of revival. If you cut it down, the stump will grow. Even if the stump gets old in the ground, at a whiff of water it will revive and send out its shoots. Humans are the converse. Once they die, they are totally helpless. In ancient times, death was often depicted as a state of total weakness, a continuation and amplification of that weakening condition that leads to the death of the body. However, Job had a different idea in mind. When a tree is cut down, it retains an unseen vitality; while humans in contrast are utterly powerless—their weakness is one from which no revival is possible. They are like water that evaporates, like a river that has dried up. Verse 11 is a quote of Isaiah 19:5, but with a different application; in Isaiah the drying up of the waters was a judgment against Egypt, as part of God working out his deliverance. Job used this verse to describe a judgment against all humanity; unlike the tree, human life cannot revive any more than the sea or the river can retrieve water that has evaporated.

The author of Job was not contemplating the possibility of a resurrection in another kind of body to another kind of world. Such ideas were familiar to him, but they did not address his problem, which was the condition of human life now in this world. His question was how to deal with the struggle of this life in the time of this life (14:1-3). In a beautiful diversion, the speech of Job turned to contemplate the possibility of a totally different kind of life in this world. Suppose human life were more like a tree—that one could die but then have hope of coming back to life again. God could set the term, and when the time of wrath had passed he would remember and there would be another chance. Job could then readily endure his struggle, and he would wait for the time of his release, when he would enjoy renewed fellowship with God. Then he would call and God would answer; this would not be in the negative sense of a call to trial (cf. 13:22) but in the positive sense of the fellowship Job desired. God would then be pleased with his own work done in such exquisite wonder (cf. 10:8-12), and instead of attacking Job as if he had made him for some sinister purpose, God would guard over his every step. Instead of constantly being vigilant for Job's sin, God would seal it up in a pouch. Sealing up stones in a pouch as a method of record-keeping is well known from ancient times (Pope 1965:109-111). God would not seal up sins for purposes of retaliation. The friends might have smeared (*tapal* [TH2950, ZH3260]) Job with lies (13:4), but God would cover over (*tapal*) Job's sin so it would not victimize him (14:17).

But Job lamented that human life is not like that of a tree. When Job asks, "Can the dead live again?" (14:14), the text presents us with the hope of new life assuming a condition contrary to fact. If it were true, then Job could wait through all his struggles. But it was not true from Job's perspective. Thus, Job said that, just as mountains fall and stones erode so God deadens the hope of another life in this world. If even heaven and earth will pass away, how much more so will human life, which depends on them. God overpowers, humans grow old, and they die. They never live to see the achievements of their children or to share with them in their ignominy. While in their body, they have pain; while they have breath, they have sorrow (in striking parallel lines the poet refers to the totality of the human person, both body and desire). The reality of life in this world cannot be altered.

◆   ## H. Eliphaz: A Defense of Wisdom (15:1-35)
1. God grants no secret revelation (15:1-16)

Then Eliphaz the Temanite replied:

2 "A wise man wouldn't answer with
  such empty talk!
  You are nothing but a windbag.
3 The wise don't engage in empty chatter.
  What good are such words?
4 Have you no fear of God,
  no reverence for him?
5 Your sins are telling your mouth what
    to say.
  Your words are based on clever
    deception.
6 Your own mouth condemns you, not I.
  Your own lips testify against you.

7 "Were you the first person ever born?
  Were you born before the hills were
    made?
8 Were you listening at God's secret
    council?
  Do you have a monopoly on wisdom?

9 What do you know that we don't?
  What do you understand that we
    do not?
10 On our side are aged, gray-haired men
   much older than your father!
11 "Is God's comfort too little for you?
   Is his gentle word not enough?
12 What has taken away your reason?
   What has weakened your vision,*
13 that you turn against God
   and say all these evil things?
14 Can any mortal be pure?
   Can anyone born of a woman be just?
15 Look, God does not even trust the
     angels.*
   Even the heavens are not absolutely
     pure in his sight.
16 How much less pure is a corrupt and
     sinful person
   with a thirst for wickedness!

15:12 Or *Why do your eyes flash with anger;* Hebrew reads *Why do your eyes blink.*   15:15 Hebrew *the holy ones.*

NOTES

15:2 *A wise man wouldn't answer with such empty talk!* The Heb. is in the form of a question: "Should a wise man answer empty talk?" It is ambiguous as to whether the wise man is Job who has answered with blustering words (so NLT; "you are . . . a windbag"), or Eliphaz who, as a wise man, must respond to this tirade. Should a wise man answer such heated speech? If Eliphaz refers to himself as the wise man, he says that in his response to Job he will fill his own "belly with the east wind" (KJV); that is, his own emotions will get the best of him.

15:4 *Have you no fear of God?* The cryptic Heb. poetry only has the word "fear." It is normally understood to be an ellipsis for "fear of God" or reverence, but it may be taken simply as "fear." Wolfers (1994a:382, 385) suggests that Eliphaz was exhorting Job to discount his fears.

no reverence for him? The Heb. word translated "reverence" usually has a negative connotation of complaint or grief. Eliphaz may have been asking Job to "restrain his complaint" rather than accusing him of "diminishing reverence."

15:5 *Your sins.* The Heb. word *'awon* [TH5771, ZH6411] can be "sin," "guilt," or "punishment." Taken as "punishment," the line would be an exhortation: "let your punishment teach you."

clever deception. The Heb. word *'arum* [TH6175, ZH6874] can be positive or negative. Eliphaz may be exhorting Job to "choose sensible words."

15:11 *his gentle word.* The translation "is there any secret thing with thee" (KJV) is based on a homonym of the word *la'at* meaning "cover." "Gentle" (cf. Isa 8:6, *'at* [TH328, ZH0351]) is correct, continuing the thought of the first line.

15:12 *weakened your vision.* The word *razam* [TH7335, ZH8141] is otherwise unknown. It is usually assumed that the word should be *ramaz* [TH7419.1, ZH8141] (metathesis—the reversal of two letters—is a common problem), which may have the sense of "weaken" (derived from Arabic) or of "giving a signal by use of the eyes" (based on the Aramaic). In the latter case, it could refer to eyes flashing in anger.

15:14-15 These verses should be compared with 4:17-20, for the author presents the same argument with some creative variations. In this second instance the author speaks of the "heavens" not being pure (15:15b) as opposed to God charging "his messengers with foolishness" (4:18b). The difference may not be of great significance. The heavens might be the rich blue sky, the kind of purity that appeared under the feet of God in a theophany (Exod 24:10), or this may be a reference to the heavenly bodies. The latter is more likely, since it would indicate a second type of heavenly being. In ancient thought, the heavenly bodies were often personified, so in effect the "heavens" would be parallel to "messengers," "servants," or "holy ones." In the first account of the vision, the author referred to the weakness of human mortality in terms of "people made of clay" (4:19); here he calls attention to them as not only being weak but culpable—they are abhorrent and corrupt (15:16). These changes provide a type of intensification of the main point.

COMMENTARY

The second speech of Eliphaz is a repetition of what he said the first time, but it is more severe. In the first speech Eliphaz had addressed the question "Can a mortal be innocent before God?" (4:17). Now with a blustering introduction, Eliphaz vilified Job for his thoughts on suffering (15:3-6), then attacked him for challenging wisdom (15:7-13). He returned directly to the question of the vision he had first introduced: "Can any mortal be pure?" (15:14; cf. 4:17a). In this speech the change of speaker is clearly marked. The question "What has taken away your reason . . . that you turn against God?" (15:12-13) was addressed by Eliphaz to Job. The "blasphemous" words of Job are repeated (15:14-16) and then Eliphaz responds: "If you will listen, I will show you" (15:17). The import of the question is that we cannot live our lives with such purity that we can control our own destiny. As has been observed, Job himself asked this question (cf. 9:2)—it is a word he received from God (cf. 6:10) and found most painful (6:25). The message is a direct affront to traditional wisdom, which assumes that retribution is a straightforward principle: those who so choose can be righteous before God and will always be rewarded accordingly. Eliphaz was rather agitated that his exposition of this principle had not been accepted and the question silenced.

In his first speech Eliphaz somewhat patiently explained that "we reap what we sow" (4:1-11). Evil is the root of trouble (5:1-7), evil will be judged (5:8-16), and the righteous will be delivered (5:17-27). Earlier, Eliphaz seemed confident that Job was among the wise; Job's relapse, he reasoned, was simply an inability to apply that wisdom to himself. No such confidence is evident in this second speech. Eliphaz insisted that Job's continued challenge of divine retribution, an ideological tenet of conventional wisdom, was sheer folly (15:1-16). The awful fate of the wicked is described in uncompromising terms (15:17-35), and Job must agree that he will not share in their fate. How then can Job continue to assert that the righteous are not really pure before God and not in control of their future? Job had allowed his thoughts to lead him into absurdity; his passions had overcome him.

Job had twice made reference to himself as a man of wisdom (12:3; 13:2), probably in response to Bildad, who had called him "empty-headed" (11:12). Eliphaz derided this claim of Job; wisdom ought to be more than "hot air"; he said that the sirocco (*qadim* [TH6921, ZH7708], 15:2), a searing eastern desert wind, serves as a very vivid metaphor for Job's speech. Job's was not the talk of a wise man or even the kind of talk a wise man should respond to lest he be made a fool himself (Prov 26:4). One ought not to argue with idiots; they drag you down to their level, and then beat you with experience. The very fact that Eliphaz deigned to respond is an indication of his loyalty and his confidence that there was still hope for Job. Eliphaz had certainly become less charitable toward Job, but he could not believe that Job was beyond understanding.

The brevity of the poetry creates a certain ambiguity as to the harshness of Eliphaz's response. As indicated in the notes (see 15:4-5), Eliphaz may not have been condemning Job so much as exhorting him: Job should break away from his fear, restrain his complaint, learn from his punishment, and choose to speak with prudence. Job was condemning himself in his argument—it was not a matter of what the friends had to say. This more compassionate interpretation adopts an established meaning for all the terminology involved. It is possible that Eliphaz was trying to give encouragement, but he was very distressed by Job's argument, which he called "heated wind." Job was unforgivably audacious in challenging wisdom in that fashion. Thus, Eliphaz pointed out the outrageous claims Job was making for himself and proceeded to correct Job with the logic of those truly wise.

Eliphaz first asked: "Were you the first person ever born?" This goes back to the belief that Adam, or perhaps a supernatural "original man," was the apogee of wisdom and perfection. The prophet Ezekiel charged the king of Tyre as claiming to be this "original man," full of wisdom and beauty (Ezek 28:12-14), and the psalmist charged that the corrupt judges of the earth had fallen from the high calling of wisdom to which they were originally ordained (Ps 82:6-7). Eliphaz was referring to a claim of revelation Job had made for himself, the words of Job he is about to repeat (15:13-16), the words that were a part of the vision in the first speech of Eliphaz (cf. 4:12-16). These words disagree with the traditional wisdom of Eliphaz, since the question asserts that mortals cannot inevitably bring about blessing for themselves by their own righteousness. Job was claiming a special wisdom for himself.

At this point, Eliphaz delivers the most decisive argument for the truth of wisdom in the ancient world: wisdom is synonymous with age. Original wisdom has been lost forever, but wisdom has been preserved in the traditions of the elders. Wisdom does not come through secret revelations in strange dreams. Job could not legitimately claim to know something that was foreign to the aged. It was preposterous that he should challenge those who were the means of preserving what wisdom there is in this world.

This arrogance of Job, as perceived by Eliphaz, had resulted in a deeper problem. Job was not satisfied with the gentle word of wisdom; he was ungrateful for the comfort of God's presence. His denial of the divine mercy was an indication of his rebellion against God and his refusal to accept divine providence in his life. Job's wild ideas had inflamed him; it was as if he was beside himself. Anger is dangerous when it assumes control; it can lead to an attack on God and result in blasphemous words. This was the only explanation Eliphaz could provide for Job's arguments.

From the viewpoint of traditional wisdom, the argument of 15:14-16 is most certainly blasphemous. In effect, it says that the heavenly beings, and even the heavens themselves, are not so pure that they can escape divine censure. This cannot be a willful failure on their part; it can only be an indication of their finite status before the most holy Creator and their inability to determine their own future. If these "holy ones" are unable to be so pure as to avoid divine rebuke, then how much less humans who are "abhorrent and corrupt"? Mortals know they "drink wickedness like water." How can such creatures ever presume to control goodness for their lives? For traditional wisdom this is a much too capricious portrayal of justice. It is completely unfair to think that humans in this world should be subject to punishment outside of their control. This is an affront to the very nature of God.

◆   ## 2. The wicked receive retribution (15:17-35)

17 "If you will listen, I will show you.
I will answer you from my own experience.

18 And it is confirmed by the reports of wise men
who have heard the same thing from their fathers—

¹⁹from those to whom the land was given
long before any foreigners arrived.

²⁰"The wicked writhe in pain throughout
their lives.
Years of trouble are stored up for
the ruthless.
²¹The sound of terror rings in their ears,
and even on good days they fear the
attack of the destroyer.
²²They dare not go out into the darkness
for fear they will be murdered.
²³They wander around, saying, 'Where
can I find bread?'*
They know their day of destruction
is near.
²⁴That dark day terrifies them.
They live in distress and anguish,
like a king preparing for battle.
²⁵For they shake their fists at God,
defying the Almighty.
²⁶Holding their strong shields,
they defiantly charge against him.

²⁷"These wicked people are heavy and
prosperous;
their waists bulge with fat.
²⁸But their cities will be ruined.
They will live in abandoned houses
that are ready to tumble down.

²⁹Their riches will not last,
and their wealth will not endure.
Their possessions will no longer
spread across the horizon.
³⁰"They will not escape the darkness.
The burning sun will wither their
shoots,
and the breath of God will destroy
them.
³¹Let them no longer fool themselves
by trusting in empty riches,
for emptiness will be their only
reward.
³²Like trees, they will be cut down in
the prime of life;
their branches will never again
be green.
³³They will be like a vine whose grapes
are harvested too early,
like an olive tree that loses its
blossoms before the fruit can
form.
³⁴For the godless are barren.
Their homes, enriched through
bribery, will burn.
³⁵They conceive trouble and give birth
to evil.
Their womb produces deceit."

15:23 Greek version reads *He is appointed to be food for a vulture.*

NOTES

15:17 *If you will listen.* Following the quotation of the vision, the Heb. is abrupt and forceful: "Let me tell you—listen to me!" Eliphaz was somewhat impatient in his response.

15:23 *Where can I find bread?* This word "where" in unpointed, pre-Masoretic Hebrew texts would have only had the letters *'yh*; pronounced *'ayyeh* [TH346, ZH372] this would ask "where"; pronounced *'ayyah* it would mean "vulture." In this case, either can make sense, and the Gr. translator took it in the sense of the latter (see NLT mg). It is fairly certain that the Heb. used by the Gr. translator also had a different word at the beginning of the line, which he translated as "appoint" (Orlinsky 1964:71-73; cf. the MT's *nadad* [TH5074, ZH5610], "wander"). Still, the Heb. of the MT can be read as "he wanders about as food for the vulture" or "he is cast out as food for the vulture" (*nuddad*). This sense of "food for the vulture" is much more appropriate than "wandering for food." The wicked are the rich, who would not be looking for food but would be fearful of being prey, as indicated by the previous verse. They fear the day of darkness and feel they are marked for the sword.

15:26 *they defiantly charge.* The Heb. is an unusual metaphor: "He runneth upon him, *even* on *his* neck" (KJV). The closest parallel is Ps 75:5, which warns against boasting by "sticking out the neck" (KJV); there, the phrase is parallel to "lifting up the horn" (i.e., defiantly asserting power). It is an act of hubris for someone to "stick out his neck" against God.

15:29 *across the horizon.* This is a paraphrase for "across the land." The word "land" (*'erets* [TH776, ZH824]) can refer to the underworld, as in 38:18, in which case the thought would be that the rich cannot retain their possessions in death (cf. Ps 49:18-20). This is unlikely in spite of the reference to death in the next verse; the problem of the wicked is their wealth in this life.

15:30 *The burning sun.* This is probably a metaphor for scorching heat, which withers plants. This is parallel to the reference to wind ("breath") in the next line.

the breath of God. This is almost certainly the correct interpretation of the Heb., which simply refers to "the breath of his mouth." Some translations (e.g., RSV, NRSV, NEB, NJB) have been misled by the LXX, which says, "his blossom will fall." These translations assume the word "flower" (*perakh* [TH6525, ZH7258]) rather than "his mouth" (*piw* [TH6310, ZH7023]). However, it is most likely that the Gr. follows a different text in this instance. The Gr. translator was following his version of 14:2a, and it will influence him again in this chapter at 15:33b (Heater 1982:61-62). This third line interprets the metaphor of the flower in the second line while repeating the words and the idea of the first line of the verse: he will not escape the darkness, he will wither like a shoot in the flame (the searing east wind), and he will not escape the blast of God's mouth. This last line is probably an allusion to the familiar words of Isa 11:4: "The earth will shake at the force of his word, and one breath from his mouth will destroy the wicked." God exercises his judgment against the wicked by simply speaking the word. The darkness in this verse is that of death. Cf. the image of the danger of darkness in 15:22.

15:32 *they will be cut down.* The translation has changed the metaphor. This verse returns to the wilting of a plant. The verb in the first line is a homonym; it can mean either "whither" or "cut off." In this case, it introduces the second line, which says that their shoot will not be lush. The first line says they will whither before their time, which is illustrated in the next verse with the grapevine and the olive tree.

COMMENTARY

Eliphaz began his reply in fashion much like that found in Psalm 49, a wisdom poem that is very similar in its condemnation of the arrogant rich and its warning that they will lose all their possessions as death overtakes them. The message of the wise was universally applicable (Ps 49:1-4); its truth was like a physical law operative in the same manner for all people in the world. This wisdom, however, was not a philosophical argument but an exercise in deductive logic. It began unapologetically from the premise that this view of the universe was correct. The task of wisdom was to convey this view in convincing rhetoric, to cast it in unforgettable metaphors, to express it in enigmas that give pause for thought (Ps 49:4). In this respect, Eliphaz was an accomplished wise man.

Wisdom was based on cumulative experience. Eliphaz quite naturally began with that which he had seen, which confirmed what those of his generation had taught him, which were the truths they, in turn, had received from the generation that had gone on before them. The wise looked back to a time of pristine purity, the "good old days" when culture and religion had not become utterly confused by the infusion of foreign and corrupt ideas. Eliphaz did not have in mind a particular historical circumstance when he referred to the time before foreigners arrived. He was probably thinking of his own home country, so there is no reference to events in the land of Israel. Eliphaz was providing a polemic for the authority of wisdom. There is one thing in this world that is pure, and that is wisdom, which has been passed on through tradition, untarnished by human corruption.

Further, what Eliphaz had to say about the wicked was true. He expressed in potent words the confession of the psalms concerning the wicked, the warnings against the rich imbedded in the pithy sayings of proverbs. The problem with Eliphaz was his failure to understand the limitations of his knowledge. He thought this truth concerning the wicked could account for all the pain in the world. This was the point he intended to drive home to Job, and he mustered the best of human eloquence in his attempt to do so.

Eliphaz began with a discussion about the deception of the apparent tranquility of the wicked rich. They have ease because they have material abundance, which they are very successful at protecting. In reality, the wicked rich live in a constant state of paranoia. They have much to lose, and they have many enemies. There is no time when fear does not grip them; the sounds of terror are continually in their ears. There is no place where they are secure, for the assassin may be lurking anywhere (15:22). Their life is marked for violent death—it is only a matter of time. The day of darkness has already been prepared for them. The vulture is circling over their heads, for it knows its prey is at hand (15:23).

The problem is not riches; the problem is arrogance against God. The wicked have despised God; they have no faith in God (cf. Ps 49:6). They defiantly shake their fist at God; they boast in their own security. Such a boast is hollow, as the paranoia of the wicked proves. Distress and anguish terrify them; they are overpowered by their fears. They live like kings under continual threat of attack. Their real enemy is God (15:26). They charge at God behind the thick shield of their riches. Their wealth is evident in their fat faces and their wide hips. Their wealth, however, will prove to be a very ineffective shield against their enemy. Against a human enemy such a shield might suffice. However, their wealth is no match for the one who owns the earth and its fullness, the world and all those who dwell in it (Ps 24:1). Their mighty cities will be destroyed; their houses will be abandoned heaps of ruin (15:34).

Wealth is temporary for all who have it because no one can escape the day of death. In 15:22-24 Eliphaz speaks of darkness to point to the impending death of the wicked, as is evident from his analogies to plants dying before their time. His point is that death is feeding on the wicked, even while they live in wealth—the same point made by other wise men about the rich (Ps 49:13-14). The wicked rich are like a shoot dried up by the "flame" (15:30; KJV, RSV); they are like a frail green leaf blasted by the hot dry east wind. The wind Eliphaz refers to is the blast of God's mouth; it is his word of the judgment of death against the wicked; it is a destiny they cannot escape. The wicked have deceived themselves; their investments in wealth were investments in nothing—they will vanish like a vapor. They are a plant withered before it can bear fruit. This plant is not by the rivers of water (Ps 1:3), bearing its fruit in its season. The wicked are the chaff, they are the grapevine stripped before the fruit ripens, and they are the olive tree where the blossoms were shed before the fruit could form.

Eliphaz saved his most devastating words for last: the wicked would have no legacy and their family will be cut off—it will be as if fire consumed their tents. This should not be surprising because they conceive trouble, carry deceit in their womb, and give birth to iniquity. They are not giving birth to the legacy of a family that will carry on their good name and be revered in the years to come. All they have given birth to is violence, and that violence will destroy them and all their children.

Death comes to all, but for the wicked, death is a sinister demise. The lives of the righteous will continue to bear fruit (Ps 1:3); the Lord knows their way, and they will not be cut off from him (Ps 1:6). The ungodly are not so. The ungodly are those who rage against God and imagine vain things (Pss 2:1-4; cf. Job 15:25-26). God has nothing but scorn for them; they will perish in their ways (Pss 1:6; 2:12; cf. Job 15:34). Eliphaz stands in the best of the teaching of the wise when he declares that there is nothing as tragic as the godless wicked in the hands of an angry God.

Truth is the most powerful of weapons, and in this case Eliphaz meant it to hurt. The pain of truth may be the means to healing, which is what Eliphaz intended. Truth, however, is like a sharp knife. Used correctly it is the surgeon's scalpel; used incorrectly it is a mutilating instrument causing pain or death. The speech of Eliphaz was a surgery that could only injure the patient further. Eliphaz missed the mark. Job had not been in defiance of God by trusting in his own wealth. The opposite was true; his faith was in God alone, and he had used every possible means to express it. Job had to make clear to Eliphaz that though he was right, he was ever so wrong.

◆ I. Job: Hope for a Sufferer (16:1–17:16)
1. God as an adversary (16:1-17)

Then Job spoke again:

2 "I have heard all this before.
What miserable comforters you are!
3 Won't you ever stop blowing hot air?
What makes you keep on talking?
4 I could say the same things if you were in my place.
I could spout off criticism and shake my head at you.
5 But if it were me, I would encourage you.
I would try to take away your grief.
6 Instead, I suffer if I defend myself,
and I suffer no less if I refuse to speak.

7 "O God, you have ground me down and devastated my family.
8 As if to prove I have sinned, you've reduced me to skin and bones.
My gaunt flesh testifies against me.
9 God hates me and angrily tears me apart.
He snaps his teeth at me
and pierces me with his eyes.
10 People jeer and laugh at me.
They slap my cheek in contempt.
A mob gathers against me.
11 God has handed me over to sinners.
He has tossed me into the hands of the wicked.

12 "I was living quietly until he shattered me.
He took me by the neck and broke me in pieces.
Then he set me up as his target,

¹³   and now his archers surround me.
     His arrows pierce me without mercy.
     The ground is wet with my blood.*
¹⁴Again and again he smashes
        against me,
     charging at me like a warrior.

16:13 Hebrew *my gall.*

¹⁵I wear burlap to show my grief.
   My pride lies in the dust.
¹⁶My eyes are red with weeping;
   dark shadows circle my eyes.
¹⁷Yet I have done no wrong,
   and my prayer is pure.

NOTES

16:4 *spout off criticism.* The Heb. is not clear as to whether the speech is positive or negative. The word *khabar* [TH2266, ZH2489] has the meaning "bind," which could be taken metaphorically as "stringing arguments together." However, it has been established that there are two other Semitic words with the same spelling that refer to speech, and it is possible one of them is used here. The word *khabar* is found in contexts such as the Flood account, where the uproar or clamor is part of the violence that causes the Flood. If this is the word intended, Job would be referring to the speeches as a noisy argument (harangue). Yet another option arises since the word *khabar* is also found in Arabic, used in reference to eloquent speech. There are disadvantages to all three possibilities. The word "bind" is an unusual metaphor for speech or argumentation. The word meaning "contentious" or "noisy argumentation" is well established with some clear biblical uses (e.g., Prov 21:9; 25:24). The difficulty is that the nodding of the head found in the parallel lines—Job 16:4b (*nu'a* [TH5128, ZH5675]) and 16:5b (*nid* [TH5205, ZH5764])—is used elsewhere in Job of a sympathetic action rather than a condemning one (2:11; 42:11). Further, it would be contradictory for Job to speak of haranguing his friends if they were in his place, for then he would be no better than they are. The problem with the word meaning "eloquent speech" is that it is known only in late Arabic as a development from a word referring to something bright or colorful. In the larger context, the friends attempted to correct Job and to be sympathetic at the same time. It seems that Job speaks of the friends as attempting to "bind words on him," even as they try to console him with a nodding head.

16:5 *I would encourage you.* The Heb. verb (*'amets* [TH553, ZH599]) simply means "to make strong"; applied to language, it refers to "fortifying speech." Eliphaz used this word to speak of how Job formerly encouraged the despondent (4:4), and Job here says he would do the same thing for the friends were he in their place.

try to take away your grief. The Heb. is difficult, but it appears to say that "sympathy would silence my lips." If this is the correct understanding, the verse makes reference to two critical aspects of consolation: speaking words of comfort (16:5a) and being present in silence (16:5b) when the pain is too deep for words.

16:8 *As if to prove I have sinned . . . My gaunt flesh testifies against me.* The Heb. offers a vivid metaphor in court terminology: The gaunt figure of Job is evidence for a conviction of guilt.

16:11 *tossed me into.* The sense is rather that Job was pushed down by the hands of the wicked. Job described himself as cast down (12:5); Eliphaz described the misfortunate as fallen (4:4).

16:13 *wet with my blood.* Job pictured himself as being attacked by a warrior. The arrows have found their mark in his inner organs (lit. "kidneys," but used generically for the digestive organs) and split them open. The description is that of a burst gallbladder with the bile running on the ground.

16:15 *I wear burlap to show my grief.* Lit., "I have sewed sackcloth to my skin." Job's state of lamentation was so permanent that he never took off the garments of sorrow.

My pride lies in the dust. Lit., "I have buried my horn in the dust." The horn of an animal was representative of its strength, power, and nobility. Job had lost every semblance of human dignity and worth in life.

16:16 *dark shadows circle my eyes.* Lit., "shadow of death"—it is a way of saying "the deepest of all darkness" or even "death." Dark eyes (deep bags under the eyes) are a sign of excessive worry and sorrow.

COMMENTARY

Eliphaz had responded to Job by deriding his claims to wisdom (15:2-3) and had introduced his own theology with the bombastic claims of the wise (15:17-19). All this was familiar to Job, and its repetition was not merely redundant—it was injurious. The conventional application of wisdom did not work in Job's situation, but Job seemed to acknowledge that their intent was noble, that they wanted to be sympathetic, and that they wanted to restore. Job could use wisdom in this way if he were in the place of his friends; Eliphaz himself had said that Job was known for just such encouragement (4:4). This knowledge in itself should give these "miserable comforters" pause. Job had been the master of the teachings of their brand of wisdom, but now he had encountered a situation where the old analysis of wisdom was not sufficient. They should not simply conclude that Job could not apply his own medicine to himself, as Eliphaz had done (4:5); they should consider the possibility that more is at work in Job's situation than they can account for.

At this point, Job expressed his lament to God (16:6-17). Though the friends must hear it if they were to learn wisdom, Job had to address God, for God was the source of the problem, and he should provide the solution. One of the most important therapies for all sufferers is the freedom to unreservedly express their complaint to God. These words of Job are like those found frequently in Psalms, the kind of lament Job's author probably knew very well.

Job knew that complaining would not relieve the pain, but silence would not help either. God had worn Job down to the point where his earthly existence had been virtually exterminated. His family had been decimated, and his body was emaciated. All this appeared to be clear evidence of his sin, but there was no sin, no explanation. Job could only reiterate the situation in his complaint. God had attacked him, torn him apart in anger; God gnashed his teeth at Job and pierced him with his gaze. In part, Job perceived this through the treatment he received from those around him in that they held him in contempt and gaped at him with open mouths, if not actually striking him in the face (16:10). It was a verbal lynching. Their judgment was that Job should accept the testimony of his decimated situation, for God had banned Job to the company of those who do wrong.

Job was secure and at peace when, without warning, God attacked him the way a warrior assaults his enemy (16:12). God's archers had found their mark; his gallbladder had been pierced and the bile was flowing on the ground. The reference to

internal organs was a way of Job expressing the torment he felt. The kidneys were
the organ used to express emotion, much the way "heart" is used in English. In our
words, Job had a broken and crushed heart, expressed here as the arrows of a warrior dashing through his innards and spilling their content on the ground. Job was
attacked blow after blow, so he was in a perpetual state of lamentation—it was as if
the clothes of mourning were sewn to his body. He had no pride left—it was buried
in the soil. His face was inflamed and red from weeping; his eyes were black from
stress and pain. Job concluded this lament in words that seem to deliberately recall
the suffering servant of Isaiah (cf. 16:17; Isa 53:9b)—and all this, though he had
done no violence and his praise of God was pure.

The most visible side of suffering is physical pain, which Job described in terms of
his battered body. It would be a mistake, however, to read this lament as though the
physical pain were the worst of his suffering. Job spoke of his bowels to make it
clear that it was the emotional torment that was the most unbearable. This was not
only caused by the loss of his family; in addition, he was being despised by friends
who assumed that God had attacked him because of his sins. He knew that he had
been stricken, smitten, and afflicted by God, but he also knew that it was not because of his sins.

Eliphaz had it wrong; he had described the arrogant rich, those who substituted
faith in wealth for faith in God. Job was not that kind of man. He knew it to be true
even if his friends could not accept it. Job knew his friends would never understand
the truth without an explanation. The deepest anguish is when there are no answers
and others turn away. In some sense, Job had become an enemy to God. Such
knowledge tore at his insides, especially because there was nothing that he could do
to change his status.

All that was left for Job was to lament his case to God, the one who had attacked
him. But in all this, Job could not turn against God because God was all he had.
Though God may attack him, God was the one he must turn to as a witness and a
friend, for God alone knew the truth. Job remained confident that truth would prevail.

2. God as an advocate (16:18–17:16)

¹⁸"O earth, do not conceal my blood.
   Let it cry out on my behalf.
¹⁹Even now my witness is in heaven.
   My advocate is there on high.
²⁰My friends scorn me,
   but I pour out my tears to God.
²¹I need someone to mediate between
      God and me,
   as a person mediates between
      friends.
²²For soon I must go down that road
   from which I will never return.

CHAPTER 17
¹"My spirit is crushed,
   and my life is nearly snuffed out.
   The grave is ready to receive me.
²I am surrounded by mockers.
   I watch how bitterly they taunt me.

³"You must defend my innocence, O God,
   since no one else will stand up
      for me.
⁴You have closed their minds to
      understanding,
   but do not let them triumph.

⁵They betray their friends for their own
  advantage,
  so let their children faint with
  hunger.

⁶"God has made a mockery of me
  among the people;
  they spit in my face.
⁷My eyes are swollen with weeping,
  and I am but a shadow of my former
  self.
⁸The virtuous are horrified when they
  see me.
  The innocent rise up against the
  ungodly.
⁹The righteous keep moving forward,
  and those with clean hands become
  stronger and stronger.

¹⁰"As for all of you, come back with a
  better argument,

though I still won't find a wise man
  among you.
¹¹My days are over.
  My hopes have disappeared.
  My heart's desires are broken.

¹²These men say that night is day;
  they claim that the darkness is
  light.
¹³What if I go to the grave*
  and make my bed in darkness?
¹⁴What if I call the grave my father,
  and the maggot my mother or
  my sister?
¹⁵Where then is my hope?
  Can anyone find it?
¹⁶No, my hope will go down with
  me to the grave.
  We will rest together in the
  dust!"

17:13 Hebrew to Sheol; also in 17:16.

NOTES

16:20 *My friends scorn me.* The uncertainties of the flow of thought and the ambiguity of the vocabulary of this verse have led to various translations. The older English versions (KJV, RSV) are followed by some more recent versions (NRSV, NLT) in moving the thought back to mocking friends in contrast to the advocate before God in heaven. This, however seems to be an unwarranted disruption of thought. Job has declared that his advocate is in heaven (16:19), and his weeping eyes look to this advocate to defend his case with God (16:20b-21). It is unlikely the intervening line refers to mocking (assuming *melitsay* is a participial form of the verb *lits* [TH3887, ZH4329]). It is more probable the verse continues the thought of an advocate (*melits* [TH3887B, ZH4885]), the same sense of the word used by Elihu (33:23). The problem then is the identity of the advocate. Rather than meaning "friend," *rea'* [TH7453, ZH8276] may be an Aramaic loanword meaning "thought" or "intention" (Koehler and Baumgartner 4:1171). The latter word is assumed in the Gr. translation and various modern versions (REB, NJB): the argument (or prayer) of Job will act as an advocate for him. This would be the same thought Job had expressed earlier (13:15-16): his salvation would be that he could make his case before God so that truth might prevail. However, Job was advancing that thought in this speech. If truth is to prevail, there must be a witness to the truth. That witness is in heaven (16:19), and that witness can be none other than God, for he alone knows the whole truth. In tears Job looks to God (16:20), for God is the advocate in heaven who must plead his case. Rather than "my friends mock me," we must translate "my advocate is my Friend." Though God has treated Job as an enemy, Job declares that God is yet his friend and will defend his case (16:21). Job's faith advances as the dialog progresses.

17:5 *They betray their friends.* This verse is an illustration of those whose thinking is irrational, but the nature of it is not clear. "He that speaketh flattery" (KJV) is a common meaning for the noun *kheleq* [TH2506A, ZH2749] (see Prov 7:21), but this has no obvious relevance to the hungering children (lit., "the eyes of his children languish"). The noun *kheleq* may also refer to a share of property, in which case the "proclaiming" (*yaggid* [TH5046, ZH5583]) might be a denouncing of friends in order to receive a share of property (RSV, NRSV, NLT) or an invitation to friends to share in it (NJB). A third proposed meaning for *kheleq* is "destruction," in which case, a good rendering is "one denounces friends to their ruin" (REB). Finally, instead of "friend" (*rea'* [TH7453, ZH8276]) we may read the word "evil" (*ra'* [TH7451A, ZH8274]) and make it the subject: "my lot (*kheleq*) is described as evil" (NAB). The verse is a proverbial saying now obscure to us. The most likely sense of the saying is "they invite their friends to a feast while their own children long for food." The point is that a proclamation of receiving a portion of something (*kheleq*) is made to others before the eyes of one's own needy children.

17:12 *These men say that night is day.* The subject could be those proclaiming false wisdom who "set the night to day." However, the dashed hopes of Job are the immediate antecedent, and the logical sequel is that Job had plans and dreams that could have "turned the night to day."

they claim that the darkness is light. In the Heb. this line complements the first with a further reference to "light," but the syntax is obscure: "out of darkness light is near." The general sense is that "only in darkness can light come near" or "as light comes near the darkness grows distant" (Koehler and Baumgartner 3:1063). In the mouth of the friends, this would be an attempt at encouragement; they would be saying "the longer the night, the nearer the dawn." For Job, this would be a false hope (NLT), for they did not understand the kind of darkness that engulfed him. If, however, the plans and wishes of Job were the subject of the first line, the second would have quite a different sense: These hopes could have brought light out of darkness.

COMMENTARY

Job had lamented his lonely situation, where the best of people insulted and assaulted him (16:10), saying he was deserving of his punishment. The deepest of the lament psalms have a similar sentiment; friends abandon and despise the sufferer (e.g., Ps 22:6-8). The lament psalms declare confidence and faith in God in a remarkable way, even when it would seem God had abandoned and forsaken the psalmist (e.g., Ps 22:1-5, 21-22). Faith in such circumstances can exacerbate the pain, as expressed in the first section of Psalm 22. It is certain that God is faithful and fair, so his silence in such painful circumstances aggravates the anguish. Job was in an even more desolate situation. God had been his adversary, mercilessly attacking him (16:12-14) for reasons Job could not understand. Even so, in such circumstances all one can do is turn to God, even if he is the adversary. Job could not stop having faith in God, for God was his advocate and friend. Having been abandoned by his friends, Job could not let the matter rest (16:18). Injustice was crying out from the earth (cf. Gen 4:10; Isa 26:21), and it could not be silenced before the God of justice. All the pain could not take away this faith from Job.

There was only one witness who knew the truth and could give testimony on behalf of Job. He was in heaven, and he was an advocate for the truth (16:19). Job poured out his grief to God because he was certain God would come to his defense, just as any other person would for a friend. Job had earlier expressed the certainty that truth must prevail. Job would make his case before God though it cost him his life (13:15); his salvation was to come before God to make such a case (13:16), a privilege the ungodly do not have, for they cannot come into the divine presence. In this response, Job was advancing this confidence further—a faith that will crescendo in his next response to Bildad (cf. 19:25). Not only was Job assured that the case of his righteousness would be known, but he was sure that God was his advocate and friend. The author of Job would not have considered this to be more contradictory than the laments of the psalms he knew so well. If they could cry out to the God who had forsaken and abandoned them, Job could cry out with that same confidence to the God who had attacked him. Job, at least, had no doubt that God was fully aware of his presence and his plight.

Job hoped that righteousness would prevail, but he did not have any hope for his present life. His time was short, his spirit broken, his life snuffed out—all that remained was the grave, and in the meantime he must endure the mockers and leave his life to God. It was not that others, who had abandoned Job, were really at fault (17:4)—they simply didn't know the truth. Job had a proverb for them (17:5): they were like those who invite friends to a feast while their own children languish in famine. God had treated Job in such a way that he himself had become an object of proverbial mocking—he was a hissing and a byword among the people who said, "Remember Job!" Such words were spit in the face of Job and there was nothing he could do about it. His eyes were exhausted from weeping; his body was wasting to a shadow. All Job could do was wait for the end and trust that God would vindicate him.

Good and morally upright folk were appalled when they saw Job in his situation. All they could conclude was that some excessive wickedness had been responsible for such a plight. They, being righteous, were horrified. Job was a powerful moral example for them; they would be more determined than ever to live as they knew they should, more resolute in the purity of their ways. Job invited them all to come and observe; let them go on thinking what they cannot help but think. Job, however, knew there was not one wise person among them (17:10). There are truths in the secrets of heaven Job did not understand, but at least he knew they are there. That gave him a wisdom unknown to the righteous. The upright were not quite "pure in heart," for their ignorance had left them bereft of meekness. They did not know that they did not know—such was the tragedy of their plight.

As for Job, there was nothing left in this life (17:11). Though hope can turn night to day (see note on 17:12), Job had lost his hope—his dreams and life-goals would not be realized, his future was the grave. As far as enjoyment in this life was concerned, there was nothing to wait for. If you lose money, you lose a lot; if you lose friends, you lose more; if you lose hope, you lose everything. The likelihood was that there would be no return in this life for Job. He faced this, abandoning any false hopes.

False hope was the bedeviling curse the friends had repeatedly tried to foist on Job. He would have none of it. Hopelessness for his life was not faithlessness, as the friends had presumed. Job did have faith; God was his friend, his advocate, his witness, and Job needed nothing more.

◆ J. Bildad: Punishment for the Wicked (18:1-21)

Then Bildad the Shuhite replied:

2 "How long before you stop talking?
Speak sense if you want us to
answer!
3 Do you think we are mere animals?
Do you think we are stupid?
4 You may tear out your hair in anger,
but will that destroy the earth?
Will it make the rocks tremble?

5 "Surely the light of the wicked will be
snuffed out.
The sparks of their fire will not
glow.
6 The light in their tent will grow dark.
The lamp hanging above them will
be quenched.
7 The confident stride of the wicked will
be shortened.
Their own schemes will be their
downfall.
8 The wicked walk into a net.
They fall into a pit.
9 A trap grabs them by the heel.
A snare holds them tight.
10 A noose lies hidden on the ground.
A rope is stretched across their
path.

11 "Terrors surround the wicked
and trouble them at every step.

12 Hunger depletes their strength,
and calamity waits for them to
stumble.
13 Disease eats their skin;
death devours their limbs.
14 They are torn from the security of
their homes
and are brought down to the king
of terrors.
15 The homes of the wicked will burn
down;
burning sulfur rains on their houses.
16 Their roots will dry up,
and their branches will wither.
17 All memory of their existence will fade
from the earth,
No one will remember their names.
18 They will be thrust from light into
darkness,
driven from the world.
19 They will have neither children nor
grandchildren,
nor any survivor in the place where
they lived.
20 People in the west are appalled at
their fate;
people in the east are horrified.
21 They will say, 'This was the home of
a wicked person,
the place of one who rejected God.'"

NOTES

18:2 *you.* The Heb. has Bildad using the plural, though presumably he is only speaking to Job. The Gr. is in the singular, but this is no indication of a difference in text (Orlinsky 1958:269-270). There are other examples of the use of the plural when apparently only one person is being addressed (Gordis 1978:190), so it may be a particular Heb. style.

stop talking. The Heb. is emphatic: "put an end to speech." Though *qenets* [TH7078, ZH7874] is the only occurrence of the Aramaic spelling of the word "end" (*qets*) in the Heb. Bible, the Aramaic translation from Qumran "put an end to words" (*tsw' swp lml'*) assures us this is the correct interpretation (van der Ploeg and van der Woude 1971:12). The speculative meaning "snare," based on Arabic (Gordis 1978:190; cf. RSV, NRSV), and the even more speculative emendation to "bridle" (Driver 1969:79; cf. REB) are to be disregarded.

18:3 *we are stupid?* The translation is speculative (Grabbe 1977:71-74), based on a cognate word meaning "stopped up," having the metaphorical application of "dense" in mental aptitude. "Reputed vile" (KJV) signals repudiation, which is expressed by being considered unclean and by being regarded as stupid like an animal. The emendation of "to be

unclean" (*tame'* [TH2930, ZH3237]) to "being like" (*damah* [TH1819, ZH1948]) in order to supply
the thought "are we nothing but brute beasts" (REB, NEB, NJB) is questionable, but it does
have the support of 11QtgJob. The LXX appears to translate another word *damah* [TH1820,
ZH1949], which has the meaning "be silent"; this may lend further support to the idea of
a Heb. text with a variant reading.

18:4 *will that destroy the earth?* The Heb. reads, "Should the earth be abandoned because
of you?" Job had never suggested the earth be deserted on his account—only that it might
be altered on his behalf, as suggested by the next line. Dahood (1959:306), using Ugaritic
support, made a case for a second word *'azab* meaning "rearrange" [TH5800A, ZH6441] rather
than "abandon" [TH5800, ZH6440]. Though this second use of *'azab* seems to have declined
in later times, Williamson (1985:84-85) concedes it may well be this word that is used in
Exod 23:5, attesting to its use in Heb.

18:11 *trouble them at every step.* The unusual Heb. expression ("scatter their feet")
is probably an idiom now lost (Grabbe 1977:76), as indicated by the ancient versions.
A suggested Arabic parallel meaning "make water," suggesting urination caused by fear
(REB), is best described as "a concession to the spirit of the times" (de Wilde 1981:202).

18:15 *burning sulfur rains on their houses.* Earlier translations reflect the vocalization of
the MT: "In his tent dwells that which is none of his" (*mibbeli-lo*) (RSV; cf. KJV, NIV mg).
This may be syntactically acceptable, but is hardly the thought in context, as observed by
Driver (1969:79). Dahood (1957:312-314) has shown that this verse and the next draw on
ancient motifs found in Ugaritic writings. "None of his" (*mibbeli-lo*) is parallel to "sulfur"
(*goprith* [TH1614, ZH1730]) and should be repointed to the word "flood" (cf. *mabbul* [TH3999,
ZH4429]), which is used with reference to a rain of fire. The analogy in the next verse of the
tree drying up is also found in Ugaritic writings.

COMMENTARY

Bildad begins his second speech as he had the first (cf. 8:2), with the question "how
long?" Bildad had no patience with the idea that the innocent may suffer. Bildad
saw life in black and white as far as morality and suffering were concerned. There
are two kinds of people, the good and the bad, and they experience life accordingly.
Bildad made it clear in his introduction (18:2-4) that the world is not a safe and stable place if we allow it to be mucked up with gray.

Like Eliphaz, Bildad was annoyed that Job should claim some superior sort of
wisdom (cf. 15:9). Bildad believed, as did Eliphaz, that the wisdom of the sages
would side entirely with the argument of Job's friends (cf. 15:10-11). To disagree
with this clear-cut view of life was tantamount to being insane (cf. 15:12-13); it
means treating the wise as brute beasts. There is no doubt that Bildad felt slighted,
for Job had challenged the traditional view that the righteous never suffer.

Bildad argued that it was only anger that made Job think the wise were wrong,
and Job's anger would not rearrange the world; the mountains would remain safely
in their place. But Job argued that God is not so predictable; without warning, God
may shake the mountains, even the very foundations of the earth, or he may stop
the sun from shining. Bildad could not imagine such a world. Even the suggestion
that there is unpredictability was distressing and insulting.

In his first speech, Bildad had used analogies with plants to describe the demise
of the wicked, but he had also sprinkled his speech with hope for the righteous. The

end of the story of Job would be better than the beginning: God would yet fill Job's mouth with laughter (cf. 8:6-7, 21). Now Bildad makes no appeals for Job to turn to God (cf. 8:5). It is not that Bildad has lost hope for Job but that it is quite distressing to Bildad that Job could be so recalcitrant in his thinking, so defiant of traditional authority. Bildad's fear was not a fear for Job—he would yet come around; but the ideas Job expressed were to be feared and rebutted. Thus, in this speech, Bildad focused on the death of the wicked, not so much as a warning to Job but as a correction of his thinking.

What Bildad lacked in insight he compensated for in eloquence. He was among the best of the wise in describing the death of the wicked. Bildad again turned to analogies from nature. He also used the imagery of mythology (18:13-14) to evoke the horror of death stalking the wicked all their lives. Sarna (1963:315-317) has shown that the terminology comes from the myths of the gods known at Ugarit, which are also variations of the Babylonian myths. Though these myths recount the deeds of false gods, a true believer in God can use mythology to portray truth and to bring conviction to those who hear it. Job had used mythology in his reference to Leviathan in his opening lament (3:8) when he appealed to the powers that could overcome chaos to change his world. Bildad responded with the mythology of Mot, the god of death. He referred to the "first-born of death" (18:13, RSV) and to the "king of terrors" (18:14, RSV). In Canaanite mythology Mot held the rank of first-born of the chief god El and was the one who ruled supreme in the kingdom of the dead. Firstborn is a title of rank; Mot was not only king of the nether world, but he also was able to temporarily displace Baal as the ruler over the earth. Mot voraciously devours his prey on earth (cf. Ps 49:14); life fails wherever he goes. Bildad vividly described the terrors of life, which feed on the wicked even while they live. These terrors are the work of the king of the nether world, already at work in this world. Their activity is evident for all to observe.

Bildad began by describing death as the extinguishing of a light (18:5-7). The first sign of a lifeless dwelling is when the light fails to come on. The dwelling of the wicked may be an impressive mansion, but death is already at work to curtail this march for wealth. The schemes of the wicked cannot halt this advance. Shortly these very plans will cast these rich down to the ground.

Death is a trap from which there is no escape (18:8-10). Six different words for trap are used in these verses to illustrate the inevitability of death for the rich. Their feet will be entangled in a net as they go, or they will walk over the covered pit. These types of traps were used to catch animals as ferocious as a lion or a crocodile. Animals were also caught by means of a rope or cord, set as a noose or a snare. The snare of death is set in the path of the wicked rich. The rope will snare them in their way. The more they struggle, the tighter it will grip them, eventually strangling their life.

Bildad then described the activity of death itself (18:11-14). The terrors of death are all around, putting the rich to flight, but there is no escape. The more they run, the more they will find that their vigor is depleted; their strength and wealth have become need and want. Their fall from wealth is at hand; calamity is there waiting for it to happen. Disease is already evident on their skin. There is no home that will keep them safe from the predator, the king of terrors. This predator will mercilessly snatch them right out of the security of their abode and march them down to their final home.

Bildad went on to describe what is left once the predator of death has come. The once proud dwellings of the rich are consumed by a flood of fire. Brimstone ("burning sulfur," 18:15) is noted for its inflammable character, burning easily in the air and forming noxious sulfur gas. It is the characteristic description of judgment on the properties of the wicked. The death of the wicked rich results in the dissipation of all that characterized their lives, both their properties and their families. These whither away like the roots and branches of a dying tree. The wicked will shortly be forgotten, no property will be attached to their name.

Bildad concluded his description by returning to the theme of light (18:18) and reiterating the fate of the wicked (18:19-20). Death is to be thrust into darkness, to be driven from this world. The wicked are left without descendants; none of their family survives where they once lived. The day of their death is an astonishment to all—shock reigns from east to west.

Bildad outdid himself in providing a description fitting to Job. Here was a man whose vast properties had been stolen and consumed by fire and whose progeny was extinct. In a world of black and white, there was no need to state the obvious. Job was still alive; he knew his situation and he knew what he must do. In his darkness, the light was near, as Job himself knew (cf. 17:12). Bildad was trying to get Job to cease his talk of hopelessness and claim the destiny of the righteous.

◆   ## K. Job: My Redeemer Lives (19:1-29)
1. Friends and family fail (19:1-22)

Then Job spoke again:

2 "How long will you torture me?
How long will you try to crush me
with your words?
3 You have already insulted me ten
times.
You should be ashamed of treating
me so badly.
4 Even if I have sinned,
that is my concern, not yours.
5 You think you're better than I am,
using my humiliation as evidence
of my sin.
6 But it is God who has wronged me,
capturing me in his net.*
7 "I cry out, 'Help!' but no one
answers me.

I protest, but there is no justice.
8 God has blocked my way so I cannot
move.
He has plunged my path into
darkness.
9 He has stripped me of my honor
and removed the crown from my
head.
10 He has demolished me on every side,
and I am finished.
He has uprooted my hope like
a fallen tree.
11 His fury burns against me;
he counts me as an enemy.
12 His troops advance.
They build up roads to attack me.
They camp all around my tent.

¹³"My relatives stay far away,
  and my friends have turned
    against me.
¹⁴My family is gone,
  and my close friends have
    forgotten me.
¹⁵My servants and maids consider me
    a stranger.
  I am like a foreigner to them.
¹⁶When I call my servant, he doesn't
    come;
  I have to plead with him!
¹⁷My breath is repulsive to my wife.
  I am rejected by my own family.
¹⁸Even young children despise me.

When I stand to speak, they turn
    their backs on me.
¹⁹My close friends detest me.
  Those I loved have turned against
    me.
²⁰I have been reduced to skin and bones
  and have escaped death by the skin
    of my teeth.

²¹"Have mercy on me, my friends, have
    mercy,
  for the hand of God has struck me.
²²Must you also persecute me, like God
    does?
  Haven't you chewed me up enough?

19:6 Or *for I am like a city under siege.*

NOTES

19:4 *Even if I have sinned.* There is a sense of incredulity in the Heb. expression *'ap 'amnam* (like some uses of "really?" and "really and truly" in English). When Sarah is told she will have a child in her old age, her thoughts of disbelief are introduced in a similar manner (Gen 18:13).

19:6 *capturing me in his net.* Cf. "a city under siege" in the NLT mg. The word *metsud* [TH4685A, ZH5179] can refer to a fortified or besieged city (as in the famous name Masada), though the more usual word for a city under siege is *matsor* [TH4692, ZH5189] (an almost negligible difference in Heb. spelling). More commonly, the word *matsod* [TH4685, ZH5178] (net) is used to translate this verse: "God has cast his net around me" (NLT, cf. KJV, RSV, REB, NAB, NJB). Though Job's description of himself includes the analogy of a city under siege, this passage does not seem to be a single sustained metaphor. Bildad had described the wicked as being caught in the trap of death (18:8), a message that was meant to be a barb at Job. A hearer could not help but make an association of this word with the earlier passage, as this exordium (19:2-6) is a response to Bildad's charge.

19:17 *I am rejected by my own family.* "I intreated for the children's sake" (KJV) assumes the common meaning of *khanan* [TH2603, ZH2858], "to be gracious." This does not make sense in Job's complaint about his isolation. Most translations consider this to be another verb, known in Arabic and meaning "stink," which fits the context much more suitably: "I stink to my children."

my own family. The reference to family has caused difficulty, since Job no longer has a family. The literal "children of my belly" was translated in the LXX as "the sons of my concubines." Dhorme (1984:277-278) takes this to be Job's own children, assuming this is poetic hyperbole, which does not require reconciliation with the introductory story. However, the book is otherwise consistent concerning the life story of Job. It is more likely that Job was referring to those who were born from the same womb—i.e., his brothers and sisters (RSV).

19:18 *they turn their backs on me.* The Heb. would seem to say "they speak against me" (KJV), but virtually all modern translations have assumed another root meaning "turn away." Clines (1989:429) observes that the philological weakness of the latter translation has been disregarded for the benefit of improved sense.

19:20 *I have been reduced to skin and bones.* The Heb. has the enigmatic "my bones cling to my skin and flesh." This is coupled with a second enigmatic line, which has become an

English idiom: "I escaped by the skin of my teeth." The English idiom means "a narrow escape," but it is not at all clear that this is the sense of the Heb. from which the expression is derived. The Old Greek rendered it "my bones cling by my teeth," and a later revisor (Symmachus) offered the scarcely more intelligible "I stripped my skin with my teeth." Though Driver (1969:80) defended the latter as an acceptable translation of the Heb. with the sense "I gnawed my upper lip" (cf. REB), the effort is hardly convincing. Symmachus would not have gone through the syntactical contortions offered by Driver, and the result is completely unsatisfactory as a climatic finale to Job's complaint. The suggestion that skin (hardly to be associated with teeth) be eliminated from this line to provide the translation "I have escaped with my flesh between my teeth" (NAB) is not an improvement. Countless similar efforts have proven that a satisfactory understanding is not to be gained by investigations and revisions of this type. Idioms work on a different order and make no sense once the original analogy is lost.

The question is whether Job is describing his physical state or a psychological condition using physical metaphors. Physical breakdown often happens as a result of emotional distress. Job had previously described his distress as a burst gallbladder (16:13) and an inflamed face (16:16). In this passage, Job was complaining about his extreme sense of isolation, so it would be somewhat surprising if in this one verse he should focus attention on his physical maladies. It is possible that Job was talking about physical emaciation (NLT); if so, it is the result of his anguish and not a description of his illness.

19:22 *Haven't you chewed me up enough?* Lit., "Can you never have enough of my flesh?" A Semitic idiom for slander and accusation is to "eat the flesh," found in the Heb. at Ps 27:2 (cf. RSV text and mg) and in Aramaic at Dan 3:8 and 6:24 [25]. In English we sometimes refer to a severe reprimand as "tearing a strip off of" someone or as "taking a pound of flesh" (i.e., the demand exacts a high price). Interpreted, Job would be asking "Can you never malign me enough?" This would be the logical question after his pleas for mercy in the previous verse. It would be merciful for them to stop their accusations against him.

COMMENTARY

In this dialog, the patience of Job has been tried as much as that of the friends, and Job responds in kind, using the exact words of Bildad (19:2; cf. 18:2) in his own complaint of how he had been treated. Job was bitter at not being understood, but he was not about to capitulate to these arguments. He was almost embarrassed on behalf of his friends, who so lacked a sense of humility that they shamelessly abused him as much as "ten times," which is a metaphor for "full measure" (cf. Gen 31:7; Lev 26:26), perhaps by analogy to the number of fingers and toes. Job was a proud man who would not bend. There was integrity to his pride, for he knew that he was not guilty as charged. The response of the friends to this pride had been an attempt to humiliate him. Even if the humiliation was successful, it did not bring humility, only emotional pain—not the desired result. The friends were, therefore, wrong on every count. Even if there were some truth in their accusations, their conduct condemned them, for it would not bring about the restoration they deemed necessary.

Job addressed the grievous presumptuousness of the friends concerning his situation. Zophar had accused him of not knowing his own guilt; he claimed Job had erred beyond what he could know. Job agreed that this could be true in the sense that a person can sin inadvertently and then discover this later and subsequently make reparation (cf. Lev 4:2, 13, 22, 27; 5:14-19). Job had earlier challenged the friends to show him such error (6:24), but no charges were forthcoming. If Job was unconsciously guilty, and no one else knew anything about it, that responsibility rested with him. He would suffer the consequences, and he would need to make the reparation. The friends should not pretend to read his mind. In such a case, it must be the responsibility of the individual before God to become more fully aware of the significance of such actions and to respond accordingly.

Job's friends had attempted to overpower him, to convict him on the basis of the shame that had come upon him. Bildad had done this in the previous speech by describing the wicked in the exact terms of Job's situation. Bildad had said that the wicked would be caught in the trap of death (cf. 18:8-10). Job knew that God had cast such a net around him. Pope (1965:131) points out the function of such a net in Babylonian mythology; in the "Net Cylinder" one of the sanctions against violating a treaty is that the god Ningirsu will capture the culprit in a giant net. There is a particular irony in Job being caught in such a net inasmuch as he had maintained uncompromising integrity in his covenant with God. The circumstances of his being trapped are not what Bildad had assumed. God had not caught Job in his sin, but God had acted perversely (*'awath* [TH5791, ZH6430]) against Job (19:6). This word may hark back to Bildad's earlier speech, where he had twice repeated this verb in his question (8:3): "Does God twist justice? Does the Almighty twist what is right?" Such a question is self-evidently rhetorical; God is righteous in all his ways. In contrast to perverse human judges (Ps 82:1-2), he is the one who will arise and judge the earth in its crooked ways. Job blatantly confronted Bildad's self-assured assertions by saying God wronged him. It is not that Job thought God was an unjust judge. His point is that God had caused the trouble for no known reason; therefore, the situation was completely out of Job's control. Contrary to what Bildad asserted, Job could not change his life.

The poetic author introduces Job's lament (19:7) with words consciously reminiscent of the complaint of Habakkuk. The burden of Habakkuk was the pervasive violence and injustice in the land, a chaos that resulted in the continual depreciation of the Torah and the perpetual failure of justice (Hab 1:2-4). Habakkuk knew that God saw evil clearly and that he found it intolerable (Hab 1:13); he could understand that evil within his nation would be judged. However, Habakkuk found it intolerable that the more wicked nation should swallow up the one more righteous. He began his protest with the cry "violence" (Hab 1:2), but the cry seemed to fall on deaf ears. For the poetic author, the problem of evil in the life of Job had its parallel in the violence and injustice experienced in the nation of Israel. He could do no better than to show the precedence for Job's complaint. There was no justice for him; his cry "violence" seemed to go unheard. Like Habakkuk, he had to cry out to God even if silence was the only response.

The first half of Job's complaint (19:7-12) contains a series of examples that portray the violence that had come upon him. He had been fenced in, and his life was engulfed in darkness. This essentially repeats what Job had said earlier (cf. 3:23).

There was no road of life for Job to travel. Job's dignified garments had been stripped away, and the crown had been torn from his head. He was bereft of the dignity of human life. Job may have had in mind the humiliation of a deposed king, though he had never been a king. More probably, Job was remembering that the dignity of human life, the significance of being "crowned . . . with glory and honor" (Ps 8:5) as the image of God, is to exercise dominion within the divine kingdom. Job had been the model of honoring God with a life of integrity, but there was no honor left for him. His life had been demolished like a building torn down on all sides. Job would go the way of all flesh, the way from which none return (16:22). His life was like a tree torn up by the roots (19:10). If you cut a tree down, there is hope (14:7-9), for at a whiff of water its roots will sprout again. However, if a tree is torn up by the roots, there is no possibility of renewal; for Job there was no hope (17:15-16). God continually stirred up his anger against Job and attacked him like an enemy (cf. 16:12-14). In a most grotesque picture, Job conceived of God as marshalling an army and building up ramparts to attack his solitary tent. All the "hounds of hell" had risen up against Job—in this respect Bildad was right (cf. 18:11-14)—all the threats of death seem to have been arrayed against Job like an army.

The second half of Job's complaint (19:12-20) focuses on the isolation and loneliness that were upon him. Laying aside the eloquent metaphors of traditional wisdom, Job gave a description of his solitary exile that exhibits the tragic pathos of his situation. The outward appearance may be more tranquil, but there is no denying the violence of withholding esteem and affection. The most painful aspect of his suffering was his estrangement. When he cried out to God, he was greeted with silence; this apparent alienation from divine providence had also separated him from all normal human interaction so critical to health and well-being. His kinfolk, his neighbors, his intimate friends, the servants of his household, his wife, and his own brothers avoided him; and if they had to come in contact with him they found him abhorrent.

Not long before, Job had been a highly respected individual; due deference was accorded his status in society; his influence demanded a high respect for his opinions. It is not that Job arrogantly flaunted these privileges; he had always known they were fragile and temporary, and he had always taken precautions for any wrongs that might be present. He did not lament the loss of such privilege; all he asked was that he at least be given the dignity every individual deserves by virtue of being human. Now, through no fault of his own, he was despised by all. Bereft of all his possessions and his health, suddenly he was treated as though he was a worm and not a man (Ps 22:6), despised and rejected (Isa 53:3) because he had been smitten and afflicted by God. His suffering was not a heroic sacrifice that would achieve some noble end; he did not choose it, and he was not seeking personal affirmation. He was not even seeking sympathy; no one else could understand his situation in any case. All Job was seeking was some of the normal human interaction that should be accorded one still present on this earth.

Job did not receive normal human respect; he was treated as repulsive, which, physically, he may have been. But worst of all, he was spurned and forgotten by those who should have had some sense of obligation to him. His own servants refused to recognize him or respond to him. His own brothers and his wife seemed to be unable to see past the rotting frame of his body to the person within. Not even his age was respected; juveniles openly disparaged him. Those who were once his "inner circle" (19:19), the confidants who shared his concerns and sought his advice, found him detestable. Though Job loved his family and all his friends and acquaintances as he always had previously, they turned away from him.

The lament concludes with an enigmatic saying, which may have been somewhat ambiguous from the beginning: "I have been reduced to skin and bones and have escaped death by the skin of my teeth." The author intended his saying to be an unforgettable and repeatable finale to his description of the plight of the lonely sufferer. Clines (1989:450-452) is almost certainly correct in taking this to be physical language as a metaphor for a mental state. "My bones hang to my flesh" is an expression used by the psalmist (Ps 102:5 [6]) to describe the anguish of one so tormented he has neglected to eat. Strong bones are a sign of health and vigor; they give shape to a body that can be said to be "lovely in its bones." The effect of extreme distress is said by Habakkuk to be a "rottenness entering the bones" (Hab 3:16, KJV); the knees collapse and the body totters. When the bones cease to function, their role in relation to the skin is reversed. Only the skin is left to hold the body together, and the bones cling to it as a kind of appendage. Such was the condition of Job. When Job said he "escaped by the skin of his teeth," he meant that, in reality, he did not escape at all. Teeth have no skin to which they can cling. Job meant that he did not have a life, a point he made repeatedly and in different ways. He had no hope—the worm was ready for him (17:14-15), the hopes that could have turned the night to dawn (17:12) were dead. His friends described his present life as an escape from worse peril, but they were wrong. The separation of death was but a breath removed from the isolation that Job already experienced.

◆   ## 2. God will vindicate (19:23-29)

23 "Oh, that my words could be recorded.
     Oh, that they could be inscribed on
     a monument,
24 carved with an iron chisel and filled
     with lead,
     engraved forever in the rock.

25 "But as for me, I know that my
     Redeemer lives,
     and he will stand upon the earth
     at last.
26 And after my body has decayed,
     yet in my body I will see God!*

27 I will see him for myself.
     Yes, I will see him with my own
     eyes.
     I am overwhelmed at the thought!

28 "How dare you go on persecuting me,
     saying, 'It's his own fault'?
29 You should fear punishment
     yourselves,
     for your attitude deserves
     punishment.
     Then you will know that there
     is indeed a judgment."

19:26 Or without my body I will see God. The meaning of the Hebrew is uncertain.

NOTES

19:23 inscribed on a monument. The Heb. word used here for "monument" (seper [TH5612, ZH6219]) commonly means a book (so KJV). The author is apparently archaizing here, using the word seper (book) in its original sense of a writing surface. Writing began on hard surfaces on which words were engraved, so a "book" (seper) in more ancient times was an inscription in material such as stone (Gehman 1944:305).

19:24 filled with lead. The function of lead in ancient inscriptions is not specifically known. The letters may have been traced with lead before they were incised in a rock; the lead then would function together with the chisel to produce the inscription, a sense perfectly compatible with the Heb. (Blommerde 1969:89). The lead may have been molded into the inscription to give it a metallic luster (NLT), which suits the sense of the context well. This technique is known to have occurred in the famous inscription of Darius I at Behistun, where the cuneiform signs of the names of the king above his head were inlaid with lead. De Wilde (1981:213) thinks the poet may have deliberately made reference to this famous inscription, engraved in the rock high above the road for all travelers to see. A fifth-century papyrus fragment of an Aramaic translation of the inscription has been found at Elephantine in Egypt, indicating that it would have been well known in Palestine around the time Job was written.

19:25 my Redeemer lives. These words, as found in the Authorized Version, have become the best known in the book of Job and were chosen by Handel (1741) to express the triumph of salvation in *The Messiah*. They are an unremarkable translation of the Heb., but have generated much discussion. The difficulty is that it seems unusual that Job would think of his enemy (God) as being his redeemer. Holman (1994:377-378) provides a litany of suggested alternatives, including "champion" as the personification of the cry of Job's blood (16:18), which will act as his "living" savior. The author of Job naturally thinks of God as the redeemer of Israel, as he is so often depicted in the Scriptures (e.g., Exod. 15:13). That God would become the redeemer as the incarnate Son of God was a later revelation not contemplated by the author of Job.

at last. The question is whether this is a reference to the distant future or to what will take place as the final event of Job's earthly existence. Job's desire for an inscription might suggest that his case is to be preserved for a final judgment, but this seems inadequate. Job had demanded that he must be vindicated while he lived (e.g., 16:19-22). Holman (1994:378-381) makes a case for this being a name for God: "And I know that my Redeemer is [the] 'Living,' and [the] 'Last' will stand against the dust." Though "dust" may refer to humans against whom God takes his stand, in Job it elsewhere has reference to the earth (cf. 41:33) and is almost certainly to be understood that way here.

19:26 my body has decayed, yet in my body. The Heb. cannot yield a comprehensible translation without some change in the text or the postulation of otherwise unknown functions for certain words. The first line refers to the stripping of the skin, the second to seeing God from the body: "and after my skin has been thus destroyed, then from [or apart from, i.e., without] my body I shall see God" (cf. RSV and notes). The simplest and therefore most preferable change is a rearrangement of the words, as proposed by Sutcliffe (1950:377-378): "though my skin be stripped from my body, even after that, I will see God." This would express a hope compatible with what Job desired. He had been reduced to nothing; he might come to the extremity of losing even his skin, but he would not lose confidence in the justice of God. This would explain "the last" of the previous verse. God may delay his deliverance to the last point of physical debilitation, but before Job died, he hoped that God would appear and be propitious. The textual change is justified by being minimal and by providing intelligible Heb. and consistency in the speeches.

19:27 *overwhelmed at the thought!* Job here describes his all-consuming desire—he wants to see God.

19:29 *punishment yourselves, for your attitude.* Pope (1965:135) calls these lines "a jumble of verbiage," but the matter is not that serious. The friends are warned to fear for the sword, for such anger is a crime deserving the sword. The anger is that of the friends, and the expression "crime of the sword" is identical in sense to "sin of judgment" (31:11, 28)— that is, sin deserving judgment. Though it may seem harsh to speak of the wrath of the friends as worthy of death, false testimony is to receive the same penalty that would have been given the accused (Deut 19:16-19). Words can kill; false testimony that leads to death is deserving of the sword.

there is indeed a judgment. The second expression of this verse is difficult, as indicated by the uncertain vocalization in the MT. The written letters would suggest "to judge" or "a judge" (*sheddayyan* or *sheddin* [TH1777/1781, ZH1906/1908]) which would be a contraction for "there is a judge" or more preferably "there is judgment." Others have related this to *shadday* [TH7706, ZH8724], a name for God used frequently in Job, and this may be indicated by the Gr. translation (Orlinsky 1965:41); but as he says, the Heb. defies "convincing interpretation."

COMMENTARY

Having concluded his lament, Job again addressed his friends directly, first asking them for mercy (19:21-22) and then warning them about the judgment in store for them (19:28-29) because of the way they maligned him. Job spoke assuredly of the judgment that would come on his friends because he believed God would vindicate him. Job had moved beyond the confidence that God would be his advocate (16:19-20) to the assurance that God would act as his redeemer. Though God had treated Job as an enemy, Job did not doubt that there is justice and that justice is maintained as part of the divine order of the world.

The plea of Job for mercy from his friends was not to ask for sympathy from them. The request for mercy (*khanan* [TH2603, ZH2858]) finds its fulfillment in an objective and concrete response of something given (e.g., Ps 37:21—"the godly are generous givers"). Mercy is not realized in mere feelings of compassion. Further, it is quite evident that the friends do not have the capacity to give sympathy to Job. All but the friends have forsaken Job, so in a sense they, at least, are more noble than the rest. It is best to be loved; it is next best to be hated; it is worst to be ignored. Their presence shows that they had some concern for Job, but their response was too full of anger. Job asked that their diatribe cease; this would be mercy.

The friends were unable to understand that God had struck (*naga'* [TH5060, ZH5595]) him (19:21). In saying this, Job unknowingly used the very word used by the Accuser in his challenge (1:11): "[strike (*naga'*)] everything he has, and he will surely curse you." Job knew explicitly what is implicit in the story: God was the source of his sorrow. The friends should not have put themselves in the place of God, for the works of God belong to another dimension. Their attempt to defend God by persecuting Job put them in danger of becoming the enemies of God themselves. They should be merciful and just be silent.

The friends would be silenced if only the facts of the case could be known. Job, at this point, longed that his life not be forgotten, that a record of what had happened be preserved for posterity (19:23-24). He imagined a monument inscribed with an account of his life. Such an inscription would be quite a contrast with those that have been preserved. Kings prefer to leave a legacy of their heroic deeds and conquests. The record of Job would show how a righteous man who had helped many (4:3-4) had suffered immeasurably and come to an unhappy demise. This record would vindicate his life.

As Job considered his situation, his faith advanced to another level of confidence and trust. It was not sufficient that he be vindicated in the future because a monument to his life had been preserved. Job desired to present his case to God. Job longed for an arbitrator (9:32-33), for the opportunity to defend himself directly before God (13:13-15). Job was confident that such a hearing would be his salvation (13:16), for there can be no doubt about the justice of God. Job had declared that God would actually take up his case (16:19-21); God would be his advocate because the facts of his life were fully known to him. There must be a better defense than his own assertions recorded in writing forever—"not the indelible letters of a dead man, but a living person will defend and vindicate his character: none other than the living God Himself will at last free his name from reproach" (Driver and Gray 1921:1.171). God must be more than a fair judge before an arbiter, more than an advocate before his accusers; he is a redeemer who will take his stand upon the earth. The earth belongs to God, and it is those of clean hands and a pure heart, those who have not sworn deceitfully (Ps 24:1-4) who will stand on his holy hill. Job had spoken truly; he had never compromised the oath of his covenant. God may have attacked Job as an enemy, but God would be his redeemer because he is redeemer of all the righteous.

We must distinguish between the God of the three friends and the God Job believed in firmly: "The LORD will help those they persecute; he will give justice to the poor" (Ps 140:12). Job had already expressed this assurance: "God might kill me, but I have no other hope. I am going to argue my case with him. But this is what will save me—I am not godless. If I were, I could not stand before him" (13:15-16). Job would leave some mysteries to faith; he did not know why God had become his enemy, but he knew God would save him because God was also his redeemer.

Given its context, it would seem too much to think that Job was expressing hope in the resurrection when he expressed his desire to see God. True, the belief that physical death did not end life was familiar to the author of the book of Job, not only from the surrounding cultures but from his own Scriptures. The righteous would not be cut off from the presence of God; even their body could dwell secure (Ps 16:9-11) as they would dwell in the house of the Lord forever (Ps 23:6). But, in his arguments, Job had never contemplated his vindication coming in a future life after a resurrection. Such a vindication would do nothing to settle the question of his guilt with his accusers. Rather, we see from the context that Job was certain he was at the end of physical life (17:15-16), with no future to emerge from the darkness (17:11-12). Job was almost gone, but not quite. He had been stripped of everything but his body, which was also slipping away (19:20). Nonetheless, he was confident that before he disappeared entirely, his Redeemer would appear. Though he lost the skin off his back, yet from this body he would see God (19:26). Job was referring to his then present, suffering body. The longing that consumed him had to be realized; with his own eyes he had to see the only one who could save him.

The appearance of the Redeemer would be bad news for the accusers. They had been saying all along that Job was the problem: "It's his own fault" (19:28). The Redeemer would put that charge to rest, and they would need to answer for their words. Their words had been harsh and condemning, words to threaten life itself. According to the law, those who testify falsely will suffer the punishment they would have brought to their victim (see note on 19:29). If the anger of the friends has inspired testimony deserving of the punishment that comes by the sword, then they had better fear the sword.

Those who persecute the righteous are the enemies of God. Throughout the Psalter, the assurance of receiving mercy is given on the basis that those pursuing the righteous will face divine judgment (e.g., Ps 7:1-6). In Job, there is a double irony on this motif. God had become the enemy in pursuing innocent Job. In their attempt to defend God, the friends had attacked an innocent and righteous man. In so doing, they had made themselves enemies of God and would face his wrath.

L. Zophar: The Wicked Will Die (20:1-29)
1. Arrogance endures for a moment (20:1-11)

Then Zophar the Naamathite replied:

2 "I must reply
because I am greatly disturbed.
3 I've had to endure your insults,
but now my spirit prompts me
to reply.

4 "Don't you realize that from the
beginning of time,
ever since people were first placed
on the earth,
5 the triumph of the wicked has been
short-lived
and the joy of the godless has been
only temporary?
6 Though the pride of the godless
reaches to the heavens
and their heads touch the
clouds,

7 yet they will vanish forever,
thrown away like their own dung.
Those who knew them will ask,
'Where are they?'
8 They will fade like a dream and not
be found.
They will vanish like a vision in
the night.
9 Those who once saw them will see
them no more.
Their families will never see them
again.
10 Their children will beg from the
poor,
for they must give back their stolen
riches.
11 Though they are young,
their bones will lie in the dust.

N O T E S
20:2 *greatly disturbed.* Zophar was expressing his agitation, but the Heb. vocabulary is rare and uncertain—cf. "my thoughts answer me, because of my haste within me" (RSV). The word for "thoughts" also seems to mean "branch" and is spelled in several ways, but

the semantic process of the connection is not known. In each occurrence, the word signifies disturbing thoughts (cf. 4:13; Pss 94:19; 139:23). "Because of my haste" is hardly suitable; most recent translations assume another word with the same spelling (*khush*), which expresses feelings (cf. "agitation," NRSV; "impatience," NJB). In later Heb. and Aramaic, the latter word is used for "pain" or "troubled thoughts" (Jastrow 441).

20:7 *like their own dung.* The Heb. word for "dung" has been contested, since the Gr. says "the wicked man perishes just when he is established." Heater (1982:68-69) shows that the Gr. interpretation is based on its own earlier translations of "the fate of the wicked" (cf. 15:21; 20:22) and is not providing an alternate meaning of the Heb. word. "Dung" is correct, but it is referring to fire fuel rather than the excrement of the wicked (see commentary below).

20:10 *will beg.* The sense of the verb *ratsah* [TH7521/7521A, ZH8354/8355] is ambiguous in this verse. It can mean "favor" and have the idea of receiving satisfaction or of repaying (paying off), but it is uncertain how either meaning relates to the children of the rich and to the poor. There are two main possibilities. It could be that the children will be required to make amends to (i.e., repay, show favor to) the poor, in which case 20:10b refers to the children restoring the ill-gotten gains of their parents to those who were defrauded. This is a rather awkward way to speak of the rich losing their wealth since it happens vicariously through their children and not in their own lifetime. The other possibility is that the children of the rich will seek satisfaction or favor from the poor— i.e., they will be reduced to begging (NLT) as the poorest of the poor. This is presumably because their parents had to give up that which they robbed from the poor (20:10b).

COMMENTARY

Zophar responded to Job with traditional wisdom expressions in his rebuttal, but in this instance they have a direct connection to Job's protest. Job had complained of being utterly insulted and abused (19:3) because his accusers had no sense of shame. Zophar protested that he had to endure an offensive castigation that had caused him to be painfully agitated. However, he was determined to respond on the basis of reason and not emotion. While Job had been crushed and exhausted by his suffering, Zophar was invigorated by his expressions of traditional wisdom. His "reason" was the undiluted and uncontaminated views of the ancients, without any original thoughts of his own.

Zophar's question "don't you realize?" (v. 4) may well be a rebuke to Job's claim of what he said he knew: "I know that my Redeemer lives" (19:25). Zophar appealed to the original wisdom, that which went back to Adam himself, as a defense for what he had to say. His argument was even less debatable than that of Eliphaz, who claimed that the wicked live in torment all their days (15:20), or that of Bildad, who claimed that the life of the wicked is surrounded by snares (18:8-10). "For Zophar's truth about the wicked corresponds to no psychological reality within the wicked (as Eliphaz's), nor to any metaphysical reality that surrounds the wicked (as Bildad's), but solely to the observer's own estimation of time: if you can be as patient as the wisdom of the ages would have you be, you will see that however long the wicked prosper it is only for a moment, for this is the kind of time that is weighed, not measured" (Clines 1989:485).

Zophar depicted the wicked as proud, rich, and oppressive. Their hubris has no limit, and nothing can satisfy their greed. Their appetite is like the mouth of death, which can never be satisfied. Zophar's fundamental point is expressed with similar vocabulary in Psalm 73. The wicked speak derisively; they set their mouth in heaven and their tongue laps up everything on earth (Ps 73:8-9). The wicked defy God, for there is no evidence he is paying any attention (Ps 73:11). It seems that the righteous have maintained their integrity in vain, for it has brought no benefit to life (Ps 73:13). The wicked are in a slippery place; in a moment they will be destroyed, they will vanish like a dream, and they will be despised (Ps 73:17-20). Zophar may have even been referring to Job's own words when he spoke of the place of the wicked not being found and the eye that had seen them not seeing them anymore (20:7, 9). Job had used similar words to describe himself (7:8). Zophar's message was not subtle; if Job did not change, he would find that the fate of the wicked had overtaken him.

For Zophar, the loss of the wealth of the wicked was swift in comparison to that which matters and endures. It can be seen as life progresses. The wicked perish like dung. It is not likely that he has in mind here the dung of the wicked themselves (cf. KJV, RSV, REB, NLT), since Zophar did not seem to be describing the offensiveness of the wicked in his analogy but rather the rapidity of their demise. It is more likely his analogy is to the use of dried dung as fuel for burning, a practice carried on even in pioneer times on the North American prairies where fuel was scarce. The speed is not that of decay but that of incineration.

The impoverishment of the wicked, according to Zophar, is the work of justice. The wealth of the wicked is gained by the exploitation and abuse of others. In due course, the wicked will be forced to give up the wealth they obtained by violence; when justice takes over, they will find themselves impoverished, even to the point of their own children begging for food. The virility of the wicked is like a mirage. Their power does not really exist. A little further down the journey of life and all their youthful vigor will have disappeared; it will lie in the dust with them.

◆   ## 2. Wealth is poison to the wicked (20:12-29)

12 "They enjoyed the sweet taste of wickedness,
    letting it melt under their tongue.
13 They savored it,
    holding it long in their mouths.
14 But suddenly the food in their bellies turns sour,
    a poisonous venom in their stomach.
15 They will vomit the wealth they swallowed.
    God won't let them keep it down.
16 They will suck the poison of cobras.
    The viper will kill them.
17 They will never again enjoy streams of olive oil
or rivers of milk and honey.
18 They will give back everything they worked for.
    Their wealth will bring them no joy.
19 For they oppressed the poor and left them destitute.
    They foreclosed on their homes.
20 They were always greedy and never satisfied.
    Nothing remains of all the things they dreamed about.
21 Nothing is left after they finish gorging themselves.
    Therefore, their prosperity will not endure.

²² "In the midst of plenty, they will run
   into trouble
   and be overcome by misery.
²³ May God give them a bellyful of
   trouble.
   May God rain down his anger
   upon them.
²⁴ When they try to escape an iron
   weapon,
   a bronze-tipped arrow will pierce
   them.
²⁵ The arrow is pulled from their back,
   and the arrowhead glistens with
   blood.*

20:25 Hebrew *with gall.*

The terrors of death are upon them.
²⁶ Their treasures will be thrown into
   deepest darkness.
   A wildfire will devour their goods,
   consuming all they have left.
²⁷ The heavens will reveal their guilt,
   and the earth will testify against
   them.
²⁸ A flood will sweep away their house.
   God's anger will descend on them in
   torrents.
²⁹ This is the reward that God gives the
   wicked.
   It is the inheritance decreed by God."

NOTES

20:17 *streams of olive oil.* The Heb. appears to have two words for "rivers" (cf. "the floods," KJV; RSV deletes the word). The line, however, requires a parallel with milk and honey; it is probable that *nahar* [TH5102A, ZH5642] (shine) refers to oil rather than a river, providing the usual combination of oil, milk, and honey to describe abundance.

20:18 *They will give back everything they worked for.* The Heb. returns to the metaphor of consumption already introduced: "they will vomit the wealth they swallowed" (20:15). The point seems to be that the rich were unable to make full use of their wealth.

20:20 *They were always greedy.* The Heb. resumes the metaphor of eating—i.e., "there was no contentment in his belly."

20:23 *rain down his anger.* Alternate translations are numerous: "rain [wrath] upon him while he is eating" (KJV) or "rain [wrath] upon him as his food" (RSV); "rain down his missiles of war" (NAB) or "hurling against his flesh a hail of arrows" (NJB). The root *lakham* [TH3894/3894A, ZH4302/4303] is common throughout the Semitic languages, either in the sense of "food," "flesh," "eat," or with the sense of "anger" or "fighting." There may be an intended double meaning in this verse; Grabbe (1977:77) notes that both senses have a great deal to be said for them. Zophar has used the metaphor of eating throughout, so it makes perfectly good sense that God's wrath becomes their food. At the same time, the sound of the word would evoke images of a rain of war or wrath, particularly following the immediately preceding words of God sending his wrath against them.

20:25 *The arrow is pulled.* This is the reading of the MT, but it is evident the Gr. translator had a different Heb. reading (Orlinsky 1964:74) which apparently became corrupted to the present text (the change is most easily explained if the Gr. is the original). The Gr. refers to a weapon such as a javelin which goes out from the back of the wicked, a logical parallel to the attack from the bow (20:24b). However, the Heb. text also makes good sense.

20:26 *deepest darkness.* The Heb. refers to the deepest darkness as the treasure (something hidden) that is preserved (hidden away) for the wicked.

wildfire. A fire outside of human initiation, such as lightning—the kind of fire that originally struck Job's sheep and shepherds.

20:28 *flood.* The word *yebul* [TH2981, ZH3292] would normally refer to the produce of the field, which would not be kept in a house. "Possession" (RSV) is hardly the sense of the term; "flood" is certainly the idea required. There is evidence for a second root meaning "watercourse" (cf. Isa 30:25; 44:4; Jer 17:8).

COMMENTARY

In this section, Zophar describes the wicked in terms of self-destructive consumption (20:12-23); greed is its own worst enemy. Beyond the destructive power of greed is the judgment of God decreed for greedy persons (20:24-29). The earth will reveal the guilt concealed within it, and all the wealth hoarded upon it will be swept away.

In modern Western society, the term "consumer" has a positive sound. Humans by nature must be consumers; consumption is the basis of a good economy and a life that is satisfying for all. There is, however, a very sinister side to consumption. The problem is insatiable desire; those who have the power to pursue physical satisfactions rob others of basic human necessities. This is wickedness, and Zophar depicts it as the chief characteristic of evil persons who bring the judgment of God upon themselves.

Eating is the most regular and fundamental aspect of consumption. Zophar chose the uncontrolled appetite as the one image that portrays all the excesses of the rich. The decadence of the rich is like food that is sweet and dissolves around the tongue. The titillating sensation is prolonged as long as possible, but eating cannot be an end in itself; food is for the body. Once food is swallowed, the sensual aspect of the experience comes to an end. Too much food leads to heartburn and considerable discomfort. Zophar chose an experience common to all who have occasionally overindulged as a means of illustrating the evil that comes to those who rob others in pursuing their own excesses. The wealth they savor becomes bile in their belly; it is a poisonous venom. It forces them to vomit. And though this may be quite a natural response, it is part of the natural order as a divine judgment. Too late the wicked realize that they have ingested a lethal poison into their system; what they found so savory becomes as fatal as a snakebite.

The irony of the whole situation is that indulgence in the diet of wickedness prevents the wicked from ever enjoying wholesome food. They will never experience the smooth taste of cream, the sweetness of honey, and the cool sensation of curdled milk. The wicked disgorge what they cannot keep down; they are never able to enjoy any return on their wealth as they had expected. In 20:19 Zophar specifies what he means by the "food of the wicked"; it is wealth obtained at the cost of oppressing the poor. In their zeal for acquisition, the wicked crushed the poor and abandoned them—so much so that they robbed them of the ability to make their own living. One particular example is the confiscation of a house to live in, the most basic of human needs. Foreclosing on property is done in the name of "good business," but economic power is readily open to abuse. According to Isaiah, the judgment that would reduce prosperous Judah to a war zone of rubble was because of those "who buy up house after house and field after field, until everyone is evicted and [they] live alone in the land" (Isa 5:8). Zophar said that this is the way of the wicked (20:20); the belly of the indulgent will never be satisfied. In their attempt to satisfy all their desires, nothing is left. Their prosperity cannot last. While stuffed to the full, great hardship will come upon them.

Zophar concluded his picture of the self-immolation of the indulgent rich by making it clear that theirs is a divine judgment. God is the one who fills their belly; but the food God grants is his wrath, the manna he rains upon them is destruction. Two points may be drawn from Zophar's concluding words. The first is the wisdom theme that the righteous are in control of their own life and will experience the rivers of oil, honey, and milk. The second is that the righteous should never envy the wicked, for their destruction is happening even as they savor the satisfactions of their wealth.

The judgment of the wicked comes in the day of God's wrath, from which there is no escape. Amos had given the same warning to the wealthy wicked nation of Jeroboam's day; he called the day of God's wrath the "day of the LORD." It is a time of terror and certain demise. It is like fleeing from a lion and meeting a bear, and then escaping the bear only to lean on the wall of your house and be bitten by a deadly snake (Amos 5:18-20).

The wicked live with paranoia; they feel terror constantly, for they have much to lose that they cannot keep. They can savor it in their mouth for a while, but they cannot retain their wealth. Darkness is stored up for the wicked; that is the only lasting treasure for all the things they hoarded. Fire will consume their goods like lightning. This has nothing to do with human revenge; it is simply the arrival of the day of divine wrath. The heavens will expose their guilt and the earth will rise to testify against them. They can never outlive the witnesses of their wickedness. Their portion and their inheritance—that which is the legacy of one's life on this earth—will be total darkness and complete loss.

◆ M. Job: The Wicked Prosper (21:1-34)
1. The wicked grow wealthy and old (21:1-16)

Then Job spoke again:

2 "Listen closely to what I am saying. That's one consolation you can give me.
3 Bear with me, and let me speak. After I have spoken, you may resume mocking me.

4 "My complaint is with God, not with people. I have good reason to be so impatient.
5 Look at me and be stunned. Put your hand over your mouth in shock.
6 When I think about what I am saying, I shudder. My body trembles.

7 "Why do the wicked prosper, growing old and powerful?

8 They live to see their children grow up and settle down, and they enjoy their grandchildren.
9 Their homes are safe from every fear, and God does not punish them.
10 Their bulls never fail to breed. Their cows bear calves and never miscarry.
11 They let their children frisk about like lambs. Their little ones skip and dance.
12 They sing with tambourine and harp. They celebrate to the sound of the flute.
13 They spend their days in prosperity, then go down to the grave* in peace.
14 And yet they say to God, 'Go away. We want no part of you and your ways.
15 Who is the Almighty, and why should we obey him?

What good will it do us to pray?'
16 (They think their prosperity is of their
    own doing,

but I will have nothing to do with
    that kind of thinking.)

21:13 Hebrew *to Sheol.*

NOTES

21:16 They think their prosperity is of their own doing. The initial particle (*hen* [TH2005/
2005A, ZH2176]) is ambiguous in the context of this line. It may be an asseverative, in which
case Job asserts that the wicked are wrong. Read this way, Job seems to contradict the point
he had just made—namely, the wicked live very well by schemes of their own making.
Alternately, the line can be read as a rhetorical question affirming the defiance of the
wicked. The particle makes it emphatic: "Is not the prosperity of the wicked in their own
hands?" (REB; cf. RSV, NRSV). Job observed that the wicked live with security and self-
determination, though the thought made him shudder (21:6). Gordis (1978:230) emends
the possessive pronouns to make this a concluding statement of the wicked: "Indeed, our
prosperity is not in His hands."

but I will have nothing to do with that kind of thinking. This line, which will be repeated
by Eliphaz (22:18), seems incongruous with the thought of the speech. The verse "makes
excellent sense of itself, but attempts to fit it into the context without twisting the translation have been eminently unsuccessful" (Pope 1965:145). Fohrer (1989:338) deletes the
verse as a gloss intended to clarify verse 14, since it cannot be Job's own words; and if he
were citing an opponent there would need to be a rebuttal. Tur-Sinai (1967:328) follows
the LXX in a change to the third person: the schemes of the wicked are far from him (i.e.,
God). Job complained that God pays no attention to the plots of the wicked and does
not punish them (cf. 21:9). But the emendation is arbitrary, and the temptation must be
avoided, even if it does accommodate a fitting conclusion to the description of the wicked.
It does not fit what we know of Job, and at face value the line is a disclaimer (Habel
1985:328). Job would have no part of the rationalizations of the wicked, though the
friends have at least implicitly accused him of such thinking.

COMMENTARY

The closing speech of this second cycle is exemplary of the dialog in Job. This chapter contains a most direct response to the preceding one. Zophar had argued that
the wicked will self-destruct because of their greed. Job argues that they live in grand
style and end up with a fine funeral. Five arguments of the friends are quoted and
rebuffed by Job. One is a direct quote (21:17), and one is explicitly attributed to
Job's friends ("you will tell me," 21:28); the others (21:19, 22, 30) recall what the
friends have said. Then Job gives his reply. Job was not saying that everything the
friends think was wrong. They had the psalms and the prophets on their side. But
they were wrong in the way they had universalized these truths and applied them in
his case.

    Job's friends needed to look at him again; they needed to see what had become of
the man who was their confidant and friend. It was an appalling situation, one that
should have left them dumbfounded, but they kept talking on and on and never got
to the heart of the matter. Job was horrified by his situation. He had to make another attempt at being heard. The best consolation he could receive from his friends
would be to know that they had heard his agony and his confusion. His real

complaint, however, was not with them, for it was obvious that they could not understand him. God was the real cause of his exasperation. God knew Job; he was fully aware of the desolate condition of his life.

It is an anguishing thought that a man of integrity should suffer as Job did. It makes one shudder to realize that at the same time Job was suffering, the wicked were living in luxury and security. If one strips away the platitudes about time, as rationalized by Zophar, the reality is frightening. There is no observable judgment for the wicked. They live long, and the older they get, the wealthier they become. Their families are well established, they see them regularly, and they live long enough to enjoy their grandchildren, perhaps even great-grandchildren. Their homes are safe and their herds are healthy and reproduce without fail. Their children have no danger; they are free to go as they please. Music and joy fills their life. It is true that they slow down with age, that their bodies wear down, but they still enjoy their prosperity. The wicked already seem to enjoy the life the prophet Isaiah had promised God's chosen in the new heaven and the new earth (Isa 65:17-22), where there is no such thing as suffering or premature death. Isaiah said that the chosen of the Lord will enjoy the work of their hands (Isa 65:22); their life will endure like a tree. The word "enjoy" (*balah* [TH1086, ZH1162]) normally conveys that which wastes away with age (cf. 13:28) and disappears. Isaiah used the word to describe an endurance that will not suffer the normal ravages of time, but will continue to enjoy the benefits of work. Isaiah also spoke about the security of the coming generations (Isa 65:23); families will live on together, as parents enjoy children and grandchildren. Job did not go so far as to say that the wolf and the lamb feed together in the pastures of the rich (Isa 65:25), but short of that the wicked live about as ideal a life as can be possible in this world. These are not God's chosen; rather, they have spurned God (21:14); they have no place for God or for the way of wisdom God has ordained for the world. Why would they turn to God? What more could they hope for?

The observations of real life in this world are stunning; they fill us with dismay. The friends had tried to see it differently, but they were living in denial. Job was about to take up their arguments and show them to be wrong. But before he did this, he brought his own description of the wicked to a close (21:16). His words have a certain incongruity, no matter how they are taken. Perhaps Job meant it to be that way. According to Job, the wicked are openly defiant, yet they live their lives without receiving any judgment from God. Their lives are entirely in their control, unlike Job's life, which was completely out of his control and was continually under divine chastisement. In conclusion, Job asked one question only: "Is their prosperity not really in their own power?" Every observation answers in the affirmative. Yet at the same time, we know that Job did not believe this to be true. Calamity is not a respecter of persons; it does not invariably exempt the wicked. Job's question in 21:16, then, must be making something of a disclaimer: "Surely their prosperity is not in their own strength." Job would have nothing to do with the rationalizations of the wicked. The wicked are wrong in their thinking, though apparently it does them no harm.

Ironically, Job's integrity was not doing him any good. Thus, Job had a problem with God (21:4), for there was a contradiction and the consequences of it were appalling.

2. The platitudes of wisdom are wrong (21:17-34)

17 "Yet the light of the wicked never
    seems to be extinguished.
  Do they ever have trouble?
  Does God distribute sorrows to them
    in anger?
18 Are they driven before the wind like
    straw?
  Are they carried away by the storm
    like chaff?
  Not at all!

19 "'Well,' you say, 'at least God will
    punish their children!'
  But I say he should punish the ones
    who sin,
  so that they understand his
    judgment.
20 Let them see their destruction with
    their own eyes.
  Let them drink deeply of the anger
    of the Almighty.
21 For they will not care what happens
    to their family
  after they are dead.

22 "But who can teach a lesson to God,
  since he judges even the most
    powerful?
23 One person dies in prosperity,
  completely comfortable and secure,
24 the picture of good health,
  vigorous and fit.

25 Another person dies in bitter poverty,
  never having tasted the good life.
26 But both are buried in the same dust,
  both eaten by the same maggots.

27 "Look, I know what you're thinking.
  I know the schemes you plot against
    me.
28 You will tell me of rich and wicked
    people
  whose houses have vanished
    because of their sins.
29 But ask those who have been around,
  and they will tell you the truth.
30 Evil people are spared in times of
    calamity
  and are allowed to escape disaster.
31 No one criticizes them openly
  or pays them back for what they
    have done.
32 When they are carried to the grave,
  an honor guard keeps watch at their
    tomb.
33 A great funeral procession goes to the
    cemetery.
  Many pay their respects as the body
    is laid to rest,
  and the earth gives sweet repose.

34 "How can your empty clichés comfort
    me?
  All your explanations are lies!"

NOTES

21:17 *the light of the wicked never seems to be extinguished.* In the Heb. this verse is a question, which recalls a metaphor from Bildad (18:6): "The lamp hanging above [the wicked] will be quenched." The verse challenges Bildad's assertion that calamity has prepared herself for the fall of the wicked (18:12). The irony of the question is continued in 21:18—"are they driven before the wind like straw?"

21:20 *their destruction.* The Heb. word *kid* [TH3589, ZH3957] is an alternate spelling for the common word *kad* [TH3537, ZH3902] (Grabbe 1977:79), which is something like a jug or a big cup. Dahood (1957:316) is correct in finding here a synonym for "cup" often used as a symbol for judgment (e.g., Ps 75:8), since the next line uses this very metaphor. "Destruction" is based on an Arabic parallel but is less suitable in this line.

21:22 *he judges even the most powerful.* The NLT agrees with most translations here, but a title for God is an expected parallel to the first line of this verse (Gordis 1978:232; Pope 1965:146; Dahood 1957:316-317), which is about judging the "most high" God rather than about God judging "those on high" (KJV, RSV, REB, NJB). The word rendered "most powerful" (*rum* [TH7311, ZH8123]) is the same for "Most High," a common title for God (Pss 99:2; 138:6; Isa 6:1). It is indicated by various words in Scripture (*'elyon* [TH5945B, ZH6610]; *gaboah* [TH1364, ZH1469]; *nissa'* [TH5375, ZH5951]). Aufrecht (1985:58-62), on the basis of 11QtgJob and the Gr., makes a case for the original being "God judges the deceivers," but it is based on homonyms in both Heb. and Aramaic and can be considered only a possibility.

21:24 *picture of good health.* The Heb. provides a verbal picture of the body: "his hips are round with fat (*khalab*), his bones rich with marrow." "Hips" (*'atin* [TH5845, ZH6489]) is otherwise unknown and its meaning is debated. The Masoretes took it to be a body part filled with milk (*khalab* [TH2461, ZH2692]), as a parallel to "bones filled with marrow" (*moakh* [TH4221, ZH4672]) in the next line. The Targums translated *'atin* as "teat," and consequently *'atin* is the word for "teat" in modern Heb. However, the translation "his breasts are full of milk" (KJV) is somewhat incongruent in describing a male. Some have offered "pail" or "trough" as the meaning (BDB 742; HALOT 1:814), which eliminates the gender inconsistency (cf. ESV), but this is based on conjecture. Other versions took *'atin* to be a body member filled with fat (*kheleb* [TH2459, ZH2693]) rather than milk, though the translations may have been based on context only. A fragment of 11QtgJob may have a part of the word for "limbs" (van der Ploeg and van der Woude 1971:20-21), but the text is defective, so it is not certain whether the letters belong to this verse or the preceding. The Aramaic word *'tm* refers to the flank or haunches (Jastrow 1063), and it is probable that this is the word to be found here (cf. NRSV, REB, NJB).

21:28 *rich and wicked.* The rich man (*nadib* [TH5081A, ZH5618]) is generally spoken of in a very positive sense. He is the opposite of the fool (*nabal* [TH5036A, ZH5572]) who is stingy and ignorant; the nobleman is a generous patron of good society (Gerleman 1974:156-159), but may be untrustworthy (Pss 118:9; 146:3). Only in this text is he said to be among the wicked.

21:30 *Evil people are spared in times of calamity.* The Heb. says that evil people are kept *for* the day of calamity and delivered *to* the day of wrath (cf. NASB, KJV). The syntactical combination is exactly the same as in 38:23: snow and hail are kept "as weapons for the time of trouble, for the day of battle and war." This verse has caused translators great difficulty because it says the opposite of what Job will argue—that the wicked live to have a splendid memorial. Most translations, like the NLT, conform the verse to Job's argument (cf. NIV, RSV, ESV).

are allowed to escape. The Heb. says, "they will be brought (*yabal* [TH2986, ZH3297]) to the day of wrath." Many translators (Fohrer 1989:338; Driver and Gray 1921:2.151; de Wilde 1981:229) emend the verb to "rescue" (*yutsal* [TH5337, ZH5911]) and make it continuous with the thought of the previous verse: "do you not accept their testimony . . . that he is rescued in the day of wrath?" (RSV, NRSV, NJB). Another option is to delete this line as a duplicate of verse 32a, which is then introduced at this point: "on the day he is carried to the grave (32a) who will charge him . . . (31)?" (NAB). Other translations resist such changes and supply a supplementary idea: "a wicked person is . . . conveyed to safety before the day of wrath" (REB).

Both lines of 21:30 are best understood if we recognize that Job was again making reference to the doctrine of his friends in conventional wisdom language (Gordis 1978:234-235; Tur-Sinai 1967:333). The friends have been specifically identified by a change of speaker (21:28) and that point has been refuted (21:29). This verse introduces a final argument, which Job discredits (21:31-33) in showing the utter emptiness (21:34) of the arguments of the friends.

COMMENTARY

Job would never adopt the philosophy of the wicked, who neglect God because they are secure in their own wealth and power. But none of the answers of conventional wisdom could satisfy Job's requirements for justice, nor could they silence his protest against God. Bildad had asserted that the light of the wicked will be snuffed out (18:6), that their vigor will become want, that calamity is awaiting them (18:12). Job asked how often that really happens (21:17), the implicit answer being that it almost never happens that way. The wicked are not like the chaff the wind drives away, as expressed in the traditional wisdom song introducing the Psalter (Ps 1:4). Judgment does not come to the wicked, so far as Job could tell.

For traditional wisdom, the temporary prosperity of the wicked was always observable to all, and it was evident that they often did not experience judgment in their own lifetime. This did not mean they had escaped judgment, only that it had been delayed—it would come upon their children. This point had been made in the first response of Eliphaz (5:4) and in the most recent response of Zophar, who had said the children of the wicked would become so impoverished they would end up begging from the poor (20:10).

This accorded with the adage that the punishment of sin would extend to the third and fourth generations (Exod 34:7; Num 14:18), but this statement was never meant to suggest that children would be punished for their parent's sin (Deut 24:16; Jer 31:29; Ezek 18). Rather, since extended households of three or four generations would live together, sin within their group disrupted their relationships and became a continual judgment upon them. This warning never did apply in the sense asserted by Zophar—that the rich would have to repay their plunder of the poor and their own children would go begging. Further, if it were true that the children of the rich were impoverished because of the sins of the parents, it would only compound the injustice. The wicked must themselves drink the cup of God's wrath right down to the dregs. How does the fate of their children affect them after they are gone? Though the wicked might fear for the future of their children, what they fear is already the experience of the children of the righteous. How can that be a punishment to them? In other cases, like that of Job's, the parents outlive the children in suffering and sorrow. The potential future poverty of the children of the rich cannot in any sense be thought a fair judgment of their sins.

Wisdom would allow that some situations in this world seem to contradict the divine order. There is a mystery to wisdom that goes beyond human understanding. As Zophar had said (11:5-12), we cannot even presume to know ourselves. This was not to call into question the divine order as understood by wisdom, it simply meant to say that humans do not know enough about their situation. Job could verify only what his eyes saw. Seeing is believing because if we deny what our senses tell us, we become totally illusory. One enjoys perfect health, obviously has a good diet, is at ease and untroubled. Another has nothing but trouble and never enjoys any success. Both have the same fate: they end up in the grave, consumed by worms. What distinguishes these diverse experiences? There are no consistent empirical criteria to determine who has a good life; life just happens. Job's conclusion was that we cannot live so that we can determine what the fate of our life will be.

Wisdom offers a rhetorical question in 21:28, literally, "Where is the house of the tyrant (*nadib* [TH5081A, ZH5618])?" The point is that their houses are no more (cf. NLT). There is no doubt some irony in the use of the word *nadib*. Normally, this word in Hebrew was used of the generous and God-fearing patron—a prince and the very opposite of the stingy fool. Yet too often, such generosity is given out of that which has been stolen by confiscating property or by other violations of fair dealing. Such benefactors really belong to the wicked, in spite of their charity; they should not be trusted. People may not even recognize that such people are wicked and therefore assume that they deserve their fine house. Zophar had said these arrogant rich would perish like dried dung used for fire (20:7), that they would vanish like a dream (20:8), that no one would recognize where they had lived (20:9). Job, however, thought this was a hostile rationalization (21:27) and had a different answer for the question about the tyrants' houses: You can ask any traveler about where these wicked rich live, and they can tell you. Their properties stand against the horizon in a blaze of glory.

Though the property of the rich might be there in all its glory, wisdom still asserted that the wicked were going to lose all that glory when God's judgment would come (Ps 1:5-6). Traditional wisdom said that God made everything for its own purpose, even the wicked for the day of trouble (Prov 16:4). Job knew that and said exactly the same thing (see note on 21:30)—perhaps he even believed it, but he knew that it is not observable in life. No one confronts evil people, and no one makes them pay for what they have done. In the end they have grand funerals with huge processionals and great memorials that are constantly protected. Death for the wicked was the coronation of an indulgent life. How could Bildad say that death was a terrible terror that feeds on the wicked even while they live (18:11-14)? Death for the wicked was a grand finale, unlike the righteous who come to an ignominious end after a life of struggle. Wisdom has no answers for Job. All its assertions are vain (21:34), and its affirmations a betrayal.

◆   N. Eliphaz: Job Is a Guilty Sinner (22:1-30)
         1. Wealthy Job is wicked (22:1-11)

Then Eliphaz the Temanite replied:

2 "Can a person do anything to help God?
   Can even a wise person be helpful to him?
3 Is it any advantage to the Almighty if you are righteous?

Would it be any gain to him if you were perfect?
4 Is it because you're so pious that he accuses you
   and brings judgment against you?
5 No, it's because of your wickedness! There's no limit to your sins.

⁶"For example, you must have lent
    money to your friend
  and demanded clothing as security.
  Yes, you stripped him to the bone.
⁷You must have refused water for the
    thirsty
  and food for the hungry.
⁸You probably think the land belongs to
    the powerful
  and only the privileged have a right
    to it!

⁹You must have sent widows away
    empty-handed
  and crushed the hopes of
    orphans.
¹⁰That is why you are surrounded
    by traps
  and tremble from sudden fears.
¹¹That is why you cannot see in the
    darkness,
  and waves of water cover you.

NOTES

22:2 *Can a person do anything to help God?* The Heb. verb *sakan* [TH5532, ZH6122] is capable of many meanings. Habel adopts a second usage common in later Heb., "Can a hero *endanger* El?" (1985:332). The intent of Eliphaz in this line is made clear by the next verse; the goodness of a righteous person does not contribute anything to God.

be helpful to him. The verb *sakan* (be helpful, profitable) is repeated from the previous line, but it is not clear exactly how this line is to complement the first. It could be synonymous and provide a heightened emphasis (NLT, NRSV, REB), but the object is ambiguous. It is more likely that Eliphaz is saying a wise man should be of benefit to himself (KJV, RSV, NAB, NJB). This would be in harmony with other statements about Job. According to Elihu (34:9), Job had said it is of no benefit to be in favor with God. At some point, Job had asked what benefit there had been for him for having stayed away from sin (35:3). The wise, Eliphaz says, benefit themselves.

Gordis would make this verse completely parallel to 34:9 (1978:244); he shifts the meaning of the verb in this line to "be in harmony" and subordinates it to the first: "does one benefit God when one wisely is in harmony with him?" The two verses complement each other in sense, but they are not synonymous. The conjunction of the second line in 22:2 (*ki* [TH3588, ZH3954]) is used to state a contrast after a negative sentence (Gesenius §163a; cf. Gen 18:15; 19:2). In this case, the question expects a negative answer; the next line is joined as a response. One cannot be of benefit to God, but surely a wise person would benefit himself.

22:8 *You probably think.* The Heb. does not explicitly indicate that Eliphaz views these words as Job's thoughts; this is gathered from the context. 11QtgJob has the words "you think" here (van der Ploeg and van der Woude 1971:22-23).

22:9 *crushed the hopes of orphans.* The LXX and many modern versions make Job the subject of the verb "crush," but the Heb. is the equivalent of the passive, implying that the strength of the orphans has been crushed because Job has sent their widowed mothers away empty-handed, giving them no assistance.

22:11 *That is why you cannot see.* Many translations say "your light is darkened, so that you cannot see" (RSV, REB, NJB). The change is based on the addition of one letter to the Heb. to create the word "light" and is usually justified on the basis of the Gr. text. Though the LXX has the word "light," it is not evidence of a textual variant; this is simply another example of the translator being influenced by the Gr. translation of other verses (Heater 1982:72-73).

COMMENTARY

This last speech of Eliphaz inadvertently raises a crucial question about an area where traditional wisdom lacks consistency: If human righteousness is of no interest to God (22:3), then why should human iniquity be of such a concern to God?

Job had earlier raised this very question (7:20-21); at the very minimum, God should be able to forgive the sin of short-lived mortals. Eliphaz did not allow that point to enter the discussion (Hermisson 1996:339); evil is a matter of justice and God metes out the penalties accordingly. The reader, however, knows that Eliphaz is wrong. If iniquity affects God, then righteousness does as well. If righteousness is of concern to God, then it is not so certain how God will deal with the righteous. This is at the heart of Job's main question, which Bildad is about to repeat (25:4; cf. 4:17; 9:2; 15:14), and it is at the heart of the scene in heaven in which the Accuser had challenged God. The last speech of Eliphaz shows that traditional wisdom has no awareness of the possibility that God may bring suffering to the righteous because he takes an active interest in their righteousness. This point will be taken up by Elihu as he seeks to correct both the friends and Job.

In the meantime, we need to examine Eliphaz's final speech more closely. Eliphaz had begun his previous speech by asking whether a wise man should respond to useless words (15:3). It would seem to be a deliberate choice to begin this speech with the same word about "usefulness," but now attached to another theme. According to Eliphaz, if Job would lay aside his useless arguments and consider his situation in the light of wisdom, he would not need to suffer this pain. Job was a fool (*nabal* [TH5036A, ZH5572]); he was not a wise person either in the sense of being a noble patron (*nadib* [TH5081A, ZH5618]) or a person with knowledge (*maskil* [TH7919, ZH8505]). According to the Scriptures, "Only fools say in their hearts, 'There is no God'" (Pss 14:1; 53:1). Since Job thought that God was far off in the heavens and knew nothing (22:13), he was obviously the fool described by the Psalter. The wise not only seek God, but they derive a benefit from doing so. Job needed to lay aside his useless words, become wise, and derive some benefit for himself.

Furthermore, Eliphaz argued, there is a reason for suffering; and it must be self-evident to all that one does not suffer because of excessive righteousness. These words were meant to taunt Job. One axiom of traditional wisdom is that righteousness results in blessing; Job could benefit himself (see note on 22:2). Though the wicked might be temporarily wealthy, it was unthinkable that the righteous could be temporarily poor. The reasoning of Eliphaz cannot countenance anything of what had transpired in the heavenly places. His certainty blinded him entirely to his error, and, more grievously, compelled him to charge Job with guilt. The only basis he had for such charges was Job's suffering, but he felt solidly supported by the prophets in condemning Job. He told Job that he must have committed some sin that brought God's judgment upon him. Eliphaz reiterated the law that says it is wrong to take as security an item required as a necessity for life—like a millstone (Deut 24:6) or clothing (Deut 24:17); should the loan default, the creditor might then be endangering someone's life. This was the worst of the sins of the wealthy, which brought the judgment of God upon Israel (Amos 2:8) and Judah (Ezek 18:12). Not only had Job committed such heinous sins, he had confiscated such pledges for no reason at all. He deserved everything that had happened. The care for the dependent, particularly widows and orphans, was a constant concern of the

prophets. Isaiah names injustice to the widows and orphans as the primary manifestation of covenant violation, which brought God's curse (Isa 1:17). Special care
was to be taken to be sure the widow and orphan received both justice (Deut 10:18)
and charity (Deut 14:29; 16:11, 14). Eliphaz reasoned that Job had both defrauded
and despised the poor (22:9); he had utterly crushed them in his greed. The land belonged to the mighty men in the thinking of tyrants such as Job. He was the wicked
wealthy patron he had complained about (cf. 21:28). His house was gone, so the
truth of wisdom had been proven once again—Job himself was the best example of
the truth his friends had been expounding.

According to Eliphaz, Job had no one but himself to blame for his situation. Job
had given a correct description of his life (3:24-25); everything he feared had come
upon him—groaning was his food and sighing was his water. Eliphaz knew that Job
was in fear, in darkness, and swept away by a flood (22:10-11), but he said Job
should not be surprised by these things—Job had thought God was not watching,
but he was wrong. According to the larger context of the narrative, however, Eliphaz
could not be more wrong. God had observed Job scrupulously, and Job had always
known that was the case (7:17-18).

2. The distance of God is deceptive (22:12-20)

12 "God is so great—higher than the
  heavens,
  higher than the farthest stars.
13 But you reply, 'That's why God can't
  see what I am doing!
  How can he judge through the thick
  darkness?
14 For thick clouds swirl about him, and
  he cannot see us.
  He is way up there, walking on the
  vault of heaven.'

15 "Will you continue on the old paths
  where evil people have walked?
16 They were snatched away in the prime
  of life,
  the foundations of their lives
  washed away.

17 For they said to God, 'Leave
  us alone!
  What can the Almighty do
  to us?'
18 Yet he was the one who filled their
  homes with good things,
  so I will have nothing to do with
  that kind of thinking.

19 "The righteous will be happy to see
  the wicked destroyed,
  and the innocent will laugh in
  contempt.
20 They will say, 'See how our enemies
  have been destroyed.
  The last of them have been
  consumed in the fire.'

NOTES

22:16 *snatched away.* Job had used this same verb (*qamat* [TH7059, ZH7855]) to describe his
emaciated appearance (16:8), and it is not surprising that Eliphaz would depict the wicked
with this same word. He was referring to either premature aging or death. Later Heb. regularly used this verb to mean "wrinkled" (Jastrow 1384); the same word is used in Aramaic
and Arabic with the meaning "seize." These are the only two occurrences of this word in
biblical Hebrew.

the foundations of their lives. The same expression is found in the vision of the first speech of Eliphaz (4:19). It seems to refer to the basis of life, perhaps the dust from which humans were created (cf. 10:9; 33:6) or the earth on which humans depend. It is often thought that the foundations' being "washed away" is an allusion to the Flood.

22:20 our enemies. The word *qim* [TH7009, ZH7799] is otherwise unknown. It seems to be related to the word for "stand" or "endure" (*qum* [TH6965, ZH7756]). This word is used to describe an enemy (*qam* [TH6965A, ZH7756]) who stands up and resists. The root may refer to substance, "that which endures," namely wealth or possessions. The LXX has translated it as "wealth"; this requires a change of the possessive, since the righteous are speaking: "surely their wealth is destroyed."

The last of them. That which is "left over" can be the last of the enemies or the wealth and the property that enemies leave behind. The reference to fire might suggest properties.

COMMENTARY

According to Eliphaz, wicked fools assume that God is not watching, that the heavens are so distant or the earth so obscured that people can do as they please. This contention of the wicked is expressed by the prophets (e.g., Isa 29:15; Ezek 8:12) and by the wisdom writers, such as the writer of Ecclesiastes. One of the problems in this world for the author of Ecclesiastes is the delay of justice and retribution (Eccl 8:11-13); the patience of God with the deeds of sinners encourages them to continue in their sin. Evil endures in this world because of the delay of judgment. Eliphaz knew that though there may be delay, there would also be judgment. The wicked waste away before their time (22:16), the foundation of life on which they depend will erode. The whole earth might be judged, as in the time of Noah, but more often war and devastation would take away all sustenance of life (e.g., Isa 3:1-6). Not only did war destroy crops and means of produce, it also robbed nations of leadership, leaving the people in chaos and preventing a return to normal life. Eliphaz knew that the wicked are fools, especially the oppressive rich who lived complacently in their luxury. These were the most culpable of all, for they ignored the instruction of wisdom and the warnings of the prophets, which were directed towards them continually.

Delay in judgment brings defiance against God (22:17). Though it has often bothered commentators that Eliphaz should say the same thing as Job (cf. 21:14), there is no reason for them not to agree on this point. Eliphaz had already explicitly made reference to what Job said (22:13; cf. 21:15). They were not in disagreement about the attitude of the wicked, only about their fate. There was no shortage of examples of the wicked telling God to turn away. The priest at Bethel told Amos to go home (Amos 7:12), they did not need someone telling them that their funeral had already taken place because of the cruel injustice they had perpetuated (Amos 5:1-17). There was not enough room in Israel for a prophet like Amos. What had God done to deserve this response? He was their provider, he filled their house with good things (22:18). This was especially the case for the wicked of Israel and Judah. Micah laid out the dispute God had with his people (Mic 6:1-8). God had brought them up from Egypt and led them into the Promised Land. For all this beneficence, what God received was their injustice and disregard of his covenant.

Micah had told them what was good: to seek justice and love mercy (Mic 6:8). As far as Eliphaz was concerned, Job had fallen into the kind of thinking condemned by the prophets. At this point, he stole a line from Job (21:16). Eliphaz understood the disclaimer Job had made for himself; they had a certain fundamental agreement about the wicked. The wicked can defy God (21:15; 22:17) because judgment is delayed.

The agreement of Eliphaz with Job does not diminish their fundamental disagreement on two critical points. The first is the destiny of the wicked and the righteous. Job said the wicked die wealthy; Eliphaz insisted that the righteous will live to laugh at the haughty arrogance of the wicked (22:19-20). The enemies of the righteous will be destroyed and their wealth consumed by fire. Judgment had always come, as the prophets had said. The second point of disagreement is the assessment of Job's life: he was not innocent. Even those God had chosen to be his people could be his enemies. God had called Jerusalem his enemy (Isa 1:25), an enemy that he would avenge and purge. Job, too, was regarded as an enemy; his time was up, his property had been burned, even his body was emaciated to the point that little remained.

◆ 3. A repentant Job would prosper (22:21-30)

21 "Submit to God, and you will have peace;
  then things will go well for you.
22 Listen to his instructions,
  and store them in your heart.
23 If you return to the Almighty, you will be restored—
  so clean up your life.
24 If you give up your lust for money
  and throw your precious gold into the river,
25 the Almighty himself will be your treasure.
  He will be your precious silver!

26 "Then you will take delight in the Almighty
  and look up to God.
27 You will pray to him, and he will hear you,
  and you will fulfill your vows to him.
28 You will succeed in whatever you choose to do,
  and light will shine on the road ahead of you.
29 If people are in trouble and you say, 'Help them,'
  God will save them.
30 Even sinners will be rescued;
  they will be rescued because your hands are pure."

NOTES
22:21 *Submit to God, and you will have peace.* Eliphaz came back to a point he had made at the start of his speech (22:2); there is a benefit to the wise who live righteously. The same verb (*sakan* [TH5532, ZH6122]) is here translated "submit." Eliphaz reminds Job that he can be a benefit to himself and "have peace." It must be remembered that "peace" (*shalom* [TH7965, ZH8934]) is much more inclusive of well-being than simple harmony. The rest of the verse would suggest that prosperity is the main emphasis; cf. REB: "you will prosper; that is the way to mend your fortune."

COMMENTARY

Eliphaz had never thought that Job was beyond redemption. He had always believed otherwise, and he continued to be assured that Job would return to his former state and thereby enjoy the benefits of the wise and prosper again. All he needed to do was take the teaching of the wise to heart; he needed to regain the perspective he had lost. He needed to lay aside his pride and his excessive desire for wealth and let God be his source of security. Then, days of joy would come to Job.

Furthermore, Job would be restored to his former state to the extent that he would again have the kind of influence he used to have on others (cf. 4:3-4). His life would have benefits that extended far beyond himself (22:28-30). Here Eliphaz invoked the principle of "horizontal responsibility" (Gordis 1965:94-95). According to the doctrine of "vertical responsibility," the sins of an individual would bring a curse to the third and fourth generations. According to the doctrine of "horizontal responsibility," the righteousness of an individual could bring about good and prevent disaster. Abraham pleaded for the deliverance of Sodom on this basis (Gen 18:17-33); Ezekiel had warned that the righteousness of the three most noble men would not be sufficient to deliver Jerusalem from judgment (Ezek 14:12-16). The righteous are the salt of the earth. Eliphaz believed that Job was such a person and that, once restored, his word would again carry conviction, he would help those who were despairing, and he would even rescue the guilty. Job was no less than the great man he once was. His present circumstance, according to Eliphaz, was an aberration—he was not like those the prophets condemned, who would die in their sins. The restoration of the influence of Job would be the proof that the way of wisdom was right and that the Lord knows the way of the righteous.

◆   O. Job: God Is Hidden (23:1–24:25)
    1. God answers no questions (23:1-17)

Then Job spoke again:

2 "My complaint today is still a bitter one,
   and I try hard not to groan aloud.
3 If only I knew where to find God,
   I would go to his court.
4 I would lay out my case
   and present my arguments.
5 Then I would listen to his reply
   and understand what he says to me.
6 Would he use his great power to argue with me?
   No, he would give me a fair hearing.
7 Honest people can reason with him,
   so I would be forever acquitted by my judge.
8 I go east, but he is not there.

I go west, but I cannot find him.
9 I do not see him in the north, for he is hidden.
   I look to the south, but he is concealed.
10 "But he knows where I am going.
   And when he tests me, I will come out as pure as gold.
11 For I have stayed on God's paths;
   I have followed his ways and not turned aside.
12 I have not departed from his commands,
   but have treasured his words more than daily food.
13 But once he has made his decision,
   who can change his mind?

Whatever he wants to do, he does.	When I think of it, terror grips me.
¹⁴So he will do to me whatever he has planned.	¹⁶God has made me sick at heart; the Almighty has terrified me.
He controls my destiny.	¹⁷Darkness is all around me;
¹⁵No wonder I am so terrified in his presence.	thick, impenetrable darkness is everywhere.

NOTES

23:2 *today*. The Heb. suggests the passage of time: "also today." This is perceived to be a difficulty because the dialog makes no other references to the passage of time. Gordis (1978:260) treats the co-ordinate (*gam* [TH1571, ZH1685]) as concessive in relation to the following clause ("though my complaint is bitter his hand is heavy"). Perhaps we should allow the poet a subtle nuance. A dialog on matters so fundamental should have intervals of reflection.

***is still a bitter one*.** According to the Heb. text, Job's complaint was defiant (*meri* [TH4805, ZH5308], lit. "rebellious") and not just bitter (*mar* [TH4751, ZH5253]). The distinction may be important. Job had said that his complaint was not with people who cannot understand; it was with God (21:4). He was impatient with a God who remained silent; Job was not just bitter—he was defiant.

***I try hard not to groan aloud*.** The multiple translations of this line indicate its difficulty. De Wilde lists sixteen modern translations of the verse that have significant variables (1972:368-369). The phrasing in the MT, "my hand is heavy upon my groaning," has been interpreted to mean that Job did his best to exercise self-control over his desire to complain, but it is doubtful the Heb. could have been understood with that sense. "My stroke is heavier than my groaning" (KJV) expresses a rabbinic interpretation found in the Targums, which translated "my hand" as "my punishment" (Aramaic *mahati*). "His hand is heavy in spite of my groaning" (RSV) makes a change of person that seems to be required. On the basis of northwest Semitic grammar (Ugaritic and Phoenician), Blommerde argues that a textual emendation is not required to read the suffix as third person (1969:8, 99). Though poetry may retain ancient and somewhat foreign terms, the suggestion remains speculative. It is doubtful such forms could have been distinguished in later Heb. The change, however, is minimal, and certainly seems to be the sense required. Job had previously mentioned the burden of God's hand (13:21; 19:21), and the burden of grief is elsewhere expressed by David with these very words (Ps 32:4). If this be allowed, Job would seem to be saying that the hand of God intensified his sorrow. De Wilde (1972:373) emends extensively: "I have a bitter complaint against the Almighty, he is deaf to my groaning." The virtue of such changes becomes their liability; this makes such good sense, it is impossible to know how it could have become so confused.

23:3 *I would go to his court*. This is not the usual word for court, but a somewhat rare word taken to be a place prepared for rule or judgment. It is related to the verb *kun* [TH3559, ZH3922] (cf. 29:7; Pss 9:7; 103:19).

23:9 *he is hidden*. Translations using the words "work" (KJV) and "turn" (REB) have mis-identified the word *'asah* (cf. HALOT 1:893). "I turn to the south" for the next line (RSV, NRSV, REB, NJB) is also incorrect. Job was unable to see God because he was hidden, not because of his motion. "Hidden" is an established meaning for *'asah* (Driver 1954:243), which is parallel to the next line of the verse. Job could not see God in the south (or "to the right" in some translations) because he was "covered" (*'atap*) there as well (KJV, NAB; the same use of *'atap* [TH5848, ZH6493] is found in Pss 65:13; 73:6).

23:10 *he knows where I am going*. The "way" of Job refers to his course of life, a common metaphor in wisdom writings. The word "way" is not qualified, making the line ambiguous. Job may be thinking of his own noble conduct as expressed in the well-known translation of the KJV: "he knoweth the way that I take" (KJV). It would be more logical, though, for Job to be expressing his confidence in the way that God had chosen for him (NLT); even if he cannot find God, he was assured God knew what he was doing.

23:12 *treasured his words more than daily food.* This is a rendering of the MT. By contrast, the Gr. translation is, "I have treasured his words in my heart," which in this case is correct (Orlinsky 1964:74). The medieval commentators based the translation of the MT on Prov 30:8. The problem began with the corruption of the preposition *be-* (in) to *me-* (more than). The metaphor is essentially the same as that used by Eliphaz (22:22): "store [his words] in your heart."

23:17 *Darkness is all around me.* The MT has a negative, which might suggest the reason why Job is fainthearted: "Because I was not cut off before the darkness" (KJV). This is difficult to reconcile with the next line, though it might be done if darkness is made the subject: "The darkness having failed to destroy me, I am plunged back into obscurity by him" (NJB). Other translations have the negative function for both lines (KJV, REB). It is possible that rather than being negative the particle is emphatic (Gordis 1978:262): "for I truly have been overcome by darkness" (cf. NLT). In any case the line must complement the dismay expressed in the previous verse.

COMMENTARY

The dialog between Job and his friends has broken down entirely because none of the parties have been willing to reconsider their assumptions. Though Job has insisted that his situation cannot be fitted into the paradigm of traditional wisdom, he has not been heard. Eliphaz has construed his assessment of Job so that Job's life has become a reinforcement of what wisdom has to say. Job kept pondering the riddle of his own situation and kept reflecting on how God deals with humans generally. The question was not only about his personal suffering, but also about why so many victims of wickedness suffer, while God seems to remain indifferent or inactive. The inability of traditional wisdom to answer these questions means the dialog cannot continue in any meaningful sense.

As we look at this particular passage, we realize that whatever time has passed has not changed the perspective of any of the parties involved. The friends, led by Eliphaz, had maligned Job on the basis of their philosophy. Job would not be intimidated, though; he remained adamant in his position. Earlier Job had summoned the courage to formulate a bold challenge against God for bringing him into trial (10:2). Job had carefully considered his inadequacy in the divine presence (9:14-16), and he longed for a mediator who could resolve the conflict (9:32-35). But there was a problem: God is elusive; his place of justice cannot be found. If Job knew where to go, he would prepare his case and lay it out before God. He expressed confidence that God would hear him and be reasonable, that he would be acquitted by the judge forever. The accusation of Eliphaz may have had the opposite effect of what he intended. Job was surer than ever that he was upright, and he was resolved that God would hear his case and be reasonable. As an innocent man, he would be vindicated by the supreme judge.

Job said he had gone in every direction in his quest to find God: forward, backward, left, and right. This language is another way of referring to the four directions of the compass, starting from the traditional orientation, where "forward" is equal to "east." God was not found in any direction, not even in the traditional places where he is revealed. God is hidden on the left—that is, in the north where the divine residence is to be found. In the ancient legends, such as the Greek *Odyssey* and the Mesopotamian *Gilgamesh*, the home of the gods is beyond the waters of death in the north (Grelot 1958:47-64). In the later book of *Enoch*, this is developed more specifically—beyond the waters of chaos in the north is the garden of justice, and beyond that the divine residence. This belief about the divine residence influenced later Hebrew groups such as those who lived at Qumran. The bodies in their cemetery were buried with their heads to the south in anticipation of the resurrection, when they would be raised facing the divine presence as God emerged from his home in the north. In the ancient religions of Canaan, the home of the gods was on the northern mountain, alluded to in Psalm 48 as "the far north" (Ps 48:2 [3]; cf. NLT mg). The author of Job somewhat enigmatically alluded to this belief about the divine home by speaking about being unable to find God in his usual place of residence. Continuing his search, Job thought that perhaps God could be found to the south.

In Hebrew tradition, the revelation of God was at Mount Sinai in the southern desert. There the mountain had trembled and shook; it was covered with smoke and blazed with fire. The prophet Habakkuk referred to the divine presence in both the north and the south. Yahweh is the God of the heat and the plague associated with the desert storms of the south (Hab 3:3-7), and the God of the thunderstorms and the mountains associated with the Canaanite traditions of the north (Hab 3:8-12). Like Habakkuk, Job recognized that the divine presence should be found in the north and the south, in the storm and the heat, but his efforts to find God were in vain. God did not reveal himself in either the north or the south but remained hidden.

In all of this, Job expressed his confidence that his present trials would be for the good because of the integrity of his life. He would be the wise man who receives benefit with God (see notes on 22:2, 21), as Eliphaz had urged, but the benefit will not come in the way Eliphaz had imagined. The benefit would come through his trials, not through some feigned repentance. Job knew the life he had lived, and he was confident that whatever way God was dealing with him, in the end he would emerge as pure gold. The metaphor does not indicate that Job was purified; instead, the test shows that he had been gold all along. It was not a matter of him laying his gold in the dust, as Eliphaz had said (22:24-25); the character of Job was his real gold, which is precious to God. Job has not lived his life in pretense, with only the external appearance of righteousness. Job has made his treasure the words God had spoken. Job knew he was upright, and that has its reward.

In spite of this confidence Job was faint and fearful. Though he did not understand how God was dealing with him, he did know that God would not be dissuaded from the path he had chosen. God would fulfill the "decree" (*khoq* [TH2706, ZH2976]) that he had for Job. Earlier, Job had spoken about the "limit" (*khoq*) God had set for life (14:5)—the fixed time that could not be changed. There Job had pleaded that he be left alone to complete this time that God had fixed. Here he acknowledges that God will have his way; God will fully accomplish his purpose for Job and all the plans he has designed. The thought of it brought Job to a state of terror. Darkness was all around him; gloom enveloped his life entirely.

◆   ## 2. The wicked are unpunished (24:1-17)

1 "Why doesn't the Almighty bring the wicked to judgment?
Why must the godly wait for him in vain?
2 Evil people steal land by moving the boundary markers.
They steal livestock and put them in their own pastures.
3 They take the orphan's donkey and demand the widow's ox as security for a loan.
4 The poor are pushed off the path; the needy must hide together for safety.
5 Like wild donkeys in the wilderness, the poor must spend all their time looking for food,
searching even in the desert for food for their children.
6 They harvest a field they do not own, and they glean in the vineyards of the wicked.
7 All night they lie naked in the cold, without clothing or covering.
8 They are soaked by mountain showers, and they huddle against the rocks for want of a home.
9 "The wicked snatch a widow's child from her breast,
taking the baby as security for a loan.

10 The poor must go about naked, without any clothing.
They harvest food for others while they themselves are starving.
11 They press out olive oil without being allowed to taste it,
and they tread in the winepress as they suffer from thirst.
12 The groans of the dying rise from the city,
and the wounded cry for help, yet God ignores their moaning.
13 "Wicked people rebel against the light.
They refuse to acknowledge its ways or stay in its paths.
14 The murderer rises in the early dawn to kill the poor and needy;
at night he is a thief.
15 The adulterer waits for the twilight, saying, 'No one will see me then.'
He hides his face so no one will know him.
16 Thieves break into houses at night and sleep in the daytime.
They are not acquainted with the light.
17 The black night is their morning.
They ally themselves with the terrors of the darkness.

NOTES

24:1ff The closing poem of Job's speech (ch 24) is generally regarded as being in complete disarray and possibly out of place. Commentators have rearranged verses or regarded them as being unintelligible. These procedures may be observed in the NAB. Others have been more radical in providing a different arrangement of chs 24–27, assuming the disorder extends to the entire section. In an attempt to recreate another full cycle of the dialog, de Wilde (1981:245-266) has arranged portions of ch 24 to be a response to a third speech of Bildad which he has expanded with a portion of ch 26. Portions of chs 24 and 27 are made to be a third speech of Zophar, and a final brief speech of Job is created from the introductory sections of chs 26 and 27. It is evident that no two critics could independently come to the same conclusions in this type of re-creation. There is no warrant for such changes from the LXX or the oldest Aramaic Targum from Qumran. We must assume that the text we possess is reasonably intact, was so structured by the author, and was so preserved because it carried meaning in that form.

The abrupt shifts of topic in ch 24 are due to the fact that Job was interacting with sayings of traditional wisdom concerning the evil of the wicked and the misery of the poor (Gordis 1978:531-534). The procedure is somewhat like that used by Job in refuting traditional arguments in his final response to Zophar (cf. 21:17-34). Job no longer responded with logical arguments to his friends, since the dialog was breaking down, but he turned his reflections to the sayings of wisdom. His thoughts are more in the form of a lament, as found in other wisdom writings. The Egyptian stories of "The Eloquent Peasant" and the "Dispute over Suicide" and the Mesopotamian "Dialogue of a Master and a Slave" and "Dialogue about Human Misery" (Gordis 1965:56-59) are examples of such laments.

24:1 *wait for him in vain.* This is the correct sense of a somewhat unusual conditional sentence. "Why, since the times are not hidden to God, do those who know him never see his day?" The "times" refers to the time set for justice and punishment, and his "day" is the day of the Lord, when he intervenes in judgment to bring salvation.

24:4 *The poor are pushed off the path.* The poor are forced from the way, which might mean they are driven off the roads by robbers, or that they are deprived of their proper way of life.

24:5 *Like wild donkeys.* It is usually assumed that this metaphorical description of the poor (24:5-8) is an independent poem, which interrupts the connection of "the poor" in v. 4 to the "bereaved widows" in v. 9 (Loretz 1981:264). Though v. 9 takes up the thought of v. 4, the misery of the poor naturally follows the description of victimization.

searching even in the desert. This translation requires a change from the line division of the MT, which says "the wilderness [must yield] food for their children." The difficulties have led to conjectural translations: "they work till nightfall, their children go hungry" (NEB); "searching from dawn for food, and at evening for something on which to feed their children" (NJB). These extensive changes are unwarranted.

24:6 *they do not own.* This translation divides the letters differently than the MT; the Gr. translator also read the text as "a field not their own." This is to be preferred (cf. NRSV) over "gather their fodder" (RSV) or "harvest at night" (NAB).

they glean. In later Heb., the verb *laqash* [TH3953, ZH4380] means "to be late" (Jastrow 719), which might mean the poor work long hours for food. The common word *malqosh* [TH4456, ZH4919] refers to the late rains, which might mean the poor glean from less desirable, late crops for their children (Driver and Gray 1921:2.166).

24:11 *without being allowed to taste it.* The paraphrase is the correct idea based on the parallel of the next line. The Heb. refers to pressing the oil between the "rows," the same word that means "walls" (cf. KJV, REB, NJB); "terraces" (NRSV) is an excellent suggestion, more suitable than "olive rows" (RSV).

24:12 *rise from the city.* The word for "city" ('*ir* [TH5892/5892B, ZH6551/6552]) can also mean "agitation" as in "terror" or "fury" (cf. Jer 15:8; Hos 11:9). Since the "city" is not otherwise significant in this verse, the word may indicate that the dying groan in terror. This is the same problem as the ambiguity of "way" in v. 4.

God ignores their moaning. The poet picked up a word (*tiplah* [TH8604, ZH9524]) from the prologue (see note on 1:22) to say that God considers nothing wrong, he lays no blame. Since the word is a virtual homonym with prayer, the nuance is that God pays no attention to their cries.

24:14 in the early dawn. The passage is about the activities of the night, which makes "at the light" (la'or [TH216, ZH240]) surprising. Many expand this to a negative by adding an additional aleph (lo' 'or [TH3808, ZH4202]) to mean that there is no light (cf. RSV, REB, NAB, NJB). Later Heb. suggests 'or is an elliptical idiom for evening (i.e., at the end of light).

24:16 sleep in the daytime. Lit., "sealed during the day." This seems to be an idiom for houses the thieves marked out during daylight (KJV, REB); this is a better sequel than suggesting they shut themselves up by day (RSV, NRSV).

COMMENTARY

Not only is God so hidden that Job cannot bring his case before him, God seems to be oblivious to all the other evil that goes on in the world. Job reasoned that his case was not unique. The world is full of miserable and weak people, suffering at the hands of the wicked who carry on unpunished. Job knew that the times of judgment are not hidden from God. Since this is so, why is it that those who know God never live to see a day of reckoning? The godly are "those who know him," which means they are those who know righteousness (see Isa 51:1, 7). They are also described as those who seek the Lord (Isa 51:1) and those who have the teaching of the Lord in their minds (Isa 51:7). These are inseparable concepts. "Knowing righteousness" is not merely the practice of righteousness, it is to know salvation, to know the way God brings righteousness into the world. Though the prophets pronounced that the day of righteousness and salvation was near (Isa 51:4-7), it seemed to Job that in the meantime those who know the Lord are suffering in vain. Their lot is miserable even though their situation is not hidden from God. Job could not share the confidence of Eliphaz that the righteous live to scorn the wicked in their day of judgment (22:19-20). Job observed that the wicked continue to plunder, leaving their victims in misery.

Theft and injustice occur in many ways; often they are legal, but they are never moral. Job did not bother to distinguish the legal, but it may be assumed they were among the violations he named (24:2-4), since all of these can be manipulated to give the appearance of right. The violation of property was always listed as among the most insidious of evils. Moving boundary markers was a cardinal sin in the biblical law (Deut 19:14; 27:17; Prov 22:28; 23:10) and in the laws of other peoples of the ancient Near East. Not only might the properties be taken but also the livestock that were on them. The outward appearance might change little, but the moving of a boundary would disenfranchise the poor of what little possession was left to them. Confiscation of possessions taken as security—even possessions that were necessary for the livelihood of the owner—was the very sin Eliphaz had used (cf. 22:6) to accuse Job of deserving all the suffering that had come upon him. The poor were driven into hiding either because they were driven from the way of justice or because they were driven off the road by robbers. Both happen and both leave folk in the misery that Job was about to describe.

The poor are driven to live like the wild animals of the field. Landless, they become scavengers trying to find food for their children, the same way a wild donkey roams in search of pasture. What harvest they receive is from a field they do not own—probably the gleanings that were left behind after the harvest was over (Deut 24:19-21; Ruth 2:2). They have no choice but to gather the late harvest that is sparse and poor—or it may be that they have to work late in the vineyards of the tyrant just to gather sufficient food for their family (see note on 24:6). Without adequate shelter and bereft of clothes, possibly because their garments had been confiscated by wicked creditors, they shiver in the cold (24:7-8). The landless are the homeless; they have no means to earn adequate food or shelter. All this is through no fault of their own. It is because the rich are allowed to carry on in their ruthless tactics of absorbing lands and properties.

According to Job, the violations of the wicked in collecting debts were extreme. They could take an orphaned infant from its mother as security for a loan to its widowed mother, then take the child to be a slave when the widow could not pay. Landowners were supposed to care for widows; instead, they were taking their children as perpetual slaves. The poor are reduced to perpetual slavery and drudgery. Without adequate clothing or food they harvest the grain, press the oil from the olives, and squeeze the juice from the grapes for wine. The poetic compression heightens the impact: without clothes they walk; hungry they carry sheaves; between the rows they press oil; thirsty they tread for wine; they groan in terror; wounded they cry out. The closing of verses 9-12 is notable as an extra line in the stanza: God considers nothing wrong; he does not lay any blame. The same thought with the same rare word (*tiplah*, 24:12) was used to describe Job in the prologue (1:22): Job did not give any blame to God. No doubt there is deliberate irony: though Job did not blame God for his suffering, it is a problem that God does not blame the wicked for the suffering they cause to others.

Life belongs to God, and to violate life was always understood to be a violation against God himself. The summary of the covenant, or Ten Commandments, begins with a commitment to God himself, requires honor for those who gave us earthly life, and then in three staccato sentences summarizes how the lives of others must be respected: do not kill, do not commit adultery, do not steal. It is these three most direct violations of life that summarize the activities of the wicked at night (24:13-17). Light is the usual metaphor for a good and peaceful life (see 17:12; 22:28), and its loss is a judgment on life (18:5, 18; 21:17). Walking in the light (Isa 2:5) means participating in such a life. The analogy is natural; all those with vision associate consciousness with light. Those activities that destroy life are works of darkness, but it is also true that they are usually done in the night.

In his closing description of wickedness, Job moved away from the activities of social deprivation to those that viciously disrupt peaceful relations—the activities of criminals. There is a tendency of translations to rearrange the lines so murder, adultery, and theft are grouped in order (REB, NAB, NJB), but this is an arbitrary procedure. There was never any need to follow a particular order of the fundamental violations (cf. Rom 13:9) nor any need to make them individual topics. They are all variations on the same theme. Those who do not know how to follow the paths of light arise at night (24:13); they kill—especially victimizing the poor, who are most vulnerable (cf. Ps 10:9-10)—and they steal. Their theft may be another man's wife (24:15) or they may steal his goods, breaking into a house they've marked as a target by day—that is all the use they have for light. They are the ones who turn light to darkness and darkness to light (Isa 5:20), whether by taking advantage of the weak or by sheer violence.

◆   ## 3. Traditional assertions are wrong (24:18-25)

18 "But they disappear like foam down a river.
Everything they own is cursed, and they are afraid to enter their own vineyards.
19 The grave* consumes sinners just as drought and heat consume snow.
20 Their own mothers will forget them. Maggots will find them sweet to eat.
No one will remember them. Wicked people are broken like a tree in the storm.
21 They cheat the woman who has no son to help her.

They refuse to help the needy widow.
22 "God, in his power, drags away the rich.
They may rise high, but they have no assurance of life.
23 They may be allowed to live in security,
but God is always watching them.
24 And though they are great now, in a moment they will be gone like all others,
cut off like heads of grain.
25 Can anyone claim otherwise? Who can prove me wrong?"

24:19 Hebrew *Sheol*.

NOTES
24:18 *they disappear like foam down a river.* Or, "they are swift [light] on the surface of the waters." The lines in this poem are concise and metaphorical. The image seems to be the volatility and vulnerability of foam.

24:19 *The grave consumes sinners.* The best that can be said is that this verse is very elliptical; words seem to stand almost independently. Though poetry can sometimes "name ideas" for the reader to construct into sentences, it is probable there has been some disruption of the text here.

24:20 *Their own mothers will forget them.* In the words of the poetic imagery, "the womb forgets him, the worm finds him sweet." This line is regularly emended to "the squares of the town forget them" (RSV), a reference to death found elsewhere in Job (7:9-10). Burns (1989) defends this conjecture on the basis of its restoration of the mythological reference of the text. The folly of this widely accepted change is that it actually removes the mythological reference of the text (Geyer 1992). Womb, maggot, and tree are present in other judgment oracles and are deliberately brought together here, no matter how incongruent they may seem to an uninitiated reader. The sinner (24:19) is a tyrant of the type described in Isa 14:4; in place of his luxury will be the maggot, and the womb will forget him because he will have no descendants (24:20, 22). Ezekiel spoke of a tree whose branches are in heaven and whose roots are in the abyss, a tree better than any in Eden (Ezek 31:8-15). This tree, representing the tyranny of the nations, will be cut down. All nations will desert the tree (i.e., it will not be remembered) and it will descend to Sheol.

24:22 *God, in his power.* The Heb. has "the mighty one" (*'abbirim* [TH47, ZH52]), but the Gr. has "the powerless one," probably a translation of *'evyon* [TH34, ZH36] (poor). The Gr. indicates a textual variant, which may likely be original (Orlinsky 1964:75-76) since it would continue the thought of the previous verse. Job 24:22 would then read: "he pulls down the poor in his power, he may rise but has no assurance in life." In this case the verb *mashak* [TH4900, ZH5432] ("prolong"; cf. RSV, ESV) must be taken in the sense of "seize," much as in the prayer of David in Ps 28:3 ("do not drag me away with the wicked").

24:23 *may be allowed to live in security.* The Heb. lacks the word "live" (*shebeth* [TH3427, ZH3782]), no doubt as part of poetic technique, which is easily understood. This kind of abbreviation is part of the difficulty in understanding other less clear lines of the poem.

24:24 *like all others.* The Heb. *kakkol* ("like all") has always been regarded as unusual and banal, especially with the metaphor of a plant in the closing line. Both the Gr. and 11QtgJob make reference to a plant. The mallow (RSV, NRSV, REB) is based on the Gr. *moloche*, but it is not certain it is related to the Latin *malva*, from which the English is derived. A number of Semitic languages have a base form of *kll* as the name for a plant with an umbel (Reider 1935:273-275); the term seems to refer to the umbel itself. The Arabic is used for either of two plants, one with a cluster of yellow flowers in a semi-circle at the end of a branch, the other with large branches spreading on the earth with a small circular cluster of yellow and white flowers at the end. The late Heb. and Aramaic word for crown (*kelila'*; Jastrow 642) is a derivative. The line says the wicked are bent and withered like a flower cluster; the next line corresponds with this.

COMMENTARY

The closing poem depicts the destruction of the wicked in pictures that would give comfort to one in sorrow. As happens with poems of this type, the allusions of some of its lines have become obscure over time, and some may have been deliberately elusive. This has also created some problems with its transmission. This was not deemed a weakness but rather a normative aspect of the way of wisdom, which was filled with riddles (Prov 1:6). This is part of the communicative technique. Wisdom did not present a worldview in deductive propositions. Wisdom assumed a worldview and attempted to teach harmony with it. Its method was to draw comparisons; the basic meaning of "proverb" (*mashal* [TH4912, ZH5442]) is to create an analogy. The power of analogies lies in the ambiguity they provide for the hearer. Hearers are able to make them specific to their own thought; the images create change according to the frame of mind of the individual concerned.

The poem describes what everyone imagines for the cruel, for those who have no respect for others or their property. Their own properties should be cursed. Their time should be cut short like the snow in the heat of the sun. You want to forget they were born; they should have no descendants or legacy. The worm should relish their dead body; there should be no memory left of them. The bigger they are, the harder they should fall, like a giant tree overcome by twisting winds (24:20). How can anyone feel sorrow for those who "feed" on widows who have no family to protect them? No good can ever come from such cruel people. These tyrants, like all tyrants, are more bluster than real power; they live with paranoia. Though they can overpower others in their might, they are quite aware that there is always someone who can overpower them. Who should trust them, when they have no respect for anyone? They have no assurance of anything for all their might; the higher they rise, the more vulnerable they become (24:22-24). The wicked in all their power can never escape the mighty one who will pull them down. They may secure themselves and provide for themselves, but they can never escape the watchful eye of God. Their glory lasts for a short time, and like everyone else they receive the fatal blow and are silenced. Eliphaz had said that God would shut the mouth of evil (5:16); the closing of this poem (24:24) uses the same unusual word (*qapats* [TH7092, ZH7890]) to describe the silencing of the wicked. The wicked dry up as quickly as a plant. In this life power and glory last but a moment, and the more one has possessed, the more fearful is its loss.

Poems such as Job's in 24:18-25 were not unusual. Perhaps one of the best examples is the second chapter of Habakkuk. The taunt song against the Assyrians (Hab 2:6-20) was not to make those cruel monsters shake in their boots. Every Assyrian monarch lived in fear; the boasts and the lies of their annals are a window into their terror and insecurity. The taunt song of Habakkuk was intended to encourage the faithful, those who knew the Lord was in his holy Temple. The song was to exhort God's people to keep an eye on tyrants. Before long they are silenced and dry up; if their name is remembered at all, it is remembered in ignominy and scorn.

Job knew all of this was true (24:25) in more than one sense. Such taunt songs are the true words of the prophets, but they are also the words abused by the wise. However, not all those who suffer the fate he just described are wicked, and no one could prove him wrong on this point either. Further, the fate of the wicked just described does nothing to justify the pathetic misery of those who suffer under their tyranny, whose pain is never alleviated, who spend their whole lives in struggle. No word of wisdom could undo his words about the poor (24:5-8, 10-12).

At this point, the dialog between Job and his friends has fully come to an impasse and nothing has been resolved. The friends were impressive in articulating traditional truths, but Job remained adamant that these discourses did not address his situation. In his final speech, Eliphaz advanced his position with vigor: the righteous do not suffer at God's hands; therefore, Job is not righteous. Eliphaz tried to identify Job's sin (22:9); it was the usual accusation of social injustice so common in the prophets. According to Eliphaz, Job had assumed that his deeds were hidden because God is so far off in the heavens (22:12-14), but Job was wrong. God is very aware of what happens on earth, and he would yet respond to Job's prayer (22:27). Job countered in chapters 23-24 with points he had made before: God is far away, he is hidden, he answers no questions, and the wicked continually go unpunished. The righteous suffer; they gain nothing from their piety. Bildad will come back to the question about righteousness before God (ch 25), but that will be the end of the dialog. He will not get to respond further; there is nothing more to be said for his view of the world. His speech is broken off by Job's long monologue (chs 26-31). In it Job ponders the mysteries of the world, the mysteries of wisdom, and his own integrity.

▶ P. Bildad: An Unanswered Question (25:1-6)

Then Bildad the Shuhite replied:

2 "God is powerful and dreadful.
He enforces peace in the heavens.
3 Who is able to count his heavenly
army?
Doesn't his light shine on all
the earth?

4 How can a mortal be innocent
before God?
Can anyone born of a woman
be pure?
5 God is more glorious than the moon;
he shines brighter than the stars.
6 In comparison, people are maggots;
we mortals are mere worms."

NOTES

25:1ff It is difficult to find a commentator who thinks this chapter should stand independently. Yet the Old Greek translation, which regularly omits lines (14 in the previous chapter, including all of 24:14b-18a), has this chapter in the same form as the Heb. The Aramaic Targum of Qumran is also unambiguous; fragment eight consists of portions of lines from 24:25–26:2, so we know it is a translation of the same Heb. text that has been preserved. Though the Aramaic has an extra line for v. 3, it is uncertain if this is an expansion or if the translator had a longer text. Regarding the position of ch 25, we can be confident we have the composition as the author intended it.

25:3 *his heavenly army.* Job earlier described his suffering as an attack by the heavenly troops (19:12). Bildad used the same term here to say there is no limit to the heavenly army. Bildad was speaking of the awe-inspiring rule of God that has power to keep peace in the highest places. The phrase that follows this, "doesn't his light shine on all the earth," must be a reference to the coming of divine justice and salvation rather than to the realm of the stars, although some commentators suggest that Bildad is referring to the stars by the phrase "heavenly army" here. The stars are the divine hosts created by God and completely under his power (Ps 33:6; Isa 40:26; 45:12), but the stars as heavenly bodies are not associated with divine warfare. Isaiah was the first to speak of the day when God will bring judgment against the hosts on high (Isa 24:21) that oppose him, which might be a reference to heavenly powers, but not as heavenly bodies. The Gr. and 11QtgJob (apparently) did not find here any reference to stars.

Doesn't his light shine on all the earth? The Gr. has this as: "on whom will his ambush not arise?" The subject pronoun in the Aramaic (which is all that remains in the Targum fragment; van der Ploeg and van der Woude 1971:28-29) is feminine, suggesting that the translator did not have the masculine word for "light" (*nehor* [TH5094B, ZH10465]). It is possible the Heb. "his light" (*'orehu* [TH216, ZH240]) was corrupted to "his ambush" (*'orevu* [TH693, ZH741]), but it should not be followed, as sometimes suggested (see REB).

25:5 *God is more glorious than the moon.* Though most translations treat the brightness of the heavenly bodies in contrast to God, both the context and a comparison with parallel passages suggest the point is the divine control over the heavenly luminaries. The Heb. is abbreviated, but can quite naturally be read "he orders the moon, and it does not shine" (Gordis 1978:277). The LXX renders this sense. Bildad was still on the theme of divine justice and was pointing out its universal extent.

COMMENTARY

What can Bildad say after Job has recited a poem on the demise of the wicked? He can hardly say that Job was just a blustering wind (8:2) or that he considered his friends to be as unintelligent as animals (18:3). It is evident that Job understood the sovereignty and justice of God, but he had doubts about the way in which it was exercised. Wickedness prevails and innocent victims suffer. Bildad begins with the question of God's dominion. His rule is awe-inspiring; God keeps peace in "his high places," whether these are the high places of power on earth or the high places of the heavens. There is no possibility of escaping divine judgment. The wicked are judged. The suffering of the innocent is a separate question.

The doxology of Bildad, as this is sometimes called, is not one that gives praise to God for his creative power. His focus is divine dominion and in particular the rule of God that inspires fear and brings about submission. His reference to God making "peace in his high places" has its counterpart in the prophets. Isaiah spoke of the day when God would bring judgment upon all the evil troubling the earth. In that day Yahweh "will punish the host of the high ones on high" (Isa 24:21, ASV). The highest of powers may go beyond earthly powers (if this is apocalyptic language), but the high places are not to be associated with the stars. Bildad used similar language. God has his troops, which cannot be counted. Since no one can escape his attack, the wicked will be judged. Bildad did not have in mind a great future judgment, but he did mean universal judgment. The light of divine justice and salvation (cf. Isa 58:8; 60:1-2) will rise and shine upon all.

The affirmation of judgment brought Bildad back to a question that had been addressed twice by Eliphaz (4:17; 15:14). The language of the question itself is the same in each instance, but there is some variation on the sequel. In the first instance Eliphaz referred to the impossibility of the divine emissaries being pure; in the second he referred to the divine assembly and the heavens. Bildad referred specifically to the moon and the stars (25:4-6). Eclipses and other heavenly disruptions serve well to illustrate that nothing stands outside of divine control and that everything is affected by it. Perhaps by stating the sequel this way, Bildad had made his point. If even the immortal moon and stars in the purity of the heavens are sometimes disrupted, how much more will it happen to mortal humans? Everyone born of woman will become food for the maggot; they can hardly expect their life to proceed without suffering. This must not become an indictment against divine justice.

Either Bildad was interrupted or he had nothing more to say. We know his viewpoint because we have heard it from Eliphaz: Divine providence is always beneficent for the righteous and brings judgment on the wicked. The mortality of humans does not change that truth. For Job, however, this was insufficient. He wondered if the righteous could really control their own lives by their righteousness.

◆ III. Monologue (Job): The Failure of Retribution (26:1–31:40)
    A. The Unsearchable God (26:1–14)
        1. Wisdom has no answers (26:1–4)

Then Job spoke again:
²"How you have helped the powerless!
  How you have saved the weak!
³How you have enlightened my
  stupidity!

What wise advice you have offered!
⁴Where have you gotten all these wise
  sayings?
Whose spirit speaks through you?

NOTES

26:3 *my stupidity*. According to the Heb., Job did not speak in personal terms. The nouns in these lines are collective; Job belonged to a class of people needing wisdom.

***What wise advice*.** The Heb. has been interpreted as "plentiful" advice (cf. RSV) or "much good advice" (NRSV); both translations assume the presence of the noun "abundance" (*rob* [TH7230, ZH8044]). Gordis (1978:286) proposes the pronunciation *rab*, meaning "youth" or "apprentice" (Jastrow 1442). This provides a balance with the other questions: "What insight have you given the inexperienced?"

COMMENTARY

The harsh questions of Job for Bildad have their roots in what he had said in his previous speech (Wolfers 1994b:390). Job had declared that there are two classes of people in this world: the oppressed, terrified, and slaughtered poor (24:5-8, 10-12) and the tyrants who oppress them (24:13-17). In all of this, God does not seem to find anything amiss (24:12). Job had thrown down the gauntlet in asking who would prove him a liar (24:25). Bildad had responded by talking about the dreadful dominion of God's rule, about the legions of God's armies, about the way God makes peace in the highest places. Job had described the activities of the night in which violence happens to the poor. Bildad asserted that there was no one on whom God's light, that is his salvation, did not shine. Job responded with very direct words. How do such platitudes about the divine rule help the weak? How does such counsel give any encouragement to those who struggle with the violence of losing their property and livelihood? These despised of society need answers that will give them wisdom, a view of the world that will help them carry on.

Bildad had come back to the question of the standing of mortals before God. His view of it seemed to be that evil must come upon all; certainly death comes upon all and therefore even the innocent will suffer. The problem for Job was that he had not been able to dissuade his friends from the false opinion that the poor will benefit from their righteousness in this life. The righteous do not bring goodness to their lives through their fear of God. The benefit that had been urged by Eliphaz (22:2-3, 21) does not materialize. The poor do not experience the divine light, and they cannot bring prosperity to their lives by following the covenant. Where then is the benefit of wisdom, and how do these words help anyone?

The source of wisdom is a critical issue (26:4). Eliphaz had challenged the source of Job's wisdom (5:1) and had told Job he was completely misguided (15:12-13). Job returned the question to his friends. They had claimed to have tradition on their side (15:9-10), but was this the wisdom of God? Job, in turn, was assured that he had received a divine truth, one that he will not deny (6:10).

◆   ## 2. God's ways are unknowable (26:5-14)

⁵"The dead tremble—
　those who live beneath the waters.
⁶The underworld* is naked in God's
　presence.

The place of destruction* is
　uncovered.
⁷God stretches the northern sky
　over empty space

and hangs the earth on nothing.
⁸ He wraps the rain in his thick clouds,
and the clouds don't burst with
the weight.
⁹ He covers the face of the moon,*
shrouding it with his clouds.
¹⁰ He created the horizon when he
separated the waters;
he set the boundary between
day and night.
¹¹ The foundations of heaven tremble;
they shudder at his rebuke.

¹² By his power the sea grew calm.
By his skill he crushed the great
sea monster.*
¹³ His Spirit made the heavens beautiful,
and his power pierced the gliding
serpent.
¹⁴ These are just the beginning of all
that he does,
merely a whisper of his power.
Who, then, can comprehend the
thunder of his power?"

26:6a Hebrew *Sheol.*   **26:6b** Hebrew *Abaddon.*   **26:9** Or *covers his throne.*   **26:12** Hebrew *Rahab,* the name of a mythical sea monster that represents chaos in ancient literature.

NOTES

26:5 *The dead tremble.* Language about the regions of the dead is drawn from surrounding religions. The word "shades" (RSV, REB, NAB) has its origin as a term for dead ancestors. If the term "shades" (*repa'im* [TH7496, ZH8327]) is related to the word "heal" (*rapa'* [TH7495, ZH8324]), it would mean these ancestors were thought to be healers. The veneration of ancestral leaders was regarded as important to the prosperity of the state. Names associated with these ancestors indicate that a cult for the dead began with the Amorite dynasties of the middle of the second millennium BC. Royal ancestors were honored at ritual banquets for the dead in order to insure the fecundity of their descendants. The Heb. uses the term *repa'im* for ancient ancestors of the past (Gen 14:5; Deut 2:11, 20). The term *repa'im* is also used for the shadowy existence of those in the place of the dead in some contexts (cf. Ps 88:10; Isa 14:9; 26:14, 19). It is not certain what relationship existed between the "giants" of ancient time and the "shades" of the dead, but the Greeks called the ancestors of their ancient past "giants" (*gigantes,* nom. pl.), which led to the same term being used in the LXX for the present verse.

26:9 *He covers the face of the moon.* Many translations (RSV, NRSV, REB, NAB, NJB, NLT) take *kisseh* [TH3677A, ZH4060] to be full moon (as in Ps 81:3), but more logically this is a variant spelling of "throne" (*kisse'* [TH3678, ZH4058]—so NLT mg) inasmuch as "some important fact relating to the structure, or more permanent order, of heaven and earth would be expected" (Driver and Gray 1921:2.179).

26:10 *created the horizon.* This is the correct interpretation of setting "a boundary for the waters at the outer limits of light and darkness" (cf. RSV, NAB, NJB). In the creation accounts, the earth and sky are formed by separating the waters into their respective spheres. The horizon is the place where light and darkness meet.

26:13 *His Spirit made the heavens beautiful.* Though "beautiful" is a common meaning for the root *shpr* in Aramaic, the line has also been understood to say that the winds of God "clear" the skies (REB). An Akkadian parallel would suggest the correct sense is that God stretched out the heavens. These lines (26:12-13) describe the origin of the universe when the "great sea monster" was crushed and the "gliding serpent" (NLT) was pierced. In ancient mythical terminology, the disorderly waters were described as a dangerous monster. The monster serpent (called *rahab* [TH7293, ZH8105] in this passage) was crushed, and the waters were separated into their proper spheres by the breath (Spirit) of God (Gen 1:2-8).

COMMENTARY

Bildad had repeated the vision that had come to Job (25:4; cf. 4:12-21), that truth which had come in secret of which his ear had caught but a whisper (4:12). In this speech Job responds to that vision. Job recounts the vast mystery of the ways of God and then comes back to the point that everything we can know is but a faint whisper (26:14) of his truth. The connection to the vision is augmented by the repetition of the rare word "whisper" (*shemets* [TH8102, ZH9066]), found only in the conclusion of this poem (26:14) and in the original vision (4:12). This poem on creation is unique, even in a book that frequently refers to the creative works of God, because of the way it describes the immeasurable breadth, depth, and height of the work of creation (Gros 1990:76), which shows the incomprehensibility of the divine power. If we know but a whisper of the ways of God, how can Bildad make his rash assertions about where and how the light of God shines? Bildad was not given a chance to respond to the question about mortality and righteousness. No one knows about the depths of death or the height of light—least of all the wise, such as Bildad, who must fit everything into their own schemes. Bildad must take the vision more seriously.

This poem on creation is itself a creative innovation on the familiar account of Genesis 1. Its point is to stress the majestic sovereignty of God over every realm. It begins with the watery depths, but in a sense quite different from that found in Genesis. The depths below are inhabited by the dead. Nothing is said about the conscious existence of the dead; it is depicted as a place constantly exposed to divine scrutiny. There is no possibility of hiding from God, as expressed by the psalmist in Psalm 139:8-12. The name Abaddon (RSV, REB) means destruction and may mean in particular the place of the destruction of evildoers, as opposed to Sheol, or "the underworld" (26:6), which is the name for the domicile of all those who have died. It is evident from the poem that "below" is not to be thought of in spatial terms. It is familiar terminology for a sphere of creation not open to human investigation. "Below" cannot be a spatial reference, for the created world itself is hung upon nothing. The north is the home of the gods (cf. 23:9), which is the origin, or genesis, of creation. The expanse of the north where God resides is empty; there is nothing there to support the earth. In more mythical terminology, the earth stands on great pillars sunk in the depths (cf. Heb. for 9:6; Pss 24:2; 75:3). In this poem such language is abandoned so as to remove any mental conceptions of a foundation for the world. Instead, a word from Genesis is adopted. In the beginning (Gen 1:2) the earth was without form and empty (*tohu* [TH8414, ZH9332]); here God stretches the north over this emptiness (26:7) and hangs the earth on nothing. The waters are confined to the clouds, where their weight cannot break through. Beyond the atmosphere and the clouds is the divine throne, hidden from view. Again this is not spatial terminology but a way of describing another sphere or realm from the limitations of an earthly perspective. Somewhere beyond the horizon God has set the limits, literally "drawn a circle," so the forces of chaos cannot enter into creation. His throne is there, though it cannot be seen, and from it the divine order extends to every sphere.

In contrast to Genesis 1, nothing is said about the act of creating; instead, the focus is on God's power over all that exists.

Mythical terminology is used in the summary of creation. The foundations (26:11; lit., "pillars") of heaven are the great mountains that sustain the sky. Creation came about through the conquest of chaos or disorder depicted as a great monster or serpent (cf. Ps 74:13-17; Isa 27:1). The divine rebuke ended the battle and the chaos, and that same power then dominated all the created order. This is what little we know about the ways of God in creation. We are forced to resort to metaphors in talking about the mystery of creation. How then should we expect to understand that rebuke when it thunders in all its force? There is no use in wisdom asserting it has the power to explain how God's sovereignty operates in the world of people any more than it can explain the earlier mystery—creation itself.

◆   B. Bankrupt Wisdom (27:1-23)
    1. Maintaining integrity (27:1-6)

Job continued speaking:

2 "I vow by the living God, who has
   taken away my rights,
   by the Almighty who has embittered
   my soul—
3 As long as I live,
   while I have breath from God,

4 my lips will speak no evil,
   and my tongue will speak no lies.
5 I will never concede that you are right;
   I will defend my integrity until I die.
6 I will maintain my innocence without
   wavering.
   My conscience is clear for as long
   as I live.

NOTES

27:1 *Job continued speaking.* Job's monologue is twice marked by a heading (here and 29:1), which must mean something other than "responded," since the speaker does not change. Most commentators say it was added by an editor conscious of the inordinately long speech by Job, which came about because of the dislocation of the third cycle. However, it is a perfectly logical expression, which could be the work of the author, just as well as a clever editor. Either way, it informs the reader that Job is continuing his thoughts on wisdom (his *mashal* [TH4912, ZH5442]). This expression for "wisdom" is usually translated "proverb," though it is not simply a traditional wise saying. It describes a teaching of values by means of analogy (Gordis 1965:199-202), by comparison of one aspect of life with another. The famous chapter on wisdom (ch 28), which compares finding wisdom to finding precious metals and jewels, is exemplary of the method. A comparison that requires thought or that can be made in various ways is called a riddle. The whole book of Job contains this kind of wisdom; the previous chapter on the wonder and mystery of creation was just such a comparison; it teaches us that understanding life is as elusive as understanding other wonders of the universe. Wisdom speech is an expression of a worldview in a particular poetic style, referred to generally as "proverb" (*mashal*).

27:6 *My conscience is clear.* The Heb. expression seems to mean "my mind will never reproach God" (cf. Jastrow 505); that is to say, Job will not even think anything blasphemous, nor will he allow an inappropriate thought against God. Since the object must be supplied, it can also say "my conscience will not reproach me." In short, Job has a clear conscience.

COMMENTARY

This confession of Job is a confirmation that he considered God to be his redeemer, and that he was not asking for an intermediary to be judge between him and God. In the previous chapter, Job frankly acknowledged that the ways of God are hidden—we catch but a glimpse of them in the mysteries of the universe that we observe. If this is true in the material world, it is even truer in the world of human relationships. Job knew that God had deprived him of his rights (27:2). A judge is supposed to render a decision that becomes the right of the plaintiff. A just judge will render decisions to guarantee victims their rights. Job regarded God as the supreme judge, but he viewed his judgment as unfair—it robbed him of his rights. However, this would not discourage Job from placing his trust in God. Job would not harbor bad thoughts against the God who he believed had wronged him (cf. note on 27:6). The Accuser in the council of God had been completely in error in his charge that Job served God for personal benefit (1:9-11). No one can swear by the God who injures him and appeal to him for justice apart from a pure love for him. The accusation in the heavenly council was silenced by these words of Job.

Job would not compromise his faith or his integrity as long as he had breath. Job had previously recognized that God was his Creator (10:3); therefore, it was illogical that God should attack that which he himself had made. In this speech, Job acknowledged not only the work of God as Creator in giving the breath of life (27:3; cf. Gen 2:7), but also as the one who sustains life by continually providing him with breath (cf. Ps 104:29-30). His devotion to God kept him from betraying that trust in the God of life. This devotion extended to his thoughts and his speech. If he retained integrity in his thoughts and mind, there could never be a false word, a lying tongue. Job especially vowed to retain this integrity in his thoughts about God. This is why he could never acquiesce to the charges of his friends. To allow them to be right in even the slightest way would be a lie against himself and against God. This would destroy everything he was as a person. Job could have no confidence in his friends. But he had complete confidence in God, and this only because he did not try to explain God's ways. The knowledge that God is Creator and sustainer of all life was sufficient to assure Job that he would be his redeemer as well.

◆   2. Meaningless thoughts (27:7-23)

7 "May my enemy be punished like the wicked,
   my adversary like those who do evil.
8 For what hope do the godless have
      when God cuts them off
   and takes away their life?
9 Will God listen to their cry
      when trouble comes upon them?
10 Can they take delight in the Almighty?
   Can they call to God at any time?

11 I will teach you about God's power.
   I will not conceal anything
      concerning the Almighty.
12 But you have seen all this,
   yet you say all these useless
      things to me.

13 "This is what the wicked will receive
      from God;
   this is their inheritance from the
      Almighty.

14 They may have many children,
but the children will die in war
or starve to death.
15 Those who survive will die of a plague,
and not even their widows will
mourn them.

16 "Evil people may have piles of money
and may store away mounds of
clothing.
17 But the righteous will wear that
clothing,
and the innocent will divide that
money.
18 The wicked build houses as fragile
as a spider's web,*

as flimsy as a shelter made
of branches.
19 The wicked go to bed rich
but wake to find that all their
wealth is gone.
20 Terror overwhelms them like a flood,
and they are blown away in the
storms of the night.
21 The east wind carries them away,
and they are gone.
It sweeps them away.
22 It whirls down on them without mercy.
They struggle to flee from its power.
23 But everyone jeers at them
and mocks them.

27:18 As in Greek and Syriac versions (see also 8:14); Hebrew reads *a moth.*

NOTES

27:8 *takes away their life.* The translation "takes away" assumes one of two possibilities for the obscure Heb. *yeshel* [TH7953, ZH8923]: it may be an abbreviated orthography for (1) the verb "ask, demand" (*sha'al* [TH7592, ZH8626]; omission of the aleph; cf. 6:14) or (2) the verb "have peace [in death]" (*shalah* [TH7951, ZH8922]; cf. 3:26). Neither of these requires a modification, but the form is unusual.

27:11 *about God's power.* The Heb. says "in the hand of God," most commonly a metaphor for divine power, as expressed in most translations. However, Job had never been concerned about God's power but rather his justice (Gordis 1978:289). Job was responding to Eliphaz's claim that he spoke for God in instructing Job (22:26-27), a connection already made by the translator of the LXX (see comment below). Job protested that he had received the word of God and that he would not hide it—the same claim he had made earlier (6:10). Thus we should read that Job was their teacher "on behalf of (*be'ad* [TH1157, ZH1237]) God," which is a close phonetic equivalent of "in the hand (*beyad* [TH3027, ZH3338]) of God." (The use of *beyad* for *be'ad* is found in the Amarna letters of Canaan and is also probable at 8:4.) The second line confirms this interpretation.

concerning the Almighty. This clause, lit., "what is with the Almighty" (RSV, NASB), is a way of referring to that which God is thinking. Job would not conceal the divine truth God had revealed to him—anything concerning *the thoughts* of the Almighty.

27:13 *receive from God.* The Heb. text says this is the destiny of the wicked "with God." The prepositional phrase is the same as in 27:11b, where it was noted that it expresses what is in the mind of God. In this verse it indicates the plans God has in mind for the wicked. Many commentators regard this as a textual error (Fohrer 1989:387; Pope 1965:172; BHS), and emend the phrase to say "from God," making it formally parallel with the second line of v. 13 (so NLT). This is preferable for poetic parallelism; the emendation involves the removal of one letter, which may have been accidentally copied twice.

27:18 *fragile as a spider's web.* The Heb. word (*'ash* [TH6211, ZH6931]) normally means "moth," an insect not noted for house-building. The use of the word in related Semitic languages suggests it may mean other insects (Grabbe 1977:90), or an insect at the larva stage while it is in its cocoon (NIV). The ancient versions all indicate some type of insect. Other translations relate this to another Semitic word (*'ushun*) meaning "nest" (NRSV, REB).

27:19 but wake to find. The Heb. word *ye'asep* could be from the root *'asap* [TH622, ZH665] and mean "gather" (KJV), which might be taken as a reference to burial—i.e., the wicked will not receive a proper burial. The following line, however, suggests the word is a variant spelling of *yasap* [TH3254, ZH3578] (continue); this is also how the LXX takes it. The resulting idea is that their "riches will not continue" (cf. "wealth is gone"; NLT, RSV, NIV, REB, NJB); those who go to bed rich will one day open their eyes and find nothing remains.

27:20 Terror overwhelms them like a flood. The Heb. has "waters," probably meant in the sense of floodwaters (cf. RSV, NIV, REB), but other versions change this to "terror assails him in broad daylight" (NJB), so as to form a parallel with "night" in the next line.

COMMENTARY

In this section, Job points out the preposterous logic of his friends. They were false accusers, as is evident in their empty and vain ideas (27:12). They claimed that Job was the enemy of God; he was a sinner and therefore was being punished accordingly. At the same time, Eliphaz had urged Job to get his peace from God (22:21), to find his delight in God (22:26), to pray to God (22:27) and fulfill all his vows. But can an enemy of God pray to God and find delight in God (27:10)? The very idea of telling an enemy under divine judgment to pray is preposterous. When the time of judgment comes, the time for prayer will have passed; at that point, the punishment can no longer be averted. Job could wish that his enemies were the wicked, that all his enemies were the enemies of God; he would then be assured of their fate, for they would have no hope under God's judgment. Life comes from God, and God recalls the life of the wicked. He will not hear their cry of distress when the day of judgment comes upon them.

Now the friends must listen. Their thinking is nothing but empty rationalization; their logic is completely useless. Job would now teach them on behalf of God. The friends had presumed they would teach Job about God's ways; Eliphaz in particular had instructed Job how to bring light back into his life (22:26-28). This connection to the words of Eliphaz was evidently recognized long ago by the Greek translator, who used the same paraphrase in both instances (22:26-27; 27:10) for the same Hebrew words. Eliphaz claimed to know about the justice of God, but he made a fool of himself in trying to apply his ideas to Job. Job knew about the justice of God, and he understood retribution. Once retribution comes upon the enemy of God, the time of reconciliation is past, as Job eloquently explained in his description of the wicked (27:13-23). If Job was such an enemy, there was no point in his friends telling him to find divine favor. And if Job was not such an enemy, there was no point in accusing him of being a sinner under judgment. Either way, the friends were wrong. Understanding the mind of God must mean that bad things can happen to good people.

Judgment upon the wicked is swift and sure, as Job had said previously (24:18-24), in spite of his observations that the wicked often go unpunished in the present time (21:17-34; 24:1-17). Life may seem to drag on forever for the sufferer, but the wicked are living in a fool's world. God has a plan for them; before they know it, their fate will have been executed. No one escapes war, famine, and plague, which sweep away whole families. A wicked man may have had the luxury of many wives and children, but his widows (the Heb. is plural, though, implying that a rich man is being described) will be too stunned too weep at the loss of their children. Polygamy was always confined to the rich for both economic and biological reasons. However, a large family was no protection in times of war and disease. Amos described just such a time in pronouncing judgment against the wealthy of Israel (Amos 6:9-10); war would decimate their cities, so there would scarcely be anyone left to gather them for burial.

The wealth and the homes of the rich are no better than a spider's web or a temporary shelter in a field (27:18); one day the wealthy will wake up to find everything is gone. If it is not war, then natural disaster will strike without warning (27:21-22). It happens so quickly that others whistle in amazement. When wealth is all a person has in this world, then its sudden destruction means the loss of everything. No matter how long the wicked may live, this will be their fate.

Wealth was not all that Job had in this world. Job had devotion to God, a devotion that was loyal throughout his distress (27:2-5). Though it seemed to Job that God had regarded him as an enemy, he was sure that his Redeemer lived (19:25). True wisdom kept him from accepting false explanations for his suffering. Such wisdom is hard to find. Even the best of the wise, represented in his friends, had missed the mark and become fools. Humans can be clever yet fail to understand what they really need to know about life.

◆ C. Hymn to Wisdom (28:1-28)

1 "People know where to mine silver
   and how to refine gold.
2 They know where to dig iron from
   the earth
   and how to smelt copper from rock.
3 They know how to shine light in the
   darkness
   and explore the farthest regions
   of the earth
   as they search in the dark for ore.
4 They sink a mine shaft into the earth
   far from where anyone lives.
   They descend on ropes, swinging
   back and forth.
5 Food is grown on the earth above,
   but down below, the earth is melted
   as by fire.
6 Here the rocks contain precious lapis
   lazuli,
   and the dust contains gold.
7 These are treasures no bird of prey
   can see,
   no falcon's eye observe.

8 No wild animal has walked upon these
   treasures;
   no lion has ever set his paw there.
9 People know how to tear apart flinty
   rocks
   and overturn the roots of mountains.
10 They cut tunnels in the rocks
   and uncover precious stones.
11 They dam up the trickling streams
   and bring to light the hidden
   treasures.

12 "But do people know where to find
   wisdom?
   Where can they find understanding?
13 No one knows where to find it,
   for it is not found among the living.
14 'It is not here,' says the ocean.
   'Nor is it here,' says the sea.
15 It cannot be bought with gold.
   It cannot be purchased with silver.
16 It's worth more than all the gold
   of Ophir,

greater than precious onyx or lapis
lazuli.
¹⁷ Wisdom is more valuable than gold
and crystal.
It cannot be purchased with jewels
mounted in fine gold.
¹⁸ Coral and jasper are worthless in
trying to get it.
The price of wisdom is far above
rubies.
¹⁹ Precious peridot from Ethiopia* cannot
be exchanged for it.
It's worth more than the purest
gold.
²⁰ "But do people know where to find
wisdom?
Where can they find understanding?
²¹ It is hidden from the eyes of all
humanity.
Even the sharp-eyed birds in the
sky cannot discover it.
²² Destruction* and Death say,

'We've heard only rumors of where
wisdom can be found.'
²³ "God alone understands the way
to wisdom;
he knows where it can be found,
²⁴ for he looks throughout the whole
earth
and sees everything under the
heavens.
²⁵ He decided how hard the winds should
blow
and how much rain should fall.
²⁶ He made the laws for the rain
and laid out a path for the lightning.
²⁷ Then he saw wisdom and evaluated it.
He set it in place and examined it
thoroughly.
²⁸ And this is what he says to all
humanity:
'The fear of the Lord is true wisdom;
to forsake evil is real
understanding.'"

28:19 Hebrew *from Cush.*   28:22 Hebrew *Abaddon.*

NOTES

28:1ff This chapter is a poem on wisdom that is perfectly comprehensible as an independent composition. We will never know if it was written as part of the rest of the poetry or was written independently and was integrated into the poetic speech of Job. It is usually considered unoriginal to Job and is thought by many to be an awkward insertion into the larger poem—though perhaps the best possible location for a poem the author or later copyists did not wish to omit. Gordis says the poem "obviously does not belong here since it anticipates the theme of the God speeches" (1978:298); it would be "strange to make God into an afterthought" (Geller 1987:177). At the end of the book, the poem would be superfluous. It is acknowledged by all that this poem has a close affinity to the book of Job, and must have been composed by the author or a close imitator. The use of identical Heb. words or phrases (cf. 28:3b and 11:7; 26:10; cf. 28:10-11 and 12:22; cf. 28:1, 12, 23 and 38:12, 19; cf. 28:26b and 38:25b) and even the similar use of prepositions show that in some sense it is part of the work of Job.

28:1 *where to mine silver.* The verse seems to have primary reference to the refining of metals. The literal "place where silver emerges" is usually thought to be a mine, but as a technical term, it refers to the emergence of the metal as the ore is smelted. This technical use is found in Heb. (cf. Prov 25:4) and related languages (Van Leeuwen 1986:112-113). The opening line introduces the subject with the finished product (cf. 28:1b), and the first section of the poem describes the quest to find its source.

28:3 *shine light in the darkness.* The poem is describing the place where ore is found rather than the process by which it is retrieved. The general sense of this and the following verses is evident, but no precise meaning can be obtained. "Miners put an end to darkness" (NRSV) supplies a subject absent in the Heb. Tur-Sinai follows older Jewish commentators who take God to be the subject with reference to creation (1967:396-397), but humans are the most likely subject (Geller 1987:178), with reference to a mining excavation executed far from human habitation. The place is emphasized again (28:6), and the application of the mining analogy is to the place where wisdom may be found (28:12, 20).

farthest regions of the earth. The Heb. may be rendered "stone of deep darkness and shadow of death." The last two words have earlier been used to refer to the underworld (10:22), and it is probable that they again describe the source of the stone (NLT). If so, that source would seem to be something other than a mine shaft, for it is described as a place of extreme heat (28:5). This stone of the depths and the heat seems to be a reference to lava (Gordis 1978:305; Wolfers 1994c:275), which would be described by the ancients as emerging from the nether regions.

28:4 *They sink a mine shaft.* The Heb. word translated "mine shaft" (*nakhal* [TH5158, ZH5707]) commonly means the gully of an intermittent stream. If it is correct that there is a reference to lava in the previous verse, then this verse refers to the mountainous uninhabited regions where volcanoes erupt and the lava sometimes flows down a ridge as a stream. This idea (as opposed to that of a vertical mine shaft) is further supported by the fact that mining excavations in the ancient Near East were usually horizontal, though vertical shafts are known to have existed. Alternately, if God is the subject of v. 3, this could be a reference to the valleys of creation, or to God creating the world with volcanic eruptions.

swinging back and forth. Diverse meanings are possible due to the uncertainty of what sense is present in the Heb. words. Though the meaning "dangle" is a defensible meaning of the word *dallu* [TH1809A, ZH1938], it is quite uncertain, particularly since it is only by inference that a mine shaft is present at all. As it stands, the word has the form meaning "they were few" (cf. Gesenius §67bb), which continues the thought of the uninhabited mountainous regions bereft of people. The lava breaks out in a stream near some wanderer, far from a traveled path, a scarcely inhabited place where few ever go.

28:5 *Food is grown on the earth above.* Though the words are logically construed this way, the idea is very awkward in the context, which is about a sterile uninhabited land. The place where rock below is melted as by fire is not one in which crops are grown. Rather than "bread" (*lekhem* [TH3899, ZH4312]) it would seem there is a reference to "heat"; Gordis (1978:306) connects it to another form of this word (*lekhum* [TH3894A, ZH4303]), previously used for heat or rage (cf. 20:23), but Tur-Sinai (1967:398-399) slightly emends the text to obtain the normal word meaning heat (*khom* [TH2527, ZH2770]). "A land where heat pours forth" is much more satisfactory in context, though the support for the meaning heat is not strong.

the earth is melted as by fire. This may refer to the ancient technique of using fire to dislodge rock in an excavation.

28:8 *no lion.* The terminology for "lion" interchanges with "serpent" in Semitic languages. Since the verse is speaking about places inaccessible to humans, some commentators (e.g., Pope 1965:179-180; Geller 1987:179-180) think the reference is to a snake or reptile.

28:11 *dam up.* The Heb. "bind" (RSV) is a metaphor for overcoming the obstacles in arriving at the distant sources. The word "bind" (*khibbesh* [TH2280, ZH2502]) is phonetically close to the Heb. word "search" (*khippes* [TH2664, ZH2924]), which is chosen by many translators (NIV, NRSV, NJB) and may have been used as a pun to bring both concepts to mind.

trickling streams. It is now known from Ugaritic that this word (*mabbakh* [TH4009.1, ZH4441]) is used mythologically to refer to the sources of the rivers where the gods dwell. The miner has reached the farthest regions in the search for treasure. It is possible some of the other terminology of these verses is also mythological, referring to secret, inaccessible places. "Dam up" is an expression that refers to restraining the primeval powers (Geller 1987:181).

28:27 *set it in place.* Some manuscripts read "he understood it" (*hebinah* [TH995, ZH1067])
instead of "set in place" (*hekinah* [TH3559, ZH3922]); since the other verbs in the context are
those of cognition, it may be preferable to follow the minority reading (cf. REB).

28:28 *And this is what he says to all humanity.* It seems to many that this conclusion—
with a traditional wisdom statement (cf. Prov 3:7; 9:10)—subverts the beauty of the poem
and is "a standard affirmation and formulation of the conservative school . . . appended
as an antidote to the agnostic tenor of the preceding poem" (Pope 1965:183). Such judgments are presumptuous in that they attribute to the composition what the critic deems it
be required to say. The distinct form of the final line, including the book's only occurrence
of the term "Lord" (*'adonay* [TH136, ZH151]), obviously intends to distinguish the application
of wisdom but cannot serve to show it is secondary and intrusive. This hymn distinguishes
the different kinds of wisdom: that which we find and follow (Prov 3:13-18) and that
which is inaccessible (28:13, 21). This distinction is not confined to the book of Job nor
to this chapter in Job (Oorschot 1994:200), which makes the closing verse of the poem
indispensable as a reflection on wisdom.

COMMENTARY

This poem breaks down into three very distinct sections: (1) humans successfully
search for hidden treasure (28:1-11); (2) humans do not know the place of wisdom, which is the greatest treasure of all (28:12-22); (3) God knows the source of
wisdom and by wisdom created the universe (28:23-28). These three sections can
be observed to have a correspondence to the comprehensive structure of 3:1–42:6,
as Job and his friends search for wisdom, Job and Elihu reflect on its worth, and
finally, God appears in the storm (Zimmermann 1994:98). The author skillfully
unites the manifold and futile efforts of the friends and Job to find wisdom with the
positive anticipation of the speeches of God. This poem on wisdom must be recognized as a component the author used as a bridge to his later reflections on the role
of wisdom for understanding the providence of God in creation. In his final speech,
Job recognized both the potential and the limits of wisdom when dealing with the
mysteries of God. As a component of the final speech of Job, it prepares the way for
his repentance (42:1-6) concerning the presumptuous assertions he had made in
his demands for divine justice.

As indicated in the translation notes, this poem can be read with a considerable
diversity of meaning in the first section, though the significance of the whole is not
in doubt. In part, this is the power of poetry and is a strength rather than a weakness. Poets create images; they stimulate the mind of the reader in various and diverse ways. As Geller points out (1987:158), a realistic meaning is submerged in a
"vibrant complex of imagery." Some variety in interpretation and impact is legitimate, though verse 4 is particularly obscure to the contemporary reader. The older
Jewish commentaries may be right in setting the quest for metal ores (28:1-6) in the
context of the wonder of creation (28:3-4). The Hebrew does not tell us directly
who puts an end to darkness (28:3), but in an absolute sense it is only God who can
do so—particularly the deep darkness found outside the natural sphere. An analogy
may be inferred between the way God puts an end to darkness, searching out every
stone in creating the desolate valleys, and the way a miner puts an end to darkness

in excavating the rocks created by God. The poem is about the work of humans within the work of God. Verse 5 alludes to melted rock, such as that of a volcano, which erupts from the lower regions of the earth, mysterious both in creation and in the technology of mining. The "stone of the shadow of death" (see note on 28:3) evokes the image of those regions outside of human activity but where the effect of divine activity may be observed. In the natural world, humans probe these mysteries with wonderful results. Precious stones and metals are found and refined. The result is tangible and satisfying, especially because of the effort and skill required for success. The miner goes to the "sources of the rivers," an image of the home of the gods, in his search for treasure (see note on 28:11). He confines all the powers that might stand in his way. The mysteries of the natural world may be pursued successfully to the most remote and uncharted regions.

Precious metals are frequently mentioned in the Old Testament, particularly gold and silver. Gold can be found in a relatively pure state in nature and can be worked effectively. Silver was separated from the ore through a process called cupellation, in which the lead, tin, and other minerals were liquified and blown away with a blast of air, with some of the residue absorbed in a porous base, leaving the silver. This process of refining silver is a frequent metaphor for purification from evil. Though gold is mentioned the most often, it is actually the least found in archaeological excavations, though it is always the best preserved. Sapphire is not the modern transparent blue stone, which was first used in the Roman period, but what we call lapis lazuli, a semi-precious, opaque, deep-blue stone associated with the colors of royalty.

The second section of the poem is marked by an inclusio—the ending (28:20-22) recapitulates the lines at the beginning (28:12-14). It accentuates the transcendent nature of wisdom with the repetition of a question (28:12, 20) that postulates the impossibility of the quest to find wisdom. No one knows the way to wisdom because it is not within the land of the living (28:13, 21); the very best of skill or perception is insufficient to find it. Even outside the world of ordered creation, there is but a rumor of the home of wisdom (28:14, 22); the netherworld, the deep, and the sea declare that she is not there. The place of death can only report rumors about wisdom.

The more difficult an object is to obtain, the greater is its worth; because pure gold, silver, and stones such as blue sapphire, black or white onyx, opaque shiny crystal, bright coral and yellow chrysolite (topaz) are difficult to obtain, they are very expensive. Yet, as to its worth, wisdom is not to be compared with any of these precious jewels. The wisdom of creation is not accessible within creation; therefore, nothing within creation can be compared in worth with wisdom.

God alone understands wisdom, knows its source, and has evaluated and approved it. The forces of creation such as wind, rain, and storm were set in place and are governed by wisdom. Wisdom was the means by which the orders of the natural world were achieved (cf. Prov 8:22-31). This kind of wisdom is inaccessible to humans. In the final line of the poem, "wisdom" is distinguished from "the wisdom" described in the previous lines by the absence of the article. Absolute wisdom, designated by the use of the article (Gordis 1978:538-539), is denied to humans, but humans have access to a more limited form of wisdom. The wisdom of humans is to fear the Lord and to know about morality, life, and appropriate conduct. Humans should know this kind of wisdom, but the wisdom of God concerning the ultimate order of the universe is a wisdom humans often wish they could know but cannot—their attempts to find it may well leave them self-deceived.

The fear of the Lord is trust in combination with full recognition of his power and judgment. There is reason for real terror unless there is complete confidence in his integrity and character. The God speeches (chs 38–41) are a lesson on the fear of the Lord. God's ways may appear to be violent and are sometimes incomprehensible, but he can be fully trusted. Job is first silent in response to the challenge, then repentant that he should have expressed a lack of trust in God's justice by his demands that God justify his ways to a suffering man.

◆ **D. Reflections (29:1–31:40)**
   1. Days of dignity (29:1-25)

Job continued speaking:

2 "I long for the years gone by
   when God took care of me,
3 when he lit up the way before me
   and I walked safely through
      the darkness.
4 When I was in my prime,
   God's friendship was felt in my
      home.
5 The Almighty was still with me,
   and my children were around me.
6 My cows produced milk in abundance,
   and my groves poured out streams
      of olive oil.

7 "Those were the days when I went
   to the city gate
   and took my place among the
      honored leaders.
8 The young stepped aside when they
      saw me,
   and even the aged rose in respect
      at my coming.
9 The princes stood in silence
   and put their hands over their
      mouths.
10 The highest officials of the city stood
      quietly,
   holding their tongues in respect.

11 "All who heard me praised me.
   All who saw me spoke well of me.
12 For I assisted the poor in their need
   and the orphans who required help.
13 I helped those without hope, and they
      blessed me.
   And I caused the widows' hearts
      to sing for joy.
14 Everything I did was honest.
   Righteousness covered me like
      a robe,
   and I wore justice like a turban.
15 I served as eyes for the blind
   and feet for the lame.
16 I was a father to the poor
   and assisted strangers who needed
      help.
17 I broke the jaws of godless oppressors
   and plucked their victims from their
      teeth.

18 "I thought, 'Surely I will die
   surrounded by my family
   after a long, good life.*
19 For I am like a tree whose roots reach
      the water,
   whose branches are refreshed with
      the dew.
20 New honors are constantly bestowed
      on me,

and my strength is continually
renewed.'

21 "Everyone listened to my advice.
They were silent as they waited for
me to speak.

22 And after I spoke, they had nothing
to add,
for my counsel satisfied them.

23 They longed for me to speak as people
long for rain.

They drank my words like a
refreshing spring rain.

24 When they were discouraged, I smiled
at them.
My look of approval was precious
to them.

25 Like a chief, I told them what to do.
I lived like a king among his troops
and comforted those who
mourned.

29:18 Hebrew *after I have counted my days like sand.*

NOTES

29:3 *when he lit up the way before me.* The verse should be understood to say that God was actively lighting the way for Job with his lamp. God had not simply left his light to shine but was making it shine continuously.

29:4 *When I was in my prime.* Though Job had grown children, he was not an old man but what we would call middle-aged—the time of highest productivity. The translation "my autumn days" (RSV) means the season of productivity and prosperity, not the end of life.

God's friendship. A number of translations (REB, NAB, NJB) provide the thought of protection, which requires an emendation to the verb "shut in" (*sakak* [TH5526, ZH6114]; cf. 1:10) or an additional meaning for the Heb. root *swd* [TH5475, ZH6051] based on cognate languages. The LXX follows this interpretation.

29:17 *I broke the jaws of godless oppressors.* In Heb., this is not quite the equivalent of our hitting someone in the jaw. This expression was always used in connection with slanderous or fraudulent speech (e.g., Pss 3:6-7; 58:3, 6), where punishment to the mouth was a kind of logical consequence. Very ancient Sumerian documents trace this expression about breaking the teeth of the wicked back to the language of contracts in purchasing a house (Hackett and Huehnergard 1984:268-273). House-purchasing records were written on a clay nail (or attached to the house by one) as a record of the transaction. If the seller was not the rightful owner of the property, the penalty would be that the clay nail that retained the record of the sale would be driven into the teeth that had made the false claim of ownership. The breaking of the teeth may have been a literal penalty in original practice—at least, it was deemed a suitable consequence for lying speech and fraudulent claims. It came to be an expression for executing a penalty on those who were dishonest.

29:18 *I will die surrounded by my family.* The literal "I shall die in my nest" (RSV, NRSV, KJV) might seem to be a simple metaphor for family, except for the question of how it relates to the next line, which seems to refer to a bird in the Heb. It has been translated as "I shall multiply my days as the sand" (RSV, KJV) or "as the phoenix" (NRSV, NAB). Ancient legend known to the rabbis held that a bird of bright plumage did not eat the forbidden fruit and lived a thousand years. When its nest was burned by fire, a small piece of the bird the size of an egg was preserved, and from it the bird was reborn (*Genesis Rabbah* 54:9). In another rabbinic legend, Noah blessed it with immortality because it alone did not torment him for food in the ark (*b. Sanhedrin* 108b). It is now known from Ugaritic that the Heb. letters for "sand" (*khol* [TH2344, ZH2567]) also mean "phoenix" [TH2344A, ZH2568] (Dahood 1974:86-87); in combination with the word "nest," it is most probable that the author was referring to the ancient legend as the rabbis assumed. The legend of a long-lived or immortal bird was known in Egypt in early times. Job had imagined he would live as long as the famous bird.

COMMENTARY

Job returned to his thoughts on wisdom, particularly his reflections on what wisdom must mean for his life in particular. The mystery of the hidden wisdom of God remained inaccessible to him, as well as to all other mortals. The necessity of applying the fear of God to his life was more compelling than ever. His thoughts turned first to what the fear of God had meant for his life in times past. This memory is set in stark contrast with what the fear of God means to Job in the present. Purity of life and fear of God do not determine what kind of life we may have, but this does not decrease their importance. Job concluded his speech with a soliloquy on what kind of man he wanted to be (29:19-25), not because it would determine the fate of his life but because that is the wisdom of the fear of God.

Job remembered, first of all, his days of prosperity (29:2-6). This was the time when God was an intimate friend. At that time, God was among his confidants, that inner circle of trusting friends with whom he could share anything. If verse 4 is read with the Greek translation (see note on 29:4), then there is an allusion here to the days when God protected Job from harm (1:10) by setting up a fence around him. In those days, Job enjoyed the presence of his family and abundant prosperity. It was as if he washed his feet with milk (because of the production of his herds), and it was as if the rocks poured streams of olive oil because his vineyards yielded so well.

More important than prosperity was the respect Job had enjoyed, and it was also well deserved. Job made justice his first priority, particularly for the disadvantaged and for the poor who had been wronged by fraud. Job spoke about investigating such cases of fraud for the poor, even for those who did not know him. If cheating had taken place, Job would execute the appropriate penalty; it was like rescuing a sheep from the jaws of a lion. Carnivorous animals use their teeth to capture their victims, and being taken in a business scam is much like being caught in the teeth of a monster. As the dignified and respected elder of the city, Job took on the task of settling such questions of injustice and making sure that appropriate recompense was made. His very presence brought about silence from young and old, small and great. His counsel was uncontested, and he was blessed by all those that he had helped.

Job had not expected this state of affairs to change; there was no reason why it should. He had expected he would grow to a great old age, like the legendary phoenix that renewed its life continuously. He would be like a tree that lives almost indefinitely because its roots reach down to the water. The irony was that Job knew the wicked would live to a good old age with their families (cf. 21:7-13), while Job had lost the family, health, honor, and wealth that was rightfully his. Job returned to the theme of respect (29:21-25) because it is the most painful reminder of the greatest loss of his life. He was now maligned as a wicked man just because of a change in fortunes. In earlier times he was regarded with awe; when he smiled at others, they could scarcely believe it because honored, dignified men in Job's day did not smile. He was a leader and a comforter; now he was despised and in need of comfort himself.

◆   2. Days of derision (30:1-31)

"But now I am mocked by people youn-
    ger than I,
by young men whose fathers are not
    worthy to run with my sheepdogs.
2 A lot of good they are to me—
    those worn-out wretches!
3 They are gaunt with hunger
    and flee to the deserts,
    to desolate and gloomy wastelands.
4 They pluck wild greens from among
    the bushes
    and eat from the roots of broom
    trees.
5 They are driven from human society,
    and people shout at them as if they
    were thieves.
6 So now they live in frightening
    ravines,
    in caves and among the rocks.
7 They sound like animals howling
    among the bushes,
    huddled together beneath the
    nettles.
8 They are nameless fools,
    outcasts from society.

9 "And now they mock me with vulgar
    songs!
    They taunt me!
10 They despise me and won't come
    near me,
    except to spit in my face.
11 For God has cut my bowstring.
    He has humbled me,
    so they have thrown off all restraint.
12 These outcasts oppose me to my face.
    They send me sprawling
    and lay traps in my path.
13 They block my road
    and do everything they can to
    destroy me.
    They know I have no one to help me.
14   They come at me from all directions.
    They jump on me when I am down.
15   I live in terror now.
    My honor has blown away in the wind,
    and my prosperity has vanished like
    a cloud.

16 "And now my life seeps away.
    Depression haunts my days.
17 At night my bones are filled with pain,
    which gnaws at me relentlessly.
18 With a strong hand, God grabs my
    shirt.
    He grips me by the collar of my
    coat.
19 He has thrown me into the mud.
    I'm nothing more than dust and
    ashes.

20 "I cry to you, O God, but you don't
    answer.
    I stand before you, but you don't
    even look.
21 You have become cruel toward me.
    You use your power to persecute
    me.
22 You throw me into the whirlwind
    and destroy me in the storm.
23 And I know you are sending me to
    my death—
    the destination of all who live.

24 "Surely no one would turn against
    the needy
    when they cry for help in their
    trouble.
25 Did I not weep for those in trouble?
    Was I not deeply grieved for the
    needy?
26 So I looked for good, but evil came
    instead.
    I waited for the light, but darkness
    fell.
27 My heart is troubled and restless.
    Days of suffering torment me.
28 I walk in gloom, without sunlight.
    I stand in the public square and
    cry for help.
29 Instead, I am considered a brother
    to jackals
    and a companion to owls.
30 My skin has turned dark,
    and my bones burn with fever.
31 My harp plays sad music,
    and my flute accompanies those
    who weep.

NOTES

30:3 flee to the deserts. This meaning is much superior to "gnaw the dry land" (RSV, NRSV, NJB). The word for "gnaw" (*'araq* [TH6207, ZH6908]) is commonly used in later Aramaic for "flee" (Jastrow 1123), a meaning also attested by the later Targums and later Gr. It is likely there is some disarray in the Heb. text in this verse. The usually literal Qumran Targum (11QtgJob) is variant at this line (van der Ploeg and van der Woude 1971:41); though fragmentary, the preserved words read "in hunger they desired the green of the desert." The word *'araq* is found only in this verse and in 30:17, and "gnaw" does not fit well in either instance but is based on Arabic and Syriac (the Ugaritic evidence is dubious).

desolate and gloomy wastelands. "By night in desolate waste" (Pope 1965:193) is an attempt to understand the Heb. that shouldn't be dismissed, as it is an evident alliteration. The Heb. for "by night" (cf. NLT's "gloomy") usually means "yesterday" (cf. KJV, "former time") but might indicate the previous night or the coming of darkness.

30:4 They pluck wild greens from among the bushes. The outcasts gather edible desert plants described lit. as "salty leaves on the shrubs." These are usually identified as saltwort, a low, straggling bush with thick, sour tasting leaves, eaten only by those on the edge of starvation. The mallow (KJV, RSV), an annual herb whose fruit, leaves, and seed were used as food, is not meant here (it may be referred to in 6:6, see the note there).

eat from the roots of broom trees. This is not the correct meaning; there is no reference to food (KJV, NAB) in this phrase. Rather than using the roots "for food" (*lakhmam* [TH3899, ZH4312]), we must read "for heat" (*lekhummam* [TH2552, ZH2801]); the heat was used to prepare the "wild greens" mentioned in the preceeding line. The text should be read this way because the plant mentioned (*rothem* [TH7574, ZH8413], "broom tree") is famous for the heat its roots produce when burned (cf. Ps 120:4), but those roots are nauseous and even poisonous and cannot be eaten. The broom tree is a desert shrub that grows 4 to 12 feet high and has straight long branches and small leaves.

30:5 driven from human society. They are driven from the community, from the midst of the people.

30:8 nameless fools. They are of ill repute and "whipped out of the land" (Roth 1960:402). The fool (*nabal* [TH5036A, ZH5572]) is one who does evil, reaps the reward of evil deeds, and is driven from society as an outcast. "Fool" always has the connotation of godlessness, someone outside the covenant, and therefore also someone ostracized from the community.

30:11 bowstring. The metaphor of a "tent cord" is preferable to "bowstring," though the Heb. word is used for both. Life is compared to a tent that collapses (cf. 4:21; Isa 38:12), not to a bow.

thrown off all restraint. They "let loose the bridle" (KJV), a vivid image of an unrestrained, runaway animal.

30:13 do everything they can to destroy me. The text does not say "they have no helper" (KJV, NIV), which makes no sense here. Many translations (RSV, NRSV, REB, NAB, NJB) read along the lines of "restrain" (*'atsar* [TH6113, ZH6806]), a minor emendation from the phonetically equivalent word, "help" (*'azar*) [TH5826, ZH6468]; Gordis (1978:334) on the basis of Arabic says *'azar* can mean either "help" or "prevent." The change from "them" (*lu*) to "me" (*li*) is also a minor emendation (NLT). The disarray of 11QtgJob on this verse (van der Ploeg and van der Woude 1971:42-43) suggests the Heb. was already problematic in the first century BC.

30:15 My honor has blown away in the wind. The difficulty of the grammar has led to various translations: "my honor is pursued" (RSV) simply changes the form of the Heb. verb, while "swept away" (REB) or "dispersed" (NJB) assumes a change of verb.

"My dignity has disappeared as the wind" fits the comparison to wind and the vanishing prosperity of the next line, though this meaning for the verb is somewhat conjectural (Koehler and Baumgartner 4:1112).

my prosperity. The word can refer to material prosperity or the power to bring justice and deliverance, namely rank and position. Since respect and honor are central themes in the chapter, the latter may be more appropriate.

30:17 *gnaws at me relentlessly.* The dubious meaning "gnaw" (cf. 30:3) makes it more likely that a body part is meant, which is parallel to bones in the first line, which are said to be "pierced." Here, the Gr. says the sinews or tendons are sundered, but "sundered" departs from the Heb., which says "had no rest" (cf. NLT's "relentlessly"). "Veins" (REB) is based on an Arabic comparison. The Arabic may confirm the Gr., since veins, sinews, and nerves are not sharply distinguished in ancient terminology (de Wilde 1981:295). 11QtgJob is only partially extant here, but it translates this verse as a "burning in my bones" and possibly "tendons" (van der Ploeg and van der Woude 1971:42-43). The evidence of the translations presents a case of double jeopardy, since the translator may have had a different text than the MT and may have been paraphrasing as well. In this case, however, the versions are as good as any other evidence we have for the meaning of the MT.

30:18 *grabs my shirt.* This is actually an alteration of the Heb., which speaks about a change in the garment (*khapas* [TH2664, ZH2924]) rather than the garment being seized (*tapas* [TH8610, ZH9530]). The subject is the garment, though God may be inferred as the one who changes or seizes the garment. The symbolic reference to clothing in the previous chapter (29:14) may be the clue to the appearance of clothing in this lament (Wolfers 1994d:571-572), since the complaint of Job in his suffering is set in deliberate contrast to his former state. This line can be paraphrased "my clothing has changed completely."

grips me by the collar of my coat. NJPS translates this as "the neck of my tunic fits my waist." Interpreted this way (which is scarcely even a paraphrase of the Heb.), the metaphor describes a loss of weight so severe the garments are completely out of proportion to the body. The question is whether there is a reference to collar or neck at all; the word "mouth" (*peh* [TH6310, ZH7023]) is used once to refer to the opening for the head in a garment for a priest (Exod 28:32), but ancient garments did not have a collar or even what we would call a neck. The expression used here (*kepi*) indicates comparison everywhere else, and it should not be taken differently in this line. The line may be paraphrased "my garment clings to me like my underwear," resuming the subject from the previous line. The meaning of this must be in reference to the metaphorical use of garments (cf. 29:14).

30:24 *no one would turn against the needy.* This is the sense of the verse, which appears to be textually defective. Attempts to restore it (e.g., Driver and Gray 1921:2.219) have not produced a consensus of any kind. The problem is as old as the earliest translations (Grabbe 1977:101-102 provides a convenient list). The later Targums actually provided two translations, and the manuscripts are not consistent on the pronouns. It is best to work with the Heb. as it is; "needy" is a translation of the word "ruined" (*'i* [TH5856, ZH6505])—the word used for the city Ai (ruin) in Joshua. "Sending the hand" is always in a hostile sense, so Job is saying that one should not strike the ruined.

cry for help in their trouble. "Yet no beggar held out his hand to me in vain for relief" (REB) assumes an unusual meaning for the expression "stretch out the hand," a conjectured form of the word "help" (Reider 1952:129), and other textual changes. The Heb. is elliptical but can be translated either as "in disaster there is a cry from them" (cf. NLT, NRSV, NJB) or "in disaster there is consequently a cry."

COMMENTARY

In this section, Job describes the bitter existence of the outcasts of society, those who live on the fringe of physical subsistence. He referred to youthful vagabonds, the type unworthy to be trusted with the sheepdogs. Dogs were not "man's best friend" in ancient Israelite society but a despised, scavenging creature howling on the outskirts of the city (Ps 59:6, 14) and prowling about for fresh blood (Ps 68:23)—one's enemies were often likened to dogs. These vagabonds were despicable urchins, not worthy to run with the dogs. They taunted people like Job without respect for his age or the person he had been. Such people were unemployable, pitiful to be sure. In their desperation, they were driven to the desert, a dark, foreboding wasteland. There they scavenged for the bitter leaves of the saltwort, one of the few plants of the desert at least partially edible. According to rabbinic legend, it was eaten by the generation in the wilderness that was occupied with building the Tabernacle (*b. Qiddushin* 66a). These outcasts dug up the roots of the broom tree (30:4), a fitting name for a shrub with long thin branches; the roots of the shrub were famous for their heat, which was useful for warmth and for cooking. No one trusted these "bush people"; they were driven out like thieves. No doubt, in their need, these people would sometimes steal, aggravating their fortunes and their fate. They were driven to find shelter wherever they could among the rocks and ravines of the desert. They sounded like wild animals as they would shout to each other and congregate among the thorny desert shrubs.

Job described these as fools, "outcasts from society" (30:8). The term "fool" always has an ethical component. The fool rejects the covenant and its way of life, the ethics and moral conduct required by it. Their rejection of God and of the respect for others demanded by a godly way of life means they became outcasts. That is the consequence of being unable to function within a respectful society. Their choices exposed them to physical hardship and to the contempt and condescension of those who chose to live in ordered society. It might seem that Job expressed a negative attitude toward them, one that is inconsistent with his own affirmations of the equality of all humanity (cf. 31:13-15). Often, the roles we occupy in life may be in conflict with the ideals we hold. Thomas Jefferson, the author of the Declaration of Independence, with its ringing affirmation of the right of all to life, liberty, and the pursuit of happiness, was a slaveholder all his life, though considered humane and considerate. To some extent, the larger forces of society have the power to coerce conformity to that which we despise. Job was not denying his desire for equality; he was describing a reality. In this case the rejection of the outcasts was, in part, a consequence of their own actions and irresponsibility.

By contrast, Job's misfortunes came through no fault of his own. To make matters worse, these despicable, culpable, disrespectful fools had made him the object of their contempt, as if they had something to flaunt. They abhorred him and did not hesitate to spit at him. His life had collapsed, the sky had fallen, and the tent cord of his life had been cut, so the uncouth monsters had opportunity to molest without restraint (see note on 30:11). These "birds" did their best to trip him up and direct him down a course of disaster. They attempted to thwart his plans and trouble him, with no one to resist their devious behavior. Job had no defenses—it was as if there was a large breach in what should have been a protective wall so that the trouble-makers just streamed through. They charged in and created havoc in a situation that was already in turmoil. All terror had broken loose; there was not a trace of dignity or respect left. At one time, Job had held a position where he could act on behalf of those who truly needed help, but the order of his social world has disintegrated. The disgraced of society shamed him without restraint.

Job's life had been turned upside-down. In a vivid word picture (30:16-19), Job described the reversal that had transpired. He was suddenly living in physical agony as a social outcast; trouble and need had him in their grip. His bones were on fire; his nerves gave him no rest. Job had been cast into the mire and was like dust and ashes. Dust and ashes could symbolize the physical deterioration caused by disease or the encroachment of death as the disease progressed. But, most likely, dust and ashes have their usual significance of representing affliction (Fohrer 1989:420) and/or lamentation (cf. 2:12). In a grotesque extension of this symbolism, Job says that his whole being has disintegrated to dust and ashes. Sorrow is not an event in his life; his whole existence is nothing but pain and grief. This anguish is much more than just physical misery; it is the pain of his life as a social outcast, which he has just de-scribed (30:8-15). Job described the change in terms of clothing (30:18), mysterious both in terms of the image itself and of its symbolism for the life of Job. Though the image could be that of God throwing Job into the mud, as he had said previously (cf. 9:31), the application here is quite different. At the end of chapter 9, Job was speak-ing of the filth of his guilt, but that is not the topic at hand. Here Job is speaking about the changed circumstances of his life in society. The Hebrew says that Job's garment has changed (see note on 30:18), which is most logically understood in ref-erence to what Job's garment had been in his former state (cf. 29:14). According to chapter 29, Job had been a respected man who could exercise judgment on behalf of those who were wronged; his garment was righteousness and his turban was justice. These had been stripped from him; a protective and beautiful robe had been reduced to an undergarment clinging to him. Job had lost the robe that would have distin-guished him as a judge. He had no robe at all; he had been deprived of even the pro-tective garment to which everyone is entitled. All Job had left was his undergarment—he was among the poorest of the poor, and he was despised. His clothing was nothing but humiliation and rejection, instead of dignity and respect.

The symbolism of clothing is particularly striking. In society, clothing is a mark of status and position. Uniforms and clothing styles are a critical aspect of how we present ourselves and how we are perceived. A friend or family member is trans-formed into an athlete, a law enforcer, a cleric, a pilot, a doctor, a judge, or any number of distinct roles with a change of uniform. Once the uniform is removed, the person's status is in a sense reduced to that of an "ordinary Joe." Clothes are more than symbolic; they are also necessary for function and protection. Job's refer-ence to his change of clothes refers to both aspects. Not only had he lost his dignity, he had no protection from the elements around him. His burning fever made him a victim to the heat of the day and the cold at night. It was as if he had no clothes. His deprivation left him to be scorned by those who were outcasts, who had no place in society at all. This dramatic change of life had taken place as quickly and completely as a change of clothes.

Job could do nothing to change his situation. He could cry out or he could be silent; either way, the result would be the same. He had been dealt a cruel blow; he had been treated as an enemy. His life had been swept away by the wind and dissolved in the deluge of a storm. Death was all that was left for him. The injustice of it all was inexplicable. No one would strike someone who had already become a heap of ruin. Everyone, especially Job, would have mourned with those who had experienced disaster and would help those who are needy.

Some would argue that every society needs its scapegoats (i.e., those individuals who must bear the guilt that everyone else recognizes in themselves). Girard (1985:17) uses this chapter to argue that the three friends made Job just such a scapegoat in their insistence that he was responsible for the misfortunes that had come upon him. The scapegoat is ostracized from society as the person charged with the guilt of all the others. Though the isolation was the most painful aspect of Job's situation—as opposed to the honor he had held previously—it cannot be said that Job's life was a story of his being made an outcast (Levine 1985:131-133). It was not the well-being of the community that was at stake in the life of Job; rather, it was the problem of how God had dealt with Job and how Job understood divine providence. The lament of Job, however, is a reminder of how we can sometimes isolate those who are most in need of help. It is not that they are made a scapegoat, as though they must bear the weaknesses or guilt of others—it may be a simple matter of ignorance or fear. It is difficult to know how to include them, and there may be a fear that including them will reduce the benefactors to being like them. Not knowing what to do may bring avoidance. Worst of all is arrogance, which is all too common. Like the friends of Job, we may assume that the sufferers were responsible for their own misfortunes, and rather than help we may humiliate. What Job described is even worse; it is the ridicule of those who belittle anyone in a position more vulnerable than their own. This is perhaps even more despicable than creating scapegoats who can take our blame.

Job brought his lament to a close with a summary of his pitiful situation. Waiting and hoping had not been of any help (30:26); he had not mounted up with the wings of an eagle (Isa 40:31). His stomach churned and affliction confronted him constantly. His days were dark—the sun never rose in his life. He cried out openly to all who would hear, but he was driven from society to live with the jackals and ostriches of the desert. Job was not actually in the desert, but he was ignored and humiliated so that he became like the desert outcasts he had once despised. To those passing by, his pleas sounded like the wailing of the desert creatures. His disease was frightful. Illness had made his skin turn dark; fever was with him constantly. The music had gone out of his life; all that was left was mournful lamentation.

3. Code of honor (31:1-40)

1 "I made a covenant with my eyes
  not to look with lust at a young
  woman.
2 For what has God above chosen for us?
  What is our inheritance from the
  Almighty on high?
3 Isn't it calamity for the wicked
  and misfortune for those who do
  evil?
4 Doesn't he see everything I do
  and every step I take?

5 "Have I lied to anyone
  or deceived anyone?
6 Let God weigh me on the scales of
  justice,
  for he knows my integrity.
7 If I have strayed from his pathway,
  or if my heart has lusted for what
  my eyes have seen,
  or if I am guilty of any other sin,
8 then let someone else eat the crops I
  have planted.
  Let all that I have planted be
  uprooted.

9 "If my heart has been seduced by a
  woman,
  or if I have lusted for my neighbor's
  wife,
10 then let my wife belong to* another
  man;
  let other men sleep with her.
11 For lust is a shameful sin,
  a crime that should be punished.
12 It is a fire that burns all the way to
  hell.*
  It would wipe out everything I own.

13 "If I have been unfair to my male or
  female servants
  when they brought their complaints
  to me,
14 how could I face God?
  What could I say when he
  questioned me?
15 For God created both me and my
  servants.
  He created us both in the womb.

16 "Have I refused to help the poor,
  or crushed the hopes of widows?
17 Have I been stingy with my food
  and refused to share it with orphans?
18 No, from childhood I have cared for
  orphans like a father,
  and all my life I have cared for
  widows.
19 Whenever I saw the homeless without
  clothes
  and the needy with nothing to wear,
20 did they not praise me
  for providing wool clothing to keep
  them warm?

21 "If I raised my hand against an
  orphan,
  knowing the judges would take my
  side,
22 then let my shoulder be wrenched out
  of place!
  Let my arm be torn from its socket!
23 That would be better than facing
  God's judgment.
  For if the majesty of God opposes
  me, what hope is there?

24 "Have I put my trust in money
  or felt secure because of my gold?
25 Have I gloated about my wealth
  and all that I own?

26 "Have I looked at the sun shining in
  the skies,
  or the moon walking down its silver
  pathway,
27 and been secretly enticed in my heart
  to throw kisses at them in worship?
28 If so, I should be punished by the
  judges,
  for it would mean I had denied the
  God of heaven.

29 "Have I ever rejoiced when disaster
  struck my enemies,
  or become excited when harm came
  their way?
30 No, I have never sinned by cursing
  anyone
  or by asking for revenge.

31 "My servants have never said,
    'He let others go hungry.'
32 I have never turned away a stranger
    but have opened my doors to
    everyone.

33 "Have I tried to hide my sins like
    other people do,
    concealing my guilt in my heart?
34 Have I feared the crowd
    or the contempt of the masses,
    so that I kept quiet and stayed
    indoors?

35 "If only someone would listen to me!
    Look, I will sign my name to my
    defense.
    Let the Almighty answer me.

Let my accuser write out the
    charges against me.
36 I would face the accusation proudly.
    I would wear it like a crown.
37 For I would tell him exactly what
    I have done.
    I would come before him like
    a prince.

38 "If my land accuses me
    and all its furrows cry out together,
39 or if I have stolen its crops
    or murdered its owners,
40 then let thistles grow on that land
    instead of wheat,
    and weeds instead of barley."

Job's words are ended.

31:10 Hebrew *grind for.*   31:12 Hebrew *to Abaddon.*

NOTES

31:5 *Have I lied?* This question is introduced with a particle expecting a negative answer (Gesenius §150i). It should not be translated as a conditional clause (RSV, NIV), making the following verse parenthetical.

31:7 *any other sin.* Lit. "if anything has stuck to my hands," an expression similar to the English idiom "sticky fingers." The sin in question is stealing the movable property of another person in any manner.

31:12 *wipe out everything I own.* Lit., "uproot all my produce." For poetic effect, the image of crops is continued from 31:8. Gordis (1978:347) is correct in recognizing a metaphor for children here as the "produce" (*tebu'ah* [TH8393, ZH9311]) of a marriage that has been "uprooted" by lust.

31:13 *If I have been unfair.* The Heb. can be ambiguous between a conditional and an interrogative. The following questions (31:14) suggest that this may be a question.

31:15 *God created both me and my servants.* The translation involves a revocalization of the MT that agrees with the LXX.

31:18 *cared for widows.* "Cared" is the correct meaning, as is indicated by Arabic and Akkadian parallels to this Heb. verb. "Guide her [the widow]" (KJV, RSV, REB, NJB) is not the sense intended here. "Widow" is appropriately supplied because this verse summarizes in poetic fashion the previous references to the orphan and the widow (31:16).

31:23 *facing God's judgment.* McCarter (1973:410-411) has made a case for the language of this verse being that of the ancient river ordeal. In Mesopotamia, when evidence was insufficient, the trial was conducted by submerging the suspect into the rushing waters of a river to determine guilt or innocence. (Only the innocent would resist and survive the rushing water.) The "judgment" (*'eyd* [TH343, ZH369]) is a reference to the turbulent waters that serve as a trial by the gods. The "rising" (majesty in most translations) is then a reference to the waters overcoming the victim in the trial. Such trials would have been familiar in Canaan, providing very vivid language for the danger of the guilty being tried by God.

31:31 *My servants have never said, "He let others go hungry."* This verse has been diversely interpreted due to the ambiguities of the sequence and the meaning of the word *basar* [TH1319, ZH1413] (flesh), which could refer to meat for eating or to a person's physical body. As is evident from the next verse, the context is focused on hospitality. Pope (1965:207-208) compares these two verses with the story of Sodom (Gen 19). Job had not abandoned anyone to the streets, where they would be vulnerable to sexual predators. On the basis of linguistic parallels in various texts, he thinks that the literal "fill ourselves with his flesh" (v 31b) is a reference to sexual gratification. On this interpretation, Job disavows that males of his household ever desired relations with him. It is doubtful that such associations would have been made in this context; the verses are about food and lodging (so NLT). Jongeling (1974:38-40) has solid grammatical support for taking this as an impersonal question requiring a negative answer; those of Job's household have well said, "Were we ever not filled with his food?" He compares 14:4, "Who can bring purity out of an impure person? No one!"

31:33 *like other people.* The Heb. word (*'adam* [TH120, ZH132]) is the same as the name Adam; it is possible there is an allusion to the Genesis story.

31:35 *Let my accuser write.* This is a change of tense from the Heb., which is required by the context. Other commentators assume a line is missing.

31:39 *murdered its owners.* Rather than this idea or the expression "cause the death of its owners" (RSV), the translation should be "broken the spirit" (NIV). It is not that their breath is taken away, but they are driven to despair (cf. note on 11:20).

COMMENTARY

In this chapter Job catalogs fourteen transgressions that are a temptation to those in positions of influence and power. The offenses are presented in a variety of ways—sometimes with a question, sometimes with a conditional, and sometimes the Hebrew could be either. The variation is deliberate; attempts to create a uniformity in form are misguided. The number fourteen is deliberate literary style, in which items are given in a series of seven or its multiples. The organization of this code of honor does not correspond to other ethical lists, but it is a conscious exposition of what it means to live by the code of God's covenant. These are not high crimes but acts of misconduct that victimize vulnerable people—despicable behavior for persons in positions of trust. Job swore that he had not committed any of these, calling an appropriate curse upon himself if he should be found guilty in any way.

Citizens from every age have become familiar with people in powerful places ruining their reputation by their personal conduct. They may make grandiose promises of justice in political pronouncements, but they are abusive in relationships with those around them. It is sometimes argued that misconduct by modern politicians appears worse to us because we live in an age where the media rigorously scrutinizes individuals. This chapter in Job reminds us that there always has been scrutiny.

There is another matter worth our attention in this chapter—that is, it is founded on the values of the Decalogue much more directly than is generally recognized (Oeming 1994:363-366). In this chapter Job was examining the thoughts and attitudes that generate crime and sins against others; as such, Job was expanding upon and heightening the values found in the Ten Commandments. The Ten Commandments (the Decalogue) is the best-known summary of ethics in the Hebrew Bible

(Exod 20:1-17; Deut 5:6-21). It is a summary of the covenant code, the values that must govern human relationships with God and with other people.

It is unfortunate that the Decalogue is often conceived of as only being laws, for in reality it is a summary statement of the covenant relationship. In the Hebrew, it is said to be "the words" (*hadebarim* [TH1697, ZH1821]) that God granted to his people (Exod 20:1). Treating them as laws, we make the first to say "you shall have no other gods," when the words begin with the positive "I am the LORD your God." Expressed this way, it is clear that the primary requirement of the covenant is knowledge of the Creator and submission to him. A correct understanding of the lordship of the Creator demands a reverence to him and a respect for all of his creation. The emphasis on attitude may be seen most clearly in the final word, which says "you shall not covet." This directly addresses the thinking that precipitates violations against others, such as taking their life, their wife, their property, or speaking false words against them. It addresses our attitude towards God who demands uncompromising allegiance in how we represent him (word two), in the integrity of our speech (word three), in how we perform the work of God within his creation (word four), and in our attitude towards those who give us life and prepare us for life (word five).

It is not surprising that the legalistic Saul of Tarsus began to realize the problem of his sin beginning with covetousness (Rom 7:7-12), for through it he recognized his violation of all the other relationships. As a legalist Saul had been righteous, for he could keep the rules. When he understood that the covenant requirement was more than a list of rules, he recognized his sin. Job was fully alive to the starting point of right conduct—the attitude of his mind in relation to God and others. Job was concerned about his attitudes and words in human relations, but these cannot be separated from his attitude toward creation and the Creator. The sequence of the first four words is discernible in a major section of his code of honor (31:24-32). A violation in any area is an indication of a more fundamental problem of integrity in our relationship with God and others.

In this chapter, Job began with the last of the ten words (31:1), which said you should not covet the wife of your neighbor (Exod 20:17; Deut 5:21). Job heightened and expanded this warning against lust; he would not even cast his eyes longingly on an unmarried woman. Intercourse with an unmarried woman was not considered to be adultery, since men, particularly in positions of power, could have more than one wife. Such an act required the man to take the woman as a wife (Exod 22:16-17) or give her the dowry if her father refused her in marriage. Job held to the ideal. Sexual relations must be in the context of marriage commitment, and anything less is a violation of a woman. Job reflected on the design that God has for human relations, recognizing that there is punishment for those who do wrong and that God is aware of every action. A man of honor begins with the control of his mind.

A man of honor should also consider his children before committing adultery. Quite naturally, children want to grow up with both of their parents. Lust for the wife of another (31:9-11) destroys the very foundations of human development.

Lust burns like the fires of hell with destructive power, causing one to lose every-thing, which is expressed as having a crop uprooted. In this context, "crop" is a refer-ence to the family that is uprooted and destroyed by a broken marriage.

In ancient times, servants were also a part of the extended family. There was a ten-dency for people to take advantage of them and not protect their rights. Job would not do this (31:13-15). He knew God would treat servants fairly, for they were cre-ated equal and deserve the same consideration as anyone else. Every human life has an equal dignity before God.

The concept of the Sabbath is present only to the extent that the sign of redemp-tion has implications for the poor. The Sabbath was a sign of the covenant (Exod 31:12-14) of those who were holy—that is, those set apart into a redemptive rela-tionship with God. It was a sign of those whom God had redeemed from bondage (Deut 5:14-15) and had been given the freedom of a new life. The specifics of its ob-servance are never given, for they vary with the times, but the principle is that it must signify redemption from the slavery of life. This redemption pertains to all, regardless of status; it is for the servants as well. Meeting the needs of servants, or-phans, and widows is one way of observing the sign of the Sabbath, since its pur-pose is to signify "rest" for those who are burdened. Sabbath rest was a cycle of days, a cycle of years, and a cycle of a series of years (the Jubilee) in which provision was made for the poor (Lev 25:1-55; Deut 15:1-18). The Jubilee addressed the problem of the landless—the homeless who have inadequate shelter and clothing. Job made special mention of these (31:19-20), for this is a critical part of living the life of the covenant before God. It is easy to become irritated with "street people" because they tend to violate the properties of others. If Job had ever "raised his hand against them" (even in his thinking), he asked that his arm be wrenched from its socket. Job took seriously the spirit of the Sabbath requirements, rather than limiting him-self to satisfying the letter of the law or the expectations of the community about what activities he should do at certain times.

The observance of the Sabbath has its basis in a total commitment to the rule of the Creator, a subject Job addressed at length (31:24-32). The first "word" (com-mandment) requires that our confidence be in God alone, so that nothing else may compete for that position of trust. Job declared that he had never made wealth his security (31:24-25). There was also a tendency to become enamored with the cre-ated universe to the point of worshipping it. In modern times this has extended to the point of deifying it in whole (pantheism) or in part (panentheism). Environ-mentalism is a necessary aspect of stewardship, but to worship the tree is to distort the proper relation of the various aspects of creation. Some people do not have the ability to distinguish between proper use of the tree and its worship, between ani-mal rights and the subversion of human rights. Job declared that he knew how to let God be God (31:26-28), that he understood what it means to be a representative (image) of God within the created order.

Job's next meditation led him to the whole notion of oath-taking (addressed in the third commandment). One of the limitations of humans is their ability to know

the truth about what others say or do. They deal with this by taking oaths by some
higher authority. The use of the name of God was the highest authority by which an
oath could be taken, but it could be used in a double respect. One can call a curse
upon oneself if the truth is not spoken, or one can call a curse upon others because
we believe them to be devious. Job had not called any such curse upon his enemies
(31:29-30); he was scrupulous about showing love for his enemy in the sense that
their ultimate well-being was his concern. He had been careful to show hospitality
to all (31:31-32), a requirement of the highest order wherever there are no hotels.
Hospitality had its dangers, particularly with strangers (some of them were violent
criminals), but to leave someone without shelter exposed them to the violence of
criminals in the area and was itself a kind of crime.

Job concluded with two affirmations of his integrity before God. His life had
been an open book. He had not been afraid to live his faith before others (31:33-
34), with the attendant danger that he would be ridiculed or even denigrated and
ostracized. He had lived by the dictum that the Lord is the king of all kings and he
must fear no other. Divine approval had been his highest goal (31:35-37); the
deeds of his life were his signature. What Job desired was the verdict of the one who
had tested him. He could wear that verdict confidently as testimony to his life. He
would gladly account for every step he had taken. Job had the ground as a witness to
this testimony of his life (31:38-40). Figuratively, the ground is a witness to everything that happens upon it; the murder of Abel was known because the ground
cried out in protest (Gen 4:10). Job was unafraid of anything the ground might have
to say, for his every step upon it had been taken with integrity.

These words of Job have been compared with those of a posthumous tribunal
(Griffiths 1983:200-204). The parallels to Egyptian texts are remarkable, but there
is no comparison to the context in which these statements are made. The Egyptians
were concerned about the balance of deeds done in a tribunal before the gods after
death. Job was giving testimony to a life lived before God, a life that is a witness to
his covenant commitment. It was God's judgment that was important to Job. That
judgment showed that he had lived by faith in the One who says, "I am the LORD
your God."

IV. Response (Elihu): Suffering as a Discipline (32:1–37:24)
A. Divine Revelation (32:1–33:13)
1. The voice of youth (32:1-22)

Job's three friends refused to reply further to him because he kept insisting on
his innocence.

²Then Elihu son of Barakel the Buzite,
of the clan of Ram, became angry. He was
angry because Job refused to admit that
he had sinned and that God was right in
punishing him. ³He was also angry with

Job's three friends, for they made God*
appear to be wrong by their inability
to answer Job's arguments. ⁴Elihu had
waited for the others to speak to Job because they were older than he. ⁵But when
he saw that they had no further reply, he
spoke out angrily. ⁶Elihu son of Barakel
the Buzite said,

"I am young and you are old,
so I held back from telling you what
I think.
⁷I thought, 'Those who are older should
speak,
for wisdom comes with age.'
⁸But there is a spirit* within people,
the breath of the Almighty within
them,
that makes them intelligent.
⁹Sometimes the elders are not wise.
Sometimes the aged do not
understand justice.
¹⁰So listen to me,
and let me tell you what I think.

¹¹"I have waited all this time,
listening very carefully to your
arguments,
listening to you grope for words.
¹²I have listened,
but not one of you has refuted Job
or answered his arguments.

¹³And don't tell me, 'He is too wise for us.
Only God can convince him.'
¹⁴If Job had been arguing with me,
I would not answer with your kind
of logic!
¹⁵You sit there baffled,
with nothing more to say.
¹⁶Should I continue to wait, now that
you are silent?
Must I also remain silent?
¹⁷No, I will say my piece.
I will speak my mind.
¹⁸For I am full of pent-up words,
and the spirit within me urges me on.
¹⁹I am like a cask of wine without a vent,
like a new wineskin ready to burst!
²⁰I must speak to find relief,
so let me give my answers.
²¹I won't play favorites
or try to flatter anyone.
²²For if I tried flattery,
my Creator would soon destroy me.

32:3 As in ancient Hebrew scribal tradition; the Masoretic Text reads *Job.*   32:8 Or *Spirit;* also in 32:18.

NOTES

32:1 *insisting on his innocence.* A few MT mss, the Gr., and the Syriac say Job was inno-cent in the opinion of the friends. Dhorme (1984:472) considers this to be the original reading, since it indicates the reason for the end of the dialog. Elihu then speaks because he is unable to tolerate this surrender. However, there is nothing to suggest that Job had prevailed over the friends to convince them of his righteousness. They may have been silenced by Job (32:13-16), but that does not mean they were convinced.

32:2 *Barakel the Buzite, of the clan of Ram.* Unlike the names of the three friends, which may be regarded as more Edomite in their connections, most of Elihu's elaborate name is Heb. in origin. Ram is one of the ancestors of David (Ruth 4:19; 1 Chr 2:9, 25); Buz is the brother of Uz, a nephew of Abraham (Gen 22:21). Barakel is found in business documents of the Persian period. It is the name of several people from the Murashu family in the reign of Artaxerxes I (Hilprecht 1898:52).

refused to admit that he had sinned. Job had not said he was sinless, but he had said his sins should be forgiven (e.g., 7:20-21). Job declared himself either to be just before God (the expression "before God" is similar in syntax to 4:17, cf. Num 32:22) or that he has been right rather than God (cf. Gen 38:26 where Tamar is in the right rather than Judah).

32:3 *for they made God appear to be wrong.* The present Heb. text says the three friends had condemned Job (cf. NLT mg). Some translations (NLT, REB, NJB) follow an emenda-tion to the Heb. text defended in rabbinic tradition. The tradition concerns deliberate changes to the text called *tiqqune sopherim.* In each instance, the change involved a removal of reference to God, presumably because it might be considered irreverent. In this case, the tradition of the rabbis was that the text originally said the three friends had condemned God. Since God ought not to be condemned, this was changed to say the friends con-demned Job and so it reads in the present MT.

Various ancient commentaries on books of the Heb. Bible mention a total of eighteen deliberate changes made by copyists (*tiqqune sopherim*). In this instance, the rabbinic tradition that the text originally read "God" may have been because they could not understand why the friends should have condemned Job. If the three friends had no answer to the claim that Job was righteous, it seems strange to say that they would then condemn Job. Their failure to prove Job wrong would mean they were then condemning God. In the previous verse, Elihu had declared Job to be wrong because he justified himself. It would seem that Elihu would then condemn the friends for declaring God to be wrong since they had been unable to convict Job.

The evidence for the original text is ambiguous (McCarthy 1981:115-120). The earliest translations used a Heb. text different from that of the rabbinic tradition, but none of them read "God" in this verse. The more difficult reading is the name "Job," which is a good reason to consider it the original wording. In that case, Elihu condemns the friends because they were unable to refute Job and yet declared him to be wrong (cf. KJV, RSV, NIV).

32:4 *Elihu had waited for the others to speak.* The Heb. includes a reference to Job, but it is phrased awkwardly. The least amount of change is to say Elihu waited with Job while the friends spoke to Job (REB, NJB). A more radical change is to say Elihu waited to speak to Job (RSV, NRSV, NIV), implying Elihu's intent to correct Job rather than the friends.

32:8 *there is a spirit within people.* The word "spirit" (*ruakh* [TH7307, ZH8120]) refers to thoughts (cf. Ezek 11:5, "I know every thought"). Elihu was making the point that the ability to think is a gift of God, but this is not limited to those who possess God's Spirit in some particular way.

32:14 *If Job had been arguing with me.* This is the simplest interpretation of the Heb. but requires reading a conditional (*lu'*) by revocalizing the negative (*lo'*) of the MT, which says "he has not directed his words against me" (RSV, NRSV, NIV). The MT reading does not flow as well with the next line. Others revise more radically; "I shall not string words together" (REB) is an unwarranted change.

32:15 *You sit there baffled.* The Heb. has the third person: "they sit there baffled." Rather than direct address, it seems Elihu was telling them about his thoughts when they fell silent, which continue in the next verse.

32:22 *if I tried flattery.* The Heb. construction is a condition contrary to fact (cf. the Heb. of Isa 1:9) rather than a negative (cf. NIV; contra RSV, REB, NJB).

COMMENTARY

Elihu has not been well received by many readers of Job. In the seventh century, Gregory the Great in his *Moralia in Iob* described Elihu as a haughty presider under the pretense of being a faithful teacher (Adriaen 1985:1146 [23.4]). Martin Luther made no reference to Elihu in his sermons or lectures, but in his *Table Talk* he made note of him as an "empty gas bag" (Luther 1912:1.68 [¶142]). In recent times Edwin Good, in his *Reading of Job with a Translation*, describes Elihu as a pompous, intensive bore and an opaque thinker with pretentious language that is often quite unintelligible (1990:321).

Elihu has not fared better in the analysis of literary critics attempting to understand the development and meaning of the composition of Job. They have generally concluded that Elihu's speeches must be an addition to the book. Elihu makes no appearance in the epilogue, his speeches interrupt the continuity between the dialog and the response of God, and he contributes almost nothing to the content or movement of the book. Many believe these speeches were composed by the same author; and if it was not the same author, it must have been someone not only acquainted with the content of the dialog but steeped in its thought patterns and modes of expression as well. Freedman (1968:55-57) has compiled dozens of parallels, allusions, and correlations. His explanation of Elihu's speeches is that they were originally separate compositions that the author intended to insert within the dialog of Job with his friends in order to refute or counterbalance Job. The author apparently did not realize the enormity of the task of adding this fourth character to the dialog, or he abandoned it as unsatisfactory, but other copyists preserved his work by inserting the whole speech after the dialog. Such literary observations about the close relationship between the dialog and Elihu are very helpful, but explanations as to how it could have come to its present form remain completely speculative. Wahl provides a helpful review of studies in the "historical-critical" epoch (1993:8-23), but it cannot be said these have led to a better understanding of the book of Job. It has been impossible to establish a more satisfactory arrangement of the book, let alone provide an explanation for how it came into its present form. It is true that ancient copyists sometimes preserved more than one form of a work, as is well known in Jeremiah,[1] but each version is both comprehensible and a literary masterpiece as it was preserved. The same is true for the book of Job in the only version in which we have received it.

A further error with the book of Job is to read it as if it were constructed as a theodicy to answer an intellectual problem. Abraham Ibn Esra in his *Hiobkommentar* in the twelfth century attempted to provide a positive assessment of the Elihu speeches. He interpreted the Elihu speeches as a basic solution to the great question of Job concerning the compatibility of divine justice and the suffering of the righteous. The Elihu speeches develop a theology of the purpose of suffering; suffering can be a punishment for sin and become a means to prevent further offense, or it can secure a blessed future in the life to come. The great medieval exegete was correct in his observations, which were developed extensively in subsequent times, but this still does not resolve the question of the present structure of the book. In the end, Elihu does not provide a solution to the suffering of Job, and the author could not have intended it to be the solution to the mystery of human suffering generally.

Appreciating great literature is somewhat like appreciating great music. The progression of the piece is determined by certain patterns familiar to the people of the time of the composition. Music history is an important aspect of enjoying music because without it a great masterpiece in music may seem redundant, pretentious, and tedious. In the times of Gregory the Great and Martin Luther, there was little recognition of the original literary milieu of ancient composers, so to them Elihu seemed to be a "windbag" (cf. 15:2). The author of Job had shaped his profound and compelling poetry around the structure of a dialog with elements of a dispute or legal case. Job had demanded a hearing (9:3), he longed for an arbiter (9:32-34), and he wanted a chance to defend himself directly before God (13:13-15). The dispute could not be complete without an arbiter, one who presided over the case and recommended a resolution for the problem. At the beginning of his speech, Elihu points out that there has been no arbiter for Job (32:12) who can answer for the charges he has made against God. This seems to be the role Elihu fills. His task is unlike that of any other dispute, since no arbiter could be more qualified than the disputants in this case. Though a resolution may be impossible, there must be a viewpoint outside that of the litigants themselves.

There are two disputes in the dialog, one between Job and his friends and the other between Job and God. Both of these are set against the dispute in the councils of heaven between God and the Accuser. In all of this, Job had been denied a fair hearing; false charges were laid against him, most specifically by Eliphaz (22:5-9), and he had been condemned. It was up to Elihu to be sure Job received an impartial trial against the charges that he had lived as a tyrant in a position of power. Such arbitration naturally follows the code of honor (ch 31) that Job maintains has been the rule of his life. As an arbiter for Job, Elihu must also deal with his charges against God, which is what the friends had failed to do. It would seem presumptuous that anyone should speak for God against the wise who also represent God. As observed by Habel (1984:88-92), the poet subtly portrays this arbiter as a brilliant young fool. Eliphaz protested that a wise man does not answer with empty talk (15:2), yet that is exactly what Elihu intended to do (32:17-20); he uncorked himself and let his words gush forth. This pretentious modesty is a reminder that there is no intellectual solution to the problem of Job, which began in the councils of heaven, or to the problem of human suffering in this world.

In this opening section of Elihu's speech, Elihu is introduced with an elaborate Hebrew family pedigree. The meaning of the names is of particular significance. Barakel means either "bless God" or "God has blessed." Ram means "highly exalted" and Buz means "scorn" or "contempt." This is an excellent description of the intruder, who is scornful of his elders and conscious of his noble role as the defender of God. The name Elihu is of the greatest significance. It is the same name as the prophet Elijah; the difference in pronunciation of *'eliyahu* [TH452/452A, ZH488/489] (Elijah) for *'elihu* [TH453/453A, ZH490/491] (Elihu) first appears in the medieval ages in the Masoretic Text.[2] The name means "Yah is my God"; Yah is the abbreviated form of the name Yahweh, as in the Hebrew word "hallelujah." This name is most appropriate, since Elihu was the defender of God, just as Elijah was in the prophetic story in 1 Kings 17-18.

Elihu introduces himself in a reluctant manner (32:6-22), saying almost nothing at all and finding it necessary to repeat it several times. In spite of the caricature created in this "seemingly windy chapter about windy words" (Skehan 1969:380), a formal structure is evident in the repetition of particular words. The phrase "tell you what I think" is repeated three times with the same Hebrew words (32:6, 10, 17). The whole poem, accordingly, is divisible into three stanzas, each of which begin and end with the same words. Elihu thought age should speak, but now he must speak, and the aged friends must listen. Elihu waited for them to give an answer, and then waited when they fell silent. Elihu decided that he must answer so that he might receive relief. The three stanzas are introduced with the announcement that Elihu will speak his mind, and Elihu concludes this first speech by saying that he will not flatter anyone. The poem is a formal rhetorical exercise introducing a reticent individual who has something he must say in spite of his age and inadequacy.

There is a progression in the introduction of Elihu. The prose section presents the compelling reasons why this speech is necessary. The friends had utterly failed to bring a resolution to the dispute. As the silence fell, Job had been vindicated and God was condemned. Job was still demanding that God answer him; he maintained he was right rather than God. The friends had failed to answer Job and yet they condemned him (according to the MT), or else the friends had condemned God by not refuting Job (according to rabbinic tradition's proposed emmendation; see note on 32:3). Either way, it is evident that God was in need of defense more than ever as silence descended on this scene. The argument came to a halt and appeared to end with God as wicked and Job as righteous. Such a conclusion was an outrage to Elihu; it demanded intervention to set the record straight.

As an arbiter in such a situation, Elihu had to consider his role and his limitations carefully, and he had to proceed with utmost caution. He dare not speak before those who were the most qualified and whose status granted them the privilege of being heard. At the same time, he dare not let his fears silence him completely. God granted the gift of intellectual ability to all humans regardless of age. The aged are not always wise and there comes a time when they must listen to a bit of wisdom. On this basis, Elihu insisted he must speak and they must give him a hearing.

Elihu had dutifully, and perhaps with difficulty, waited until those in the dispute had utterly exhausted everything they might have to say. They had shown beyond doubt that they could not refute Job, which means they had been unable to pass fair judgment in the dispute. Elihu used a technical legal term for one who corrects the injustice of a situation. The term is found frequently outside the Scriptures to describe the procedure of arriving at an impartial decision (Wahl 1993:49-50). An Akkadian hymn to the sun god describes him as the prince of his palace who acts as an advocate of the weak, refuses bribes, and makes fair decisions. Job did not have such a mediator. The friends failed in their accusations against Job, which means they had not judged him correctly. Now they dare not say that no one else could. Should he continue to wait now that they have nothing more to say? Could he be the kind of judge needed in this situation?

Elihu could contain himself no longer; he was like a balloon ready to burst. He may have been unwitting in describing himself as pent up with wind ready to explode (Habel 1985:444), or perhaps he was preempting the friends by saying what they were thinking before they could ridicule him. Foolish as he may appear, his words had to be heard. Elihu intended to avoid favoritism and to be an impartial arbiter, but in the end his speech offered more than his introduction promised.

He took up three major contentions Job had made (Gordis 1965:105) and refuted them in reverse order. Job had said he was innocent (33:8, 9), that God's persecution was an act of base power and injustice (33:10-11), and that God had

ignored his suffering by refusing to answer him (33:12-13). Elihu, the defender of
God, began by explaining that God had spoken and was speaking (33:14-26) in various ways. Elihu contended that God as the creator plays no favorites (ch 34) and
that he does not pervert justice. Finally, he said it was foolish to think that somehow
our actions affect God for good or ill (ch 35). The problem with humans is that they
suffer from their own base perversity.

ENDNOTES

1. Jeremiah in the Greek Bible, used by the eastern Orthodox churches, has a different
   arrangement; the section of prophecies against the nations (chs 46–52 in the MT) is
   quite logically placed immediately after the announcement of the destruction of Babylon (Jer 25:13). The Gr. version is also shorter throughout. The shorter version of Jeremiah is found in the Heb. manuscripts of Qumran, along with the longer version. The
   Christians preserved the shorter version in Gr.; the Jews preserved the longer version
   in Heb. Protestant translations of Jeremiah are from the Heb. MT, usually without reference to the other version.
2. The pronunciation in the other occurrences of Elihu is the same even though the spelling may be 'elihu' [TH453A, ZH491] (1 Sam 1:1; 1 Chr 12:20) or 'elihu (1 Chr 26:7; 27:18).
   Elijah is consistently given a distinct pronunciation.

▶ 2. An arbiter for Job (33:1-13)

¹"Listen to my words, Job;
   pay attention to what I have
      to say.
²Now that I have begun to speak,
   let me continue.
³I speak with all sincerity;
   I speak the truth.
⁴For the Spirit of God has made me,
   and the breath of the Almighty
      gives me life.
⁵Answer me, if you can;
   make your case and take your stand.
⁶Look, you and I both belong to God.
   I, too, was formed from clay.
⁷So you don't need to be afraid of me.
   I won't come down hard on you.

⁸"You have spoken in my hearing,
   and I have heard your very words.
⁹You said, 'I am pure; I am without sin;
   I am innocent; I have no guilt.
¹⁰God is picking a quarrel with me,
   and he considers me his enemy.
¹¹He puts my feet in the stocks
   and watches my every move.'

¹²"But you are wrong, and I will show
      you why.
   For God is greater than any human
      being.
¹³So why are you bringing a charge
      against him?
   Why say he does not respond to
      people's complaints?

NOTES

33:3 I speak with all sincerity. The first line lacks a verb in the Heb. Many commentators
(e.g., Fohrer 1989:454; Driver and Gray 1921:2.239) have felt it necessary to supply one,
often to say "my mind overflows." However, this misses the point of the verse, which
emphasizes the purity of Elihu's thought. The expression "uprightness of mind" is found in
a number of other occurrences (cf. Deut 9:5) and is to be preferred here (Jenni and
Westermann 1971:1.794). The use of a noun clause is to give the attribute a certain emphasis (Gesenius §141c)—in this case, the quality of the words Elihu is about to share. Gordis
(1978:371) says the line is "far-fetched and awkward."

33:4 gives me life. The Gr. says that the breath of the Almighty "teaches me" (*tekhawweni* [TH2331, ZH2555]) rather than "gives life" (*tekhayyeni* [TH2421, ZH2649]). The Gr. repeats the same thought as expressed earlier by Elihu (cf. 32:8) and is fitting in the context. Though the Gr. may have had a variant text (Orlinsky 1965:46-47), it is also suspect as a borrowing of the translation from the earlier reference (Heater 1982:100).

COMMENTARY

In this section, Elihu begins with a direct address to Job. Though he also spoke to the friends, Job was the focus of his attention. No one had answered Job's challenge to God, which put God in the wrong. If Elihu could successfully answer Job, he would accomplish what the friends failed to do—he would establish the justice of God.

Elihu claimed to have the genuine words of God but at the same time did not presume that he was superior to Job. He spoke with a pure mind and authentic knowledge, even though he—like Job—had been made from clay. The idea that Elihu was given life by the breath of God fits the Creation story (Gen 2:7 has the same word), but the idea that God has instructed Job, as the Greek says, would be virtually equivalent with what Elihu earlier affirmed (cf. 32:8). The point important to Elihu is that the work of creation provided humans with intellectual ability. Furthermore, Elihu did not consider himself to have any knowledge superior to Job's. They were on an equal footing before God, so the arguments of Elihu need cause no alarm. Elihu was making a deliberate reference to an earlier plea Job had made (13:20-21) in his desire to confront God. Job had asked that God remove his heavy hand and not terrify him with dread. Elihu was about to impart the truth of God to Job from a pure mind, but Job need not be threatened in any way.

Elihu went on to speak of particular claims he thought Job had made (33:8-13). He heard Job make the claim that he was sinless, that his life was pure. Job, on different occasions, had acknowledged his sin. He had used the term "pure" (*zakh* [TH2134, ZH2341]) only in relation to his prayer (16:17) and protested only that his punishment was monstrously disproportionate to his sins. Job had said that God was always seeking out his sin (10:6), that he had made Job's life bitter with punishment from the sins of his youth (13:26). Job has certainly claimed to live a life of integrity (9:20-21) and without compromise, but that is not the same thing as claiming he was without sin. Secondly, Elihu argues that Job has said God acts out of wanton power and injustice. In 33:11 Elihu quotes Job's words from 13:27, Job's complaint that God had made him an enemy and pursued him the way a leaf is driven in the wind (13:24-25). Finally, Elihu points out that Job had complained that God is so far superior to humans that he can simply overwhelm them or ignore them. Job had been frustrated by the divine silence. God is so great you might not even know it when he passes by (9:10-11), no one asks him what he is doing when he plunders (9:12), and even one in the right cannot make a case (9:15). God continually expressed his displeasure (16:9) and violated Job (19:6-7) without any response to his protests. Elihu insists that in this charge Job was wrong (33:12). God does speak to humans in more than one way, as Elihu would explain—God speaks through visions and he speaks through suffering in order to rescue people from the punishment of death.

B. The Words of Correction (33:14-33)

14 For God speaks again and again,
   though people do not recognize it.
15 He speaks in dreams, in visions of
   the night,
   when deep sleep falls on people
   as they lie in their beds.
16 He whispers in their ears
   and terrifies them with warnings.
17 He makes them turn from doing
   wrong;
   he keeps them from pride.
18 He protects them from the grave,
   from crossing over the river of
   death.

19 "Or God disciplines people with pain
   on their sickbeds,
   with ceaseless aching in their
   bones.
20 They lose their appetite
   for even the most delicious food.
21 Their flesh wastes away,
   and their bones stick out.
22 They are at death's door;
   the angels of death wait for them.

23 "But if an angel from heaven
   appears—
   a special messenger to intercede
   for a person
   and declare that he is upright—

24 he will be gracious and say,
   'Rescue him from the grave,
   for I have found a ransom for his
   life.'
25 Then his body will become as healthy
   as a child's,
   firm and youthful again.
26 When he prays to God,
   he will be accepted.
   And God will receive him with joy
   and restore him to good standing.
27 He will declare to his friends,
   'I sinned and twisted the truth,
   but it was not worth it.*
28 God rescued me from the grave,
   and now my life is filled with light.'

29 "Yes, God does these things
   again and again for people.
30 He rescues them from the grave
   so they may enjoy the light of life.
31 Mark this well, Job. Listen to me,
   for I have more to say.
32 But if you have anything to say,
   go ahead.
   Speak, for I am anxious to see
   you justified.
33 But if not, then listen to me.
   Keep silent and I will teach you
   wisdom!"

33:27 Greek version reads *but he [God] did not punish me as my sin deserved.*

NOTES

33:14 *again and again.* The verse is an enumeration often used in poetic style (Steinmann 1995:294): "God speaks one way, even two ways." Elihu began his response to the charges Job had made by naming two ways that God speaks: dreams and illness.

33:16 *terrifies them with warnings.* "[He] sealeth their instruction" (KJV) is not the sense required here, though it is a possible rendering of the Heb. "Frightens him with appari-tions" (NJB) is based on the LXX. The translation commonly adopted (NLT, RSV, NIV, REB) requires only the revocalization of the MT.

33:17 *makes them turn from doing wrong.* The line says that the warning "turns one away from a deed," which in context must mean "evil deed" or "evil work." Usually, the phrase is emended to specify that God will "turn man aside from his deed" (RSV)—that is, the particular intended action of an individual, which was averted before it could actually take place.

33:18 *crossing over the river of death.* The translation "perishing by the sword" (KJV, RSV, NIV) is a common meaning of the word *shelakh* [TH7973, ZH8939] but is a poor parallel in this verse. A parallel expression later in the chapter (33:28) makes it clear that a crossing into the place of death is meant. The word *shelakh* is also a water canal used in ancient Semitic writings to speak about the river of the netherworld (Tsevat 1954:43-45), which properly complements "grave" earlier in this verse.

33:23 *angel from heaven . . . special messenger.* These two Heb. terms refer to one intermediary. The first is simply "messenger," sometimes designating a heavenly messenger as in the expression "the angel of the LORD." The second term may refer to an interpreter (Gen 42:23), a mediator (Isa 43:27), or an ambassador (2 Chr 32:31). Only on this occasion in the Heb. Bible does it refer to a heavenly being said to be "one in a thousand." On the basis of Semitic usage, the significance of "one in a thousand" can be established to be one from a numerous body of heavenly intermediaries (Gevirtz 1990:147-153) who act as advocates or agents for humans.

33:26 *God will receive him with joy.* The Gr. has an excellent paraphrase of the Heb. idiom (Orlinsky 1959:160-161) that says the person who has found mercy will appear before God to worship with joy. Though the expression is often used of appearing at the Temple, the sense here is only that of being alive in God's favor.

restore him to good standing. Since the person has already been described as accepted before God, it seems unnecessary to say he has been restored. Some translations omit this line (REB, NAB), and others connect it to the following verse as a confession of restored salvation (RSV, NJB). If the word "restore" is given the sense of "pay tribute" (Gordis 1978:378-379), it forms a pleasing poetic parallel with the following line.

33:27 *it was not worth it.* The precise meaning of the Heb. idiom is uncertain. "It was of no worth to me" is a common later idiom (Jastrow 1532), which is suitable here. Other translations say the penalty was not inflicted as deserved (RSV, NIV, NRSV, NJB).

33:29 *again and again.* Lit. "two, even three times." See note on 33:14.

COMMENTARY

God speaks three ways to people in order to rescue their lives from death. The first two are ordinary; God speaks through dreams (33:14-18) and God speaks through illness (33:19-22). The third means is supernatural; it happens through a divine messenger who intervenes and saves guilty persons from the punishment of the grave (33:23-24) so that their health is restored and they are saved from death (33:25-28). God continually does these things to spare people from "the pit." It will be observed that the reference to the grave or the pit occurs five times in this section as Elihu explains the ways in which God responds to suffering. In conclusion, Elihu challenged Job to answer him if he could (33:31-33).

Night is often the time for reflections that are otherwise preempted by the busyness of the day. These reflections stay within our subconscious throughout the day and then surface later during sleep. Elihu maintained that sometimes these thoughts are a divine warning about the way in which people are prone to choose their own path rather than the way God has chosen. The decisions that Elihu has in mind are moral issues, matters of right conduct. Moral failure is a matter of pride, for it assumes we know better than God about what is right or at least that we can escape the harm that comes from such actions. Every sin in some sense has its origin in the hubris of humans who think that they can be their own god. The original temptation (Gen 3:4-5) was the promise of human autonomy, the thought that humans can do as they please without accountability. This kind of arrogance leads to death, but God intervenes to warn against this destructive thinking (33:16). God turns people from their arrogant ways before they can follow through on their ideas of independence. As expressed in a Hasidic proverb (Gordis 1978:375), it is better to be a sinner who knows that he is a sinner than to be a saint who knows that he is a saint. No doubt, Elihu had in mind the days when Job was a revered and powerful man and was reminding him that God warns such people in their thoughts about their proper position before him.

Sometimes God speaks to people through pain (33:19). Pain can be tormenting and seemingly endless. Pain robs sufferers of appetite; they can become so emaciated that their bones protrude, so they are unsightly. Illness may take them right to the door of death where the emissaries of the world beyond "the river" await to bear the dead across. Yet even this can be a correction. God has not abandoned such individuals; they may be restored to health. Job was convinced that only the grave was left for him, but Elihu did not believe this was so.

Elihu believed that God has his intermediaries, thousands of them, who may intervene and spare a person from death. A belief in such messengers is common in other ancient writings, but there is little reference to them in Scripture. Elihu did not have in mind the divinities that belonged to the pantheons of other religions, nor does he mean the "angels of death" (33:22), who have quite a different function. It is true that the Greek translation has linked the "death-bearers" with the "advocates," but it is quite periphrastic at this point. The Greek translator was not necessarily assuming there was no positive function for angels as mediators (Gammie 1985:5-6), but he may have linked these intermediaries to the death-bearing function of the Accuser in the prologue. The "special messenger" (NLT) is certainly to be distinguished from the "angels of death" in the text (Mach 1992:107-108), and the dark view of angels that threaten harm was not determinative for the later concept of fallen angels as demons. Elihu was not thinking about the kind of messenger seen in the prologue because he considered these to be advocates rather than accusers. They will declare that a person is upright (33:23, NLT, NRSV). It is not that they will declare to a person what is right (NIV, RSV, REB, NAB, NJB); Elihu is not talking about moral rehabilitation but about physical rehabilitation, the restoration of the sick. The heavenly advocate will declare the upright state of those threatened by death, and they will be spared. They will find favor with God and will give him praise in the great assembly, as is often affirmed in the Psalms (e.g., Ps 22:19-24). They will make confession of the destructive power of their sin, recognizing that their decisions were of no worth. Their life will come to be enlightened as they experience again the blessing of God.

God does these two and three things continuously to protect his people from slipping into the grave, where they can no longer praise him. These "two and three" things are a poetic technique to create parallel lines, not a precise tabulation (see note on 33:29). Though three actions may be distinguished, it is obvious that at least the last two relate to each other. The correction that comes through illness is achieved through the mediation of God's grace and may be considered two aspects of the same thing. God desires that the lives of people be filled with light, a point that is repeated (33:28, 30). God does not design a punishing illness simply to bring one to death. Elihu was confident that Job could not refute this argument, though he would give Job opportunity to defend his charge that God had made him an enemy and consigned him to death. Ironically, Elihu says that he wants to show that Job is right; this is a way of saying that he was not trying to win an argument for argument's sake. Elihu simply wanted truth to prevail. Though he invited Job to speak, he was so confident that Job could have nothing more to say that he immediately asked for silence so he could make his next point.

◆   ## C. The Work of Justice (34:1-37)

1. Job's charge of injustice (34:1-9)

Then Elihu said:

2 "Listen to me, you wise men.
Pay attention, you who have knowledge.
3 Job said, 'The ear tests the words it hears
just as the mouth distinguishes between foods.'
4 So let us discern for ourselves what is right;
let us learn together what is good.
5 For Job also said, 'I am innocent,

but God has taken away my rights.
6 I am innocent, but they call me a liar.
My suffering is incurable, though I have not sinned.'
7 "Tell me, has there ever been a man like Job,
with his thirst for irreverent talk?
8 He chooses evil people as companions.
He spends his time with wicked men.
9 He has even said, 'Why waste time trying to please God?'

NOTES

34:6 *they call me a liar.* The MT says "I am a liar." This is interpreted to mean "I am counted a liar" or interrogatively as "shall I lie?" Other translations emend the text: "my judge is treating me cruelly" (NJB) expresses what Job had said (cf. 30:21). The LXX indicates that this may be another deliberate change of the scribes (*tiqqune sopherim*) to protect the name of God (McCarthy 1981:209-211). According to that translation, the Heb. text used by the translator said "he [God] has lied about my case." The ancient rabbinic explanation for the textual difference is that it was deliberately changed to eliminate the inference that God could lie.

My suffering is incurable. The Heb. more lit. says "his arrow inflicts an incurable wound" (NIV), a reference to Job saying that God has pierced him with his arrows (6:4). There is no need to emend "arrow" (*khets* [TH2671, ZH2932]) to "wound" (*makhats* [TH4273, ZH4731]), since Job had described his pain as God attacking him with the weapons of war (16:13-14).

COMMENTARY

Elihu proceeded to take up the second charge he had heard Job make (33:10-11), that God had unjustly faulted him and made him an enemy. Elihu had founded that charge by reference to Job's statements that God had pursued him and imprisoned him as an enemy (cf. 13:24, 27), indicting him with trumped up charges (13:26) of sins long past. Before taking up that charge, Elihu affirmed that he had wisdom to impart (34:2-4) and established that Job had taken up the way of the sinner (34:5-9) in his charges against God.

Elihu began with a wisdom proverb (34:3) that Job had quoted earlier (12:11), which appears to have been a common saying. Its point is that wisdom is gained through analogies with observable phenomena. Just as good food is judged through the sense of taste, so truth is discerned through the sense of hearing. The senses are channels through which we come to know the order of the world. Job had quoted the proverb as part of a series of wisdom sayings in order to challenge the usual assertions of wisdom. According to convention, wisdom belonged to the aged (12:12), who have heard its truths from previous generations. Job had argued that there was a disorder, particularly in society (12:14-25), that wisdom did not acknowledge or understand. Elihu returned to the appeal of conventional wisdom (34:3-4). It is possible to discern what is right and what is good. Though the words "right" and "good" are parallel terms in two poetic lines, there is a distinction to be made between them (Wahl 1993:75-76). The right (*mishpat* [TH4941, ZH5477]) refers to that knowledge of correct order against which every particular situation must be evaluated. Determining the "right" is often a matter of legal decision. The "good" is a knowledge of that which is beneficial and useful so that an individual may avoid that which is harmful. Knowledge of the good is the basis for personal decision. Job had presented a view of the world that was almost a form of anarchy; the wise, the rulers, and the priests (12:17-19) could all be robbed of the ability to fulfill their respective roles. Job considered himself to be a victim of this kind of injustice. Elihu would take up this charge of anarchy and argue that Job was wrong to consider God's governance perverse, as he had implied.

Job considered himself to be a victim of a breakdown in social order because he knew he was innocent (34:5). Furthermore, God had robbed him of justice (*mishpat*) and God had taken away his rightful place in society. Job 34:5 quotes part of Job's complaint that the Almighty had removed justice from him and that he had made his life bitter (27:2). Job had said that his protest of innocence (*mishpat*) had only led to him being branded a liar (34:6). His version was that God had assailed him with arrows of pain that shot through his body (cf. 6:4; 16:13-14), for which there was no reason and no relief. Elihu wondered what kind of man could make such assertions. When Eliphaz reported Job's vision of the relationship between humans and God (15:14-16), he had said that humans "thirst for wickedness" (15:16). Elihu apparently did not think much of the vision or of Job's ideas. He said that Job drank sacrilege like water (34:7)—that Job had no respect for the justice and dignity of God. Job was traveling the way of the sinner (34:8), the very path the wise warned against (Ps 1:1, 6). The wise had said that those who followed God's ways would be blessed (Ps 1:2-3), but Job had said there was no particular benefit to piety (34:9). Job had made this point at various times (cf. 9:22; 10:3) but most specifically in talking about the way the wicked escape punishment (21:7, 15). Eliphaz had responded by saying that humans cannot benefit God (22:2), but people can certainly benefit if they will follow God's ways (22:21-22). Elihu intended to make his own case against the assertion that there is disorder and chaos in the way God governs his world.

◆   2. Job's views condemned (34:10-37)

10 "Listen to me, you who have
   understanding.
Everyone knows that God doesn't
   sin!
The Almighty can do no wrong.
11 He repays people according to their
   deeds.
He treats people as they deserve.
12 Truly, God will not do wrong.
The Almighty will not twist justice.
13 Did someone else put the world in his
   care?
Who set the whole world in place?
14 If God were to take back his spirit
   and withdraw his breath,
15 all life would cease,
   and humanity would turn again
   to dust.

16 "Now listen to me if you are wise.
Pay attention to what I say.
17 Could God govern if he hated
   justice?
Are you going to condemn the
   almighty judge?
18 For he says to kings, 'You are wicked,'
   and to nobles, 'You are unjust.'
19 He doesn't care how great a person
   may be,
and he pays no more attention to
   the rich than to the poor.
He made them all.
20 In a moment they die.
In the middle of the night they pass
   away;
the mighty are removed without
   human hand.

21 "For God watches how people live;
he sees everything they do.
22 No darkness is thick enough
   to hide the wicked from his eyes.
23 We don't set the time

when we will come before God
   in judgment.
24 He brings the mighty to ruin without
   asking anyone,
and he sets up others in their place.
25 He knows what they do,
and in the night he overturns and
   destroys them.
26 He strikes them down because they
   are wicked,
doing it openly for all to see.
27 For they turned away from following
   him.
They have no respect for any of
   his ways.
28 They cause the poor to cry out,
catching God's attention.
He hears the cries of the needy.
29 But if he chooses to remain quiet,
who can criticize him?
When he hides his face, no one can
   find him,
whether an individual or a nation.
30 He prevents the godless from ruling
so they cannot be a snare to the
   people.

31 "Why don't people say to God, 'I have
   sinned,
but I will sin no more'?
32 Or 'I don't know what evil I have
   done—tell me.
If I have done wrong, I will stop
   at once'?

33 "Must God tailor his justice to your
   demands?
But you have rejected him!
The choice is yours, not mine.
Go ahead, share your wisdom
   with us.
34 After all, bright people will tell me,
and wise people will hear me say,

³⁵'Job speaks out of ignorance;
   his words lack insight.'
³⁶Job, you deserve the maximum
   penalty
   for the wicked way you have talked.

³⁷For you have added rebellion to your
   sin;
   you show no respect,
   and you speak many angry words
   against God."

N O T E S

34:14 *take back his spirit.* The Heb. has a double reading for this verse; expressed fully it
says "If it were his intention and he withdrew his spirit and breath" (NIV), but this is clearly
overloaded. There are two Masoretic traditions for the first verb of the verse (Gordis
1978:388). "If he were to turn his thoughts inwards" (REB) is a translation of the western
Masoretic tradition for the first line of the verse, but it has likely come about by a copyist
error. The eastern Masoretic tradition (followed by NLT) forms a natural parallel with the
second line.

34:18 *he says to kings.* The MT appears to have the interrogative "is it not he who says . . ."
(NIV, KJV), but the vocalization is anomalous; the form contains an article and not an
interrogative, as is recognized by most translations.

34:20 *In a moment they die.* The reference is specifically to the wicked—that is, the rich
tyrants who receive no favors from God (34:19).

34:23 *We don't set the time.* This verse is often interpreted to make the subject of this line
"he [God]" and say that God has not appointed a time for mortals to come into judgment
(RSV, NRSV, NAB), which is sometimes interpreted to mean that God has no need to call
mortals before him for judgment (NIV) or that there is no opportunity for mortals to present cases before God (REB). Neither of these interpretations fits the argument of Elihu.
Job's complaint has been that God's time of reckoning remains unknown to mortals
(24:1), and his demand was that retribution be swift (21:19, 30-31). In order to defend
God's governance of the world, Elihu must insist that mortals do not determine the time
when God will judge. The first line of the verse carries the sense that it is not proper or not
permitted for humans to set the time.

34:24 *without asking anyone.* The expression "which cannot be searched out" in later
Heb. is an idiom for something that has no limit or number. Both the Gr. and the Qumran
Targum (11QtgJob) translate it in its idiomatic sense. The Gr. is periphrastic at this point,
adapting its earlier translations of the phrase (cf. 5:9; 9:10) where it means the same thing
in reference to the works of God.

34:29 *whether an individual or a nation.* Other translations either join this phrase to the
next verse (NIV), incorporate it between the verses (RSV, NRSV), paraphrase it completely
(REB, NJB), or omit it and the next verse completely (NAB). A section of this chapter
(34:29-33) has been disrupted from an early period, apparently before the time of the first
translations. Though 11QtgJob is too fragmentary to be of help, what remains can be read
as an interpretation of our present text (van der Ploeg and van der Woude 1971:60-61).
The Gr. has omitted the entire section (34:28-33), probably in part because it was difficult
and in part because it seemed to repeat previous arguments (Cox 1985:46). Driver and
Gray (1921:1.300) justly say that these verses (34:29-33) are "as a whole unintelligible,
the details being . . . very ambiguous, and the ambiguities, in the face of the extreme uncertainty of the remainder, insolvable."

34:30 *He prevents the godless from ruling.* This is the sense that can be discerned from
the Masoretic reading of the Heb. Gordis (1978:392-393) revocalizes the verse to say God

allows a godless person to rule because of the sins of the people. This explains the result of God hiding his face.

34:31 *Why don't people say to God.* Wahl (1993:89-90) follows Fohrer and others in making God the subject: should God say to you "I have erred, but I will do wrong no longer." Job charged God with wrong. Is it reasonable to think that the Creator should be judged by the creature? This interpretation is a speculative emendation of the text, but it has the advantage of clarifying the subject of the next verses as a development of Elihu's argument against Job.

34:33 *you have rejected him.* Job has either rejected God or is rejecting the judgment of God against the evildoers.

34:34 *wise people will hear me say.* It is wise people who heard Elihu, who will then speak words to Job. The closing section is the words of the wise (as a class) directed to Job.

34:37 *added rebellion to your sin.* The translation "he claps his hands among us" (RSV, NRSV, NIV) assumes an expression for derision (cf. 27:23). It is more likely that, rather than "clap" (the word "hands" is not present in Heb.), the verb means to "furnish" or "supply" (Jastrow 1016), as it commonly does in later Heb.

COMMENTARY

Job had said that the way God governs the world is unfair because the wicked prosper without suffering (21:7-13). He had found the arguments of wisdom against this state of affairs (21:17-33) to be hollow and without substance. He had further said that God had mistreated him personally, removing justice (27:2) and twisting (*'awath* [TH5791, ZH6430]) what was right for him (see commentary on 19:6). Bildad had asserted that God could not be accused of twisting (*'awath*) justice (8:3), and Elihu began with that same affirmation (34:12). Answers to life's mysteries must arise from certain unshakable premises. It was unquestionably true that God must be good and just, but Job had challenged these basic ideas. For this reason, Elihu began by establishing the foundation of these truths (34:10-15). God is the Creator of the world and upholds it constantly in his care. If God should withdraw that constant provision for his world, everything would die, just as the psalmist had said (cf. Ps 104:27-30). God is certainly not going to wrong the world he created and sustains. People who violate the order God has for his creation will find that punishment comes to them, for they have violated the work God does in sustaining life in creation. At this point, the argument has advanced little. This had been the very mystery Job had expressed (10:3-7): how could God take pleasure in afflicting the work of his own hands?

Elihu hereby laid down the first premise in his argument concerning the justice of God in his rule of the world. Elihu then called for the attention of the wise to a further premise that could not be questioned: God does not show favoritism to anyone, for all are the work of his hands. God will call the most powerful king a scoundrel, no matter what his influence and prestige. If God governs this world with impartiality and without compromise, it is a given that we must be careful what we say about the leaders of this world. God could not govern if he were unjust, for then he would violate the equality that is the very foundation of created order. It is blasphemous to condemn the judge, who is the Creator, as being unjust. If God is this kind of judge and this kind of ruler, it is obvious he will demand the same standard of all other rulers. If rulers violate the law of God's order that all are equal, then they will be swept away in judgment themselves. Nothing these people do will escape God's notice. Since God is constantly at work in sustaining the world, he sees every step that everyone takes. There is no hiding place from the divine scrutiny, not even in death. The thick darkness described as the "shadow of death" is a reference to the place of the dead. Again, it is as the psalmist had said (Ps 139:7-12); even the place of death (Ps 139:8) does not escape the watchful eye of God.

Elihu was getting closer to closing his argument about justice. Job had complained that the day of reckoning does not come (24:1); in the end, the wicked get away with everything they do (21:19, 30-33), living a luxurious life and having a grand funeral. Elihu said that Job was asking for too much in thinking that he should be the one to set the times of judgment (34:23). In demanding to see the Day of Judgment, Job was setting a limit on how God rules his world. God cares about the poor and the needy and hears their cries (34:28). Those who have caused the poor to cry out in this way have placed themselves under judgment. God will crush even the most powerful ruler who has acted in such a harsh manner. The order of equality God has for creation cannot be violated without cost. Powerful leaders need to be especially careful to act with justice because this is the way of God. This is true for God, and it is true for all who represent his rule in his world. Job's trouble was the mistaken thought that he should be able to determine when this judgment takes place.

Elihu concluded his argument about God's governance of his world with a very strong statement that humans cannot determine when and how this judgment of the powers that be in this world will take place. When God grants peace, there will be no trouble, but there are also those times when God hides his face—when his light does not shine. At such times, the wicked may rule over a nation and over all of its people. He may allow the godless to rule because of the evil of the people. This is, at least, one interpretation of Elihu's argument (see note on 34:31). This is like saying that we who live in democracies get the kind of government we deserve, but God will eventually judge the wicked. A mortal does not stand in a position to determine what that judgment should be. The time and manner of judgment remain solely in God's control.

Elihu brought the inescapable conclusion of his argument to a close with the words "but you have rejected" (34:33). The underlying Hebrew is somewhat enigmatic in this context, but within the composition it should be expected that it will apply to Job. Job had used this verb in a similar expression on two occasions (7:16; 9:21) to say that he would not accept his life as it was after his inexplicable calamity. Unlike the friends, Elihu never condemned Job for particular transgressions. He did say that Job was wrong in thinking that he could pass judgment on what is right or best for his life. No one can determine when and how the judgment of God should come, and that was also true for Job and for his own situation. Elihu argued that Job had no right to say he refused his life as he did in his opening speech (ch 3) and his later statements. How could mortals begin to have such a presumption about judgment? How could one person reject or choose the time of judgment over against another? If mortals are in no position to decide such ordinary matters as when, where, and by what amount the rain should fall, how much less are they in a position to declare the weighty matters of judgment. If Job knew something about this, then it was time for him to speak up. Elihu does not think for a minute that Job could have anything to say about this argument.

Elihu concluded his lengthy presentation of the justice of the divine order with an affirmation that he had presented the teaching of wisdom; it could not be contravened. When the story of Job is all told, wisdom will be on Elihu's side. Elihu had said that judgment on leaders was the result of turning away from following God (34:27). In conclusion, he said that Job had not spoken with insight—his words lacked understanding. It was no wonder that Job had to be tested to the limit. Job's response—with respect to his ideas about what is just and right—had been that of the wicked. In this attitude he heaped sin upon sin, for he had continued to speak against the justice of God in contradiction to the very fundamental principles of equity within creation. Job had virtually put himself in the place of God in his demands for justice. No mortal belongs in the place of the Creator of all mortals. Job was wrong. There would not be an end to his suffering so long as he persisted in this kind of thinking. Only when Job allowed God to be God could there be a change in his circumstances.

◆   ## D. The Watcher of Mankind (35:1-16)
1. Our good does not benefit God (35:1-8)

Then Elihu said:

2 "Do you think it is right for you to claim,
'I am righteous before God'?
3 For you also ask, 'What's in it for me?
What's the use of living a righteous life?'

4 "I will answer you
and all your friends, too.
5 Look up into the sky,
and see the clouds high above you.
6 If you sin, how does that affect God?
Even if you sin again and again,
what effect will it have on him?
7 If you are good, is this some great gift to him?
What could you possibly give him?
8 No, your sins affect only people like yourself,
and your good deeds also affect only humans.

NOTES
35:2 *righteous before God.* Job never declared himself to be more righteous than God (KJV), and Elihu was not concerned that Job be cleared by God (NIV). Job did say that God had wronged him (19:6) so that he was right rather than God (32:2). It is this claim of innocence in this circumstance that Elihu was addressing.

COMMENTARY
Elihu was convinced that he had something to say to both Job and the friends concerning the relationship of God with mortals. He did not like the stance that Job had taken concerning his own righteousness, but neither was he happy with the

assertion of Eliphaz that the benefit to being righteous is that it will bring prosperity and blessing (22:2, 21). For Elihu, the retribution principle did not explain the divine relationship with mortals. Job had taken this to an extreme in his assertion that there is no difference to being righteous or evil because God treats them all the same in the end (9:22-24).

Furthermore, Job's complaint was that God gave far too much attention to mortals (7:17-20). Job had become a target (7:20), an object of persecution, as if he were a particular problem to God. It seemed to Job that God watched mortals every moment (7:17-18) just so he could test them and punish them. The perspective of the psalmist (Ps 8:6-9) that God had anointed humans as his representatives in the care of creation was of no comfort to Job.

Elihu wanted to correct these assumptions about God. Job had assumed that God was immediately responsible for his suffering because, in his own way, Job had overestimated his importance to God. Elihu argued that God was high above the earth; he was not watching Job every moment. It made no difference to God if Job was a sinner—in the sense that it would not harm God in any way. Conversely, God does not benefit in any way if Job is righteous. It is wrong to think, as Eliphaz did, that to be righteous would assure a particular benefit from God (22:2, 21). God does not govern his world by responding to particular cases moment by moment. That does not mean that the actions of humans are a matter of indifference. Our actions do affect others moment by moment; there are consequences that are good or bad. These effects in human relations are important to everyone and should be a concern at all times, but it is wrong to assume that God directly intervenes each time someone does something wrong or is directly concerned that each action follow his prescribed order.

Elihu did not deny that God cares about the world, and he had already affirmed that it was sustained by his constant care (34:13-15). God does care about mortals, but Job and the friends had made the mistake of placing themselves at the center of God's concerns for justice. What happens in the world is more than the sum total of the concerns of all of its particular individuals. It is right to assume that God will be just toward all because he made them all equal (34:19), but it is wrong to assume that this equity can be seen from the viewpoint of any individual at every point in time.

◆ 2. Our pride keeps us from God (35:9-16)

9 "People cry out when they are
oppressed.
They groan beneath the power of
the mighty.
10 Yet they don't ask, 'Where is God my
Creator,
the one who gives songs in the
night?

11 Where is the one who makes us
smarter than the animals
and wiser than the birds of the sky?'
12 And when they cry out, God does not
answer
because of their pride.
13 But it is wrong to say God doesn't
listen,

to say the Almighty isn't concerned.
¹⁴You say you can't see him,
  but he will bring justice if you will
  only wait.*
¹⁵You say he does not respond to
  sinners with anger

and is not greatly concerned about
  wickedness.*
¹⁶But you are talking nonsense,
  Job.
  You have spoken like a fool."

35:13-14 These verses can also be translated as follows: 13*Indeed, God doesn't listen to their empty plea;* / *the Almighty is not concerned.* / 14*How much less will he listen when you say you don't see him,* / *and that your case is before him and you're waiting for justice.* **35:15** As in Greek and Latin versions; the meaning of this Hebrew word is uncertain.

NOTES

35:11 *smarter than the animals.* Pope (1965:229) thinks that this is too banal even for Elihu and says God teaches humans by means of the animals. This would be in harmony with traditional wisdom teachings, but Elihu's point concerns human status in relation to the animals.

35:12 *because of their pride.* It is ambiguous as to whether it is the pride of the sufferer or that of the evil tyrant. The thought seems to be that the cry is only because of the pride of the tyrant, with no concern for the rule of the Creator.

35:13 *it is wrong to say.* Translations tend to apply the literal Heb. phrase "surely it is vain" to the cry that is not answered, saying that the cry is "empty" (RSV, NRSV, NIV), "trivial" (NJB), or "to no purpose" (REB). Instead, the phrase should be applied to the line of which it is a part—namely, it is vain to think that God does not hear (NLT, NAB). The cry of the oppressed is real, and it is not in vain.

35:15 *he does not respond to sinners with anger.* The interpretation of 35:15-16 depends on the relationship of this line to the preceding lines. Many translations make this a part of Job's accusations and a reason why God will not listen to him (NLT, NIV, NJB), while others subordinate it to 35:16 with the lack of punishment for the wicked being the cause of Job's protest (RSV, NRSV, REB). It seems more likely that Elihu was pointing out that the sufferers, like Job, cry impatiently, and, in anger, God does punish (NAB).

COMMENTARY

Job had charged God with injustice because the innocent suffer at the hands of the wicked and God does not intervene (24:2-11). When the groaning and the dying cry for help, God does not respond (24:12); it is as if nothing is wrong. Elihu must demonstrate that God is not indifferent to the cries of those oppressed by tyranny. The problem is related to what he had said before. It is the tendency of mortals to expect divine justice to operate according to their immediate personal needs. They never think beyond themselves to ask about what justice might mean from the perspective of the Creator. They want relief from their suffering immediately. They forget that they are but one aspect of the wonder of God's creation. The "songs in the night" (35:10) is a reference to creation, when the pillars of the earth were set and the stars of the morning sang for joy (38:6-7). At the time God made humans, he gave them a particular role that was greater than that of the other creatures (35:11) so that they might exercise dominion on behalf of their Creator. Such a status did not exempt humans from their subordination to divine sovereignty or their direct participation in the order of creation. In their pride, however, humans somehow think creation should be ordered to their desires and that their suffering should be eliminated at the moment of their cry. The sufferers cry out because they want the evil pride of the tyrant to be cut short but not because they have any concern that the glory of the Creator be known in the world. Sufferers are not concerned to represent the rule of God in the world; they only want relief from their pain. Since they have no interest in living out the ways of God in this world, their cries are met by silence.

Job had come to the conclusion that God did not answer him because he was not concerned about his suffering; therefore, it was vain to cry out. Job could cry out urgently for help (19:7), but there was no answer and there was no justice. But Job was wrong to think that God is indifferent to the cries of the persecuted and that God does not notice when justice is being violated. Job may not see the judgment of God (35:14), but he should not come to the conclusion that God is indifferent to the order of justice. Elihu had been emphatic on the point that God does judge the mighty (34:24-26); they are crushed publicly for their wickedness so that all may see. Judgment rests with God, but it comes in his time, so it is necessary for people to wait. As he had said previously, it is not up to mortals to decide when these times of reckoning may come (34:23). Impatience has a price; because Job and sufferers like him cannot wait, they experience judgment for their failure.

Furthermore, Elihu argued that God is very concerned about sin (35:15; see note)—both the sins of those who enslave, as well as the sins of those who would dictate to God how his justice should operate. Through Elihu, the author was probably applying the message of the prophets. In exile Israel had complained that God did not notice their suffering (Isa 40:27); the prophet had to remind them that those who waited, trusting God (Isa 40:31), would experience renewal and strength. Elihu's message is much the same (35:14)—sufferers must wait—but he also gives the warning that failure to wait brings a judgment of its own.

Job had spoken nonsense (35:16), not because he had failed to see punishment come upon the wicked (cf. 35:15 in RSV, REB, NJB) but because he had failed to understand the order of justice in the world. He was among the impatient sufferers who never pause to reflect on their proper place in the way God governs his world (35:9-11).

◆   E. The Lessons of Justice (36:1–37:24)
      1. Discipline is redemptive (36:1–21)

Elihu continued speaking:

2 "Let me go on, and I will show you the truth.
      For I have not finished defending God!
3 I will present profound arguments for the righteousness of my Creator.

4 I am telling you nothing but the truth,
      for I am a man of great knowledge.

5 "God is mighty, but he does not despise anyone!
      He is mighty in both power and understanding.
6 He does not let the wicked live
      but gives justice to the afflicted.

⁷He never takes his eyes off the
innocent,
but he sets them on thrones
with kings
and exalts them forever.
⁸If they are bound in chains
and caught up in a web of trouble,
⁹he shows them the reason.
He shows them their sins of pride.
¹⁰He gets their attention
and commands that they turn
from evil.
¹¹"If they listen and obey God,
they will be blessed with prosperity
throughout their lives.
All their years will be pleasant.
¹²But if they refuse to listen to him,
they will be killed by the sword*
and die from lack of understanding.
¹³For the godless are full of resentment.
Even when he punishes them,
they refuse to cry out to him for help.
¹⁴They die when they are young,
after wasting their lives in immoral
living.

¹⁵But by means of their suffering, he
rescues those who suffer.
For he gets their attention through
adversity.
¹⁶"God is leading you away from danger,
Job,
to a place free from distress.
He is setting your table with the
best food.
¹⁷But you are obsessed with whether
the godless will be judged.
Don't worry, judgment and justice
will be upheld.
¹⁸But watch out, or you may be seduced
by wealth.*
Don't let yourself be bribed into sin.
¹⁹Could all your wealth*
or all your mighty efforts
keep you from distress?
²⁰Do not long for the cover of night,
for that is when people will be
destroyed.*
²¹Be on guard! Turn back from evil,
for God sent this suffering
to keep you from a life of evil.

36:12 Or they will cross the river [of death]. 36:18 Or But don't let your anger lead you to mockery.
36:19 Or Could all your cries for help. 36:16-20 The meaning of the Hebrew in this passage is uncertain.

NOTES

36:3 *present profound arguments.* Elihu says he will derive his knowledge from far away. Wisdom represented the legacy of many generations; the mysteries of wisdom were learned from experiences in the most distant places.

36:5 *does not despise anyone.* The poet had a number of favorite words; he used the word "reject" (*ma'as* [TH3988, ZH4415]) on a number of occasions (e.g., 5:17; 8:20; 9:21; 10:3), four times without an object (7:16; 34:33; 36:5; 42:6). This verb occurs without an object only in Job. One of the ways poetry provides emphasis is by ellipsis, the deliberate omission of a word. The object of God's rejection in the present verse may be either "anyone" (the poor and afflicted) or "the righteous." The righteous and the afflicted are both the subject of the passage; they constitute the group Elihu is describing.

mighty in . . . understanding. "Mighty" occurs in both lines of the verse as a title for God. "Strong in mind" (cf. "understanding," NLT) is a distinct expression but should not be regarded as unusual (Diewert 1989:77) or emended to "pure in mind," as is often suggested. In this context, it must mean resolution of decision rather than breadth of understanding. Elihu was emphasizing that God would resolutely bring justice.

36:8 *trouble.* In one other passage (Ps 107:10) the word *'oni* [TH6040, ZH6715] logically means "captivity" (Thomas 1965:444-445), a meaning supported by the Arabic and a verb form in the Heb. (Ps 105:18).

36:12 be killed by the sword. The reference may be to the river of death (*shelakh*; see note on 33:18); death is also the subject of the second half of this verse.

36:16 leading you away from danger. Some translations give the sense of "allure" (RSV, NRSV) or "woo" (NIV), but the verb means to persuade toward either a good or bad end.

He is setting your table with the best food. The Heb. of vv. 16-19 is difficult; the NAB omits the entire section. The general intent as an application of the principle of suffering to Job is very clear. This verse is metaphorical: Job has lived without being "squeezed," his life has been free from trouble and struggle, his table has been set with rich food.

36:17 the godless will be judged. The difficulty with this interpretation (cf. RSV, NRSV, NIV, NJB) is that the verb for "judgment" always means to act on behalf of someone rather than against them, which is not logical with "godless" as the subject. The REB avoids the problem by paraphrasing it, "you are occupied with the business of law." A simple redivision of the letters yields "you did not judge the case of the poor" (cf. Gordis 1978:416), which is considerably preferable to the Masoretic word division.

36:18 But watch out. As has long been recognized, this verse contains an Aramaic word for "beware" (RSV, NJB) and does not have a reference to "wrath" (KJV) or "wine" (REB).

36:19 all your wealth. The Heb. (*shu'a* [TH7769A, ZH8782]) must be read as "wealth" (as in 34:19) rather than the homonym "cry" (*shu'a* [TH7769, ZH8780]) as vocalized in the MT (cf. RSV, NRSV).

COMMENTARY

Elihu had responded to the three charges he had heard against God (33:8-13). He demonstrated that God does speak, that he does judge justly, and that the righteous are too often concerned with their own righteousness. He drew his speech to a close by recapitulating his views, showing how God deals equitably with all people. As usual, in introducing his speeches, he called for silence as he propounded further truth as the defender of God. This time he emphasized that his words were spoken on behalf of God, and his call was abbreviated because he had no need to recall the invalid arguments he had heard. He spoke in good wisdom tradition as he stressed in his own way that his knowledge came from afar, both in terms of time and place (see note on 36:3). The wisdom teachers accumulated their knowledge over generations of time and from the most distant places. Elihu did not mean that his wisdom derived directly from God, for knowledge does not come in that fashion. What he had to share was an interpretation of experience, which he assured his listeners was true—unlike the arguments of the dialog that had gone on before.

Elihu began with a summary of the justice of God in relation to suffering (36:5-15). He gave the explanation of suffering in a single poetic strophe (36:15): God redeems the afflicted by means of their suffering, and he gets their attention through adversity. His first premise in this argument is that God is resolute in his administration of justice (36:5-7). God does not reject anyone, especially those who might think God has neglected them, namely those who are suffering. The wicked will cross the river into the pit (36:6), but the afflicted will receive their rights. God never loses sight of the devout but elevates them to their proper status with kings. Affliction serves the purpose of correction. Even the pious become oblivious to the error that has crept into their way of life, so God has to do something to get their attention. Suffering is not to be thought of as punishment, for that is reserved for the wicked who go the way of no return. Suffering is a discipline; it serves the purpose of correction. Those who receive it properly will be ever grateful for it. The two possible responses to suffering differentiate the meek from the rebellious and the proud. The submissive will hear the word of God, and they will experience a life that is prosperous and pleasant. The years may not always be easy, but they can be seen to be good. Those who do not hear are the proud—they are those who resent God and elevate themselves instead of allowing God to elevate them. The wicked remain stubborn; they resent God's discipline and keep up their anger against God. Without knowing what has happened, these wicked die in shame before their time. The poet used an expression of idolatrous prostitution for "immoral living" (36:14), describing simultaneously their unfaithfulness to God and society. God is just. Suffering is not evil of itself; if it serves as a corrective, it is actually good. It is all a question of submission to the God of justice.

Elihu left nothing to chance but made the application to Job very explicit in the form of a warning (36:16). Job had been among the privileged. God had led him away from trouble; he had given him great freedom in life and taken care of all his needs. In such a privileged position, he had a responsibility to protect the less fortunate. Elihu believed Job had failed (see note on 36:17). He thought Job had been lured away by the power of money, which had prevented him from taking care of the poor as he should or had led him to protect his own interests first and foremost. While God had led (*suth* [TH5496, ZH6077]) Job into a good life (36:16), Job had been lured (*suth*) into the deception of using his wealth for his own interests (36:18). The power of wealth is deceptive; all the efforts one may make for security will not provide the security and the good life everyone desires. The wicked look for the security of the night to protect them, but the night is also a time of great danger.

In light of all this, Elihu argued that Job's suffering had the potential to be of great service in calling him back to the way of honor. To reject this suffering was to choose the way of evil. Suffering would then end in the judgment of punishment rather than the correction of discipline. In making his false charges against God, Job was in great danger of choosing punishment instead of the correction that God had for him.

◆   ## 2. Discipline is like the seasons (36:22–37:24)

22 "Look, God is all-powerful.
    Who is a teacher like him?
23 No one can tell him what to do,
    or say to him, 'You have done
    wrong.'
24 Instead, glorify his mighty works,
    singing songs of praise.
25 Everyone has seen these things,
    though only from a distance.

26 "Look, God is greater than we can
    understand.
    His years cannot be counted.
27 He draws up the water vapor
    and then distills it into rain.
28 The rain pours down from the clouds,
    and everyone benefits.
29 Who can understand the spreading of
    the clouds

and the thunder that rolls forth
from heaven?
[30] See how he spreads the lightning
around him
and how it lights up the depths
of the sea.
[31] By these mighty acts he nourishes*
the people,
giving them food in abundance.
[32] He fills his hands with lightning bolts
and hurls each at its target.
[33] The thunder announces his presence;
the storm announces his indignant
anger.*

CHAPTER 37

[1] "My heart pounds as I think of this.
It trembles within me.
[2] Listen carefully to the thunder of
God's voice
as it rolls from his mouth.
[3] It rolls across the heavens,
and his lightning flashes in every
direction.
[4] Then comes the roaring of the
thunder—
the tremendous voice of his majesty.
He does not restrain it when he
speaks.
[5] God's voice is glorious in the thunder.
We can't even imagine the
greatness of his power.

[6] "He directs the snow to fall on the
earth
and tells the rain to pour down.
[7] Then everyone stops working
so they can watch his power.
[8] The wild animals take cover
and stay inside their dens.
[9] The stormy wind comes from its
chamber,
and the driving winds bring the cold.
[10] God's breath sends the ice,
freezing wide expanses of water.
[11] He loads the clouds with moisture,
and they flash with his lightning.

[12] The clouds churn about at his direction.
They do whatever he commands
throughout the earth.
[13] He makes these things happen either
to punish people
or to show his unfailing love.

[14] "Pay attention to this, Job.
Stop and consider the wonderful
miracles of God!
[15] Do you know how God controls the
storm
and causes the lightning to flash
from his clouds?
[16] Do you understand how he moves the
clouds
with wonderful perfection and skill?
[17] When you are sweltering in your
clothes
and the south wind dies down and
everything is still,
[18] he makes the skies reflect the heat
like a bronze mirror.
Can you do that?

[19] "So teach the rest of us what to say
to God.
We are too ignorant to make our
own arguments.
[20] Should God be notified that I want
to speak?
Can people even speak when they
are confused?*
[21] We cannot look at the sun,
for it shines brightly in the sky
when the wind clears away the
clouds.
[22] So also, golden splendor comes from
the mountain of God.*
He is clothed in dazzling splendor.
[23] We cannot imagine the power of the
Almighty;
but even though he is just and
righteous,
he does not destroy us.
[24] No wonder people everywhere fear him.
All who are wise show him
reverence."

36:31 Or he governs.   36:33 Or even the cattle know when a storm is coming. The meaning of the Hebrew is
uncertain.   37:20 Or speak without being swallowed up?   37:22 Or from the north; or from the abode.

NOTES

36:27 *distills it into rain.* The poet chose the rare word *'ed* [TH108, ZH116] to describe the rain, a term found elsewhere only in the Creation story (Gen 2:6). It is now known to be a Sumerian word (Speiser 1955:10-11), where it seems to be the underground streams that break through and water the fields. Pope (1965:236) thinks there is a cosmic reference, much like that of the Flood story, where the rain is drawn from the great reservoirs above and below. However, the word seems to have undergone a shift in meaning (Grabbe 1977:114) and is used by Elihu to describe the waters of the storm.

36:30 *See how he spreads the lightning.* This verse has generated various interpretations. The word "light" (*'or* [TH216, ZH240]) does not usually mean lightning, and it is difficult to know how lightning might "cover the depths of the sea" (as in the second half of the verse). It is often suggested that the word "light" is really a reference to "floodwaters" (*'ed* [TH108, ZH116]) or "mist" (Fohrer 1989:480; Wahl 1993:115; Dhorme 1984:555), though it is doubtful that the late versions support this as claimed. It may be helpful to draw on the imagery found in the Psalms. There the Heb. says that God "spreads out his light like a garment" and "makes the clouds his chariot, walking upon the wings of the wind" (Ps 104:2-3). Job 36:29 has described the clouds as God's dwelling ("pavilion"; cf. "heaven," NLT); his glory or light is present in the clouds covering the great depths of the seas. The spreading of God's light may be seen in the lightning in the clouds, but this is more than a lightning bolt, for which the word *baraq* [TH1300, ZH1398] is used (cf. 38:35). The second half of the verse is enigmatic. The familiar words seem to say God covers himself with the depths of the sea, but the idea that the "roots of the sea" refer to the storm clouds concealing God's throne is unsatisfactory. The verse is often emended or interpreted to say God's glory reveals or "lights up the depths of the sea" (NLT).

36:31 *he nourishes the people.* The NLT mg reads, "Or *he governs* [the people]." The feeding of the people in the second half of the verse has led scholars to change "judge" (*din* [TH1777, ZH1906]) to "support" or "nourish" (*zun* [TH2109, ZH2315]) as is found in standard lexicons (Koehler and Baumgartner 1:256). Such a judgment may be premature. Dahood (1972:540) has found several poetic parallels where judging and nourishing are found in sequence. The poet was thinking of the clouds as bearing God's throne; from within them God both judges and feeds his people.

36:32 *He fills his hands.* "Hands" may be correct here, but it is also possible that the poet had in mind the word "arch" (from *kippah* [TH3712, ZH4093]) instead of "hand" (*kap* [TH3709, ZH4090]), since the heavens were often thought of as layers of great arches (Jastrow 635) or a vaulted chamber. The idea would then be that God fills the arches of the heavens with lightning.

36:33 *the storm announces his indignant anger.* A recognition of the late form of the words allows this sensible reading without any alteration of the consonantal text. Instead of the Masoretic reading, "the cattle also tell of his coming up," we have words for "indignant anger" and "storm." The phrase "upon going up" (*'al 'oleh* [TH5927, ZH6590]) is the same spelling as the single word "storm" (*'al'olah*), common in Aramaic (Jastrow 1085). The word for "cattle" (*miqneh* [TH4735, ZH5238]) is actually a nominative form of the verb "be jealous" (*qana'* [TH7065, ZH7861]), here used together with "wrath" (*'ap* [TH639, ZH678]).

37:6 *tells the rain to pour down.* Instead of "his strength" (*'uzzo* [TH5797, ZH6437]), translated as "the great rain of his strength" (KJV), "his heavy shower of rain" (NRSV), the line requires a verb. "Be strong" (RSV) is an emendation to the verb *'ozzu* (BHS; Koehler and Baumgartner 3:764). In Heb. the verb *'uz* [TH5756, ZH6395] in certain contexts takes on the distinct nuance of "taking flight" (Exod 9:19-20; Jer 4:6; 6:1). Taking this as the verb here, the line means that at God's command the shower and rain "rush down" (cf. Ps 104:7).

37:11 flash with his lightning. The vocabulary of this verse is obscure. Some translators use "lightning" (REB) or "hail" (NAB) in the first line and "light" in the second, but it is surprising that the clouds should spread light. "Light" in the second line refers to "lightning," as in the previous verses (36:32; 37:3), and the first line refers to "moisture" (*ri* [TH7377, ZH8188]) from the root meaning "saturate" (*rawah* [TH7301, ZH8115]) rather than "brightness" (*bar* [TH1249, ZH1338]), "lightning" (*baraq* [TH1300, ZH1398]), or "hail" (*barad* [TH1259, ZH1352]).

37:12 throughout the earth. This translates a Heb. phrase in which two words for "earth" (*tebel* [TH8398, ZH9315] and *'erets* [TH776, ZH824]) are used together. The two are always used as synonyms, resulting in translations such as "surface of the earth" (NAB) or "earthly world" (NJB); but the use of the two words together here has particular significance and should be understood as all the "habitable earth" (cf. RSV, REB). Use of the word *tebel* for "earth" is less common than the word *'erets*; in the Heb. Bible *tebel* is found almost exclusively in poetry. An examination of passages where the word is used shows that it refers to the inhabited world (Stadelmann 1970:129-130).

37:13 makes these things happen. The MT of this verse has the enigmatic phrase "or to his land" following the statement about punishment; so it appears to say that the wrath of the storm (36:33) comes as a punishment for the earth. It may also be interpreted to say that the storm has the dual purpose of being both a punishment and a provision for the earth (RSV, NRSV). Other translations omit the word "earth" altogether (REB, NAB, NLT), since it does not fit an application where the lessons of the teacher (36:22) are for individual people. Two classes of individuals are meant, those out of favor with God and those loyal to God. Rather than "or for the earth" (*'im le'artso* [TH776, ZH824]), the word division should be "if they are not in favor" (*'im lo' ratsu* [TH7521, ZH8354]).

37:16 moves the clouds. The unusual word *miplas* [TH4657, ZH5146] is often related to "scale" (*peles* [TH6425, ZH7144]) as a way of speaking about the way the clouds hang in the sky, weighted with moisture. The expression is the phonetic equivalent of the "spreading of the clouds" (36:29) and is probably the same word. The previous description was that of clouds spreading into thick, heavy layers; here the description is that of clouds spreading out to leave the bright sky.

37:24 wise show him reverence. Some translations take this line as negative, saying that God has no regard for the "wise in heart" (KJV, RSV, NRSV). Such an interpretation must be rejected because the expression "wise in heart" is never used in the sense of conceit, which is to be "wise in one's *own eyes.*"

COMMENTARY

Elihu concluded his speech by pointing to the majesty of God as seen in the tempest, a reminder that the just will emerge from the storm of adversity into the light of divine favor. Instead of a narrow personal concern about present suffering, Elihu wanted to call our attention to the wonder of the works of God. It is the duty of mortals to exalt his glory (36:22-26) and not to focus on themselves. God is the exalted teacher, and no one ever tells him he is wrong (36:23). No one can presume to hold God accountable for what he does. Instead, it is the responsibility of mortals to sing the praises of the great things God has done (36:24)—though admittedly humans see these only from a distance, and it is not always clear what he is doing. While God is on high (36:26), humans are limited to an earthly perspective. There is no limit to God's years, while the years of mortals are very few. The greatness of God is conceivable, but it is not comprehensible (Andersen 1976:263). Failure to understand this greatness must not lead people to challenge it or deny it.

The storm expresses a finite visible presence of the majesty of God (36:27-33). It is destructive and productive at the same time. The water is gathered up in the clouds and pours down upon all peoples. God is not to be identified with these great forces of nature, as happened among the people all around Israel, but these forces of nature are understood as a direct result of the activity of God. In ancient Canaan, Baal was the rider of the clouds. The Israelites described God as the one who rides the clouds and sets his throne in their midst (Ps 104:2-3). It was common in ancient times for kings to have a movable throne, one set on wheels that could transport the royal presence from place to place. Such thrones were a sort of formal, royal chariot. In some sense, the clouds are this royal throne for God, the place from which his voice is heard. Who can understand the billowing, darkening clouds (36:29) from which God's rule emanates? From them he judges as he wills and provides food in abundance (36:31). The lightning is but a small token of the glory of his light, which is sheltered within his great pavilion (36:32). The lightning brightens the whole sky. God directs it to its target as he chooses. The mighty storm is both a blessing and a warning. The destructive power of the thunder and lightning (36:33) is an ever-present reminder of the wrath and rule of God.

The fierce winter storms are sufficient to set the heart pounding (37:1), either from fear or awe of the majesty of God. These storms are one of the ways the great Teacher (36:22) gives his lessons for those who are out of his favor and for those who are loyal (37:13). No matter how secure we may make our buildings, occasionally we are reminded that the great forces of the storm (37:2-4) are greater than what we can control. Buildings and whole communities can be swept away, along with human life. Our failure to adequately predict or prepare for these great meteorological forces is a reminder of the mystery of their great power (37:5). Though moderns may analyze the forces of weather as a self-contained system, the whole is governed by God (37:6), who compels the snow and rain to fall. The forces of weather are not self-determined natural powers but are governed by God as a part of his care for his world. The ancients were fully aware of the cycles of nature and the seasons (37:9-12), but they were also impressed with how these matters are quite outside of human control. The wind whistles with a piercing cold, turning the waters into ice, as if it were the very breath of God. The clouds loaded up with water and lightning make their circuits under God's direction over the surface of every inhabited area of the earth. The wind and the storm perform their tasks precisely as directed by God. Sometimes the destructive powers of the storm come as a corrective discipline for those who have determined to be their own god and go their own way. At other times, these mighty forces that subordinate all creatures to their power serve as a provision to those loyal to God. In every case, events such as the rain and the wind are experienced exactly as God intended. Elihu considered these things to be not just a part of providence but divine instruction.

Elihu thought of the providence of God for the world particularly in terms of its effect on humans. He probably considered humans to be the primary object of divine care, as expressed in the Scriptures (e.g., Gen 1:26-31; 2:4-25; Ps 8). This concern for how storms affect humans is seen in his sequential use of two words that mean "earth" (see note on 37:12) and are correctly translated as "habitable world" (RSV, NRSV, REB). The use of the two terms together emphasizes that God's providence and care are at work wherever people live. The implication is that Job should not describe God as attacking him—rather, God may be correcting him.

The storms of winter and the latter rains of spring are followed by the hot summer sun (37:14-18). These also have lessons for Job, and he should pause to ponder them. Just as God orders the thick black clouds with their frightful thunder and piercing lightning (37:15), so also in his perfect knowledge (37:16) he spreads them out so the sun burns and scorches the earth. In the hot summer, clothes are needed as a shield from the burning heat. The sky turns hard like a mirror of glass as the clouds spread around and the wind stops. Elihu's argument is that Job cannot say he understands any of these great activities of God, and he certainly has no part in their taking place. Further, they do not take place simply for the benefit of his personal concerns. Job is but one person in the vast area of the earth. God cares for them all, and Job is a part of that care. Neither the storm nor the sun always comes to his liking, but that does not mean there is anything wrong with the way they are carrying out the divine orders. Job had the capability of controlling his relationship to God, but he did not have the power to understand or control the great powers that are a part of the world in which we all live.

Finally, Elihu summarized the main lesson (37:19-24). God is concerned that his glory be known by those he created to know him (37:24). God does not accomplish this by simple retribution for bad and good deeds; rather, he acts as a great teacher who knows so vastly much more than his students that they do not always understand his methods. The seasons and the weather do not happen according to their liking, but they do happen according to their good. If these students have nothing to say about the elements of their environment, how much less do they have to say about the great moral questions of the governance of the world? If Job thought he had some wisdom on this, let him speak (37:19) and teach everyone else. Elihu wondered exactly how Job thought he was going to address his teacher—God. Should God be warned that someone had a point to make (37:20)? Would this Teacher suddenly be surprised and confused about something he never thought of before? Job would do well to think again about the storm, the wind, and the sun (37:21). Job should look again to the sky, after the storm clouds clear away and the sun bursts through with golden rays. This is the garment of the majestic God who cares for Job. Job may demand that God answer his particular questions, but the God we are to fear is beyond the reach of our limited knowledge. His care for the world assures us of both his power and his justice. The righteous can be sure he does not afflict them. The righteous will learn to fear him.

Elihu had brought another dimension to the discussion. He has made clear that the governance of the world involves more than the immediate interests of particular individuals. Each one must learn to submit to God. Failure to submit will lead to divine correction. Those who experience divine providence as a chastisement must not think they are simply being punished. Chastisement is an indication that lessons need to be learned so that all will come to fear God (37:24). Even with this new dimension to the dialog, however, it is evident to the reader that Elihu has not solved the problem. Job knew that his desire in every respect had been to live in submission to God. The agony he had suffered was not fair in relation to the others he saw around him.

◆ V. Challenge: God Asks the Questions (38:1–42:6)
  A. The First Challenge: Understanding the Universe (38:1–40:6)
    1. Question: what do you know? (38:1-3)

Then the LORD answered Job from the whirlwind:

2 "Who is this that questions my wisdom with such ignorant words?

3 Brace yourself like a man, because I have some questions for you, and you must answer them.

NOTES

38:1 *the LORD*. Except for the quotation from Isa 41:20 in Job's speech at 12:9, the name of God has not appeared since the prologue. Even in the common expression "the fear of the Lord" (28:28), the name of God was avoided and the title used instead. The appearance of the name in the God-speeches (cf. 40:1, 6) and the epilogue (42:1, 7, 9-12) provides a connection with the prologue and a reminder that it is the God of the covenant who cares for Job and the world.

whirlwind. Elihu had spoken of the storm as the primary phenomenon in which the work of God can be seen (36:26–37:6). Humans and animals give confession to the awesome work of God as they scurry for shelter when it approaches (37:7-8). Job had reason to fear storms. It was a mighty wind that had taken away his children (1:19), and the very thought that he should encounter God led Job to the fear he would be crushed in a whirlwind (9:17).

38:2 *my wisdom*. This is often translated "darkens my counsel" (KJV, RSV, NRSV, NIV, REB), but the word *'etsah* [TH6098, ZH6783] carries the sense of "plan" or "purpose" (Fohrer 1962:15). Job had challenged God concerning the order of creation. God now demands that he answer the questions about the divine purpose (NJB) for the world, and the plans (NAB) by which it is carried out. The word "wisdom" (*khokmah* [TH2451, ZH2683]) is also used in this sense of purpose for the world (12:13; Prov 8:12, 14).

COMMENTARY

The Elihu speeches have a pivotal role in preparing the reader for the challenge from God. The book could not be complete without a response from God, since it is entirely about God in its exploration of the mystery of the world and the world's relationship to the Creator. God has not spoken since the prologue, and the questions about him remain unanswered. God must speak in his own defense because all of his defenders have proven to be unequal to the task. By the end of the dialog and Elihu's monologue, it is completely unclear what God could say on his own behalf that would be of help in resolving the questions that have been raised. It is obvious that God's response will not be in the form of answers but that it will bear the unique perspective of the Creator toward his world.

When silence descended at the termination of the dialog, Elihu came forward as God's defender. His role was to prepare for the divine response. The effect of Elihu's speeches was to show that the divine government of the world cannot be viewed from the particular interests of each of the individuals within it. Job had shown that there was something wrong with justice in the world in the present—this has not only been true for the helpless and the poor (ch 24) but especially in Job's personal experience (chs 29–31). The problem with Job's argument was his assumption that justice must be answered by means of "immediate retribution." Elihu had said that sufferers must wait (35:14); he had refused mortals any limits to determine when times of judgment may come (34:23). Elihu did not suggest that judgment is outside of the present world, but he did deny mortals the privilege of perceiving it within this world.

Elihu had shown that the present revelation of God will restrain human pride and deliver mortals from premature death (33:14-30). He had also established that the wicked will receive their due (34:12-33) and that God will treat all with equity. As for Job's protest that he himself is righteous (33:8-9), Elihu can only say that Job is somewhat too concerned about his own righteousness (35:2-8). Though God is concerned about all those who suffer, those who suffer are too little concerned about God (35:9-12) and are too impatient with their present lot (35:13-15). The world is bigger than they realize.

The speeches of God develop the thought that Elihu had introduced. The speeches of Elihu do not detract from God's speeches but provide an orientation so their impact can be fully appreciated. It is not just the seasons that provide a full complement to the beauty of the world. In the entire natural world as we know it, danger and death are an integral part of the great beauty that constitutes the whole; even in the present time, "all things work together for good." No individual can hope to grasp their part within it at all times. Each individual can only submit to the Creator, as Job will come to understand (42:6). The Almighty God is sufficient in strength to govern every aspect of this majestic mysterious universe justly and equitably.

Now it is God's turn to speak, and he does so "from the whirlwind." The force and power of the wind are symbolic of the majestic and holy presence. Rather than danger, the storm signifies divine immanence and intervention, somewhat like the storm upon Mount Sinai when God committed himself to the salvation of his people through the covenant (Exod 20:18-19). The narrative makes it clear that the transcendent divine being who speaks from the whirlwind is Yahweh, the Lord of the covenant, the one who had taken an oath promising to save his people. This is the same Lord that Job had served without compromise (1:1-5), the Lord who had paid close attention to Job and spoken of his integrity to the Accuser (1:6-8). It is somewhat striking that God never spoke of himself by his personal name but used a variety of generic names (38:41; 39:17; 40:2, 9, 19). The speeches are a reminder that the God of Israel is the God of the cosmos, whose dominion extends far beyond the concerns of Job, of Israel, and even of all humanity. At the same time, it is this God who chose to make himself known to Israel and to be present in their midst. In the end, Job can say that he had seen God (42:5). Job was belittled (Williams 1984:268) in the sense that he was reduced to insignificance in the great scheme of things—he was simply a creature with the other beasts and monsters. At the same time, Job was distinguished as the recipient of the divine speech. He was the one who could hear God's voice and see him, receiving a direct response to the challenge he had given.

◆   ## 2. Joy and beauty at the birth of the universe (38:4-21)

4 "Where were you when I laid the
foundations of the earth?
Tell me, if you know so much.
5 Who determined its dimensions
and stretched out the surveying
line?
6 What supports its foundations,
and who laid its cornerstone
7 as the morning stars sang together
and all the angels* shouted for joy?

8 "Who kept the sea inside its
boundaries
as it burst from the womb,
9 and as I clothed it with clouds
and wrapped it in thick darkness?
10 For I locked it behind barred gates,
limiting its shores.
11 I said, 'This far and no farther will
you come.
Here your proud waves must stop!'

12 "Have you ever commanded the
morning to appear
and caused the dawn to rise in the
east?
13 Have you made daylight spread to the
ends of the earth,

to bring an end to the night's
wickedness?
14 As the light approaches,
the earth takes shape like clay
pressed beneath a seal;
it is robed in brilliant colors.*
15 The light disturbs the wicked
and stops the arm that is raised
in violence.

16 "Have you explored the springs from
which the seas come?
Have you explored their depths?
17 Do you know where the gates of death
are located?
Have you seen the gates of utter
gloom?
18 Do you realize the extent of the earth?
Tell me about it if you know!

19 "Where does light come from,
and where does darkness go?
20 Can you take each to its home?
Do you know how to get there?
21 But of course you know all this!
For you were born before it was all
created,
and you are so very experienced!

38:7 Hebrew the sons of God.   38:14 Or its features stand out like folds in a robe.

NOTES

38:7 *angels.* This is a reference to the members of the heavenly court around the throne of God just as in the prologue (1:6; 2:1).

38:14 *it is robed in brilliant colors.* The coming of the dawn is described as the dyeing of a garment. The Heb. form is the word *tsaba'* [TH6646.1, ZH7388], meaning "dye" (Jastrow 1259), and not the word "stand" (*yatsab* [TH3320, ZH3656]) as is found in the KJV, NAS, REB, NIV.

38:18 *the extent of the earth.* The word "earth" (*'erets* [TH776, ZH824]) is one of the names used for the underworld (Stadelmann 1970:167-168); this section of the poem is about the extent of the place of death (38:16-18), described as the "gates of the shadow of death" (cf. NLT's "utter gloom").

COMMENTARY

The first speech of God directly addressed the original lament of Job concerning the day of his birth (Alter 1984:34-37). Job had complained that creation was flawed in that it included one day too many. He began by insisting that the dawn of the day he was conceived should never have taken place (3:3-9). God begins by asking Job about the day in which creation was born (38:4-7). When God put the earth in its place and made it stable in the universe, all the stars of the morning sang for joy. How could Job wish that the stars of the day he was born be concealed and never be seen (3:9)? How could he wish that it be enveloped in darkness forever? Job had wished that Leviathan, the great chaos monster, would have been successful on that day (3:8) so that it would have been cursed forever. That way, Job never would have emerged from the womb into a world of trouble (3:10). God gave his attention to the birth of the sea (38:8-11). The sea burst forth joyfully from the womb of darkness. The sea was no dangerous monster at all. God laid down the limits of its power, the shoreline which it could never break; thus, the rest of creation was safe from its powerful waves. Job needed to understand that God opened the womb for his purpose and created birth entirely in accordance with his plan.

Job had further complained of the evil in the world—especially, the way in which the tyrants could be masters over the slaves (3:13-19) so that no one had peace. He longed for death where all would be free from this oppressive society. Job did not wish to see the light any longer (3:20). God responded by asking Job about the morning and about the light (38:12-15). What did he know about the arrival of the dawn? Was he in a position to determine the goodness of the arrival of each morning, which brings about a transformation of all the features of the earth as they become visible under the red rays of the early sun? The arrival of each morning curbs the power of wicked people, such as those that had taken away many of Job's possessions. Each morning God shakes the wicked out of their haunts and destroys their power. They do not have free reign within the world. Job thought that death would be preferable to life in this world, but what did he really know about the place of the dead (38:16-18)? Did he know anything about the seas and the vast underworld? Had he seen the gates to the place of death? Had he wandered about and explored its expanses? Job seemed to think that he knew all about these things.

Then God asked Job about the origins of the light (38:19-20), which he so wished would be taken away from him. Could Job go out to the boundaries of light and darkness? Could he trace the light back to its home? Was he in a position to declare when the light should shine and who should see it? Job seemed to think he had lived long enough to understand all these mysteries—God asked if, perhaps, he was around when it all began.

The lament of Job at the loss of all his property and family was understandable.

His assumption that this somehow was an indication of a flaw in divine providence was presumptuous. Creation is bigger than Job and his concerns. It is not that the concerns of Job were unimportant to God, for it is evident that God had heard his complaint. However, God's plans for Job within this vast universe extend beyond his ideas of what constituted a proper and good life.

◆   ## 3. Beauty and mystery in the heavens (38:22-38)

22 "Have you visited the storehouses of the snow
or seen the storehouses of hail?
23 (I have reserved them as weapons for the time of trouble,
for the day of battle and war.)
24 Where is the path to the source of light?
Where is the home of the east wind?

25 "Who created a channel for the torrents of rain?
Who laid out the path for the lightning?
26 Who makes the rain fall on barren land,
in a desert where no one lives?
27 Who sends rain to satisfy the parched ground
and make the tender grass spring up?

28 "Does the rain have a father?
Who gives birth to the dew?
29 Who is the mother of the ice?
Who gives birth to the frost from the heavens?

30 For the water turns to ice as hard as rock,
and the surface of the water freezes.

31 "Can you direct the movement of the stars—
binding the cluster of the Pleiades
or loosening the cords of Orion?
32 Can you direct the sequence of the seasons
or guide the Bear with her cubs across the heavens?
33 Do you know the laws of the universe?
Can you use them to regulate the earth?

34 "Can you shout to the clouds
and make it rain?
35 Can you make lightning appear
and cause it to strike as you direct?
36 Who gives intuition to the heart
and instinct to the mind?
37 Who is wise enough to count all the clouds?
Who can tilt the water jars of heaven
38 when the parched ground is dry
and the soil has hardened into clods?

NOTES

38:24 *the source of light.* Though the Masoretes read this as the word "light" (*'or* [TH216, ZH240]), it is clear that it should be read as "heat" (*'ur* [TH217, ZH241]), a word known elsewhere in the Scriptures (cf. Isa 44:16; 47:14). The origin of the light has already been mentioned (38:19), and this section is about elements of the weather. Both the Gr. and apparently the Qumran Targum (11QtgJob) read this as something other than light.

38:30 *turns to ice.* The expression, "the waters are hid as *with* a stone" (KJV), seems to be exactly what the Heb. says (Grabbe 1977:118-120). None of the attempts to make the Heb. word "hide" (*khaba'* [TH2244, ZH2461]) mean something like "congeal" can be regarded as viable. The poet seems to be describing the way the formation of ice conceals the waters below.

38:31 *Pleiades or . . . Orion.* The precise identification of the ancient names with these constellations is not possible. These are the ones generally accepted.

38:32 *the sequence of the seasons.* The verse is about the movements of the stars, as is evident from the second half of the verse. The *mazzaroth* [TH4216, ZH4666] ("Mazzaroth"; KJV, RSV, NRSV, NAB) is otherwise unknown but must refer to some aspect of the constellations.

38:36 *heart . . . mind.* Lit., "ibis . . . rooster." The mention of the ibis (*tukhoth* [TH2910, ZH3219]) and the rooster (*sekwi* [TH7907, ZH8498]) in this verse has been made clearer by the discovery of a seal at Nimrod dating from the eighth century before Christ. The ibis as the bird of the Egyptian god Thot is well known as announcing the flooding of the Nile. Ancient Jewish and Christian tradition has associated the rooster with the announcement of coming rain. This idea has been confirmed by an eighth-century seal from Calah that has an image of the rooster with the water jars of heaven (Keel 1981:221-222). The ibis and the rooster were believed to have wisdom, for they predicted the coming of the rain.

COMMENTARY

No less mysterious than the creation of the world is God's governing of that creation. God directs Job's attention to meteorological phenomena. Precipitation in all its forms (38:22-30), the associated movements of the stars in their seasons (38:31-33), and the coming of the storms (38:34-38) are all described. Sometimes precipitation arrives as snow and ice, which may function as more than just moisture for the ground. The plagues (Exod 9:18) and the conquest of the Promised Land (Josh 10:11) are two of the best-known examples of hail being sent by God for judgment (38:23), but hail and frost are present in other times of judgment as well (Ps 78:47; Hag 2:17). The deserts are beaten into parched dusty sands by the hot east winds; the deserts are uninhabitable places, being absolutely desolate and barren. Even such arid deserts are periodically turned green by the cloudbursts; the grass sprouts from the place where it had been hidden. The seasons run their courses according to unfailing laws. Ice forms upon the water, hiding it and trapping it beneath its grip.

The constellations make their rounds in a perfectly predictable fashion. No mortal can link the seven stars in Pleiades or disassociate the stars of Orion. The movements of the stars and planets are so perfectly regular that it is possible to use notations of eclipses in ancient history to calculate the very day on which certain events took place. Though telescopes transmitting images from outside the atmosphere have enabled astronomers to peer into the wonders of space beyond what the poet of Job could have imagined, the forces of the stars and planets have only proved to be more mysterious and marvelous than humans can know. An advanced technological age is still completely dependent on the rain clouds to bring moisture in its time. Scientists are not capable of raising their voices to the clouds to get them to respond. It is still true that the animals have a better sense for when the rain will come than the weather forecaster, and, in spite of many irrigation techniques, farmers still rely on the rain more than anything else for the growth of successful crops.

It is often thought that birth imagery is present in this section as well, in that it notes God as the father of the dew and the rain (38:28) and the mother of the ice and frost (38:29). The form of the question, however, indicates that the rain does not have a father. The point is the mystery of the origin of rain and snow (Vall

1995:509-513). In ancient religions the nature deities were responsible for precipitation and fertility. In those contexts, dew had a father and ice had a mother. When God asked the question, he was challenging such assumptions. The arrival of snow and rain is a mystery, and questions about its origin are a riddle. Yahweh, the God who was speaking, must not be compared in any sense to the nature deities who supposedly bring about fruitfulness. God alone is the one responsible for the beauties and wonders of the earth.

◆   **4. Power and danger among the animals (38:39-39:30)**

39 "Can you stalk prey for a lioness
   and satisfy the young lions'
      appetites
40 as they lie in their dens
   or crouch in the thicket?
41 Who provides food for the ravens
   when their young cry out to God
   and wander about in hunger?

CHAPTER 39

1 "Do you know when the wild goats
   give birth?
   Have you watched as deer are born
   in the wild?
2 Do you know how many months they
   carry their young?
   Are you aware of the time of their
   delivery?
3 They crouch down to give birth to
   their young
   and deliver their offspring.
4 Their young grow up in the open
   fields,
   then leave home and never return.

5 "Who gives the wild donkey its
   freedom?
   Who untied its ropes?
6 I have placed it in the wilderness;
   its home is the wasteland.
7 It hates the noise of the city
   and has no driver to shout at it.
8 The mountains are its pastureland,
   where it searches for every blade of
   grass.

9 "Will the wild ox consent to being
   tamed?

Will it spend the night in your stall?
10 Can you hitch a wild ox to a plow?
   Will it plow a field for you?
11 Given its strength, can you trust it?
   Can you leave and trust the ox to
   do your work?
12 Can you rely on it to bring home your
   grain
   and deliver it to your threshing
   floor?

13 "The ostrich flaps her wings grandly,
   but they are no match for the
   feathers of the stork.
14 She lays her eggs on top of the earth,
   letting them be warmed in the dust.
15 She doesn't worry that a foot might
   crush them
   or a wild animal might destroy
   them.
16 She is harsh toward her young,
   as if they were not her own.
   She doesn't care if they die.
17 For God has deprived her of wisdom.
   He has given her no understanding.
18 But whenever she jumps up to run,
   she passes the swiftest horse with
   its rider.

19 "Have you given the horse its strength
   or clothed its neck with a flowing
   mane?
20 Did you give it the ability to leap like
   a locust?
   Its majestic snorting is terrifying!
21 It paws the earth and rejoices in its
   strength
   when it charges out to battle.

²²It laughs at fear and is unafraid.
    It does not run from the sword.
²³The arrows rattle against it,
    and the spear and javelin flash.
²⁴It paws the ground fiercely
    and rushes forward into battle
    when the ram's horn blows.
²⁵It snorts at the sound of the horn.
    It senses the battle in the distance.
    It quivers at the captain's commands
    and the noise of battle.

²⁶"Is it your wisdom that makes the
    hawk soar

and spread its wings toward the
    south?
²⁷Is it at your command that the eagle
    rises
    to the heights to make its nest?
²⁸It lives on the cliffs,
    making its home on a distant,
    rocky crag.
²⁹From there it hunts its prey,
    keeping watch with piercing eyes.
³⁰Its young gulp down blood.
    Where there's a carcass, there you'll
    find it."

NOTES

39:9 *wild ox*. The mistaken rendering "unicorn" in the KJV is derived from the Gr. translation. The term may have arisen from a profile showing a single horn. The animal in question was a powerful bovine that mingled with buffalo. Hunting this dangerous creature was a favorite sport of royalty. Shalmaneser III had it portrayed among the items of tribute on his famous Black Obelisk.

39:13 *ostrich*. The bird is not actually named but described as making "piercing cries" (*renanim* [TH7443, ZH8266]). The ancient versions have various renderings, describing the bird as "making itself joyful" or "pompous" (Müller 1988a:91-96), which may be the result of edifying paraphrases. There is no real doubt the bird meant is the ostrich, identified here by poetic description rather than its more usual description as "the singing (wailing) bird."

***feathers of the stork*.** The line consists of three nouns, the last of which could be either "plumage" or "hawk" (cf. NJB). As a poetic complement to the previous line, it contrasts the noisy wings of the ostrich—useless in flight—with the silent power of birds that soar. Conceptually, however, the contrast is between the stork as a tender, loving bird (cf. RSV) and the ostrich as a bird that is indifferent and cruel towards its young (cf. Lam 4:3).

39:24 *It paws the ground fiercely*. The word is not related to "swallow," as is assumed by most translations (RSV, NRSV, REB, NIV, NAB, NJB), but rather to the Aramaic word "scrape" or "make a hole" (Jastrow 223), as is readily seen in the translation of the Targums.

39:27 *eagle . . . make its nest*. 11QtgJob and the Gr. have the word "vulture" in the second line, complementing the first line: the eagle soars and the vulture builds its nest on high. Grelot (1972:489) proposes that the "eagle" of the MT is a corruption of an original reference to a scavenger bird.

COMMENTARY

This poem is quite an unsentimental treatment of the animal world. It begins with images of how the carnivorous creatures care for their young after they have given birth. The lioness crouches for her prey determined to satisfy the craving of her young for flesh (38:39-40). The raven seeks its food from God when its young wander about hungry (38:41). The sequence closes with the piercing eye of the eagle looking for unsuspecting animals to bring back to her brood, which will eagerly gulp their blood (39:29-30). Wherever there is a carcass, you will find the eagle.

It may seem strange that God should speak about his creation in such a manner, but violence and the peculiar beauty of violence are the very point of what God has to say to Job (Alter 1984:38). The animal realm is non-moral, and its sharp paradoxes make us see the inadequacy of human moral calculus. Violence in the natural world does not conform to the explanations that Job's friends give for suffering, but neither does it fit Job's protesting his integrity in the face of his anguish and loss. In the animal world, the tender care of young means gulping the blood of freshly slain creatures; it is "a daily rite of sustaining life that defies all moralizing anthropomorphic interpretation" (Alter 1984:38). In this strange manner, divine providence cares for all of these esoteric creatures. Fecundity and violent destruction are twin forces working together in the imponderable mysteries of how God cares for his world.

This care for creation begins with the time of birth in the case of animals. Job had declared that his time of birth should never have appeared among the months of the year (3:6); now God asks Job about the birth of the mountain goat and the deer (39:1-4). Under the watchful eye of God, these creatures of the wild spaces gestate and give birth at just the right times so that their young not only survive but are healthy and quickly independent. Birth in the wild is as strange as it is wonderful. In Job's day, the ostrich still roamed in the Syrian Desert, and some of its strange nesting habits were known to the poet. She lays her eggs in a shallow nest scooped out of the ground, often scattering some of the eggs around outside the nest. The ostrich crushes some of her own eggs and may deliberately trample them if the nest is discovered. Some of the eggs are broken as food for the chicks when they hatch. By night the ostrich leaves her eggs to the care of the male. Their strange practices may seem to lack wisdom, but God takes care of them so that they flourish. The timing of gestation or incubation enables each of the animals to sustain and propagate their species. Job must rest content that God may know something about the time of his birth, as well.

The gangly and timid ostrich is a considerable contrast to the frightful and seemingly fearless warhorse. The warhorse impatiently snorts and paws the ground, confident in its strength and speed. It impatiently awaits the blast of the ram's horn; when no longer restrained, it charges off into battle, oblivious to spears and arrows. Even battle holds no terrors for the warhorse, yet strangely enough, the ostrich makes sport of it (39:18). With a height of up to 8 feet and strides 12 to 15 feet long, the ostrich can reach speeds of up to 40 miles an hour. The warhorse holds no terrors for the ostrich.

The animal world in which Job lived defies all categories of right. An immense, imponderable play of power is at work in all of creation. The discourse began with discussion about a beast of prey, the lion, followed by a scavenger bird, the raven (38:39-41). The ravens come around to clean up what is left of the carcass the lion has killed. All of this is in the interest of care for their young. The mountain goat and the deer bear their young and send them off into independence in this brutal and merciless world (39:1-4). These animals live and thrive in freedom, though death is all around them. The donkey (39:5-8) and the wild ox (39:9-12) were both animals domesticated and cared for by humans. The wild donkey and wild ox defy such domestication; they want no help from humans nor would they allow themselves to serve humans. The ostrich defied logic, leaving its eggs in the sand (39:13-18). The warhorse scoffed at the routine danger to its life and left chaos and destruction in its wake (39:19-25); the carcasses would become food for the eagles and other vultures.

There is a kind of cycle in this description of the animal world (Miller 1991:419-421), and the portrayal seems to be significant for the particular role that it gives to humans. The wild donkey and the wild ox are at the center of the description of the eight animals, both of them resistant to human power over their lives. The warhorse is trained by humans but with the sole purpose of destroying other humans. And humans, by their wars, create food for the vultures in this great cycle of the natural world. "The world is a constant cycle of life-renewing and nurturing life, but it is also a constant clash of warring forces" (Alter 1984:39). There is a role for humans in this world, but it does not fit into the straightforward moral categories that were the basis of Job and his friends' dialog.

The warhorse, the only creature in the group subject to human manipulation, betrays a condition of excitement and confusion that typifies the human world of moral ambiguity (Odel 1993:166-167). It paws the ground, quivering as it is restrained, impatient for the sound of the horn, so it can charge into battle. Deafening noise is all about in the battle. There is the thunder of the hoofs, the blast of the bugle, and the clash of spears and arrows with the metal shields. The inner compulsion of the horse makes it oblivious to fear in the midst of all this noise and violence, so it will charge directly into battle contributing to the violence. The horse charges forth in its own strength, yet that power itself is vulnerable to the danger all about. War is supposedly fought in the interests of justice, but its action is violent and destructive. The horse is in some sense a willing and eager participant in this violence, yet at the same time a victim of it. As the only human intervention in the animal world mentioned in the poem, this exemplifies the moral ambiguities Job had challenged. These now become a challenge to him.

◆ ## 5. Response: the silence of Job (40:1-5)

Then the LORD said to Job,

2 "Do you still want to argue with the Almighty?
You are God's critic, but do you have the answers?"

3Then Job replied to the LORD,

4 "I am nothing—how could I ever find the answers?
I will cover my mouth with my hand.
5 I have said too much already.
I have nothing more to say."

NOTES

40:2 *Do you still want to argue . . . ?* This line is parallel in form to the next—the expression "you are God's critic" has its parallel in "you argue with God." The form *yissor* [TH3250, ZH3574], often treated as an adjective and translated as "faultfinder" (RSV) or "opponent" (NJB), should be read as a verb: "will the one who lays charges against God teach him?"

40:5 I have said too much already. The Heb. employs the poetic device of numerical parallelism: "I have spoken once but will not answer, twice but I will not continue." Steinmann thinks this is meant to be an enumeration (1995:395-396), referring to Job directly addressing God in cursing the day of his birth (ch 3) and in his oath of integrity (chs 29–31). This seems to be forcing the point. Job has addressed God repeatedly, and now he recognizes he has said too much.

COMMENTARY

The storm of divine questions and descriptions brings Job to the end of his quest for wisdom. The silence that follows God's question can be considered an attentive listening rather than a fearful dread or a hushed humility (Dailey 1993a:194). Job was being moved to consider again his place in this vast universe. The universe was not created exclusively for human use, so its Creator cannot be judged solely by human standards and goals. Job was beginning to appropriate the divine wisdom being offered to him; he was beginning to appreciate more of the divine design and plan for the world, which he had so vigorously challenged.

The divine questions develop the shift of perspective initiated by Elihu. Elihu had said Job was much too concerned about his righteousness (35:6-7), which was not the primary issue for God. The questions focus upon what Job knew, rather than upon what kind of person he presumed to be. The questions forced Job to confess his exceedingly limited knowledge. This is a surprising turn in the function of wisdom (Crenshaw 1992:80), since the purpose of wisdom is to increase knowledge. In this case, the increase of knowledge comes in knowing which things one cannot know. This is a great gain, for there is nothing so damaging as presumptuousness, as the friends have amply demonstrated. The most dangerous situation of all is to not know that one does not know. Job had been demanding answers but came to recognize that he must live within the confines of what he did know.

◆   B. The Second Challenge: Understanding Justice and Power
         (40:6–41:33)
         1. Question: can you bring justice? (40:6–14)

⁶Then the LORD answered Job from the whirlwind:

⁷"Brace yourself like a man,
    because I have some questions
        for you,
    and you must answer them.

⁸"Will you discredit my justice
    and condemn me just to prove you
        are right?
⁹Are you as strong as God?
    Can you thunder with a voice like his?
¹⁰All right, put on your glory and
        splendor,

your honor and majesty.
¹¹Give vent to your anger.
    Let it overflow against the
        proud.
¹²Humiliate the proud with a glance;
    walk on the wicked where they
        stand.
¹³Bury them in the dust.
    Imprison them in the world
        of the dead.
¹⁴Then even I would praise you,
    for your own strength would
        save you.

NOTES

40:12 *walk on the wicked.* Dahood (1968:509-510) proposes that the otherwise unknown Heb. verb for walk (*hadak* [TH1915, ZH2070]) is actually the word for "your glory" (*hwdk* [TH1935, ZH2086]) with defective or abbreviated spelling. He bases this on the grammatical parallelism of the lines and the continuity of thought with God challenging Job concerning his glory. The translation "by your splendor terrify the wicked" is grammatically defensible and enhances the poetic effect.

40:13 *Imprison them.* This is the correct sense of the word *khabosh* as used in Aramaic (Jastrow 423; cf. NAB, NJB on this verse). It is not that their faces are bound (RSV, NRSV) or shrouded (NIV, REB). The word *taman* [TH2934, ZH3243] (hide) in this verse is a euphemism for "bury [in a grave]." The metonymy of using "their faces" to represent the people suggests an indignity that accompanies the disaster of death: it is as if their faces were pushed down into the grave where they lie imprisoned in death.

COMMENTARY

While there was truth to the assertion of Elihu that discipline is redemptive (36:1-15), his application to Job (36:16-21) was still wide of the mark. Job had taken an oath of integrity (ch 31), in which he affirmed that he had not abused any of his privileges of power. The fact remained that injustice and violence are observable in the world. In this section, God challenged Job to propose his own solutions to all that is not right in the world. He confronted Job with the violence of the world of animals in which the nurture and care of the young of the lion or the eagle means the death of other creatures. Furthermore, humans occupy a peculiar position in that world; the warhorse is a reminder of how they endanger animals in pursuit of their own causes of justice. If Job was in a position to convict God concerning his own circumstance of losses, then he must have some proposals as to how justice should be exercised. Twice in the exact same words God challenged Job to observe the proud (40:11-12); could Job humiliate the proud and bring them to the dust, as he desired (40:13)? If so, then his challenge to God was appropriate and he should be praised. If he had no solution for the proud and the wicked, then he must withhold his challenge to the one clothed in glory and majesty. Job may vent his frustration, but his charges of injustice against God were out of place.

If Job could bring about justice, then his "strength" (40:14) would deliver him. Such a power would take the place of God in redemption. Justice came against the proud Egyptians when the right arm of the Lord, clothed in power and majesty, shattered the enemy (Exod 15:6). This was testimony to the eternal reign of God (Exod 15:18). This great redemptive event served as the basis for hope in a new song (Ps 98:1), a time when the right arm of God would again act on his behalf to bring about his rule. In that day the mighty thunder of God, like the roaring of the sea, will go before the Lord as he comes to judge the whole world (Ps 18:7-9) and bring righteousness to it. Job did not have this kind of thunder (40:9); he was powerless to bring about the subjugation of the wicked (40:12) who live in their own pride. As a finite mortal he had no place in protesting against the divine rule of the world. Under the rule of God there is righteousness for this world, and Job would do well to affirm the confessions of the psalmist in waiting for that salvation.

Job had struggled with coming to an understanding of the divine-human relationship. The question God posed to Job demanded a response to that very issue.
Earlier, Job had complained, in the explicit terminology of Psalm 8, that God would
not leave him alone (7:17-18) but tormented him every moment. Later, Job complained that God could not be found, though he searched in every direction of the
compass (23:3-9). Job needed to know how God would respond to his complaint
as a human. For Job, God was both too close and too far away. Justice eluded him
because God was always testing him and because God never answered any questions. Now God asked Job if he was adorned in majesty (40:10)—if he was clothed
in glory and honor. The parallel to Psalm 8 in the second half of the verse is too
close to be accidental (cf. Ps 8:5) and must be a rejoinder to Job's complaint that he
was so significant to God that he was tested every moment. As Gradl has observed
(1991:74-79), this is one of a series of word parallels in this section (40:9-14) that
contrast the glory of God with the human condition of Job.

From the beginning, the primary problem of humans has been their inablilty to
accept dependence on God while, at the same time, having the status of representing God. Being representatives of the divine rule does not grant humans the status
of determining that rule. The representative of God does not have the power to
determine justice in this world. Thus, when the section closes with the ironic statement that God might praise mortals (40:14), the point is clear: it is man's place to
submit to God rather than the other way around.

◆   **2. Power and beauty: Behemoth (40:15-24)**

15 "Take a look at Behemoth,*
    which I made, just as I made you.
    It eats grass like an ox.
16 See its powerful loins
    and the muscles of its belly.
17 Its tail is as strong as a cedar.
    The sinews of its thighs are knit
      tightly together.
18 Its bones are tubes of bronze.
    Its limbs are bars of iron.
19 It is a prime example of God's
      handiwork,
    and only its Creator can threaten it.

20 The mountains offer it their best food,
    where all the wild animals play.
21 It lies under the lotus plants,*
    hidden by the reeds in the marsh.
22 The lotus plants give it shade
    among the willows beside the
      stream.
23 It is not disturbed by the raging river,
    not concerned when the swelling
      Jordan rushes around it.
24 No one can catch it off guard
    or put a ring in its nose and lead
      it away.

40:15 The identification of Behemoth is disputed, ranging from an earthly creature to a mythical sea monster
in ancient literature.   **40:21** Or *bramble bushes;* also in 40:22.

NOTES

40:15 Behemoth. This animal is almost universally identified as the hippopotamus. The
term *behemoth* [TH930, ZH990] generally refers to cattle, but in at least one other Scripture
it almost certainly has reference to the hippopotamus (Isa 30:6, translated "animals" in
NLT). The attempt to make it the crocodile (NEB, REB) must be judged a failure; Leviathan
(41:1) is the crocodile. The identification of Leviathan as a whale (so that Behemoth can be

the crocodile) requires the rearrangement of the text so that the description of it as a creature of the water (41:1-6) follows that of the eagle (39:30) as in the NEB and REB.

40:17 *Its tail is as strong as a cedar.* The language of this verse is obscure, in part because it contains euphemisms for sexual organs. The use of "tail" (*zanab* [TH2180, ZH2387]) to refer to a phallus is well known in Heb. (Jastrow 406). The reference to loins in the previous verse is an indication that the reference is to a sexual organ; in Heb. "loins" are the seat of male procreative power. The belief that this is a reference to procreative power is ancient. In the Middle Ages, Christian theologians like Albertus Magnus conceived of Behemoth as a symbol of sensuality and sin.

sinews of its thighs. The modern adoption of the meaning thighs for the otherwise unknown Heb. word *pakhadayw* (following the Qere in the MT) is based on Arabic. The use of Arabic as the only basis for meaning is always precarious. A study of the versions indicates that the ancients understood this to be a reference to the sexual organ parallel to that in the previous line (Wolters n.d.:4-7). The Aramaic term *pakhad* [TH6344, ZH7066] is attested in the Targum of Leviticus (21:20), a reference where it almost certainly means "testicle." A second Targum translation of Job uses the word *gbryh* (the common word for "penis"), along with another word that appears to refer to the sexual organs generally. The Latin translation unambiguously makes *pakhadayw* the "testes."

40:19 *only its Creator can threaten it.* In the Heb. this line makes reference to the Creator and a sword, often taken to mean only God can come near it with a sword (KJV, RSV, NRSV, NIV). It may be that instead of "sword" (*khereb* [TH2719, ZH2995]) we should read "companion" (*khaber* [TH2270, ZH2492]), an interchange of two letters. In that case the hippopotamus is said to be a tyrant among his fellows (REB, NAB). Though this change is not extensive, it hardly yields a more suitable thought since the hippopotamus is not a predator.

40:23 *the swelling Jordan.* The Heb. verb (*'ashaq* [TH6231A, ZH6943]) usually means "to rob or oppress." The verb has either been emended by some or given a second root based on Akkadian to mean "strong" (Koehler and Baumgartner 3:849), and the image is then assumed to be the tranquility of the hippopotamus in rushing waters (cf. NIV, NASB, CEV). The vocabulary, however, suggests a different picture of the great beast in the normally calm Jordan River: the enormous creature literally robs (*'ashaq*) the stream of water as it rushes (bubbles, swells) to his mouth.

40:24 *catch it off guard.* The Heb. has the phrase "in his eyes," but this is enigmatic in this context, since it is hard to know how the eyes are related to the idea of capture in the following line. "Eyes" are sometimes taken as meaning "a ring" or "a hook" (RSV, NRSV), but it is more likely that it should be read as to capture it "by its eyes," the meaning being that since only the nose and eyes of the hippopotamus are visible in the stream, it is impossible to catch him (cf. REB, NJB, NIV).

COMMENTARY

The identity of Behemoth as the hippopotamus is generally accepted but is dependent upon the interpretation of the description. The creature can hardly be a hippopotamus if "its tail is as strong as a cedar" (40:17), but this has not been the ancient interpretation of that verse, and it seems most probable that the ancients were correct. The great beast is described in terms of its massive loins and belly (40:16) and its powerful legs (40:18), making it most unlikely that the intervening reference is to its tail. The outstretched phallus of the hippopotamus is impressive indeed, and virility is always closely associated with power (see note on 40:17). The creature is described as being in the shade of water plants (40:21-22) and is apparently submerged under the water so that only its eyes and nose are visible (40:24) as it quietly robs the stream of its water (40:23). The hippopotamus best fits this description.

The hippopotamus does not belong to the horse family, as might be suggested by the Greek derivation of the name (lit. "river horse"); rather, it belongs to its own family in the animal kingdom. It is a mammal native to Africa, and in the era of the poet would still have been found in the Nile, where it constituted a considerable danger to crops along the river (Herrmann 1992:263-264). The poet had no doubt seen them there, but betrays his Palestinian homeland when he makes reference to the Jordan River, not the Nile (40:23). The hippopotamus is a bulky creature that will grow as large as 9,000 pounds and about 12 feet in length. It is "nude" in that it has no hair covering; instead, a thick layer of fat protects its body from loss of fluids. It has a larger mouth than any animal except the whale. It has huge, sickle-like teeth used for cutting reeds, tall grasses, and various aquatic plants. The largest teeth may weigh up to seven pounds, serving as protection against crocodiles. Its bulging eyes are high on its head and its nostrils on top of its nose so that it can see and breathe with very little of its face exposed above the water. The air escaping from its lungs makes a metallic sound. It can walk on the bottom of rivers and lakes and can remain completely submerged for up to thirty minutes. It is a fast swimmer, though it can also float like a log. It spends most of the day sleeping in the shade in dense thickets of reeds. It is basically an aquatic creature and rarely strays more than a mile from its sleeping quarters.

Both the vagueness of the identification and the grandeur of the portrayal indicate that the poet had moved from the descriptive to the hyperbolic, from the concrete to surreal imagery. The hippopotamus is on the border between the natural and the supernatural. It has been suggested that the poet is describing an animal larger than life, like Paul Bunyan and his blue ox, Babe, in American folklore. It is true there was no shortage of mythical imagery available to the poet and his audience. Ugaritic texts make reference to a great bovine creature killed by the war goddess Anat, which may be the great bull of El, the chief Canaanite god. The monstrous bullock of the Ugaritic myths may be connected with the Sumero-Akkadian "bull of heaven" (Pope 1965:269-270) slain by Gilgamesh and Enkidu in the Gilgamesh epic. The later mythical allusions of *1 Enoch* 60:7-9, as well as *4 Ezra* 6:49-52 and the *Apocalypse of Baruch* 29:4, where the two beasts of Job are said to be created as food in the messianic age, are later developments from Job. It is most unlikely that the poet intended any identification at all with these mythic creatures. The Behemoth is not described as bovine but rather as aquatic and herbivorous.

In spite of the poet's hyperbole, however, Behemoth should be read as a reference to a real-world animal because it better fits the point of the speech. It would destroy the point of the poet to move from the world of the Creator to the mythic world, for the message from God was directed to the world in which Job lived. The speeches of God are a hymn of joy to creation, an invitation for Job to revel in the delights of his world. The speech appeals to both understanding and emotion, so that Job may live wisely in a world that is a miracle as well as a mystery (Gordis 1978:560). The hyperbolic intensity heightens the emotional impact. It is true that the hippopotamus was hunted successfully with spears and hooks, but that does not take away from the description of the giant beast as unassailable, except by God, as it lies peacefully and undisturbed, draining the waters of the river in its giant mouth. Poetic license always allows exaggeration for effect.

In the hippopotamus is found a paradoxical union of peace and power. He is an herbivore peacefully resting in the shade of the lotuses on the riverbank, but he is unassailable because of his terrific power. His bones are like tubes of bronze and bars of steel. The incredible power of his muscles and his sexual potency make him a marvel. He is a complete contrast to the next creature (ch 41), which is a violent carnivore. He can live peacefully in the same waters because of his great strength and mastery over his own domain.

3. Danger and beauty: Leviathan (41:1-34)

1 *"Can you catch Leviathan* with a hook
or put a noose around its jaw?
2 Can you tie it with a rope through
the nose
or pierce its jaw with a spike?
3 Will it beg you for mercy
or implore you for pity?
4 Will it agree to work for you,
to be your slave for life?
5 Can you make it a pet like a bird,
or give it to your little girls to play
with?
6 Will merchants try to buy it
to sell it in their shops?
7 Will its hide be hurt by spears
or its head by a harpoon?
8 If you lay a hand on it,
you will certainly remember the
battle that follows.
You won't try that again!
9 *No, it is useless to try to capture it.
The hunter who attempts it will be
knocked down.
10 And since no one dares to disturb it,
who then can stand up to me?
11 Who has given me anything that
I need to pay back?
Everything under heaven is mine.

12 "I want to emphasize Leviathan's limbs
and its enormous strength and
graceful form.
13 Who can strip off its hide,
and who can penetrate its double
layer of armor?*
14 Who could pry open its jaws?
For its teeth are terrible!
15 Its scales are like rows of shields
tightly sealed together.
16 They are so close together
that no air can get between
them.
17 Each scale sticks tight to the next.
They interlock and cannot be
penetrated.

18 "When it sneezes, it flashes light!
Its eyes are like the red of dawn.
19 Lightning leaps from its mouth;
flames of fire flash out.
20 Smoke streams from its nostrils
like steam from a pot heated over
burning rushes.
21 Its breath would kindle coals,
for flames shoot from its mouth.

22 "The tremendous strength in
Leviathan's neck
strikes terror wherever it goes.
23 Its flesh is hard and firm
and cannot be penetrated.
24 Its heart is hard as rock,
hard as a millstone.
25 When it rises, the mighty are afraid,
gripped by terror.

²⁶No sword can stop it,
   no spear, dart, or javelin.
²⁷Iron is nothing but straw to that
   creature,
   and bronze is like rotten wood.
²⁸Arrows cannot make it flee.
   Stones shot from a sling are like
   bits of grass.
²⁹Clubs are like a blade of grass,
   and it laughs at the swish of
   javelins.
³⁰Its belly is covered with scales
   as sharp as glass.

It plows up the ground as it drags
   through the mud.

³¹"Leviathan makes the water boil with
   its commotion.
   It stirs the depths like a pot of
   ointment.
³²The water glistens in its wake,
   making the sea look white.
³³Nothing on earth is its equal,
   no other creature so fearless.
³⁴Of all the creatures, it is the proudest.
   It is the king of beasts."

41:1a Verses 41:1-8 are numbered 40:25-32 in Hebrew text.   **41:1b** The identification of Leviathan is disputed, ranging from an earthly creature to a mythical sea monster in ancient literature.   **41:9** Verses 41:9-34 are numbered 41:1-26 in Hebrew text.   **41:13** As in Greek version; Hebrew reads *its bridle?*

NOTES

41:1 [40:25] *Leviathan.* Like the former creature, this one is also ambiguous, being given the name Leviathan, the mythical creature mentioned in the first lament of Job (3:8) and later under the name Rahab (9:13; 26:12-13). There is no doubt that the description is based on a crocodile, found in the same river as the hippopotamus. In Job, the name Leviathan immediately brings to mind the forces of chaos overcome by God at creation. The crocodile, dragon, or sea monster is the creature used to represent the forces of chaos that oppose the created order. The commentary below treats this animal as a crocodile.

41:5 [40:29] *give it to your little girls.* Lit., "bind him for your maidens." The word *na'aroth* [TH5291, ZH5855] would normally mean "servant girls" and not "children." But it is unusual that Job should have a pet for his servants, and the poetic pattern in the verse would call for a reference to another bird here. The context suggests that, rather than "maidens," a Semitic word for "sparrow" is found here (Thomas 1964:115-116) and that it should be translated as "can you confine it as one of your sparrows?" (Gordis 1964:492-494).

41:10 [2] *who then can stand up to me?* The first person reference to God is striking, and many translations choose to change it to a third person reference to Leviathan (NRSV, REB, NAB, NJB). The MT has a little sermon from God at this point (41:9-12), which interrupts the description of the animal. Though there are variations among the versions, none of them is consistent; and on the whole they support the MT, which should be left unchanged.

41:11 [3] *Who has given me anything that I need to pay back?* The Heb. says, "who will confront me and I must repay." The apostle Paul quoted a form of this verse in his hymn of praise to the great wisdom of God in bringing salvation (Rom 11:34-35). There he joined it with a quote from Isa 40:13. It is notable that the Isaiah quotation is almost exactly as in the LXX, but the one from Job is not. It is almost certain that these verses were joined in a hymnic text before the time of the apostle Paul (Johnson 1989:166-168) in a traditional form of the text. The old Greek translation of Job should not be followed in changing the last phrase to "remain safe" (from Gr. *hupomenō*). The point of the verse is that none can stand before God and demand that he pay accordingly (KJV, NIV, RSV), though many translations follow the LXX (NRSV, REB, NAB, NJB).

41:12 [4] *Leviathan's limbs.* The interpretation of the phrase "his limbs" is a crux in determining the role of this verse in relation to the preceding. The Heb. word *bad* [TH905A, ZH963] has been used in Job to mean a body part such as limbs (18:13), but a homonym has been used to mean "boastful speech" (11:3) *bad* [TH907, ZH966]. Some lexicons list this reference under both words (Koehler and Baumgartner 1:104-105), since it could be interpreted either way. There are a number of verbal associations in this short sermon from God (41:9-12) with words Job has said to God (Gibson 1992:137-138; see commentary below), and this may indicate that this verse is part of the sermon rather than the description of the crocodile. In that case it would be translated "will I not silence his [Job's] boasting?"

its enormous strength and graceful form. The interpretation of this line flows from that of the previous line. The literal words "grace of its order" can refer either to the body of the crocodile or to the words Job had said he would use to make his case in protest to God.

41:13 [5] *double layer of armor.* The word "bridle" (KJV, NIV) has been replaced in most translations with "coat of mail," as found in Gr. The Gr. translator apparently read *siryono* [TH5630, ZH6246] (coat of armor) instead of the MT *risno* [TH7448, ZH8270] (bridle), which is not really comprehensible with the word "double."

41:20 [12] *pot heated over burning rushes.* It is not certain how the reeds, or "rushes," relate to the pot. The word "reed" (*'agmon* [TH100, ZH109]) is often abbreviated to *'ogem* [TH97.1, ZH105] meaning "heat" or "boil." Another possibility is that "reed" is metonymy for "marsh" [TH98, ZH106] and two metaphors are present (Gordis 1978:486): "like a boiling pot or a steaming marsh."

41:24 [16] *heart . . . hard as a millstone.* Heart must mean the "breast," just as Aaron wore the breastplate on his "heart" (Exod 28:29). In this case, the outer appearance of the animal is evidence of its harsh or "cruel" nature. The lower millstone was not fixed so it could not be moved; the scales of the crocodile in the same way are fixed and cannot be penetrated through to the skin.

41:25 [17] *gripped by terror.* It is uncertain how the word "shatter" (*sheber* [TH7667, ZH8691]) should be interpreted. Sometimes it means "waves of water," and it is sometimes thought to mean that here (cf. 41:17, NAB, NJB); this can also be translated as his "thrashing" (NIV) , "crashing" (NRSV), or "lashings of his tail" (REB). "Shatter" is also used to describe being terrified, collapsing in fear. The verb is similarly ambiguous; the root *khata'* [TH2398, ZH2627] means "miss" and is the common word for sin. It is in the reflexive form and could mean "lose the way" or "become confused" (RSV, NRSV), but it is also taken as "falling back" or "withdrawing" (NIV; 41:17 in NAB, NJB). Between the variables of the two words, the translations have a considerable diversity, all equally defensible.

COMMENTARY

The crocodile is the surviving legacy of the great and ferocious dinosaurs that once roamed the world. It is fitting as the last creature in God's tribute of praise to his creation. Like Behemoth, it is portrayed as an animal larger than life, invulnerable in its own domain. Though the poem distinctly says it cannot be captured, crocodiles were taken by hunters with ropes and hooks as described in the opening lines. Keel (1981:223-224) gives several examples depicting the ancient capture of a crocodile. A papyrus fragment from the middle of the first millennium depicts a twisting crocodile held by a rope through its jaw, about to be slaughtered by a man with a giant knife. It illustrates a saying of the Egyptian Book of the Dead, which contains numerous portrayals of the killing of crocodiles. However, the killing of crocodiles in the context of the Book of the Dead does not depict hunting for sport or commerce. The crocodile is portrayed there as the ancient enemy and opponent of the correct order of life in this world. The caption of this papyrus fragment suggests that the crocodile has come because a spell of death was cast upon the individual, and the incantation was to remove this curse into the realm of the underworld.

As the poet of Job concluded his portrayal of beauty and danger in creation, he used a majestic but dangerous creature of the wild to point towards the greater forces of evil in the world. His description of the crocodile as a kind of "fire-breathing dragon," that can turn the waters into a boiling cauldron, is more than just poetic hyperbole; it is also symbolic. Evil is greater than just those forces observable within creation.

The use of the name Leviathan cannot help but recall for the reader Job urging Leviathan to rise up and destroy the day of his birth from creation (3:8). The eyes of the crocodile, described as red in the water like the dawn (41:18), are a further allusion to Job's demand that Leviathan destroy his day so it never see the first, red light of dawn (3:9). The speech of God began with a description of the birth of creation (38:4-21) as a reminder to Job of his complaint about his own birth. Now at the close of the speech, God speaks of the creature that Job had requested remove his day from the months of the year. With this orientation, the short, direct sermon from God to Job (41:9-11) is understandable, and translators have been wrong in emending it away. Though the vocabulary can be made to fit a bodily description of the crocodile, it is deliberately drawn from the passages in which Job launched his challenge against God (Gibson 1992:133-138). Job had dared to "rouse Leviathan" (3:8), but in presenting the crocodile to Job, God asked if he would wish to rouse this earthly creature. If just rousing the crocodile was a hazardous task, should Job be so ready to rouse Leviathan? Further, if Job was tenuous about standing before the crocodile, should he be so insistent on standing before the Creator of the crocodile, as he had demanded (13:15; 23:4)? Job had said he was prepared to take his life in his hands (13:14), confident that God would be his savior (13:16). Most importantly, God asked Job about his boasting (41:12; see note), as Zophar had already pointed out (11:3). Job had twice declared he would prepare his case before God (13:18; 23:4), which he regarded as being irrefutable. Did Job really think God would not silence such boasts (41:11)?

God had confronted and conquered the chaos and disorder that the Leviathan represents, and in place he left but a living representation of that disorder and violence—the crocodile. If that representative overwhelmed Job, he must reconsider his demands before the Almighty God who fully controlled this creature. In another song in praise of creation, the psalmist described Leviathan as merely one of the creatures of the sea (Ps 104:26) fully dependent on God for his sustenance, playful, and making sport in the waters. The poet described it as a creature that played with its attackers—"it laughs at the swish of javelins" (41:29).

In an age when the greatest of water creatures, the whales, have been declared an endangered species, the effect of the poetic description of the Leviathan (or crocodile) might seem to lose its edge. Humans have fashioned weapons and equipment that can control the greatest and most powerful beasts of the animal kingdom. It would be unwise, however, to assume that the point of the poet has lost its relevance. Environmentalists constantly warn that we are destroying ourselves by making our own habitat uninhabitable. Though the poet did not intend to present an ethical base for ecology, he has in fact done so (Gordis 1985:199). Humans take their place among the other living creatures, all of whom are the handiwork of God and have a right to live on his earth. An evolutionist has no basis for ecological concern as far as ethics is concerned,[1] since by their view of the world the elimination of species is the way in which progress happens. The creationist has an entirely different point of view. If God created all the creatures and put them under the care of humans, then it is their responsibility to care for them all, even at some sacrifice to themselves. The poem, at the same time, is a reminder that the destiny of the world is not in the hands of humans. Humans are totally dependent creatures, although they control other creatures and, to a certain degree, their environment. But they must be careful that they do not jeopardize their own existence. The crocodile must be feared and respected by modern humans just as by the ancients.

The final speech of God is the culmination of the argument that the universe was not created for human wishes to govern the way in which it operates. People must rethink the outrage they feel at the things they perceive to be out of order. The world is an immense arena of power and beauty amidst awesome, warring forces. This world is permeated with the order of divine providence, but it presents to humans a "welter of contradictions, dizzying variety, energies, and entities that man cannot take in" (Alter 1984:41). This realization makes the fact that God spoke to Job and confronted him even more remarkable. God asked Job who would dare to stand before him (41:10). According to the prologue, the members of the heavenly court do so, but according to the divine speech, it is also the one whom God favors, such as Job (Williams 1984:271). The pulsating life of the cosmos was his heritage, even though he was unable to comprehend it any more than he could follow the foaming wake of Leviathan as it churned the water into a boiling cauldron. The grandeur of creation is the place where mortals meet God. The home of humans displays the face of a foreign and fascinating divinity. They cannot understand his creation, much less his divine nature. Rather than challenge what they do not know about themselves in their world, they are invited to live in its mystery and to know they stand before its Creator.

ENDNOTES

1. Environmentalist evolutionists are quite aware of this problem. One response is a kind of pantheism that asserts that there is something divine in the entire universe of which we are a part, and therefore we must revere it, including ourselves. A second response is to elevate the importance of humans as somehow being a most desirable stage of evolution. Implicitly this is a demand that the progress of evolution as described must now be altered. David Suzuki, in a call-in show sponsored by the Canadian Broadcasting Corporation (May 1999), insisted that since we have evolved to become rational beings, it is now our responsibility to act as morally responsible beings and to preserve the world the way it is, insofar as it is within our power to do so. "Morality" is to care about your descendants, as he does for his grandchildren, because we feel they are important. The relative importance of human beings is precisely the question raised in the speeches of God but from an entirely different worldview.

◆   ## 4. Response: the submission of Job (42:1-6)

Then Job replied to the LORD:

² "I know that you can do anything,
and no one can stop you.
³ You asked, 'Who is this that questions
my wisdom with such ignorance?'
It is I—and I was talking about
things I knew nothing about,
things far too wonderful for me.

⁴ You said, 'Listen and I will speak!
I have some questions for you,
and you must answer them.'
⁵ I had only heard about you before,
but now I have seen you with my
own eyes.
⁶ I take back everything I said,
and I sit in dust and ashes to
show my repentance."

NOTES

42:6 *I take back everything I said.* This enigmatic phrase has been read in many different ways. The verb, lit. meaning "reject" (*ma'as* [TH3988, ZH4415]), does not have an object, leaving it open to various interpretations as to what is rejected. It must be understood in connection with the previous references to Job's life (7:16; 9:21) and with his confession of repentance. Dailey (1993b:207-209) thinks that Job rejected this earthly life and then repented of that rejection. The poet scarcely intended Job's final word to be so ambiguous. It is not novel for him to omit the object (cf. 7:16; 34:33), and there are good reasons for doing so in this instance. The omission provides emphasis by absence, and allows the rejection to be inclusive of Job rejecting his legal claims and his attitude about his life.

I sit in dust and ashes. The Heb. should be read "I recant and repent, a child (*'ul* [TH5764, ZH6403]) of dust and ashes" (Wolters 1990:116-117). This requires only the change of one vowel from the MT. Both the Gr. and the Aramaic Targum interpret the phrase along these lines, with Job poetically equating himself (in the Gr.) or his children (in the Aramaic Targum) to dust and ashes as opposed to describing himself as "upon (*'al*) dust and ashes." This makes the point intended by God's speeches—that Job must humble himself before God as a child and allow God to direct his life. This same change from *'al* to *'ul* is made in 24:9 where the text speaks of taking the child of a poor person in pledge for a debt.

COMMENTARY

Job's final response was to acknowledge the divine order he had so vigorously challenged. Job had never doubted that God was sovereign, but he now had a better perspective on his own place within the purposes of God. This place may not be to his liking, and from his perspective it was not just, but the world and the divine purpose in it are greater than he could ever know. Job was compelled to answer the divine question (38:2) with a frank confession (42:3). He was the one who had spoken in rashness and ignorance about things that were much beyond his ability to understand.

Job had "seen God," which means he had an immediate encounter with God that was unprecedented in its immanence. Job had not been crushed by the arrival of the divine presence as he had feared (9:17), but he had been overcome. He was unable to answer, just as he had anticipated (9:15), but he could not say he had not been heard (9:16). He was not as right as he assumed (9:15), for the questions of justice were more than he knew. Now Job must repeat the words "I reject" (see note on 42:6), though he does not say what it is that he rejects. Earlier he had rejected his life explicitly (9:21) and implicitly (7:16), but now he has been transformed. Did he reject his legal claim, his attack on God, or his perspective on the world? The omission of the object allows the rejection to be inclusive of all the previous aspects of his challenge to God. As Kuyper (1959:94) points out, Job rejected all the arguments and demands based on what he did not know. He did not reject his life, as he previously had, for the appearance of God had affirmed his place in the world and in the divine presence. Job had now found wisdom, which led him to repentance and submission before God. He now understood that he could not dictate to the Creator what is just and right for his life. Neither could Job determine what is right for his life—in comparison to what happens in the lives of other people. All his comparisons and points of reference were finite and inadequate in his attempt to understand justice.

Job came to realize that he was but a child of dust and ashes. The message from the whirlwind had reminded Job that he came from the dust and he would return to the dust. From the beginning, it has been the folly of humans to make too much of themselves in this world, attempting to be their own god (Gen 3:5) and masters of their own destiny. In his own way, Job had also demanded that he determine what was acceptable for his own life. Now he understood that he, too, was a child of this world, and as such a child must accept his lot within the order of this earth. This is not to suggest there is no distinction between the divine purpose for Job and all the rest of the creatures. Yet Job was not distinguished from them in such a way that he could determine justice for himself or even understand it in relation to the whole world of which he was a part. Instead of rejecting his limitation as a child of dust and ashes, Job finally affirmed it and submitted himself as clay in the potter's hand.

◆ VI. Epilogue: The Fortunes of Job (42:7-17)
A. God's Vindication of Job (42:7-10)

⁷After the LORD had finished speaking to Job, he said to Eliphaz the Temanite: "I am angry with you and your two friends, for you have not spoken accurately about me, as my servant Job has. ⁸So take seven bulls and seven rams and go to my servant Job and offer a burnt offering for yourselves. My servant Job will pray for you, and I will accept his prayer on your behalf. I will not treat you as you deserve, for you have not spoken accurately about me, as my servant Job has." ⁹So Eliphaz the Temanite, Bildad the Shuhite, and Zophar the Naamathite did as the LORD commanded them, and the LORD accepted Job's prayer.

¹⁰When Job prayed for his friends, the LORD restored his fortunes. In fact, the LORD gave him twice as much as before!

NOTES
42:7 *have not spoken accurately.* This is not to say that what the friends have said about God was wrong. It is not that it was complete folly, but it was not adequate to deal with reality as they presumed it to be.

42:8 *seven bulls.* The use of the number seven for the sacrifices conforms to the symbolic significance of completeness. This use of the number seven is consistent in the prologue and the epilogue (cf. 1:2, 3; 2:13).

treat you as you deserve. God said he would not expose them according to their "folly," a term that often refers to making profane the sacred. Their attempts to defend God were foolish and disgraceful.

COMMENTARY

The book of Job has deliberate symmetry. The story of the man Job begins and ends the book. In the prologue the Accuser twice confronted God with the suggestion that the piety of Job was strictly self-serving. In the dialog, Job became the accuser, insisting on his righteousness and his right to a hearing before the divine judge. Job was granted his wish to the extent that God twice responded to his accusations. The first response brought Job to silence, the second brought him to a confession of sub-mission. Job learned nothing about his own personal case, but the divine response had made that quite unnecessary. There are mysteries in the marvel of the universe far greater than the disasters that befell Job, and all of them may be left safely in God's hands. The dialog is introduced by a transitional passage that tells of the arrival of the three friends to comfort and console Job (2:11-13). In the end they were all "miserable comforters" (16:2), whose only interest was to defend God according to their own traditional perspective of justice. The only perspective they had to offer was to condemn Job. In the conclusion of his address, God now speaks to the three friends (42:7-10) and renders a divine decision on their efforts to defend justice in the world. Once the three friends have been addressed, the epi-logue brings the book to a conclusion with the end of the story of the man named Job.

The verdict on the three friends is not favorable. Their position has been one of doing nothing more than defending their own wisdom. In the interests of defend-ing their inadequate understanding of the universe, they had wronged both Job and God. They had wronged Job by wrongly accusing him of guilt. They had wronged God by reducing his order of the world to their simple principles of retribution—a mere mortal understanding (or misunderstanding) of them. Job had been wrong in assigning to himself a far more central role of importance than was warranted, but he had spoken truly of those things he knew. Job had challenged the divine order but always with the assurance that his salvation rested in the One he knew as the Creator (13:16)—and always in the assurance that the Creator was his redeemer (19:25). The challenge of Job to the divine order is now made clear: his redemption is not based on the principles of retribution, for Job knew that a mortal cannot be righteous before God (9:2). It is those who have integrity of faith that will stand before God and receive divine favor. In this, Job had spoken correctly about God.

◆ B. God's Restoration of Job (42:11-17)

¹¹Then all his brothers, sisters, and for-mer friends came and feasted with him in his home. And they consoled him and comforted him because of all the trials the LORD had brought against him. And each of them brought him a gift of money* and a gold ring.

¹²So the LORD blessed Job in the second

half of his life even more than in the beginning. For now he had 14,000 sheep,
6,000 camels, 1,000 teams of oxen, and
1,000 female donkeys. ¹³He also gave
Job seven more sons and three more
daughters. ¹⁴He named his first daughter
Jemimah, the second Keziah, and the
third Keren-happuch. ¹⁵In all the land no

women were as lovely as the daughters of
Job. And their father put them into his
will along with their brothers.

¹⁶Job lived 140 years after that, living
to see four generations of his children
and grandchildren. ¹⁷Then he died, an old
man who had lived a long, full life.

42:11 Hebrew *a kesitah;* the value or weight of the kesitah is no longer known.

NOTES

42:14 Jemimah . . . Keziah . . . Keren-happuch. The first name means "dove," the second
is the name of a perfume, and the third is the name of a black powder used to adorn the
eyes. The names of Job's daughters and the description of their beauty indicate the special
status they received as part of the restoration God granted to Job.

42:16 140 years. This is double the normal span of a full life—expressed as a multiple
of seven (cf. Ps 90:10)—in keeping with the restoration of all the rest of Job's fortunes.

COMMENTARY

It might seem that the conclusion of the book of Job is a reversal of everything the
book has said in that it appears that Job's restoration is proportionate to his righteousness. But it is wrong to think that this is nothing more than the operation of
the principles of retribution. In light of God's speeches, the restoration cannot be
understood as a matter of divine blessing for righteousness. Rather, it shows that
God provides for those who submit themselves to him. More importantly, the
blessing is an expression of God's grace toward those who trust him (Müller
1988b:231); it is not a reward on the basis of ethical obligation. The notion of
divine providence on the basis of an ethical obligation had been overturned, and so
it should now be understood that divine providence is based on divine gracious-
ness. The critical question about whether one can be righteous before God (4:17;
9:2; 15:14; 25:4) is no longer relevant. Divine grace in human affairs cannot be predicted or controlled, but it will end favorably for those who have found favor with
God. Everything under the whole heaven belongs to God, and, by his grace, he gives
it as he wills.

The philosophical problems remain unresolved, but what Job and all his readers
receive is much better than a logical solution to the question of theodicy. The restoration of Job is symbolic of the hope mortals always have before their Creator. Believers understand the responsibility they have here and now before their gracious
God, but as mortals their success can only be assured by the gift of God; it is based
on hope. It is a hope that humans will be transformed in a manner appropriate for
them. This pragmatic truth cannot assure the prospect of success in human terms,
nor does it serve to bring about ethical correction. It is an assurance that the
Creator of all creatures is also their redeemer and that their trust in him will be
rewarded.

BIBLIOGRAPHY

Adriaen, M., editor
1985 Gregorius Magnus *Moralia in Iob* Libri XXIII-XXXV. Corpus Christianorum Series Latina, vol. 143B.

Albright, W. F.
1954 Northwest Semitic Names in a List of Egyptian Slaves from the Eighteenth Century BC. *Journal of the Oriental Society* 74:225, 232.

Alter, Robert
1984 The Voice from the Whirlwind. *Commentary* 77:33-41.

Andersen, Francis I.
1976 *Job: An Introduction and Commentary.* Downers Grove: InterVarsity.

Aufrecht, Walter E.
1985 Aramaic Studies and the Book of Job. Pp. 54-66 in *Studies in Job.* Editor, W. E. Aufrecht. Studies in Religion Supplements 16. Waterloo: Wilfred Laurier University Press.

Barr, James
1971 The Book of Job and Its Modern Interpreters. *Bulletin of John Rylands Library* 54:28-46.

Block, D.
2005 What has Delphi to do with Samaria? Ambiguity and Delusion in Israelite Prophecy. Pp. 185-212 in *Writing and Ancient Near East Society: Essays in Honor of Alan Millard.* Editor, P. Bienkowski. Edinburgh: T & T Clark.

Blommerde, Anton C. M.
1969 *Northwest Semitic Grammar and Job.* Biblica et Orientalia 22. Rome: Pontifical Biblical Institute.

Brueggemann, Walter
1985 Theodicy in a Social Dimension. *Journal for the Study of the Old Testament* 33:3-25.

Burns, John Barclay
1989 Support for the Emendation *Rehob Meqomo* in Job XXIV 19-20. *Vetus Testamentum* 34:480-484.

Cheney, Michael
1994 *Dust, Wind and Agony: Character, Speech, and Genre in Job.* Coniectanea Biblica Old Testament Series 36. Stockholm: Almqvist & Wiksell International.

Clines, David J. A.
1981 Job 5:1-8: A New Exegesis. *Biblica* 62:185-194.

1985 False Naivety in the Prologue of Job. *Hebrew Annual Review* 9:127-136.

1989 *Job 1–20.* Word Biblical Commentary 17. Waco: Word.

1995 Why Is There a Book of Job? Pp. 122-144 in *Interested Parties: The Ideology of Writers and Readers of the Hebrew Bible.* Journal for the Study of the Old Testament Supplement 205. Sheffield: Sheffield Academic Press.

Cooper, Alan
1990 Reading and Misreading the Prologue to Job. *Journal for the Study of the Old Testament* 46:67-79.

Cox, Claude E.
1985 Elihu's Second Speech According to the Septuagint. Pp. 36-53 in *Studies in Job.* Editor, W. E. Aufrecht. Studies in Religion Supplements 16. Waterloo: Wilfred Laurier University Press.

1986 Methodological Issues in the Exegesis of LXX Job. Pp. 79-89 in *VI Congress of the International Organization for Septuagint and Cognate Studies.* Editor, Claude E. Cox. SBL Septuagint and Cognate Studies 23. Atlanta: Scholars Press.

Craigie, Peter C.
1985 Job and Ugaritic Studies. Pp. 28-35 in *Studies in Job.* Editor, W. E. Aufrecht. Studies in Religion Supplements 16. Waterloo: Wilfred Laurier University Press.

Crenshaw, James L.
1981 *Old Testament Wisdom: An Introduction.* Atlanta: John Knox Press.

1992 When Form and Content Clash: The Theology of Job 38:1-40:5. Pp. 70-84 in *Creation in the Biblical Traditions.* Editors, Richard J. Clifford and John J. Collins. Catholic Biblical Quarterly Monograph Series 24. Washington: Catholic Biblical Association of America.

Cross, Frank Moore
1973 *Canaanite Myth and Hebrew Epic: Essays in the History of the Religion of Israel.* Cambridge, MA:
Harvard University Press.

Dahood, Mitchell
1957 Some Northwest-Semitic Words in Job. *Biblica* 38:306-320.

1959 The Root *'zb* II in Job. *Journal for Biblical Literature* 78:303-309.

1968 *HDK* in Job 40:12. *Biblica* 49:509-510.

1972 Is the Emendation of *yadin* to *yazin* Necessary in Job 36:31? *Biblica* 53:539-41.

1974 *hol* 'Phoenix' in Job 28:18 and in Ugaritic. *Catholic Biblical Quarterly* 38.85-88.

Dailey, Thomas F.
1993a Theophanic Bluster: Job and the Wind of Change. *Studies in Religion* 22:187-195.

1993b And Yet He Repents—On Job 42:6. *Zeitschrift für die Alttestamentliche Wissenshaft* 105:205-209.

Day, John
1985 *God's Conflict with the Dragon and the Sea: Echoes of a Canaanite Myth in the Old Testament.*
Cambridge: Cambridge University Press.

Delekat, L.
1964 Zum Hebräischen Wörterbuch. *Vetus Testamentum* 14:7-66.

De Wilde, A.
1972 Eine Alte Crux Interpretum: Hiob XXII, 2. *Vetus Testamentum* 22:368-374.

1981 *Das Buch Hiob.* Leiden: Brill.

Dhorme, Edouard
1984 *A Commentary on the Book of Job.* Translator, Harold Knight. Nashville: Thomas Nelson.

Diewert, David
1989 Job XXXVI 5 and the Root of M'S II. *Vetus Testamentum* 29:71-77.

Driver, G. R.
1954 Problems and Solutions. *Vetus Testamentum* 54:225-245.

1968 Isaiah i-xxxix: Textual and Linguistic Problems. *Journal for Semitic Studies* 13:36-57.

1969 Problems in the Hebrew Text of Job. Pp 72-93 in *Wisdom in Israel and in the Ancient Near East.*
Editors, M. Noth and D. Winton Thomas. Supplement to Vetus Testamentum III. Leiden: Brill.

Driver, Samuel Rolles and George Buchanan Gray
1921 *A Critical and Exegetical Commentary on the Book of Job.* 2 vols. International Critical Commentary.
Edinburgh: T & T Clark.

Eaton, J. H.
1985 *Job.* Sheffield: Sheffield Academic Press.

Emerton, J. A.
1989 The meaning of the verb *hamas* in Jeremiah 13,22. Pp. 19-28 in *Prophet und Prophetenbuch.* Editors,
Volkmar Fritz, et al. Beiheft zur Zeitschrift für die alttestamentliche Wissenschaft 185. Berlin:
Walter de Gruyter.

Fitzmyer, Joseph A.
1979 The First-Century Targum of Job from Qumran Cave XI. Pp. 161-182 in *A Wandering Aramean:
Collected Aramaic Essays.* Society of Biblical Literature Monograph Series 25. Chico, CA:
Scholars Press.

Fleming, Daniel E.
1994 Job: the Tale of Patient Faith and the Book of God's Dilemma. *Vetus Testamentum* 44:468-482.

Fohrer, Georg
1962 Gottes Antwort aus dem Sturmwind, Hi. 38–41. *Theologische Zeitschrift* 18:1-24.

1989 *Das Buch Hiob,* 2 Auglage. KAT XVI. Gütersloh: Gütersloher Verlagshaus Gerd Mohn.

Fox, M. V.
1980 The Identification of Quotations in Biblical Literature. *Zeitschrift für die Attestamentliche
Wissenschaft* 92:416-431.

Freedman, D. N.
1968 The Elihu Speeches in the Book of Job. *Harvard Theological Review* 61:51-59.

1969 Orthographic Peculiarities in the Book of Job. *Eretz Israel* 9:35-44.

Gammie, John G.
1985 The Angelology and Demonology in the Septuagint of the Book of Job. *Hebrew Union College Annual 56:1-19.*

Gehman, Henry S.
1944 *Seper,* an Inscription in the Book of Job. *Journal of Biblical Literature* 63:303-307.

Geller, Stephen A.
1987 'Where is Wisdom?' A Literary Study of Job 28 in Its Settings. Pp. 155-88 in *Judaic Perspective on Ancient Israel.* Editors, Jacob Neusner, Baruch Levine, and Ernest Frerichs. Philadelphia: Fortress.

Gerleman, Gillis
1974 Der Nicht-mensch. Erwägungen zur hebräischen Wurzel *nbl. Vetus Testamentum* 24:147-158.

Gesenius, W., E. Kautzsch and A. E. Cowley
1910 *Gesenius' Hebrew Grammar.* Oxford: Clarendon.

Gevirtz, Stanley
1990 "Phoenician *wšbrt mlsm* and Job 33:23," *MAARAV* 5-6:145-158.

Geyer, J. B.
1992 Mythological Sequence in Job XXIV 19-20. *Vetus Testamentum* 42:118-120.

Gibson, J. C. L.
1975 Eliphaz the Temanite: Portrait of a Hebrew Philosopher. *Scottish Journal of Theology* 28:259-272.

1992 A New Look at Job 41:1-4 (English 41:9-12). Pp. 129-39 in *Text as Pretext: Essays in Honour of Robert Davidson.* Editor, Robert P. Carroll. Journal for the Study of the Old Testament Supplement 138. Sheffield: Sheffield Academic Press.

Ginsberg, H. L.
1969 Job the Patient and Job the Impatient. *Vetus Testamentum Supplements* 17:88-111.

Girard, Ren
1985 'The Ancient Trail Trodden by the Wicked': Job as Scapegoat. *Semeia* 33:13-41.

Good, E. M.
1990 *In Turns of Tempest: A Reading of Job with a Translation.* Stanford: Stanford University Press.

Gordis, Robert
1964 Job XL 29—An Additional Note. *Vetus Testamentum* 14:491-494.

1965 *The Book of God and Man.* Chicago: University of Chicago Press.

1978 *The Book of Job: Commentary, New Translation, and Special Studies.* New York: Jewish Theological Seminary of America.

1985 Job and Ecology (and the Significance of Job 40:15). *Hebrew Annual Review* 9:189-202.

Grabbe, Lester L.
1977 *Comparative Philology and the Text of Job: A Study in Methodology.* Society of Biblical Literature Dissertation Series 34. Missoula, MT: Scholars Press.

Gradl, Felix
1991 Ijobs Begegnung mit Gott: Anmerkungen zu Ijob 40,6-8.9-14. Pp. 65-82 in *Ein Gott, Eine Offenbarung: Beiträge zur biblischen Exegese, Theologie und Spiritualität.* Editor, F. V. Reiterer. Würzburg: Echter Verlag.

Gray, John
1970 The Book of Job in the Context of Near Eastern Literature. *Zeitschrift für die Alttestamentliche Wissenschaft* 82:251-269.

1974 The Masoretic Text of the Book of Job, the Targum and the Septuagint Version in the Light of the Qumran Targum, 11QtargJob. *Zeitschrift für die Alttestamentliche Wissenschaft* 86:331-350.

Grelot, Pierre
1958 La géographie mythique d'Hénoch. *Revue Biblique* 65:33-69.

1972 Note de Critique Textuelle sur Job xxxix 27. *Vetus Testamentum* 22:487-489.

Griffiths, J. Gwyn
1983 The Idea of Posthumous Judgment in Israel and Egypt. Pp. 186-204 in *Fontes atque Pontes: Eine Festgabe für Hellmut Brunner.* Editor, Manfred Görg. Ägypten und altes Testament: Studien zu Geschichte, Kultur und Religion Ägyptens und des alten Testaments 5. Wiesbaden: Otto Harrassowitz.

Gros, Heinrich
1990 Die Allmacht des Schöpfergottes: Erwägungen zu Ijob 26,5-14. Pp. 75-84 in *Die alttestamentliche Botschaft als Wegweisung: Festschrift für Heinz Reinelt*. Editor, Josef Zmijewski. Stuttgart: Verlag Katholisches Bibelwerk.

Habel, Norman C.
1984 The Role of Elihu in the Design of the Book of Job. Pp. 81-98 in *In the Shelter of Elyon: Essays on Ancient Palestinian Life and Literature*. Editors, W. Boyd Barrick and John R. Spencer. Journal for the Study of the Old Testament Supplement 31. Sheffield: JSOT Press.
1985 *The Book of Job: A Commentary*. The Old Testament Library. Philadelphia: Westminster.

Hackett, Jo Ann and John Huehnergard
1984 On Breaking Teeth. *Harvard Theological Review* 77:259-275.

Heater, Homer
1982 *A Septuagint Translation Technique in the Book of Job*. The Catholic Biblical Quarterly Monograph Series 11. Washington: Catholic Biblical Association of America.

Hermisson, Hans-Jürgen
1996 Von Gottes und Hiobs Nutzen: Zur Auslegung von Hiob 22. *Zeitschrift für Theologie und Kirche* 93:331-351.

Herrmann, Wolfram
1992 Eine Notwendige Erinnerung. *Zeitschrift für die Alttestamentliche Wissenschaft* 104:262-264.

Hilprecht, H.V., and Rev. A.T. Clay, editors
1898 *Babylonian Expedition of the University of Pennsylvania*, Series A: Cuneiform texts, Vol. IX. Business documents of Murashû, sons of Nippur, dated in the reign of Artaxerxes I (464-424 BC).

Holman, Jan
1994 Translation of Job 19, 25. Pp. 377-81 in *The Book of Job*. Editor, W. A. M. Beuken. Bibliotheca Ephemeridum Theologicarum Lovanienium CXIV. Leuven: Leuven University Press.

Hölscher, Gustav
1935 Hiob 19:25-27 und Jubil 23:30-31. *Zeitschrift für die Alttestamentliche Wissenshaft* 53:277-283.

Hurvitz, A.
1974 The Date of the Prose-Tale of Job Linguistically Reconsidered. *Harvard Theological Review* 67:17-34.

Jacobsen, Thorkild
1976 *The Treasures of Darkness: A History of Mesopotamian Religion*. New Haven: Yale University Press.

Janzen, J. Gerald
1994 On the Moral Nature of God's Power: Yahweh and the Sea in Job and Deutero-Isaiah. *Catholic Biblical Quarterly* 56:458-478.

Jastrow, Marcus
1903 *A Dictionary of the Targumim, The Talmud Babli and Yerushalmi, and the Midrashic Literature*. New York: Judaica Press (reprinted 1982).

Jenni, Ernst and Claus Westermann
1971 *Theologisches Handwörterbuch zum alten Testament*. Vol. 1. Zurich: Theologischer Verlag.
1976 *Theologisches Handwörterbuch zum alten Testament*. Vol. 2. Zurich: Theologischer Verlag.

Johnson, Elizabeth
1989 *The Function of Apocalyptic and Wisdom Traditions in Romans 9-11*. Society of Biblical Literature Dissertation Series. Atlanta: Scholars Press.

Jongeling, B.
1974 L'expression *my ytn* dans l'ancient testament. *Vetus Testamentum* 24:32-40.

Kaufmann, Yehezkel
1972 *The Religion of Israel: From Its Beginnings to the Babylonian Exile*. Translator, Moshe Greenberg. New York: Schocken Books.

Keel, Othmar
1981 Zwei kleine Beiträge zum Verständnis der Gottesreden im Buch Ijob (xxxviii 36 f., xl 25). *Vetus Testamentum* 31:220-225.

Kelly, Balmer H.
1961 Truth in Contradiction. *Interpretation* 15:147-156.

Koehler, Ludwig and Walter Baumgartner
1967, 1974, 1983, 1990, 1995 *Hebräisches und Aramäisches Lexikon zum alten Testament.* 5 vols.
Leiden: Brill.

Konkel, A. H.
1992 Wisdom as the Way to Knowing God. *Didaskalia* 4/1:15-25.

Kuyper, Lester J.
1959 The Repentance of Job. *Vetus Testamentum* 9:91-94.

Lambert, W. G.
1963 *Babylonian Wisdom Literature.* Oxford: Oxford University Press.

Levine, Baruch
1985 René Girard on Job: The Question of the Scapegoat. *Semeia* 33:125-133.

Loretz, O.
1981 Philologische und Textologische Probleme in Hi 24,1-25. *Ugarit-Forschungen* 12:261-266.

Luther, Martin
1912 *Tischreden,* Band 1. In *D. Martin Luther's Werke: kritische Gesamtausgabe* Abteilung 2. Weimar:
H. Böhlau Nachfolger. (Orig. pub. c. 1530)

Mach, Michael
1992 *Entwicklungsstadien des jüdischen Engelgloubens in vorrabbinischer Zeit.* Texte und Studien zum
Antiken Judentum 34. Tübingen: J .C. B. Mohr.

McCarter, Paul Kyle
1973 The River Ordeal in Israelite Literature. *Harvard Theological Review* 66:403-412.

McCarthy, Carmel
1981 *The Tiqqune Sopherim and Other Theological Corrections in the Masoretic Text of the Old Testament.*
Orbis Biblicus et Orientalis 36. Göttingen: Vandenhoeck & Ruprecht.

Michel, W. L.
1984 *SLMWT,* 'Deep Darkness' or 'Shadow of Death?' *Biblical Research* 29:5-20.

1994 Confidence and Despair: Job 19, 25-27 in the Light of Northwest Semitic Studies. Pp. 157-81 in
The Book of Job. Editor, W. A. M. Beuken. Bibliotheca Ephemeridum Theologicarum Lovanienium CXIV.
Leuven: Leuven University Press.

Miller, James E.
1991 The Structure and Meaning of the Animal Discourse in the Theophany of Job (38,39-39,30).
Zeitschrift für die Alttestamentliche Wissenshaft 103:418-421.

Moore, Rick D.
1983 The Integrity of Job. *Catholic Biblical Quarterly* 45:17-31.

Müller, Hans-Peter
1988a Die sog. Straussenperikope in den Gottesreden des Hiobbuches. *Zeitschrift für die Alttestamentliche
Wissenshaft* 100:90-105.

1988b Gottes Antwort an Ijob und das Recht religiöser Wahrheit. *Biblische Zeitschrift* n. s. 32:210-231.

Murphy, R. E.
1981 *Wisdom Literature: Job, Proverbs, Ruth, Canticles, Ecclesiastes, and Esther.* Forms of Old Testament
Literature XIII. Grand Rapids: Eerdmans.

Nel, Philip
1978 A Proposed Method for Determining the Context of the Wisdom Admonitions. *Journal of Northwest
Semitic Languages* 6:33-39.

Noth, Martin
1951 Noah, Daniel und Hiob in Ezechiel XIV. *Vetus Testamentum* 1:251-260.

Odel, David
1993 Images of Violence in the Horse in Job. *Prooftexts* 13:163-173.

Oeming, Manfred
1994 Hiob 31 und der Dekalog. Pp. 362-68 in *The Book of Job.* Editor, W. A. M. Beuken. Bibliotheca
Ephemeridum Theologicarum Lovanienium CXIV. Leuven: Leuven University Press.

Oorschot, Jürgen van
1994 Hiob 28: die verborgene Weisheit und die Furcht Gottes als Überwindung einer generalisierten *hkmh*. Pp 183-201 in *The Book of Job*. Editor, W. A. M. Beuken. Bibliotheca Ephemeridum Theologicarum Lovanienium CXIV. Leuven: Leuven University Press.

Orlinsky, Harry
1957 Studies in the Septuagint of the Book of Job. *Hebrew Union College Annual* 28:53-74.
1958 Studies in the Septuagint of the Book of Job. *Hebrew Union College Annual* 29:229-271.
1959 Studies in the Septuagint of the Book of Job. *Hebrew Union College Annual* 30:153-167.
1961 Studies in the Septuagint of the Book of Job. *Hebrew Union College Annual* 32:239-268.
1962 Studies in the Septuagint of the Book of Job. *Hebrew Union College Annual* 33:119-151.
1964 Studies in the Septuagint of the Book of Job. *Hebrew Union College Annual* 35:57-78.
1965 Studies in the Septuagint of the Book of Job. *Hebrew Union College Annual* 36:37-47.
1991 Some Terms in the Prologue to Ben Sira and the Hebrew Canon. *Journal of Biblical Literature* 110:483-490.

Peel, Paul
1997 The Function of Virtual Quotation in the Dialog of Job. Unpublished master's thesis, Providence Theological Seminary, Otterburne, Manitoba.

Ploeg, J. P. M. van der and A. S. van der Woude
1971 *Le Targum de Job de la Grotte XI de Qumran*. Leiden: E. J. Brill.

Pope, Marvin H.
1965 *Job: Introduction, Translation, and Notes*. Anchor Bible 15. Garden City: Doubleday.

Reider, J.
1935 Contributions to the Hebrew Lexicon. *Zeitschrift für die Alttestamentliche Wissenshaft* 53:270-277.
1952 Etymological Studies in Biblical Hebrew. *Vetus Testamentum* 2:113-130.
1954 Etymological Studies in Biblical Hebrew. *Vetus Testamentum* 4:276-295.

Roth, W. M. W.
1960 NBL. *Vetus Testamentum* 10:394-409.

Rowley, H. H.
1970 *Job*. The Century Bible. Greenwood, SC: Attic Press.

Sarna, Nahum M.
1957 Epic Substratum in the Prose of Job. *Journal of Biblical Literature* 76:13-25.
1963 The Mythological Background of Job 18. *Journal of Biblical Literature* 82:315-318.

Sheppard, Gerald T.
1980 *Wisdom as a Hermeneutical Construct: A Study of Sapientializing of the Old Testament*. New York: Walter de Gruyter.

Skehan, Patrick W.
1969 I Will Speak Up! (Job 32). *Catholic Biblical Quarterly* 31:380-382.

Skladny, U.
1961 *Die ältesten Spruchsammlungen in Israel*. Berlin: Vandenhoek & Ruprecht.

Smith, Gary V.
1990 Job IV 12-21: Is it Eliphaz's Vision? *Vetus Testamentum* 40:453-463.

Speiser, E. A.
1955 'ed in the Story of Creation. *Bulletin of American Schools of Oriental Research* 140:9-11.
1963 The Stem *pll* in Hebrew. *Journal of Biblical Literature* 82:301-306.

Stadelmann, Luis I. J.
1970 *The Hebrew Conception of the World: A Philological and Literary Study*. Analecta Biblica 39. Rome: Pontifical Biblical Institute.

Steinmann, Andrew E.
1995 The Graded Numerical Saying in Job. Pp. 288-97 in *Fortunate the Eyes that See*. Editors, Astrid B. Beck, Andrew H. Bartelt, Paul R. Raabe, and Chris A. Frank. Grand Rapids: Eerdmans.
1996 The Structure and Message of the Book of Job. *Vetus Testamentum* 46:85-100.

Sutcliffe, Edmund F.
1950 Further Notes on Job, Textual and Exegetical. *Biblica* 31:365-378.

Thomas, D. Winton
1964 Job XL 29b: Text and Translation. *Vetus Testamentum* 14:114-116.
1965 Hebrew *'oni* 'Captivity.' *Journal of Theological Studies* 16:444-445.

Torczyner, N. H.
1967 *The Book of Job: A New Commentary.* Jerusalem: Kiryath Sepher.

Tov, Emanuel
1992 *Textual Criticism of the Hebrew Bible.* Minneapolis: Fortress Press.

Treves, Marco
1995 The Book of Job. *Zeitschrift für die Alttestamentliche Wissenschaft* 107:261-272.

Tsevat, Matitiahu
1954 The Canaanite God *salah. Vetus Testamentum* 4:41-49.
1980 The Meaning of the Book of Job. Pp. 1-37 in *The Meaning of the Book of Job and Other Biblical Studies.* New York: Ktav.

Tur-Sinai, N. H.
1967 *The Book of Job: A New Commentary.* Jerusalem: Kiryath Sepher.

Vall, Gregory
1995 'From Whose Womb Did the Ice Come Forth?' Procreation Images in Job 38:28-29. *Catholic Biblical Quarterly* 57:504-513.

van der Ploeg, J. P. M. and A. S. van der Woude
(See Ploeg, J. P. M. van der)

Van Leeuwen, Raymond
1986 A Technical Metallurgical Usage of *ys'. Zeitschrift für die Alttestamentliche Wissenschaft* 98:112-113.

van Oorschot, Jürgen
See Oorschot, Jürgen, van

Wahl, Harald-Martin
1993 *Der gerechte Schöpfer: Eine redaktions- und theologiegeschichtliche Untersuchung der Elihureden— Hiob 32-37.* Beihefte zur Zeitschrift für die Alttestamentliche Wissenschaft 207. Berlin: Walter de Gruyter.

Waltke, Bruce K. and M. O'Conner
1990 *An Introduction to Biblical Hebrew Syntax.* Winona Lake, IN: Eisenbrauns.

Williams, James G.
1981 *Those Who Ponder Proverbs: Aphoristic Thinking and Biblical Literature.* Sheffield: Almond Press.
1984 Job's Vision: The Dialectic of Person and Presence. *Hebrew Annual Review* 8:259-272.

Williams, Ronald J.
1985 Current Trends in the Study of the Book of Job. Pp. 1-27 in *Studies in the Book of Job.* Editor, Walter E. Aufrecht. Studies in Religion Supplements 16. Waterloo: Wilfrid Laurier University Press.

Williamson, H. G. M.
1985 A Reconsideration of *'zb* II in Biblical Hebrew. *Zeitschrift für die Alttestamentliche Wissenschaft* 97:74-85.

Wolfers, David
1993 The Speech-Cycles in the Book of Job. *Vetus Testamentum* 43:385-402.
1994a Job 15,4.5: An Exploration. Pp. 382-386 in *The Book of Job.* Editor W. A. M. Beuken. Bibliotheca Ephemeridum Theologicarum Lovanienium CXIV. Leuven: Leuven University Press.
1994b Job 26: An Orphan Chapter. Pp. 387-391 in *The Book of Job.* Editor W. A. M. Beuken. Bibliotheca Ephemeridum Theologicarum Lovanienium CXIV. Leuven: Leuven University Press.
1994c The Stone of Deepest Darkness: A Mineralogical Mystery (Job xxviii). *Vetus Testamentum* 44:274-276.
1994d The 'Neck' of Job's Tunic (Job XXX 18). *Vetus Testamentum* 44:570-572.
1995 *Deep Things out of Darkness.* Grand Rapids: Eerdmans.

Wolters, Al
1990 'A Child of Dust and Ashes' (Job 42, 6b). *Zeitschrift für die Alttestamentliche Wissenschaft* 102:116-119.

n. d. The 'tail' and 'thighs' of Behemoth (Job 40:17). Unpublished paper. Redeemer College, Ancaster
    Ontario.

Zimmermann, Ruben
1994 Homo Sapiens Ignorans: Hiob 28 als Bestandteil der ursprünglichen Hiobdichtung. *Biblische Notizen*
    71:80-100.

Ecclesiastes

TREMPER LONGMAN III

INTRODUCTION TO
Ecclesiastes

ECCLESIASTES IS AN ENIGMATIC BOOK. What other book in the Bible puts such an emphasis on the meaninglessness of this present life (see 1:2 and throughout) or advises readers not to be either "too good or too wise" (7:15-18)? This is a book that seems, on the surface, to have internal tensions—if not contradictions. Should we enjoy life (2:24-26), or should we take a sober or even somber attitude toward it, perhaps preferring death (7:1-4)?

Even though there are many questions concerning the interpretation of this book and, consequently, numerous disagreements among the commentators on certain details, the main message is rarely lost: Apart from God, there is no true meaning in life. Likewise, the final advice of the book is clear and beyond debate:

> Here now is my final conclusion: Fear God and obey his commands, for this is everyone's duty. God will judge us for everything we do, including every secret thing, whether good or bad. (12:13-14)

This small, admittedly difficult book is an important one for us to hear today. The issues of life haven't changed all that much since the time the book was first written in antiquity. Today we still face the question, where can we find the meaning of life?

AUTHOR

"Ecclesiastes" is the Latin translation of the Hebrew name *Qoheleth* (sometimes written Kohelet), which the NLT translates as "the Teacher." Accordingly, both "Qoheleth" and "the Teacher" will be used to refer to this person in this commentary. The Hebrew *Qoheleth* literally means "one who assembles (a group)" and may refer to assembling a group of students to hear one's teaching (as recorded in 1:12–12:7). Interestingly, this name likely intends to associate the Teacher with Solomon, since the verb *qahal* [TH6950, ZH7735], on which the name Qoheleth is formed, occurs a number of times in 1 Kings 8, which is Solomon's speech at the dedication of the Temple. As a matter of fact, there are a number of characteristics of the Teacher's description that cause one to think of Solomon. He is called "David's son, who ruled in Jerusalem" in the superscription (1:1). As he later searches for meaning "under the sun," he describes his great wealth, wisdom, and the numerous women who were his. This fits in well with what we know of the historical Solomon from 1 Kings 3–11. Even so, it is unlikely that the Teacher actually was Solomon.

A number of texts, for instance, dissociate the Teacher from the royal throne (4:1-3; 5:8-9; 10:20). Indeed, if the Teacher was Solomon, what purpose would be served by using a nickname (Qoheleth, meaning "Teacher") rather than simply stating that fact? Solomon's name was associated with such wisdom and authority as to merit a wide audience—certainly preferable to any nickname. The view that Solomon is not the author of the book has been held by other conservative commentators in the past (Luther, Moses Stuart, Delitzsch, Young, and Kidner—to name a few). However, in the interests of fairness, it should be pointed out that some conservative scholars consider this opinion to be incorrect (most notably in recent days, W. Kaiser). (See the Bibliography for each of these authors' commentaries.)

Furthermore, the Teacher, even if he was Solomon, is clearly not the author of the book of Ecclesiastes, in spite of some popularly held interpretations that insist on this view. There is a second voice in the book—that of an unnamed wise man who uses the Teacher's words and life story to teach the dangers of embracing "under the sun" perspectives (12:12). This unnamed wise man talks about the Teacher in 1:1-11 and 12:8-14. By contrast, the Teacher's distinct voice can be recognized by the fact that he speaks in the first person in 1:12–12:7. The second wise man, whose words frame the Teacher's speech, could be called the "frame narrator" (Fox 1977). The authorial voice is more closely connected with this second wise man, who chose not to give his name.

Thus, in the final analysis, the book of Ecclesiastes, like many other Old Testament books, is anonymous. Due to its presence in the canon, though, we can affirm that its ultimate author is God himself, because he speaks through the human author.

Notwithstanding, the implicit references to Solomon in the book are not to be ignored. The association of the "Teacher" with Solomon serves an important function in the book. Temporarily, the Teacher assumes the character of Solomon (with no intention to deceive since it is so clearly marked by the Teacher's dissociation from royalty; cf. 4:1-3; 5:8-9; 10:20) in order to explore areas of potential meaning. From the historical record in 1 Kings, we know that Solomon had more of everything than anyone else did, yet he still turned against the Lord and ended up splitting the kingdom. He had it all, but his life ended in meaninglessness.

It should also be noted that the Teacher, whose words form the central section of the book, can be characterized as a confused wise man. He is someone who knows the wisdom teachings of Israel well but has set out to understand life on his own and is frustrated and confused by life's incongruities and mysteries. This being the case, it is not surprising that in some cases we see the Teacher contradicting himself, as he turns sometimes to his knowledge of traditional wisdom for answers and at other times to his own anecdotal observations of life (e.g., 3:16-22; 7:3-9; 11:9).

DATE AND OCCASION OF WRITING

As we have seen above, the book of Ecclesiastes is anonymous. Since we do not know who the author is, its date is unknown. Due to the extensive associations with Solomon in the book, it clearly could not have originated before Solomon

(c. 960 BC). The language of the book is unusual, and some scholars argue that its Hebrew is like post-biblical Hebrew and therefore points to a late date for the book, perhaps sometime after the fourth century BC. This viewpoint is often supported by the presence of what look like Greek and Persian loanwords and a similarity in terms of language and grammar to Aramaic. An interesting twist on this argument is the viewpoint that the difficult Hebrew of Ecclesiastes should be explained as the product of someone who was thinking in Greek and writing in Hebrew (Buhlman 2000). DeJong believes that Qoheleth's argument describing human limitation fits best in the Jewish Hellenistic period when there was too much ambition (1994). These data could well point to a late date, but we are actually in the dark about many aspects of the development of the Hebrew language. The unique nature of the Hebrew of the book could be due to its use of a dialect or vernacular, rather than literary, form of Hebrew. It is best to remain "agnostic" about the date of the book, especially since it is unimportant to its interpretation.

AUDIENCE

Since we cannot date the book, we cannot be specific about the audience to whom it is addressed. The way the book is written, the second wise man is speaking to his son (12:12) concerning the dangers of speculative thinking—that is, thinking apart from God ("under the sun"). In a sense, then, other readers find themselves in the same place as the son, learning a lesson about living without God and his revelation: Apart from God, life is meaningless. This warning serves to undermine the tendency of all God's human creatures to create their own meaning for their lives. Wisdom, relationships, power, money, influence, and other areas are all put under a microscope, and the conclusion is that "all is meaningless" without God.

CANONICITY AND TEXTUAL HISTORY

With few and minor exceptions, the Hebrew Masoretic text of Ecclesiastes is without problems; it is supported by the Greek, Latin, and Syriac versions. The Aramaic Targum characteristically is an interpretive paraphrase and in the case of Ecclesiastes in particular is a witness to early exegesis. Fragments of Ecclesiastes were discovered at Qumran, and they also essentially agree with the Masoretic Hebrew tradition.

Ecclesiastes was one of five books that had their canonicity questioned by some early rabbinic authorities. Doubts arose because it was felt that Ecclesiastes contradicted itself, as well as other Scripture. For instance, the Talmud gave voice to the thought that Ecclesiastes 2:2, which teaches that pleasure is useless, contradicted 8:15 where the Teacher commends pleasure (b. Shabbath 30b). More seriously, some felt that 11:9, which literally encourages the reader to "follow the ways of your heart and the sight of your eyes," contradicted Numbers 15:39, which literally admonishes people to "not prostitute [themselves] by going after the lusts of [their] own hearts and eyes" (Midrash Rabbah, Kohelet).

Some rabbis also accused Ecclesiastes of being secular inasmuch as one hears the incessant refrain "everything is meaningless." However, the predominant opinion was that Ecclesiastes indeed was canonical, and it is found in all the major early lists of authoritative books. The fact that it was found at Qumran implies that it had achieved that status before the time of Christ. In other words, though the canonicity of Ecclesiastes was questioned by some, it was never rejected by the mainstream Jewish communities.

GENRE AND LITERARY STYLE

One of the most important keys to interpreting a biblical book is the identification of its literary genre, which often includes structure. We can tell this from modern examples. We expect different things from a novel than we do from a biography and, therefore, we read them differently. In the Bible there are many different genres represented, including history, law, wisdom, prophecy, gospel, epistle, and poetry. (For information on how to read the different genres of the Bible, see Longman 1997.)

It is therefore appropriate to ask what kind of book we have when we begin to read the book of Ecclesiastes. As was noted in the section above under "Author," one important observation is that there are two voices in the book. The largest part of the book (1:12–12:7) contains the voice of a person who goes by the nickname "the Teacher" (Heb., *Qoheleth*). However, in the beginning of the book (1:1-11) and at the end (12:8-14), someone is speaking to his son (12:12) *about* the Teacher. These words provide a kind of literary frame around the Teacher's words.

In comparison with other ancient writings, I have elsewhere identified the Teacher's words as a kind of reflective autobiography (see Longman 1991). Thus, the book as a whole may be called a framed autobiography. As we will see below, the most important insight we can derive from this literary observation is that the authoritative teaching of the book comes from the words of the voice in the frame. That voice directs us as to how to understand the thoughts and opinions of the Teacher, much like the authoritative voice of the book of Job is that of God who, at the very end of the book of Job, guides our understanding of the thoughts of the human characters of the book.

The book of Ecclesiastes is composed of both prose and poetry. The formatting used in some versions (such as the NIV and NJB) gives the wrong impression that there is more poetry in the book than is really there. The NLT redresses this imbalance.

The Hebrew of the prose is difficult, but we do not know whether that is the result of the style or a particular dialect of the language. The poetry is most often associated with the proverbs that are found throughout the book (1:15, 18; 7:1-14). The famous poem that begins "For everything there is a season, a time for every activity under heaven" is rightly put in poetic format (3:1-8). The striking images that are found throughout the book will be unpacked in the commentary.

MAJOR THEMES

The structure of Ecclesiastes has three parts. In the prologue (1:1-11), an unnamed wise man (see above under "Author") introduces the Teacher and sets the mood for his conclusion. As we will see, the tone is quite depressing. It anticipates the Teacher's conclusions by introducing some of his favorite phrases such as "everything is meaningless" (1:2) and "under the sun," where nothing is "truly new" (1:9). The second section is the longest. It is the autobiography of the Teacher in which he talks about his futile search for meaning and gives some advice to those who listen to him (1:12–12:7). The structure of the autobiography itself is not very clear-cut. We can delineate distinct units of his teaching, but he keeps coming back to the same subject. The confusion of the structure of his speech may well reflect the confusion in his thinking as he grapples with the apparent conflict between Israel's tradition and the suffering of the righteous. The last part is, in a number of ways, the most important part of the book. In the epilogue (12:8-14), we again hear the words of the unnamed wise man who is commenting on the Teacher's words to his son. We need to read the Teacher's comments in the light of the evaluation of the second wise man in much the same way that we read the speeches of Job's three friends in the light of the Yahweh speeches at the end of the book of Job. The epilogue affirms the fact that life under the sun is difficult; but then in the last two verses of the book, the wise man turns his son back to the foundational teachings of the faith: fear God, obey the commands, and expect a future judgment. Because of this structure, we need to differentiate the major themes in the speech of the Teacher from the major themes in the words of the second wise man who comments on the Teacher's thinking.

Major Themes of the Teacher. One cannot read the Teacher's comments in 1:12–12:7 without coming away with the impression that everything is "meaningless" (*hebel* [TH1892, ZH2039]). He looks for meaning in a number of different areas of life (work, pleasure, wisdom, wealth, relationships) and comes up empty. Half of the occurrences of the word *hebel* in the Old Testament are found in Ecclesiastes. It means literally "breath, breeze, vapor," but the word is always used in a metaphorical way, signifying either the meaninglessness of a thing or its transitory nature. A minority of scholars think that the word has the latter sense and translate "everything is transitory," giving the book of Ecclesiastes a radically different sense (see Fredericks 1993). But this is not the way the ancient versions (the LXX and Vulgate) understood it. Also the New Testament almost certainly contains an allusion to the *hebel* of Ecclesiastes in Romans 8:20, and there the sense is clearly "meaninglessness" or "frustration" (Gr. *mataiotēs* [TG3153, ZG3470]), rather than "temporary."

Some scholars, while taking *hebel* in the sense of meaninglessness instead of transitory, argue for a more specific meaning. Fox (1989) takes it as "absurd," Staples (1955) as "mysterious" and Ogden (1987:22) as "enigmatic," but none of these arguments are persuasive. It is best to stick with the general translation of "meaninglessness" (for a fuller discussion see Longman 1998:61-64).

A second important theme for the Teacher is represented by the phrase "under the sun." This phrase indicates the scope of the Teacher's inquiry into meaning. It is analogous to saying "under heaven" (2:3; 3:1) or "on earth" (5:2). In other words, the Teacher is restricting his inquiry to what he can see and experience. He makes no appeal to revelation or to God for his knowledge.

The Teacher also reflects at length on death (3:16-22; 9:1-12; 12:1-7) and the inability to control or read the "times." Death renders everything meaningless, since there is nothing after death. As for the inability to control or read the "times," this is particularly frustrating for a wise man who needs to say the right thing and do the right thing at the right time. According to 3:1-15, God has established a right time for everything, but he has not let human beings in on it (see esp. 3:11). Death and the inability to control time are two factors that lead the Teacher to conclude that everything is meaningless.

The other major contributing factor to this conclusion is the Teacher's conclusion that good people suffer, while bad people prosper. That is not the way it is supposed to be, but that is what he observes "under the sun" (see 7:15-18; 8:9-15).

Major Themes of the Second Wise Man. While the second wise man speaks much less than the Teacher (1:1-11; 12:8-14), his words are significant because they evaluate the significance of the Teacher's words and provide the normative teaching of the book.

The most important themes of the second wise man and the book are found in 12:13-14, the last two verses of the book. Here the wise man tells his son (12:12) that the most important things in life are to "fear God and obey his commands." It is true that the Teacher used the same words (3:14; 5:7; 7:18; 8:12) but with doubtful conviction. Here there is no doubt but that he intends his son to "fear God" in the sense of Proverbs 1:7—that is, to respect, honor, and worship the Lord. This attitude leads to a grateful obedience of God's commandments. This attitude is also to be held in the light of the coming judgment of God.

THEOLOGICAL CONCERNS

The book of Ecclesiastes, though we cannot precisely date it, deals with issues that are perennially relevant, both during the entire period of the Old Testament as well as today. The Teacher expresses what we today would call a crisis of faith. Of course, as a person living in ancient Near Eastern society, he did not question God's existence, but he did wonder about his fairness and also about the purpose of life. In a word, he struggled with life as he saw it "under the sun," by which he meant "life from a human perspective." From an "under the sun" perspective, our earthly life is all we have, which is why he expressed doubt, if not denial, about the idea of an afterlife (3:16-22; 9:3-7; 12:1-7). Furthermore, as he looks at life on earth, he sees it is unfair that the wicked often prosper, while the righteous suffer (7:15-18 and throughout). Is God fair if he does not reward the righteous in this life or the next? Accordingly, he concluded that all is "meaningless" (throughout, but see especially the summarizing statements in 1:2 and 12:8).

However, the Teacher's perspective is not the final viewpoint of the book. We should understand his speech (1:12–12:7) as a lengthy quotation, which is framed by a second wise man speaking to his son (see "Author" above). It is the second wise man's perspective on the Teacher that gives us the normative teaching of the book.

In essence, he is using the Teacher's speech as a tool in order to teach his son about the dangers of "under the sun" thinking (which is limited to human perception).

In the epilogue (see commentary on 12:8-14), the father tells his son that the Teacher is right if you restrict your vision to life "under the sun." Life is hard, with only momentary glimpses of joy, and then you die (cf. the so-called "seize the day" passages: 2:24-26; 3:12-14, 22; 5:18-20; 8:15; 9:7-10). But to restrict one's vision in this way is dangerous, and the father warns his son about dwelling too long on such viewpoints: "But, my child, let me give you some further advice: Be careful, for writing books is endless, and much study wears you out" (12:12). The intention of the book, then, can be summarized as a warning against speculative thinking that leads to the conclusion that everything is meaningless and an encouragement toward the "final conclusion: Fear God and obey his commands, for this is everyone's duty. God will judge us for everything we do, including every secret thing, whether good or bad" (12:13-14).

Ecclesiastes and the New Testament Above, we have seen that the book of Ecclesiastes contains two voices; one is that of the Teacher, and the other is that of the unnamed wise man who is using the Teacher's words to teach his son about the dangers of "under the sun" thinking. The Teacher has looked life on earth square in the face and has concluded, "Life is hard, and then you die." The second wise man, in essence, agrees that this is true "under the sun," but then at the very end points his son to what is truly important—fearing God by obeying his commandments in the light of the coming judgment (12:13-14).

The New Testament never quotes Ecclesiastes at length, but an allusion in Romans 8:20 is very important for us to see how we should understand the book in the light of the coming of Jesus Christ. In that verse, Paul reminds us that God had subjected the world to "God's curse." The Greek word Paul used (*mataiotēs* [TG3153, ZG3470]) is the same word used in the Septuagint to render the Hebrew for "meaningless" (*hebel* [TH1892, ZH2039]). Comfort's (1993:322) comments on this are appropriate: "Nowhere in the NT is the kind of futility described in Ecclesiastes so clearly reflected as in Romans 8:20. When Paul speaks of the creation being subjected to futility, he is focusing on the inability of creation to attain the goal for which it was originally designed. When humanity sinned, God subjected creation to the curse of futility and decay (cf. Gen 3:17-19)."

In the context of the whole canon, we understand with new depth the fact that when the Teacher was talking about life under the sun, he was giving us insight into the effects of the Fall on all things in creation. In the broader context of Romans 8, Paul is telling us that God subjected the creation to the curse in hope of a future redemption. Hope is centered on Jesus; that is the message of the New Testament. Jesus subjected himself to the fallen world and experienced its meaninglessness in order to free us from the curse of the Fall (Gal 3:13). In particular, Jesus died in order to free us from the curse of death (1 Cor 15:20-28).

As we review the story of Jesus' life as found in the Gospels and interpreted in the Epistles, we can see how this worked out. Jesus was God himself but did not hesitate to humble himself by taking on human form (Phil 2:5-11). When he was born, he was born not in grandeur but in a manger. He was the one through whom the creation came into being, but the world did not recognize him (John 1:10).

Toward the end of his life, we see how he was deserted by his broader group of followers and his closer circle of disciples, betrayed by Judas, and denied by Peter. Finally, as he was hanging on the cross, he cried out, "My God, my God, why have you abandoned me?" (Mark 15:34). At this point, Jesus experienced the meaninglessness of this world in a way that Qoheleth could not imagine. Jesus did this in order to break the curse of that meaninglessness in our life. His resurrection infuses life with new meaning. In short, Jesus, the Messiah, is the answer to the problem expressed by the Teacher's cry, "meaningless, meaningless, everything is meaningless."

OUTLINE

COMMENTARY ON
Ecclesiastes

◆ Superscription (1:1)

These are the words of the Teacher,* King
David's son, who ruled in Jerusalem.

1:1 Hebrew *Qoheleth;* this term is rendered "the Teacher" throughout this book.

NOTES

1:1 *the Teacher.* The Hebrew is *Qoheleth* (cf. NLT mg). This word is the participle of a
verb that means "to assemble (a group)." The traditional translations of "the Teacher"
or "the Preacher" derive from the idea that the group is either a classroom or a congrega-
tion. Indeed, the name of the book, Ecclesiastes, comes from a Gr. word that means "the
Preacher." In actuality, though, the use of *Qoheleth* as a name or title is intended to further
the Solomonic fiction described in the Introduction (see "Author"), because the verb "to
assemble" occurs frequently in connection with Solomon's actions in 1 Kings 8.

COMMENTARY

The superscription acts like the title page of the book. Here it identifies in general
terms the form of the message that follows ("these are the words"), as well as the
source of the teaching that is found in 1:12–12:7 ("the Teacher"). For more about
this superscription, please consult the "Author" section in the Introduction.

◆ I. Frame Narrative: Prologue (1:2-11)

2"Everything is meaningless," says the
Teacher, "completely meaningless!"
    3What do people get for all their hard
work under the sun? 4Generations come
and generations go, but the earth never
changes. 5The sun rises and the sun sets,
then hurries around to rise again. 6The
wind blows south, and then turns north.
Around and around it goes, blowing in
circles. 7Rivers run into the sea, but the
sea is never full. Then the water returns
again to the rivers and flows out again to
the sea. 8Everything is wearisome beyond
description. No matter how much we
see, we are never satisfied. No matter how
much we hear, we are not content.
    9History merely repeats itself. It has
all been done before. Nothing under the
sun is truly new. 10Sometimes people say,
"Here is something new!" But actually it is
old; nothing is ever truly new. 11We don't
remember what happened in the past,
and in future generations, no one will
remember what we are doing now.

NOTES

1:2 *meaningless*. This word occurs over 35 times in this short book, marking it as a major theme, particularly of the body of the book (1:12–12:7). As a matter of fact, the refrain "Everything is meaningless . . . completely meaningless" may be seen as the Teacher's bottom line since the second wise man (see "Author" in the Introduction) introduces the Teacher's thoughts with this refrain here and then summarizes them similarly in 12:8. The basic meaning of the Heb. word is "vapor" or "bubble," but in Ecclesiastes it is used metaphorically to mean "devoid of meaning." Attempts to make the word suggest the brevity of life (see Fredericks 1993) are unpersuasive.

1:3 *What do people get?* Lit., "What profit is there for a person?" What is the ultimate end once all our activities cease? Is there any significance to our work, including our work at searching for meaning? This rhetorical question assumes the answer is "nothing"—people get nothing for all their hard work.

hard work. This renders a phrase (see also 2:18) that might be lit. translated "my toil that I toil." The Heb. root (*'amal* [TH5999, ZH6662]) occurs here in noun and verb form, which serves to emphasize its importance for the thought of the verse. The word usually has negative connotations and is well translated by "hard work," "toil," or "drudgery."

under the sun. The Teacher's thought may be characterized as "under the sun" thinking— that is, thinking apart from the revelation of God. It is not that he completely leaves God out; after all, he reflects on who God is and gives advice about a relationship with him in ch 5. However, his thinking about life is restricted to what he sees happen on earth and is not based on what he learns from Israel's prophets.

1:5 *hurries*. Lit., the verb *sha'ap* [TH7602, ZH8634] means "to pant." The sun can hardly keep up with its daily cycle. The picture supports the Teacher's point that in spite of all the strenuous effort, nothing meaningful is accomplished in the world.

1:6 *The wind blows south, and then turns north*. The Heb. utilizes a literary device that is called delayed identification. The subject "wind" is actually toward the end of the verse. Thus, as the verse describes something going south, north, and round and round, the reader is not certain until the end that the author is describing the wind. Such a device grabs the attention of readers and gets them involved, but, as with many Heb. literary devices, it is hard to reflect it in a modern translation without sounding wooden.

1:9 *History*. Heb. does not have a word for history as such, but this translation is a good one for the literal but vague "that which was."

COMMENTARY

As was explained in the introduction, the first part of the book contains the words of someone who is speaking about Qoheleth ("the Teacher"). Although the same is true of the epilogue (12:8-14), most of the book represents the words of Qoheleth speaking in the first person about himself.

The prologue (1:2-11) is the second wise man's introduction before the reader encounters the Teacher's speech. It essentially sets the mood for what follows, giving a foretaste of the conclusion that the Teacher reached in his exploration for meaning in this world. The tone is somber and expresses the conclusion that while there is a lot of activity in the world, it is tedious. To use a modern image, we are like rats on a wheel, running constantly but getting nowhere.

It begins by expressing the Teacher's final conclusion: "Everything is meaningless." As we will see in the chapters that follow, the Teacher looked for lasting significance in many different areas of life and came up empty. In 1:3 he asks a rhetorical question that he will repeat elsewhere in his reflections (see 3:9; 5:16). He asks what people get for all their hard work, and the assumed answer is "absolutely nothing." There is no profit to life. Indeed, according to 1:4-8, this is true not only for individuals but also for corporate humanity, nature, and even history. In 1:4, he takes the long view—a consideration of the ebb and flow of humanity from one generation to another—and concludes that nothing changes.

He then turns to nature, where change seems obvious at first glance, but closer inspection shows its insignificance. The sun moves through the sky, certainly, but it is the same every day, rising and setting, rising and setting. The wind blows, suggesting progress or change, but actually it simply blows in a circle getting nowhere (1:6). The same natural circular movement is seen with water (1:7). The water flows down the river to the sea, but the sea never gets full. Why? Because it simply recycles into the river, which flows back down into the sea, back to the river again, *ad infinitum*. After observing and commenting on all this motion that actually goes nowhere, the Teacher confesses his boredom with it all (1:8). Life is truly unsatisfying.

In 1:8-11 the Teacher reflects on the realm of human action. It again is characterized by constant motion, but on closer reflection he realizes that here, too, there is no real progress. Nothing is really new; history just repeats itself. If something strikes people as an innovation, it is only because they have forgotten something that actually happened in the past. A little research will show that it was an illusion; nothing is new. This paragraph also introduces another theme that wears heavily on the Teacher—forgetfulness. What we do today seems new and exciting to us, but it is not really new and will not be remembered in the future. Such an insight takes all the steam out of living and so-called creativity. The present loses out to the past and the future.

◆ II. The Teacher's Autobiography (1:12–12:7)
Introduction (1:12)

¹²I, the Teacher, was king of Israel, and I lived in Jerusalem.

NOTES
1:12 *I, the Teacher, was king of Israel, and I lived in Jerusalem.* The body of the book, beginning with this verse, contains the reflections of the Teacher. It is cast in autobiographical form and is framed by the words of a second wise man who introduces the Teacher and his thought (1:2-11), evaluates what he said (12:8-12), and concludes by emphasizing what is truly important in life (12:13-14).

COMMENTARY
The Teacher's reflections on life begin with a self-introduction. This verse is a typical introduction to an ancient Near Eastern autobiography, as we know them from Mesopotamia and Egypt (e.g., the Cuthaean Legend of Naram-Sin; the Sin of Sargon;

the Adad-guppi inscription; see Longman 1991:97-130). His description of himself as king over Israel in Jerusalem is part of his identification with Solomon. However, he also signals to his readers that this is a literary and not an actual identification by using the nickname "Teacher" (Heb., *Qoheleth*) and by using the past tense "I . . . was king." According to the book of Kings, Solomon was king until his death; there never was a time he could look back on his life and say "I was king." However, the Targum, which is admittedly a late work (second half of the first millennium AD), may witness to early legends that Solomon left the throne at the end of his life and searched for meaning (see Levine 1978:28). The book of Ecclesiastes may have been exploiting these legends for its own purpose of pointing out the meaninglessness of life.

◆ ## B. The Teacher's Search for the Meaning of Life (1:13–2:26)

1. Beginning thoughts (1:13-18)

¹³I devoted myself to search for understanding and to explore by wisdom everything being done under heaven. I soon discovered that God has dealt a tragic existence to the human race. ¹⁴I observed everything going on under the sun, and really, it is all meaningless—like chasing the wind.

¹⁵What is wrong cannot be made
   right.
   What is missing cannot be
   recovered.

¹⁶I said to myself, "Look, I am wiser than any of the kings who ruled in Jerusalem before me. I have greater wisdom and knowledge than any of them." ¹⁷So I set out to learn everything from wisdom to madness and folly. But I learned firsthand that pursuing all this is like chasing the wind.

¹⁸The greater my wisdom, the greater
   my grief.
   To increase knowledge only
   increases sorrow.

NOTES

1:13 *I devoted myself.* Lit., "I gave my heart." This phrase is used by the Teacher to indicate his whole-hearted devotion to the task of finding meaning in this world.

under heaven. This phrase has the same sense as the more frequent refrain "under the sun" (see note on 1:3). It points to the Teacher's intention to look at life apart from the revelation of God.

1:14 *I observed.* This phrase occurs regularly in the speech of the Teacher, particularly the first two chapters. What follows is a real-life description of the world that, at least in his mind, often conflicts with what he has been taught. The latter is signaled by the phrase "I know."

1:15 *What is wrong cannot be made right.* The Heb. is more lit. rendered "what is bent/crooked cannot be straightened." The NLT translation assumes a moral sense to the phrase, which certainly is in keeping with the Teacher's later explicit assertions that there is injustice under the sun about which little, if anything, can be done (4:1-3). However, it is not absolutely certain that this phrase has a moral sense. In any case, there is no doubt about his assessment that the world has problems.

1:16 *I said to myself.* This phrase (lit., "I spoke with my heart") and its variants signal self-reflection (see note on 2:1). The Teacher tries to honestly get a read on himself and his attitudes toward the world and ultimately God.

COMMENTARY

After introducing himself in good autobiographical style, the Teacher then alerts his hearers to his intention to "search for understanding and to explore by wisdom everything being done under heaven" (1:13a). The Teacher is trying to discover something that makes life worth living, but he is also restricting his vision to that which takes place on earth. He no sooner tells us of his intention than he informs us of his unhappy conclusion. He doesn't hold back when he states that it is God who has "dealt a tragic existence" to his human creatures. Certainly, as he will concede later, we can find some joy in this world and maybe even some relative purpose in life, but to find absolute meaning—that is beyond us. Life in this world is like "chasing the wind" (1:14). The wind seems substantial, but we cannot grab hold of it. This phrase, which will recur in the book, is a perfect illustration of meaningless activity. He concludes his first paragraph with a proverb about futility (1:15). There is something wrong with the world, and it cannot be fixed no matter how hard we try. Later on in his speech, the Teacher will go so far as to directly name God as the cause of the world's inadequacy (7:13).

In the next paragraph, the Teacher begins by asserting his qualifications to conduct a search into the matter of the meaning of life under the sun. In 1:16, he associates himself with Solomon, again in a way that also signals to us that he is not really Solomon (see "Author" in the Introduction). Solomon, of course, had legendary wisdom (1 Kgs 3-4). But, if this really were Solomon, the statement that he was wiser than any king who ruled before him in Jerusalem (1:16) would make little sense, since only one other Israelite king ruled before him in Jerusalem, namely David. The point is that the wise man in the first part of the book explores different areas of life where meaning might be found by adopting the persona of Solomon. After all, no one had more wisdom, women, money, status, and pleasure than Solomon, and where did it get him? He ended his life an apostate, and the kingdom split in half! As the proverb that concludes the final paragraph of the chapter suggests, wisdom only brought him increased trouble in life.

◆   ## 2. Searching for meaning in pleasure (2:1-11)

I said to myself, "Come on, let's try pleasure. Let's look for the 'good things' in life." But I found that this, too, was meaningless. ²So I said, "Laughter is silly. What good does it do to seek pleasure?" ³After much thought, I decided to cheer myself with wine. And while still seeking wisdom, I clutched at foolishness. In this way, I tried to experience the only happiness most people find during their brief life in this world.

⁴I also tried to find meaning by building huge homes for myself and by planting beautiful vineyards. ⁵I made gardens and parks, filling them with all kinds of fruit trees. ⁶I built reservoirs to collect the water to irrigate my many flourishing groves. ⁷I bought slaves, both men and women, and others were born into my household. I also owned large herds and flocks, more than any of the kings who had lived in Jerusalem before me. ⁸I collected great sums of silver and gold, the treasure of many kings and provinces. I hired wonderful singers, both men and women, and had many beautiful concubines. I had everything a man could desire!

⁹So I became greater than all who had lived in Jerusalem before me, and my wisdom never failed me. ¹⁰Anything I wanted, I would take. I denied myself no pleasure. I even found great pleasure in hard work, a reward for all my labors. ¹¹But as I looked at everything I had worked so hard to accomplish, it was all so meaningless—like chasing the wind. There was nothing really worthwhile anywhere.

NOTES

2:1 *I said to myself.* Lit., "I said to my heart," a variant of 1:16, also indicating self-reflection.

2:4 *for myself.* This prepositional phrase is repeated eight times in 2:4-8, after most of the main verbs. The NLT does not translate it in every instance for fear that it would be overly repetitive. We must not miss the point, however, that the Teacher does everything described in this section for his own pleasure. There are no philanthropic intentions involved with his actions here.

2:5 *parks.* The Heb. word is *paredes* [TH6508, ZH7236], which the attentive reader can see is related to the English word "paradise." The language of this verse (see also next note) implies that the Teacher is trying to recreate the conditions of paradise—that is, Eden itself. Brown (2000:38) points out that ancient, as well as more recent, kings gloried in their gardens. Their ability to tame "raw nature," he observes, goes with their ability to wage war and to control society.

all kinds of fruit trees. This language is reminiscent of the language used to describe Eden in Gen 1:11, 29; 2:9 (see Verheij 1991).

2:8 *many beautiful concubines.* The Heb. word (*shiddah* [TH7705, ZH8721]) that refers to these women is rare, but is probably related to the word "breast" (*shad* [TH7699, ZH8716]) and thus is a crude expression referring to a woman by reference to her sexual parts.

2:9 *all who had lived in Jerusalem before me.* This reference, with a number of others, is odd in the mouth of Solomon, since it implies a number of people, if not generations, had lived in Jerusalem before the Teacher. However, the city of Jerusalem was captured and incorporated into the kingdom by Solomon's father, David (2 Sam 5:6-16), and so there was only a short Israelite history in this city by the time of Solomon. This verse is just one of many signals that the Teacher is simply adopting the persona of Solomon for the purpose of mentally exploring potential areas of meaning.

COMMENTARY

In this section, Qoheleth searches for meaning in pleasure. Perhaps life's ultimate significance can be found in simply indulging the senses. As we will see, this avenue leads to a dead end. There must be something more to life, and if there isn't, then perhaps it is not worth living.

Pleasure is the first of a number of specific areas where the Teacher attempts to find the meaning of life. In modern terms, he experiments with hedonism. The relevance of the book of Ecclesiastes may be seen in that even today many people live for pleasure. The booming entertainment industry is testimony to the draw of pleasures of all types. Modern pleasure seekers need to listen closely as the Teacher announces his intention to investigate pleasure for possible meaning and then tells us his sad conclusion: the "good things" in life turned out to be meaningless. In the final analysis, they are useless. While there may be a momentary thrill in pleasure, there is no lasting significance. Therefore, pleasure is not ultimately satisfying.

After talking in general about this phase of his search, the Teacher goes on to specify the variety of areas in which he explored pleasure. The first type of pleasure that he sought was with wine. Could the happiness induced by alcohol give him a reason for life? Interestingly, the Teacher tells us that he drank wine with the particular intention of testing its value for providing life with meaning. While the sensuous pleasure of drinking is the only joy many people find in this life, he found it inadequate. He thus moved on to other possibilities.

The Teacher then describes a different type of pleasure, pleasure that only great wealth can provide. Many people think they would enjoy life if only they had a lot more money than they do right now. However, the Teacher, by reminding us of the Solomonic experience of having everything but ending up as an apostate who lost the kingdom, debunks this illusion. The Teacher describes his attempt at finding happiness and satisfaction by building a huge home surrounded by luxurious gardens. Furthermore, he hired a staff to support it, and he indulged his desires by having entertainment (singers) and many beautiful women at his beck and call (2:4-8). In a sense, we may say that the Teacher was trying to recreate the experience of Eden (see notes on 2:5) but again to no avail. In his evaluation of this experience recorded in 2:9-11, he asserts that no one had more than he had, and he had everything that he could possibly want. He tried and had the means to fulfill his every desire—money and law were not obstacles. Furthermore, he did not indulge mindlessly in this way. He still worked hard (2:10)—that is, he carried out his experiment wisely, in other words self-reflectively (2:9). Nonetheless, the conclusion that he anticipated in 2:2 rings out loud and clear once again. No matter how hard he tried, everything remained meaningless. Pleasure was a dead end! It could not grant life the significance for which the Teacher searched with such eagerness.

◆ ## 3. Searching for meaning in wisdom (2:12-17)

12So I decided to compare wisdom with foolishness and madness (for who can do this better than I, the king?*). 13I thought, "Wisdom is better than foolishness, just as light is better than darkness. 14For the wise can see where they are going, but fools walk in the dark." Yet I saw that the wise and the foolish share the same fate. 15Both will die. So I said to myself, "Since I will end up the same as the fool, what's the value of all my wisdom? This is all so meaningless!" 16For the wise and the foolish both die. The wise will not be remembered any longer than the fool. In the days to come, both will be forgotten.

17So I came to hate life because everything done here under the sun is so troubling. Everything is meaningless—like chasing the wind.

2:12 The meaning of the Hebrew is uncertain.

NOTES

2:12 *I decided.* More lit., "I turned my attention to." The Teacher uses this verb (*panah* [TH6437, ZH7155]) to indicate a shift in subject.

foolishness and madness. This pair could be treated as a hendiadys and simply translated "mad folly."

2:15 *I said to myself.* Cf. notes on 1:16 and 2:1. This expression indicates self-reflection.

2:17 *I came to hate life.* Whybray (1989:60-61) points out that other "wisdom figures" in the Bible express a similar frustration with life (cf. Job in Job 3 and Ahithophel, the wise man who committed suicide according to 2 Sam 17:23).

COMMENTARY

One might suspect that the Teacher would find meaning in wisdom, which is the object of his next search. After all, he was a wise man. While Solomon, whose persona the Teacher draws on, was endowed with great wisdom by God, he still ended up making a fool of himself by worshipping other gods and goddesses. The Teacher, too, will discover that acquiring wisdom is not the answer to the question of the meaning of life.

This relatively short unit, a self-reflection (Murphy 1981:35), epitomizes in many ways the Teacher's thought as he pursues meaning in this world. The unit also concerns wisdom, a subject that would be dear to the Teacher's heart and life since, after all, he was a wisdom Teacher. In other words, if he is to find meaning anywhere, we would expect that he find it here. However, a quick reading of the section reveals to the reader that he does not successfully find meaning in wisdom, and a closer examination tells us why.

He examines wisdom, interestingly enough, by comparing it with its opposite, foolishness. The Teacher does not give us a definition of wisdom; but from elsewhere in the Bible, particularly the book of Proverbs, we learn that wisdom is applying God's truth to life. It is a practical intelligence, a kind of skill in living. Today, it might even be called emotional intelligence (see Goleman 1995). Indeed, from the Teacher's description of wisdom's advantage over foolishness, we can see that he has this concept in mind. The Teacher quickly concludes that wisdom is better than foolishness because a wise person can navigate the obstacles of life more efficiently than the fool can. He uses the metaphor of sight to communicate this. The wise person is like someone who walks with eyes wide open, whereas the fool does not see the obstacles in the way. It is clear that the Teacher prefers wisdom over foolishness. So far, so good. The Teacher, though perhaps not sharing the enthusiasm of Proverbs for wisdom, certainly agrees that wisdom is a relatively good thing.

This positive picture is soon disturbed, however, by the thought of death. Verse 14 says that the wise person and the fool share the "same fate," which the next verse makes abundantly clear is death. Wisdom may help one navigate life, but it cannot spare a person from death. This realization leads the Teacher to question the ultimate value of wisdom and to again conclude that life is essentially meaningless.

This conclusion, the Teacher would claim, goes well beyond his own situation and is true of everyone, including those of us who are reading it today. The parenthetical remark at the end of 2:12 indicates this. He asks rhetorically, "Who can do this better than I, the king?" If the Teacher—taking on the persona of King Solomon, the wisest person of all—cannot find meaning in wisdom, we don't stand a chance! Solomon was given great wisdom from God himself, and look how he ended his life—a dead fool.

The unit ends with a strong expression of the Teacher's exasperation (2:17). It says that he came to "hate life" because it is full of trouble and ultimately meaningless. Not only will death come to both wise and foolish, but both will be ultimately forgotten (2:16), a fate that is equally tragic to the Teacher.

◆   ## 4. Searching for meaning in work (2:18-23)

¹⁸I came to hate all my hard work here on earth, for I must leave to others everything I have earned. ¹⁹And who can tell whether my successors will be wise or foolish? Yet they will control everything I have gained by my skill and hard work under the sun. How meaningless! ²⁰So I gave up in despair, questioning the value of all my hard work in this world.

²¹Some people work wisely with knowledge and skill, then must leave the fruit of their efforts to someone who hasn't worked for it. This, too, is meaningless, a great tragedy. ²²So what do people get in this life for all their hard work and anxiety? ²³Their days of labor are filled with pain and grief; even at night their minds cannot rest. It is all meaningless.

NOTES

2:18 *hard work.* See note on 1:3.

on earth. A variant English rendering of Qoheleth's idiom "under the sun" (cf. note on 1:3). Its basic theological meaning is "apart from the revelation of God."

2:19 *And who can tell whether?* Lit., "And who knows?" As Crenshaw (1987:274-288) points out, this is a rhetorical question with the implicit answer, "No one knows!"

2:21 *Some people work wisely.* Lit., "There was a person who worked wisely"; the phrase introduces an anecdote that illustrates the Teacher's point about the futility of work. The NLT appropriately gives a dynamic equivalent rendition of the phrase that communicates its message well.

COMMENTARY

The Teacher now explores work to see if he might find life's meaning in that area. We can see why he might be attracted to this possibility. Through work, we get something done. A contractor builds a house; a plumber repairs a leaky faucet. A writer completes an essay; a minister delivers a sermon and hopes that the world will be changed for the better. Through work, we get what we need to survive and even thrive. In our modern world our work earns money, which we can use to obtain homes, clothes, cars. Yes, for reasons similar to these, work must have attracted the Teacher's attention as a possible avenue to significance.

Surprisingly, though, the Teacher reaches the same stark conclusion as he did with pleasure and wisdom: work is meaningless. He reaches his negative verdict for a reason similar to that of the previous section. Death renders one's work worthless. In the light of death, there is no ultimate meaning to one's work. He envisions himself working hard all his life with good results; his labor will indeed bear fruit. But it comes at great cost (anxiety, pain, grief; 2:22-23), and what will happen when he dies? He cannot be sure. He cannot control his wealth beyond the grave. It may be inherited by a fool (2:19)! It will certainly go to someone who has not worked for it

(2:21). This realization led the Teacher to despair and to hate his work. Why bother, if the results are so temporary?

As a wisdom figure, the Teacher would have been amazed with the results of his inquiry. After all, the book of Proverbs is very optimistic about the rewards of hard work and the suffering of lazy people (see Prov 6:6-11). The Teacher's reflection on the topic of work again calls the value of wisdom into question (cf. 2:12-17).

◆   ## 5. Grab all the gusto you can! (2:24-26)

24So I decided there is nothing better than to enjoy food and drink and to find satisfaction in work. Then I realized that these pleasures are from the hand of God. 25For who can eat or enjoy anything apart from him?* 26God gives wisdom, knowledge, and joy to those who please him. But if a sinner becomes wealthy, God takes the wealth away and gives it to those who please him. This, too, is meaningless—like chasing the wind.

2:25 As in Greek and Syriac versions; Hebrew reads *apart from me?*

NOTES

2:24 *there is nothing better than.* This formulaic statement communicates a note of resignation and occurs in three other places in the book (3:12, 22; 8:15).

than. Most translations, including the NLT, understand that there is a minor textual problem in this verse, and so the comparative idea (represented in the English "than") must be restored to the text. It has dropped out of the Heb. text due to a very common textual error called haplography, where a letter occurring twice in a row was copied by a scribe only once. In this case, the one letter was a *mem,* a common contraction of the Heb. comparative that should be supplied here. The detailed argument may be found in Delitzsch (1975:251).

2:26 *sinner.* The NLT and most translations (cf. NIV, NASB, KJV) understand the Heb. word *khote'* [TH2398, ZH2627] here in its narrow theological sense, which is certainly possible. Some commentaries (see Longman 1998:109-110) take the word in its broader sense as "one who offends God." This reading is argued for on the basis of the context and tone of the Teacher's argument. It suggests that God plays favorites, according to the Teacher's "under the sun" perspective on God.

COMMENTARY

This section is a concluding paragraph to the Teacher's argument from 1:13–2:23. So far, the Teacher has looked at pleasure, wisdom, and work in the attempt to find the ultimate meaning of life. He has been disappointed with each and has concluded that everything is meaningless. In the present section, he asserts that under such conditions we ought to grab whatever pleasure comes our way. Ecclesiastes 2:24-26 is the first of six so-called *carpe diem* passages (the others are 3:12-14; 3:22; 5:18-20; 8:15; 9:7-10). In other words, they encourage the reader to "seize [the pleasures] of the day." They should be read with a tone of resignation. After all, the passage begins with "there is nothing better than . . ." In other words, this is the best that a person can hope for in this life that will end with death.

The joys that the Teacher specifies here are eating and drinking and work. These are areas (eating and drinking subsumed under pleasure) that the Teacher has already told us cannot sustain ultimate meaning, but they can create a diversion from the harsh reality of life (this point will be particularly developed in the *carpe diem* passage found in 5:18-20).[1]

In the interest of fairness, it should be pointed out that some scholars hold a different view on these *carpe diem* passages. Kaiser (1979:463-466) and Whybray (1982) both suggest that these passages really represent the Teacher's ultimate conclusion and that we should read him as more orthodox than the present commentary is suggesting. However, as one continues in the book, one observes that the Teacher himself finds no peace in eating, drinking, or work. In the present passage (2:24), he admits that even these simple pleasures are God's gift; but from his tone and what he says to follow, we are led to conclude that this is a gift that he himself did not receive. The fact that the *carpe diem* passage ends with another expression of the meaninglessness of life also supports the idea that his conclusion is a pessimistic one—not that one should enjoy the simple pleasures of life.

ENDNOTES
1. Brown (2000:39) makes an interesting connection with the advice of the witch of Endor. In 1 Sam 28:21-25 the witch encourages Saul, who has just heard that he will die in battle, to enjoy a last meal.

◆ C. The Search Continues (3:1–6:9)

1. A time for everything (3:1-15)

For everything there is a season,
a time for every activity under heaven.
[2] A time to be born and a time to die.
A time to plant and a time to harvest.
[3] A time to kill and a time to heal.
A time to tear down and a time to build up.
[4] A time to cry and a time to laugh.
A time to grieve and a time to dance.
[5] A time to scatter stones and a time to gather stones.
A time to embrace and a time to turn away.
[6] A time to search and a time to quit searching.
A time to keep and a time to throw away.
[7] A time to tear and a time to mend.
A time to be quiet and a time to speak.
[8] A time to love and a time to hate.
A time for war and a time for peace.

[9] What do people really get for all their hard work? [10] I have seen the burden God has placed on us all. [11] Yet God has made everything beautiful for its own time. He has planted eternity in the human heart, but even so, people cannot see the whole scope of God's work from beginning to end. [12] So I concluded there is nothing better than to be happy and enjoy ourselves as long as we can. [13] And people should eat and drink and enjoy the fruits of their labor, for these are gifts from God.

[14] And I know that whatever God does is final. Nothing can be added to it or taken

from it. God's purpose is that people should fear him. ¹⁵What is happening now has happened before, and what will happen in the future has happened before, because God makes the same things happen over and over again.

NOTES

3:1 season . . . time. The two Heb. words rendered here are close in meaning, though probably not identical. Unfortunately, at our historical distance we cannot determine the exact difference in nuance between them. That explains why some versions like the NIV have these two words in the opposite order. The NLT chose to move from the more general to the more specific English word. The second word (*'eth* [TH6256, ZH6961]), here translated "time," is also the Heb. word that is repeated like hammer blows throughout the poem that follows.

3:9 The rhetorical question found in this verse is nearly identical to the one in 1:3. There are some minor changes in grammar and vocabulary, but the basic thrust of the verses is identical. The implicit answer is that people get nothing for all their hard work.

3:10 burden. The Heb. root behind this word (*'inyan* [TH6045, ZH6721]) has been debated in terms of its precise meaning. The verbal root we associate the noun with determines its precise meaning. This explains why some versions (NRSV) translate the word something like "business" or "task." The context, though, makes it clear that no matter how one translates the word it has negative connotations. "Burden" can be defended on linguistic grounds (see Longman 1998:80, where I argue for "task," though I would agree that "burden" brings out the connotation more effectively here).

3:11 God has made everything beautiful. This section echoes Gen 1, though it uses different vocabulary. "Beautiful" (*yapeh* [TH3303, ZH3637]) seems to be an alternate way of describing creation as "good," as in Gen 1. "Appropriate" (NASB) also gives the sense of this Heb. word here in Ecclesiastes.

eternity. The meaning of this word (*'olam* [TH5769, ZH6409]) is much discussed. The most common meaning of this word by far in the Hebrew Bible is "eternity," but some think it too abstract a concept in this context and suggest another possible meaning like "darkness," which they suggest fits the context better (see Crenshaw 1974:40; Whybray 1989:73-74). However, this seems a desperate suggestion since it is based on a rather tenuous connection with a cognate word in Ugaritic. But what does it mean to place "eternity" in the heart? The commentary below understands it to mean "a sense of eternity," which fits the context quite well.

COMMENTARY

Ecclesiastes 1:13-2:26 contains the first cycle of the Teacher's search for ultimate meaning and his conclusion that everything was meaningless under the sun. In this next section of the book (3:1-6:9), the search continues as the Teacher explores new territory for meaning in life (for instance, relationships and political power) and in the process finds himself drawn back into looking at certain areas, such as work, a second time. This search will cause him to look deeper into the problems of death and injustice. In this section, we will also find his most profound, though ambivalent and sometimes disturbing, thoughts about God. After all is said and done, however, the Teacher once again concludes that meaning is not to be found in this life. And as for a life beyond the grave, who knows whether there is such a thing as eternal life (3:21-22)?

One of the most important themes in the Teacher's speech (1:12–12:7) has to do with his inability to discern or control the "times." It was very important for a wisdom Teacher to know the right time for the right action or the right word. Wisdom was all in the timing. Remember Proverbs 15:23: "Everyone enjoys a fitting reply; it is wonderful to say the right thing at the right time!" To the Teacher, knowing the right time was crucial to his ability to function with wisdom.

Our passage begins with optimism. The first eight verses constitute the most well-known passage in the book—indeed, one of the most well-known passages of the Bible. (This passage is even known to many who do not read the Bible through the Byrds' musical rendition of it in the mid-1960s.) It seems to exude confidence; but as we will soon see, it does so only when read apart from the evaluation that follows in 3:9-15. Nonetheless, 3:1-8 is a poem that affirms the truth that there indeed is a time or a season for everything that happens. In verse 11 the Teacher even affirms the fact that it is God who has made everything beautiful or appropriate for its time.

The poem lists fourteen areas of activity by citing their polar opposites, a literary device called a merism. For instance, there is a time to be born and a time to die, thereby citing the beginning and the end of one's earthly existence. By citing the two extremes of life, it assumes that life as a whole has its appointed time. Another observation to make about the structure of this powerful, mesmerizing poem is that the fourteen opposites break up into seven groups of two, and for almost all of the seven pairs there is a clear linkage. This use of seven groupings is another marker indicating the totality of life that the poem describes. After the first colon that speaks of birth and death comes a second that applies birth and death to plant life, planting and harvesting. In 3:3 the first pair is "kill" and "heal," and the second pair applies that to architecture—"tear down" and "build up." In verse 4, crying and laughing lead to the more specific grieving and dancing.

Verse 5 presents us with a conundrum of sorts. Is there a deeper significance to the surface meaning of scattering and gathering stones? This question has occupied interpreters for centuries, and we cannot be dogmatic in our answer. Some people suggest that it refers to the military defeat of a city, where the stones of houses and public buildings would be destroyed and scattered as during the destruction of Jerusalem when they were defeated by Babylon (in 586 BC). Others look at its "pair" in the next colon ("embrace" and "turn away") and detect a parallel with rabbinic language concerning sexual intercourse. Gathering stones would be refraining from sex, while scattering stones was apparently a rabbinic euphemism for male ejaculation (*Midrash Rabbah Kohelet*). Of course, the rabbinic idiom was much later than the Old Testament, so we cannot be certain about this interpretation.

The poem continues with four more opposite pairs (search/quit searching; keep/throw away; tear/mend; be quiet/speak) and then concludes with the climactic: "A time to love and a time to hate. A time for war and a time for peace" (3:8).

In the light of this last verse, let me make one more general observation about the poem before continuing into the second part of our passage with its evaluation of the contents of the poem. That is, the poem is descriptive and not prescriptive at least in the following sense: it may not be used to justify any particular emotion or action. In other words, it is not legitimate to use this concluding verse to justify any particular war. Participants cannot simply say that "there is a time for war" and conclude that their warfare is right and just. Indeed, the Teacher is here affirming that God has a right time for everything, but in the following verses he is going to question whether human beings can have any certain knowledge of these times.

Following the poem, the Teacher begins his questioning by asking the same rhetorical question (though there are some minor changes in grammar and vocabulary) that we earlier encountered in 1:3, "What do people really get for all their hard work?" (3:9). The assumed answer to this question is "Nothing—people get nothing from all their hard work!" This immediately qualifies any positive reading of the poem, and as the paragraph continues, we see that it only confirms our understanding that the Teacher himself found no comfort in the idea that there was a time or a season for everything.

Verses 10-11 tell us more directly what the trouble is. Certainly God made everything beautiful or appropriate for its own time, but he has not clued human beings in on his grand scheme. He has given human beings a sense of something beyond themselves ("eternity in the human heart"), but it creates a sense of expectation that is not fulfilled. It frustrates the Teacher that "people cannot see the whole scope of God's work from beginning to end." It doesn't lead him to a sense of mystery and awe. After all, the Teacher was a wise man, and as we have pointed out already, wisdom depends on the ability to discern the right time, the correct circumstance, for the right word and the right actions. Not knowing the times paralyzes wisdom and renders it ultimately worthless. This is why the Teacher refers to the "burden" that God has placed on humanity. Having a sense of something beyond us, but no ability to get at it, is exasperating to the Teacher.

This unhappy situation, this "burden," leads the Teacher to express resignation ("there is nothing better than") for a second time (see 2:24-26); he expresses this in yet another *carpe diem* passage (3:12-13). The relative good is to be "happy" and find enjoyment in life at every available opportunity. Again, as in the earlier *carpe diem* passage, the specific areas of enjoyment are food, drink, and work. We might call these the simple pleasures in life. In the *carpe diem* passage at the end of chapter 5, we will see precisely how these pleasures function to make life better by distracting us from the harshness of reality.

The concluding verses (3:14-15) make it clear that the Teacher does not for a moment doubt God's control and sovereignty. No one can change the world he has created and placed us in, no matter how bereft of ultimate purpose it is. He has placed eternity in our hearts and given us a sense that there are "right" times, but he has not allowed us access to that information. Furthermore, what God has done is "final" (3:14). Things are not going to change; they are going to be the same in the present as they were in the past, and the future will follow suit. Again, God has made it that way; after all, "nothing under the sun is truly new" (1:9).

2. Where can we find justice? (3:16-22)

[16]I also noticed that under the sun there is evil in the courtroom. Yes, even the courts of law are corrupt! [17]I said to myself, "In due season God will judge everyone, both good and bad, for all their deeds." [18]I also thought about the human condition how God proves to people that they are like animals. [19]For people and animals share the same fate—both breathe* and both must die. So people have no real advantage over the animals. How meaningless! [20]Both go to the same place—they came from dust and they return to dust. [21]For who can prove that the human spirit goes up and the spirit of animals goes down into the earth? [22]So I saw that there is nothing better for people than to be happy in their work. That is why we are here! No one will bring us back from death to enjoy life after we die.

3:19 Or *both have the same spirit.*

NOTES

3:16 courtroom . . . courts of law. Lit., "place of justice" and "place of righteousness," respectively.

3:17 In due season. This phrase is to intentionally remind us of the similar phrases in 3:1 and thus binds the two sections together.

3:18 proves. This is a suggested extended meaning of the Heb. root *barar* [TH1305, ZH1405], which normally means "to separate, select out." For a full discussion, see Crenshaw (1987:103).

3:20-21 they came from dust and they return to dust . . . the human spirit goes up. According to Gen 2:7, humans were created from the dust of the ground and the breath or spirit of God. Thus, to say that the dust returns to the ground and that the spirit either goes up or down is a way of describing the reversal of the process of creation, that is, death. There is no hint here of even the slight possibility of continued conscious existence. Qoheleth's thought is quite simply that death for animals and death for humans signifies exactly the same thing: the end.

3:21 who can prove . . . ? Lit., "who knows?" Crenshaw (1986) definitively shows that this marks a rhetorical question with the assumed answer, "No one knows."

COMMENTARY

The Teacher passes now from one frustration to another. In the previous section (3:1-15), he expressed his unhappiness over humans' inability to know the "times." This, in essence, is a crisis of control. In the present section, he raises a second major problem with finding meaning in this life—the problem of death. He comes to the problem of death through the issue of retribution: Do people get what they justly deserve in life? All three of these issues—control, death, and retribution—reverberate throughout the Teacher's autobiography. This section also demonstrates how the Teacher's thinking will occasionally waffle between what he has learned through tradition and what he observes in real life—that is, "under the sun."

In terms of real life, the Teacher begins by stating that he finds evil in a place where he expected to find justice, namely, the courtroom. The court is a human institution, but according to the Old Testament, it was to be run by godly kings, priests, and other leaders. The court was a place where wrongs were to be righted, victims helped, and sinners/criminals punished. In the Teacher's estimation, though, this institution was "corrupt." We will see this message repeated elsewhere; good people are treated as if they are wicked and wicked people are rewarded as if they are righteous!

At this point, though, the Teacher remembers his past theology lessons. If retribution does not come from fellow humans, at least it will come from God (3:17). God will give people what they deserve!

However, as soon as the Teacher expresses this idea, he throws a question mark over it. In the concluding paragraph to this chapter, he raises the specter of death. In 3:18-19 he certainly does not deny the idea of the afterlife, but he also does not warmly support it. His view, at first, is an agnostic one: Who knows? He begins by comparing people and animals, not to the advantage of animals but rather to point out that humans are like animals. They both live by breathing, but they also both end their lives by ceasing to breathe. This leads the Teacher to the sad conclusion that "people have no real advantage over the animals," and, thus again, life is ultimately meaningless (3:19). So, while at first he seems to be agnostic about the afterlife, the final verse seems to deny it altogether. His ultimate denial of the afterlife fits in with his other teachings on the subject, in chapters 9 and 12.

This assessment leads the Teacher to a third *carpe diem* expression (3:22). He again resignedly suggests that the best we can do is try to find happiness in work, something that he has already pointed out as having no ultimate significance (2:18-23).

◆   3. I'd rather be dead (4:1-3)

Again, I observed all the oppression that takes place under the sun. I saw the tears of the oppressed, with no one to comfort them. The oppressors have great power, and their victims are helpless. ²So I con-cluded that the dead are better off than the living. ³But most fortunate of all are those who are not yet born. For they have not seen all the evil that is done under the sun.

NOTES

4:2 *I concluded.* Lit., "I praised" (*shabakh* [TH7623, ZH8655]). He praises the dead more than the living. The NLT has rightly captured the sense of this verb, which is awkward if translated as "praised" in English.

the dead are better off than the living. In this verse, Qoheleth uses the first of a number of "better-proverbs" (Ogden 1977). The function of the form is simple: it takes one thing or a relationship between two things and compares it favorably with another thing or another relationship. In this case, Qoheleth reacts to the pervasive oppression that he observed on earth by favoring death over life.

COMMENTARY

The Teacher now passionately bemoans the oppression that he observes in the world. Though he is obviously sickened by the suffering, it is telling that he talks about it as if it is happening to someone else. Even more interesting is the fact that he talks about it as one who cannot alleviate the suffering that he observes. We hear this tone in other places in the Teacher's speech, and it is an indication that he is not someone who can do anything about the suffering. In other words, this section again lends strength to our conclusion that the Teacher is not actually Solomon. Solomon, after all, could have done something about the oppression of the people. As a matter of fact, according to the testimony of those who lived under Solomon's reign up to the time of his death, he horribly oppressed his own people in order to complete his monumental building projects (1 Kgs 12:4). Solomon himself was an oppressor and not a sympathizer of those who were oppressed.

In any case, when the Teacher sees the oppressed, it does not prompt him to action; rather, he concludes that death is better than life. As a matter of fact, he says that it would be best not to have been born. Non-existence is preferable because one wouldn't have to experience life at all. Job expresses a similar sentiment in his lament found in Job 3.

4. Searching for meaning in work, again (4:4-6)

⁴Then I observed that most people are motivated to success because they envy their neighbors. But this, too, is meaning-less—like chasing the wind.

⁵"Fools fold their idle hands, leading them to ruin."

⁶And yet,

"Better to have one handful with quietness
than two handfuls with hard work and chasing the wind."

NOTES

4:4 *most people are motivated to success because they envy their neighbors.* Lit., "all toil and all success in work results from envy of one's neighbors."

4:5 *leading them to ruin.* The Heb. is much more vivid and concrete: "consuming their own flesh." The idea is that when the lazy fool does not work, there is no income; so the fool will have to rely on resources that he or she already has. Ultimately, these resources will run out.

COMMENTARY

The Teacher has already explored work as a potential avenue of meaning and come up empty (2:18-23). He returns to the topic of work, but this time with an eye toward those who work hard in order to be successful. Is there meaning in success? The Teacher makes the insightful observation that striving for success is fueled by envy, or the desire to get ahead of one's neighbor. The NLT gives the impression (see note on 4:4) that the Teacher thought that some people sought success for other motivations, but this is not correct. According to the Teacher, all who seek success do so out of envy. He also continues by saying that such an effort is ultimately meaningless. After all, there is always someone who is ahead of us in some way. The richest person alive may be dreadfully unsuccessful in relationships; a person successful in relationships may be quite unathletic or even physically weak. No one has it all, and so everyone will keep striving until death. The Teacher wants none of that, so he imparts advice in the form of two proverbs. What is interesting is that these two proverbs appear to give contrary counsel.

The first proverb ("Fools fold their idle hands, leading them to ruin"; 4:5) recommends work by chiding the fool who is lazy and does not work. No work leads to no income at all and eventual destruction. This proverb reflects a major theme in the book of Proverbs 10:4-5; 14:23; 19:15; 20:4, 13; 21:25; 24:30-34). But then the second proverb ("Better to have one handful with quietness than two handfuls with hard work and chasing the wind"; 4:6) chides those who work too hard and never rest. What they seek is beyond them. It is like trying to catch the wind, which is the Teacher's favorite phrase about futility.

These two proverbs are not contradictory, but they push from both sides and basically counsel moderation. Work hard enough to earn an income and survive, but not so hard that there is no time to rest. After all, as the Teacher said in the first verses of this unit, working to attain success is ultimately meaningless and driven by envy. If there is tension, it is between Qoheleth and Proverbs (see Spangenberg 1991:25).

◆   ## 5. The lonely miser (4:7-8)

⁷I observed yet another example of something meaningless under the sun. ⁸This is the case of a man who is all alone, without a child or a brother, yet who works hard to gain as much wealth as he can. But then he asks himself, "Who am I working for? Why am I giving up so much pleasure now?" It is all so meaningless and depressing.

NOTES

4:7 *another example.* This phrase signals to the reader that Qoheleth is about to relate an anecdote or brief story that will support one of his central ideas, in this case the futility of work when someone has no vital relationships. From here on in the book, anecdotes will increasingly characterize Qoheleth's style. There are no names given in the story, just a description. By keeping the story general in this fashion, it becomes easier for readers to think of their own acquaintances and say, in effect, "I know somebody like that."

COMMENTARY

The next two sections, this one and 4:9-12, are associated by their shared theme of relationships or friendship. As we will see, the Teacher does think that relationships are a solace in a difficult world. He never says that people can find ultimate meaning in relationships, but one gains the strong impression that he feels that this hard world is much better off with friendship. However, some of the Teacher's later comments make one wonder exactly how many good relationships he himself enjoyed.

In any case, the present unit is an anecdote, a story about "a man," which illustrates the difficulty of a life without relationship. He tells the story of an anonymous man who does not have any relatives but works hard to gain wealth. The man simply asks, "Why?" Work involves abstaining from other pleasurable activities, and it strikes him as sad that someone might devote their life to the simple acquisition of personal wealth.

◆   ## 6. It's great to have friends (4:9-12)

⁹Two people are better off than one, for they can help each other succeed. ¹⁰If one person falls, the other can reach out and help. But someone who falls alone is in real trouble. ¹¹Likewise, two people lying close together can keep each other warm. But how can one be warm alone? ¹²A person standing alone can be attacked and defeated, but two can stand back-to-back and conquer. Three are even better, for a triple-braided cord is not easily broken.

NOTES

4:12 *a triple-braided cord.* A rope made out of multiple strands braided together is stronger than a single strand or even two. In this way, the Teacher informs us that the more good relationships a person has in life, the better off he or she will be. Shaffer (1967; 1969) has shown that this is a reference to an ancient Near Eastern proverb, one that is found quoted in the Gilgamesh Epic.

COMMENTARY

In the previous section, the Teacher described the travails of the person who is all alone by presenting an anecdote about a lonely miser. Why should such a person work so hard when there is no one to share it with? In the present section, he now expresses the relative advantages of relationship. It is clear that relationships are important to him. Nonetheless, we should also take note of his lack of enthusiasm. While finding a relative advantage, he is not claiming that ultimate meaning may be discovered in relationship. Gordis (1968:242) takes this too far, though, when he says that the Teacher is actually putting relationship down by giving it faint praise.

One question that scholars discuss in this section is precisely what kind of relationship the Teacher is talking about here. Gordis (1968:242) believes that he is speaking only about marriage, but there is nothing in the text that specifically identifies the relationship here in that way. The Teacher's comments may indeed include the marriage relationship, but would also include friendship (Delitzsch 1975:277). I believe the Teacher's comments include marriage, friendship, business associates, and more. I subsume all these under the general topic of relationship.

In any case, relationship has a number of advantages over being alone. For one thing, two people can help each other get ahead and be successful. Two people can protect and defend each other from dangers. In a particularly touching example, the Teacher says that two can keep each other warm on a cold night.

As a final emphasis on the relative advantage of relationship, the Teacher affirms that if two are better than one, then three are better than two. This is probably to be related to what is called a number proverb (Watson 1984:282) in the ancient Near East. It is a way of saying the more friends, the better.

◆   ## 7. Even political power lets you down (4:13-16)

¹³It is better to be a poor but wise youth than an old and foolish king who refuses all advice. ¹⁴Such a youth could rise from poverty and succeed. He might even become king, though he has been in prison. ¹⁵But then everyone rushes to the side of

yet another youth* who replaces him.
¹⁶Endless crowds stand around him,* but
then another generation grows up and
rejects him, too. So it is all meaningless—
like chasing the wind.

4:15 Hebrew *the second youth.* 4:16 Hebrew *There is no end to all the people, to all those who are before them.*

NOTES

4:13 better . . . than. The Teacher again uses a distinctive grammatical form (the better . . . than construction) in order to communicate his ideas concerning relative, though not ultimate, meaning in life (see Ogden 1977).

4:15 another youth. Lit., "second youth" (see NLT mg). There are some who believe this refers to the poor but wise youth already mentioned, and so understand second to mean second to the king (Ginsburg 1970:333). Rudman (1997) suggests that the phrase is to be translated "young lieutenant," but his interpretation struggles with the fact that this person succeeds the king. I agree with Whybray (1982:90-91), Crenshaw (1987:113-114), and Fox (1989:207-208) that the second youth is a third character in the anecdote.

COMMENTARY

This unit gives us an anecdote that illustrates the advantages of wisdom over folly. It thus tells us a story that incarnates the principle enunciated in a passage like 2:12-17, which is that wisdom has a relative but not absolute value. Thus, it has only a distant connection with the immediately preceding sections that discuss social relationships (contra Ginsburg 1970:330).

Some of the details of this anecdote are confusing to the modern reader, but it is hard to say, along with Irwin (1944:255), whether this is a result of ambiguity in writing or distance from the original text. In either case, it is unclear whether there are two or three characters in the anecdote. I think the phrase translated as "another youth" in 4:15 suggests a third character, and my interpretation will proceed with that assumption.

As with the other anecdotes that the Teacher constructs (see 4:8-9 and 9:13-16), it is a little difficult to see whether he had specific people in mind behind the story. Some people see a connection between Joseph and the "poor but wise youth" who rises even from a prison to be king (see Ogden 1980). However, whether or not there is such historical specificity really does not affect our understanding of the passage.

The initial contrast is between a "poor but wise youth" and an "old and foolish king." We see that three polarities are being contrasted here. In the first place, there is youth versus age. In an ancient Near Eastern context, age was considered an asset over youth. After all, an older person did have more experiences that would help them know how to navigate life. Then there is a contrast between "poor" and "king." There are two contrasts hidden here, and they are related. First, there is an economic contrast. Kings, of course, were rich, and the youth is explicitly said to be poor. Then there is a social contrast between a king and a poor commoner (who at one point was even in prison). Needless to say, in an ancient, as well as a modern society, social status and wealth were considered more attractive than the low status of poverty. However, the anecdote judges the poor youth as better off than the rich, old king. Why? Because wisdom trumps everything! The king does not have wisdom, so he is not considered well-off, in spite of his riches and his power.

In the early part of his reign, Solomon got it exactly right (1 Kgs 3). Faced with an invitation from God to request and receive anything he wanted, Solomon asked for wisdom. God was pleased with his response, and gave him power and wealth in addition. Of course, his wisdom left him later in life when he very foolishly married foreign women who led him away from the exclusive worship of Yahweh, the God of Israel.

Returning to the Teacher's anecdote, we observe first that wisdom has a definite advantage over foolishness, so much so that this youth might actually become king. However, it is a limited benefit, according to the second half of the story, for there is "another youth" (see note on 4:15) who replaces the first youth. Though the first youth was wise, his wisdom apparently is soon forgotten. The implication of the Teacher is that even this second youth will be forgotten; the cycle will continue on and on and on, so that "it is all meaningless—like chasing the wind" (4:16).

◆ 8. God is distant (5:1-7)

1*As you enter the house of God, keep your ears open and your mouth shut. It is evil to make mindless offerings to God. 2*Don't make rash promises, and don't be hasty in bringing matters before God. After all, God is in heaven, and you are here on earth. So let your words be few.

3 Too much activity gives you restless dreams; too many words make you a fool.

4When you make a promise to God, don't delay in following through, for God takes no pleasure in fools. Keep all the promises you make to him. 5It is better to say nothing than to make a promise and not keep it. 6Don't let your mouth make you sin. And don't defend yourself by telling the Temple messenger that the promise you made was a mistake. That would make God angry, and he might wipe out everything you have achieved.

7Talk is cheap, like daydreams and other useless activities. Fear God instead.

5:1 Verse 5:1 is numbered 4:17 in Hebrew text.   5:2 Verses 5:2-20 are numbered 5:1-19 in Hebrew text.

NOTES

5:1 [4:17] *It is evil to make.* The NLT collapses the last two clauses of the Heb. for readability's sake. A more word-for-word translation of the Heb. text of the last clause would be: "For they do not know to do evil." The reference is to those who offer the mindless offerings, and does not denote their inability to do evil, but rather that "they do not know that they are doing evil." Those who perform mindless offerings are so foolish they do not know that what they are doing is evil. For a defense of this understanding of the verse, see Ogden (1987:76) over against Driver (1964:79) and Schmidt (1940–1941).

mindless offerings. The NLT interprets the Heb. expression that is lit. "the sacrifice of fools." The text is ambiguous as to whether the expression refers to a certain type of sacrifice or a sacrifice offered with a particular mind-set, or lack thereof, or if it is referring to all sacrifices as foolish, since "God is in heaven" and therefore unaffected by human sacrifices. In either case, as the section below will explain, the Teacher does not take an enthusiastic view of OT worship practices in this section. At best, he is urging great caution because of the potential dangers of these acts, as well as the minimal benefits.

5:2 [1] *rash promises.* The Heb. reads "do not be quick with your mouth." The reference here is not specifically to promises made to God, which is the subject of 5:4-7 [3-6]. The topic of this verse and the next is prayer, not specifically promises.

5:4 [3] *promise.* The promise is specifically a vow (*neder* [TH5088A, ZH5624]), a formal promise to God that necessitates a payment of some sort, like a sacrifice, when fulfilled.

5:6 [5] *Temple messenger.* The Heb. has "messenger" only; the NLT and NIV supply "Temple" and thus indicate that they follow the tradition of interpreting this passage as instruction about what to do when the Temple authorities send out a priestly messenger to pick up that which one has promised/vowed at the time that God fulfills his part of the obligation (see Salters 1978). Another line of interpretation understands the messenger to be an angel sent by God—so the Gr. translations by Aquila, Theodotion, and Symmachus (see also Ginsberg 1952:340-344).

COMMENTARY

The Teacher now turns his full attention to the question of how we ought to relate to God. He certainly believes that God exists and that he is powerful. The question, though, is whether or not God is someone who can help, someone to whom we ought to get close. The Teacher seems wary of too much intimacy with God and advises his hearers to be extremely careful as they approach him. His comments about relating to God are specifically connected to formal worship. It must be remembered that in the Old Testament God made his presence known to his people only in special locations. The sanctuary was the preeminent place where one encountered God during the Old Testament period, and so it is that the Teacher specifically talks about how to behave when going to God's house, another name for the sanctuary. In particular, he refers to three acts that take place in the house of God—sacrifice, prayer, and taking vows.

In the first verse, the Teacher cautions the worshipper to be very careful when entering God's house. In particular, the worshipper should not speak needlessly, if at all. He should keep his ears open, or more literally "listen." To "listen" in this type of context means to obey (so Perdue 1977:182). The sanctuary was a holy place where God made his special presence known. A mistake could be very costly indeed. The seriousness of being in the presence of God is illustrated by the fact that even the High Priest is warned that unwanted intrusions into the divine presence could result in death (Lev 16:2). If one offers a sacrifice, it had better be done right and with the right heart or else the consequences could be worse than not offering any sacrifice. Exactly what a "mindless sacrifice" entails is difficult to determine exactly (see note on 5:1), but it probably refers to a sacrifice not done according to divine instruction (Lev 1-7) or one done with the wrong heart attitude (Ps 40:6-8). Micah 6:6-8 contrasts sacrifice with a right attitude and behavior and concludes: "The LORD has told you what is good, and this is what he requires of you: to do what is right, to love mercy, and to walk humbly with your God." However, the Teacher's thought is more biting than what we read in Psalm 40 and Micah 6. The broader context leads us to the opinion that to the Teacher all sacrifices are mindless and to be avoided at all costs. After all, according to 5:2 God is in heaven and people are on earth, a phrase that indicates the Teacher's view that God is not very involved in people's lives.

The Teacher is similarly cautious about praying to God. In 5:2, the Teacher is not warning against rash promises in particular, but against speaking any words (that is, prayer) before God. The motivation is clear; God is not around to hear your prayer. He is in heaven, and you are on earth. This is not a statement of piety as much as it is a denial of God's intimate involvement with his people. The Teacher gets no solace from God throughout the book, and this verse gives us one reason why. Again, this is not a denial of the existence of God but an extreme statement concerning the distance that the Teacher feels from him. Keep words to a minimum, he advises. Otherwise, as 5:3 indicates, one lives in a fantasy world. That verse is a proverb that sets up a comparison. Just like much activity leads to restless dreams, so too many words toward God makes you a fool. Why a fool? The comparison indicates that it is because people are dreaming if they think the words will have any effect. Again, God is in heaven, not on earth, to hear and respond to your prayers.

The third and longest section (5:4-7) has to do with vows, here called promises to God. Like sacrifice and prayer, a vow was a cultic tribute to God. When taking a vow, worshippers committed themselves to undertake some kind of action, often a sacrifice, if God would answer a specific request (Gen 28:20-22; Judg 11:30-31; 1 Sam 1:11) or simply to curry God's favor (Ps 132:2-5).

The Teacher begins with the warning that a vow should not be broken. This caution fits in with broader Scriptural teaching (Deut 23:21; Prov 20:25). It is dangerous and wrong to break a promise to God. To do so defines a person as a fool, one who does not know how to live life rightly or successfully. Indeed, not only should a person follow through on their vows to God, but they had better not delay or put it off! Worse yet, according to 5:6, one who vows will encounter huge problems in their relationship with God if the Temple has to send a "collector," here called a "messenger," to collect on the vow. The Teacher believes that if the messenger is turned away, then God will retaliate by wiping out everything that the person who took the vow has accomplished.

So, once again, as with prayer, the Teacher advises his listeners to take few, if any, vows. The more vows one takes, the more responsibility one bears before God. Furthermore, the Teacher never describes God as merciful or redemptive. Indeed, not only here, but elsewhere in his speech, he gives the impression of a rather vindictive God, a God to be avoided rather than sought after. Again, God is in heaven, and you are here on earth (5:2).

As with 5:3, so this second part of the unit (5:7) ends with a proverb-like statement that compares talk (and by implication of the context specifically talk directed to God) with dreams. A person is dreaming if they think their chatter before the distant God is going to do them much good.

In summary, our understanding is that the Teacher is not positively inclined toward God. He does not think that God helps much, and indeed he might be more trouble than help. He is best avoided or at least approached at a minimum. In this context, as in other contexts within the speech of the Teacher, we thus understand his admonition to "fear God," not in the sense of respect, but rather in the sense of being afraid of a God who could hurt a person (cf. Mavis 1999).

◆ 9. Oppression (5:8-9)

8Don't be surprised if you see a poor person being oppressed by the powerful and if justice is being miscarried throughout the land. For every official is under orders from higher up, and matters of justice get lost in red tape and bureaucracy. 9Even the king milks the land for his own profit!*

5:9 The meaning of the Hebrew in verses 8 and 9 is uncertain.

NOTES

5:9 [8] *Even the king milks the land for his own profit!* The NLT gives an accurate and colorful rendition of the Heb. here, though it is perhaps guilty of collapsing two clauses into one sentence. The Heb. is more lit. translated as "The profit of the land is taken by all; even the king benefits from the field." I understand the problem described by the Teacher in this section as government officials fleecing their subjects, though two alternative interpretations may also be mentioned. First, some commentators, like Delitzsch (1975:293) understand the relationship to be between officials fleecing each other. Second, Hitzig (see his view cited in Ellul 1990:80-81) and others suggest that the government officials protect each other with the intention of getting gain from others. In any case, the verse describes governmental bureaucracy gone haywire to the detriment of the broader society.

COMMENTARY

The translation of 5:8-9 is extremely difficult, a fact to which the NLT text note bears witness. The general topic, though, is certainly political oppression. The Teacher has already observed the suffering of the masses (in 4:1-3); here he attributes this problem to hierarchical governments. Modern democracies like those in the United States, Canada, and other countries have their share of bureaucracy and oppression, but the situation was potentially much, much worse in a radically hierarchical system like the monarchy of Israel. Monarchy is not inherently evil or wrong—after all, God instituted kingship in Israel (1 Sam 8–12)—but the potential tendency toward oppression was always there. Samuel—the one God commanded to anoint the first king, Saul—made this clear to the Israelites when he told them:

This is how a king will reign over you . . . The king will draft your sons and assign them to his chariots and his charioteers, making them run before his chariots. Some will be generals and captains in his army, some will be forced to plow in his fields and harvest his crops, and some will make his weapons and chariot equipment. The king will take your daughters from you and force them to cook and bake and make perfumes for him. He will take away the best of your fields and vineyards and olive groves and give them to his own officials. He will take a tenth of your grain and your grape harvest and distribute it among his officers and attendants. He will take your male and female slaves and demand the finest of your cattle and donkeys for his own use. He will demand a tenth of your flocks, and you will be his slaves. When that day comes, you will beg for relief from this king you are demanding, but then the LORD will not help you. (1 Sam 8:11-18)

With such a warning, there is no doubt as to why the Teacher said, "Don't be surprised if you see a poor person being oppressed by the powerful and if justice is being miscarried" (5:8). When a hierarchical society like Israel's goes haywire, the consequences can be more than frustrating. Everybody, from lower functionaries to the king himself, seeks their own good, and the common person gets the short end of the stick. The Teacher brought up this issue to remind us again just how difficult life is. Kidner (1976:54) is correct to compare the Teacher's comments here to the descriptions that Franz Kafka (as, for instance, in the novel *The Castle*) provided of bureaucracy in the early twentieth century.

◆ 10. Searching for meaning in money (5:10-6:9)

[10]Those who love money will never have enough. How meaningless to think that wealth brings true happiness! [11]The more you have, the more people come to help you spend it. So what good is wealth—except perhaps to watch it slip through your fingers!

[12]People who work hard sleep well, whether they eat little or much. But the rich seldom get a good night's sleep.

[13]There is another serious problem I have seen under the sun. Hoarding riches harms the saver. [14]Money is put into risky investments that turn sour, and everything is lost. In the end, there is nothing left to pass on to one's children. [15]We all come to the end of our lives as naked and empty-handed as on the day we were born. We can't take our riches with us.

[16]And this, too, is a very serious problem. People leave this world no better off than when they came. All their hard work is for nothing—like working for the wind. [17]Throughout their lives, they live under a cloud—frustrated, discouraged, and angry.

[18]Even so, I have noticed one thing, at least, that is good. It is good for people to eat, drink, and enjoy their work under the sun during the short life God has given them, and to accept their lot in life. [19]And it is a good thing to receive wealth from God and the good health to enjoy it. To enjoy your work and accept your lot in life—this is indeed a gift from God. [20]God keeps such people so busy enjoying life that they take no time to brood over the past.

CHAPTER 6

There is another serious tragedy I have seen under the sun, and it weighs heavily on humanity. [2]God gives some people great wealth and honor and everything they could ever want, but then he doesn't give them the chance to enjoy these things. They die, and someone else, even a stranger, ends up enjoying their wealth! This is meaningless—a sickening tragedy.

[3]A man might have a hundred children and live to be very old. But if he finds no satisfaction in life and doesn't even get a decent burial, it would have been better for him to be born dead. [4]His birth would have been meaningless, and he would have ended in darkness. He wouldn't even have had a name, [5]and he would never have seen the sun or known of its existence. Yet he would have had more peace than in growing up to be an unhappy man. [6]He might live a thousand years twice over but still not find contentment. And since he must die like everyone else—well, what's the use?

[7]All people spend their lives scratching for food, but they never seem to have

enough. ⁸So are wise people really better
off than fools? Do poor people gain anything by being wise and knowing how to
act in front of others?

⁹Enjoy what you have rather than desir-
ing what you don't have. Just dreaming
about nice things is meaningless—like
chasing the wind.

NOTES

5:12 [11] *the rich seldom get a good night's sleep.* The Heb. is fuller and reads "the abundance of the rich does not permit them to get a good night's sleep." The NLT shortens the
idea and does not fully convey the fact that it is particularly the abundance of the rich that
limits their sleep. The next question is whether we can precisely determine what is meant
by "abundance." If we go back to the first part of the verse, it refers to the eating of workers.
Since they work, it does not make any difference how much they eat. So, I suggest that
abundance here refers specifically to the fact that the rich eat too much and then try to
sleep without having worked and find it difficult to do so.

5:13 [12] *There is.* The Heb. word is *yesh* [TH3426, ZH3780]; it introduces an anecdote or
story used to illustrate or further a point (see also 2:21).

serious problem. This translation of *ra'ah kholah* [TH7451B/2470, ZH8288/2703] is possible but
probably a little soft for the Heb. The NIV comes closer with "grievous evil." The Teacher
finds it sickening that wealth does not benefit the wealthy or his offspring. This is because
the rich person hoards his money. The Teacher likely saw nothing wrong with growing
rich. What disgusts him is that often accumulated wealth does not lead to the desired end.
If v. 13 is treated alone (and the conjunction between vv. 13 and 14 translated as "or"),
then the harm of hoarding is that it is never used for the person's enjoyment. If, as seems
more likely, it should be read with v. 14, then the hoarding was done by investment and
the harm came when the money was lost.

5:14 [13] *risky investments.* This translation is appropriate and contemporary. However,
the Heb. is simply "wealth lost in an evil situation."

5:16 [15] *serious problem.* See note on 5:13.

5:17 [16] *they live under a cloud.* Lit., "they eat in darkness." The Heb. image is clear but
strikes a modern audience as strange and therefore difficult to grasp. The NLT has substituted an analogous popular image for the ancient Heb. one.

6:1 *There is.* The Heb. word is *yesh* [TH3426, ZH3780]; it introduces an anecdote or story used
to illustrate or further a point (see also 2:21 and 5:13[12]). In this case, Qoheleth's point
has to do with how difficult it is to find joy in life.

serious tragedy. The MT simply has "tragedy" (or "evil"), though many other Heb. manuscripts add "sickening" (*kholah* [TH2470, ZH2703]) as in the next verse (as well as in 5:13
[12]).

weighs heavily. The Heb. word (*rab* [TH7227, ZH8041]) is derived from a verbal root that may
either denote qualitative greatness (thus the NLT translation) or quantity. If the latter, then
Qoheleth states that what he is about to describe is frequently found as part of the human
condition.

6:2 *honor.* The NLT appropriately translates the Heb. term *kabod* [TH3519, ZH3883]. An alternative approach suggests that the term is simply another way of referring to riches. Salters
(1979) argues that the word should be understood in this sense and believes that it is more
compatible with the verb.

A literal translation of the second part of this verse is, "But God does not allow them to eat
of it, but a stranger will eat of it. This is meaningless, and it is a sickening evil." The NLT
rendition provides the reason why the person cannot eat it when it translates, "They die,

and someone else, even a stranger, ends up enjoying their wealth!" Certainly death is the obvious reason why someone might not enjoy their wealth, but other reasons are also imaginable (a depressive personality, for instance).

6:3 might. This reflects the fact that a conditional particle (*'im* [TH518, ZH561]) begins this verse.

born dead. The Heb. word (*nepel* [TH5309, ZH5878]) means "stillborn" and occurs three times in the Bible. In Ps 58:8 it is the wish of the psalmist that his enemies might be like a still-born (parallel to a slug melting away). Thus, to be stillborn was considered by the psalmist to be a tragedy. In Job 3:16, Job declares that he preferred to be stillborn rather than to be in his present state of misery; Eccl 6:3 utilizes the metaphor in a similar way.

6:7 spend their lives scratching for food. This is the NLT's colorful translation of the pro-verbial statement "all toil of humans is for their mouth." Humans spend their energy just to satisfy their needs. The search for contentment is never ceasing, and so is the speaker's frustration. Ackroyd (1967) and Dahood (1968) wrongly argue that the "mouth" for which one labors is the "mouth of death." Though the "mouth of death" is a known ancient Near Eastern metaphor and the idea fits in with Qoheleth's thoughts elsewhere about death, it seems a strange idea to import into this particular text.

6:9 Just dreaming about nice things. The Heb. behind this phrase is simply "this." It is typical for Qoheleth to use pronouns with an indefinite antecedent. I believe this is part of his strategy of emphasizing that everything is meaningless. The NLT takes the phrase "desir-ing what you don't have" (6:9a) as the antecedent and expresses that concept here in place of "this."

COMMENTARY

There is some debate over the extent of this section. Some scholars, like Whybray (1989:98), believe the section comes to a conclusion with the *carpe diem* passage at the end of chapter 5. But even he recognizes the theme of money continues into the next section. I think the connection is so close that the first part of chapter 6 ought to be treated with the last part of chapter 5, as I have done here.

The focus of this large section is on money. Can money provide life with mean-ing? Needless to say, this topic is of continued relevance. Even if on an unconscious level, many people today work all their lives to get money to live or even to amass wealth. What does the Teacher say about this?

The first point he makes is that no one ever makes enough money. People often live under the illusion that if they could just make a given sum of money, they would be happy. The Teacher insightfully points out that everyone wants just a little bit (or even a lot) more. Part of the problem is that the more money one has, the more people there are around to spend the money (5:11).

A second problem with money is that it leads to worry. The Teacher is not clear on exactly what it is about money or wealth that fuels the type of worry that causes someone to lie awake in bed at night, but we can guess. For one thing, the contrast is with those who work (5:12a), so the Teacher may have in mind the lazy rich who don't exert enough energy during the day to fall asleep at night. This could be com-pounded by worry about money—keeping it or protecting it. In any case, it is again obvious to the Teacher that money is not an answer to problems but rather the ori-gin of trouble. A third problem that the Teacher sees, which may lead to the anxiety he has already commented on, is that no matter how hard one tries to protect money, it can be lost in an instant through risky investment. The kind of investment that the Teacher may have in mind is a trading expedition (see comments on 11:1-6). Today we can see the same sort of problem with investing in the stock market. It's risky, especially if one invests in just one volatile section of the stock market. In a moment, it is all gone, one dies with nothing, and there is no legacy to pass on to one's children (5:14). Naked we come into the world, and naked we leave it. As a matter of fact, even if someone dies with lots of money, they can't take it with them to the grave (5:15). It will do them no good there.

In 5:16-17 the Teacher comes to the conclusion that hard work for the purpose of earning money or amassing wealth is pretty much a hopeless endeavor. People end up with nothing one way or the other. One gets the definite feeling that the Teacher is talking concretely here and not hypothetically. He himself is "frustrated, discouraged, and angry" (5:17).

This section now continues with yet another *carpe diem* passage, the fourth in the series (5:18-20). As with the others, this one expresses ultimate frustration with the attempt to find meaning in life. Like most of the other *carpe diem* passages, this one finds comfort in what we might call the simple pleasures of life. What is "good" is to eat, drink, and enjoy work. However, the limitation of the "good" that these three pleasures might impart is communicated in a number of ways in the passage. For one thing, the work is described as "under the sun," a phrase that means "on this earth" but also implies the idea of life apart from God. Furthermore, to talk about work "under the sun" also conjures up the image of labor in the intense heat. In addition, this pleasure is circumscribed by the time that people have on this earth. Indeed, the Teacher says it is a "short life." This implicitly reminds us of death, which we have seen is a major issue for the Teacher. Notice that it is God who has given us this short life with its limited enjoyment and lack of substantial meaning. Finally, besides eating, drinking, and working, it is also "good" to accept our lot in life (5:18). That is, we will only be happy if we give up the quest for something greater than is offered in the *carpe diem* passages.

In the next few verses, however (extending into the following chapter), the Teacher points out that it is not easy to enjoy even these simple, limited pleasures in life. For one thing, a person needs money and health to participate in work (5:19). When we move to the first few verses of the next chapter, we will see additional conditions, also provided by God, that are necessary for people to find some enjoyment in life.

The most startling statement of all, however, is found in the final verse of the chapter. Here, the Teacher gives us a window into the benefit of the enjoyment of eating, drinking, and working. It is simply that in this way people are distracted from the "past," or more literally and accurately "the days of one's life." Fox put it well: "Pleasure is an anodyne to the pain of consciousness" (1989:73). In other words, in this way God keeps people from thinking too much about the harsh realities of life. Life is hard, and then comes death. That is the ultimate truth that the Teacher sees about life under the sun. How do these activities operate as an anesthetic to the pain of life? We all know people who avoid problems by going from party to party or by devoting themselves to work. They find happiness in their busy-ness, distracted from trouble.

So far Qoheleth has said that ultimate meaning is elusive and joy is hard to come by. A person needs money to enjoy life ("it is a good thing to receive wealth from God and the good health to enjoy it," 5:19), and money comes with all kinds of problems that make it hard to hold on to. As we begin the sixth chapter, we see that even having money is not enough. Qoheleth introduces the new problem by means of another anecdote, marked by the Hebrew word *yesh* (see note on 6:1; for another example of an anecdote, see note on 2:21). In this way, he will present yet another situation for our consideration. However, even before he tells us the situation, he evaluates it. Qoheleth pronounces that it is a "serious tragedy" and adds the pon-derous and dark "under the sun" expression to accentuate his unhappiness about it. Furthermore, it "weighs heavily" (or "is frequent," see note on 6:1) on humanity.

What is this tragic situation? It is the fact that even people who "have it all," including wealth and honor, may not find joy in life! Thus, money and honor are necessary but not sufficient conditions to experiencing joy in a meaningless world.

To compound the pathos of this section, Qoheleth attributes this "serious trag-edy" to none other than God himself! He is the subject of 6:2; he is the one who gives some people wealth and honor, but not the chance to enjoy it. The NLT sug-gests that this is because the wealthy person dies before enjoying it, and so it goes to someone else to enjoy. This is a possible interpretation but not certain (see note on 6:2). For whatever reason (death or something else, perhaps a depressive personal-ity), not all wealthy people have been given the gift of enjoying what they have.

The next paragraph gives a concrete example of the principle expressed in 6:1-2. In the ancient Near East, a long life and a large family were considered to be a bless-ing from heaven. In the book of Proverbs, for instance, life is the consequence of wisdom (Prov 3:2; 9:6) and death the result of foolishness (Prov 9:18). And as for children, in particular sons, Psalm 127:3-5 proclaims:

Children are a gift from the LORD;
   they are a reward from him.
Children born to a young man
   are like arrows in a warrior's hands.
How joyful is the man whose quiver is full of them!
   He will not be put to shame when he confronts his accusers at the city gates.

Long life and many children would be a concrete example of God giving some-one ". . . honor and everything they could ever want" (6:2). But this person, even the man with the hyperbolic one hundred children of 6:3, will not necessarily find joy in life. Such a person may not find satisfaction with his life, probably an allu-sion to someone who does not find meaning. Furthermore, even if a person has children and has a long and happy life, improper burial will ruin everything! A decent burial in ancient Israel would involve family members placing their loved one in a grave, taking good care of the grave, and periodically visiting it. In this way, the memory of the deceased was carried on in the family group. An indecent burial might involve public exposure or neglect. Later, Qoheleth will complain that evil people have decent burials that they have not deserved (8:10).

The point is that no matter how long people might live, it will ultimately end in death (6:6). Indeed, Qoheleth again waxes hyperbolic: a person may live two thousand years but still die, rendering life and its achievements meaningless. That long life may never find satisfaction either. Qoheleth considers this a great tragedy as well.

Such a person—that is, one who can find no satisfaction in life or decent burial at death—is worse off than a stillborn child. These are harsh words and are meant to leave a bad taste in our mouths. It is a sad tragedy when, after nine long months of expectation, a baby is born dead; but the Teacher says that that loss is nothing compared to the plight of the person who lives without finding meaning. The stillborn would have no consciousness of its loss, but the struggling long-lived person would not only ultimately die but also have to experience the sadness of life.

This thought leads Qoheleth to question the value of wisdom itself. Life is a rat race of survival that no one escapes. "All people spend their lives scratching for food" (6:7). This struggle for survival is not restricted to fools but also involves the wise. So why bother? He questions in particular the benefit of poor people trying to better themselves through wisdom. Qoheleth's skepticism seems directed at the wisdom of the book of Proverbs itself, where we read statements such as "The LORD will not let the godly go hungry, but he refuses to satisfy the craving of the wicked" (Prov 10:3).

The Teacher then ends this long section with a bit of practical advice that sounds in some ways similar to the *carpe diem* passages that we have already encountered (6:9). He advises that his listeners or readers enjoy what they have and not spend their lives desiring what they don't have. The desire for something that is not in our possession is "like chasing the wind"—fruitless!

◆   ## D. The Teacher's Advice (6:10–12:7)

1. Who can know the future? (6:10-12)

[10]Everything has already been decided. It was known long ago what each person would be. So there's no use arguing with God about your destiny.

[11]The more words you speak, the less they mean. So what good are they?

[12]In the few days of our meaningless lives, who knows how our days can best be spent? Our lives are like a shadow. Who can tell what will happen on this earth after we are gone?

NOTES

6:10 *Everything has already been decided.* Lit., the Heb. says "everything has already been named." In the OT, "naming" captures the essential nature of a person or thing. To name is to have knowledge and control over something or someone. Adam's naming of the animals (Gen 2:19-20) was more than applying a label; it was assigning function and expressing dominion.

no use arguing with God. The NLT rightly interprets the more enigmatic Heb. expression "no one may argue with one stronger than they are." This is an indirect but recognizable reference to God; the NLT makes this explicit.

C O M M E N T A R Y
We are now at the exact midpoint of the book according to an ancient scribal notation in the Masoretic Text. In addition, we have a change of course in the content of the Teacher's thought. Up until now the emphasis has been on the search for meaning in life. What makes life here on earth ("under the sun") ultimately worth living? Qoheleth tried to find meaning in work, pleasure, money, relationships, religion, and success but came up empty. At this point in the book, Qoheleth subtly shifts gears and begins to emphasize advice. How does one live in such a world? This is not an abrupt transition from search to advice with the sections being exclusively devoted to one of the two. We have already seen some advice in the first part. For instance, we have seen instances of the *carpe diem* passages (which will continue in the second half of the book) that urge the realization that in an ultimately meaningless world, there is nothing better to do than to eat, drink, and do one's best to enjoy life (though even this may be unattainable for many). Nonetheless, in terms of emphasis, there is no question that Qoheleth begins a trend at this point toward serving up advice.

In the admonitions and proverbs to follow, we get a window into Qoheleth's value structure. What does he think is important? What does he think is the correct way to live life? We will see that, at least occasionally, his advice may be contrasted with that which we find in the book of Proverbs.

Who Can Know the Future? This first section in the second half of Qoheleth's autobiography is a short transitional statement. It looks back to the first part of the book and provides a frame for understanding the advice to come. Verse 10, for instance, reminds us of the Teacher's idea that there is "nothing new under the sun" (cf. 1:9; 3:15). It is a fairly strong statement of divine determinism. Everything is out of human hands. "Everything has already been decided." No one has any freedom to create themselves; God has fixed people's destinies.

The idea of our destiny being in the hands of God brings peace and confidence to many, but not to the Teacher, who seems to chafe against the idea. His statement that there is no use arguing with God presumes that he imagines that argument would be naturally a human (and certainly his own) reaction. Since there is no use in arguing with God about our destiny, we might as well save our breath (6:11). The more words we speak, the more we increase meaningless chatter; so he begins his advice by warning us to avoid high expectations.

The final verse (6:12) of this section emphasizes what we have seen to be Qoheleth's two most vexing questions. He is disappointed in life for two reasons; it is meaningless while we live, and it ends in death. It is meaningless, in particular, because we cannot control or know the future. He raises the specter of death by comparing our lives to a shadow. A shadow is there, but barely. The metaphor of the shadow is used elsewhere in the Bible (1 Chr 29:15; Job 8:9; 14:2; Ps 144:4) to indicate the fragility of life. He then underlines the human inability to predict and control one's life through the two rhetorical questions of the verse: "Who knows how our days can best be spent?" and "Who can tell what will happen on this earth after we are gone?" Both questions presume a negative answer. Notice, too, that especially the first question throws into doubt the advice that will follow. For the most part, though, we will see that Qoheleth avoids absolute pronouncements and will instead give advice about what kind of behavior is better, relatively speaking.

◆   2. Advice (7:1-14)

A good reputation is more valuable
      than costly perfume.
And the day you die is better than
      the day you are born.
² Better to spend your time at funerals
      than at parties.
   After all, everyone dies—
   so the living should take this to
      heart.
³ Sorrow is better than laughter,
   for sadness has a refining influence
      on us.
⁴ A wise person thinks a lot about
      death,
   while a fool thinks only about
      having a good time.

⁵ Better to be criticized by a wise person
      than to be praised by a fool.
⁶ A fool's laughter is quickly gone,
   like thorns crackling in a fire.
   This also is meaningless.

⁷ Extortion turns wise people into fools,
   and bribes corrupt the heart.

⁸ Finishing is better than starting.
   Patience is better than pride.

⁹ Control your temper,
   for anger labels you a fool.

¹⁰ Don't long for "the good old days."
   This is not wise.

¹¹ Wisdom is even better when you
      have money.
   Both are a benefit as you go
      through life.
¹² Wisdom and money can get you
      almost anything,
   but only wisdom can save your life.

¹³ Accept the way God does things,
   for who can straighten what he has
      made crooked?
¹⁴ Enjoy prosperity while you can,
   but when hard times strike, realize
      that both come from God.
   Remember that nothing is certain
      in this life.

NOTES

7:1 *A good reputation is more valuable than costly perfume.* The first proverb illustrates the presence of sound and word play that runs through this section. In Heb. it reads *tob shem mishemen tob*, literally rendered "Better/good a name than oil good." The two outside words are identical, while there is a close sound connection between the two middle words (*shem* [TH8034, ZH9005], "name"; and *shemen* [TH8081, ZH9043], "oil").

7:6 *quickly gone.* These two words don't occur in the Heb. This verse may be lit. rendered, "For like the sound of thorns under the pot, so is the laughter of a fool. This is also meaningless" (cf. NIV, NASB). The NLT aims to make the enigmatic first part of the verse explicit by answering the question: in what way is the laughter like the sound of thorns presumably burning under the pot? The rendition of the NLT is defensible with

its emphasis on the fact that thorns would burn intensely but briefly. However, there
may be other or additional nuances of the image that are intended. For instance, the
loud crackle of the thorns might communicate the actual sound of the laughter and thus
signal that it is irritating to hear.

7:7 This verse is actually connected to the previous one in the Heb. by the conjunction
"for," though this is left untranslated in some versions such as the NLT and NIV. This
misses the connection with the context that is discussed in the commentary below.

7:11 *money*. Lit., "inheritance" (*nakhalah* [TH5159, ZH5709]). During most of the history of
the ancient Near East, money as we know it was not in existence. Coins were an innovation
of the Persian Empire. While the book of Ecclesiastes may have come from a time as late
as this, the Heb. word in this verse does not properly designate any kind of currency.

7:12 *Wisdom and money can get you almost anything*. The NLT collapses the metaphor
of this verse to make it more understandable to a modern audience. The protective nature
of both wisdom and money is communicated by speaking of the shadow of wisdom and
the shadow of money. The NIV captures this by translating it, "wisdom is a shelter as
money is a shelter." Again, "money" does not refer to currency as we know it. The Heb.
word here is simply "silver" (*kesep* [TH3701, ZH4084]).

COMMENTARY

Qoheleth continues by giving advice through a series of proverbs. These proverbs
follow at least indirectly from his life experience with its conclusion that life is ultimately meaningless. We learn about Qoheleth's values in this section, and it is no
accident that he frequently uses the so-called "better than" proverbial form (see
Ogden 1977). Since he does not find anything that is absolutely meaningful and
good as he looks "under the sun," he is reduced to suggesting that some things are
only better than others. Even here, we must admit, the Teacher surprises us by
his view on things, at least if we compare his thought to other parts of the Old
Testament.

It may be right to see this section in connection with the rhetorical question at the
end of chapter 6, "In the few days of our meaningless lives, who knows how our
days can best be spent?" Two themes dominate the proverbs: death (7:1b, 2, 4, and
perhaps 7:8) and wisdom and folly (7:4, 5, 6, 7, 9, 10, 11, 12). These two themes
and the proverbial form combine to provide a sense of unity to this section as well.
A kind of literary unity is also expressed and felt through repetitive words (good/
better, wise/wisdom, fool, and anger, among others) in this section.

The first twelve verses of this section are proverbs, and the last two verses (7:13-
14) conclude the section with two admonitions. The first verse has two parts that
seem unrelated, at least at first glance. The first half expresses a thought that is similar to that found in Proverbs 22:1. "A good reputation is more valuable than costly
perfume." Exactly what would constitute a good reputation for Qoheleth is not
clearly stated, but we might imply from his own behavior that it means, at least in
part, taking a long, hard look at reality and living in the light of the fact that everything is meaningless under the sun. Perhaps that is in part the connection, if there is
one, with the second half of the verse. This second proverb is not one that would be
found in the book of Proverbs, a book that associates life with wisdom and death

with folly. Here Qoheleth boldly states that death is better than birth. This theme will continue in the next few verses and seems to point to the value of living life in the face of reality and not repressing one's awareness of the inevitable end.

Another possible connection between the two proverbs in 7:1 is that the reputation that is so precious is the one that is fixed when death occurs. The Targum at this point states that the righteous rejoice at the time of their death because their reputation is secure (see Levine 1978:37-38).

The advice in 7:2 follows from that in the preceding verse. If death is better than birth, then it is not too surprising to hear that it is better to go to "funerals" than "parties." Why? Because it is more in keeping with reality. Parties are celebrations of life; funerals are reminders that everyone dies. Notice that this is out of keeping with the advice that Qoheleth gives in the last verses of chapter 5. There he said God gives a gift to some people to allow them to enjoy life so much that they become too busy "to brood over the past." In other words, God allows them to party so much that they don't have time to worry about the problems of life, including life's ultimate problem, which is death. Throughout Qoheleth's speech we see him going back and forth between wishing for death and fearing it. This is one reason why I characterize Qoheleth as a confused wise man (see the Introduction) as he looks at life under the sun—that is, apart from God.

The same kind of tension arises with the third proverb of the chapter (7:3). Here Qoheleth promotes "sorrow/sadness" over "laughter." We should first point out that the NLT and most English translations (cf. NIV, KJV, NASB, RSV) render the verse in the direction of sadness where the Hebrew suggests anger (it is the same word in 7:9b). Note the following more literal translation: "Anger is better than laughter, for in a troubled face the heart is made well."

We may quickly see the logic behind Qoheleth's thinking. Anger is better because, like a funeral, it is more in keeping with reality. Life is difficult, and then we die. What place does laughter have in such a view of the world? Indeed, he says that anger has a refining influence on us. That means we don't live an illusion, rather we live in the knowledge that death ends it all. Notice though, again, what Qoheleth says in 5:18. Here he does not seem to advocate anger but rather enjoyment. This provides even more evidence to the confusion that Qoheleth expresses as he grapples with the world apart from God.

The fourth proverb brings this same idea home once again. Wisdom dwells on "death"; folly on "having a good time" or, as the Hebrew more literally expresses it, "joy" (7:4).

As the proverbs of Qoheleth continue, they further the promotion of looking bravely and soberly at the true state of things rather than hiding behind foolish fantasies about life (7:5). One who is "praised by a fool" is tempted to believe what they hear because it makes them feel good. However, by virtue of the fact that the praise comes from a fool, it is unlikely that his words reflect reality. Though they hurt, it is better to listen to the criticisms of a "wise person." They reflect reality and remind one of the serious nature of life. As pointed out by Whybray (1989:114-

115), Qoheleth's teaching reflects that of Proverbs at this point (Prov 13:1; 15:31; 17:10; 25:12; 26:9), though the type of rebuke Qoheleth has in mind may be different. A wise person's rebuke, for instance, may fit in with Qoheleth's broader approach to life and be a wake-up call to depressing reality. In other words, the Teacher's own writing may be such a rebuke to those who are living sheltered lives.

The Teacher's sixth proverb (7:6) is an observation on the brevity of the "laughter" of the fool (so the NLT translation, see note on 7:6). The comparison is made to "thorns crackling in a fire." A fire fueled by thorns would be bright but short, burning out quickly. The context leads us to think that the short-lived nature of the fool's laughter may be the result of the fact that fools live in a fantasy world. Once their bubble is burst—that is, when they confront reality—the laughter ceases. At the end of this sixth proverb, the Teacher adds the phrase so often repeated in the first part of the book: "This also is meaningless." As before, the antecedent to "this" is not altogether obvious. Does it refer specifically to the fool's laughter or to all the proverbs that precede it? In either case, it shows that even with these proverbs Qoheleth has not transcended the meaninglessness of the world under the sun.

The next verse (proverb 7 in 7:7) seems clear in isolation from the context. It states that "extortion" or a "bribe," or presumably any kind of illicit monetary gain, will spoil wisdom. Indeed, it has the effect of taking a wise person and making them a fool. How is this possible? Wise people make judgments based on the merits of a case; they make a decision based on the right principle for the right situation and the right people. A bribe or extortion, however, rules all of that out; the decision is made for one reason only—money. This much is clear, but what is the connection with what precedes? It is true that proverb collections tend to be loose in their structure as witnesses the arrangement of the individual proverbs in Proverbs 10–31. However, here we should take seriously the conjunction "for" that begins the verse (see note on 7:7). This suggests that a reason is being given for the preceding statement. The best explanation is that it is spelling out why "this is meaningless." Verse 7:6 stated that fools and their laughter are meaningless. Here we learn that even wise people are not beyond corruption. Even a wise person can be made a fool when they are blinded by money.

Proverb 8 (7:8) is another "better than" statement that reveals Qoheleth's relative values. In the first part, he states that finishing is to be preferred to starting. This may be connected to the earlier statements on death regarding the end of life being preferred to its beginning (7:1). In Qoheleth's view of life, the beginning of a matter does not imply potential but rather the start of a struggle that ends in meaninglessness. The second half of this proverb may be connected to the first part in the sense that "patience" is a more realistic and helpful character trait than "pride" in such a meaningless world. Pride presumes accomplishment, and that is not possible in a meaningless world. Patience, though, is a virtue in a world where there is no end but death.

The ninth proverb (7:9) seems to be contrary to the third. This is not at first evident in the English but becomes clear when it is understood that the Hebrew word translated "sorrow" in 7:3 is translated as "temper"/"anger" in the present verse (*ka'as* [TH3708, ZH4088]). The NLT is following the lead of some interpreters and many translations (cf. NIV, KJV, NASB) that seek to harmonize the apparent tension by understanding the word to have two different senses in these two closely connected verses. This seems a desperate move to me, and I think it is better to take the word as meaning "anger" in both instances (as noted in the discussion of 7:3). This bit of contradiction fits in with a broader pattern of tension within Qoheleth's thinking that leads me to characterize him as a confused wise man. Back to the meaning of the proverb—we should note why anger exposes a person as a "fool." The answer lies in the previous verse. Anger arises from a lack of patience and perhaps an exalted sense of oneself, which is pride. If someone gets angry, then they reveal that they do not understand this and therefore are a fool. Note that the same sentiment may be found in Proverbs 14:29.

The tenth proverb may connect with the idea that endings are better than beginnings, finishing better than starting. He quotes what was quite possibly a common saying in his day to the effect that the past times were the "good old days." We even hear this today as people are nostalgic for a simpler, quieter, safer time—such as the idyllic 1950s. Qoheleth would respond by calling such people fools. The past is no better than the present, and the future will not bring any improvement. He has struck this note time and time again, saying, "Nothing under the sun is truly new" (1:9; 3:15). These "glorifiers of times past" (so Luther 1972:117) are fools because they deny reality. They wish for a time that has never been.

Qoheleth's jaundiced view of life comes to the fore in the eleventh proverb (7:11). In the book of Proverbs, we hear that wisdom far surpasses precious jewels or metals (Prov 3:13-15). Previously, the Teacher has admitted that wisdom is better than folly. This holds true—at least before one takes into account everyone's impending death (2:12-17). Here, he also expresses his appreciation of wisdom in very subdued terms, when he claims that "wisdom" is much better when one has "money." Proverbs might suggest that it is only through wisdom that one can get and keep money (Prov 10:2, 16, 22). But here Qoheleth brings wisdom down to the same level as money, giving them both their due as helping one navigate life. This proverb is closely linked with the twelfth proverb (7:12), which again has a world-weary ring to it as Qoheleth says that wisdom and money can provide everything. Granted, he concludes by saying that "only wisdom can save your life." Indeed, one's money is no help if one is attacked; it might even make attacks more likely. However, a person could get out of a jam by virtue of his wit.

This section of the book ends with two bits of advice that are presumably related to the proverbs that precede them. The first admonition advises that one simply bow to the way God has shaped circumstances. This verse echoes a thought from 1:15, but here God is named as the agent who has made life's circumstances "crooked." And since he is the one behind it, there is no use in trying to change things. Thus, the second admonition follows from the first. Enjoy life when God allows it, but then when "hard times" arrive, roll with the punches. Again, one cannot straighten what God has made crooked. As the Teacher looks at it from his finite, human point of view, he concludes that one cannot guess when good times would come or hard times arrive because "nothing is certain in this life." Again, Qoheleth expresses the idea that, though God may know the times (3:11), from a human point of view "chance" rules all (9:11).

◆   3. Wisdom and righteousness don't help (7:15-22)

¹⁵I have seen everything in this meaning-less life, including the death of good young people and the long life of wicked people. ¹⁶So don't be too good or too wise! Why destroy yourself? ¹⁷On the other hand, don't be too wicked either. Don't be a fool! Why die before your time? ¹⁸Pay attention to these instructions, for anyone who fears God will avoid both extremes.*

¹⁹One wise person is stronger than ten leading citizens of a town!
²⁰Not a single person on earth is always good and never sins.
²¹Don't eavesdrop on others—you may hear your servant curse you. ²²For you know how often you yourself have cursed others.

7:18 Or *will follow them both.*

NOTES

7:15 *good.* The NLT translates the Heb. word *tsaddiq* [TH6662, ZH7404] and its related forms as "good" in this passage, which is certainly fitting in the context. However, the word is often translated "righteous" (e.g., 9:2; Gen 6:9) and has a broader sense (though difficult to define). It implies not only good behavior but also a right relationship with God.

7:16 *don't be . . . too wise.* The Heb. verb here (*khakam* [TH2449, ZH2681]) is based on the hitpael stem and has given rise to considerable controversy. Some scholars have argued that the hitpael stem here indicates pretense, that is "don't pretend to be wise" (see Kaiser 1979:85-87; Whybray 1978). Seow provides the right response in his study of this word when he simply says in response to this conclusion: "The Hithpael of *khakam* never indicates pretense anywhere" (1997:253). For an extensive discussion of this issue and this passage, see Strange (1969).

COMMENTARY

The overarching teaching of this section of Qoheleth's speech is that, though wisdom has some benefit in relationship to other human qualities and attributes (7:19), it really does not help in the final analysis. Thus, one should not have too high an expectation of wisdom.

This teaching begins in 7:15-18, which clearly forms a paragraph and makes an argument for moderation. What is surprising is that it is a case for moderation in the pursuit of wisdom and righteousness! One would not find such attitudes expressed in Proverbs. Hear what the sage says in Proverbs 2:1-8:

My child, listen to what I say,
    and treasure my commands.
Tune your ears to wisdom,
    and concentrate on understanding.

Cry out for insight,
and ask for understanding.
Search for them as you would for silver;
seek them like hidden treasures.
Then you will understand what it means to fear the LORD,
and you will gain knowledge of God.
For the LORD grants wisdom!
From his mouth come knowledge and understanding.
He grants a treasure of common sense to the honest.
He is a shield to those who walk with integrity.
He guards the paths of the just
and protects those who are faithful to him.

In the book of Proverbs, wisdom is integrally connected to righteousness and is highly desired because it leads to life. So why does the Teacher here advise, "Don't be too good or too wise!" Quite simply, he gives this advice because his observation and experience have led him to believe that wisdom and goodness have no reward. That's his point in 7:15. As he has looked at life, which he has time and time again concluded is meaningless, he has seen that good people die young and wicked people live a long time. Of course, not every good person dies young and not every wicked person lives long, but the point is that a superficial reading of Proverbs might lead one to believe that every good person should have a good, long life.

If one isolates individual proverbs out of the book and treats them as universally true laws, then one could rationally conclude that the righteous would never be harmed. Take for instance, Proverbs 10:3, which declares, "The LORD will not let the godly go hungry, but he refuses to satisfy the craving of the wicked."

As we look at this and similar sounding proverbs, we must be careful to keep in mind that the proverb form does not state law but, rather, generally true principles. They are not always true, but they describe behaviors that are normally true and advise living according to those principles. It is much less likely, the proverb suggests, that people will go hungry if they follow God (which would include not being lazy, see Prov 10:4-5) than if they turn their backs on him. Indeed, there are other proverbs that acknowledge that the wise sometimes suffer, at least for a period, and the wicked prosper (see the excellent article by van Leeuwen [1992]).

A problem develops if one understands the wisdom tradition of the Bible to teach that the wise or righteous are invariably blessed with material wealth and health and the wicked are not. We may take the three friends of Job—Eliphaz, Bildad, and Zophar—as a case in point. As they saw the sufferings of Job (who we know from the first two chapters of the book is innocent), they applied a rigid formula. "Sin is punished by suffering. Therefore, if one suffers, then one is a sinner." The inevitable conclusion for them was that Job was a sinner.

Qoheleth seems to have shared the position of the three friends of Job regarding the ability of wisdom to guarantee reward or retribution, but when he observed that life did not bear this out, he questioned the value of wisdom. Wisdom is supposed to bring life, but too many wise people die young for that to be true. So, he concludes, what good is it ultimately to be wise? Indeed, to be too wise or righteous might bring attention to oneself and perhaps cause trouble. As he argues for an avoidance of extremes, he turns right around and, in 7:17, counsels that one avoid folly and wickedness as well. The bottom line of his advice seems to be to reach for moderation and avoid the extremes of both wisdom (or goodness) and folly (or wickedness). He specifically advises those who "fear God" to "avoid" the "extremes." Qoheleth seems to use this phrase "fear God" in the oddest places (5:7; 8:12-13—the phrase also occurs in 12:13, but Qoheleth is not the speaker there). The phrase for Qoheleth does not have the sense of respect and awe, but of utter terror of God who is in absolute control and doesn't always reward wisdom and punish wickedness. At this point, we need to remember that Qoheleth is reflecting the skeptical point of view of a confused wisdom teacher. His views will be evaluated by the second wise man whose words we hear in the epilogue (12:8-14, see "Author" in the Introduction).

In spite of his negative views on the ultimate effects of wisdom, it is interesting that the very next proverb (7:19) asserts the value of wisdom, at least in comparison with other human capacities and abilities: "One wise person is stronger than ten leading citizens of a town." Wisdom is better, therefore, than political power. He has made this point with an anecdote in 4:13-16 as well: a poor but wise youth is better than an old, foolish king. However, that anecdote went on to show how even that youth's life and contribution was ultimately meaningless. Again, he will return to this subject in 9:13-16, where the point will be made that although wisdom outstrips political strength in its benefit to people, even wisdom is ultimately meaningless.

Verse 20 then asserts the limits of human ability. Qoheleth sounds like Paul in Romans 3:9-20, where the apostle quotes from a number of Old Testament books, especially from Psalms. Qoheleth denies that anybody on the face of the earth is righteous—that is, "always good" and without sin. Perhaps this is another reason for the advice in 7:16. If one cannot be consistently good, why put so much effort into it? This understanding of human nature may lead to the advice given in 7:21-22. It is a warning not to eavesdrop on the talk of a servant. A servant might curse his master. The verse may be implying that if the master hears it, he will be tempted to punish the servant; but then again, if the master thinks about it, he will remember that he has cursed others himself. "Let the one who is without sin cast the first stone"—after all, no one is "always good and never sins" (7:20).

◆   ## 4. Wisdom is hard to come by (7:23-24)

23I have always tried my best to let wisdom guide my thoughts and actions. I said to myself, "I am determined to be wise." But it didn't work. 24Wisdom is always distant and difficult to find.

NOTES

7:24 *Wisdom is always distant and difficult to find.* The NLT gets to the point but in a rather prosaic fashion. The Heb. is more enigmatic and may be translated something like, "Far away is that which is, and deep, deep, who can find it?" Fox and Porten (1978:28) argue that "that which is" refers to reality, though George Barton believes it refers more to "the reality below all changing phenomenon" (1908:146).

COMMENTARY

Wisdom is a key theme in the book of Ecclesiastes. Qoheleth is a wise man; however, he has already spoken of the limits of wisdom. It is nothing in the face of death (2:12-17); the fool and the wise man will both die. In the present passage, he addresses the issue of the inaccessibility of wisdom. As a wise man, he has always tried to live his life by the tenets of wisdom. However, no matter how hard he tries, he must concede to failure. Wisdom seems beyond him.

Wisdom involves more than memorizing proverbs. The book of Proverbs itself recognizes that the principles embodied in the individual proverbs are only relevant at the right time and in the right circumstance. It takes a wise person to know the right thing to say at the right time. "A proverb in the mouth of a fool is as useless as a paralyzed leg" (Prov 26:7). "A proverb in the mouth of a fool is like a thorny branch brandished by a drunk" (Prov 26:9). "Everyone enjoys a fitting reply; it is wonderful to say the right thing at the right time" (Prov 15:23). The sad truth, though, has already been revealed in Ecclesiastes 3:11—"Yet God has made everything beautiful for its own time. He has planted eternity in the human heart, but even so, people cannot see the whole scope of God's work from beginning to end." In other words, the so-called wise person cannot reliably determine the right time to apply wisdom principles. Wisdom indeed is inaccessible.

Job 28 teaches this same truth in a more positive vein. There it is seen that wisdom is indeed hard to find, indeed impossible for unaided humans. However, wisdom can be found if one finds God. Qoheleth's frustration does not lead him to recognize and express such a sublime truth. Qoheleth remains a confused wise man.

◆   5. Seeking and not finding (7:25-29)

²⁵I searched everywhere, determined to find wisdom and to understand the reason for things. I was determined to prove to myself that wickedness is stupid and that foolishness is madness.

²⁶I discovered that a seductive woman* is a trap more bitter than death. Her passion is a snare, and her soft hands are chains. Those who are pleasing to God will escape her, but sinners will be caught in her snare.

²⁷"This is my conclusion," says the Teacher. "I discovered this after looking at the matter from every possible angle. ²⁸Though I have searched repeatedly, I have not found what I was looking for. Only one out of a thousand men is virtuous, but not one woman! ²⁹But I did find this: God created people to be virtuous, but they have each turned to follow their own downward path."

7:26 Hebrew *a woman.*

NOTES

7:26 seductive woman. As the NLT mg indicates, the simple word "woman" has been interpreted as "seductive woman" here, which is a vast improvement over the Living Bible's "prostitute," but is still a bit misleading. Qoheleth is not leaving any women out of this category as if there are non-seductive women. Indeed, in this very section, he claims that there is not a single woman who has virtue (7:28). As we will see below, this passage is meant to be understood not only on a literal level but also on a metaphorical level, since, in wisdom literature, wisdom is represented by a woman. Garrett (1988) is right when he says that Qoheleth's object here is women in general and not a specific type of evil woman. However, Garrett is wrong to say that the point is about the difficulty of marriage relationships.

7:28 is virtuous. The Heb. in this verse does not specify virtue when it says, "I found one man out of a thousand, but I did not find a woman among all these." However, the NLT is clearly right in its interpretation when it supplies virtue. This is an instance of delayed identification, which intends to get the reader interested. What does he mean that he has found one man in a thousand and no women? The qualification "virtue" is supplied in 7:29. To us, this kind of literary device can be confusing, so the NLT does the reader a service by supplying it.

COMMENTARY

This passage is filled with enigmas and strange sayings, strange even for such an unpredictable speaker as Qoheleth. Before looking at some of Qoheleth's startling comments, we should observe the very clear central theme of these verses: "seeking and not finding." The NLT translates the verb baqash [TH1245, ZH1335] twice as "search" and the verb matsa' [TH4672, ZH5162] three times as some form of "to find" and twice as "to discover." Interestingly, there are actually two other occurrences of the root mts' that the NLT chose not to make explicit because it would sound so redundant in English style. These statistics, however, point out just how major the theme of searching and not finding is in this section.

As we study the passage, we see that the emphasis is on not finding anything of importance. The details will show that he claims to discover some things, but what he finds is really not worth the effort.

Verse 7:25 states what the Teacher really wanted to find. He wanted to "find wisdom and to understand the reason for things." As a good wisdom teacher, he also wanted to "prove . . . that wickedness is stupid and that foolishness is madness." All we have to do is to read anywhere in the book of Proverbs to see that wisdom is praised and folly is demeaned. However, we have also already observed more than once (and as recently as 7:23-24) that in spite of his determination to find wisdom, he ultimately found it inaccessible. Thus, in 7:28 he concludes: "Though I have searched repeatedly, I have not found what I was looking for." That is, he did not find wisdom or prove that foolishness is madness.

What is difficult in this passage, though, is his sudden shift to the topic of women. He speaks in very negative terms about women in 7:26 and 28. What's the connection?

The answer to this question is debated (see note on 7:26); however, it is suggestive to turn our attention to the book of Proverbs again. After all, that book has much to say about women. The addressee, the young son, is urged to avoid the strange, seductive woman and to embrace the wife of his youth (Prov 5:18-20; 7:1-27). Moreover, and perhaps more pointedly for our purposes, wisdom and folly are both personified as women (see in particular Prov 8-9). The "Woman Wisdom" represents God's wisdom and ultimately God himself, while the "Woman Folly" represents the "wisdom" of idolatry (see Longman 2002:28-36). In Proverbs, finding wisdom is equivalent to finding the right woman, while going with the wrong woman is indicative of folly.

Thus, Qoheleth talks both figuratively and literally about his discovery that a woman is "a trap more bitter than death" in 7:26 (see note on 7:26, where I explain why it is that all women and not just a seductive woman is meant here). To enter into relationship with a woman brings slavery since "her passion is a snare, and her soft hands are chains." Only God's will separates men from such a devastating relationship. As we saw in 5:10-6:9, God doles out the good life and the hard life on his own terms.

As we read on in 7:28, we see that Qoheleth's attitude toward women does not get any more complimentary. He looks for virtue (see note on 7:28) and claims that "one out of a thousand men is virtuous, but not one woman!" This again is an argument for seeing 7:26 as applying to all women, not just a small set of women; they all lack virtue. It is true that Qoheleth's words are not to be taken literally. He is employing a form called number parallelism (see also Amos 1:3; 2:1 NLT mg). The bottom line is simply that there are not many virtuous people in this world—perhaps a few men, but no women. However, we cannot use this insight to exonerate the claim that Qoheleth is a misogynist. He does not trust women. It is true that we must remember that he is not only condemning the vast majority of men and all women, but also he is using this language to say again that wisdom (represented by women) is inaccessible (cf. Schloesser 1990).

This is an important place to point out (see Introduction) that Qoheleth's words are not normative biblical teaching. He is a confused wise man who is being quoted at length and then commented on by a second wise man as he instructs his son concerning the dangers of living "under the sun." Even so, we find that we can agree with his final statement: "God created people to be virtuous, but they have each turned to follow their own downward path" (7:29). As a matter of fact, it seems to reflect the teaching of Genesis 1-3.

Finally, it should be noted that the central theme of this passage is "seeking and not finding." This will be of the utmost importance when we get to the epilogue and hear the second wise man tell his son that Qoheleth "sought to find" true words.

◆   6. No one is like the wise! (8:1)

How wonderful to be wise,   Wisdom lights up a person's face,
   to analyze and interpret things.   softening its harshness.

COMMENTARY

Here we see Qoheleth at his sarcastic best. We have seen again and again how he considers the wise person better than the fool—but only relatively. The wise person's abilities are severely hampered under the sun (3:11b), and ultimately both the wise and the fool will die and be no more (2:12-16). Indeed, the immediately preceding section asserted a clear comment on the impossibility of becoming wise (7:23-24).

How, then, do we interpret Qoheleth's statement, "How wonderful to be wise, to analyze and interpret things"? The Hebrew is a rhetorical question, literally rendered, "Who is like the wise man and who knows the interpretation of a matter?" The assumed answer is absolutely no one! Except, of course, God, but God isn't letting his human creatures in on the secret (3:11).

One cannot miss the sarcasm of the verse when reading the second bicolon of the verse: "Wisdom lights up a person's face, softening its harshness." We know Qoheleth much too well by this stage to miss the humor. No one is more sour than Qoheleth. How many times so far has he called out in anguish, "Everything is meaningless . . . completely meaningless"? This is not a man who goes around with a smiley face!

◆ 7. The king is supreme (8:2-8)

²Obey the king since you vowed to God that you would. ³Don't try to avoid doing your duty, and don't stand with those who plot evil, for the king can do whatever he wants. ⁴His command is backed by great power. No one can resist or question it. ⁵Those who obey him will not be punished. Those who are wise will find a time and a way to do what is right, ⁶for there is a time and a way for everything, even when a person is in trouble.

⁷Indeed, how can people avoid what they don't know is going to happen? ⁸None of us can hold back our spirit from departing. None of us has the power to prevent the day of our death. There is no escaping that obligation, that dark battle. And in the face of death, wickedness will certainly not rescue the wicked.

NOTES

8:2 *Obey the king since you vowed to God that you would.* The Heb. of this verse is extremely difficult. Lit. it would be rendered "I, the mouth of the king, guard and concerning the vow of God." The "I" may be a shortened form of "I say," which would introduce the advice Qoheleth is about to give. The "mouth of the king" is likely the commands that come from his mouth, and the imperative "guard" is the admonition to obey those commands. That is hard enough, but then how does this relate to "concerning the vow of God"? The NLT takes it as a vow to God to obey the king's command. It is also possible, and in my opinion likely, that the opening words in the Heb. of 8:3 should be read with 8:2. Thus, I think a good rendering of this opening line of our passage is: "I say: Observe the king's command, and do not rush into a vow to God." Thus, this passage is a warning not to cross the two absolute authorities in the life of the hearer, the king and God. See the treatment of this verse by Irwin (1945).

8:3 *plot evil.* Contrary to the conclusion of Waldman (1979), this phrase is broader in scope than just political insurrection and refers to all criminal activity.

COMMENTARY

It was common in ancient Near Eastern wisdom literature to instruct young nobles on how to act in the presence of the king. It would be highly unusual for a king to instruct another person how to behave before the king, and thus this passage is one of a number of passages in the book that reveals to us that Qoheleth is not to be equated with Solomon (see Introduction). The opening verse is difficult (see note on 8:2) but as rendered by the NLT is a strong encouragement to "obey the king." According to its rendition of the verse, the hearer promised God of his obedience to the throne. Furthermore, Qoheleth warns against any plot against the king. The reason is the king's absolute power ("for the king can do whatever he wants. His command is backed by great power. No one can resist or question it" [8:3b-4]).

Verses 5 and 6 strike us as very optimistic if taken literally. They grant a lot to "those who are wise," that is, those who know the right time for the right action. We saw that 3:11 and other verses show that Qoheleth believed that only God knew the right time and that we humans are kept in the dark. Strikingly, 8:7-8 appear to take back what Qoheleth just optimistically granted. If the wise will find a time and a way to do what is right, how can things be as out of control as 8:7-8 suggest? These verses clearly instruct us that we cannot control the time; events surprise us. In particular, we cannot control or predict "the day of our death." There is no escape from death and no way to predict when it will happen. This theme will be developed even further in chapter 9.

◆   8. Do bad people really get what is coming to them? (8:9-15)

⁹I have thought deeply about all that goes on here under the sun, where people have the power to hurt each other. ¹⁰I have seen wicked people buried with honor. Yet they were the very ones who frequented the Temple and are now praised* in the same city where they committed their crimes! This, too, is meaningless. ¹¹When a crime is not punished quickly, people feel it is safe to do wrong. ¹²But even though a person sins a hundred times and still lives a long time, I know that those who fear God will be better off. ¹³The wicked will not prosper, for they do not fear God. Their days will never grow long like the evening shadows.

¹⁴And this is not all that is meaningless in our world. In this life, good people are often treated as though they were wicked, and wicked people are often treated as though they were good. This is so meaningless!

¹⁵So I recommend having fun, because there is nothing better for people in this world than to eat, drink, and enjoy life. That way they will experience some happiness along with all the hard work God gives them under the sun.

8:10 As in some Hebrew manuscripts and Greek version; many Hebrew manuscripts read *and are forgotten.*

NOTES

8:10 *I have seen wicked people buried with honor.* This verse has a number of problems, perhaps the chief of which is a textual issue. The MT reads that wicked people "were forgotten in the city." This, however, would be good news to Qoheleth and those who look for justice in the world, and so, on such a reading, we don't understand why he would judge this as another example of meaninglessness. As it turns out, the ancient versions (in particular, LXX, Aquila, Symmachus, Theodotion) provide an answer, preserving what was originally in the text. We should emend the verb from a form of "to forget" (*shakakh* [TH7911, ZH8894]) to a form of "to praise" (*shabakh* [TH7623, ZH8655]) to get the translation that we have in the NLT. It must be remembered that in Heb. the difference in appearance between the letters beth (*b*) and kaph (*k*) is minute, and a scribe could easily copy one letter in place of the other.

COMMENTARY

Qoheleth is deeply troubled by the issue of justice. He has already made it clear that he does not believe the world is fair. People are oppressed, and no one can do anything about it (4:1-3). Indeed, he earlier suggested that it would be a waste of time or even dangerous to be too wise and righteous. It would be equally wrong-minded to be a fool or too wicked (7:15-18). Instead, he advised a middle course between wisdom and folly, righteousness and wickedness.

Our present text again raises questions about the fundamental fairness of the world. Of course, by implication it also raises the issue of the justice of God. Do bad people really get what is coming to them?

As we look closely at these verses, we will notice something else that is typical of the Teacher's thinking. We have seen that he is a confused wise man (see Introduction). On the one hand, he knows what his theology teaches, but on the other hand, he sees contradictions in the "real world" (what he sees "under the sun"). This passage is a prime illustration of how his mind moves between these two poles.

He begins by announcing that he again is going to reflect on the situation on earth ("under the sun"). He knows that this is a place where people can hurt other people. The question is, do abusers get away with their crimes? His initial answer is yes, they do. Verse 8:10 is one of the most difficult verses in the book to translate (see note), but the message is basically clear. Wicked people are "buried with honor." What a thought! Evil people, people who harm, not only go unpunished during their life, but even in the grave they continue to be honored. Where is the justice in this? To the Teacher, it is another example of meaninglessness that evil people can be praised after their death in the very city where they perpetuated their evil. Since there are no apparent punishments for these crimes, it just encourages more of the same. Here, we see Qoheleth struggling like the psalmist who said:

> For I envied the proud
>   when I saw them prosper despite their wickedness.
> They seem to live such painless lives;
>   their bodies are so healthy and strong.
> They don't have troubles like other people;
>   they're not plagued with problems like everyone else.
> They wear pride like a jeweled necklace
>   and clothe themselves with cruelty. (Ps 73:3-6)

The psalmist eventually saw a deeper reality and resolved his struggle with the justice of God, so that he begins his prayer with "Truly God is good to Israel" (Ps 73:1). As a matter of fact, it appears at first that Qoheleth moves in that direction. In 8:12 he affirms that "those who fear God will be better off." He seems to assert this against the obvious facts, since he says that this is true even if a person "sins a hundred times and still lives a long time." Long life was not supposed to be the reward of evil according to many of the proverbs in the book of Proverbs. The Teacher even seems to contradict himself when he says at the end of 8:13 that such wicked people will neither prosper nor live a long time ("Their days will never grow long like the evening shadows").

We see here a confused and struggling Qoheleth. We should note that when he asserts what seems the more positive, but unrealistic, statement in 8:12-13, he uses the verb "I know" rather than "I have seen" as he did in 8:10. This represents the conflict between what he has been taught ("I know"—the wicked are punished) and what he has observed in the real world ("I have seen"—the wicked are even praised after their death).

Qoheleth is not able to keep himself from the harsh real world for long. He is soon back to affirming the disparity between ethical action and suitable reward: "good people are often treated as though they were wicked, and wicked people are often treated as though they were good" (8:14). This leads him yet again to assert the fundamental meaninglessness of the world and to advocate, by means of yet another *carpe diem* passage (see commentary on 2:24-26) that the best one can do is "to eat, drink, and enjoy life." He advises his hearers to get what they can out of life, which is otherwise filled with hard work.

◆   ## 9. Not even the wise know (8:16-17)

[16]In my search for wisdom and in my observation of people's burdens here on earth, I discovered that there is ceaseless activity, day and night. [17]I realized that no one can discover everything God is doing under the sun. Not even the wisest people discover everything, no matter what they claim.

COMMENTARY

The eighth chapter ends with the Teacher returning to one of his most pervasive themes: the limitations of human wisdom. He refers to his search for wisdom, about which we learned early on (cf. 1:13 and 2:12). He is most likely describing this search when he refers to "ceaseless activity." In other words, the search is intense, but the discovery is disappointing. No matter how much wisdom one has, that person does not know everything. This limitation is a great disappointment to Qoheleth. Again, as in 7:25-29, he utilizes a search-and-discover theme in this section that will be important as we consider the epilogue in 12:10.

Lauha is correct to see that the answer to Qoheleth's frustration is divine revelation. He cites Matthew 16:17, Romans 1:19-20, and 1 Corinthians 1:21 as the New Testament solution to Qoheleth's problem. Of course, God also revealed himself, accurately though not fully, during the Old Testament period; so even from an orthodox Old Testament perspective Qoheleth's frustration is hard to understand. But as Lauha notes, "For Kohelet there are no means of revelation. History, nature, and cult are all silent in this regard according to him" (1978:162).

10. Everyone dies! (9:1-10)

This, too, I carefully explored: Even though the actions of godly and wise people are in God's hands, no one knows whether God will show them favor. ²The same destiny ultimately awaits everyone, whether righteous or wicked, good or bad,* ceremonially clean or unclean, religious or irreligious. Good people receive the same treatment as sinners, and people who make promises to God are treated like people who don't.

³It seems so tragic that everyone under the sun suffers the same fate. That is why people are not more careful to be good. Instead, they choose their own mad course, for they have no hope. There is nothing ahead but death anyway. ⁴There is hope only for the living. As they say, "It's better to be a live dog than a dead lion!"

⁵The living at least know they will die, but the dead know nothing. They have no further reward, nor are they remembered. ⁶Whatever they did in their lifetime—loving, hating, envying—is all long gone. They no longer play a part in anything here on earth. ⁷So go ahead. Eat your food with joy, and drink your wine with a happy heart, for God approves of this! ⁸Wear fine clothes, with a splash of cologne!

⁹Live happily with the woman you love through all the meaningless days of life that God has given you under the sun. The wife God gives you is your reward for all your earthly toil. ¹⁰Whatever you do, do well. For when you go to the grave,* there will be no work or planning or knowledge or wisdom.

9:2 As in Greek and Syriac versions and Latin Vulgate; Hebrew lacks or bad. 9:10 Hebrew to Sheol.

NOTES

9:2 The verse lists six pairs of opposites. Some of the pairs are obvious in their meaning (good/bad; righteous/wicked; good people/sinners), but some of them benefit from further explanation. The first such category is ceremonially clean/unclean. This refers to the laws of Leviticus where certain actions and states render someone clean—that is, able to enter into the holy place, and others render them temporarily unclean. To be unclean does not mean to be a sinner. Sometimes being unclean entails coming into contact with a holy substance such as semen or blood. At other times, it may mean coming into contact with a dead body or having a skin rash. In any case, to be clean did not prevent one from meeting the same fate as the unclean, namely death.

The Heb. behind the pair religious/irreligious has to do with sacrifices: "one who offers sacrifices / one who does not offer sacrifices." Sacrifices were required of all godly Israelites (cf. Lev 1-7). These sacrifices were a means of fellowship, as well as a gift offered to God. Most importantly they were the divinely instituted ritual by which the Israelites sought atonement for their sins. But again, Qoheleth says that offering sacrifices (i.e., being religious) does not save people from death.

Finally, we should understand that the promises that the last pair in 9:2 refers to are not any old promises but rather vows made to God. This is a subject that Qoheleth addressed in 5:4-5. We now understand even better why Qoheleth was not enthusiastic about such religious promises. There was a large downside (God's anger) if one did not follow through on the promise but little, if any, upside. Making promises and following through on them would not save a person from the grave.

9:8 *Wear fine clothes, with a splash of cologne!* The NLT uses a modern equivalent to the Heb., "Let your clothes be white at all times, and do not spare oil on your head." White garments were festive clothes during the OT time period. Qoheleth here advises his listeners to put on their best clothes and refresh themselves with oil—to take whatever enjoyment they can out of life. As the broader section concludes, there is certainly nothing else to look forward to—except death.

9:9 *The wife God gives you is your reward.* The translation "reward" is probably too positive for the Heb. word, which is better translated "lot."

COMMENTARY

Qoheleth introduces no new ideas in this section, but he dramatically reemphasizes some of the most important themes of his thought. In particular, he describes death as the ultimate end for everyone, an end that renders every accomplishment in life without value. In addition, he talks again about human inability to control one's fate and determine the right time for an action. Finally, he questions the justice of the world, indeed the justice of God. Why do the righteous, those who follow God, get no better treatment than sinners who ignore him?

Again, we must keep in mind that this speech of Qoheleth is in the middle of a quotation of his questionable teaching. We must not confuse the thoughts of Qoheleth with the instruction of the book of Ecclesiastes. Qoheleth is a questioning, confused wise man of Israel, whose speech a second wise man is quoting to his son, so he can present a more positive, God-directed viewpoint at the end of the book (cf. Introduction; commentary on 12:8-14). In the words of Qoheleth himself, he is talking about life "under the sun," that is, apart from God. The second wise man will use this negative teaching to drive his son to go "above the sun," namely, to God himself.

The passage opens on a very promising note. Most of us would be comforted by the news that "the actions of godly and wise people are in God's hands." However, this does not make Qoheleth feel better, since he believes God is arbitrary in how he treats people. "No one knows whether God will show them favor" (9:1). We should remember that for this reason he advised his hearers not to be too righteous or wise (see 7:15-18). Indeed, he goes on to say that death is the great leveler. It does not discriminate between different types of people. He then lists six different pairs of opposites (9:2):

Righteous / Wicked
Good / Bad
Ceremonially clean / Unclean
Religious / Irreligious
Good people / Sinners
People who make promises to God / People who don't

One would think that the people in the first group would indeed find favor in God's eyes, while the people in the second would not. That is not the Teacher's experience, however. The people in the first group die ("the same destiny") just like the people in the opposite group. As we continue in this section, as elsewhere in his speech (see 3:1-15; 12:1-7), we see that Qoheleth's thinking does not allow for an afterlife where everything can be worked out justly. No, to Qoheleth, good people and bad people are treated the same, and occasionally bad people have a better life and a more dignified death than good people (8:9-15).

Good and bad people die, and Qoheleth considers it "tragic that everyone under the sun suffers the same fate" (9:3). For one thing, it leads people to be bad rather than good. If one derives no ultimate benefit from one's good behavior or religious activities, why bother? Without hope, people do evil things. He does allow that the living can have hope, but notice the sarcasm. Why do the living have hope? "The living at least know they will die" (9:5). What kind of advantage is this? However, in comparison to death, it does seem like an advantage. Death leads to the end of everything. The strong emotions one feels during life (loving, hating, envying) all disappear at the time of death.

This conclusion leads the Teacher to suggest a life of superficial enjoyment. In other words, we have yet another *carpe diem* passage (see 2:24-26; 3:12-14, 22; 5:18-20). One should eat, drink, and dress for a party (see note on 9:8). One should also enjoy life with one's wife. We are left to wonder how this harmonizes with the teaching in 7:25-29, which stated that there were no virtuous women to be found; presumably, what can be had is, at best, slim pickings. The wife is your "lot" through all the meaningless days of life that God has given you. And there is nothing to come after that. In the grave, there will be "no work or planning or knowledge or wisdom."

◆ 11. Chance rules (9:11-12)

¹¹I have observed something else under the sun. The fastest runner doesn't always win the race, and the strongest warrior doesn't always win the battle. The wise sometimes go hungry, and the skillful are not necessarily wealthy. And those who are educated don't always lead successful lives. It is all decided by chance, by being in the right place at the right time.

¹²People can never predict when hard times might come. Like fish in a net or birds in a trap, people are caught by sudden tragedy.

COMMENTARY

With "I have observed something else under the sun" Qoheleth moves on to yet another depressing observation on life: it's not fair! In the preceding section, he says that one should find joy in the present because the future has nothing to offer; now he points out that there is no surefire path to a good life in the present. In other words, hard work is not rewarded. Skill and ability do not always lead to success. He looks at five different cases where the best do not win. The fastest runner may not win the race—perhaps the fastest trips and falls. The strongest warrior does not always win the battle—perhaps, while occupied with an opponent, someone shoots an arrow in his back.

The final three groups (the wise, skillful, and educated) hit closer to home for the Teacher, who himself was a wise man. The wise man may go hungry. This seems different than what we read in Proverbs 10:3: "The Lord will not let the godly [or, righteous] go hungry, but he refuses to satisfy the craving of the wicked." Again, the Teacher, looking at life "under the sun," has grown to question the connection between wisdom and success. He points out that those who have skill do not always become rich. And then, finally, he says that the educated do not always lead successful lives. Perhaps we know people with PhDs who have failed careers and hopeless relationships. Education is not an infallible path to a good life.

Qoheleth's thought here is not too far removed from that of Paul in Romans 9:16: "So it is God who decides to show mercy. We can neither choose it nor work for it." In other words, human inability drives Paul to divine grace, while Qoheleth ends up in frustration.

With these observations Qoheleth is once again raising the issue of retribution and thus questioning God's fairness. Success is determined by chance, at least from a human perspective. One needs to be at the right place at the right time to get ahead. And, as Qoheleth has already told us, God, not human beings, knows the right time and place (3:1-15). Since human beings cannot read the times, they cannot predict when hard times might come. He ends the unit with an analogy between human beings caught in a sudden tragedy and fish caught in a net or birds snared in a trap. All three are sudden, unexpected, and terrifying. Underlying the images of tragedy, net, and trap is, of course, death. No one knows when they will die. It could happen any time to old or young, healthy or not, male or female. Life—and its end—are simply unpredictable and thus uncontrollable. Humans are at the mercy of chance and fate.

◆ 12. The limits of wisdom (9:13-16)

¹³Here is another bit of wisdom that has impressed me as I have watched the way our world works. ¹⁴There was a small town with only a few people, and a great king came with his army and besieged it. ¹⁵A poor, wise man knew how to save the town, and so it was rescued. But afterward no one thought to thank him. ¹⁶So even though wisdom is better than strength, those who are wise will be despised if they are poor. What they say will not be appreciated for long.

NOTES

9:13 *I have watched the way our world works.* This is an idiomatic translation of the Heb. phrase "I observed [everything] under the sun." We have here once again the expression "under the sun," which is to be understood as "apart from the revelation of God" (see notes and commentary on 1:3).

9:14 *small town . . . few people . . . great king . . . besieged.* The Heb. emphasizes the lopsided nature of the battle. The town is small and has only a few people; the king is great and the siege engines (ramps, ladders, etc.) are huge. The NLT treats the noun phrase "huge siege works" as a verb "besieged," which is accurate but misses the nuance that supports the contrast between the size of the siege works and the size of the town.

9:15 *poor, wise man.* This verse emphasizes another contrast that the story draws between the great king of the previous verse and the poor wise man in this verse.

thank him. The NLT says that no one thought to thank the poor wise man for rescuing the town. The Heb. is the verb for "remember" (*zakar* [TH2142, ZH2349]). Part of remembrance is thanks, but we should not lose sight of the fact that to Qoheleth remembrance (and its antonym "forgetfulness") is an important theme (1:11; 2:16). In the short run, the wise man's actions were significant, but in the long run they disappeared in the oblivion of passing time. There is an alternative interpretation of the concluding clause, one that understands the verb "save" as having a "potential meaning" (Crenshaw 1987:166-167). Isaksson translates it, "Now there lived in that city a man poor, but wise, and he alone might have saved the city by his wisdom, but no one thought of that poor man" (1987:97). However, the verb "remembered" (*zakar*) makes better sense with an actual event in the past. Also the idea that the poor man actually did save the city and was not remembered heightens the depressing nature of the verse.

9:16 *those who are wise will be despised if they are poor.* The Heb. is more precisely translated "but the wisdom of the poor man was despised!" In other words, this section says nothing really about the value of poverty, it does teach that wisdom is relatively valuable, although not in the long run.

COMMENTARY

We return now to one of Qoheleth's favorite subjects: the relative value but limitation of wisdom. We first encountered his thinking in this topic in 2:12-16, where he judged that wisdom is better than folly just like sight is better than blindness, but neither the wise nor the fool can avoid the ultimate end: death. In the present text, Qoheleth makes his point by means of an anecdote, a short story with a moral at the end (see also 4:7-8).

Again, the Teacher's wisdom here flows from his observation of the world. It is unclear, however, whether the story he is about to narrate is something that actually happened or whether, like a parable, it simply is constructed in order to make his point. The fact that everyone is anonymous and no place is given a specific name seems to indicate that the latter is true. Verse 14 presents the problem: a large army led by a great king besieges a small town. The conflict seems one sided, but what sways the balance in favor of the small town is the presence of a wise man. This wise man is also described as poor in order to contrast him with the king. On the one side, we have a great king with a powerful army, and on the other side we have a small town with a poor but wise man in its midst. As we will see, the lesson of the first part of the story is that wisdom in and of itself outweighs the benefits of wealth and military power.

The story makes its point simply and without detail. The wise man knew how to save the city, and it was rescued. This illustrates the saying "the strongest warrior doesn't always win the battle" (9:11). However, after the superiority of wisdom over power is emphasized, the conclusion of the story tells of its limited value. No one expressed their appreciation to the wise man. No value accrued to him because of his wisdom. As the previous section just said, "The wise sometimes go hungry, and the skillful are not necessarily wealthy. And those who are educated don't always lead successful lives" (9:11).

◆ ### 13. Assessing wisdom (9:17-18)

[17] Better to hear the quiet words
of a wise person
than the shouts of a foolish
king.

[18] Better to have wisdom than weapons
of war,
but one sinner can destroy much
that is good.

NOTES

9:17 *quiet.* It is slightly unclear whether the verse refers to the quiet words of the wise or communicates that the words of the wise are best heard in quietness. The contrast, though, with the shouts of the foolish king in the second part of the verse strongly suggests that the NLT is right in adopting the first possibility.

9:18 *sinner.* The NLT (with the NIV, KJV, NASB) translates the participle that indicates the class of people who destroy much that is good in the moral sense as "sinner." It is very possible, though, that the word is better understood in its non-moral sense as "someone who messes up" or "someone who makes a mistake," destroying much that is useful. In any case, the basic point about the limited value of wisdom, explicated in the commentary below, still stands.

COMMENTARY

The chapter ends with two proverbs that underline the teaching of the anecdote that precedes them. Wisdom is better than folly; wisdom outstrips power. But in the end, even wisdom is no guarantee of success in life.

Qoheleth expresses this thought using one of his favorite forms—the "better than" proverb (or "better-proverb"; cf. Ogden 1977). This form is well-suited to express relative value—that is, how one thing is superior to another. The first proverb (9:17) pits the words of a wise person over against a fool and judges the wise person's words as superior. Note that, as in the anecdote, the equation seems stacked in favor of the fool. The fool is a king; the wise person is not. Further, the king speaks forcefully—that is, he shouts—whereas the wise person speaks in a quiet voice. Nonetheless, the implicit message is that the quiet words of the wise person are much more valuable to listen to than the shouts of the foolish king.

The second proverb has an interesting twist. The first part is a "better than" proverb once again, which promotes wisdom over power—here represented by weapons of war. This was concretely illustrated in the anecdote in 9:13-16. However, the second part of the verse takes the carpet out from under both proverbs—one sinner can destroy much that is good. We have a modern proverb that says essentially the same thing: "One bad apple spoils the whole barrel." The implicit message achieved by placing this line at the end is that no matter how much good or benefit can be achieved by the wise, it can all be undone by the presence of just a pinch of sin.

◆   **14. Proverbs on wisdom and foolishness (10:1-4)**

As dead flies cause even a bottle
    of perfume to stink,
so a little foolishness spoils great
    wisdom and honor.
²A wise person chooses the right
    road;
a fool takes the wrong one.

³You can identify fools
    just by the way they walk down
    the street!

⁴If your boss is angry at you, don't
    quit!
A quiet spirit can overcome even
    great mistakes.

NOTES
10:2 *right road . . . wrong one.* The NLT rightly interprets the Heb., which lit. states that the wise person takes the road to the right and the foolish person the road to the left. In many ancient cultures, the direction to the right was also associated with "power and strength" (Ogden 1987:165, who cites Gen 48:18 and Isa 41:10), and the direction to the left was without this meaning. Analogous is the Latin word *sinister*, which also means "left" as well as "wrong" or "perverse."

COMMENTARY
This unit may be a continuation of the preceding section. We will see this first of all in the fact that the first proverb talks about how a little bit of a bad thing can destroy a good thing. Then, the following proverbs have to do with wisdom, the theme of much of chapter 9. In that 10:1-4 contains proverbs, it reminds us of 7:1-14, which also contains a number of proverbial sayings. The proverbs of 9:17-18, however, differ from these in their use of the "better than" form, making a new section here a possibility.

The analogy drawn by the first proverb in this list is clear and depressing, especially when we remember that Qoheleth himself is a wise man. The smell of perfume is enticing and wonderful. However, it does not take many dead flies rotting in the perfume to destroy it. The same is true for a little bit of foolishness; it spoils wisdom and honor. Again, as in the saying in 9:18, it only takes one rotten apple to spoil the whole barrel.

This proverb is ingenious because it subtly introduces another theme in a surprising way, namely death. Just like the dead flies turn the whole batch of perfume putrid, so death destroys the lasting value of wisdom (2:12-16).

The second proverb contrasts the wise person and the fool and makes an observation on their behavior. Quite simply, there are two roads—a right one and a wrong one—and the fool takes the wrong one. The image of the road or way is a popular one in wisdom literature. The road is part of a metaphor, seeing life as a journey, and there are decisions that must be made particularly at the crossroads. Note, for instance, how the father instructs the son about how to follow the road or way of wisdom and to avoid the way of folly in Proverbs 1-9.

The third proverb says that fools are easily identified by the road they take. Fools cannot hide their identities. Folly is really a heart attitude (one that rejects the instruction of the Lord), but this heart attitude manifests itself in decisions and actions.

The fourth and final proverb of this unit gives some advice concerning how to act before an angry boss. This type of instruction is typical in the wisdom found in Proverbs, as well as in other ancient Near Eastern wisdom texts, particularly Egyptian. Quite simply, the proverb encourages a calm reaction to an angry boss. The proverb does imply that the employee may have made a mistake and that the boss is not irrationally angry, but the point is that a quiet spirit overcomes these mistakes.

◆   15. The world upside down (10:5-7)

⁵There is another evil I have seen under the sun. Kings and rulers make a grave mistake ⁶when they give great authority to foolish people and low positions to people of proven worth. ⁷I have even seen servants riding horseback like princes— and princes walking like servants!

NOTES

10:6-7 These verses describe an unstable society. Ecclesiastes is not the only ancient Near Eastern book to describe the world as topsy-turvy. The theme may be found in other ancient Near Eastern wisdom books as well. Van Leeuwen (1986) describes this literary topos well and cites examples from some Twelfth Dynasty Egyptian texts including the "Prophecy of Neferti," "The Complaints of Khakheperre-Sonb," and "The Admonitions of Ipuwer."

COMMENTARY

This text provides yet another anecdote or illustration of why the world is as messed up as it is. The Teacher keeps bombarding the reader with examples of problems in the world, that is, under the sun. In this brief section, he describes a world gone awry. He describes social chaos by saying that incompetent, unprepared people assume leadership roles and those who are leaders are put in the position of servants.

The Teacher's world was an aristocratic one. Thus, he describes the topsy-turvy world as one where those born to privilege like kings and princes assume the role of servants and vice versa. His point is that the world is simply not functioning correctly. Proverbs 30:21-23 echoes this sentiment:

> There are three things that make the earth tremble—
>   no, four it cannot endure:
> a slave who becomes a king,
>   an overbearing fool who prospers,
> a bitter woman who finally gets a husband,
>   a servant girl who supplants her mistress.

◆   16. The "accidents" of life (10:8-11)

⁸When you dig a well,
    you might fall in.
When you demolish an old wall,
    you could be bitten by a snake.
⁹When you work in a quarry,
    stones might fall and crush you.
When you chop wood,
    there is danger with each stroke
    of your ax.

¹⁰Using a dull ax requires great
    strength,
    so sharpen the blade.
That's the value of wisdom;
    it helps you succeed.

¹¹If a snake bites before you charm it,
    what's the use of being a snake
    charmer?

NOTES

10:8 *you might fall in.* When reading this verse, one cannot help but think of a common expression for retribution in the Psalms, typified by Ps 7:15: "They dig a deep pit to trap others, then fall into it themselves." This is a common and vivid metaphor for the idea that those who create a problem will reap the consequences. However, Qoheleth's proverb, whether he created it or is simply quoting it, reverses this idea. It is an innocent person, who is simply doing a job, who falls prey to the dangers of the hole.

10:9 The NLT appropriately makes explicit what is implicit in the Heb. text: "The one who quarries stones may be injured by them; the one who splits trees may be endangered by them." The Heb. only suggests how those who quarry stones and split trees might be injured, but the NLT introduces the idea of getting crushed by the stones or being struck by the ax.

10:10 *Using a dull ax requires great strength, so sharpen the blade. That's the value of wisdom; it helps you succeed.* Charles Wright (1888:423) admitted that "this, linguistically speaking, is confessedly the most difficult passage in the Book of Qoheleth." The problems are ancient, as the translations of even the various ancient versions attest. The Gr. of the LXX, for instance, might be rendered: "If the ax falls and it troubles a face, then he will strengthen his strength. The advantage of man is wisdom." The NLT follows the suggestion of Frendo (1981) that there is a genitive relationship between words that are not next to each other, and this insight helps yield the translation and understanding of the verse presented here.

COMMENTARY

Qoheleth has repeatedly acknowledged the providence of God. God knows the times (3:1-15). He is in charge of how events work themselves out. On the human side, however, we are ignorant. Time and chance rule all (9:11). We do not know what God has in store for us now or in the future (9:1). In such a world ("under the sun"), our good, constructive intentions can turn disastrous, and wisdom is of limited value as we struggle with the "accidents" of life.

Ecclesiastes 10:8-9 offers four examples for our consideration. As we dig a well, we may fall in and hurt ourselves. As we take down an old wall, we could reach in and be bitten by a snake and be injured or even die. Quarry work might lead to death by crushing, while chopping wood may well result in a severed foot.

These are just people doing their occupation, and they end up getting hurt. This may well be a further comment on the fairness of the world and of God. These people have done nothing wrong; they do not deserve the injury.

The connection between 10:8-9 and 10:10-11 is not strong. Since 10:9 refers to chopping wood, it may have suggested that this would be a good place for 10:10, though it is not making the same general point. One need only read a section from Proverbs 10–31 to realize that collections of proverbs and wise sayings often have a rather random structure.

In any case, the point of the proverb seems to be the value of wisdom. To paraphrase: "If you're smart, you'll sharpen the edge of an ax before you start chopping wood—it will save your strength." Qoheleth has nowhere in the book abandoned the idea that wisdom has some value; he has only insisted on its limited usefulness. It does not help one with the big problems of life such as death. In light of this, it is not surprising that, again, what he gives with one hand, he takes away with the other. Verse 10:11 points out the limits of wisdom and knowledge in the face of death.

A snake charmer is someone who knows how to handle snakes. The charmer keeps the potentially dangerous animal mesmerized so it can do no injury. This is a great skill, requiring sophisticated wisdom. By a simple question, however, Qoheleth undermines the wisdom of snake charmers, showing their limits. In effect he says, "Fine and good, but once bitten the charmer can do nothing. Snake charming has its obvious limitations." Of course, Qoheleth's point about danger and limitations is not restricted to snake charming; he intends to apply it to the use of any type of wisdom.

Thus, this section, though difficult to interpret in detail, makes two very clear points. Life is dangerous and prey to accidents. Though wisdom has some limited value, it does not ultimately help the one who possesses it.

◆ 17. Fools (10:12-15)

¹²Wise words bring approval,
but fools are destroyed by their
own words.

¹³Fools base their thoughts on foolish
assumptions,
so their conclusions will be wicked
madness;
¹⁴ they chatter on and on.

No one really knows what is going
to happen;
no one can predict the future.

¹⁵Fools are so exhausted by a little
work
that they can't even find their
way home.

NOTES

10:12 *fools are destroyed by their own words.* The Heb. is actually more specific and vivid than the NLT translation reveals. The verse talks about how "the lips of the fool swallow him."

10:13-14 Some ambiguity attends the relationship between the poetic lines of these two verses. The debate centers on whether the first line of 10:14 ("they chatter on and on"; Heb. "And the fool multiplies words") concludes the thought of 10:13 or opens 10:14. The latter is actually more likely, though the NLT and NIV have opted for the former. However, it is also possible that this line is what is sometimes called a pivot pattern and is to be read with the verse before it and the poetic bicolon after it. The only really important point to make for our reading is that 10:14 concerns the fool, as do the other three proverbs in this section, though this is not immediately obvious from the NLT's formatting.

COMMENTARY

These proverbs are associated because of their common focus on fools. They make fun of the fool and show the negative consequences of such behavior. While the Teacher admits the limitations of wisdom many times in his writing, he has no respect or appreciation for the opposite class of people, the fool.

No strong connection exists between this group of proverbial sayings and the one that it follows (10:8-11). Ecclesiastes 10:10 does assert the value of wisdom, though its limits are also pointed out, and it is this that may provide reason for this placement of these proverbs about the fool.

While many of Qoheleth's proverbs seem different from those of the book of Proverbs, here we can note some similarities in the importance of words, as seen in this section and in the idea of the self-destructive nature of the fool. The wisdom literature of Israel and of the entire ancient Near East was concerned with the use of words. The list of proverbs that talk about the value of saying the right thing at the right time and the danger of the ill-timed word is long. The book of Proverbs teaches that wise words build up, but foolish ones tear down·

A gentle answer deflects anger,
    but harsh words make tempers flare. (Prov 15:1)

Everyone enjoys a fitting reply;
    it is wonderful to say the right thing at the right time! (Prov 15:23)

Proverbial wisdom also noted the self-destructive nature of the fool. Fools fall into their own trap; they hurt themselves. Some proverbs, like the first proverb of this section (10:12), relate to a fool's words and his self-destruction:

The wise are glad to be instructed,
    but babbling fools fall flat on their faces. (Prov 10:8)

The words of the godly encourage many,
    but fools are destroyed by their lack of common sense. (Prov 10:21)

A fool's proud talk becomes a rod that beats him,
    but the words of the wise keep them safe. (Prov 14:3)

The second proverb (10:13) points out that fools begin their thinking with stupid assumptions. This is bad but does not immediately appear to us as dangerous. However, the Teacher's proverb goes on to say that these foolish assumptions lead to conclusions that can be characterized as wicked madness. As Psalm 14:1 states, "Only fools say in their hearts, 'There is no God.'" The wise, though, understand that "fear of the LORD is the foundation of true knowledge" (Prov 1:7). With these two statements, we see the most basic assumptions of the fool and the wise. It is no wonder, then, that the Israelite sage felt that a fool's assumptions would lead to wicked madness.

This proverb, at first, seems awkward in the writings of a confused wise man like Qoheleth. But again, Qoheleth is no fool. He does not reject the idea of God. He rather questions his fairness in the world that he is examining "under the sun."

In any case, as the NLT structures this section, these fools are more than willing to share their harmful conclusions. They chatter on and on. "Chatter" captures the low quality of their communication, as well as its annoying nature. However, as mentioned in the notes above, it is more likely that the first line of 10:14 goes with the proverb that follows. That means that the endless chatter about which the proverb complains has to do with their talk about the future. Qoheleth has already expressed his opinion that no one can know the future (6:12; 7:14; 8:7). By definition, then, people who talk about the future do not know what they are talking about.

The final proverb in this section (10:15) makes fun of the fool for his laziness. It says that when fools work, it exhausts them so much that they are not alert enough to follow directions to get home. The fool is similarly characterized by laziness in the book of Proverbs, for instance: "A wise youth harvests in the summer, but one who sleeps during harvest is a disgrace" (Prov 10:5).

◆   18. The king: blessing or curse? (10:16-17)

16 What sorrow for the land ruled
    by a servant,*
the land whose leaders feast
    in the morning.
17 Happy is the land whose king
    is a noble leader

and whose leaders feast at the
    proper time
to gain strength for their work,
    not to get drunk.

10:16 Or *a child.*

NOTES

10:16 *servant.* The verse mourns for the land whose king is a *na'ar* [TH5288, ZH5853], translated, not inappropriately, by "servant." The Heb. word can denote either a young person or a person in a subservient position. The latter is more likely in the present context because the contrast drawn in the next verse is with a noble person. In either case, whether understood as servant, youth, or immature, the *na'ar* has no business being on the throne. The situation will lead to the deterioration of the land.

COMMENTARY

These verses treat a royal theme and in that regard are similar to verse 20. Some commentators (Ogden 1987:174-175) treat 10:16-20 as a unit dealing with wisdom concerning kings, but this does not take into account that 10:18-19 has nothing to do with the king, so we will treat 10:16-20 in three separate sections.

Verses 16-17 first present a dirge over the land with a king who is immature or who is a follower rather than a leader, and they follow this with a blessing upon a land with a king who is responsible and fit for rule.

Verse 16 is an example of a theme found in many wisdom texts in antiquity. It describes a topsy-turvy world, where followers are leaders and leaders are followers. To have a land where the king is a servant means certain distress. Such a king will not be responsible, and the leaders of the country will start the day with a feast and never get to the work of administrating the country. Nothing will get done and the land will deteriorate. Similarly, Proverbs 30:21-23 includes this idea of a "slave who becomes a king" in a list of horrible situations.

In contrast, verse 17 presents a positive picture where everything is as it should be. The king comes from the nobility, not from the servant class. He eats at the right time and not to dissolution. The warning about leaders drinking too heavily reflects the advice King Lemuel received from his mother, according to Proverbs 31:4-7:

It is not for kings, O Lemuel, to guzzle wine.
    Rulers should not crave alcohol.
For if they drink, they may forget the law
    and not give justice to the oppressed.
Alcohol is for the dying,
    and wine for those in bitter distress.
Let them drink and forget their poverty
    and remember their troubles no more.

◆   19. More wisdom (10:18-19)

18 Laziness leads to a sagging roof;   19 A party gives laughter,
    idleness leads to a leaky   wine gives happiness,
    house.   and money gives everything!

NOTES

10:18 *idleness.* This translates two words in the Heb. text that are in a genitive relationship: "lowering of hands." This pictures the idea of inactivity, and so the NLT has rightly captured the sense of the phrase.

10:19 *A party gives laughter.* The Heb. of the first line is more lit. "making bread for laughter." However, bread (*lekhem* [TH3899, ZH4312]) often stands for food and in this case refers to a feast or, in modern parlance, a party (see Salters 1977).

COMMENTARY

The previous section (10:16-17) provides a wise observation concerning kings, and the following section (10:20) returns to this royal subject matter, but 10:18-19 interposes two proverbs on two miscellaneous issues, laziness and fun. What to us is a rather haphazard organization is rather typical of proverbial collections, as anyone can tell by simply reading Proverbs 10–31. Some people create what I think is a false connection between 10:18 and the preceding section by suggesting that the neglected house of 10:18 is the "land" of 10:16-17. In this interpretation, 10:18 concerns the immature king allowing the land to disintegrate by virtue of neglect. This connection seems quite far-fetched and does not take into account the random nature of most proverb collections.

Verse 18 is an observation that implicitly criticizes lazy people. This topic is frequent in the book of Proverbs (cf. Prov 6:6; 10:4; 12:27; 26:15-16). In Proverbs, as here, the lazy person is a fool. In this verse, lazy people are criticized by describing the consequences of their actions. The image is vivid: a lazy person doesn't expend the energy to repair the roof of his house, and the result is that the roof sags and eventually leaks—an undesirable consequence.

While verse 18 fits in with a well-established wisdom tradition concerning the lazy person, verse 19 appears to be unique and may even undermine the previous proverb. It extols a life of material enjoyment. It encourages one to go out and grab all the pleasure one can, a goal that could lead to the neglect of responsibilities like fixing up one's house.

The verse is a typical three-part parallelism where each line builds on the previous one, and the last line provides a kind of climactic statement. We can understand how a party might lead to laughter and fun. Wine, through its intoxicating powers, imparts a sense of happiness, but how does money give everything? Perhaps we are to understand Qoheleth to say that one can only give a party or buy wine with money. Money is the necessary condition for the other two. No money, no party!

Of course, we need to raise the question of what tone of voice we are to imagine as this line is being delivered. Is it a serious assertion? If so, then it fits in with the frequent *carpe diem* passages that we have seen throughout the book (2:24-26; 3:12-14, 22; 5:18-20; 8:15; 9:7-10). In other words, good times are the best that life has to offer, so make sure to have some. However, we might imagine that the proverb is delivered with a sarcastic tone. In that case, it would fit in with Qoheleth's overall teaching that life is meaningless and also conform better to 10:18.

◆ **20. Advice concerning the king (10:20)**

20 Never make light of the king, even in your thoughts.
And don't make fun of the powerful, even in your own bedroom.

For a little bird might deliver your message
and tell them what you said.

COMMENTARY
Here we return to the topic of the king that was also the subject of 10:16-17. In good ancient Near Eastern wisdom fashion, the wise Teacher instructs his pupil how to act in front of royalty and other politically powerful people. In a word, he tells them to beware—to watch their backs. People must even be so careful as to guard their private thoughts and speech about such powerful individuals. After all, the king is sovereign (8:2-4) and the other leaders are people with whom lesser mortals must reckon. These people are so powerful that they have agents all over the place (a little bird); furthermore, they can act in their displeasure to bring great harm or even death to those who upset them.

◆ **21. Risk and the uncertainty of life (11:1-6)**

Send your grain across the seas, and in time, profits will flow back to you.*
2 But divide your investments among many places,*
for you do not know what risks might lie ahead.

3 When clouds are heavy, the rains come down.

Whether a tree falls north or south, it stays where it falls.
4 Farmers who wait for perfect weather never plant.
If they watch every cloud, they never harvest.

5 Just as you cannot understand the path of the wind or the mystery of a tiny baby growing in its mother's womb,* so

you cannot understand the activity of God, who does all things. ⁶Plant your seed in the morning and keep busy all afternoon, for you don't know if profit will come from one activity or another—or maybe both.

11:1 Or *Give generously, / for your gifts will return to you later.* Hebrew reads *Throw your bread on the waters, / for after many days you will find it again.* 11:2 Hebrew *among seven or even eight.* 11:5 Some manuscripts read *Just as you cannot understand how breath comes to a tiny baby in its mother's womb.*

NOTES

11:1 *Send your grain across the seas, and in time, profits will flow back to you.* This translation is an interpretation of the Heb. that is lit. rendered, "Throw your bread on the waters, for after many days you will find it again" (cf. NLT mg). Needless to say, this seems a strange statement to modern ears. One imagines a soggy piece of Wonder Bread coming back to the shore after a few days at sea. We must first of all recognize that the Heb. word "bread" (*lekhem* [TH3899, ZH4312]) often stands for food of all kinds. The NLT understands the idiom as referring to a commercial venture based on this verse's relationship to 11:2, a difficult verse in its own right, but one seemingly concerned with business. The main rival interpretation understands the verse to refer to charity. The NLT mg also gives this interpretation: "Give generously, for your gifts will return to you later." This, however, does not fit in with the context, which gives no hints that charity is the subject.

11:2 *divide your investments among many places, for you do not know what risks might lie ahead.* The NLT is interpretive in its translation in the interests of clarity. A more literal rendition of the Hebrew is, "Give a portion to seven, even to eight, for you do not know what evil may occur in the land" (cf. NLT mg). The numerical progression of "seven, even eight" is a typical number parallelism attested not only in the Bible (Prov 30:15, 18, 21, 29; Amos 1:3, 6, 9, 11, 13; 2:4; Mic 5:5) but in Canaanite poetry as well. It is not to be taken literally (see Roth 1962). As in the NLT's translation, it means "many," not literally seven or eight.

11:3 *north or south.* This is an ancient Heb. rhetorical device called a merism, whereby two opposites are cited to include everything in between. In this case, north and south imply "whatever direction" it falls (Fox 1989:275).

11:4 *who wait for perfect weather.* Lit., "who watch the wind." It refers to farmers who would watch for the wind to cease and put off planting for fear that the wind would blow away the seed that they were sowing, just as the rains would ruin the harvests (11:4b). Thus, this verse looks at both ends of the agricultural cycle.

COMMENTARY

Qoheleth has already told his readers that "it is all decided by chance, by being in the right place at the right time" (9:11). The present section gives advice about how to navigate a risky world or, as Roland Murphy expresses it, the unit is composed of "sayings about the uncertainty of human industry" (1992:147).

The first two verses compose the opening salvo. The first verse urges that the reader send grain across the sea, which is most likely (see note on 11:1) a reference to commercial ships that are involved in trade for profit. As one does so, then profits from this activity will come back to the investor. It is interesting to note first of all that, though Qoheleth believes chance ultimately rules all, he advises action and not resignation here. In 11:2 he goes on to advise the one who invests in this commercial venture, however, not to "put all your eggs in one basket." Since life is risky, one had better diversify to avoid the risk of total collapse. Let's say someone is involved in commercial shipping and puts everything they have in one ship. What if a freak storm causes that ship to sink? That would result in financial disaster. But if that person were involved in other investments, then the ship going down, though a setback, would not completely destroy one's livelihood.

Verses 3-4 form a kind of unit. The two parts of verse 3 speak to the "inevitability" and "randomness" of life (Whybray 1989:159). The first colon observes that it rains when the clouds are heavy. Besides "inevitability," this may also speak to human inability to control life. No human can determine when the clouds are going to be heavy and, therefore, rain. Randomness, with the inability to control what happens in the world, is the meaning of the second colon as well. Who can control the direction in which a tree falls? Where it falls, there it stays!

With this in the background, we now read verse 4. Farmers who try to control their circumstances will never get anywhere. Perfect weather never comes; as a result, they do not get a harvest. The implicit message is not to let our inability to control circumstances paralyze our actions. The farmer who does this may very well starve to death.

Verse 5 implies that these seemingly random events that appear to be beyond human control are actually under the control of God. The Teacher describes two more earthly phenomena that are beyond human control and comprehension. The first is the direction of the wind. We feel it, but we do not see it, and we certainly cannot control it. The second is a growing fetus. We need to place ourselves in the time before sonograms and other methods of looking into the human body. Something is clearly happening in the woman's body, but what and how? It is beyond human observation and control. The same is true of God's ways in the world. We do not see him acting explicitly, nor can we control it. One might think this is a comforting thought, but we have already seen from earlier expressions of this idea by the Teacher that it does not lead him to joy but rather to frustration (3:11; 8:17; 9:12).

All of his teaching and illustration of human inability to control circumstances leads us finally back to the point made in 11:1-2. In such a world, it is wise to cut your risks by diversity of investment. In this agricultural context, the lesson is to plant not just in the morning or just in the afternoon but at both times. After all, who knows which of these two times will prove productive? So cover your bases. (This is sort of the ancient equivalent of the modern investor's dollar cost averaging.) This agricultural illustration is likely to stand for all human activity. The Teacher is skeptical about life to be sure. From a human perspective, all of life is random and uncontrollable, but that should not lead to passivity; it should lead to action.

◆   22. Youth, old age, and death (11:7-10)

7Light is sweet; how pleasant to see a new day dawning.
8When people live to be very old, let them rejoice in every day of life. But let them also remember there will be many dark days. Everything still to come is meaningless.
9Young people,* it's wonderful to be

young! Enjoy every minute of it. Do everything you want to do; take it all in. But remember that you must give an account to
God for everything you do. ¹⁰So refuse to

worry, and keep your body healthy. But
remember that youth, with a whole life
before you, is meaningless.

11:9 Hebrew *Young man.*

NOTES
11:9 *Do everything you want to do; take it all in.* While the NLT has rightly captured the
sense of the Heb. here, this idiomatic translation may cause one to miss an echo from Num
15:39 to be discussed below. A literal translation would be: "Follow the ways of your heart
and the sight of your eyes."

COMMENTARY
This unit of text begins the transition to Qoheleth's final topic, death, which he will
more fully develop in 12:1-7. The passage begins on an optimistic, even happy
note, but we should notice that in every instance where he says something positive,
he soon presents the negative side. He gives with one hand and takes away with
the other.

He starts with what certainly looks like a strong affirmation of life. Light is sweet,
he says. In the context, this reference is certainly to the light of the sun. After all, he
goes on to talk about the pleasure of a new day. This is not the first time that
Qoheleth affirms life over death (9:4-6), though he has also earlier protested that
he hated life (2:17). However, in the next verse (11:8), we see that this rosy picture
has a dark lining. He encourages elderly people to enjoy every day they possibly
can but also to keep in mind the dark days to come. Why? Because, meaninglessness rules here on earth. One would love to interview Qoheleth to ask him what he
has in mind here. Does he really expect people to enjoy life even with the anticipation of dark days and a recognition of the meaninglessness of life? It is perhaps
more likely that he is being sarcastic as he talks about the sweetness of life.

The likelihood that the Teacher is being sarcastic is supported by looking at
11:9-10, which he addresses to young people. He encourages the young to enjoy
life to the fullest. He also provocatively tells them to do what they want to do. What
Qoheleth gives with one hand, however, he takes away with the other. The young
should do what they want to do but also remember that a judgment is coming! (It
may also be noted here that Qoheleth contradicts himself by referring to a sure
judgment. This again shows him to be a confused wise man, often talking out of
both sides of his mouth as mentioned in the Introduction.)

Interestingly, it was this verse more than any other that troubled the ancient rabbis. To some, its advice seemed to contradict the Torah where in Numbers 15:39 it
says, "You will remember and obey all the commands of the LORD instead of following your own desires [lit. "the lusts of your hearts and eyes"] and defiling yourselves, as you are prone to do" (see note on 11:9). Perhaps the rabbis were thrown
off by the extent of Qoheleth's sarcasm: On the one hand, he says almost flippantly,
"Don't worry. Do what you want." But then on the other hand, he takes away what

freedom he has given by saying that youth, and indeed life as a whole, is meaningless. This provides a transition to Qoheleth's final topic, which is death.

◆ **23. Youth, old age, and death, continued (12:1-7)**

Don't let the excitement of youth cause you to forget your Creator. Honor him in your youth before you grow old and say, "Life is not pleasant anymore." [2]Remember him before the light of the sun, moon, and stars is dim to your old eyes, and rain clouds continually darken your sky. [3]Remember him before your legs—the guards of your house—start to tremble; and before your shoulders—the strong men—stoop. Remember him before your teeth—your few remaining servants—stop grinding; and before your eyes—the women looking through the windows—see dimly.

[4]Remember him before the door to life's opportunities is closed and the sound of work fades. Now you rise at the first chirping of the birds, but then all their sounds will grow faint.

[5]Remember him before you become fearful of falling and worry about danger in the streets; before your hair turns white like an almond tree in bloom, and you drag along without energy like a dying grasshopper, and the caperberry no longer inspires sexual desire. Remember him before you near the grave, your everlasting home, when the mourners will weep at your funeral.

[6]Yes, remember your Creator now while you are young, before the silver cord of life snaps and the golden bowl is broken. Don't wait until the water jar is smashed at the spring and the pulley is broken at the well. [7]For then the dust will return to the earth, and the spirit will return to God who gave it.

NOTES

12:1 *your Creator.* As discussed below in the commentary, the reference to God the Creator seems odd in this context. It is certainly not impossible, but there are other indications that there is something wrong with the MT text at this point. In terms of the word itself, it is most surprising that it is actually plural in the Heb. ("your creators"). The versions (Latin Vulgate and Greek LXX) either reflect a correct and original Heb. text or, more likely, correct the Heb. text for theological reasons, having the singular (*creatoris* and *ktisias* [TG2937, ZG3232] respectively). It is also possible that the plural here is a kind of "plural of majesty," and thus does not intend to communicate a plurality as such. Because of these possible explanations, we stay with the MT and understand it as a singular reference, but this explains why some scholars resort to emendations at this point. For instance, Crenshaw (1987:185) repoints the text to mean "your well" and takes this as a metaphor for a wife. In other words, Qoheleth is advising his readers in good wisdom fashion to enjoy one's wife during youth. This emendation, however, is quite speculative and therefore I reject it. Another approach to this issue is simply to say that a later, more pious editor came along and added this reference to God to sort of soften the message of Qoheleth. But making an appeal like this to the work of a redactor is much too convenient. In any case, there is no persuasive reason to reject the Heb. text as it stands, and therefore I assume a reference to God, the Creator, in line with the NLT.

12:2 *Remember him.* The Heb. text does not repeat the introductory admonition to remember God. In fact, this imperative stands at the very beginning of 12:1. In the NLT, however, the translators rendered this first instance as "honor him" for variety and supplied "remember him" in 12:2, 3 (two times), 4, 5 (two times), and 6.

to your old eyes. This phrase is not in the Heb. and is added by the NLT. This is unfortunate in my opinion since it makes the verse sound as if it has to do specifically with losing eyesight in old age. The comparison is more general between growing old and the onslaught of a rainstorm.

12:3-6 The NLT has taken some liberty with the Heb. text here resulting in a highly interpretive rendition of the Heb., which is an extended metaphor that primarily compares a deteriorating house and its inhabitants with the human aging process (12:3-5). For that reason, I will here provide a translation that is more literal in relation to the Heb. text and that may be compared with the NLT and used while reading the commentary below. (For a detailed defense of this translation, see Longman 1998:264-265, 269-270).

> On the day when the house guards tremble and the landowners bend, and the women grinders cease because they are few, and those women who look through the window grow dim; the doors in the street are shut, when the sound of the mill decreases, and one rises at the sound of a bird, and all the daughters of song are brought low. Moreover, they are afraid of heights and the terrors in the path. The almond tree blossoms and the grasshopper drags itself along and the caperberry is useless. For humans go to their eternal home, and mourners walk about in the street.

12:5 *dying grasshopper.* "Dying" is not in the Heb. text but is an interpretation of the state of the grasshopper. Alternatively, the grasshopper (*khagab* [TH2284, ZH2506]) may be in an early stage of development.

COMMENTARY

We now come to Qoheleth's final words. The last section of the book (12:8-14) returns to the speech of the second wise man, whose words frame Qoheleth's (see 1:1-11). Considering the tone of Qoheleth's words overall, we are not surprised that his last topic is death. He has already reflected on death and its implications for life throughout his speech. Death, to the Teacher, renders everything meaningless. But he, nonetheless, takes this final opportunity to drive home his belief that death has the final word.

He does this by using three metaphor complexes. First, he likens growing old and death to an oncoming storm (12:1-2), then he evokes the picture of an old and decaying house (12:3-5), and finally he refers to the destruction of precious objects (12:6-7). We will look at each in turn.

In these three sections, the reader is advised to pay close attention to the notes. The NLT has interpreted the metaphors of the Hebrew text as allegory. This is generally accurate in my view, but it bypasses some of the meaning of the text. The point of the text is not lost, but the reader misses some of the fine nuances of the writer here. The notes will alert the reader to some of these.

Qoheleth begins by reminding his hearers to remember God their Creator while young. This advice seems odd for a number of reasons. In the first place, he has just encouraged young people to be carefree in their approach to life. In the second, there seems to be no motivation to remember the Creator. How does it help? According to Qoheleth's view of things, it is not as if God will take the sting of death away or restore meaning to life. Thirdly, there are some grammatical problems with this reference that have caused some interpreters to conclude that there is no reference to God in the verse (see note on 12:1). This is not the approach taken here. I understand the reference as a pious, but fairly empty, impersonal, and objective reference to God as the Teacher introduces the real subject of his concluding section—death.

Verse 2 is the first metaphor for growing old and dying. Life is like a sunny day where expectations are high, but these are dashed by the approach of a storm. Metaphor, like all imagery, evokes emotion as well as intellectual content. This image intends to depress us concerning our aging and eventual death.

The second metaphor concerning growing old and dying is found in 12:3-5. The depressing storm is still in the background as we read the description of the deteriorating house and its languishing inhabitants. The NLT takes these verses as an allegory (i.e., the language is taken as symbolic even when an explicit comparison is not made). In actuality, however, this is a very rich passage that is a metaphor before it is an allegory. The Hebrew text describes a deteriorating house with four classes of inhabitants, each of which is languishing. The four classes of inhabitants may be divided into two male and two female. Each of the genders has a master/servant division as well. The male servants (the guards) are mentioned first, followed by the male owners (strong men). The Hebrew term for the next group, the servants who in the NLT are compared to teeth, is feminine, as is the term for the women of leisure, the "women looking through the windows." This comparison of the body with a household of slowly deteriorating inhabitants reminds us that as we age, we grow weaker and weaker until we die.

I agree with the NLT, against some opposition, that this metaphor is also an allegory. It is most clear in regard to the female servants, who in the Hebrew are literally called "the grinders." How can we miss here a specific reference to the teeth? The idea that these servants are few is reminiscent of the fact that the older one gets, especially in an ancient society without advanced dental care, the fewer teeth one has left. Furthermore, it is hard to ignore the connection between the women who look through the windows and our eyes. As we age, our eyesight grows progressively worse.

Those who are critical of the allegorical interpretation of these verses point to the two classes of men in the passage. There seems to be more ambiguity concerning the connection between the guards and the strong men and any particular type of degeneration. The NLT fits in with a major tradition of interpretation when it associates the former with the legs and the latter with the shoulders. As we age, our legs grow weaker and our backs begin to stoop.

There will continue to be debates concerning the exact interpretation of the details of these verses. However, there is no doubt that they provide an interesting poetic reflection on the processes of aging and death. Qoheleth seems mesmerized by the idea of death here and throughout his writings.

Verses 4-5 take us from inside to outside of the house. Again, the NLT translation brings out much of the meaning of the text, but it also obscures the metaphor. Therefore, it is useful to compare the translation provided in the note to 12:3-6. In anticipation of the oncoming storm, mentioned in 12:2 and in the background throughout the section, the house is shut down, the work at the mill stops, and one successively rises at the sound of the bird, but then their sounds grow increasingly silent.

In verse 4, the NLT has interpreted the metaphor of the closing doors to the house as a reference to life's opportunities. It is more likely, since the deteriorating house of the previous verse is compared with the body, that the doors refer to those orifices that connect our body with the outside world: ears, eyes, mouth, and so forth. It is a function of aging that these orifices cease to work as well as they did in youth. This interpretation seems supported by the rest of the verse, which seems to speak poetically of the ravages of age on the sense of hearing (being startled at the chirping of birds, but sound growing faint). In either case, however, it is clear that Qoheleth is deeply and negatively affected by the idea of aging.

Verse 5 continues a description of what goes on outside of the house. It continues the metaphor of an aging person's diminishing capacities, as afraid of heights and dangers in the streets. The NLT rightly and immediately applies this to an aged person's fears of falling and running into danger. This is all part of the loss of control that confronts an elderly person.

A comparison with the literal translation of the rest of 12:5 in the note above will show how far the NLT has departed from the metaphor of the Hebrew. Though I believe the NLT is right in its allegorical interpretation, the metaphorical point that is missed by its translation is the idea that life outside of the house is going on as if nothing is happening at all. While death is approaching inside the house, there is an almond tree blossoming outside, there is a grasshopper moving itself along—as if the deterioration of the house and the languishing of its inhabitants were not happening. That is, while a person ages and grows near death, the world still goes on. The most catastrophic event of our lives—its end—will, Qoheleth imagines, have virtually no effect on the world.

However, while the metaphor operates on this level, it also has the allegorical overtones suggested by the NLT translation. The white blossoms of the almond tree suggest the whitening of the hair; the dragging of the grasshopper might invite a comparison with the halting gait of an older person; and the uselessness of the caperberry, a well-known aphrodisiac in the ancient world, points to a fading sexual desire. Lastly, he mentions that final, eternal home—the grave. Qoheleth, who does not have a firm belief in the afterlife, asks his listeners to imagine their own funerals. A sad picture indeed, but it is not over. There is yet one more metaphor for death.

We have observed that the NLT has given an interpretive translation of 12:3-5. By contrast, the translation of 12:6-7 is much more subdued and stays closer to the Hebrew because it is felt that the metaphors are fairly clear. There is one interpretive addition in 12:6. In the expression "the silver cord of life," the phrase "of life" is added. And, indeed, it is true that the images of the silver cord, the golden bowl, the water jar, and the pulley are all images of life. These are all items that are valuable but when destroyed are rendered useless. Qoheleth is saying the same thing about life, and this message is consistent with his overall understanding. Life is valuable, even precious, as far as it goes; but it only goes as far as death, and then everything we thought was valuable is useless. Life has some relative meaning, perhaps, but no enduring significance, since death wipes it out.

The Teacher's last words are a reversal of the creation seen in Genesis 2:7: "Then the LORD God formed the man from the dust of the ground. He breathed the breath of life into the man's nostrils, and the man became a living person." What God has put together let no person pull asunder! But that is what Qoheleth says happens with death. The dust returns to the earth, and the spirit returns to God. It is absolutely impossible to take this as any kind of belief in the continuation of a spiritual consciousness; it is instead a destruction of the creation process. Qoheleth ends his speech on a very depressing note. Praise God that it is not the last word in the book!

◆ III. Frame Narrative: Epilogue (12:8-14)

8"Everything is meaningless," says the Teacher, "completely meaningless."

9Keep this in mind: The Teacher was considered wise, and he taught the people everything he knew. He listened carefully to many proverbs, studying and classifying them. 10The Teacher sought to find just the right words to express truths clearly.*

11The words of the wise are like cattle prods—painful but helpful. Their collected sayings are like a nail-studded stick with which a shepherd* drives the sheep.

12But, my child,* let me give you some further advice: Be careful, for writing books is endless, and much study wears you out. 13That's the whole story. Here now is my final conclusion: Fear God and obey his commands, for this is everyone's duty. 14God will judge us for everything we do, including every secret thing, whether good or bad.

12:10 Or *sought to write what was upright and true.*   12:11 Or *one shepherd.*   12:12 Hebrew *my son.*

NOTES

12:10 *The Teacher sought to find just the right words to express truths clearly.* This verse is difficult in terms of its syntax and meaning and thus is debated. One can see the disagreement by comparing the NLT translation with the NIV: "The Teacher searched to find just the right words, and what he wrote was upright and true." The grammatical issue is what the relationship is between the main verb "sought" and the word that is translated "wrote" in the NIV and "to express" in the NLT. In other words, is the frame narrator saying that Qoheleth *sought* to write or express the truth or that he indeed *did* write truth? As one can tell from the notes below, I side with the NLT. (The technical issues in this debate require a working knowledge of Hebrew grammar; those interested in the details can see my reasoning in Longman 1998:275, note 65.) Even if I am wrong about the translation and the NIV is correct, it does not radically affect my overall understanding of Qoheleth. Below, I will argue that in a limited sense Qoheleth does write the truth when he says, "Life is hard and then you die." After all, he is talking about life "under the sun." His problem is that he does not go beyond this worldly perspective. The frame narrator will do that in the last two verses.

12:11 *painful but helpful . . . a shepherd drives the sheep.* These phrases are not in the Heb., which refers simply to "goads" and "well-driven nails" and concludes "they are given by a shepherd." The NLT interprets these images and extends the imagery, making explicit what is implicit in the comparison between the words of the wise and cattle prods and the collected sayings (of the wise) and a nail-studded stick. Most commentators agree with the interpretation offered in the translation and expanded upon in the commentary that this refers to the painful, yet helpful messages of the words of wise teachers like Qoheleth.

For comparison, a literal translation of this verse reads: "The words of the wise are like goads, and like firmly implanted nails are the masters of collections. They are given by a shepherd."

a shepherd There is a debate about the reference to the shepherd in this verse. It begins with the fact that the Heb. has the word *'ekhad* [TH259, ZH285] modifying shepherd. This can either be translated as the number one, thus "one shepherd," or understood to be an indefinite pronoun "a shepherd." This explains the difference between the translation in the NLT text and one given in the margin. There is a further interpretative disagreement over the referent of this shepherd. Some who take it as "one Shepherd" capitalize the word and thus show that they understand this to point to God who shepherds his people. The NIV takes the passage in this direction, but this seems awkward in the context, and it is much more likely that the reference points to the wise teachers who are mentioned in the first part of the verse, each one of whom is "a shepherd."

COMMENTARY

We can easily see that Qoheleth is no longer speaking in these last few verses because now he is referred to in the third person ("says the Teacher"). Someone is speaking about Qoheleth in these last verses of the book. As we stated in the Introduction, this is the unnamed wisdom teacher who is using Qoheleth's confused wisdom speech as an instruction to his son (12:12). It is this "frame narrator" who is the authoritative voice in the book, so it is vitally important we listen to what he says.

First of all, he parrots the Teacher's own words by means of summary. "Everything is meaningless, completely meaningless." He cites this characteristic phrase in order to give us what he considers to be Qoheleth's bottom line. This is Qoheleth's final conclusion. The frame narrator's comments here should be determinative as we have sought to understand Qoheleth's sometimes rambling and confused comments in the body of the book. Though sometimes we see what seems to be a glimmer of hope when we isolate a verse or two, we are certain, because of the frame narrator's summarizing statement here, that Qoheleth's final conclusion admits the ultimate meaninglessness of life. In the light of this statement, it is also impossible to follow scholars like Kaiser (1979) and Whybray (1982), who say that Qoheleth's *carpe diem* passages (those passages when he says there is nothing better than to eat and drink and enjoy life, see 2:24-26; 3:12-14, 22; 5:18-20; 8:15; 9:7-10) are really Qoheleth's final conclusion. No, the final conclusion is "everything is meaningless, completely meaningless." Indeed, in this regard it is also significant that the frame narrator began his introduction to the Teacher's speech with exactly the same words, thus 1:2 and 12:8 form a kind of envelope structure around the body of the book.

After this restatement of Qoheleth's final conclusion about the meaninglessness of life, the frame narrator continues by evaluating Qoheleth and his writings. Again, though he is not mentioned until 12:12, we should keep in mind that the frame narrator is speaking to his son. This is typical of ancient Near Eastern wisdom texts, as we can see in the book of Proverbs (particularly chs 1–9) as well as in Egyptian and Mesopotamian wisdom texts. As later readers, though, we stand in the place of the son. We are the ones being instructed.

The frame narrator begins with a respectful but reserved tone toward Qoheleth. He calls him wise. More exactly, the Hebrew says that he is a wise person (*khakam* [TH2450A, ZH2682]). It would be a mistake to read too much of a positive evaluation into these words. It is easy to make that mistake because, if we have read the book of Proverbs, we know that wisdom is associated with all kinds of virtues such as righteousness, honesty, prudence, discipline, and—most importantly of all—piety ("the fear of the LORD is the beginning of wisdom"). However, outside of Proverbs, wisdom and its related terms do not necessarily carry such positive overtones. One does not have to be pious to be wise. Indeed, there are evil wise men recorded in the historical books. One need only think of Jonadab who used his wisdom to teach Amnon how to trick his half-sister Tamar into his bed (2 Sam 13:3-5); or else remember Ahithophel the wise man, who told Absalom how to wage war against his father David (2 Sam 16:15–17:29). In other words, these men were shrewd. They knew how to get things done, even if those things were not honoring to the Lord.

My point is not that Qoheleth was an evil, shrewd man like Jonadab or Ahithophel. It is simply to say that by calling Qoheleth a wise man, the frame narrator is not affirming everything he says as gospel truth. Indeed, when he then goes on to further describe Qoheleth's role as a wise man, it is interesting that he cites rather mechanical actions ("He listened carefully to many proverbs, studying and classifying them," 12:9). What is interesting is that there are only a handful of proverbs that are cited in Ecclesiastes (e.g., 1:15, 18). Proverbs are traditional material, and the wise teachers of Israel were the ones who collected them and transmitted them, but again I believe it is significant that the frame narrator first focuses on this role rather than mentioning Qoheleth's incredible insight into life. The frame narrator is being respectful but not glowing in his comments thus far.

This tone continues into the next verse, where we must pay careful attention to the choice of the main verb "sought." The NLT has rightly captured this in a way that other translations have not (cf. NIV, KJV, RSV). The Hebrew does not say that Qoheleth found the right words but that he sought to find them. There is a world of difference between the two. It is one thing to seek and another to find. This is especially the case as we remember the use of these words in 7:25-29. There Qoheleth talks about his vain search for something significant. He sought but did not find ultimate meaning.

In this way, the frame narrator is being both respectful and critical toward Qoheleth as he evaluates his words for his son. Why respectful and critical? He is respectful because he knows that Qoheleth is right "as far as he goes"—that is, Qoheleth reads the world quite correctly "under the sun." It is true that life is difficult and then you die—"under the sun." After all, according to Genesis 3, the world, created good by God, has been thrust into meaningless futility by human sin. The rebellion of Adam and Eve brought the whole world under God's curse. They were ejected from Eden to live in the harsh world that we know from our own experience. Death became a reality in human experience for the first time. However, as is explained below in connection with 12:13-14, he is critical of Qoheleth's thinking because Qoheleth remains under the sun; he does not look beyond this world toward heavenly realities.

Before we proceed to 12:13-14, we need to comment on 12:11-12. Here is where the frame narrator's critical stance becomes more explicit. The NLT again does an excellent job in capturing the sense of 12:11 (see note for literal translation and issues). The narrator broadens his comments to include not just the words of Qoheleth but of other wisdom teachers as well, and he judges them painful but helpful like "cattle prods." A prod is painful to cattle, but it also keeps them going in the right direction. In this case, Qoheleth has helped because he has rightly described what this fallen world is like under the curse (life is frustrating and then you die). This message, however, is also painful, and, as I have already suggested from the broader context, it does not go far enough since it does not take us beyond an "under the sun" perspective. The second analogy has the same force. Wisdom sayings are also painful but helpful, "like a nail-studded stick with which a shepherd drives the sheep." These sticks were used to drive the sheep toward food and away from danger, but they certainly hurt.

In verse 12 the narrator admits that his son might get too much of a good thing. It is good to be exposed to a thinker like Qoheleth who tells it like it is in a frustrating and frustrated, sin-cursed world; however, this view is pretty bleak and is not the final word, so the narrator tells his son not to get too engrossed in such studies, lest they wear him out.

With that, the frame narrator proceeds to his "final conclusion" (12:13-14). We have already observed that Qoheleth's final word was "Everything is meaningless." Now it is the frame narrator's turn, and he makes quite a different statement. The Hebrew is very abrupt as he turns to this final statement. It is almost as if he is saying: "We've heard enough of Qoheleth, now let me state clearly what is really important."

There are three parts to his final conclusion, and each part is packed full of significance. They are (1) "fear God," (2) "obey his commands," and (3) realize that "God will judge us." Certainly, we have seen glimmers of this teaching even in Qoheleth himself but in a different context. When he spoke of the fear of God, it was a horror that led him to avoid God's presence (see Spangenberg 1996:59). The voice here in the epilogue is more positive.

As a matter of fact, these three statements are a reaffirmation of the basic teaching of the Old Testament. To fear God is to establish a right relationship with God. Imposing an anachronistic theological phrase on it, we might call it the doctrine of justification. To obey his commandments is to maintain that relationship in a way that is pleasing to God. We might call this sanctification. Then, finally, the remembrance of God's coming judgment gives the whole statement a future-oriented (or eschatological) edge to it.

Furthermore, this threefold statement also is a very clear affirmation of the three main parts of the Hebrew Bible. The exhortation to fear God certainly reminds us of the wisdom literature of the Old Testament (see especially the motto statement at Proverbs 1:7: "Fear of the LORD is the foundation of true knowledge"). The call to obey God points us to the Torah, the first five books of the Bible, which contain the Ten Commandments and the other laws that flow from them. Then the expectation of a future judgment connects us with the prophets. The law, the prophets, and the wisdom books are a threefold, traditional Hebrew way of referring to what Christians today call the Old Testament.

In this way, the frame narrator, who is the controlling voice of the book of Ecclesiastes, concludes the book. He has exposed his son to the "under the sun" thinking of a confused wise man in Israel. He has not written him off by any stretch of the imagination. Qoheleth rightly understood the frustration of a world under the effects of the Fall. Life is hard, and then we die. However, the frame narrator has not let the story conclude with an affirmation of the meaninglessness of the world—he has rather reaffirmed the need for a good relationship with God and in so doing has reaffirmed the entire body of authoritative literature that we today know as the Hebrew Bible or the Old Testament.

As is explained more fully under "Theological Concerns" in the Introduction, the story does not stop even with the words of the frame narrator. Paul also reflects on the world that has been subjected to the effects of the Fall (Rom 8:18-21) and indeed alludes to, if not quotes from, Ecclesiastes. Paul knew and proclaimed that the release from all futility was accomplished by Jesus Christ's death and resurrection. Christ is the one who, although he was God, voluntarily subjected himself to the curse of the covenant in order to free us from that curse. Because of his death and resurrection, we may indeed find meaning in life in this world, even though we experience its hard knocks. Even though death still affects our lives, we know that Jesus has defeated death so it no longer holds us forever. He died so that we may live.

BIBLIOGRAPHY

Ackroyd, P.
1967 Two Hebrew Notes. *Annual of the Swedish Theological Institute* 5:82-86.

Barton, G. A.
1908 *The Book of Ecclesiastes.* International Critical Commentary. Edinburgh: T & T Clark.

Brown, W.
2000 *Ecclesiastes.* Interpretation. Louisville: Westminster John Knox.

Buhlman, A.
2000 The Difficulty of Thinking in Greek and Speaking in Hebrew (Qohelet 3:18; 4:13-16; 5:8). *Journal for the Study of the Old Testament* 90:101-108.

Comfort, P. W.
1993 Futility. Pp. 320-322 in *Dictionary of Paul and His Letters.* Editors, G. Hawthorne, R. Martin, and D. Reid. Downers Grove: InterVarsity.

Crenshaw, J. L.
1974 The Eternal Gospel (Eccl 3:11). Pp. 23-55 in *Essays in Old Testament Ethics.* Editors, J. L. Crenshaw and J. T. Willis. New York: KTAV.

1986 The Expression *mi yodea'* in the Hebrew Bible. *Vetus Testamentum* 36:274-288.

1987 *Ecclesiastes.* Philadelphia: Westminster.

Dahood, M. J.
1968 Hebrew-Ugaritic Lexicography. *Biblica* 49:368.

DeJong, S.
1994 Qohelet and the Ambitious Spirit of the Ptolemaic Period. *Journal for the Study of the Old Testament* 84:85-96.

Delitzsch, F.
1975 *Proverbs, Ecclesiastes, Song of Solomon.* Translator, M. G. Easton. Grand Rapids: Eerdmans. (Orig. Pub. 1872)

Driver, G. R.
1964 Once Again Abbreviations. *Textus* 4:76-94.

Ellul, J.
1990 *Reason for Being: A Meditation on Ecclesiastes.* Translator, J. M. Hanks. Grand Rapids: Eerdmans.

Fox, M. V.
1977 Frame-Narrative and Composition in the Book of Qohelet. *Hebrew Union College Annual* 48:83-106.

1989 *Qohelet and His Contradictions.* Journal for the Study of the Old Testament Supplement 71. Sheffield: Almond Press.

Fox, M. V. and B. Porten
1978 Unsought Discoveries: Qohelet 7:23-8:1a. *Hebrew Studies* 19:26-38.

Fredericks, D. C.
1993 *Coping with Transience: Ecclesiastes on the Brevity of Life.* Sheffield: Sheffield Academic Press.

Frendo, A.
1981 The "Broken Construct Chain" in Qoh. 10:10b. *Biblica* 62:544-545.

Garrett, D. A.
1988 Ecclesiastes 7:25-29 and the Feminist Hermeneutic. *Criswell Theological Review* 2:309-321.

Ginsberg, H. L.
1952 *Studies in Qoheleth.* New York: Jewish Theological Seminary of America.

Ginsburg, C. D.
1970 *The Song of Songs and Cohelet.* Editor, H. M. Orlinksy. New York: KTAV. (Orig. Pub. 1861)

Goleman, D.
1995 *Emotional Intelligence.* New York: Bantam.

Gordis, R.
1968 *Qoheleth—The Man and His World.* 3rd ed. New York: Schocken.

Irwin, W. A.
1944 Ecclesiastes 4:13-16. *Journal of Near Eastern Studies* 3:255-257.
1945 Ecclesiastes 8:2-9. *Journal of Near Eastern Studies* 4:130-131.

Isaksson, B.
1987 *Studies in the Language of Qoheleth.* Studia Semitica Uppsaliensia 10. Uppsala: Uppsala University Press.

Kaiser, W.
1979 *Ecclesiastes: Total Life.* Everyman's Bible Commentary. Chicago: Moody.

Kidner, D. A.
1976 *A Time to Mourn and a Time to Dance.* Downers Grove: InterVarsity.

Lauha, A.
1978 *Kohelet.* Biblischer Kommentar Altes Testament 19. Neukirchen-Vluyn: Neukirchener Verlag.

Levine, E.
1978 *The Aramaic Version of Qohelet.* New York: Sepher-Hermon.

Longman, T., III
1991 *Fictional Akkadian Autobiography.* Winona Lake: Eisenbrauns.
1997 *Reading the Bible with Heart and Mind.* Colorado Springs: NavPress.
1998 *Ecclesiastes.* New International Commentary on the Old Testament. Grand Rapids: Eerdmans.
2002 *How to Read Proverbs.* Downers Grove: InterVarsity.

Luther, M.
1972 Notes on Ecclesiastes. Pp. 3-193 in *Luther's Works*, vol. 15. Editor and translator, J. Pelikan. St. Louis: Concordia. (Orig. Pub. 1532)

Mavis, R. S.
1999 The Epilogue of Ecclesiastes and the Meaning of the Book. PhD diss., Westminster Theological Seminary.

Murphy, R.
1981 *Wisdom Literature: Job, Proverbs, Ruth, Canticles, Ecclesiastes, and Esther.* Grand Rapids: Eerdmans.
1992 *Ecclesiastes.* Word Biblical Commentary. Dallas: Word.

Ogden, G. S.
1977 The 'Better-Proverb' (Tob-Spruch), Rhetorical Criticism, and Qohelet. *Journal of Biblical Literature* 96:489-505.
1980 Historical Allusion in Qoheleth iv 13-16? *Vetus Testamentum* 30:309-315.
1987 *Qoheleth.* Sheffield: Journal for the Study of the Old Testament Press.

Perdue, L.
1977 *Wisdom and Cult.* Missoula: Scholars Press.

Roth, W. M. W.
1962 The Numerical Sequence x/x+1 in the Old Testament. *Vetus Testamentum* 12:300-311.
1965 *Numerical Sayings in the Old Testament: A Form-Critical Study.* Vetus Testamentum Supplement 13. Leiden: Brill.

Rudman, D.
1997 A Contextual Reading of Ecclesiastes 4:13-16. *Journal of Biblical Literature* 116:57-73.

Salters, R. B.
1977 Text and Exegesis in Koh 10:19. *Zeitschrift für die Alttestamentliche Wissenschaft* 89:423-426.
1978 Notes on the History of the Interpretation of Koh 5:5. *Zeitschrift für die Alttestamentliche Wissenschaft* 90:95-101.
1979 Notes on the Interpretation of Qoh 6:2. *Zeitschrift für die Alttestamentliche Wissenschaft* 91:282-289.

Schloesser, S.
1990 "A King is Held Captive in Her Tresses": The Liberating Deconstruction of the Search for Wisdom from Proverbs through Ecclesiastes. Pp. 205-228 in *Church Divinity 1989-90.* Edited by F. S. Tebbe. Donaldson, IN: Graduate Theological Foundation.

Schmidt, J.
1940-1941 Qoheleth 4:17. *Zeitschrift für die Alttestamentliche Wissenschaft* 17:279-280.

Seow, C. L.
1997 *Ecclesiastes*. Anchor Bible. Garden City: Doubleday.

Shaffer, A.
1967 The Mesopotamian Background of Qoh 4:9-12. *Eretz Israel* 8:246-250.
1969 New Information on the Origin of the "Threefold Cord." *Eretz Israel* 9:159-160.

Spangenberg, I. J. J.
1991 Quotations in Ecclesiastes: An Appraisal. *Old Testament Essays* 4:19-35.
1996 Irony in the Book of Qohelet. *Journal for the Study of the Old Testament* 72:57-69.

Staples, W. E.
1955 Vanity of Vanity. *Canadian Journal of Theology* 1:141-156.

Strange, M.
1969 The Question of Moderation in Ecclesiastes 7:15-18. D.Sac.Th. diss., Catholic University of America.

Stuart, M.
1851 *Commentary on Ecclesiastes*. New York: G. P. Putnam.

Van Leeuwen, R.
1986 Proverbs 30:21-23 and the Biblical World Upside Down. *Journal of Biblical Literature* 105:599-610.
1992 Wealth and Poverty: System and Contradiction in Proverbs. *Hebrew Studies* 33:25-36.

Verheij, A. J. C.
1991 Paradise Retried: On Qohelet 2:4-6. *Journal for the Study of the Old Testament* 50:113-115.

Waldman, N.
1979 The *dabar ra'* of Eccl 8:3. *Journal of Biblical Literature* 98:407-408.

Watson, W. G. E.
1984 *Classical Hebrew Poetry*. Journal for the Study of the Old Testament Supplement 170. Sheffield: Journal for the Study of the Old Testament Press.

Whybray, R. N.
1978 Qohelet the Immoralist (Qoh 7:16-17). Pp. 191-204 in *Israelite Wisdom: Theological and Literary Essays in Honor of Samuel Terrien*. Editors, J. G. Gammie, W. A. Brueggemann, W. L. Humphreys, and J. M. Ward. Missoula: Scholars Press.
1982 Qoheleth, Preacher of Joy? *Journal for the Study of the Old Testament* 23:87-98.
1989 *Ecclesiastes*. Grand Rapids: Eerdmans.

Wright, C.
1888 *The Book of Qoheleth*. London: Hodder & Stoughton.

Young, E. J.
1949 *An Introduction to the Old Testament*. Grand Rapids: Eerdmans.

Song of Songs

TREMPER LONGMAN III

INTRODUCTION TO
Song of Songs

"KISS ME AND KISS ME AGAIN, for your love is sweeter than wine" (1:2). With this passionate expression, the Song of Songs opens. The woman expresses her intense desire to be in the intimate presence of her man. As we read on, we encounter not only expressions of desire and passion but also the rapturous sighs of their union.

So what is such a book doing in the canon of Holy Scripture? What has intimacy between a man and a woman to do with our knowledge of God? These are the questions that have concerned the church through the centuries and will concern us in the following pages of this commentary. As we reflect on these issues, it will soon become apparent that such a book does belong in the Bible. After all, God loves us as whole people, not as disembodied souls. He created us with body and soul integrally united together. He gave his people—male and female—the precious gift of sexual enjoyment within the parameters of marriage. This gift comes to life in the Song of Songs.

AUTHOR
The book begins, "This is Solomon's song of songs, more wonderful than any other" (1:1). Contrary to popular understanding, this superscription does not clearly claim Solomonic authorship of the whole book. The book of Proverbs begins with a similar superscription, but it also names other authors besides Solomon in the body of the text (Prov 30:1; 31:1). Both books are collections of material, either proverbs or, in the case of the Song of Songs, love poems, as I will describe below. It is possible that Solomon wrote some of the poems that are now found in the collection, but it is unlikely that he wrote them all. For one thing, when Solomon is mentioned at the end of the book, it appears as if another party is critical of him—the famous monarch created a lot of trouble because of his love life (cf. 8:11-12; 1 Kgs 11:1-13). The perspective of the description of his wedding, which is the only other certain mention of Solomon, also shows some emotional distance (3:6-11).

The Song of Songs, a sensual psalter, is composed of a number of different poems. Like the Psalms, they were written by a number of different authors and bound together into a loose literary unity by a single editor.

DATE AND OCCASION OF WRITING

Once the true nature of the Song of Songs as an anthology is identified, the question of the date of the book is seen to be complex. There are really two questions: (1) the date of the individual poems and (2) the date of the final composition, the time the book was brought together into a literary unity. Since there is no definitive statement of author or date (see the discussion under "Author"), we cannot come to a dogmatic conclusion concerning the date of the book. As an anthology, it is possible that the individual poems span a lengthy period of time, beginning with Solomon (c. 970 BC) and extending onward. The final author/editor of the whole composition did not leave clues concerning his identity or his time period, though it surely came to a close by the end of the Old Testament time period around the end of the fourth century BC. As with Ecclesiastes, it is fortunate that our inability to date the book does not impede our ability to understand it.

AUDIENCE

The Song of Songs reveals no signs of being addressed to a specific audience. Our uncertainty is heightened by the fact that we cannot date the book. At best, we can look at the contents of the book and guess who specifically is in mind. The book describes passionate love between a man and a woman. From their attitudes and expressions, it is highly probable that they were young and entering into this kind of relationship for the first time. Thus, the book might be seen as a text that is addressed to young married and marriageable men and women in Israel. Perhaps this is why the book even today is found useful in premarital counseling. However, older married couples can also find new passion in their relationship by reading the Song.

CANONICITY AND TEXTUAL HISTORY

The Hebrew text (the MT) of the Song is without major problems and is strongly supported by the Greek, Syriac, and Latin versions. The Aramaic Targum is an early interpretive paraphrase and adopts an allegorical approach to the Song. As such, it bears witness not so much to the text as to the early history of interpretation. There were four manuscripts of the Song discovered at the Dead Sea (see Abegg, Flint, and Ulrich 1999:611-622), though they rarely deviate from the Masoretic Text.

At the time of our earliest evidence, it appears that the presence of the Song in the canon was questioned due to the sexual nature of the material. According to Beckwith, it is one of five books (the others are Esther, Proverbs, Ecclesiastes, and Ezekiel) about which a minority of early rabbis expressed doubt (1985:1-2, 275-276, 282-284, 308-322). The predominant opinion, though, was articulated by Rabbi Akiba around AD 100 when he said: "God forbid!—no man in Israel ever disputed about the Song of Songs [that he should say] that it does not render the hands unclean, for all the ages are not worth the day on which the Song of Songs was given to Israel; for all the Writings are holy, but the Song of Songs is the Holy of Holies" (quoted in Murphy 1990:6). The rabbinic expression "to make the hands unclean" is a difficult one for moderns to understand. It is the idea that something is so holy that it is surrounded by taboos that protect it and involve washing the hands in a lustration ritual afterward. In other words, if something makes the hands unclean, it is especially holy.

The bottom line is that, despite some protests, Song of Songs was included in the canon according to both early rabbinic and early Christian sources. (For an example of its inclusion in the Christian canon, see the canon of Athanasius in the fourth century AD.)

LITERARY STYLE
The Song is clearly poetic. It is composed of parallel lines that are characteristically brief. There is also quite a bit of imagery in the Song. In short, the Song is made up of lyric poems celebrating love and sexuality. Our task in interpreting the Song is not to recreate a plot but rather to explain the metaphors and do our best to describe the emotions that its authors are trying to elicit from the readers. Poetry communicates truly but not precisely. What it gives up in detail of information, it makes up for in intensity of expression.

MAJOR THEME
The Song of Songs is composed of twenty-three separate love poems that have been united into a single composition through the use of refrains and common images and characters. The Song is, in this sense, a single song composed of many songs. The commentary below will comment on each of the poems independently.

The major theme of the book is human love between a man and a woman (for a detailed exploration of this theme in the Bible and in the Song in particular, see Allender and Longman 1995). Many striking images communicate that this love is sensual, intimate, exclusive, and important. Since the broader canon describes our relationship with God as a marriage, the more we learn about married love, the more we also learn about our relationship with our divine spouse.

THEOLOGICAL MESSAGE
For years, the Song of Songs has been badly misunderstood as an allegory of the relationship between God (or Jesus) and the church (or the individual Christian). In other words, this love poem has been forcibly turned into a theological tract. The man, this viewpoint advocates, stands for God and the woman is the church or believer. In an allegorical approach, the idea is that the audience is learning about who God is and his relationship with them. Indeed, the details of the poems are also pressed into service to stand for theological truths. For instance, according to one allegorical interpretation, the sachet of Song of Songs 1:13 ("My lover is like a sachet of myrrh lying between my breasts.") is understood to refer to Jesus Christ, who spans the Old and the New Testaments! Needless to say, such an approach was born out of the shock that a highly sensual book like the Song of Songs is in the canon of Scripture. But there is absolutely nothing in the book itself to suggest such an intention (see Davidson 1989).

The most natural reading of the Song of Songs is the correct one. The book is composed of love poetry. God has placed the Song in the canon, it appears, to celebrate the good gift of love and sexuality. Even though marriage is rarely mentioned in the book, its setting in the canon assumes that this couple is either moving toward marriage or already married. The type of intimacy that is spoken of is only appropriate within the context of marriage according to the divine institution of marriage in Genesis 2, as well as the law (Deut 5:18; 22:13-30).

Some readers of the book rightly understand that the book is talking about human love but make the mistake of thinking that the book tells a story. A careful reading shows that there is no plot; in order to construct one, the interpreter has to read between the lines frequently, which is always a dangerous thing to do. Indeed, those who argue that there is a plot cannot agree together on whether there are two or three characters, that is, whether the main characters include a male lover and his female lover, or whether there is a third character—hence, a lover, his beloved, and a rival. If the text is telling a story, something that basic should be quite clear.

My position is that the Song of Songs is a collection of love poems with the purpose of celebrating intimacy among God's people (for a fuller, more detailed account, see Longman 2001). Some of the poems, however, speak of continuing problems in relationships (e.g., 2:15; 5:2-8; for a careful study of this theme within the book, see Schwab 1999). This brings us to our second point concerning the intention of the book. It is part of a biblical theology of love in the Bible. When we read the Song and hear about the man and the woman naked in the garden, it is intended to remind us of Genesis 2, when Adam and Eve were in the Garden of Eden, naked and feeling no shame. However, Genesis 3 informs us of their rebellion and resultant alienation, not only from God but also from each other. They clothe themselves, revealing that they no longer are completely open to each other. Read in the light of these passages, the Song makes a statement about the redemption of sexuality (Trible 1978:144-165). A good relationship is possible, even this side of heaven. However, the negative passages remind us that it cannot be a perfect relationship.

Finally, we come full circle to the allegorical approach of interpretation, at least in part. Throughout the Bible (e.g., Ezek 16; 23; Hos 1-3; Eph 5:21-33), the believers' relationship to God is likened to a marriage. Marriage is the only human relationship that is mutually exclusive and therefore is an excellent illustration of the intimate and exclusive relationship that we have with God. Taking the allegorical approach alone, however, would not be adequate for interpretation since it bypasses the natural meaning of the book in regard to human sexuality.

OUTLINE

Superscription (1:1)

    I. First Love Poem: The Woman's Pursuit (1:2-4)

   II. Second Love Poem: Dark but Beautiful (1:5-6)

  III. Third Love Poem: Teasing Lovers (1:7-8)

  IV. Fourth Love Poem: A Beautiful Mare (1:9-11)

   V. Fifth Love Poem: Intimate Fragrances (1:12-14)

  VI. Sixth Love Poem: Outdoor Love (1:15-17)

 VII. Seventh Love Poem: Flowers and Trees (2:1-7)

VIII. Eighth Love Poem: Springtime (2:8-17)

  IX. Ninth Love Poem: Seeking and Not Finding (3:1-5)

   X. Tenth Love Poem: A Royal Wedding Procession (3:6-11)

  XI. Eleventh Love Poem: From Head to Breasts (4:1-7)

 XII. Twelfth Love Poem: The Invitation (4:8-9)

XIII. Thirteenth Love Poem: The Garden of Love (4:10–5:1)

XIV. Fourteenth Love Poem: Seeking and Not Finding, Again (5:2–6:3)

 XV. Fifteenth Love Poem: An Army with Banners (6:4-10)

XVI. Sixteenth Love Poem: In the Nut Grove (6:11-12)

XVII. Seventeenth Love Poem: The Dancing Shulammite (6:13–7:9)

XVIII. Eighteenth Love Poem: I Will Give You My Love (7:10-13)

XIX. Nineteenth Love Poem: Yearning for Love (8:1-4)

 XX. Twentieth Love Poem: Love More Powerful than Death (8:5-7)

XXI. Twenty-first Love Poem: Protecting the Sister (8:8-10)

XXII. Twenty-second Love Poem: The Owner of the Vineyard (8:11-12)

XXIII. Twenty-third Love Poem: Be Like a Gazelle (8:13-14)

COMMENTARY ON
Song of Songs

◆ **Superscription (1:1)**
This is Solomon's song of songs, more
wonderful than any other.

NOTES

1:1 *Solomon's song of songs.* The relationship between song of songs and Solomon is
expressed by a Heb. preposition that could be translated in a variety of ways (of, by, for,
to, concerning). The NLT appropriately preserves some of the uncertainty in its translation.

COMMENTARY

The superscription is like a title page in a modern book. We are introduced to the
content of what follows in the bulk of the book. Here, we learn that the composition that follows is the "song of songs." We often use this phrase as the title of the
book, and that is in keeping with the ancient practice of using the first phrase of a
text as its title. The expression "song of songs" tells us that what follows was likely
sung with musical accompaniment. The form of the expression (similar to the
phrases "Holy of Holies" and "King of Kings") indicates that, in the opinion of the
one who wrote the superscription, what follows is the most sublime song of all. The
NLT captures this idea by referring to the Song as "more wonderful than any other"
(1:1). The expression "song of songs" also informs the reader that the book is a
unity (song) composed of many different poems (of songs). The superscription also
connects this book to Solomon, Israel's third king. See the Introduction (under
"Author") for a discussion of this.

◆ **I. First Love Poem: The Woman's Pursuit (1:2-4)**

*Young Woman**
²Kiss me and kiss me again,
    for your love is sweeter than wine.
³How fragrant your cologne;
    your name is like its spreading
        fragrance.
    No wonder all the young women
        love you!

⁴Take me with you; come,
    let's run!
The king has brought me into his
    bedroom.

Young Women of Jerusalem
How happy we are for you,
    O king.

| We praise your love even more
than wine. | *Young Woman*
How right they are to adore you. |

1:1 The headings identifying the speakers are not in the original text, though the Hebrew usually gives clues by means of the gender of the person speaking.

NOTES

1:3 *your name is like its spreading fragrance.* Lit., "your name is poured out oil." The metaphor is well captured by the NLT in that this would be fragrant oil that has been spilled, its wonderful smell filling the room.

1:4 *The king has brought me into his bedroom.* Notice that in the first part of this verse, the man is addressed in the second person and then in the concluding part he is referred to in the third person. Indeed, throughout this poem, the woman uses both second and third person to address the man. This is a poetic device called *enallage*, but since modern readers are thrown off by this ancient poetic convention, the NLT often harmonizes the references to the man in this poem, rendering them in the second person.

COMMENTARY

The woman speaks first. Indeed, the woman speaks more often than the man in the Song (see LaCocque 1998:41). She is not bashful or timid. She desires the man, and she tells him of her love. Here, she wants him to kiss her and take her away into his bedroom, the most intimate of all rooms of a house. She wants to be alone with him.

We should notice how she describes his desirability in a very sensuous way. She wants the intimate *touch* of a kiss. She describes his love as sweet to the *taste*. His name, which here has the connotation of reputation, has the *smell* of cologne. Love in the Song has a very physical side; it is expressed unabashedly through the union of two bodies. In reference to taste, she compares his love to wine, a thick liquid that lingers on the palette. Furthermore, love can lift the human spirit in the same way as wine; both intoxicate.

The woman refers to the man as the king. This language is not to be taken literally or applied to the man throughout the Song of Songs. It is poetic language. In her eyes, he is king. Later, she will refer to him as a shepherd (see 1:7-8). These are not two different characters, but two different ways of referring to the man.

In this first poem, we are introduced to the young women. Here they are not named, but we detect their presence by the use of the first person plural in 1:4b. Elsewhere in the book, they are called the "young women," the "daughters of Jerusalem," and the "daughters of Zion." These women are always treated and referred to as a group. They are a group of friends of the young woman. Their presence serves different purposes in the Song. In 1:4 they function as an external attestation to the qualities of the young man. They agree with the young woman that this man is indeed desirable. Further, at the end of the poem they celebrate the love that they see existing between the two.

At the end of this poem, we see that the woman speaks one last time. She speaks to her king-lover and affirms that "they," the young women, are right when they adore him. She is not jealous but rather takes their words as a confirmation of her own judgment.

◆ II. Second Love Poem: Dark but Beautiful (1:5-6)

⁵I am dark but beautiful,
  O women of Jerusalem—
  dark as the tents of Kedar,
    dark as the curtains of Solomon's
    tents.
⁶Don't stare at me because I am dark—
the sun has darkened my skin.
My brothers were angry with me;
  they forced me to care for their
  vineyards,
  so I couldn't care for myself—my
  own vineyard.

NOTES

1:5 *but beautiful*. The NLT properly translates the conjunction *waw* [TH2050.1, ZH2256] with the adversative "but" here; the context in 1:6 indicates that the woman is unpleased with her dark complexion. The woman's unhappiness with her dark skin has nothing to do with race but rather the artificial coloring of the skin by exposure to the sun. It makes her look like a country bumpkin, a low-class laborer.

tents of Kedar . . . Solomon's tents. Kedar is a tribe of nomads from the Syro-Arabian desert, mentioned often in the Bible (Gen 25:13; Jer 49:28-29). We have no other indication of the color of their tents, but the passage here suggests that they were widely known as being dark in color, perhaps woven from brown or black goat hair, as some modern Bedouin tents are. The same could be said of the curtains of Solomon's tents.

1:6 *so I couldn't care for myself—my own vineyard*. Lit., "my own vineyard I could not guard." The NLT rightly interprets the meaning of the metaphor of guarding her own vineyard because the vineyard is a reference to her own appearance.

COMMENTARY

This poem is a self-description by the woman. She presents an apology for her appearance and explains why she has come to look the way she does. Her skin is, at least from her perspective, unattractively darkened by exposure to the sun (for a contrary viewpoint, see Pope 1978:322). This state of affairs has been brought about by her brothers, who have forced her to labor in the vineyards. They have so forced her because they were angry with her, but the text does not tell us why. Brothers played a large role in their sisters' marriage arrangements, according to ancient Near Eastern and biblical custom (cf. Gen 34). They may be angry about what they might consider their sister's rather forward relationship with the man (cf. 8:8-10).

In this poem, we are introduced for the first time to the vineyard, which is often used as an image for the woman's sexuality. Throughout the ancient Near East and the Song, the vineyard, the garden, and the orchard are all used to signify the place of lovemaking and, especially, the woman's sexuality (see Paul 1997). This does not mean that it is always a symbol of the woman. Here, the woman is working in the field, which must be understood literally first in order to explain how she got her unwanted dark skin. We are to think of real physical labor, though this may also suggest a more poetic reference—in this case, to her sex appeal. The verse seems to state that the work in the vineyard of her brothers has meant that she cannot take care of her own appearance. The NLT has rightly captured the meaning of the last sentence of verse 6 by the rendering "so I couldn't care for myself—my own vineyard." Though we feel sorry for the woman, we respect her self-assertion in the face of her brothers, who are standing in the way of her true love.

◆ III. Third Love Poem: Teasing Lovers (1:7–8)

⁷Tell me, my love, where are you
    leading your flock today?
Where will you rest your sheep
    at noon?
For why should I wander like
    a prostitute*
among your friends and their flocks?

Young Man
⁸If you don't know, O most beautiful
    woman,
follow the trail of my flock,
and graze your young goats by
    the shepherds' tents.

1:7 Hebrew *like a veiled woman.*

NOTES

1:7 *wander.* In the Heb. the woman simply asks why she should be like a prostitute. The NLT introduces the idea of wandering, since that is the implication of the comment. If the man does not give her directions, then she will have to proceed from tent to tent and look like a prostitute who is trying to get a customer.

like a prostitute. Lit., "like a veiled woman" (cf. NLT mg). The NLT rightly understands that the veil is a prostitute's veil in this context (Gen 38:14-15) and so makes the ancient implication clear to the modern reader. An alternate understanding of the line is provided by G. R. Driver (1974) and J. A. Emerton (1993). Preferring the other of the two ancient Semitic roots spelled *'th* as the source of the word *'otyah,* they interpret the phrase as indicating that the woman does not want to be left "picking lice," an expression equivalent to our "twiddling thumbs." The NEB has adopted this reading.

COMMENTARY

In this poem, we get our first interchange between the young woman and the young man. Indeed, this is the first time that we hear directly from the young man. The woman invites him to an intimate noontime meeting, and he responds with a provocative tease. Her invitation has a playful tone about it as well, with sexually charged overtones. She asks for directions as to where she might meet him at noon and then implies that she would still try to find him anyway. She fears lest she look like a paid woman (a prostitute) who goes out to the shepherds during their breaks in her attempt to find him. The man responds to her question indirectly, leaving an air of mystery, but also implying that he desires her company.

◆ IV. Fourth Love Poem: A Beautiful Mare (1:9–11)

⁹You are as exciting, my darling,
    as a mare among Pharaoh's
    stallions.
¹⁰How lovely are your cheeks;
    your earrings set them afire!

How lovely is your neck,
    enhanced by a string of jewels.
¹¹We will make for you earrings
    of gold
and beads of silver.

NOTES

1:11 *We will make for you.* Commentators have been confused by the sudden shift to the first person plural "we." S. Paul (1997) has described this shift as an indication of the man's passion.

COMMENTARY

This short love poem is a song of admiration that the man sings to the woman. He begins by comparing her to a horse, which sounds odd to a modern audience. More specifically, the Hebrew compares her to a mare among the Egyptian pharaoh's chariotry. First, the reference to Pharaoh connotes wealth and luxury. Second, we know from historical sources that Pharaoh's chariots were all drawn by stallions, not mares. So what does a reference to a mare among Pharaoh's chariots signify? Modern commentators (see Pope 1978:336-341) understand the metaphor to be built on an ancient military defensive strategy. As chariots attacked, the defenders would let a mare loose, and the hope was that the charging stallions would be distracted and thrown into confusion. The metaphor, as applied to the woman, implies that her beauty is overwhelming and distracting. She drives him crazy with love. In the next verse, he comments further on her beauty, framed as it is by jewelry; and then, finally, in 1:11, he makes known his intention to honor her with precious earrings, further enhancing her beauty.

◆ V. Fifth Love Poem: Intimate Fragrances (1:12-14)

Young Woman
12 The king is lying on his couch,
    enchanted by the fragrance of my
    perfume.
13 My lover is like a sachet of myrrh

lying between my breasts.
14 He is like a bouquet of sweet henna
    blossoms
    from the vineyards of En-gedi.

NOTES

1:12 *my perfume.* Specifically, nard, a perfume that comes from India.

1:14 *bouquet of sweet henna blossoms.* Henna blossoms, the sweet-smelling flowers of the henna shrub, are well known in the Middle East for their reddish-brown dye.

COMMENTARY

The woman now answers the man with a poem of her admiration for him. Her poem refers to a number of different sweet smells. In the first place, she refers to nard, an exotic perfume derived from far-away India. This is her perfume, the scent of which wafts to the man as he lies on a couch, a sensuous scene, to be sure. She then metaphorically refers to the man as a sachet of myrrh, another exotic substance with a pleasant scent, which hangs between her breasts. The reference to the location of the sachet communicates intimacy. He is as close to her as he can get. Then, finally, she likens the man to a cluster of henna blossoms, another reference to a sensual fragrance. Furthermore, these are not ordinary hennas but hennas from the most romantic place in all of Israel, En-gedi. En-gedi may still be visited today.

Located on the western bank of the Dead Sea, it is an oasis in the middle of desolate wilderness. It has a well, a secluded waterfall, and is filled with lush vegetation—the perfect place for a romantic tryst.

◆ VI. Sixth Love Poem: Outdoor Love (1:15-17)

Young Man
15 How beautiful you are, my darling,
   how beautiful!
   Your eyes are like doves.

Young Woman
16 You are so handsome, my love,

pleasing beyond words!
The soft grass is our bed;
17   fragrant cedar branches are the
      beams of our house,
   and pleasant smelling firs are
      the rafters.

COMMENTARY

The chapter concludes with a mutual admiration song. The man speaks first and proclaims his beloved beautiful, specifically remarking on the attractiveness of her eyes. The comparison with doves is difficult and it is hard to know for sure what the point of comparison was. It may be "the dove's softness, beauty of feathers and eyes, and affection for and faithfulness to its mate" (DBI 217). In any case, the context shows it to be a warm compliment. The woman responds with an equally warm affirmation of her attraction to the man and adds a word about their intimate location. They are embracing outdoors. Their bed is the grass, and they are surrounded by trees that provide them privacy as if they were in an actual house.

◆ VII. Seventh Love Poem: Flowers and Trees (2:1-7)

Young Woman
   I am the spring crocus blooming
      on the Sharon Plain,*
   the lily of the valley.

Young Man
2 Like a lily among thistles
   is my darling among young women.

Young Woman
3 Like the finest apple tree in the
      orchard
   is my lover among other young men.
   I sit in his delightful shade

and taste his delicious fruit.
4 He escorts me to the banquet hall;
   it's obvious how much he loves me.
5 Strengthen me with raisin cakes,
      refresh me with apples,
   for I am weak with love.
6 His left arm is under my head,
   and his right arm embraces me.

7 Promise me, O women of Jerusalem,
   by the gazelles and wild deer,
   not to awaken love until the time
      is right.*

2:1 Traditionally rendered *I am the rose of Sharon.* Sharon Plain is a region in the coastal plain of Palestine.
2:7 Or *not to awaken love until it is ready.*

NOTES

2:1 *crocus.* The NLT here translates the Heb. word *khabatseleth* [TH2261, ZH2483] as "crocus." This may be too specific a translation; we cannot be sure that the word means "crocus."

However, the crocus is a common flower that blooms in the early spring. The parallel with "lily of the valley" suggests that this plant is a wildflower common in ancient Israel. In the Bible the word is only found elsewhere in Isa 35:1, where the desert will burst into bloom with these flowers. The traditional translation, as found in the KJV, is "rose." However, this is surely incorrect since the rose was not introduced into the region until well after the OT period.

Sharon Plain. This is a plain just between the coast and the foothills of western Israel, north of Jaffa up to Athlit. Sharon was a very fertile area that was probably well known for its wildflowers (see Borowski 1988).

lily. The Heb. for "lily" is *shoshannah*. This is the origin of the name Susanna.

2:3 apple tree. Again, we encounter the problem of identifying an ancient Heb. word (*tappuakh* [TH8598, ZH9515]) with a plant name. There have been many different suggestions for this word including peach, apricot, and quince. Indeed, this ambiguity led M. Falk (1982:174) to simply translate it as "sweet fruit tree." The major English translations, however, are convinced that the word refers to the apple tree.

2:4 banquet hall. Lit., this phrase is "house of wine" (*beth hayyayin*). It appears to be similar to what in other passages is called the "house for the drinking of wine" (cf. Heb. of Esth 7:8) and the "drinking house" (cf. Eccl 7:2; Jer 16:8).

it's obvious how much he loves me. This is a rather prosaic translation of the Heb., which is more lit. rendered "his banner over me is 'Love.'" The banner (*degel* [TH1714, ZH1840]) was most likely a battle standard or emblem that identified an army (see Num 1:52; 2:2, 3, 10, 17, 18, 25, 31, 34; 10:14, 18, 22, 25). The NLT, though perhaps overly interpretive, presents the meaning of this military image accurately. The point is that he is making public how much he loves the woman. He has taken out an advertisement, to use a related (but non-military) analogy.

2:7 by the gazelles and wild deer. This enigmatic expression (cf. 3:5) is a very subtle and playful means of taking an oath. First, it is important to remind ourselves that while God's name does not appear in the book, most oaths do invoke a divine name to add force. (There seems to be an intentional avoidance of naming God in the Song.) Second, we must remember the pastoral mood that is evoked in the Song, and gazelles and deer certainly evoke a pastoral scene. Thus, the explanation for this particular expression comes from both the pastoral scene it evokes and from the fact that it sounds like another common oath expression that does include divine names. In Heb., this expression (*bitsba'oth 'o be'ayloth hassadeh*) sounds a great deal like "by (the LORD) of Hosts or by God Almighty" (*be(yhwh) tseva'oth 'o be'el shaddai*).

not to awaken love until the time is right. There is some debate over how to understand this command in its context (see de Villiers and Burden 1989 as well as Grossberg 1981). The woman may be requesting that the chorus not disturb them while they are in a lovers' embrace. In essence, the phrase would then function as a kind of "Do Not Disturb" sign posted on the outside of a hotel room door. However, if this were the correct reading, it would be more likely that the text would say "not to awaken us" rather than "not to awaken love." It is more likely that she is telling them not to hurry love in their own lives. It is a warning not to rush into intimate relationships. This refrain is also found in 3:5 and 8:4.

COMMENTARY

The woman speaks first. She likens herself to flowers, specifically the crocus—a type of common wildflower. The woman appears to be giving herself a slight self-compliment, at best. She says she is like a flower, but a common flower, one among thousands.

This love poem is a dialogue between the young woman and the young man. They compliment each other by comparing one another's delights to flowers and trees. Perhaps, however, dialogue is the wrong word. What we have here is back-and-forth banter that is not directly addressed to the other speaker. They speak in the third, not the second person. Nonetheless, it is a kind of dialogue because one speech is clearly playing off the other. The nature of poetry is such that we can have dialogue without the speakers directly addressing each other.

As an alternative to this, perhaps we are to imagine 2:5-6 as addressed to the women of Jerusalem, to whom the woman is clearly speaking in the last verse. After all, the Hebrew imperatives are in the plural. The poem ends with two refrains, one a note of bliss, the other a word of warning (2:6-7; cf. 3:5; 8:3, 4).

The young man picks up on her modest assessment of herself and situates it in such a way as to make her superior to her peers. She is a lily indeed but a lily among thorns. In his eyes, she makes all the other girls look worse than plain. The woman then returns the compliment by comparing the young man to an apple tree. The NLT rendering proclaims that he is the best apple tree among all the other apple trees of the orchard, but the contrast may be even stronger than this implies. The Hebrew text places this apple tree in the midst of a forest, most likely a forest of non-fruit trees (cf. NIV, KJV). An apple tree is special in this context for a number of reasons. For one, an apple tree is scented. It evokes the image of a pleasant place to dally. In 8:5, the apple tree is the place of lovemaking. Besides a pleasant smell, the other relevant distinctive trait of an apple tree in contrast to other trees is that it bears apples. It is fruitful and productive, showing its fertility in an obvious way.

The woman poetically describes her being in his presence as sitting in the shade of the apple tree. To sit in someone's shade in the ancient Near East means to enjoy their protection. But here, it implies intimacy, as made explicit by the next line where she relishes the idea of eating his delicious fruit. Note how the man is no longer compared to the tree but has metaphorically become the tree at this point.

In 2:4, the garden imagery is dropped, and she tells how he escorts her into the banquet hall. The banquet hall is literally the "wine house." We have already seen how wine is a sensuous liquid in both its consistency as well as in its effects (1:2). Love and wine can both make one lightheaded. The "wine house" is a public place, though, and it is here that he makes his love for her manifest. The NLT makes abstract the concrete meaning of the Hebrew in 2:4b: "it's obvious how much he loves me." As the note above regarding this phrase explains, the poem here uses military terminology. His battle standard communicates his love for the woman.

Lovemaking is strenuous emotionally and physically. The woman thus calls out for something that will revive her. She asks for raisins and apples, fruits that were thought to replenish sexual energy. The poet seems to be tastefully implying that the man and the woman are in a most intimate embrace.

The last two verses of the poem (2:6-7) are refrains that may be found elsewhere in the Song. In the first, the woman describes the man's embrace. The embrace is described in such a way (left arm *under* my head) that the couple appears to be reclining together with the man above the woman. And then finally, though she may have been implicitly speaking to the women of Jerusalem throughout, she now turns to them explicitly with what in essence is a warning. She makes them promise (see note on 2:7) not to engage in love and by implication the physical act of love-making until circumstances become appropriate. In essence, she becomes their teacher. They have just heard her speak of a beautiful, wonderful relationship filled with sensuality. She warns them not to jump into this type of relationship. As we will see elsewhere in the Song (2:15; 5:2ff), love is beautiful, but painful as well. It is not to be treated lightly.

◆ VIII. Eighth Love Poem: Springtime (2:8-17)

⁸Ah, I hear my lover coming!
He is leaping over the mountains,
bounding over the hills.
⁹My lover is like a swift gazelle
or a young stag.
Look, there he is behind the wall,
looking through the window,
peering into the room.
¹⁰My lover said to me,
"Rise up, my darling!
Come away with me, my fair one!
¹¹Look, the winter is past,
and the rains are over and gone.
¹²The flowers are springing up,
the season of singing birds* has
come,
and the cooing of turtledoves fills
the air.
¹³The fig trees are forming young fruit,
and the fragrant grapevines are
blossoming.
Rise up, my darling!
Come away with me, my fair one!"

Young Man
¹⁴My dove is hiding behind the rocks,
behind an outcrop on the cliff.
Let me see your face;
let me hear your voice.
For your voice is pleasant,
and your face is lovely.

Young Women of Jerusalem
¹⁵Catch all the foxes,
those little foxes,
before they ruin the vineyard
of love,
for the grapevines are
blossoming!

Young Woman
¹⁶My lover is mine, and I am his.
He browses among the lilies.
¹⁷Before the dawn breezes blow
and the night shadows flee,
return to me, my love, like a gazelle
or a young stag on the rugged
mountains.*

2:12 Or *the season of pruning vines.* 2:17 Or *on the hills of Bether.*

NOTES

2:9 *like a swift gazelle.* The gazelle is known for its speed and agility. It is able to traverse geographical obstacles to get to its desired location. The image as applied to the man expresses excitement and eagerness. The woman wants him to be near her, so she wishes that he might be like the gazelle, or, in the parallel, a stag.

2:15 *foxes.* The fox (or jackal; the Heb. word *shu'al* [TH7776, ZH8785] is ambiguous) is a "very small and light carnivore" (DBI 30). It is a predator and in a garden setting would have been seen as a dangerous nuisance. Most think that the fox here stands for some kind of threat to the love relationship. The identity of the threat is difficult to determine but may refer to rival suitors. That foxes were pests in a vineyard is attested by a poem of Theocritus of Comatas from approximately 275 BC: "I hate the brushtail foxes, that soon as day declines / Come creeping to their vintaging mid Goodman Micon's vines" (quoted in Keel 1994:109-110). Perhaps more relevant to the Song, Keel also alerts us to the fact that the fox represents a mischievous lover in ancient Egyptian love poetry, citing Papyrus Harris 500, group A, no. 4: "My heart is not yet done with your lovemaking, / my (little) [fox]! / Your liquor is (your) lovemaking."

vineyard. As early as 1:6, we have been aware of the use of the vineyard as a metaphor for the woman's sexuality. After all, the vine bears a fruit, the grape that can be plucked and savored. This image will recur throughout the Song and is also found in other ancient Near Eastern love poetry.

2:16 My lover is mine, and I am his. This phrase is used in 6:3 and 7:10, as well, and is one of those recurrent refrains that makes the disparate poems of the Song cohere in a final literary unity. The phrase itself is one that expresses a mutual affection and secures a bond between the man and the woman. Indeed, it is reminiscent of the covenant formula ("I will be their God, and they will be my people"—see Jer 7:23; 11:4; Ezek 34:30).

2:17 Before the dawn breezes blow. The Heb. phrase here is more ambiguous than the NLT reveals. The Heb. may be rendered more lit. "until the day blows and the shadows flee." To complicate things even further, the temporal marker at the beginning of the clause could be translated "while" or "when" rather than "until." In other words, this phrase is either pointing to the end of the day or, as the NLT has taken it, the end of the night. We might expect the nighttime to be the more appropriate time for a tryst, but there is also the possibility of an afternoon rendezvous as well. At least, we can observe (and feel) the intensity of the woman's desire for intimacy in the verse.

the rugged mountains. The word rendered "rugged" here is a debated translation. The root *btr* [TH1334, ZH1439] means "to cut into pieces" or "to cut into halves." This suggests cleavage and may indicate that the mountain stands for the woman's breasts. I think Pope (1978:410) goes too far when he identifies the cleft mounds as the woman's *mons veneris*, or love mound. Some translators (see NAB, NJB) throw up their hands and simply translate it as "mountains of Bether."

COMMENTARY

The poetic quality of Song of Songs is very evident in this poem. To treat it with crass literalism could result in the accusation that the man is a Peeping Tom (2:9). It could also lead to the ridiculous view that the woman runs out of her house (2:9) and up into the hills where she is hiding from the man in some cave (2:14). On the contrary, this poem communicates its message and expresses its emotion through various creative, yet established, poetic motifs.

The poem coheres by virtue of its springtime setting. The young man and young woman both speak, and, according to the decision of the NLT, so do the young women of Jerusalem (2:15). Regarding 2:15, the text is not crystal clear on who is speaking. It may be a continuation of the woman's speech. If so, then the "us" (cf. NIV, NASB) refers to the woman and the man. I agree, however, that it is more likely that here it is the daughters of Jerusalem referring to themselves all together as "us."

The overarching mood expressed by this poem is emotional distance and a yearning to overcome that distance. The woman begins by excitedly hearing signs that her lover is coming closer to her. His eagerness is expressed in her metaphor of a swift gazelle or young stag bounding over the mountains. The mountains are obstacles, but he is more than able to surmount them in order to reach his goal, namely, the woman. Almost instantly, he is near her home, right outside the wall, looking into the room. Rather than seeking entry, he invites her to come outside. He wants her company, her embrace, in the countryside, which is the locus of intimacies throughout.

In order to persuade her, he describes the end of winter and the onset of spring. As in our own culture, springtime apparently was considered a season conducive to love. This makes sense, since the deadness of the winter gives way to the renewed fertility of the spring. Spring is a time when people can go outdoors, remove excessive clothing, and enjoy the beautiful sights, pleasant sounds, and sweet smells of the earth. The man specifically mentions flowers, singing birds, and cooing turtledoves. The fruit-producing fig trees and vines were blossoming. The man ends his speech to the woman as it began—with an invitation to leave the house and join him in the romantic countryside.

The man's speech in 2:10-13 is embedded as a quotation within the woman's speech. She has reported to us what he told her. But now, in 2:14, we hear the man speak, and there is an abrupt shift in the woman's location. She is no longer in the house, but now she is hiding behind the rocks. If we try to picture this as an actual event, as if the woman ran from her house to play hide-and-seek with her lover, we will be confused; this is not a report of an actual event but the evocation of poetic themes.

According to 2:14, the woman is in a barren, perhaps hostile location (as in 4:8). More importantly, she is at a distance from the man. He calls to her to make herself present to him. He desires to hear her voice and see her lovely form. The next verse (2:15) involves yet another abrupt transition. The young women of Jerusalem are now speaking. The location is neither the woman's home nor the rocky cliffs but a vineyard. The women of Jerusalem issue an urgent call to catch the little foxes that are loose in the vineyard. The foxes threaten to wreak havoc on the vineyard. As explained in the notes above, the vineyard can either represent the woman's body or, as is more likely, the location of intimate activity. The foxes are obstacles and threats to the intimacy that the man and the woman share. The warning about the foxes, then, fits in with a broader theme in the book that, though a vital relationship is possible, there are still threats to perfect union.

This note of danger is not the end of the eighth poem; the poem ends rather with the soothing voice of the woman. She expresses their mutual love with an expression that echoes the great covenant formula found elsewhere in Scripture (see note on 2:16). She then contentedly says that her lover grazes among the lilies. The latter is a bit obscure to our modern understanding; however, it is clear that the phrase seems to indicate some act of intimacy. She is elsewhere likened to a vineyard or garden, and he is here partaking of it. He is a gazelle that is feeding off the garden, which is her body. This interpretation is supported by the fact that in 4:5 we have the same idiom, but there it clearly refers to her two breasts, which are like fawns that graze among the lilies. The poem comes to a close with a final expression of yearning and desire. She wants him to return to her like a gazelle or a young stag (2:17).

◆ IX. Ninth Love Poem: Seeking and Not Finding (3:1-5)

Young Woman
One night as I lay in bed, I yearned
    for my lover.
I yearned for him, but he did not
    come.
²So I said to myself, "I will get up and
    roam the city,
    searching in all its streets and
    squares.
I will search for the one I love."
So I searched everywhere but did
    not find him.
³The watchmen stopped me as they
    made their rounds,

and I asked, "Have you seen the one
    I love?"
⁴Then scarcely had I left them
    when I found my love!
I caught and held him tightly,
    then I brought him to my mother's
    house,
    into my mother's bed, where I had
    been conceived.

⁵Promise me, O women of Jerusalem,
    by the gazelles and wild deer,
    not to awaken love until the time
    is right.*

3:5 Or *not to awaken love until it is ready.*

NOTES

3:1 *yearned.* The NLT here translates a verb more lit. understood to mean "searched" (*baqash* [TH1245, ZH1335]).

COMMENTARY

Song of Songs 3:1-5 is a self-contained poem with a definite opening and closing. It is the story of a single evening as told by the young woman. Again, it is important to remember that these poems are not actual occurrences. It is a poem in which the young woman expresses her deep desire for the man, a desire that allows her to overcome large cultural and personal obstacles to go in search of her man. This "seek and not find" poem is similar in many ways to the poem that begins in 5:2, but the latter poem is much darker in atmosphere.

The woman recounts an evening when she lay in bed awake and uneasy because the man was not with her. Her intense desire for him is expressed by the verb "to yearn" (see note on 3:1). She feels empty at his absence, but her feelings of loneliness and desire do not result in his presence.

She realizes that if she is to have him, she must go out in search of him. At this point, we should note yet again how the woman takes the initiative in the relationship. She does not wait passively until he returns; rather, she sets out in hot pursuit of him. The poem expresses her determination by reporting her thoughts: "I will get up and roam the city." This is a bold and brave move. For a woman by herself, the city was a place of great potential danger in antiquity, even as it can be today.

Her initial efforts to find her lover are not successful, something that simply builds the pressure of desire. She then encounters the watchmen, those charged with preserving the safety of the community. The modern equivalent would be the police. Their role in this poem, as opposed to the poem in 5:2–6:3, is simply to be a sounding board for the woman's plaintive question: "Have you seen the one I love?" This shows her desperation for his presence, but the watchmen are not the ones who bring him into her presence.

Nonetheless, as she leaves them, she miraculously finds him. He appears out of nowhere, but how he is found is not the issue. He is in her arms, and she will not let him go. The description of her strong embrace underlines her deep affection for him and her desire to be in his presence.

But she does not just hold him; she takes him to the bedroom. The rest is left to our imagination, though our imagination is guided by the fact that this is the bedroom where her mother conceived her. It is a place of sexual activity, and she has been a good student of her mother. She, too, will enjoy her husband in a similar way.

The suggestion of intercourse turns her attention to her disciples in love—the women of Jerusalem. These are young women who have not yet experienced the pleasures of the marriage bed. In this refrain, which is repeated from 2:7 (see the commentary there for more on this verse), she warns them not to hurry love. The picture that she has drawn of intimacy with her man would certainly lead them to desire a similar relationship, but her warning is that love is not something to be entered into lightly.

◆ X. Tenth Love Poem: A Royal Wedding Procession (3:6-11)

Young Women of Jerusalem
⁶Who is this sweeping in from the
    wilderness
    like a cloud of smoke?
Who is it, fragrant with myrrh and
    frankincense
    and every kind of spice?
⁷Look, it is Solomon's carriage,
    surrounded by sixty heroic men,
    the best of Israel's soldiers.
⁸They are all skilled swordsmen,
    experienced warriors.
Each wears a sword on his thigh,
    ready to defend the king against an
    attack in the night.

⁹King Solomon's carriage is built
    of wood imported from Lebanon.
¹⁰Its posts are silver,
    its canopy gold;
    its cushions are purple.
It was decorated with love
    by the young women of
    Jerusalem.

Young Woman
¹¹Come out to see King Solomon,
    young women of Jerusalem.*
He wears the crown his mother gave
    him on his wedding day,
    his most joyous day.

3:11 Hebrew *of Zion.*

NOTES

3:6 Who is this. My view is that "what is this" is a better rendering here. The Heb. interrogative *mi* [TH4310, ZH4769] can be translated according to its usage in Akkadian as "what"

rather than "who" (cf. NRSV). The interrogative is coupled with the feminine word for
"this" (*zo't* [TH2063, ZH2271]), which corresponds in gender to the word for the carriage
(*mittah* [TH4296, ZH4753]), but does not sensibly refer to the man Solomon. The parallel
usage in 8:5 uses this same feminine construction to ask after the woman, making "who"
the natural and appropriate rendering there. Translated as "what" in this case, the question
is answered in the text: it is the carriage or palanquin of Solomon that approaches.

COMMENTARY

The emotion and tone of this tenth poem is very different from the ninth and thus
allows us to see clearly that 3:6-11 is a separate poem. The mood is ebullient; the
talk is about a wedding. This is indicated by 3:11, which refers to Solomon's wedding day. Reading this reference back, the entire poem seems to be a happy remembrance of Solomon's wedding. The opulence and grandeur of the occasion reflect
the honor and glory of the institution of marriage.

Why Solomon's wedding is highlighted is an interesting question. Some interpreters, of course, think the subject of the entire Song of Songs is Solomon's love
life, but I have expressed my reservations about such an approach in the introduction to the commentary (see "Author"). Even if we were sure that the book was
about Solomon's love life, we might still have issues with the choice of this man
to be the subject of a poem that seeks to heap honor on the marriage institution.
He was, after all, lured away from the Lord by the many foreign wives that he wed
(1 Kgs 11:1-13). It is a hard issue to resolve, but there is no doubt about the fact that
the famous king's wedding day itself was a day of great joy.

There is some debate over who is speaking the words of this poem, but the NLT is
likely correct to place all but the last verse in the mouth of the young women of Jerusalem. One problem with being certain about this is that we do not know who is in
Solomon's carriage. If the question that begins the poem is a question of *who*, it is
never directly answered (see note on 3:6). If it is a question of *what*, then the answer
is directly given: Solomon's carriage is what is coming up out of the wilderness. This
second option is more likely in my view, and though this does not directly tell us
who is in the carriage, it is fair for the reader to understand that Solomon is in his
carriage. Whether he is accompanied by the young woman is harder to answer. He
may be coming to meet her.

There are three types of settings in the various poems of the Song. First, there is
the city, which is hostile to love. Second, there is the cultivated countryside—the
garden, the nut orchard, the vineyard—which is a place of intimacy and love.
Finally, there is the rugged, untamed wilderness, which, like the city, is not a place
conducive to love. The arrival from the wilderness, a hostile countryside, probably
indicates a movement toward rather than away from intimacy. This understanding
certainly fits with the excitement and warm description of the carriage's arrival.

From a distance, the carriage is seen kicking up dust, which is poetically described
as a cloud of smoke, perhaps intentionally reminding the reader of the column of
smoke that accompanied Israel during their wilderness wanderings. If so, this may
be another subtle allusion to God (see note on 2:7 about "the gazelles and wild

deer"). As we have already seen, these love poems appeal to all the senses, including smell. As this column of smoke approaches (again, the dust kicked up by the carriage), it is described by the poetic imagination as sweet smelling incense (3:6b).

Solomon's carriage arrives in full glory. It is accompanied by sixty of Israel's finest warriors. They are fully armed and ready for any exigency. The night is mentioned specially (3:8), since the time of darkness is a time of greatest danger. Evil often operates when its movements can be concealed.

Notice that these are Solomon's soldiers and Solomon's carriage; soon the language will turn to talk of Solomon's wedding. Solomon himself, however, is never described and never speaks. Again, this is what leads to the question about who is actually in the carriage. Though the mystery persists, the passage turns to a description of the ornate carriage (3:9). The Hebrew actually uses two words here for this vehicle. One is rare ('appiryon [TH668, ZH712]; occurs only in 3:9) and the other (mittah [TH4296, ZH4753]; 3:7) indicates that the carriage would be a place where the occupants would recline. I am fairly certain that this vehicle is a litter—that is, a platform with carrying poles that would be placed on the shoulders of bearers (cf. Rundgren 1972). This would be the height of luxury in travel.

Its physical description highlights just how precious the materials of the carriage are. The wood from Lebanon was undoubtedly cedar. It was considered the finest wood in the area and was used for the construction of the Temple, as well as Solomon's palace. The posts and canopy were at least covered by those most precious metals, silver and gold (3:10). The cushions were purple, an expensive dye in antiquity that was reserved only for royalty. Finally, in a passage of debated interpretation, it says that this carriage was decorated by the women of Jerusalem and that they did it "with love." Love permeates this poem.

Now the woman speaks to her charges, the young women of Jerusalem. Whether she has just arrived with Solomon or was waiting with the young women is unclear. She invites them out for a closer look at Solomon himself, who is wearing his wedding crown. The day of his wedding is described as a day of great joy. Notice, too, that the mother of Solomon, probably at the point when he is a young lover, is mentioned. Mothers (rather than fathers) played a large role in ancient Near Eastern love poetry, as can be traced back to Sumerian times. (For a full treatment of Sumerian love songs, see Sefati 1998.)

◆ XI. Eleventh Love Poem: From Head to Breasts (4:1-7)

Young Man
You are beautiful, my darling,
  beautiful beyond words.
Your eyes are like doves
  behind your veil.
Your hair falls in waves,
  like a flock of goats winding
    down the slopes of Gilead.

² Your teeth are as white as sheep,
  recently shorn and freshly washed.
Your smile is flawless,
  each tooth matched with its twin.*
³ Your lips are like scarlet ribbon;
  your mouth is inviting.
Your cheeks are like rosy
  pomegranates

behind your veil.
⁴Your neck is as beautiful as the tower
    of David,
    jeweled with the shields of a
    thousand heroes.
⁵Your breasts are like two fawns,
    twin fawns of a gazelle grazing
    among the lilies.

⁶Before the dawn breezes blow
    and the night shadows flee,
    I will hurry to the mountain of
    myrrh
    and to the hill of frankincense.
⁷You are altogether beautiful, my
    darling,
    beautiful in every way.

4:2 Hebrew *Not one is missing; each has a twin.*

NOTES

4:1-7 Scholars refer to this poem as a *wasf*, an Arabic term meaning "description." (For more on this, see Soulen 1967:183-190, though I do not agree with his final conclusions.) The poem is one that describes the physical beauty of the woman and is the first of four such poetic passages—two others are also directed toward the woman (6:4-7; 7:1-9) and another one where the woman describes the physical beauty of the man (5:10-16). The term comes from the nineteenth century, when biblical scholars recognized the similarity between these poems in the Song of Songs and wedding songs that were sung among Arabic tribesmen (see Delitzsch 1975:162-176).

4:1 *beyond words.* This is an addition. The Heb. is actually repetitious: "Behold, you are beautiful, my darling. / Behold, you are beautiful." This repetition, however, is an intensifier, and the NLT does well to represent that by the addition of the phrase "beyond words."

falls in waves. This is an interpretive addition, not in the Heb., to help the modern reader understand the metaphor that compares the woman's hair to a flock of goats streaming down the slopes of Gilead.

Gilead. A hilly region located in the central Transjordan near the Jabbok River (modern Wadi Zarqa); a particularly beautiful landscape.

4:2 *smile is flawless.* The man compliments the woman as having all her teeth, well preserved and white. However, the reference to the flawless smile is not in the Heb. but is an English equivalent of the literal compliment: "not one [of your teeth] is missing" (cf. NLT mg).

4:3 *cheeks.* The verse in Heb. describes the woman's temples (the most likely meaning of the Heb. *raqqah* [TH7541, ZH8377]), not her cheeks, as similar to slices of pomegranate, though the NLT is most likely right in showing that the reference to the fruit is a comment on the woman's "rosy" complexion (see Rozelaar 1988).

COMMENTARY

This powerful and intriguing poem is commonly referred to by the Arabic term *wasf*, a word that simply means "description" (see note on 4:1-7). It is, after all, a description by the man of the woman's beauty, from head to breasts. After a short interlude, this description will pick up again in 4:10 and focus on the most inviting of all parts of the woman's body, using the metaphor of a garden fountain. An Arabic *wasf* is sung at a wedding and is a precursor to lovemaking; it is thus quite sensuous in its imagery. Such songs begin either with the head (like this one in the Song) or with the feet and work down or up the body respectively. The imagery, as mentioned, is quite provocative, though always tasteful, and I will try to preserve that tone in my comments.

The present poem begins with a general exclamation of the beauty of the woman. It will also conclude with such an exclamation, thus forming what is called an *inclusio*, where a similar opening and closing gives a poem or literary passage a sense of closure.

The man first compliments the beauty of his lover's eyes, comparing them to doves. On the surface, this sounds romantic, but the precise point of comparison between the woman's eyes and doves escapes us. Is it the color of her eyes? Indeed, are her eyes compared to a dove's coat of feathers or perhaps to a dove's eyes? And if the latter, what is it about dove's eyes that are so intriguing? When we come to the woman's description of the man's physical beauty, we will see that she compares his eyes to a dove, as well, in a way that seems to point specifically to his pupils (5:12).

Equally intriguing is the fact that the man sees her eyes behind the veil. This suggests a transparent veil that covers the entire face. The veil hides and reveals, it seems, and it is true that a partial glimpse of physical beauty is often more arousing than seeing the whole. The view of the part arouses the desire to see the whole.

It should also be noted that the status and purpose of veils in ancient Israelite society is not known. Was it a sign of modesty? In the reference in 1:7 (cf. NLT mg) and in reference to Tamar wearing a veil in Genesis 38, it has been suggested that a veil may indicate a woman of dubious character. That is impossible here. This woman arouses the man, but such a response is healthy and appropriate, not seedy.

The man then goes on to compliment the woman's hair. It is like a flock of goats streaming down Mount Gilead. Gilead refers to the region in central Transjordan around the Jabbok River gorge. It is a stunningly beautiful area. The idea of a mountain suggests a head and the goats that descend (which are probably to be pictured as black) suggest hair. It is interesting to reflect on how the imagery works here. Some mischievous readers have thought about single lines of goats coming down the mountain and commented that the comparison suggests that she was balding (so Soulen 1967). This view is somewhat humorous perhaps but, of course, not in keeping with the intention of the compliment.

The second verse, which turns attention to the woman's teeth, also sounds comical from a modern perspective, reminding us that we need to put ourselves in the position of the original readers to truly understand these ancient writings. Ancient peoples did not have the same expertise in dental care that we have today. To compliment the woman's white teeth was indeed a compliment and may be compared to the nineteenth century English/American compliment about a person's "pearly white teeth." However, modern men should beware of saying what the ancient Israelite lover says next in his exuberant proclamation that none of his beloved's teeth are missing (4:2, NLT mg). Indeed, a person giving such an ill-considered compliment may find some of his own teeth missing as a result! This simply reminds us that beauty is both bound by culture and sometimes found only in the eyes of the beholder.

The statement about the woman's lips (4:3) is for the most part a sensible compliment in the minds of modern readers. Red (or scarlet) lips have long been considered attractive as are full lips, suggested by the ribbon simile (as opposed to NRSV's "thread").

We may be a bit mystified by the man's comment about her temples ("cheeks" in NLT; see note on 4:3), however. Again, it is behind her veil, implying that the veil covered her entire face. The pomegranate is a reddish-orange fruit, and since women of the region were dark-skinned, the comparison probably indicates a desired skin color. This statement, whether shaped by the man's own tastes or by his culture, does not privilege any particular skin color over another. God has created beauty in every color.

Departing from the woman's face and head, the poet works down the body and next comments on her neck. Again, a literal understanding sounds somewhat ridiculous to most modern readers, though there are tribes in which extremely long necks are highly valued (e.g., the Padaung of Myanmar/Thailand and the Ndebele of South Africa). However, it is more likely that the comparison between her neck and David's tower is a reference to its majesty and dignity. We do not know for certain whether there was actually a tower known as David's tower in Israel at the time of the Song (the structure in Jerusalem that currently bears this name does not date back to the OT time period). The association with David enhances the idea of dignity, majesty, and power. The shields that ring the tower suggest an ornament of some kind, very probably a necklace. There is some evidence that military towers had places to hang ornamental shields on the outside (cf. Ezek 27:11). The fact that these shields are the shields of heroes again implies the dignity and majesty of the reference.

These poems are not prudish. The fact that he compliments her on her breasts, an intimate body part in antiquity even as it is today, shows the closeness of their relationship. It also prepares us for the later reference to her "fountain" (4:12, 15) and illustrates how these poems were uttered in anticipation of sexual union.

Her breasts, he says, are like fawns. Fawns are pastoral creatures, and throughout the Song the cultivated countryside is the place of romance. This is underlined by the fact that these fawns are grazing on lilies. Some have suggested, probably rightly, that the perspective we should adopt is from behind. As we see the fawns grazing from behind we see their rounded rumps elevated with their tiny tails suggestive of the nipples of a woman's breasts.

At this point, the man cannot continue but breaks off momentarily in a kind of rapturous whimsy. He now throws himself into the description and says he will go to the mountain of myrrh, also called the hill of frankincense. This, of course, is not an actual place. Coming after the reference to the woman's breasts, the mountains may continue the reference to that part of her body. He tastefully states his desire to fondle her breasts. Myrrh and frankincense are very expensive, sweet-smelling perfumes that enhance the sensuousness of the scene.

As mentioned at the beginning of my comments about this poem, it ends as it begins, giving the poem a sense of closure, a feeling of completion. She is indeed totally beautiful. Indeed, as he looks at her, he sees absolutely nothing wrong with her—no blemish at all. Is there any woman who ever existed who has been without blemish (or any man)? Of course not. But the rapture of love causes us to focus in on what is beautiful. Love is indeed a strange thing.

As explained in the introduction to the book, this is not an actual, specific woman, and there is not a specific man involved in this poem either. The purpose of this poem is to prod the reader to look at his beloved and find those things that attract him to her (the *wasf* in 5:10-16 will do the same for a female reader regarding her man). The poem encourages us to utter our own poetry of love. We may not be as articulate or as powerful in our imagery, but that is not what is important. What is important—and it is something that most of us need to be reminded of—is to find those points of beauty in the one we love and to express them.

◆ XII. Twelfth Love Poem: The Invitation (4:8-9)

8 Come with me from Lebanon,
   my bride,
   come with me from Lebanon.
Come down* from Mount Amana,
   from the peaks of Senir and Hermon,
where the lions have their dens
   and leopards live among the hills.

9 You have captured my heart,
   my treasure,* my bride.
You hold it hostage with one glance
   of your eyes,
   with a single jewel of your
   necklace.

4:8 Or *Look down.*   4:9 Hebrew *my sister;* also in 4:10, 12.

NOTES

4:8 *Lebanon . . . Mount Amana . . . Senir . . . Hermon.* Hermon is the well-known mountain at the northernmost reaches of Israel. It is an imposing, often snow-capped mountain that is the tallest and southernmost in the Anti-Lebanon mountain range, which extends up into Lebanon. The other peaks mentioned in this verse are Amana and Senir. According to Pope (1978:474-475), both of these peaks are also in the Anti-Lebanon Mountains.

4:9 *You have captured my heart.* This represents a single verb in the Heb. (*libabtini*), a verb formed from the noun "heart" (*leb* [TH3820, ZH4213]). The heart represented the inner person in Hebrew culture and language. She has captured the very essence of who the man is. She has aroused his emotions. Indeed, this verb could be translated more colloquially as "you drive me crazy." Regarding this verse, see Waldman 1970.

my treasure. Lit., this epithet is "my sister" (cf. NLT mg). "Sister" was a term of endearment in ancient Near Eastern society, used not only in this Israelite love poetry but also in the love poetry of Egypt (Westenholz 1995:2474). It does not imply incest. However, since "sister" is not typical of English love language and since it could be misunderstood as implying incest, the NLT has wisely employed an alternative rendition that expresses the same thought.

COMMENTARY

The woman's beauty overcomes the man, and he urges her to come to him. His urgency is communicated by the use of repetitive parallelism where he repeats his call: "come with me."

Confusion results if the reader tries to understand the geographical references literally. True, Amana, Senir, and Hermon are all peaks in the mountains of Lebanon, but she is not literally in these mountains. We are not to imagine that she is really hiding in the caves of wild animals. This is poetry, not a historical transcript. This rugged terrain represents her present distance from the man. Away from him, he implies, she is lonely and in danger. He desires that she come into his warm and protecting embrace.

He expresses his passionate love for her. He is totally enthralled by her beauty. He is like a prisoner to his love for her, but it is an enslavement that he enjoys. He expresses this by means of the epithets of love that he showers upon her. She is his "bride" and his "treasure." Indeed, it does not take much to arouse his passion—just a glance of her eye or a single jewel of her necklace.

◆ XIII. Thirteenth Love Poem: The Garden of Love (4:10–5:1)

¹⁰Your love delights me,
  my treasure, my bride.
Your love is better than wine,
  your perfume more fragrant than
    spices.
¹¹Your lips are as sweet as nectar,
  my bride.
Honey and milk are under your
  tongue.
Your clothes are scented
  like the cedars of Lebanon.

¹²You are my private garden, my
  treasure, my bride,
a secluded spring, a hidden
  fountain.
¹³Your thighs shelter a paradise
  of pomegranates
with rare spices—
henna with nard,
¹⁴ nard and saffron,
  fragrant calamus and cinnamon,
with all the trees of frankincense,
  myrrh, and aloes,
  and every other lovely spice.

5:1 Hebrew *my sister;* also in 5:2.

¹⁵You are a garden fountain,
  a well of fresh water
  streaming down from Lebanon's
    mountains.

Young Woman
¹⁶Awake, north wind!
  Rise up, south wind!
Blow on my garden
  and spread its fragrance all
    around.
Come into your garden, my love;
  taste its finest fruits.

CHAPTER 5
Young Man
I have entered my garden, my
  treasure,* my bride!
I gather myrrh with my spices
and eat honeycomb with my honey.
I drink wine with my milk.

Young Women of Jerusalem
Oh, lover and beloved, eat and drink!
Yes, drink deeply of your love!

NOTES
4:10 *Your love delights me.* The NLT well reflects the emotion and meaning of the Heb., which is more lit. rendered "How beautiful is your love." The literal translation shows the connection to the first descriptive poem, particularly verses 4:1 and 4:7.

my treasure. See note on 4:9; cf. 5:1.

4:11 Your lips are as sweet as nectar. The Heb. may be rendered "your lips drip honey(comb)." In other words, the word here rendered "nectar" may be a form of honey, but it is true that a different word is used for honey later in the line, and the NLT is right to differentiate the two. In either case the effect is the same, since both nectar and honey from the honeycomb are sweet and desirable. The reference to the honey dripping from her mouth, however, creates a more sensuous picture. The picture of the woman is positive, and the desire for her is certainly proper. The same image, however, is used in a darker context in Prov 5:3-6 where the immoral woman's lips are also described as dripping honey; but there it is a deceit, since what looks sweet is actually poisonous.

4:12 garden. For a survey of ancient Near Eastern, including biblical, references to the garden as an image of the woman's sexuality, see S. Paul (1997).

4:13 Your thighs shelter. "Thighs" renders the rare and difficult word *shelakh* [TH7973B, ZH8945], which is lit. "shoots." In the garden context, the shoots refer to the plants, but commentators differ over whether the referent is the woman's pubic hair or, as it is taken here, her legs. In any case, the aromatic plants listed immediately afterward suggest her pubic region as most desirable.

paradise. The English word actually derives from the Heb. *pardes* [TH6508, ZH7236], which itself may be borrowed from Persian. It is a word that otherwise occurs rarely and in late biblical books (Eccl 2:5, "gardens"; Neh 2:8, "forest").

4:13-14 These verses describe the garden as containing the most exotic and aromatic of all plants. The meaning of some of these words is disputed, but it is interesting to note that the English words for some of these come from the Heb.— nard (*nerd* [TH5373, ZH5948]), cinnamon (*qinnamon* [TH7076, ZH7872]), myrrh (*mor* [TH4753, ZH5255]), and aloes (*'ahalot* [TH174B, ZH189]).

4:16 north wind . . . south wind! The mention of these two winds coming from opposite directions is a merism that signifies that the woman is opening herself completely and without reservation to the man.

5:1 my treasure. See note on 4:9.

myrrh with my spices . . . honeycomb with my honey . . . wine with my milk. The use of the double objects indicates the experience of total satisfaction in his intimate encounter with the woman.

drink deeply. Or may be translated as an imperative with the meaning "Be intoxicated." Here and elsewhere in the Song, the headiness of love is often communicated by references to drinking wine.

COMMENTARY

After issuing the invitation of 4:8-9, the man resumes his description of the woman's beauty. It is not clear whether this is truly a separate poem or a continuation of the poem in 4:1-7, briefly interrupted by his spontaneous invitation for her to draw closer to him. In any case, he begins his adoration of her again by proclaiming how wonderful he finds her love (4:10). It delights him and is better than wine (cf. 1:2). Wine is a sensuous liquid that hangs heavy on the tongue. When consumed, it intoxicates but not as much as his strong passion for the woman. He invokes not just taste, however, but also smell, since pleasant spices seem bland in comparison to the scent of his beloved.

In 4:11 the man again describes particular parts of her body with suggestive metaphors that anticipate his physical touch. That her lips are sweet like nectar and that honey and milk are under her tongue indicate his desire to explore those regions. Deep kisses will do the job, to be sure. Again, the use of images that invoke the senses—in this instance taste—is notable. Like wine, honey and milk are heavy, sensuous liquids that leave a strong aftertaste—just like a kiss. In addition, we should note the fact that the beauty of the land of Israel was traditionally described by the phrase a "land flowing with milk and honey" (Deut 6:3). This connection would not be lost on the poet or his early readers. The man then makes note of another beautiful fragrance: her clothes smell like the pleasant (and majestic) cedars of Lebanon, the most renowned wood of that part of the ancient world. Pleasant smells motivate one to move closer, to become intimate. And the next section grows more intimate indeed.

The woman is now likened to a garden, a garden with a water source (4:12). As noted in my comments on 1:6, we see that the image of the garden is used in various ways. It is sometimes the place of lovemaking (and in that sense poetically contrasted with the city, which is hostile to intimacy). But in other contexts, as it is here, the garden (as with the orchard and vineyard) is an image of the woman's sexuality. That there is a spring or fountain in the midst of this garden is also suggestive of the woman's most intimate place, the locus of lovemaking, her vagina. This imagery is used throughout ancient Near Eastern love poetry and elsewhere in the Bible (e.g., Prov 5:15-19).

The NLT tastefully but clearly communicates this by understanding that the woman's garden is sheltered by her thighs (4:13). It is the most pleasant of all gardens, planted with the most fragrant and exotic plants. Its spring is the most refreshing to be imagined with the purest waters that descend from the melted snows on Lebanon's mountains. The man desires to enter—but this garden and its fountain are not open to the public! As was mentioned, they are "secluded" and "hidden" from view (4:12). This woman carefully preserves her delights. Not just anyone can enter; indeed, the implication is that no one has done so yet.

After this exotic rhapsody, the woman speaks. She has been closed up to this point, but now she will open her garden to the man. She invites him to come and taste the fruits of her garden (4:16). The man takes no time to respond (5:1). He will enter and partake of the garden. All of the garden imagery combined with talk of eating honey and drinking wine and milk is the language of physical intimacy, of sexual intercourse, and the chorus chimes in to celebrate this delicious moment (5:1c).

◆ XIV. Fourteenth Love Poem: Seeking and Not Finding, Again (5:2–6:3)

Young Woman
²I slept, but my heart was awake,
   when I heard my lover knocking and
      calling:
"Open to me, my treasure, my darling,
   my dove, my perfect one.
My head is drenched with dew,
my hair with the dampness of
   the night."

³But I responded,
"I have taken off my robe.
   Should I get dressed again?
I have washed my feet.
   Should I get them soiled?"

⁴My lover tried to unlatch the door,
  and my heart thrilled within me.
⁵I jumped up to open the door for
    my love,
  and my hands dripped with
    perfume.
My fingers dripped with lovely myrrh
  as I pulled back the bolt.
⁶I opened to my lover,
  but he was gone!
My heart sank.
I searched for him
  but could not find him anywhere.
I called to him,
  but there was no reply.
⁷The night watchmen found me
  as they made their rounds.
They beat and bruised me
  and stripped off my veil,
  those watchmen on the walls.

⁸Make this promise, O women of
    Jerusalem—
  If you find my lover,
  tell him I am weak with love.

Young Women of Jerusalem
⁹Why is your lover better than all
    others,
  O woman of rare beauty?
What makes your lover so special
  that we must promise this?

Young Woman
¹⁰My lover is dark and dazzling,
  better than ten thousand others!
¹¹His head is finest gold,
  his wavy hair is black as a raven.

¹²His eyes sparkle like doves
  beside springs of water;
they are set like jewels
  washed in milk.
¹³His cheeks are like gardens of spices
  giving off fragrance.
His lips are like lilies,
  perfumed with myrrh.
¹⁴His arms are like rounded bars of gold,
  set with beryl.
His body is like bright ivory,
  glowing with lapis lazuli.
¹⁵His legs are like marble pillars
  set in sockets of finest gold.
His posture is stately,
  like the noble cedars of Lebanon.
¹⁶His mouth is sweetness itself;
  he is desirable in every way.
Such, O women of Jerusalem,
  is my lover, my friend.

CHAPTER 6
Young Women of Jerusalem
  Where has your lover gone,
    O woman of rare beauty?
  Which way did he turn
    so we can help you find him?

Young Woman
²My lover has gone down to his
    garden,
  to his spice beds,
to browse in the gardens
  and gather the lilies.
³I am my lover's, and my lover is mine.
  He browses among the lilies.

NOTES
5:2 *my treasure.* Lit., "my sister" (see note on 4:9).

my perfect one. This Heb. term (*tam* [TH8535, ZH9447]) could also be translated "flawless." Typically, this word denotes moral wholeness (Job 8:20; 9:20-22), but in the Song (see also 6:9) it points to physical perfection.

5:3 *my feet.* "Feet" can be used euphemistically for male or female genitalia; for example, the Heb. expression "water of the feet" refers to urination (cf. uses of "feet" in the Heb. of Exod 4:25; Deut 28:57; Judg 3:24; 1 Sam 24:3; Ezek 16:25). For more on this, see NIDOTTE 3:1048.

5:4 *tried to unlatch the door.* Lit. "My lover sent (or thrust) his hand through the hole." The NLT translates the surface meaning appropriately as unlatching the door, though the fact is that "hole" (*khor*) is never used elsewhere for lock. In ancient times, "to make the tumbler locks more difficult to pick, they were mounted inside the door and reached by passing one's hand and key through a hole in the door" (King and Stager 2001:32; they cite the present verse as their only example and also assert that "the poet's double entendre is transparent throughout this passage").

Furthermore, the Heb. word translated "heart" (*me'eh* [TH4578, ZH5055]) in the second part of the verse is often used to denote the woman's erogenous zone, making sense of the verb *hamah* [TH1993, ZH2159], translated "thrilled" by the NLT but more precisely meaning "seeth" or "roil." The sentence describes the woman's growing sexual arousal.

5:5 my hands. Like "feet," "hand" was also used to refer to genitalia (Heb. of Isa 57:8-10); for other Heb. and extra-biblical evidence, consult Pope (1978:517-518) and Delcor (1967).

5:8 I am weak with love. In the above exposition, it was mentioned that the lovesickness theme in this verse could be paralleled by ancient Near Eastern equivalents. By way of demonstration, the following is a short Egyptian poem (the translation is that of Fox [1997:129]) on love sickness:

> Seven whole days I have not seen my sister.
> Illness has invaded me,
> My limbs have grown heavy,
> And I barely sense my own body.
> Should the master physicians come to me,
> Their medicines could not ease my heart.
> The lector-priests have no (good) method,
> Because my illness cannot be diagnosed.
> Telling me, "Here she is!"—that's what will revive me.
> Her name—that's what will get me up.

5:10 dark and dazzling. Perhaps this should be rendered, "radiant and ruddy." The first word signifies a healthy hue to the pigmentation of his skin. The second word means that his complexion is reddish, perhaps brownish red. Whatever exact features these words referred to, we know they were considered attractive to the original audience since the context marks them as compliments of the highest order.

5:12 sparkle. This verb is implicit in the metaphor but is not expressly in the Heb.

set like jewels. The Heb. has "sitting on fullness," which the NLT understands to be a reference to jewels. The early versions also struggled with the elliptical nature of the colon and rendered "sitting by the fullness of water" (see the early Gr. and the Vulgate).

5:14 beryl. Lit., "stones of Tarshish." Jewels and stones are hard to identify. The reference might be to chrysolite, but Zimmerli (1985:83) suggests instead black jet or golden topaz.

5:15 posture. The Heb. (*mar'eh* [TH4758, ZH5260]) has a more general meaning, something like "appearance." The more specific meaning, supplied by the NLT, is suggested by the metaphor of the cedar from Lebanon. That metaphor would also conjure up sweet smells and the notion of nobility or stateliness, since the cedars of Lebanon were renowned from the beginning of recorded history.

6:2 to browse. Or "graze" (*ra'ah* [TH7462, ZH8286]). For the use of this theme to express intimacy, see also 2:16 and 4:5.

COMMENTARY

While the previous poem celebrates the wonderful intimacy of romantic love, the poem now under consideration reminds readers that love is not easy. This fourteenth poem tells a story of misread signals. However, it also attests to the power of love to break through obstacles and achieve a desired relationship. Love is hard; but in the end, at least in this poem, the lovers are victorious.

As mentioned, the poem tells a story. Nonetheless, it is a mistake to think that it tells the story of an actual relationship. As we will see, the man and the woman often act in a way that defies motivation. This has led some to interpret the poem as a dream, but that, too, is not the point. It is a poem that tells a story to evoke certain emotions, and that is where I will put my emphasis in its interpretation.

The dream interpretation derives from a certain understanding of the first line of the poem: "I slept, but my heart was awake, when I heard my lover knocking" (5:2). What does it mean to say that she slept with an alert heart? "Heart" in Hebrew typically indicates something close to one's core personality, sometimes with an emphasis on the mind or cognitive functions. As such, this phrase could mean any number of things. It could conceivably refer to a dream, the dream indicating an active mind. I find it more believable to take it as a reference to fitful sleep or light sleep. In either case, the most important point to understand is that the sound of knocking wakes the woman up so that she hears the request of the young man.

The description of the interchange between the young man and the young woman and their conversation is full of double entendre. Their actions and their words have meanings beneath the surface. The attentive reader, especially one who knows ancient love idioms, can discern this with a little effort, but the following commentary will try to bring it out more clearly, while preserving the dignity of the language. The double entendre itself is only suggestive of sexual innuendo, so there is no need to indulge in overly graphic descriptions of the scene.

In the opening example of this double entendre, it is clear that the request that the woman open her door to let the man in suggests the desire for physical intimacy (5:2). He appeals to her while piling up terms of endearment (my treasure, my darling, my dove, my perfect one). It is also quite possible that his self-description of damp hair both gives a surface motivation for his wanting to come into her warmth and alerts us to the state of his arousal.

The woman certainly understands the sexual allusions from the man, but she is not presently ready for intimacy. In the Bible it is not uncommon for "feet" or "hands" to be used as euphemisms for male or female sex organs (see notes on 5:3 and 5:5). Her demurral that she is not ready to open the door to him is a statement that she is not willing to engage in sexual relations.

Even so, this does not stop the man from attempting to enter (5:4). A literal translation of the description of the man trying to enter reveals that there is more here than meets the eye (see note on 5:4). In any case, on all levels of reading, we see that her mind is changed and she now desires to be in the embrace of the young man. Where earlier he was wet with the dew of the night (5:2), now she is dripping with myrrh (5:5).

Inexplicably, however, he is gone! We never learn why but must assume that it is because of her initial verbal response. In such symbolic poetry, we should not look too hard for normal human motivations. The poem is making a statement about those times in an intimate relationship when only one partner is ready for physical love.

The woman's deep disappointment, as well as her new determination to pursue her lover, is expressed in 5:6. She leaves the house and goes into the city, a recurrent motif in the Song signifying forces that are inhospitable to union. Indeed, for the second time in the Song (see also 3:1-5), the woman runs into the watchmen, the ancient equivalent of the police. The watchmen are those who guard custom and propriety. And it certainly was not proper for a woman to be out in the streets at night in pursuit of a man. Once again, if we try to explain this narrative by the motivations of real life, we are at a loss. They do not question her; they simply find her, beat her, and strip her. What is especially mystifying, though, is how she responds to this severe sexual abuse without even a whimper. (The term translated veil may actually refer to an undergarment; but even if not, the forced removal of any clothing would be considered abusive.)

What is the poem saying? It is saying that not even social custom and the culture's idea of what is "right" will stand in the way of her pursuit of love.

The watchmen do not help; they only harm. She turns then to the chorus of young women of Jerusalem, who appear out of nowhere to offer their aid in the search. She makes them promise to tell the young man, should they see him first, that she is weak with love. This theme of lovesickness appears in other ancient Near Eastern love poetry as well (see note on 5:8) and is quite simply a way of expressing the intensity of her passion.

The woman's request also leads the chorus to ask a question that will segue into the next part of this long song. They ask for a description of the young man, which encourages the woman to rhapsodize about his physical beauty in yet another *wasf* (see explanation of this term in the note on 4:1-7), the first and only one where the woman speaks of the physical beauty of the man.

Typically, the descriptive poem begins with a general comment on the striking physical attractiveness of the man (5:10). He stands out in a crowd. After the general assessment, the woman then begins to compliment his appearance, beginning with his head and continuing down his body.

To say that his head is finest gold compares him to an ornate statue, perhaps of a king or even a god (5:11). In her eyes, he is more than ordinary. The man's hair is wavy and deep black. Like the woman's eyes, his eyes are also compared to a dove, a metaphor whose detail is hard to determine (see comments on 4:1). The NLT adds the comment that they sparkle in order to bring out some of the meaning possibly implicit in the image. The reference to water in connection to the eyes paints a picture of health, moist eyes being associated with life. More accessible is the image that compares his eyes to jewels washed in milk. The jewel here is clearly a reference to his pupils and the white of milk to the rest of the eye.

To understand the compliment that his cheeks are like gardens of spices, one must remember that all adult Israelite men wore beards. The garden is the beard, and these beards must have been perfumed; thus, a garden of spices is an apt image. This physical description, like the others in the Song, alludes to all the senses, not just sight. Lovemaking is an act that involves all the senses.

One might expect a taste metaphor to go with the description of his lips, but we find instead another that emphasizes smell (5:13). His lips are like lilies and they drip with myrrh, a sweet-smelling spice.

With the description of his torso and legs, we seem to return to the comparison with a statue made of precious metals and woods. His arms are gold, decorated with the precious stone beryl. The reference to gold and beryl could be a reference to his arms covered with gold bands set with jewels or else simply a way of describing how precious the man and his different parts are to the woman.

The NLT and other English translations render the next line "his body is like bright ivory, glowing with lapis lazuli" (5:14). This seems an odd progression, since "body" suggests a general comment as in 5:10 rather than the natural progression on the way to the legs at 5:15. The explanation may be found in the translators' reticence to be as specific as the text, since it is a very sensuous line. The word ivory calls to mind the tusk, and the word that the NLT translates as "body" in the general sense (me'eh [TH4578, ZH5055]) often points to the female or male erogenous zone (see note on 5:4). We have already commented on the sensuous nature of the garden fountain/spring image at the end of chapter 4. One would expect a male counterpart, and so we find it here.

The power of his legs is described by comparison to marble pillars, and the nobility of his posture by reference to the majestic and well-known cedars of Lebanon. Then, finally, she describes his mouth. Here she comments on the taste of his mouth, which of course anticipates her experience of kissing him. As we have commented before, these description poems are preludes to intimate physical touch.

At the beginning of chapter 6, the reader learns that the woman's description of the man has piqued the interest of the chorus of young women from Jerusalem. They agree to join the search. The final interchange between the chorus and the young woman is odd if judged by the standards of a real-life situation. She enlists their help to find the man, but then in answer to their question as to where they might find him, she reveals that she knows and tells them. He is in the garden. Again, we are reminded that this is not a real-life situation. It is a song that expresses emotions and, in the case of this particular poem, talks about the initial difficulty of achieving union but then (acknowledges) the power of love to overcome obstacles and find intimacy. And it is on the latter note that the poem ends. He is in the garden, and he is gathering the lilies, which is likely a reference to his enjoying the presence of the woman. She finishes by repeating the refrain that proclaims their mutual ownership of one another (2:16; 7:10).

◆ XV. Fifteenth Love Poem: An Army with Banners (6:4-10)

Young Man
4 You are beautiful, my darling,
   like the lovely city of Tirzah.
Yes, as beautiful as Jerusalem,

as majestic as an army with
   billowing banners.
5 Turn your eyes away,
   for they overpower me.

Your hair falls in waves,
  like a flock of goats winding down
    the slopes of Gilead.
6 Your teeth are as white as sheep
    that are freshly washed.
  Your smile is flawless,
    each tooth matched with its twin.*
7 Your cheeks are like rosy
    pomegranates
      behind your veil.

8 Even among sixty queens
    and eighty concubines
    and countless young women,

9 I would still choose my dove,
    my perfect one—
      the favorite of her mother,
  dearly loved by the one who bore her.
  The young women see her and praise
    her;
  even queens and royal concubines
    sing her praises:
10 "Who is this, arising like the dawn,
    as fair as the moon,
  as bright as the sun,
    as majestic as an army with
      billowing banners?"

6:6 Hebrew *Not one is missing; each has a twin.*

NOTES

6:5 *overpower.* The verb is a hiphil from *rahab* [TH7292, ZH8104] and can mean "overpower," "excite," or "unsettle" (see NIDOTTE 3:1063-1066).

6:7 **Your cheeks are like rosy pomegranates.** The verse in Heb. describes the woman's temples (the likely meaning of the Heb. *raqqah* [TH7541, ZH8377]), not her cheeks, as like pomegranates, though the NLT is likely right in implying that the reference to the fruit is a comment on the woman's complexion. The adjective "rosy" is not found in the Heb., but is added in the translation to help modern readers get a sense of what the comparison with pomegranates is intended to communicate. See note on 4:3.

COMMENTARY

In the fifteenth love poem of the collection, the man praises the woman for her outstanding beauty. Through a series of metaphors, as well as a short section of a "descriptive song" (*wasf*), the man tells his beloved that she far surpasses any other woman in his eyes.

The man begins in this poem by simply stating that his darling is beautiful, and then compares her beauty to two cities. That the man chooses cities with which to compare the beauty of the woman at all is rather surprising. After all, throughout the Song there has been a theme wherein cities are contrasted with the cultivated countryside, the former being a locale that is hostile to intimacy and love, and the latter being conducive to it. However, in this case, cities are not the setting where love is developing; they are envisioned from a distance, and it is the physical attraction of the cities that is relevant. And who can deny it? Very few things rivet the attention as much as a city. Of course, modern cities are not quite like ancient cities, but since we have only the modern experience, we may start with an experience such as many of us have had. We are driving along the highway when a large city's impressive skyline suddenly appears on the horizon. You might think of New York or Seattle or imagine passengers in a plane at take-off getting a beautiful aerial view of San Francisco and its harbor with the Golden Gate Bridge in the background. Although these experiences are not quite like the ancient one, they mirror the effect of taking the long walk to Jerusalem and coming over the Mount of Olives to see that magnificent city with its walls, Temple, and other massive public buildings. The view would indeed have been riveting, sending shivers up the spine.

Since we know little about Tirzah, we tend to focus our attention on Jerusalem. Tirzah was evidently a great and beautiful city in its own right—for a short period it was the capital of the northern kingdom. Some even think that this bit of information helps us date this particular poem to the time when Tirzah was the capital, which would be during the time of King Jeroboam in the tenth century BC (1 Kgs 14:17; 15:21, 33; 16:6, 8, 15, 17, 23), but there is not enough evidence to say this with confidence. The name Tirzah means "pleasant," and perhaps that is explanation enough for its choice here, along with the fact that it may well have lived up to its name. In any case, we note that the actual progression in the verse is from Tirzah to Jerusalem, and this is a clear heightening within the parallel line. In Hebrew poetry, the second line almost always intensifies the idea expressed in the first.

By contrast, verse 4 climaxes not with the name of a third city but with another comparison, and one that is quite unexpected. The man compares the woman to an army with billowing banners. (For more about military imagery in love poetry, see Schroeder 1996 and Meyers 1986.) The banners are likely references to battle standards of some sort. The NLT makes explicit what the translators believe is the main point of the comparison: majesty. Indeed, an army assembled for war with banners at the lead is a picture of power. Such a display can elicit fear—not only from the enemy but also from all who look at it. The woman's beauty captures the man's attention in a way that makes his knees knock. (For a different view on this verse, see Long 1996.) That these images intend to express that the man is overcome by the woman's beauty is stated plainly in 6:5. He cannot stand her gaze—not because it is repulsive but because it is just the opposite. As he looks into her eyes, he is overcome with her beauty. As we look into the eyes of another person, we not only see physical beauty, we also look into his or her soul.

Contemplating the man's experience and taking into account the many allusions to the Garden of Eden in the Song (see the Introduction), we might remember here what happened in the Garden in Genesis 3: Because of their transgression, neither Adam nor Eve could stand freely in the gaze of the other. They quickly covered themselves. As Adam felt Eve looking at him, he became aware of his imperfections and sought to hide them from her. Perhaps as the poem reflects the common human experience of being uncomfortable in another person's gaze, it picks up on this idea. However, we should not miss the main, positive point the man is making: her beauty is so great that he needs a break from it so that he does not faint from overexposure!

At this point, he describes her beauty in a short descriptive poem. Interestingly, this poem is virtually identical to 4:1-3, a portion of the longer descriptive poem found in 4:1-7. Since these sections are so similar, there will be an understandable overlap between my comments here and there.

The man begins by complimenting the woman's hair. It is like a flock of goats streaming down Mount Gilead. Gilead refers to the region in central Transjordan around the Jabbok River gorge. Gilead is a stunningly beautiful area. The idea of a mountain suggests a head, and the goats that descend (probably having black coats) suggest hair. Although some mischievous readers have thought about single lines of sheep coming down the mountain and commented that the comparison suggests that she was balding, this is clearly not the intent of the compliment.

Verse 6, which turns attention to the woman's teeth, also sounds humorous from a modern perspective, reminding us that we need to put ourselves in the position of the original readers to best understand the Song. That is, we must remember that ancient peoples did not have the same expertise in dental care that we have today. To compliment the woman's white teeth is indeed a compliment and may be compared to the nineteenth-century English/American compliment about a person's "pearly white teeth." However, modern men should beware doing what the ancient Israelite lover literally does here—that is, say that none of his beloved's teeth are missing (cf. 6:6, NLT mg). Indeed, a person giving such an ill-considered compliment may find some of his own teeth missing as a result! This simply reminds us that beauty is culturally bound, and furthermore, it is in the eye of the beholder.

We may also be a bit mystified by his comment about her temples (NLT "cheeks," see note on 6:7). These are behind her veil, implying that the veil covers her entire face. The pomegranate is a reddish-orange fruit; and since women of the region were dark-skinned, the comparison probably indicates a desired skin color. Again, beauty is in the eye of the beholder; and in the eyes of the man, the woman's skin was beautiful and enticing. The passage does not designate any skin color as the most beautiful but simply reflects the man's appreciation of what God has created.

After the "descriptive poem," the man proclaims in yet another way the woman's incomparable beauty (6:8-9). The form of this compliment is foreign to modern readers. He says that she is outstanding in comparison to sixty queens, eighty concubines, and countless young women. In order to understand the force of this compliment, we must first of all realize that these three classes of women—queens, concubines, and young women—represent all the options available to a king. Queens are primary wives with the most rights, concubines are secondary wives, and then the Hebrew word for young women ('almah [TH5959, ZH6625]) stands for all those women who are marriageable and therefore available to the king. Second, the modern reader needs to understand that this verse is built on an ancient form of poetry called numerical parallelism. We see it in Proverbs in the form x, $x + 1$, for instance: "There are three [= x] things that make the earth tremble—no, four [= $x + 1$] it cannot endure: a slave who becomes a king, an overbearing fool who prospers, a bitter woman who finally gets a husband, a servant girl who supplants her mistress" (Prov 30:21-23). The intention of the verse is not that there are exactly four things but that there are a large number. The same may be seen even more clearly in Amos (e.g., Amos 1:3), where the poet will condemn a city for three, yea four sins, but then list two. In other words, this compliment moves from sixty to eighty and then on to countless numbers of young women. This woman is number one out of all women of all classes.

We press the imagery too far if we take this reference in a literal way and say that the poet has to be Solomon, and the young Solomon at that—though we do know that at his height he had 700 queens and 300 concubines (1 Kgs 11:3). As we have already argued, the Song is not about Solomon or any actual king but uses royal imagery to enhance the prestige of the lovers. In modern Arab wedding poetry, the young bride and groom are king and queen for the day. Even in modern America, ordinary brides and grooms are transformed into something very special for their wedding day. Likewise, the man here does not actually have the many queens and concubines of a king (the references in 6:9 are similarly poetic).

The woman's mother confirms the man's choice (6:9). The mother is the one who has instructed her daughter in the ways of intimate relationship (see note on 8:2), and this girl has learned from the best. Not only that, but her rivals, mentioned in a different order—young women, queens, and concubines—actually acknowledge her superiority by praising her.

The poem climaxes with the type of rhetorical question that we saw in 3:6 and which we will revisit in 8:5. The question form grabs the attention of its hearers or readers and gets their minds involved. Who, indeed, is this? It is the woman, of course. She is described again by comparison. She arises like the dawn, bringing light to the darkness. She is the one who renews all things with hope. She is like the moon and the sun that dominate the night and day sky, respectively, with their brilliance. Finally, the poem ends as it began with the military comparison to a majestic army with its billowing banners.

◆ XVI. Sixteenth Love Poem: In the Nut Grove (6:11–12)

¹¹ I went down to the grove of walnut trees
and out to the valley to see the new spring growth,
to see whether the grapevines had budded
or the pomegranates were in bloom.
¹² Before I realized it,
I found myself in the royal chariot with my beloved.*

6:12 Or *among the royal chariots of my people*, or *among the chariots of Amminadab*. The meaning of the Hebrew is uncertain.

NOTES

6:11 *grove of walnut trees.* The Heb. word *'egoz* [TH93, ZH100] certainly means "nut" and perhaps, as suggested by the NLT, specifically the walnut. No matter what type of grove, the point made in the expository section of the commentary about cultivated countryside settings being connected with the theme of intimate union still stands. However, Pope (1978:574-578) takes the point further, by commenting that there is a connection between the nut and the genitalia of both men and women: the whole nut represents the male gland, and the open nut, the woman's vulva. Even apart from the imagery of the nut, the verse as a whole is a coy suggestion of intimate relations between the man and the woman.

COMMENTARY

The connection of these two verses to what precedes and follows is a matter of debate. In other words, my Poem Sixteen could be a continuation of Poem Fifteen or the beginning of Poem Seventeen, but there are no compelling connections with either. For this reason, I treat these two verses separately. Even if this assessment is wrong and these two verses belong to one of the other poems, it really makes no major difference to our understanding of the message of the text, since we are concerned with the exposition of the images and themes and the description of the emotions expressed, rather than being intent on recovering an elusive plot line (see Introduction).

In these verses, the woman is speaking, and she is sharing an experience. She talks about going into the grove of walnut trees and examining the new spring growth. By this time in the Song, we are well aware of the meaning of such a setting. While the city is hostile to love, any type of garden or cultivated countryside setting is conducive to intimacy. The time period specified is spring, which is a time perennially associated with love. After all, the spring follows the winter. It is a time to remove clothes, not put them on. It is a time of new fertility, also suggestive of sexuality. Spring brings wonderful fragrances into play, particularly in the garden. Indeed, this poem describes the woman as going down to see the new buds and blossoms of particularly fragrant plants like the grape and the pomegranate. Grapes and pomegranates also are edible fruits that suggest another sense, that of taste. As we have seen throughout the Song, love is an emotion that expresses itself in physical union involving all the senses.

Thus far everything is as we might expect in this short love poem. However, when we come to verse 12, we encounter an exegetical conundrum that has occupied the attention and the imagination of professional interpreters for centuries. The ancient versions, such as the Greek Septuagint and the Latin Vulgate, as well as some modern English versions (NIV, NRSV) may be compared in order to see that neither interpreters nor translators can agree on the meaning here. Even an attempt at a literal translation is difficult because there are questions about the meaning of the words, as well as their syntactical relationship. (For all the technical issues concerning this matter, see Longman 2001:184-187).

The NLT's attempt at translating this verse is as defensible as any other and more defensible than some. But if it is correct, what does it mean? We should be very hesitant to press too many of the verse's details for meaning (see Mulder 1992). The first colon of the verse ("before I realized it") expresses surprise and perhaps some confusion. Her surprise comes with the fact that she is with her beloved and in his royal chariot. Here, as throughout, we must remember that this is poetry that expresses emotions and not the report of an actual experience. If it were the latter, we would be really hard pressed to explain how she could so abruptly find herself transported from the grove of walnut trees to the chariot of the man she loves. She is in a reverie. The royal chariot perhaps ought to be compared to the "carriage" of 3:7-10. She is alone with her man, and her statement here expresses her strong passion for him.

◆ **XVII. Seventeenth Love Poem: The Dancing Shulammite (6:13–7:9)**

Young Women of Jerusalem
¹³*Return, return to us, O maid of
   Shulam.
   Come back, come back, that we may
   see you again.

Young Man
   Why do you stare at this young
   woman of Shulam,
   as she moves so gracefully between
   two lines of dancers?*

CHAPTER 7
¹*How beautiful are your sandaled
   feet,
   O queenly maiden.
   Your rounded thighs are like jewels,
   the work of a skilled craftsman.
²Your navel is perfectly formed
   like a goblet filled with mixed wine.
   Between your thighs lies a mound of
   wheat
   bordered with lilies.
³Your breasts are like two fawns,
   twin fawns of a gazelle.
⁴Your neck is as beautiful as an ivory
   tower.

Your eyes are like the sparkling pools
   in Heshbon
   by the gate of Bath-rabbim.
Your nose is as fine as the tower
   of Lebanon
   overlooking Damascus.
⁵Your head is as majestic as Mount
   Carmel,
   and the sheen of your hair radiates
   royalty.
   The king is held captive by its
   tresses.
⁶Oh, how beautiful you are!
   How pleasing, my love, how full
   of delights!
⁷You are slender like a palm tree,
   and your breasts are like its clusters
   of fruit.
⁸I said, "I will climb the palm tree
   and take hold of its fruit."
   May your breasts be like grape
   clusters,
   and the fragrance of your breath
   like apples.
⁹May your kisses be as exciting as the
   best wine,
   flowing gently over lips and teeth.*

6:13a Verse 6:13 is numbered 7:1 in Hebrew text.   6:13b Or *as you would at the movements of two armies?* or *as you would at the dance of Mahanaim?* The meaning of the Hebrew is uncertain.   7:1 Verses 7:1-13 are numbered 7:2-14 in Hebrew text.   7:9 As in Greek and Syriac versions and Latin Vulgate; Hebrew reads *over lips of sleepers.*

NOTES

6:13 [7:1] Return, return. As mentioned below, the question that is raised by this rendition is "From where?" It is possible for the root *shub* [TH7725, ZH8740] to have the meaning "turn around," and perhaps they are simply asking her to twirl around just to get a full look at her beauty or to twirl around in the dance that may be alluded to at the end of the verse.

Shulam. That the word is an epithet is seen from the fact that it has the definite article connected to it. Some, like Pope (1978:598-599) and Albright (1931-1932), mistakenly connected this name with that of a Mesopotamian deity. A better hypothesis associates the name with a town named Shunem, since in Semitic languages there is often attested an interchange between the letter "n" and the letter "l." Those who see a connection with Shunem also point out that Abishag, David's young wife in his old age (1 Kgs 1:1-4; 2:17), came from this city. However, the best hypothesis for the significance of the name Shulam is in its similarity to Solomon and the connection of both names with the Heb. word *shalom* [TH7965, ZH8934], meaning "peace" or "wholeness."

as she moves so gracefully between two lines of dancers? The NLT mg indicates how uncertain the translation of this colon is. The second marginal alternative ("as you would at the dance of Mahanaim"), though accepted by the NIV, is not likely because it treats the final word as a place name rather than as a noun. Much more likely than either of the others is the first marginal alternative ("as you would at the movements of two armies"), a rendering which would compare the mesmerizing effect of the Shulammite's movements, perhaps dance movements, with that of two armies engaged in battle.

7:2 [3] *Between your thighs.* Lit., the reference is to the woman's belly; but the metaphor, plus the location in the *wasf* description, is such that I think this is a reference to the woman's vulva. Thus, the NLT mirrors the indirect reference to this most sensitive of locations of a woman's body.

7:4-5 [5-6] *beautiful . . . sparkling . . . fine . . . majestic.* These adjectives are not found explicitly in the Heb., but the metaphors suggest the connection, so the NLT supplies them.

7:4 [5] *Heshbon . . . Bath-rabbim . . . Lebanon . . . Damascus.* These four geographical locations all appear to be outside the land of Israel proper (in the case of Bath-rabbim this is an assumption, since we cannot locate it with certainty, though Brenner [1992] associates it with the Ammonite city Rabbah, which was near Heshbon). Heshbon is a location on the east side of the Dead Sea, while Lebanon and Damascus are north of Israel. We know that Lebanon and Damascus were locations of exceptional physical beauty, and we conjecture that Heshbon and Bath-rabbim were as well.

7:5 [6] *the sheen of your hair radiates royalty.* The Heb. has "the hair of your head is like purple." The NLT communicates the sense of the passage, though, because purple was considered the color of royalty.

7:7 [8] *slender.* This word does not occur in the Heb. but is implied by the metaphor of the palm tree.

7:9 [10] *May your kisses be as exciting as the best wine.* Again, the NLT makes explicit what is implicit in the metaphor, which states, "may your palette be like fine wine."

COMMENTARY

The seventeenth poem begins with a request on the part of the young women of Jerusalem that the maid of Shulam return to them. One question that this request evokes in the reader's mind is, "Return from where?" It is possible that this poem is a continuation of the previous poem and that they are asking her to return from the chariot of her lover who has carried her off. But why would they want her to return from the bliss of that relationship? Nowhere else have they shown themselves to be obstacles to her union with the man. If this is a start of a new poem, then the question "from where" is irrelevant, and the Hebrew may actually be rendered "turn around, turn around" and be a request for her to twirl around in dance. The request is simply a statement of good feeling. Everyone loves her, and they all want to be with her (see Munro 1995:31 for the highly speculative view that the chorus here is male).

A second question that this request raises concerns the manner of address directed toward the woman. The woman is called the "maid of Shulam" for the first and only time in the Song. Throughout the rest of the book, she is simply unnamed, referred to by various terms of endearment (such as "treasure," "bride," and "perfect one"). It is this verse that provides what little justification there is for the widespread habit of referring to the woman of the Song as Shulammite. (For some detail concerning alternative understandings of the title, see the note on 6:13.). However, in the final analysis, we can fathom where the name comes from when we remember the only named male in the Song. Solomon, in Hebrew, is pronounced "Shlomo." Both Solomon and Shulammite are names derived from the Hebrew root *shalom*, meaning "wholeness" or "peace." It is no accident that these names contain the meaning of the word that expresses the consequence of the union between the man and the woman. In their intimacy, they achieve a wholeness that brings great peace or contentment.

The second part of 6:13 asks a question, but the text does not betray its speaker. The NLT assigns the question to the young man, but this, to be honest, seems odd. Why would the man ask such a question? He knows why people would want to stare at this maid of Shulam. She is captivating—overpowering! The question more likely comes from the woman. The fact that she speaks of herself in the third person presents no problem. We are to imagine the question asked with a tone of quiet humility. This explanation at least makes good sense of the first part of the question: "Why do you stare at this young woman of Shulam?" However, the real difficulty comes with the last colon. I disagree with the NLT rendering here and think that the better translation is in the footnote: "Why do you stare at this young woman of Shulam as you would at the movements of two armies?" (6:13b, NLT mg). The idea is that she notices their mesmerized looks, and she wonders what the reason for such intense interest is. Their attention is riveted as if they were watching the clash of two rival armies on a battlefield below them. We have already seen the Song liken the woman's attention-grabbing beauty to things associated with the military (see commentary on 6:4). If we understand the question as that of the woman, then when the young man starts speaking, as he does without doubt, at the beginning of chapter 7, we can see his description of her as an answer to her question.

Chapter 7 begins with a form that we are now very familiar with in the Song, the *wasf* or descriptive poem (see note on 4:1-7). This poem is different, however, in that it starts the description not with her head but with her feet. This suggests to some (including the translators of the NLT) that the woman is dancing as she is being described. Whatever the reason, the man finds his attention focused first on the woman's sandaled feet, and then moves up to her rounded thighs. When he compliments her thighs as the work of a skilled craftsman, there may be a metaphor at work, at least in this verse, comparing her to a perfectly sculpted statue.

The next verse is particularly sensuous as it works up from her thighs to her "navel." Following Pope, I think "navel" here should be understood as "vagina" (for an extended discussion of the argument, see Longman 2001:194-195). One point is that this "navel" is a well-lubricated place, suggested by the simile that it is like a goblet filled with wine. Although in the second part of the verse, some versions weakly suggest that the mound of wheat is the woman's belly, the image actually points to the most intimate place on a woman's body (see note on 7:2). The NLT appropriately and delicately suggests this by its rendering "between your thighs." The meaning of this second line reinforces the idea communicated in the first. These poems are preludes to lovemaking.

The man continues his upward trend and next describes her breasts. The description here is a shortened form of that which is found in 4:5, and the commentary there should be consulted for the full sense of the image. However, we are reminded briefly that the mention of fawns of a gazelle evoke a pastoral scene that is conducive to love. The fuller description in 4:5 indicates that we should find the connection between the fawns and the woman's breasts in the animal's rounded rears with their nipple-like tails.

From the woman's breasts, the man's description ascends to her face by means of her neck. The architectural image here is that of a tower, again a military figure (see 6:4, 10), suggesting dignity and power. This tower is constructed from ivory, a precious and smooth material. Arriving at the woman's face, he first comments on her eyes. Like the man's eyes in 5:12, their moistness is highlighted by reference to water, in this case the pools of Heshbon near the gate of Bath-rabbim. The reference seems proverbial, but we have no similar references elsewhere. Heshbon, located on the east side of the Dead Sea, was a beautiful area, but we cannot be more specific.

Today, the image of the nose as a tower that overlooks Damascus might cause people to snicker, but such a reaction would not be sensitive to its original intentions. This is a compliment and surely signifies majesty and dignity. Lebanon, as throughout, may invite the thought of fragrant smells, since Lebanon is famed for its cedars. Damascus is mentioned as the leading city of this area, just to the north of the Promised Land.

To complete his description of the woman's physical beauty, the man finally praises her head and hair. He likens her head to Mount Carmel. This refers to the magnificent range that juts out into the Mediterranean, located in northern Israel, just south of modern Haifa. Her hair literally is described as purple, but the NLT rightly captures the sense, since purple is a color reserved for royalty. It is not that she has literally dyed her hair purple but, according to the man, her hair marks her as a queen, and he, totally captivated by her, has become her king. This king, however, is powerless before her, as he has become obsessed with her beauty.

He finishes the *wasf* in the same way that we have seen earlier, with a general assertion of her beauty (7:6), but then he continues in a new direction. The other *wasf* may have implied action, but in this poem, he describes how he will now act on his love for her. He first evokes another image to describe her: the palm tree and its fruits. The palm tree is slender; its fruit, therefore, stands out all the more. The fruit clusters are appropriately likened to her breasts, and his intention to make love to her is described as his climbing up her palm-like body and fondling her fruit-like breasts. Her breath smells pleasant and refreshing like apples. Elsewhere in the Song, the apple tree is also used in connection with the lovers' intimacy (8:5). Her kisses taste like wine. His intimate union with her excites all of his senses.

◆ XVIII. Eighteenth Love Poem: I Will Give You My Love (7:10–13)

Young Woman
¹⁰I am my lover's,
    and he claims me as his own.
¹¹Come, my love, let us go out to the
    fields
    and spend the night among the
    wildflowers.*
¹²Let us get up early and go to the
    vineyards
    to see if the grapevines have budded,

if the blossoms have opened,
    and if the pomegranates have
    bloomed.
There I will give you my love.
¹³There the mandrakes give off their
    fragrance,
    and the finest fruits are at our door,
new delights as well as old,
    which I have saved for you, my
    lover.

7:11 Or *in the villages.*

NOTES

7:10 [11] *he claims me as his own.* Lit., "his desire is for me." The word desire (*teshuqah* [TH8669, ZH9592]) is of interest here. It only appears two other places in the Bible, the other two times in Genesis. It is clear that in Gen 4:7 the desire is negative; that is, sin desires to dominate Cain. The other occurrence is in the context of the Fall and is also likely negative when it says that the woman's desire will be for her husband (Gen 3:16). The present context is clearly positive, and the common idea is that all three occurrences express a strong desire, urging, or longing (see Foh 1974–1975).

7:11 [12] *wildflowers.* There is a debate over the meaning of this Heb. word. The NLT follows those who connect it to *koper* [TH3724B, ZH4110], which refers to the henna flower. But there is also a Heb. term *kapar* [TH3723/TH3723A, ZH4099/ZH4107], which means "villages." Many commentators (including Longman 2001:199) prefer the latter, but even if this is the correct reading, the effect of the poem remains the same since lovemaking takes place in cultivated countryside settings, whether gardens or villages. It is the city that is a hostile setting to love.

7:13 [14] *mandrakes.* The mandrake may be mentioned here because of its purported value as an aphrodisiac. Note the role of the mandrake in the episode between Rachel and Leah in Gen 30:14-16. Interestingly, the word for mandrake (*duda'im* [TH1736, ZH1859]) looks as though it is related to a common word for "lover" in the Heb. of the Song of Songs (*dod* [TH1730, ZH1856]).

new delights . . . old. The Heb. does not have "delights," which is supplied by the NLT translators to provide the reference with some substance. This seems appropriate and does capture the sense, but a question remains: why *new and old* delights? This is likely a merism, a literary device that cites opposite poles of a dichotomy in order to signify "all" or "everything." She has saved up every delight that she knows of for her lover.

COMMENTARY

This short poem has the woman expressing her desire for intimate union with the man. It is a monologue by the woman, who invites the man into the joys of their relationship. Many of the themes and motifs of this relatively short poem are already well established by this point in the Song, but they are used in new and engaging ways.

The poem opens with a variation of what we have already seen in 2:16 and 6:3. It is an expression of mutual affection, and the similarities among these three verses suggest that they function as a kind of refrain in the Song. The thought of this refrain is one of mutual ownership.

She then urges the man to join her in the countryside. Many times, as early as 1:6, we have observed how the cultivated countryside, its fields and gardens in particular, are the location of intimate physical relationship—in contrast to the city, a location hostile to union. The invitation, then, to go to the garden, is more than an invitation to tour of the botany of the region. This may be seen, too, in the fact that she desires to spend the night there. Nighttime settings, like countryside locales, heighten the privacy of the liaison.

The reference to budding, blooming, and the opening of blossoms is a way to communicate that the time is also conducive to love. It is springtime, and all the plant fragrances are in the air. She asserts that she will give him her love (7:12). "Love" is at least intended to indicate an emotion but also suggests more: she will surrender her body to him in love. By now in the Song, we are also well acquainted with the woman as the initiator in the relationship (cf. 1:2-4, 7-11). In this poem, she is the one who pursues the man, thus debunking any stereotype of the passive woman.

◆ XIX. Nineteenth Love Poem: Yearning for Love (8:1–4)

Young Woman
  Oh, I wish you were my brother,
    who nursed at my mother's breasts.
  Then I could kiss you no matter who
    was watching,
    and no one would criticize me.
²I would bring you to my childhood
    home,
    and there you would teach me.*

  I would give you spiced wine to drink,
    my sweet pomegranate wine.
³Your left arm would be under my head,
    and your right arm would embrace
    me.

⁴Promise me, O women of Jerusalem,
    not to awaken love until the time
    is right.*

8:2 Or *there she will teach me;* or *there she bore me.*   8:4 Or *not to awaken love until it is ready.*

NOTES
8:2 *to my childhood home.* Lit., "to the house of my mother." The NLT's idiomatic translation in this case loses sight of the fact that it is specifically the mother who is mentioned, and this may be important in light of the social customs of the day. The mother was likely responsible for teaching young girls how to behave in love relationships—that is, how to be a mother and wife (cf. 3:4; 6:9).

there you would teach me. The Heb. verb is grammatically ambiguous and could mean "you will teach" or "she will teach." The rendering in the NLT mg, "there she will teach me," is preferable to that in the text and gives the idea that the mother teaches the daughter in the ways of love and sexuality.

COMMENTARY
The first poem of the final chapter of the book begins with the woman expressing a desire that is hard for modern interpreters to explain for a couple of reasons. She

says she wishes her lover could also be her brother so they could publicly display their affection for one another. In the first place, if we are honest, we really do not know the social customs of the Old Testament time period very well; and further, such things as marriage and dating customs surely developed and changed over the near millennium during which the Old Testament came into existence. What was the relationship like between a husband and wife, between a boyfriend and girl-friend, or between a brother and sister? A second difficulty in understanding the woman's desire is our uncertainty about the status of her relationship with the man. Are we to think of them as married or courting? The rest of this poem expresses an intensity of physical relationship that would make us think the former, but was it really the case that a man and a wife could not be seen kissing in public? We simply do not have conclusive information regarding these questions.

Even with our remaining questions, we can surely appreciate that this poem is a strong expression of the woman's love for the man and her desire to give herself to him completely.

Once we get beyond these initial difficulties presented by our lack of knowledge of social relationships at the time the poems were written, we are struck with an-other question. Why does she want to bring her lover back to her childhood home, literally "the house of her mother" (see note on 8:2)? I doubt that many modern readers could resonate with this expression. In the context of seeking physical inti-macy, she wants to go home to her mother's house and embrace him! Though there is much we cannot explain due to our lack of knowledge about ancient social cus-toms, it appears that the mother was the one who instructed her daughter in matters of love and relationships (see note on 8:2). The inclusion of the girl's mother in the setting, then, is fitting for the romantic situation.

The woman next expresses her intention of giving her lover spiced wine—sweet pomegranate wine—to drink. By this point in the Song, we are well acquainted with wine as a cipher for love (as early as 1:2). Wine intoxicates, as does love and the physical touch between two people who are in love. That a physical embrace is meant here may be seen plainly in the next verse (8:3), which repeats a refrain that has served to bind Song of Songs together as a whole (2:6). This refrain is followed by the third and last admonition to the chorus of young girls not to move toward love prematurely (8:4; cf. 2:7; 3:5). As they look on the relationship between the man and the woman, they will desire its passion; but they must beware, because love is a dangerous emotion, not to be initiated prematurely (Schwab 1999).

◆ XX. Twentieth Love Poem: Love More Powerful than Death (8:5-7)

Young Women of Jerusalem
⁵Who is this sweeping in from the desert,
leaning on her lover?

Young Woman
I aroused you under the apple tree,
where your mother gave you birth,
where in great pain she delivered you.

⁶ Place me like a seal over your heart,
   like a seal on your arm.
For love is as strong as death,
   its jealousy* as enduring as the
      grave.*
Love flashes like fire,

the brightest kind of flame.
⁷ Many waters cannot quench love,
   nor can rivers drown it.
If a man tried to buy love
   with all his wealth,
   his offer would be utterly scorned.

8:6a Or *its passion.*   **8:6b** Hebrew *as Sheol.*

NOTES

8:5 *gave you birth.* The verb *khabal* [TH2254C, ZH2473] here translated "gave you birth" may rather mean "conceived you." The ambiguity in the meaning of the verb is discussed in NIDOTTE 2:12. However, the parallelism (which typically intensifies the thought of the first colon, or poetic line) would suggest a progression from arousal (first colon) to conception (second colon) to birth (third colon). Such a picture lingers on the mother's act of intimacy before moving to birth and thus heightens the romantic feeling of the image.

8:6 *brightest kind of flame.* The issue that surrounds the translation of this phrase is the particle *yah* [TH3050, ZH3363] at the end of the word for "flame." Some see here a reference to the name of God, a shortened form of Yahweh. If this is the case, the translation would be "a flame of Yahweh." The NLT is surely right, however—particularly in this book that does not mention the name of God—to take it as a superlative (cf. similar uses of God's name in Gen 23:6; Isa 51:3; Jonah 3:3).

COMMENTARY

The chorus opens the poem with a question that is similar to an earlier passage. They ask for the identity of the woman who is leaning on her lover. The reference is certainly to the young woman, and she speaks for the remainder of the poem; but instead of speaking to the chorus, she speaks again to the man.

This poem is one of the most famous of the book because of its imagery and the intensity of its expression. She begins by reminding the man of her effect on him. She has aroused him under the apple tree. The apple tree has earlier been used as a location of lovemaking in the Song (see the appearance of the apple tree and its fruit in 2:3, 5; 7:8). The apple tree evokes the pastoral countryside setting, which, in the Song, is conducive to love. The fertility of this specific tree makes it particularly evocative of love, and the fragrance of its apples and buds also makes it a particularly happy locale for intimacy.

We are not to understand 8:5 as historically factual—that is, that there is a specific apple tree in view that was the place where the man was born. No, the image captures the idea that just as the young woman was trained by her mother in matters of love (see previous poem), so too the man follows in a tradition of lovemaking. This reference to giving birth, interestingly enough, is the only place where the reproductive consequences of lovemaking are made at all explicit. The emphasis throughout the poem is on the romantic nature of physical intimacy, not on its utilitarian consequences.

In 8:6-7 the woman expresses the strength of the emotion of her love toward the man. Again, up to this point in the Song, the emphasis has been on the physical expression of love. But here, we observe just how intense the emotion of love is. It is like a seal. The seal was a common way of ascribing the ownership of things in the ancient Near East. The most common type of seal in ancient Israel was the stamp seal. The stamp seal would have a symbol and often a name written on it. By pressing it firmly on wet clay, the seal would leave an impression that showed who owned an object like a jar or who was responsible for the writing of a letter (see Hallo 1985 and Hallo 1993).

Modern men and women sometimes find this image of "ownership" objectionable because it treats a man or a woman as an object. This is not the woman's perspective. She rejoices in the thought that she might belong to the man, most likely because she understands that his desire is to be equally owned by her. That the seal would be pressed on heart and arm is surely a way of saying on his whole person, both inner and outer—thoughts and actions.

The woman then talks almost philosophically about love. Love, and certainly her love for him, is stronger than death, even more enduring than the grave (8:6). This is a very strong statement, considering just how powerful death is (Eccl 2:13-15; 3:19; 6:1-2). Indeed, in the ancient Near East, death was often personified as a god of great power. Here, the woman boldly asserts that her love is stronger than death. It is, in other words, irresistible, resolute, and unshakable.

But what about jealousy? Isn't jealousy a negative emotion? Not always, at least in the Bible. Jealousy is the energy that propels a person to protect a relationship that is in danger. It is only appropriately expressed in a relationship that admits only one partner, like marriage, and it should only be expressed in positive and non-violent ways, but it is not to be condemned as always destructive or evil (see discussion of jealousy in Allender and Longman 1993:107-132).

The woman then compares love to another mighty force, namely fire. Fire symbolizes passion, and this is the brightest kind of flame. It is a flame that cannot be quenched by "many waters." The deeper significance of the waters here is probably hidden from modern readers: The mythologies of the ancient Near East frequently represent the powers of chaos in the world as flood waters, often using the equivalent of the expression "mighty waters" to refer to these powers. Thus, she is saying that the power of love can stand up to even the mighty powers of chaos in the universe.

Finally, she states that love is so powerful that it cannot be demeaned by wealth. Just because someone has money, that does not mean they can buy another person's love (8:7).

◆ XXI. Twenty-first Love Poem: Protecting the Sister (8:8-10)

The Young Woman's Brothers
⁸ We have a little sister
     too young to have breasts.
   What will we do for our sister

if someone asks to marry her?
⁹ If she is a virgin, like a wall,
     we will protect her with a silver
        tower.

But if she is promiscuous, like
   a swinging door,
we will block her door with
   a cedar bar.

Young Woman
¹⁰I was a virgin, like a wall;
   now my breasts are like towers.
When my lover looks at me,
   he is delighted with what he sees.

NOTES

8:8 too young to have breasts. Lit., "she has no breasts." The NLT certainly captures the sense of the phrase, which is pointing to their perception that the young woman is physically and emotionally immature and needs their protection.

if someone asks to marry her? The Heb. says "on the day she is spoken for?" Again, the NLT rightly understands the phrase as a reference to the day that she is spoken for in marriage.

8:9 virgin . . . promiscuous. These two words are not in the Heb., but are the NLT's correct explanation of the meaning of the metaphors of "wall" and "door."

8:10 I was a virgin, like a wall. The Heb. has no verb here. The NLT has interpreted the comment as past, which presumes passage of time between verses 9 and 10. But most (REB, NAB, NJB, NIV, HCSB) take the verb as present ("I am a virgin, like a wall") and see this as an immediate response to the brothers' comments (see commentary below).

he is delighted with what he sees. The Heb. lit. says that in his eyes she is "like one who brings/finds peace" (*shalom* [TH7965, ZH8934]). Earlier, in the Seventeenth Love Poem, we commented on the role of the root *shalem* [TH7999A, ZH8971] in Song of Songs. Here the consequence of her relationship with the man is *shalom*—"peace," "wholeness," or "contentedness."

COMMENTARY

The twenty-first poem is a brief one of only three verses. In my opinion, the NLT should have placed a space between verses 10 and 11, indicating the break between poems, but I readily admit that the break is not a crystal clear one. This poem intends to be somewhat humorous, but it also makes a serious point.

The young woman's brothers have been mentioned as early as chapter 1, but they have not spoken until this poem. In their speech, they display their obvious concern for their sister. In particular, they indicate a desire to protect the sexuality of their sister, a function of brothers that seems to be attested elsewhere (see 1:6). The brothers speak not to the sister, but to an unnamed party. Perhaps we are to understand the addressees to be ourselves, the readers. In any case, the brothers describe their sister as immature. She is too young to have breasts. They ask how they might care for their sister in anticipation of a marriage proposal.

The answer is given, but it seems as if the brothers are answering their own question. The NLT gives an interpretation of the images that follow (see notes above) in a way that makes them easy to understand. There are two possible scenarios. If she is a wall, that is, sexually impenetrable in her chastity, then they will build a silver tower on that wall. The NLT takes the silver tower as a metaphor of protection. This is likely right, but I should also point out the fact that since the tower is silver, this likely indicates that they are also rewarding her for right behavior. However, if she is a door (see Hicks 1987), which the NLT rightly understands as a metaphor for promiscuity, then they will take steps to rein her in. They will keep her from opening herself sexually to others.

Now the woman speaks, and the humor of the passage is found in the contrast between the brothers' perception and their sister's perception. First of all, she puts their minds to rest (and perhaps she says this with some contempt at her brothers' doubts) and states that she is a virgin (that is, like a wall). Then second, she proclaims her maturity by denying her brother's presumed contention that she has no breasts by saying that her breasts are large indeed—like towers.

As a mature virgin, she knows that she is one who will bring enjoyment and happiness to her lover, to the one who will ask her to marry him.

◆ XXII. Twenty-second Love Poem: The Owner of the Vineyard (8:11-12)

¹¹Solomon has a vineyard at Baal-hamon,
  which he leases out to tenant
    farmers.
Each of them pays a thousand pieces
  of silver*
for harvesting its fruit.

¹²But my vineyard is mine to give,
  and Solomon need not pay a
    thousand pieces of silver.
But I will give two hundred
  pieces
to those who care for its vines.

8:11 Hebrew *1,000 shekels of silver.*

NOTES

8:11 Baal-hamon. This appears to be a geographical location, but we do not know it outside of this reference. It could be an actual place where Solomon was known to have vineyards. According to Snaith (1993:126-127), Jdt 8:3 mentions a place called Baalmon, possibly a Greek equivalent to Baal-hamon, which is near Dothan. In this regard, it is notable that the Septuagint translates the Song of Songs' reference as Beelamon. From another angle, the meaning of its name is "lord/possessor of tumult/crowd", and the Vulgate translates it as *quae habet populos* ("which has people") rather than as a place-name. Such a translation might support the idea of the verse that Solomon had a mass of women, whereas the ideal couple of Song of Songs has only each other. It would thus juxtapose (and implicitly favor) their monogamy over his polygamy.

which he leases out to tenant farmers. In contrast to the NLT rendering here, the Heb. word *notrim* [TH5201, ZH5757] supports the idea that he entrusted the vineyard to guards, which makes more sense within the context. This idea is more along the lines of "caretakers" (NASB) and "keepers" (RSV).

8:12 Solomon need not pay a thousand pieces of silver. This is the NLT's attempt to interpret the Heb., which simply says "the thousand is for you, Solomon." A better understanding of the statement is as a rebuke to Solomon, saying, "Keep your money; you can't buy her love."

COMMENTARY

This poem is difficult, beginning with the question of who is speaking (Alden 1988). Besides the fact that it is an individual, thus ruling out the chorus, we cannot be sure whether it is the man or the woman, and sense can be made of the passage either way. In spite of these and other difficulties, the main point is clear. The poem asserts that love cannot be bought.

Verse 11 begins by describing Solomon's vineyard. We have not heard Solomon's name since chapter 3, but here he is said to own a vineyard at a place named Baal-hamon (but see note on 8:11 regarding Baal-hamon). At this point in the Song, we are well aware of the symbolic use of the vineyard for the woman's sexuality (1:6; 2:15; 7:12). Perhaps the vineyard imagery refers to Solomon's large harem. But then what would it mean that he leases out his vineyard to farmers? It certainly could not mean that he allows any one else to enjoy his women. Keel (1994:282) offers the following helpful comment: "One must assume that verse 11de belongs only in the realm of the lender of meaning (i.e., the literal vineyard), rather than the receiver of meaning (the women). Solomon's vineyard is immense and of great value, which is also the reason he must entrust it to keepers." Thus, the passage is not saying that the guards can use the harem as a bordello but rather that Solomon's harem is impressive.

The NLT rendering here, "tenant farmers," is wrong in my opinion. Though the Hebrew can be translated in this way, it is better understood as referring to guards (see note on 8:11). He is not leasing the vineyard to farmers; he entrusts it to guards to care for it, since it is so large. Even so, questions remain about this passage.

Nevertheless, in verse 12 the speaker asserts that his (or her) vineyard does not belong to Solomon, but rather belongs to the speaker. Again, most commentators agree that the vineyard refers to the woman, whether the young man or the young woman speaks these words, and that this statement amounts to telling Solomon to keep his hands off of what is not his—the woman. Whatever Solomon does, he should not disgrace himself by trying to buy what is not his.

◆ XXIII. Twenty-third Love Poem: Be Like a Gazelle (8:13-14)

Young Man
13 O my darling, lingering in the gardens,
     your companions are fortunate to
          hear your voice.
     Let me hear it, too!

Young Woman
14 Come away, my love! Be like
     a gazelle
     or a young stag on the mountains
          of spices.

NOTES

8:14 *mountains of spices.* The reference to "mountains of spices" may contain a double reference. The mountains are obstacles that the man needs to traverse in order to be in the presence of the woman, but these perfumed mountains could, at the same time, evoke the idea of the perfumed breasts of the woman herself. In other words, she is inviting him to enjoy her sexual pleasures.

COMMENTARY

The final poem makes a very important point about love. It is never satiated, never completely fulfilled. If the Song wanted to say otherwise, it would end with a final love scene where the man and the woman would melt into each other's arms and feel perfect contentment and satisfaction. But that would not be honest or true to reality. Nowhere this side of heaven do men and women reach the point of ultimate and complete fulfillment in relationship.

Therefore, it is appropriate in a song about a love that is achievable and wonderfully intoxicating, though imperfect, to end with a statement of continuing desire to be in one another's presence. In the final poem we hear the voices of both the man and the woman expressing their desire to be in each other's presence. The man says to the woman, who is in the garden, that he wants to hear her voice. For her part, the woman once again (2:17) wants her man, like a gazelle or a young stag, quick and nimble, to traverse the mountains of spices and come to her.

Thus ends the Song of Songs. Love is a powerful emotion, a potent physical act. At first, we are surprised that God has guided his people to acknowledge such a book—one that celebrates the joys of the flesh—as worthy to be included in Holy Scripture. On further reflection, however, we find we must rejoice and thank God for the good gifts he has given us on earth, which, in a shadowy manner, anticipate the utter bliss that we will have in heaven.

BIBLIOGRAPHY

Abegg M., Jr., P. Flint, and E. Ulrich
1999 *The Dead Sea Scrolls Bible.* San Francisco: Harper.

Albright, W. F.
1931–1932 The Syro-Mesopotamian God Sulman-Esmun and Related Figures. *Archiv für Orientforschungen* 7:164-169.

Alden, R.
1988 Song of Songs 8:12a: Who Said It? *Journal of the Evangelical Theological Society* 31:271-278.

Allender, D. and T. Longman III
1993 *Cry of the Soul.* Colorado Springs: NavPress.

1995 *Intimate Allies.* Wheaton: Tyndale House Publishers.

Beckwith, R.
1985 *The Old Testament Canon of the New Testament Church.* London: SPCK.

Borowski, E.
1988 The Sharon—Symbol of God's Abundance. *Bible Review* 4:40-43.

Brenner, A.
1992 A Note on *Bat-Rabbim* (Song of Songs VII 5). *Vetus Testamentum* 42:113-115.

Davidson, R. M.
1989 Theology of Sexuality in the Song of Songs: Return to Eden. *Andrews University Seminary Studies* 27:1-19.

Delcor, M.
1967 Two Special Meanings of the Word *yd* in Biblical Hebrew. *Journal of Semitic Studies* 12:230-240.

Delitzsch, F.
1975 (ET) *Proverbs, Ecclesiastes, Song of Solomon.* Translator, M. G. Easton. Grand Rapids: Ferdmans. (Orig. Pub.1885)

Driver, G. R.
1974 Lice in the Old Testament. *Palestine Exploration Quarterly* 106:159-160.

Emerton, J. A.
1993 Lice or a Veil in the Song of Songs 1.7? Pp. 127-140 in *Understanding Poets and Prophets.* Editor, A. G. Auld. Sheffield: Sheffield Academic Press.

Falk, M.
1982 *Love Lyrics in the Bible.* Sheffield: Almond Press.

Foh, S.
1974–1975 What is the Woman's Desire? *Westminster Theological Journal* 37:367-373.

Fox, M.
1997 Love Poems. Pp. 125-130 in *The Context of Scripture*, vol. 1. Editors, W. W. Hallo and K. L. Younger. Leiden: Brill.

Grossberg, D.
1981 Sexual Desire: Abstract and Concrete. *Hebrew Studies* 22:7-25.

Hallo, W. W.
1985 'As the Seal upon Thy Heart': Glyptic Roles in the Biblical World. *Bible Review* 1:20-27.

1993 For Love is Strong as Death. *Journal of Ancient Near Eastern Studies* 22:45-50.

Hicks, R. Lansing.
1987 The Door of Love. In *Love and Death in the Ancient Near East: Essays in Honor of Marvin H. Pope.* Editors, J. H. Marks and R. M. Good. Guilford, CT: Four Quarters.

Keel, O.
1994 *The Song of Songs: A Continental Commentary.* Translator, F. Gaiser. Minneapolis: Fortress.

King, P. J. and L. E. Stager
2001 *Life in Biblical Israel.* Louisville: Westminster John Knox.

LaCocque, A.
1998 *Romance She Wrote: A Hermeneutical Essay on Song of Songs.* Harrisburg: Trinity International Press.

Long, G. A.
1996 A Lover, Cities, and Heavenly Bodies: Con-Text and the Translation of Two Similes in Canticles (6:4c and 6:10d). *Journal of Biblical Studies* 115:703-709.

Longman, T., III
2001 *Song of Songs.* New International Commentary on the Old Testament. Grand Rapids: Eerdmans.

Meyers, C.
1986 Gender Imagery in the Song of Songs. *Hebrew Annual Review* 10:209-223.

Mulder, M. J.
1992 Does Canticles 6,12 Make Sense? Pp. 104-113 in *The Scriptures and the Scrolls: Studies in Honour of A. S. van der Woude on the Occasion of his 65th Birthday.* Editor, F. Garcia Martinez. Leiden: Brill.

Munro, J.
1995 *Spikenard and Saffron: A Study in the Poetic Language of the Song of Songs.* Sheffield: Sheffield Academic Press.

Murphy, R.
1990 *The Song of Songs.* Minneapolis: Fortress.

Paul, S.
1997 A Lover's Garden of Verse: Literal and Metaphorical Imagery in Ancient Near Eastern Love Poetry. Pp. 99-110 in *Tehillah le-Moshe: Biblical and Judaic Studies in Honor of Moshe Greenberg.* Editors, M. Cogan, B. L. Eichler, and J. H. Tigay. Winona Lake: Eisenbrauns.

Pope, M.
1978 *Song of Songs.* Anchor Bible. Garden City: Doubleday.

Rozelaar, M.
1988 An Unrecognized Part of the Human Anatomy. *Judaism* 37:97-101.

Rundgren, F.
1972 'prywn: Trangsessel, Sanfte. *Zeitschrift für die Alttestamentliche Wissenschaft* 74:70-72

Schroeder, C.
1996 A Love Song: Psalm 45 in the Light of Ancient Near Eastern Marriage Texts. *Catholic Biblical Quarterly* 58:417-432.

Schwab, G.
1999 The Song of Songs' Cautionary Message concerning Human Love. Ph.D. dissertation, Westminster Theological Seminary.

Sefati, Y.
1998 *Love Songs in Sumerian Literature: Critical Edition of the Dumuzi-Inanna Songs.* Ramat-Gan: Bar-Ilan University Press.

Snaith, G. J.
1993 *Song of Songs.* New Century Bible Commentary. Grand Rapids: Eerdmans.

Soulen, R. N.
1967 The *Wasfs* of the Song of Songs and Hermeneutic. *Journal of Biblical Studies* 86:183-190.

Trible, P.
1978 *God and the Rhetoric of Sexuality.* Philadelphia: Fortress.

Villiers, D. W. de, and J. J. Burden.
1989 Function and Translation: A Twosome in the Song of Songs. *Old Testament Essays* 2:1-11.

Waldman, N.
1970 A Note on Canticles 4:9. *Journal of Biblical Studies* 89:215-217.

Westenholz, J. G.
1995 Love Lyrics from the Ancient Near East. Pp. 2471-2484 in *Civilizations of the Ancient Near East,* vol. 4. Editor, M. Sasson. New York: Charles Scribner's Sons.

Zimmerli, W.
1985 *Ezekiel 25-48.* Translator, J. D. Martin. Minneapolis: Fortress.